WHAT IS YOUR TRUE ZODIAC SIGN?

REDISCOVER WHO YOU ARE
FROM 186 TYPES

Greenstone Lobo

ISBN 978-93-81836-72-9
© Greenstone Lobo, 2015
Cover: Fravashi Aga
Layout: Chandravadan R. Shiroorkar - Leadstart Design
Printing: Dhote Offset Technokrafts Pvt. Ltd.

Published in India 2015 by
CELESTIAL BOOKS
An imprint of
LEADSTART PUBLISHING PVT LTD
Unit 25-26, Building A/1, Near Wadala RTO,
Wadala (E), Mumbai – 400 037, INDIA
T + 91 22 2404 6887 **W** www.leadstartcorp.com

All rights reserved worldwide
No part of this publication may be reproduced, stored in or introduced into a retrieval system, or transmitted, in any form, or by any means (electronic, mechanical, photocopying, recording or otherwise), without the prior permission of the Publisher. Any person who commits an unauthorised act in relation to this publication can be liable to criminal prosecution and civil claims for damages.
Disclaimer The views expressed in this book are those of the Author and do not pertain to be held by the Publisher.

To the two women in my life who believed in me morethan I believed in myself:

Mom...*thank you for teaching me that 'chasing excellence would be far more rewarding than chasing success', long before Baba Ranchoddas did.*

Darshu...*thank you for putting up with my idiosyncrasies, for allowing me to go in search of that elusive rainbow, and for being with me through the thick and thin of it all... especially...the thin!*

CONTENTS

About the Author 10
What is your true zodiac sign? 11
Astronality 186 15

1. Aries 18
2. Taurus 21
3. Gemini 24
4. Cancer 27
5. Leo 30
6. Virgo 33
7. Lbra 36
8. Scorpio 39
9. Sagittarius 42
10. Capricorn 45
11. Aquarius 48
12. Pisces 51

13. Aries-Taurus 54
14. Aries-Gemini 57
15. Aries-Cancer 60
16. Aries-Leo 63
17. Aries-Virgo 66
18. Aries-Libra 69
19. Aries-Scorpio 72
20. Aries-Sagittarius 75
21. Aries-Capricorn 78
22. Aries-Aquarius 81
23. Aries-Pisces 85

24. Taurus-Gemini 88
25. Taurus-Cancer 92
26. Taurus-Leo 95
27. Taurus-Virgo 98
28. Taurus-Libra 101
29. Taurus-Scorpio 104
30. Taurus-Sagittarius 107

31.	Taurus–Capricorn	110
32.	Taurus–Aquarius	113
33.	Taurus–Pisces	116

34.	Gemini–Cancer	119
35.	Gemini–Leo	122
36.	Gemini–Virgo	125
37.	Gemini–Libra	128
38.	Gemini–Scorpio	131
39.	Gemini–Sagittarius	134
40.	Gemini–Capricorn	137
41.	Gemini–Aquarius	140
42.	Gemini–Pisces	143

43.	Cancer–Leo	146
44.	Cancer–Virgo	149
45.	Cancer–Libra	152
46.	Cancer–Scorpio	155
47.	Cancer–Sagittarius	158
48.	Cancer–Capricorn	161
49.	Cancer–Aquarius	165
50.	Cancer–Pisces	168

51.	Leo–Virgo	171
52.	Leo–Libra	174
53.	Leo–Scorpio	177
54.	Leo–Sagittariu	180
55.	Leo–Cappricorn	183
56.	Leo–Aquarius	186
57.	Leo–Pisces	189
58.	Virgo–Libra	192
59.	Virgo–Scorpio	195
60.	Virgo–Sagittarius	199
61.	Virgo–Capricorn	202
62.	Virgo–Aquarius	205
63.	Virgo–Pisces	208
64.	Libra–Scorpio	211
65.	Libra–Sagittarius	214
66.	Libra–Capricorn	217
67.	Libra–Aquarius	220

68.	Libra–Pisces	223
69.	Scorpio–Sagittarius	226
70.	Scorpio–Capricorn	229
71.	Scorpio–Aquarius	232
72.	Scorpio–Pisces	235
73.	Sagittarius–Capricorn	238
74.	Sagittarius–Aquarius	241
75.	Sagittarius–Pisces	244
76.	Capricorn–Aquarius	248
77.	Capricorn–Pisces	252
78.	Aquarius–Pisces	255
79.	Aries-Taurus-Gemini	259
80.	Aries-Taurus-Cancer	262
81.	Aries-Taurus-Leo	265
82.	Aries-Taurus-Virgo	268
83.	Aries-Taurus-Libra	271
84.	Aries-Taurus-Scorpio	275
85.	Aries-Taurus-Sagittarius	278
86.	Aries-Taurus-Capricorn	281
87.	Aries-Taurus-Aquarius	285
88.	Aries-Taurus-Pisces	289
89.	Aries-Gemini-Cancer	293
90.	Aries-Gemini-Pisces	297
91.	Aries-Cancer-Leo	300
92.	Aries-Cancer-Pisces	303
93.	Aries-Leo-Virgo	307
94.	Aries-Leo-Pisces	310
95.	Aries-Virgo-Li	313
96.	Aries-Virgo-Pisces	316
97.	Aries-Libra-Scorpio	320
98.	Aries-Libra-Pisces	323
99.	Aries-Scorpio-Sagittarius	326
100.	Aries-Scorpio-Pisces	329
101.	Aries-Sagittarius-Capricorn	333
102.	Aries-Sagittarius-Pisces	337

103. Aries–Capricorn–Aquaris 341
104. Aries–Capricorn–Pisces 344
105. Aries–Aquarius–Pisces 347
106. Taurus–Gemini–Cancer 350
107. Taurus–Gemini–Leo 354
108. Taurus–Gemini–Virgo 358
109. Taurus–Gemini–Libra 361
110. Taurus–Gemini–Scorpio 365
111. Taurus–Gemini–Sagittarius 369
112. Taurus–Gemini–Capricorn 373
113. Taurus–Gemini–Aquarius 377
114. Taurus–Gemini–Pisces 380
115. Taurus–Cancer–Leo 383
116. Taurus–Leo–Virgo 387
117. Taurus–Virgo–Libra 390
118. Taurus–Libra–Scorpio 394
119. Taurus–Scorpio–Sagittarius 398
120. Taurus–Sagittarius–Capricorn 402
121. Taurus–Capricorn–Aquarius 406
122. Taurus–Aquarius–Pisces 410

123. Gemini–Cancer–Leo 414
124. Gemini–Cancer–Virgo 417
125. Gemini–Cancer–Libra 421
126. Gemini–Cancer–Scorpio 425
127. Gemini–Cancer–Sagittarius 428
128. Gemini–Cancer–Capricorn 431
129. Gemini–Cancer–Aquarius 435
130. Gemini–Cancer–Pisces 439
131. Gemini–Leo–Virgo 443
132. Gemini–Virgo–Libra 447
133. Gemini–Libra–Scorpio 451
134. Gemini–Scorpio–Sagittarius 454
135. Gemini–Sagittarius–Capricorn 457
136. Gemini–Capricorn–Aquarius 461
137. Gemini–Aquarius–Pisces 464

138. Cancer–Leo–Virgo 468
139. Cancer–Leo–Libra 472

140. Cancer–Leo–Scorpio 475
141. Cancer–Leo–Sagittarius 478
142. Cancer–Leo–Capricorn 481
143. Cancer–Leo–Aquarius 484
144. Cancer–Leo–Pisces 488
145. Cancer–Virgo–Libra 491
146. Cancer–Libra–Scorpio 494
147. Cancer–Scorpio–Sagittarius 498
148. Cancer–Sagittarius–Capricorn 502
149. Cancer–Capricorn–Aquarius 506
150. Cancer–Aquarius–Pisce 510

151. Leo–Virgo–Libra 514
152. Leo–Virgo–Scorpio 518
153. Leo–Virgo–Sagittarius 522
154. Leo–Virgo–Capricorn 526
155. Leo–Virgo–Aquarius 530
156. Leo–Virgo–Pisces 534
157. Leo–Libra–Scorpio 538
158. Leo–Scorpio–Sagittarius 541
159. Leo–Sagittarius–Capricorn 545
160. Leo–Capricorn–Aquarius 549
161. Leo–Aquarius–Pisces 553

162. Virgo–Libra–Scorpio 557
163. Virgo–Libra–Sagittarius 560
164. Virgo–Libra–Capricorn 563
165. Virgo–Libra–Aquarius 566
166. Virgo–Libra–Pisces 570
167. Virgo–Scorpio–Sagittarius 573
168. Virgo–Sagittarius–Capricorn 577
169. Virgo–Capricorn–Aquarius 581
170. Virgo–Aquarius–Pisces 585

171. Libra–Scorpio–Sagittarius 589
172. Libra–Scorpio–Capricorn 593
173. Libra–Scorpio–Aquarius 596
174. Libra–Scorpio–Pisces 599
175. Libra–Sagittarius–Capricorn 603

176. Libra–Capricorn–Aquaris 606
177. Libra–Aquarius–Pisces 610
178. Scorpio–Sagittarius–Capricorn 614
179. Scorpio–Sagittarius–Aquarius 618
180. Scorpio–Sagittarius–Pisces 622
181. Scorpio–Capricorn–Aquarius 626
182. Scorpio–Aquarius–Pisces 630
183. Sagittarius–Capricorn–Aquarius 634
184. Sagittarius–Capricorn–Pisces 638
185. Sagittarius–Aquarius–Pisces 642

186. Capricorn–Aquarius–Pisces 646

Select Bibliography 650
Glossary of Terms 650
Acknowledgements 652

Editor's Note: 'He' has been used as a generic, unisex indicator.

ABOUT THE AUTHOR

On a rainy day in 1986, when he was fourteen, Greenstone ducked for shelter on a sidewalk. To kill time he picked up a book with a mystifying cover; it was on astrology. His life changed forever. In a year he had learnt to read his own horoscope. When he graduated in chemistry, his notebooks were filled with more horoscopes than formulae. Today, he has a systemised personal collection of over 13,000 horoscopes, and life details, of celebrities and people from all walks of life.

Based on his extensive research into astrology, he has propounded various rational methodologies to explore longevity, widowhood, wealth, fame, marriage, family, marital discord, sex life, careers, secret areas of life, travel and death. Greenstone is one of the few astrologers in the world to have concrete works on planets like Uranus, Neptune and Pluto. He has hundreds of horoscopes to prove their exact exaltation points. He has also re-discovered four more planets, asteroids and comets along with conclusive evidence that these planetary bodies too have a major impact on the life and times of human beings. Two of these planets are the *true* rulers of the zodiac signs Taurus and Virgo.

Greenstone also makes predictions about mundane matters, politics, sports, and celebrity-related events in various fora and media. He writes a weekly column titled 'Octozone', which focuses exclusively on sporting predictions. Training is his other passion, besides astrology. As a corporate learning and development professional, he has trained over 50,000 people.

Greenstone lives with his wife, Darshana, and son, Neil, in Mumbai and can be reached at: contact@greenstonelobo.com

WHAT IS YOUR *TRUE* ZODIAC SIGN?

'What is your zodiac sign?' You will have confidently answered this question many times. But what if I tell you that your usual answer may not, in fact, be correct? Shocked? Disbelieving? Yes, it is possible. Allow me to explain...

Let us suppose that you are a Scorpio. Every time you have said this, you must have received reactions of artificial admiration or fear. You must have wondered what the fuss was all about and deliberated over the widespread gospel about Scorpios being passionate, ruthless and vengeful. In reality, you feel you are none of these things!

This may have led you to read popular books on Sun Signs either for clarification or to convince yourself that you are a Scorpio. You may have even thrown away those books thinking they are all bogus and that astrology is nothing but hogwash.

Well, think about it – a 5000-year-old science cannot be all gibberish, can it? Instead, there must be a mistake somewhere that not many have stumbled upon. Before I get into that, it is important to understand what astrology actually is.

Astrology depends to a greater extent on astronomy. A simple discovery that seasons are created by the changes in planetary positions or that high tides are caused by the moon, fuelled further explorations in astronomy. While astronomy is the science dealing with the physical aspect of everything in the cosmos, astrology is the discipline that uses the apparent positions of the celestial objects to predict future events. Astronomy has evolved and has been accepted as a science while the esoteric, mysterious and intangible aspects of astrology have been the deterrents to it being accredited as a science.

Your horoscope is the astronomical picture of the positions of all the planets and stars in the sky when you were born. Astrology interprets the implications of these positions and attempts to understand how your life or events will unfold in the future. These are extrapolations based on numerous recorded incidents from the past. It is interesting to note that most kings, queens or princes/princesses of the British Empire and Europe were born either on a new moon day or a full moon day! That includes Queen Victoria and even the current Prince William and his consort Kate Middleton.

One amazing fact I found while researching the birth dates of captains who played in the 1999 Cricket World Cup was that almost every captain of all the major countries playing in that tournament was born on a full moon day! India's Mohd. Azharuddin, England's Alec Stewart, Pakistan's Wasim Akram, South Africa's Hansie Cronje, Sri Lanka's Arjuna Ranatunga and West Indies's Brian Lara – all of them were born on full moon days! Interestingly, the tournament was won by someone not born on a full moon day – Steve Waugh. Born in 1965, Steve Waugh had an important planet placed supremely in his birth chart – Pluto – which won him the World Cup.

The three superstars of the Indian film industry, Shah Rukh Khan, Salman Khan and Aamir Khan, were born in the same year, 1965. The birth of these three most powerful people in the same year cannot be a coincidence. Planet Pluto, which I consider to be the most impactful planet in the universe, was powerfully placed in the horoscopes of these three and hence they reached where they have. Similarly, most events of our lives can be attributed to the strong or weak placement of planets in our horoscopes. All the planets, Mars, Venus, Uranus, etc., have their roles to play in our lives.

While it may be hard to believe that a planet that is many millions of miles away from us can influence us in any way, it is harder to ignore the simple fact that the psyche of a person is influenced by these very planets. While a horoscope can be read by a competent astrologer who can interpret your birth chart for you, even a novice may know the placement of the Sun in a horoscope and rattle out a few common characteristics of people born in a particular month. It is uncanny, but most people born with their Sun in Cancer tend to be emotional, sensitive, moody, loving, caring; they regard their mother with the highest respect, are extremely careful with money, and can cook.

So, what exactly is a Zodiac Sun Sign?
The **Zodiac** is a circle of twelve 30° divisions of celestial longitude that are centred upon the ecliptic. Each of these divisions forms clusters of stars to form a unique configuration, which is grouped together as a zodiac sign. The zodiac signs, which are a cluster of fixed stars grouped together, form the backdrop against which the Earth and other planets traverse in their respective orbits. The Sun, too, traverses the celestial sphere in the course of the year. In late April, the Sun enters the constellation that consists of stars like α-Arietis, β-Arietis, etc., grouped together to form the zodiac sign Aries. People born when the Sun was traversing the zodiac sign Aries will have many characteristics which are surprisingly similar.

But the point is – do *you* really know if your zodiac Sun Sign is the correct one? Maybe not!

We all know that the Earth rotates on its axis. But many of us do not know that it also wobbles while it rotates, just like a spinning top. This wobble changes the direction of the earth's rotational axis in relation to the fixed stars, which form the zodiac. The wobble is very slight and it takes hundreds of years for even a one-degree shift to occur. This concept of the gradual shift in the orientation of the earth's axis in relation to the fixed stars of the zodiac is called *precession*.

It takes approximately 26,000 years to complete one precession cycle. What it means for us is that approximately every 2000 years, there is a shift of *one* zodiac sign. Please remember that the zodiac does not move but the earth's orientation does.

The ancient Babylonians were the first to record the precession of the Zodiac. Over the last few centuries, concrete astronomical systems have been formulated to factor-in this shift in the earth's rotational axis. Astrological calculations have changed accordingly. But many Western astrologers have not adopted this system and still follow the traditional zodiacal path in their calculations.

Indian astrology is very much cognisant of the precession phenomenon and accounts for it in its calculations, which involves knowing the *ayanamsha* (the exact difference in the *fixed* zodiac used in Western astrology and the *moving* zodiac used in the Indian system). The Western method of calculation (without precession) is called the Sayana method while the Indian methodology (after subtracting the *ayanamsha*) is called the Nirayana method. The *ayanamsha* was zero around the year 293 AD. But the wobble of the earth has ensured increase in the *ayanamsha* over the centuries. Currently, it stands at about 24 degrees. A zodiac sign consists of 30 degrees, hence almost four-fifths of the people who believe they are Scorpios, are actually Librans!

The highest authority on astronomy, NASA, has a website http://ssd.jpl.nasa.gov/horizons.cgi which provides an ephemeris to know the exact position of a planet at any point in time. If you access the sun's position on the site you will be surprised to see that the sun enters the zodiac sign of Aries only by the 14th of April, every year. Therefore, most of you, who think you are Arians, are probably Pisceans.

Astrology is based on astronomy and there cannot be a deviation in the actual astronomical position of the sun and the classification of the Zodiac. Unfortunately, Western astrology does not recognise this. In my practice of astrology over two decades, I have got accurate results only when using the Nirayana method and not the Sayana method.

Another important thing to understand is – it is not just the Sun Sign that determines a person's psyche. In that case, we would have only 12 types of people in this world and Human Resource managers would have no problem in identifying their core competencies. All Geminians and Librans would be in Sales, Arians and Sagittarians in Marketing, Cancerians would cook for everyone, Virgos would manage the back office and accounts, we would have only Leo bosses and the poor Pisceans would never get promoted!

The fact is, our mental makeup is determined by the composition of the zodiac signs in which we have our Sun, Mercury and Moon. These three planets work in synchronisation to create the persona. Just as the heart, mind and soul combine to form the psyche of a person, the Sun, Mercury and the Moon combine to weave a unique personality type. If the heart can be explained by the zodiac sign in which we have our Moon, the mind is where Mercury is and the Sun denotes our soul. While the Sun rules the self and ego, the Moon rules our emotions and Mercury our mental processes. *Permutations and combinations of these three factors create 186 types of personalities*!

This means that if your date of birth is 7th of July 1981, your Sun and Mercury are in Gemini and Moon in Leo. But you may have believed all along that you were a Cancerian.

M.S. Dhoni was born on this day and it is clear why he thinks on his feet and has amazing reflexes – typical of Gemini. He took to leadership like a duck to water because he is a natural leader, *à la* Leo!

Another good example is Salman Khan, born on 27th of December 1965. No, he is not a Capricorn, people! Khan has his Sun in Sagittarius, Mercury in Scorpio and the Moon in Aquarius. Hence, he is athletic and retains the child-like charm and honesty of a Sagittarian. He is a rebel, has a distinct individualistic style, is a non-conformist and is a good friend, like most Aquarians. He never forgives or forgets those who have wronged him and is intense and passionate, like a true Scorpio. So, no, he is not a scheming, conniving, stuffy and politically correct Capricorn!

Your True Sun Sign
Now, let us come back to the question I asked you at the very beginning: 'What is your zodiac sign?' In fact, what is your *correct* zodiac sign?

To know the correct answer, get your horoscope checked using either computer software (in the Nirayana method) or by a competent astrologer. This book also provides a link which enables you to create an accurate birth chart and know your planetary positions. This way, you can understand yourself better.

Based on the Nirayana methodology and NASA's positions of planets, there is a need for the realignment of dates against popular notions of when the Sun Signs change from one to the next.

The following table gives you the sun's ACTUAL (Nirayana method) entry into the zodiac signs. This is your real Sun Sign!

14th April to 14th May	Aries	17th Oct to 15th Nov	Libra
15th May to 14th June	Taurus	16th Nov to 15th Dec	Scorpio
15th June to 16th July	Gemini	16th Dec to 13th Jan	Sagittarius
17th July to 16th Aug	Cancer	14th Jan to 12th Feb	Capricorn
17th Aug to 16th Sep	Leo	13th Feb to 14th Mar	Aquarius
17th Sep to 16th Oct	Virgo	15th Mar to 13th Apr	Pisces

This could be a huge paradigm shift for many. The aim of this book is not to break long-held views but to bring forth the truth and help you know yourself better. When you read your individual horoscopes based on all the other planets like Mars, Venus, Jupiter, Pluto, etc., you will be surprised by the accuracy of the insights into yourself.

I was introduced to astrology by the book, *Linda Goodman's Sun Signs*. I was 14 when I read it for the first time and was thrilled and overwhelmed to read the chapter on Scorpios. I felt proud to be one.

The trouble began when I started reading about my family members. My father was supposed to be a career-oriented, conservative Capricorn, but that was certainly not him. My mother was supposed to be a flamboyant, stylish Leo – again she was not. This led me to ask if I was deluding myself that I was a Scorpio and wondered if I really had those wonderful qualities Goodman described in her book. Why didn't my parents, and some others, reflect the actual qualities of their zodiac signs? The characteristics described matched a few people I knew to a T but were quite off the mark with many others.

Then I re-read the introduction to the book and understood why. According to Goodman, while the placement of the Sun in a horoscope is essential, the positions of the Moon and Mercury are equally important, as the Moon rules emotions and Mercury rules the thought process.

That struck me like a bolt of lightning!

I had my computerised horoscope made immediately and saw to my horror that my Sun was actually in Libra, my Mercury was in Scorpio and my Moon in Aquarius! I read the Libra and Aquarius chapters and realised that I actually possessed a medley of the characteristics of all these three zodiac signs, in varying degrees. I then re-read all the zodiac signs from Aries to Pisces and was certain that my personality did not reflect the qualities of any other sign, except those where my Sun, Mercury and Moon were positioned. But how could I be a Libran when I was born on the 15th of November? Moreover, according to Linda Goodman, I was a Scorpio!

It took me a while to understand the difference between the Indian and Western methods of calculation. I realised that the NASA calculations and the Nirayana calculations of Indian astrology are almost in sync and began practising the Nirayana method of astrology.

Over the next 20-odd years, I tried to verify my understanding with those I met. Whenever I was introduced to someone, I would be restless until I knew his birth date and year. Then, I would take a quick look at the positions of his Sun, Mercury and Moon and 'follow' him meticulously to reaffirm that his behaviour was indeed in accordance with the placement of these planets. My theory was working. After the painstaking compilation of over 13,000 horoscopes in 20-plus years, I was convinced that my hypothesis was correct.

In the process, I have also discovered various other planets, asteroids and bodies that influence human beings in important ways. But more on that later.

I wanted to present to people my understanding of the most basic offshoot of astrology – Astro-Psychology.

We need to demystify and deconstruct the conventional wisdom that humans can only be of 12 types, represented by the 12 zodiac signs. The fact is that almost

95 percent of human beings are born as a combination of two or more zodiac signs. Hence, there are not just 12 types of human beings, but 186 types! And these are just the basic categories!

This book helps you identify and know them all. It also provides you with insights about the people you deal with on a daily basis. It takes you on an interesting new journey into yourself. You are able to understand yourself better, become aware of your triggers, natural abilities, traits, characteristics and shortcomings. It helps you look within to your centre.

Astronality is the art of describing the personality of a person using astrology. There are 186 types of Astronalities. The Sun, Mercury and the Moon are your 'personal' planets; they form the basis of your personality. The permutations and combinations of the positions of the Sun, Mercury and Moon create all these types of personalities.

To know your zodiac combination and Astronality type, please visit www.truezodiacsign.com/calculator and fill in your birth details or those of the person whose Astronality combination you are looking for. You can also scan the image below with your smartphone to go directly to the calculator.

Suppose the birth details are as follows: 27th December 1965, 2:30 p.m., Indore (Salman Khan). You see that the Sun is in Sagittarius, Mercury in Scorpio and Moon in Aquarius. So, Salman Khan is not a Capricorn. *His Astronality combination is* **Scorpio-Sagittarius-Aquarius**. Now, go to the chapter Scorpio-Sagittarius-Aquarius to know more about Salman Khan or any other person born into this Astronality.

Interestingly, I also (re)discovered the one factor in which I disagreed with Linda. Linda and a few astrologers believe that the ascending sign also plays a role in defining a personality. The ascending sign is the first zodiac sign that rises in the horizon during a person's birth. It is the point on the ecliptic at which it intersects the eastern horizon. The horoscope consists of 12 houses representing 12 zodiac signs and the ascendant forms the first house and the rest of the zodiacal signs follow suit. In my analysis of thousands of horoscopes, I found that the zodiac sign on the ascendant has no influence at all on the personality of a person. It only influences the physical attributes of a person, not the mental, emotional or spiritual attributes. The placement of the Sun, Mercury and Moon is sufficient to give enough indications of a personality.

In fact, I would say that if at all there is another planet that affects the personality, it has got to be Venus. Venus affects the human psyche to some extent by adding some spice to the personality. Hence, in cases where the Astronality combination indicates just one or two zodiac signs, you can also add the position of Venus to get a sharper analysis. For example, if your Sun and Mercury are in Taurus, the Moon in Cancer, and Venus in Gemini, your Astronality combination is Taurus-Cancer. But you can also read Taurus-Gemini-Cancer to add perspective.

Now, before you proceed to the combination signs, I urge you to read about them individually to get a complete picture of the basic signs. For example, if you are Aries-Taurus, it would be beneficial to read about Aries and Taurus as individual signs first to get a better understanding of the combination Astronality.

If you are not sure of the exact time of birth, even partial information like 'in the morning', 'late in the evening', etc. would suffice. You can key in an approximate time of birth and go ahead with the analysis. For example, we know that Sachin Tendulkar was born on the 24th April 1973, but his time of birth is not known to all. We can key in any time from 00:01am to 23:59pm to discover that his Astronality combination remains the same, i.e. Aries-Sagittarius-Pisces. Therefore, this book gives you insights into the people you are closest to. But, you can maximise its use by also gaining insights into those with whom you have important interactions. This includes people you hire or your bosses or high-profile clients. But most importantly, this book is about *you*.

So should you now be reading your weekly predictions according to the *new* Sun Sign? Well it doesn't make a difference because 1/12th of the population of the world cannot have the same fate unfolding in their lives at any given time. It's not that simple. The synchronisation of various planets in your birth chart weaves a unique symphony about you, which is distinctly *YOU* and can never be the same for any other person in the world.

The long and intriguing journey of life starts with knowing yourself.

Bon voyage!

1. ARIES

The baby of the zodiac, a true-blue Arian always says 'me first', throws tantrums when denied, and is as easy to please and as difficult to handle as a baby. The strong Fire sign gives him a healthy disregard for the opinions of others and the cardinal strength of the Arian makes him a leader. Mars, the god of war, rules Aries and makes him violent, aggressive, and powerful.

Fearless and courageous, Arians have a warrior's temperament. Sly tactics and underhanded dealings are not for them. They are motivated by glory and applause rather than monetary gain. Arians love butting heads with the enemy for the sheer challenge of it.

The best and the worst thing about an Arian is that he is never artificial. When he is angry, he is truly angry; when generous, no one can compare to him, and if he likes you he will be your champion. This lack of tact can lead to massive misunderstandings and ego clashes. Once he realises he is wrong, he immediately apologises, but only in private. Sometimes, an Arian's fearlessness borders on foolhardiness and they lack the caution to weigh options before rushing headlong into war. Their naïveté resembles that of a child playing with fire without heed for the consequences.

The childish, 'me first' attitude leads many to misunderstand him, and to think that he is selfish but that is not true. When he needs something, he is like a baby crying for what it wants. Once all his needs are met, he becomes charming and caring once again. His generous streak is second only to a Leo's. Optimism makes him always see the glass as half-full and he never worries about the future. No matter what life brings, he is always bursting with positive energy.

When you feel hopeless, they will smile and talk of miracles. Surprisingly, most of the time, their seemingly unfounded optimism leads them on to the glory they seek. Failure never intimidates them and they are not afraid to try again. They are pioneers, the people who dream incredible dreams. This unbounded optimism comes at a price, though. They refuse to learn from their mistakes or change their behaviour.

Quick to anger, it is foolish to incite them to rage. They are capable of killing or destroying in a fury, but once the anger has gone, they are filled with remorse for their actions.

Saying exactly what they think makes them vocal in love. Arians feel that their love is exclusive and unique; that others never loved as strongly or as idealistically as them, nor have they had as perfect a partner. The Arian girl wants a perfect Prince Charming, while the boy wants a girl everybody will look at and sigh. You can be sure of drama, passion, and excitement in their love lives. Arians love truly and deeply and when their love crashes, they crash with it. They idolise their partners and if their faith is broken, they are devastated. Soon, however, their eternal optimism takes over, and they are ready to live and die for love again.

They are extremely ambitious. Their ambitions are not driven by materialistic gains but by the need for power and recognition. They crave adulation and applause. Their high energy levels ensure that they work hard to achieve their dreams. They are not methodical or meticulous, but get results through sheer vision and the intense power of their dreams.

Deep inside, every Arian is insecure, all Fire signs are. They fear they may not be good enough, strong enough or smart enough. If you understand that and hold their hand tight, they will be your friend forever.

Aries is ruled by Mars, which is the planet of war, which is probably why the children of Mars are exceptionally courageous. They tirelessly go headlong against any challenge in the world. They may lack subtlety, finesse and depth but they more than make up for that with their idealism and never-say-die attitude.

Aries rules the first house of a horoscope. The first house indicates the *self*, the ego. It shows the way we are viewed by the world. It isn't a surprise that the Arians are obsessed with their self, is it?

Aries is symbolised by the Ram – the Goat. Just like the Goat, Arians see the only way to go is up, butting their way forward passionately, not too worried about obstacles or consequences.

Aries – Kelly Clarkson

Kelly turned down recording contracts from Jive Records and Interscope Records, after winning American Idol, stating, 'They would have completely pigeonholed me as a bubblegum act. I was confident enough that something better would come along.'[1]

'I'm not nervous when I come out with a record thinking, 'Oh, how is it going to amount up to others?' I'm not nervous when I go into the studio, thinking: 'Oh, well, is this potentially radio-friendly? Is it not mainstream enough?'...I just have a good time.'[2]

We hear her self-belief. Kelly is an uninhibited and strong Aries.

Love and Marriage for Him

He is authoritative, autocratic and demanding. He demands your attention and hates to be crossed. He takes care of you and showers you with attention when his needs are met. This guy does not take well to criticism and wants a girl who loves being conquered. He lacks sensitivity and does not understand sighs and tears. But if clearly communicated to, he will come to comfort you promptly.

He needs a woman who makes him feel wonderful, pampered and looked after. Never order him around, especially in front of others. He prefers independent women to clinging vines, but always needs to be the one in control.

Do not dampen his spirits by crying and moaning. He is off to dazzle the world with his extraordinary ideas and needs a companion who will hold the fort, not let him down, and understand that behind his devil-may-care attitude, hides insecurity.

Saying *I told you so* will not make him love you. He has little control over his anger, which is aggressive and loud. Let him run out of steam before you respond; chances are he will apologise as soon as he cools down, for he holds no grudges.

The best way to handle him is sweet talk. He will be the most generous of husbands. Once he is through with the money, he will pass on whatever is left to you. If you make him feel indispensible, then you have him hooked for life.

---

[1] http://en.wikipedia.org/wiki/Kelly_Clarkson
[2] http://www.oprah.com/entertainment/Kelly-Clarkson-Interview--Oprahcom-Screening Room/3#ixzz20CuP7DVq

Though he dominates his children's early lives, he inspires them to dream and instils in them the will to reach for the stars.

Love and Marriage for Her

The Arian woman is bold and independent, and the liveliest girl around. She will be totally, madly, truly and deeply in love. She needs a stable and calm mate who can handle her temper and not grudge her the limelight. To catch her attention, act uninterested. She simply cannot resist a challenge. Highly ambitious, she expects support and always strives to succeed.

Gender will never stop her from achieving anything, so do not expect her to be a submissive wife. She is a constant challenge to live with as she is full of opposites – she demands freedom but hates granting it; she can be loud and aggressive but does not take the same behaviour from you. Despite this, she is blind when in love and sees you as her ideal. But do remember that even though she loves deeply, she will not hesitate to leave if she feels wronged.

Sentimental and passionate, she can be the easiest person to handle with flowers and flattery. But there can be no question of who is the boss. She hates being dominated. But deep inside, is a sliver of insecurity she never admits to. Highly ambitious, she expects support and will always strive to succeed. Though she acts tough, she fears failure. Hold her hand and reassure her in her time of need. She is very protective of her children and would go to war with anyone who harms them.

At the Workplace

The Arian is a fabulous worker and an asset to any organisation. He is ambitious and ready to work double for half the salary. You can pay the rest in kind by praising him in front of others. If you do that and give constructive criticism in private, he will perform the best.

He is great at delegating. Expect the ideas and bold strokes from him and leave the details to others. He has amazing energy levels and can finish in a few hours what others take days to complete. Arians are not methodical but work well when driven. More than money, the number of people under him and fancy designations motivate him. So provide the carrot and forget the stick.

The biggest problem with Arians is their lack of tact. They are capable of telling senior people that their plans are not worth a dime. He can also sulk or get angry in meetings. He needs to be told to respect experience and not treat contrary opinions as personal attacks. As a boss his biggest drawback is that he can be end up being authoritarian and hierarchical. When he believes that he is right, no one can show him he is near his downfall, because he can never see it coming.

Arians are a bundle of raw energy, full of vitality, dynamism and assertiveness, but can become confrontational, impulsive and controlling with the inability to look at their own follies.

Famous Aries Personalities

Andy Flower, Anju Bobby George, Jacques Rudolph, Jonathan Vandiar, Kelly Clarkson, Malcolm Marshall, Daniel Day Lewis, Sujatha Rangarajan.

2. TAURUS

Taurus is ruled by a yet-to-be (re)discovered and (re)named planet that I call 'Planet X' (see Glossary). It is a calm and powerful planet that endows Taureans with stability and placidity even in the most trying of circumstances.

The most obvious thing you will notice about them is their stability. They can be thin and willowy (but they will have to put in a lot of effort to maintain that look) or stocky, yet they exude the strength of mountains. You can identify a Taurean by their lazy, solid tread. They can endure anything life throws at them without giving way to depression or hysterics. Patient, calm and peaceful, they are blessed with a composure that helps them overcome problems with patience and perseverance. They are extremely non-aggressive and like to be relaxed rather than stressed out. Their sense of humour helps them in this. There is a strong streak of common sense in Taureans that is their most endearing quality. They see the obvious solutions that elude even people who pride themselves on their intelligence. Their practical nature makes them opt for things that last.

They talk in monosyllables or short sentences. Long gab-sessions are not their style. I don't mean to say that they are sombre and dull – far from it – they laugh and make jokes easily, but they use the least possible words.

Food is their first love. They love eating, especially traditional food, and also find great happiness in feeding people. They can be fabulous cooks too, and their food will be traditional rather than experimental. This love of food along with their lazy Taurean ways will make them pile on the ounces quite quickly and they will have to depend on good genetics or willpower to try and shed the kilos.

Taurus is a fixed sign and combined with the Taurean realistic thoughts and traditional views will make them stubborn. Once they believe what they say is correct – then you can move mountains but you cannot change their opinions. It's tough!

Materialism is natural to them and they like comforts and a fat bank balance. They need to be sure that they are secure financially in order to feel free. Taureans mark out family and wealth as special areas and they work to make these two areas shine in their lives. They are born traditionalists and prefer living by conventions rather than flouting rules.

Taureans are extremely sensual in nature. Their bodily senses are much heightened and they love soft fabrics against their skin, luxuries, long baths and massages. They love natural earthy aromas, and perfumes, but hate body odour. They love luxury and revel in tastes and colours, and are very close to Mother Earth. This love for the Earth also makes them extremely patriotic in nature. They are true children of the soil.

But their practicality and common sense take a back seat when they are in love. They are extremely romantic and deeply sentimental. They find it difficult to convey their feelings but they will pursue you relentlessly if they choose you.

They make wonderfully caring and sensible lovers. Once they know you are theirs, their practical self returns and they now become dependable mates. Their decisions are always well thought out. It is fabulous to be loved by Taureans for they know how to care for and protect their loved ones.

Taureans have a deeply creative streak in them. They love music and respond to it at a very deep level. Painting, dancing and singing will also attract them. They can have them as hobbies or professions but you can be sure that they enjoy their creative pursuits.

The biggest drawback or maybe even the strength of a Taurean is the lack of emotional sensitivity. They cannot read your eyes, or peek into your soul and instinctively know what you feel. That makes them a little insensitive but the same factor makes them emotionally stable. They may also be possessive, controlling, and overly concerned about money, security and creature comforts. Bullheadedness, tunnel vision, inflexibility, and imperviousness to the opinions of others are a few prominent qualities they may also display.

'Planet X', the ruler of Taurus, is probably the most powerful planet in the solar system, probably as strong as Pluto. It blesses them with immense inner strength and endurance. This is the planet that rules the second house of a horoscope, and is the indicator of wealth, material possessions, etc. – it is not surprising that Taureans go earnestly about accumulating wealth. Taurus is symbolised by the Bull; yes, they are stubborn. Look at the word 'stubborn' positively – they persevere, however tough the situation is.

Taurus – Shilpa Shetty
'People who know me well can vouch for the fact that I'm a foodie, even though I am a health freak.'
'If I set my mind on something, I want to achieve it.'
'I think if surveys say Indians are the happiest people in the world, it's because we are rooted, we stay close to our families.'[3]

The family-loving, strong and immovable Shilpa Shetty is a true Taurean. As an enterprising Taurean, she also has her eyes set on multiple business ventures ranging from a perfume brand, an IPL team, a yoga DVD, a spa salon chain and many more.

Love and Marriage for Him
He is your support system and the man you turn to for every problem. He never lets you down. This guy is a responsible family member. He loves his family wholeheartedly. He is extremely hard working, and though he may not say it, you can make out from the look in his eyes when he has had a rough day. Let him relax at home.

He does not like feminists and runs away from motorcycling, riding and body-piercing females. He is just not excited by the unconventional. His desire is for a girl who loves home and tradition. He will not be bothered if you work, as long as you pamper him when he comes home. I know it is a little old-fashioned but that's the way it is.

Money is very important to him and he likes to save. Value for money is what he looks for and not show-biz glamour. He does not spend on expensive gifts.

His conversational skills are not exemplary and, though he loves you, he may never shower praises on you. He expresses love by taking care of you and seeing that your needs are met. You will never have any complaints on the physical expressions of love, though. Food will be his favourite topic and he will not mind cooking.

---

[3] *Hello!*, June 2011

As a father, he is well prepared, calm and responsible. You can count on him to hold your hand and help when you feel overwhelmed by motherhood.

Love and Marriage for Her
She is the perfect Indian wife and daughter-in-law who follows traditions and strives to give the right values to her family. Soft-spoken and responsible, she takes on problems with a smile. Loyal and committed, she expects the same from you. The best part is that though she is the rock of the family, she lets you be the 'man' of the family and allows you to take the decisions. Her kitchen is extremely important to her and she spends hours cooking delicious dishes. She loves making food for her family.

Well-educated or a school dropout, her opinions are always heard, for they are couched in practical common sense. She takes good care of the finances. Her personal savings form an important part of her mental makeup; she carefully maintains and adds to it.

As a mother, she is absolutely hands-on. She does not give in to modern parenting fads or search parenting blogs for answers. She understands her children instinctively, although she does not understand their ideas at times. Her views might be too fixed and she will find it difficult to change with the times.

At the Workplace
Taureans excel in finance; they have an innate understanding of how money works, where to invest it and how to multiply it. At the same time, they are extremely suspicious of get-rich-quick schemes and do not believe in new investment methodologies easily.

They are extremely hard working. Taureans can be drawn to anything from art to medicine and give everything they have to their chosen professions. They are extremely good at the arts but will pursue it only if it brings them monetary gains.

Don't expect Taureans to sell or innovate, they are the dependable doers of the world. Money is essential to them; well-spaced-out increments will see them working hard for their pay. They are not very adept at matters related to thoughts and views. If they are the business heads, expect them to reign in the budget and ensure the business thrives and turns profitable.

As bosses they are fine with you taking time to learn but will show you the door if you take them for granted. They are also great at managing large-scale projects.

Every Taurean's deepest desire is to own his own business and allow reliable people to run it for him, while he goes and plays golf or relaxes in the countryside, near the river.

Dependable, earthy and practical, Taureans need to guard themselves against the extremes of being materialistic, possessive and bull-headed.

Famous Taurus Personalities
Amisha Patel, Andrew Symonds, Haroon Lorgat, Shilpa Shetty, Brooke Shields, Ilayaraja, Jonny Wilkinson, Nitish Bharadwaj, Ramanuja Aiyengar, Ronnie Screwvala, Steffi Graf, Wilhelm Steinitz, John Maynard Keynes.

3. GEMINI

Mercury, the planet of the maverick messenger god, embodies Gemini. It marks its people with a changeable nature, versatility and loads of intelligence.

They are eternally youthful and rarely look as old as they are. They have the supreme advantage of looking young despite their wrinkles. They are always learning new ideas and never allow their minds to rust, which is the secret of their youthful demeanour.

They find it very easy to understand even the most complex of ideas. They will also be able to rephrase that abstract vision into beautifully chosen words for you and me to follow. They are master communicators, the zodiac's wordsmiths, and are magicians with words. They are great linguists, and a Gemini can easily learn at least four languages.

Change is a constant in their lives. They just cannot be chained to one thought, one room or one task for a long time. They want and need change as much as they need to breathe. They may be adept at multitasking and will be multi-skilled too. The Gemini's curiosity will make them look and wonder at every task before they move to a new assignment. This lack of constancy could stop them from finding the deep truth behind each discovery for they do not know how to manage their restless nature.

Fun-filled and vivacious, Geminis have a definite charm. Sociable and vivacious, they love spending their time sharing funny jokes, mimicry and anecdotes with friends. With their quick intellect and adaptability, Geminis will seem different every two or three years. There will be a process of evolution with them. Interestingly, every Gemini loves to have a nickname or an alias.

Friends and family who tell them unhappy tales never see more than a nod of their heads before they change the topic to something more interesting. They constantly change their views and opinions and can be quite manipulative to get what they want. Their ability to lie with a straight face is their biggest negative trait. Geminis have such a wild imagination that they sincerely believe in their half-truths or outright lies and they are ready to defend these with more lies. They carry tales, and love to embellish facts with their own stories. They actually like to see the ensuing confusion and have fun at the expense of others.

Geminis can be fickle in love. The fact is that they are such changeable creatures that they can never be satisfied with the status quo for long. Geminis, sadly, spend most of their life looking for that someone who is better than the one they have. As they age they will realise the menace of their mind and they slowly understand themselves. They are frivolous and flirtatious in love and will have to learn how to lose their self-centredness for a more giving relationship.

Anger is never their failing for they always think on their feet and find a way out of any situation. They sometimes use words as weapons, resulting in being extremely sarcastic. They sulk or throw tantrums when they are upset but are back to normal as soon as they find a new interest.

Gemini is an Air sign and there is no constancy or dependability in them. But their biggest bane is their duality. They seem to be two or more people packed into one. Different people would have contrasting opinions about them. They get bored with people and things very quickly and look out for newer, more interesting options. Hence, they fall in and out of relationships; they have more than one career option; and always have a second option for almost everything in life.

Mercury, the metal that rules Geminians, does not have a permanent shape or form. Geminians exactly reflect that – they change all the time, albeit for the better. Gemini is symbolised by the Twins, which shows their duality. Gemini also rules the third house of communication – writing, journeys, etc. – the reason for their love of chatter, their command over words and their everlasting quest for *something*, even if they don't know what it is.

Gemini – Salman Rushdie
Salman Rushdie, with his flair for writing and taste for partying, is the perfect example of a Gemini. His personal life, too, matches the Gemini trait of not easily settling down. Rushdie has been married four times.[4] He does not believe in conventions, as is apparent from the following statement: 'The idea of the sacred is quite simply one of the most conservative notions in any culture, because it seeks to turn other ideas – uncertainty, progress, change – into crimes.'[5] [From a speech on 6 February, 1990.]

Salman Rushdie truly exemplifies a Gemini, with his gift for stories and maverick thoughts.

Love and Marriage for Him
Although you have him, he may not be around all the time! He is elusive. He can surprise you with sudden changes. He prefers a strong, independent woman and is not very reliable around the house. Often, he surprises you with his dexterity at handling more than one task at a time. He wants to be constantly challenged in life. The best way to handle him is to let him feel free. Clingy, teary scenes make him flee. Love him with a cool detachment; be happy when he is there and nonchalant when he is not.

The best thing about him is that he is never boring. He can keep you amused, and bemused, for hours. He is adventurous and you feel ten years younger when you are with him. You need to engage him in love – talk and express yourself as much as he does or it can become a boring one-sided conversation for him.

You need to keep him interested – keep changing the way you look and keep the moves in the bedroom intriguing too. Meet him in the most unexpected places and keep the mystery alive. Probably this will not be enough to stop him from flirting but maybe he will just keep it to words.

As a father, he is all fun and games. Responsibility can be missing in his actions. He teaches his children to think beyond the ordinary and live life with adventure and curiosity.

Love and Marriage for Her
Every Gemini girl has a dazzling, sparkling twinkle in her eyes that you can never miss. She has multiple dimensions to her personality that would take a lifetime for you to decipher. Talkative, exuberant and vivacious, she is always full of fun and games and knows how to strike up a conversation with anybody. She has more

---

[4] http://en.wikipedia.org/wiki/Salman_Rushdie
[5] http://www.notable-quotes.com/r/rushdie_salman.html

than a dozen friends. Learn to communicate well if you want this girl in your life. You will need to dazzle her with your mental abilities.

She will want to do so many things and be interested in such diverse activities that you will see her changing passions with the changing of the months. You will also see her in different avatars every time – she is many women packaged into one. From her moods to how she dresses, there is a constant kaleidoscopic change to her personality. You will never feel bored with her as every time you are meeting a new her. She will definitely keep you interested.

She does not need a lot of emotional care or sensitive handling. Despite her bubbly charm, she is prone to mood swings and can surprise you at times with her despondent answers. Don't fret; just introduce her to a new thought or bring in a new activity. Also, keeping her interested will prevent her from getting bored and looking for other excitements in life.

This lady is always ready to do more than three things at one time. She needs to be challenged and feels let down if life seems too simple. Her version of events will always be colourful and she will love adding spice to her tales; please recheck with the parties involved before taking any decisions.

As a mother, she is fun. She needs a lot of help when the children are small and starts bonding with them in earnest once they start to talk intelligently.

At the Workplace
They have the gift of the gab and careers for them must highlight this talent. They can be wonderful sales people, negotiators, coordinators and writers. Their ability to comprehend complex facts, and explain them in simple terms, makes them good teachers and trainers. Their quick thinking, adaptability, versatility and nervous, restless energy make them excel in fields as varied as sports and fashion, and even politics. Creative and talented, they shine in their fields but they need to be challenged. You can expect them to change their minds about their career many times before settling on one. More than money, it is the challenge of using their minds that keeps them interested in their career.

Geminis can enlighten the world with their views and they can also walk away from consequences without a backward glance. Air gives them flight and it also gives them a flighty temperament. The biggest lesson that they need to learn is to move beyond discussions – to actually implement.

Creative, intelligent, venturesome and adaptable – Geminis always live their lives in the stratosphere and always remain adolescents at heart.

Famous Gemini Personalities
Georgio Armani, Harrison Ford, Jessica Simpson, Paolo Maldini, Raj Babbar, Richard Hadlee, Salman Rushdie, Shaun Marsh.

4. CANCER

The waxing and waning Moon, ruler of emotions and creator of changeable moods, rules this sign. Cancer is the most loving and caring sign in the zodiac. Home, family and food top their list of desires. It is a cardinal sign; however, Cancerians never lead with aggression. They get their way by coaxing and by being persuasive.

They revere their homes and idolise their mothers. Cancerians will respect their mother's views and value her sacrifices for the family. Their regard for the mother is astonishing and unquestionable. Nurturing and caring come naturally to them. Even the males are amazingly good at cherishing friends and family. They embody the purest form of love – a mother's love. It works both ways with Cancerians. They try to be the best children to their parents; and they are definitely model parents – loving, caring, nurturing and even sacrificing.

These tender and loving creatures seem unsuited for the practical world, yet, in the depths of their personality, they hold the key to survival. Cancerians are stunningly tenacious. Just like a crab that holds on to its victim, Cancerians never abandon their mission till they achieve success. They keep driving themselves to work when everyone around them has given up the idea as lost.

They cherish the past and see it ensconced in a golden glow. Every phase of their life seems better as they pass it. As teenagers they look back at their childhood years, in their twenties they sigh about hostel life, in their thirties they raise a toast to their twenties and so on. They have sharp memories. In fact, they find strange comfort in hanging on to the past. They re-live their past and feel happy. They simply love photography as it accentuates their memories.

They have soulful eyes that clearly reflect their emotions. Their emotional intensity is something that others cannot understand. The Moon makes them extremely sensitive and touchy. The waxing and waning of the Moon affects their moods. They are at their crankiest best on moonless nights.

This extreme insecurity makes them even more sensitive to words and tones. They get hurt quickly. If your smile is a little less warm they will think you are not happy with them and get anxious. There is no way you can convince them otherwise; just be patient with their fears. Their imaginary fears are worse than true fears. The positive thing about their sensitivity is that it makes them extremely perceptive. They can read your eyes and heart; a Cancerian just needs to look into your eyes to know you.

They can develop a crippling inferiority complex. They constantly feel they are not good at something or not equipped to do something better. They always think of the worst possibilities and fret about the things that could go wrong. Insecurity makes them extremely stingy about money. They are always saving money, for they worry incessantly about the future, no matter how wealthy they are.

Cancerians make excellent friends and will always be loyal. They are the guys who care for you and feed you, and they are extremely sociable. There may be times when they wear masks of indifference or become reclusive when hurt. Dig deep and you will find total softies under the hard exterior.

Food is extremely important to them and they keep going back to their mother's cooking. They hate wasting food as they equate no food to poverty and dread being poor. Parties with them feature the choicest viands that warm the heart and fill the stomach, and lots of joy and cheer. They are not full-blown party animals, though they like to enjoy themselves with a select group of friends, preferably in the comfort of their own home. They have a fabulous sense of humour – a by-product of their sharp memories of observing small events in daily life.

Love will find Cancerians becoming deeply dippy. Loyalty, love, care and deep emotions mark their love. They can be highly romantic and create lovely romantic settings to woo their loves. Love, care and sensitivity characterise Cancerians. They shower their beloved with excessive affection, almost bordering on smothering. Their love is always for keeps. They get into anything in life, most of all love, only if there is a guarantee of permanence attached to it.

They are chocolaty-soft, yet ambitious and faithful to their goals. They will just hang in there, longing, waiting, till a goal is accomplished.

Cancer is ruled by the ever-changing Moon – which reflects the kaleidoscopic emotions of Cancerians. Cancer is symbolised by the Crab, which is known for being crabby and also tenacious. Cancer also rules the fourth house of the horoscope that indicates the home and mother.

Cancer – Suniel Shetty
Shilpa Shetty: 'He has got a macho image, but is actually a child at heart. A complete family man. A very successful businessman.'

Sanjay Dutt: 'Suniel helps everyone. He is one of the best human beings I have ever met.'

Raveena Tandon: 'He is like a security blanket. Everyone in the film industry call him 'Anna' with respect because he is like an elder brother, he is so protective about you.'

Suniel Shetty is associated with many causes related to children; he sang for a children's video, meets children of commercial sex workers and also helps cancer-afflicted children.[6]

Suniel has all the attributes of a true-blue Cancerian – sensitive, emotional, loving, caring, protective, a family man, children-loving and an excellent businessman.

Love and Marriage for Him
He is a true gentleman. This guy understands, loves, cares, makes you laugh, is extremely sentimental, remembers all the important dates and surprises you with his love and care in many ways. There is only one thing he needs – he wants you to love him the same way. The best part is that he is extremely easy to read.

He can sulk a lot. This guy does not get violently mad or abusive but just goes into a shell and refuses to come out till he is pampered and cajoled. This man will love his mother, so please don't try to force her out of his life – you won't succeed. It will be better if you make your peace and let her have that part of his heart. Plus you will never cook as well as his mother and you had better agree with that – that way, everyone will be happy.

---
[6] https://www.youtube.com/watch?v=TyU9wfHzC6s

He can worry a lot and needs you to tell him all the time that he can achieve the success he dreams of. Don't let his fears get the better of him and don't laugh at his fears. They are real for him. He has no ego issues and does not stop you from earning. On the contrary, he is happy if you are financially independent for it takes care of his fears related to money.

As a father, there is no one better. He mothers his children and is extremely protective of them. Nurturing comes naturally to him. You will need to tell him to give them a little space as they grow up for he will want to smother them in his love.

Love and Marriage for Her

She is extremely feminine, emotional, sensitive, caring, nurturing and shy. You need to give her a lot of care and attention. She needs constant appreciation to make her feel good about herself for she always frets and feels inferior to people around her. She cries a lot. She cries when sad and cries when happy, too. Her love can be overwhelming at times. If you love space in a relationship then please let her go for she can't understand that concept. She is a soft-hearted girl who needs to be treated with care.

Family is extremely important to her and she can sacrifice herself for it. Her love for her family is the value around which she weaves her whole life. She loves her photo albums and her house is full of pictures of family. She is happy just being with her family, cooking for them, feeding them, travelling with them and of course, taking photos of them! She is not extravagant and prefers saving to spending. Luxury gifts are not her only idea of romance.

She is the ideal mother. Her children are her life and she does everything for them. She is understanding, loving and nurturing. She knows how to bring them up with softness yet instil the right values in them. She finds it very difficult to handle the fact that they can get along fine without her when they grow up.

At the Workplace

Cancerians appear soft and act like kindly souls, so it is quite difficult to imagine them in leading roles. But, they are able leaders, who treat their subordinates like a parent or elder sibling would. They shine in the corporate and artistic world as they are not only ambitious but also extremely imaginative. Human resources, finance, cinema and music are good as careers for them.

They do not like professions where they need to be solitary for long periods of time or which keep them away from their families. Reward them with money for it is very important to them. You can even offer them family holidays as rewards – they will work harder! Please appreciate them too, for they need that pat on the back to feel good about themselves. If you want people who will stick around for a long time, then hire Cancerians.

As corporate honchos they will nurture their small businesses into empires, without being too flashy and by keeping strict control on the budget.

Loving, caring and protective – Cancerians are strongly tenacious and their perseverance and loyalty is unquestionable.

Famous Cancer Personalities

Charlize Theron, Halle Berry, Kishore Kumar, Suniel Shetty, Wesley Snipes.

5. LEO

The generous and proud Sun, the king of gods, rules this majestic sign. Leos are characterised by their majestic stride and a proud glow. Even if they are from the humblest of origins, their swagger is evident. They always act like royalty. Exactly like a lion in the wild, they are lazy, royal, and know that respect is due to them. They are never in a hurry or appear flustered, for such agitation is for common people, not royals.

They live life king-size; they like the spotlight and love being the centre of attraction. They don't mind being melodramatic and over-the-top to attract attention. Leos always think big, on a grand scale and have the ability to make small ideas shine like the brightest stars. Glory is their biggest need and want, and what they envisage for themselves has no boundaries.

There is fun and splendour when a Leo is around. He loves hosting parties and you can expect them to swagger into your birthday bash and say that the treat is on them. The generosity of these guys can be quite amazing. They are excellent hosts too. Leos are usually talented in some field and you do not have to coax them to show off their talents. They naturally move towards the arc lights. They love creating drama around themselves and you always feel that extraordinary things happen to them.

Leos are natural protectors and love being leaned upon. The Leo desire to help and be of value to people make them take on tasks and challenges without worrying about the outcome. The only thing they demand from you is absolute loyalty – just like a king would demand from his subjects. He will give you anything if you are true and faithful to him and adore him unconditionally. They love to give advice, whether you want it or not. They want to be the leaders of the pack with everyone else following them. They have a distinctly stylish persona and are passionate and big-hearted people.

Romance will always be in the air with a Leo. These guys know how to impress and of course the women of this sign expect nothing less when they are being romanced. They want their romance to be the most talked about and the most happening. But once they take the bait they are too lazy to be unfaithful! They always look well turned out. They spend a fortune on their pampering routine and absolutely love branded or designer clothes.

Anger management can be an issue with them for they can truly roar their opinions. They lack the sensitivity to realise it is not the time for ego bashing. They sulk when not given importance but Leos will always be ready to forgive – if you accept your mistake and accede to their point of view!

Despite their outward confidence and awe-inspiring power, there is an element of insecurity deep within them. They try and mask it with their bravado; don't ever try to pry them open. Your silent sensitive understanding will help you get brownie points with them. But never doubt or taunt their efforts when the tide is against them. The Leo ego gets easily hurt and they find it very hard to recover their lost confidence. More importantly, you would have also made a bitter enemy.

Leos are quite spiritual and religious as well. They not only like to show their big *tilaks* and *rudraksh* necklaces for effect but are also deeply in tune with their spiritual side. As they grow older, the anger and brashness of Leo makes way for a more subtle confidence and they become more accommodating of others' views. Emotional sensitivity is lacking in them, though. They find it very hard to know what's wrong with you till you spell it out.

The same confidence and positivity that makes them leaders can also turn into self-assured arrogance and make them disregard vital information in their belief of assured success. Their ego is the weak link in the chain and it can lead them astray. Leos need a stable person by their side when they achieve the success they always dreamed about, for it is very easy for them to lose their bearings in the adrenalin rush of success and become pompous personalities.

A Leo's innate desire to shine and attain glory probably originates from its ruler, the Sun, the brightest body in the solar system. Remember, all planets revolve around the mighty Sun. Leo is symbolised by the Lion, the ruler of the jungle, and naturally Leos lord it over all. Leo also rules the fifth house of love, romance, arts and pleasure. A Leo's ideal scenario would be to laze around enjoying the pleasures of life.

Leo – Robert Redford
Redford has been a vocal critic of Barack Obama for his lack of follow-through on environmental policies. He wrote, 'One reason I supported President Obama is because he said we must protect clean air, water and lands. But what good is it to say the right thing unless you act on it?'[7]

'Any time I saw people treated unfairly because of race, creed, whatever — it struck a nerve.'[8]

Robert Redford has the generous spirit, the desire to protect the weak and also the rebelliousness of a natural Leo.

Love and Marriage for Him
You need to be the milder one for there is no way a Leo can let another roar in his castle. But do not fret, for despite his high-handed ways, this guy is quite a charmer if you play your part well. He knows how to romance you with flowers, love notes and fancy getaways. This guy can be the epitome of romance if you know how to handle him. He always has an opinion on what looks good on you. Dress well, especially in public, and conduct yourself with dignity, for you are his queen.

Never seek to command; and remember, a little flattery will help you get your desires. This guy craves respect and wants to be pampered. Do not expect him to understand your tears; it will be easier on both of you if you tell him what makes you sad. He is a generous soul but he needs to be gently nudged in the right direction. He will bring excitement and glamour to the relationship while you should supply calm stability to keep the relationship going. You have to control the money, for he likes to splurge. However, please do not overrule him in public. He cannot tolerate anyone undermining his image.

As a father, he adores his children. He is sure to spoil them and cannot hear a word against his precious treasures. He also likes telling them how to lead their lives.

---
[7] http://en.wikipedia.org/wiki/Robert_Redford
[8] http://www.aarp.org/entertainment/movies-for-grownups/info-01-2011/robert-redford-unedited

Love and Marriage for Her
Stylish and regal, this lady surely likes to turn heads. If she holds your hand, feel very proud, for she does not easily look upon a person as equal. This girl is not made for domesticity and needs a lot of help in that department. She wants to move around, meet people and party. She wants to be seen and loves to see the world. You cannot keep such a vital, charming force cooped up at home. Never lord over her in public. She likes to laze around and loves getting pampered. Massages and aroma therapy remind her of her queenly destiny and she wants to have as many of them as possible. She also needs a fat bank balance to take care of her needs.

She needs lots of attention from her partner as she has a tendency to be highly demanding and controlling in love. You need to learn the subtle art of being in control without stifling her spirit or curtailing her independence.

She adores her children and never lets anyone reprimand them. She teaches them to be perfectly dressed and well mannered. She is very ambitious for them too, and makes them dream big dreams.

At the Workplace
Leos are very ambitious. They cannot start at the bottom and always think of leading. They have the self-assured confidence to make them reach the top. They love the spotlight and want to work for glory.

They need help in putting their grand plans into action and here, Virgos or Capricorns can help with their ability to flesh out ideas. Leos need a little help in deciding where to focus their brilliance. They are a little unfocused in the beginning and do not have the patience to wait for their ideas to materialise.

They need massive doses of appreciation while they do their work. Never appreciate them in private. It is much better if you praise them in public and criticise in private. They can be a little lazy too, and like to work smart rather than hard. They are good delegators who know how to pass on tedious jobs while retaining the glory for themselves.

As bosses they will be commanding but generous. They are the easiest to handle if you know to submerge your ego. If they are happy with your work they will never stop to think before rewarding you.

Leos will be generous yet arrogant, loving yet dominating and always think big. They have oodles of energy, which needs some focus.

Famous Leo Personalities
Donald Bradman, Gulzar, Jehangir Sabavala, Leo Tolstoy, Madonna, Prithviraj Sukumaran, Rajiv Gandhi, Ratnakar Shantaram Pai, Robert Redford, Sanjukta Panigrahi, Pyarelal (Laxmikant), Blake Lively.

6. VIRGO

Virgo endows a person with caring and perfectionism. The god of industriousness, 'Planet Y' (*see Glossary*), also known for his healing powers, rules over this sign and gives it the gift of medicine. Virgos know the right medicines for every ailment and always have a medicine chest ready.

Meticulous and neat, Virgos rarely look dishevelled or out of place. You never find them dressed vulgarly. Tastelessness in thought, word and deed anger them. There is a certain dignified charm about them.

Duty comes first. They love and care for their families. Though they might not be very expressive in their sentiments, they are capable of sacrificing a lot for their loved ones. They take on huge responsibilities and kill themselves worrying, yet never let their family know of their problems. Virgos are never rebellious.

They often hide their soft and caring demeanour under an aloof, precise exterior. This is because they do not feel confident enough to reveal their true feelings. They can never rid themselves of the feeling that they lack something and never really feel comfortable about their accomplishments.

Their clarity of thought is one of their most interesting traits. They state their views clearly and precisely. An oft-irritating but very useful feature of their clarity of thought is their desire to finely dissect every subject that comes their way. They can be accused of needlessly checking details but cannot stop themselves till they satisfy their intense desire to know everything there is to know about a particular subject. They are highly analytical, masters of extrapolation and deduction. Virgos never accept a fact for a fact till they exhaustively research and find the truth. They plan, sort, classify and store. They can always finely discriminate between a half-truth and truth and say so without dissembling.

They want everything around them to be neat and clean. They need friends who bring in cheer and enthusiasm into their lives or become prone to spend their time worrying, cleaning and thinking. This habit of worrying, added to their apparent love of solitude, can make them reclusive. They prefer the company of books and nature.

Routine ensnares them. They want to be bound by routine and rules, and make too many of them, to the dismay of others. They have fixed times for everything, from their meals to the time they sleep, or else feel vulnerable. Impulsive behaviour and careless extravagance has no place in their book of life.

Duty-minded and highly conscientious, they are a delight to work with on serious projects. Meticulous to a fault, perfectionist to the core, Virgos bring in high ethics to every sphere of life. Love will rarely find them willing or volatile. When they fall in love their inherent insecurity usually makes them more than willing to sacrifice their love for they see all the ineptitudes in themselves. If you love them, tell them so and never expect them to make the first move.

Health is a worrisome topic for them. Their knowledge of medicine, along with in-depth analysis of almost all the illnesses, ensures this. However, it helps them choose healthy lifestyles. Virgos are the people you can expect to stick to a strict diet without ever giving in to temptation.

They are conscientious savers and do not spend without thinking. They would rather obsessively clean and shine their clothes and boots than buy new ones. Expect them to invest wisely. They make up their minds only after reading and analysing historical data and reports.

Anger is supplanted by criticism in Virgos. They are very hard to please and are nitpickers. When Virgos get riled, they do not shout but just keep on analysing and criticising everything that troubles them. Their real challenge is to expand their perspective beyond details and look at the bigger picture. Virgos have a tendency to rehearse for life rather than live it. As they see it, they are never prepared enough to take full advantage when an opportunity presents itself.

'Planet Y' compels its children to walk the path of perfectionism and diligence. Virgo is symbolised by the Virgin, who reflects purity of thought, conscientiousness and inner health and beauty. Virgo also rules the sixth house of work and health.

Virgo – Dr P.B. Sreenivas

Dr P.B. Sreenivas has sung in Telugu, Hindi, Kannada, Tamil and Malayalam films. He dresses immaculately with a bright *srichurnam* on his forehead, a *zari* turban and a *zari* shawl casually draped over the left shoulder, and he sits surrounded by books and diaries.[9] 'Writing has been my passion and I have written more than two lakh songs of all kinds – ghazals, bhajans, verses, dohas, etc. – in many languages. I meticulously learnt to read and understand them. As a first step, I released a book titled *Pranavam,* in eight languages.'[10]

Dr P.B. Sreenivas exemplifies the perfection-seeking Virgo with his flair for learning new languages and his meticulous attention to details.

Love and Marriage for Him

He loves silently. Don't expect him to understand your sighs. If you want flowers, tell him – he will surely get them for you. Responsible and caring, he does what is expected of him. He never lets you down with careless behaviour. There is a deep thoughtfulness behind all his actions.

He prefers a wife who is rational, independent and cheerful. Tears, emotional outbursts and clinginess make him very uncomfortable. Mushy scenes and flirtatious overtones also make him very uneasy. He dislikes plunging necklines and flashy clothes. So if you are trendy and like to wear outrageous costumes, remember to overlook this guy.

He does not stop you from working. On the contrary, it helps to keep his tendency to worry at bay. He also helps out at home. You can expect him to chart out all the duties and delegate each between the two of you. He will never shirk his time at dishwashing and you too will have to follow his example. You need to understand his desire for cleanliness for he cannot live in an unclean environment.

He is an easy guy to understand for his wants are few and well-defined. He wants his food at specific times and is very particular about what he eats. If you do not show the same regard for decorum as he does, or try and boss him around, he can just leave one day. He can easily break ties and walk off without a backward glance if he feels ill-used.

---

[9] http://www.hindu.com
[10] http://www.hindu.com/fr/2008/09/19/stories/ 2008091951110200.htm

Though he doesn't part with money easily, he is not stingy on necessities either. He will be a duty-minded and responsible partner and you will never find unpaid bills when he is around.

As a father, he wants his children to excel in academics. He worries for them and his soul travels with them when they go to take important exams! He does not mind changing nappies and is exceptionally well-read on the medical emergencies of children.

Love and Marriage for Her

Gentle and hardworking, she spends her days thinking and caring for her family. She has a ladylike charm about her. She works with quiet courage and never gives up in the face of disaster. She may worry a lot but when problems do come, they find her ready with answers.

She takes care of you and is very conscientious in performing her duties. She does not laze around, especially when there is work to be done. She is always the first one to get up and start working and the last one to rest. She needs a man who is responsible, yet fun-loving. She does have a pessimistic streak and will be glad if you can show her an optimistic view. But don't expect her to thank you for that, she will still cling to her morbid thoughts and will need cheering up.

She definitely knows how to nag and criticise and you better not try the same tactic on her for she will not like being told that she is wrong. She cannot be lied to, either, for she gets to the truth with her precise questioning.

Loving and gentle, she is a good mother. She takes care to inculcate the right values in her children and brings them up with a gentle but firm hand.

At the Workplace

Virgos are hard working, analytical and good with numbers. They have no desire to outshine others and are happy doing their own work. They prefer jobs that make them think and analyse. They are blessed with superb manual skills, make fine technicians and bring in great refinement, order and fastidiousness to work.

They also have the gift for clear, concise language. They insist on the right words and hence can be good teachers. The fact is that they are always ready to learn and like doing things on their own rather than leading. Their arguments are too logical to be ignored, and if you do, you lose a good worker. They can be good actors too. With their eye for detail and keen powers of observation, Virgos will excel in any field that requires logic and analysis, and demands perfection.

Virgos can go on and on with the same precision day in and day out. They are extremely intelligent, gentle and meticulous, prudent and precise, pure-minded and conscientious. They need to know that mental preparation and rehearsals are good, but going out there and performing with power and energy is even more important.

Famous Virgo Personalities

Bishen Singh Bedi, Chris Gayle, Chellapalli Chittibabu, Hussein Khwajerwala, Kate Winslet, Lal Bahadur Shastri, P.B. Sreenivas, Prithviraj Sukumaran, Rohit Roy, Venugopal Dhoot.

7. LIBRA

Venus, the planet of beauty, grace and luxury, rules these happy people. Librans exude charm that is just right and in perfect balance. There is something about them that pulls people towards them. They attract with a witty remark or a thoughtful response. Librans are characterised by Venusian dimples and a dazzlingly sweet smile.

Air is the element of Libra. It makes their views expansive and broadens their horizons. Librans are not ruled by conventions alone. They seek a balance between tradition and revolutionary views. They analyse each thought and respect each dream without seeking to condemn.

The power of speech belongs to a true Libran. When they speak, you hear beauty, intelligence, wit and humour. They are quite honest in their dealings without being blunt for they never hurt people intentionally. Diplomacy and tact are inherent to them. They also have the ability to empathise. Sadly, this often works to their disadvantage. These poor guys, who are so hell-bent on being fair, find it very difficult to win an argument for they see exactly what you mean and know why you believe in what you believe.

They find it difficult to reach conclusions too. They are prone to over-analysis, which further confuses them. In order to take decisions fast you need to be a little biased and Librans with their ability to look at the pros and cons of everything, lack that bias. The Libran mind swings to the opposite word or idea when you tell them something, which adds to their dilemma.

Venus accentuates their creative talents. You will find that Librans will be drawn to some kind of creative field. Most Librans have a melodious voice and they can be fabulously harmonious singers. They can also be those dancers who effortlessly flow into a rhythm while smiling blissfully. Their fashion sense is quite evident in their appearance. They can carry off modern clothes in the most elegant manner. They walk with decided style. Beauty is a Libran thing. They do not understand the value of saving and in keeping with their love for shopping, can really splurge on fashion.

Love will be extremely important to Librans. They will be in love with the concept of love and will want to be in love. Romance is a Libran art. A Libran can never live without a partner. They instinctively think, breathe and live the life that their life partners want from them. This overwhelming need for love will see them go through many relationships before they find true love.

Librans like doing things with their loved ones; they like companionship and need a person to share their life with. They need a lot of attention too. They are extremely sociable creatures and like spending time with their extended families and friends.

There is an element of frivolity in them that, if left unchecked, can make them extremely shallow, leading them to pursue happiness in materialism and mindless chatter. Librans can be extremely talented yet lack the passion or drive to turn their talent into a formidable achievement. They need a stabilising force to ground them. The lazy Libra needs to understand that there is no short cut to hard work and only talk will not guarantee them success!

They like neatness around them. Their sense of aesthetics is very well-developed and they can turn a small cramped room into an elegant home. They are extremely sensitive to colours and are highly colour coordinated too. They are elegant and their dreams are elegant too.

The only flaw in this lovely sign is that it can take life easy and spend a lot of time analysing and dissecting ideas rather than working towards a better future. They run the risk of too much analysis leading to paralysis of action. Librans can also be quite lazy. They keep procrastinating till the last minute. While evolved Librans are judicious, immature Librans can be judgemental. Some love being party animals and drown themselves in the pleasures of life, ignoring their responsibilities.

Libra is ruled by Venus, the planet of love, arts and pleasure. They seek all of these in good measure. Libra is symbolised by a set of Scales, which shows their sense of fairness. Libra rules the seventh house of relationships – understandable why the Librans place a high premium on their relationships.

Libra – Katy Perry

'I'm on this extraordinary adventure, and if I have no one to talk to at the end of the night, I feel lonely.'[11]

'I'm a good girl because I really believe in love, integrity, and respect. I'm a bad girl because I like to tease. I know that I have sex appeal in my deck of cards. But I like to get people thinking. That's what the stories in my music do.'[12]

'I'm a woman who likes to be courted, strongly. Never say never, I guess you'd say. I'll let love take the lead on that.'

Creative, irrepressible and romantic, Katy Perry is the Libran who thinks differently.[13]

Love and Marriage for Him

You have a charming guy by your side. He is intelligent and witty with an attractive smile. It does not irritate him if your girlfriends turn up en masse. He likes travelling, meeting new people and discovering new thoughts with you by his side.

He does not run scared at your independence and free-spiritedness. The best thing about this guy is that he is open to new ideas without insisting on tradition. The only thing he insists on, though, is neatness around him. He cannot live in disorderly surroundings.

He needs you to be the more decisive one. He takes his time rationalising ideas and you can let him do so while you go on with your life. He does not mind so long as you listen to him, when he finally makes up his mind. Aggressive women turn him off. You will have to be the perfect balance between independent and intelligent.

You need to be the more stable one and push him to achieve his goals.

Money can be a concern. If you want investments and savings, you have to do them yourself. He can help but he can never be the propelling force in this area. Retail therapy works for him. It is your duty to ensure that he realises the problems of

---

[11] http://www.cosmopolitan.com/celebrity/exclusive/katy-perry-cover-interview-0809
[12] http://www.harpersbazaar.com/magazine/cover/katy-perry-interview-1210
[13] *DNA*, 3 Aug 2012, 'After hrs'

inordinate spending. He will always listen to reason – just couch it in appealing words.

As a father, he is loving and caring, but does not displace you from the number one position in his heart. He is fair and just, and shows his children that there are many ways to look at a problem. They learn to be more compassionate and understanding from him. Control will never be his idea of love and he will like to let them be free to choose their own path.

Love and Marriage for Her
She needs a lot of attention and needs to be told constantly that you love her. She loves to talk and fills you in on the details of her day and her thoughts. If communication is not your plus point, you have to learn to make some small talk, for she cannot bear silence for too long. She can be deeply analytical and logically astute. Her mind is sharp, and interestingly, no matter how adorably feminine she looks, works with male logic. It will not be easy to win an argument with her. If she allows you to win sometimes, it's because she is fair and also knows the 'man' in you needs to win.

Sensitive and caring, she likes to live her life with you. She does not admire lonely pursuits and can never understand if you lock yourself away in your library. She needs friends, companions and especially you around, to enjoy her life.

Money is not her strong point and budgets make her uncomfortable. She easily takes refuge in retail therapy if something troubles her for long. She is a comfort-eater and overindulges her sweet tooth.

As a mother, she is extremely loving, without losing perspective. This is a mother who knows her children thoroughly and does not overemphasise their virtues. She does not downplay their problems and is extremely fair in her judgment.

At the Workplace
Talented and communicative, Librans can hold sway over sales, marketing and even corporate training. These guys talk so well that it is a shame not to use their expressive talents. They can be great lawyers and judges too, with their penchant for seeing both sides of the problem and their love of arguments.

They are very creative and can be artists, singers and dancers, or can use their artistic temperament and fashion sense to become interior decorators and stylists.

Libra is a cardinal sign and Librans make good bosses. They are not commanding or aggressive but know how to get their work done smoothly. Whatever they do, you can be sure that they talk, express and communicate their way through it.

The Scales of Libra make this sign always seek balance. Loving yet argumentative, creative yet balanced, Librans embody charm and grace, and no one can make others work with a smile like Librans.

Famous Libra Personalities
Anu Malik, Douglas Jardine, James Franklin, Jean Shrimpton, Katy Perry, Karthik (singer), Laxmikant Berde, Narayan Dutt Tiwari, Sunil Mittal, Whoopi Goldberg, Laxmikant (Pyarelal).

8. SCORPIO

Scorpio is ruled by Pluto, the ruthless lord of the underworld. Pluto imparts strong passions and emotions in them. Being a Water sign, Scorpio is the most intense and passionate of all the signs in the zodiac with deep emotions and feather-touch sensitivity.

They have the ability to understand the emotions of anyone they meet. You find it hard to save your secrets from them and their deep penetrating gaze. There is a hypnotic quality to them and, though they usually appear controlled and reserved in public, you sense a seething volcano beneath.

Passion is very important to them. Scorpios never do anything half-heartedly. This makes them formidable adversaries for they can even put their lives at risk in order to achieve what they want.

They do not mind living in deplorable conditions and do not care for food or entertainment when they are in achievement mode. They have unbelievable endurance and are able to withstand the greatest shocks without a flicker of emotion on their faces. They either pull themselves up or waste their lives indulging in extreme emotions.

They also have the ability to change if life offers them no recourse. They hold within themselves the ability to be the scorpion with the sting in its tail, the grey lizard, or the preying eagle. The scorpion is evidently vengeful while the grey lizard will hide its emotions for years and kill itself with its poisonous thoughts. The eagle is the most evolved variety of Scorpio. It rises above base emotions and preys only for food. Metamorphosis is part and parcel of their lives and they change continuously over the years. Their emotions, however, remain the same. Scorpios are very thin-skinned and are easily and deeply hurt at the smallest of comments. This hurt is rarely seen as they show inscrutable exteriors. Look into their eyes and you may see the fire blazing.

They stand up for what they believe in. They have a strong protective streak. Their emotions make them vulnerable to the people they love. If they see someone close to them deeply hurt, they do not hesitate to try and make amends or even take up arms for them.

They do not make friends easily nor do they suffer fools, but, once they decide to include you in their hallowed circle, they stand by you forever. Loyalty is a deep Scorpio trait and the flip side of their love and loyalty will be that they will expect you to be the same.

They have the urge to explore the deepest, darkest mysteries of the world. Scorpios like learning mystical sciences and find the study of the occult familiar territory. Spirituality interests them too and they have an instinctive knowledge of forces greater than themselves. The most startling fact about them is that whatever they think, they can be.

They do not mind trying negative professions or experimenting with addictions to see if they can have a hold over them. They can either work themselves out of addictions or change their lives for the better, if they think they should, or wallow in substance abuse and sadistic, perverse and cruel acts.

Love is very important to Scorpios. They need a soul mate and someone into whose eyes they look and know that they are their long-lost life mates. There is something ethereal and supernatural about Scorpios; especially their loves. Eroticism is very important to them too and they know how to express themselves sexually. Scorpios intensely scrutinise each and every aspect of sex and it plays a major part of their mind and lives. Love will find them immensely passionate and ludicrously jealous too. Scorpios want their partner to love them body and soul and will not permit any distractions.

Anger is a very strong emotion in them. They find it hard to forgive and can carry anger in them for many years. Vindictiveness is a part of their nature and you can be sure that they have a well-thought-out plan to bring about their opponents' downfall. If you invite the wrath of a Scorpio he will surely get back at you. Until then, he will behave as if you don't exist. He mentally switches you off from his life. They also need to win; win at any cost, even their lives. They simply hate losing and the person to whom they lose. Beware.

Money is quite dear to them. They are not prone to impulsive buying and prefer saving and investing rather than squandering their money.

Scorpios have ideals and like to follow them. Their ideals can be good or bad and they follow them with an abiding passion. A ruthless Scorpio has no tinge of mercy while a Scorpio dedicated to high ideals will be utterly true.

It's a pity that astronomers choose to name a celestial body depending on its size and not by its influence. Pluto may be called a *minor planet* by them, but astrologically, Scorpio is ruled by the most powerful 'planet' in the universe, Pluto. Scorpio rules the eighth house of mysteries: sex, death and regeneration. That makes Scorpios penetrate the deepest mysteries of life and rise like a phoenix in the toughest trials of life.

Scorpio – Scarlett Johansson

Scarlett Johansson is a true Scorpio woman, absolutely aware of her sex appeal and extremely private about her life. She has been voted the sexiest woman innumerable times by different magazines.

She rarely comments on her romantic relationships (including her broken marriage to actor Ryan Reynolds) and does not sashay down a red carpet unless she has to.[14] During the filming of *Match Point*, director Woody Allen described Johansson as 'sexually overwhelming', saying that he found it 'very hard to be extra witty around a sexually overwhelming, beautiful young woman who is wittier than you are'.[15]

Love and Marriage for Him

He demands and needs your complete love. This man wants a soul mate.

If your idea of love is friendly companionship and you like ribbing your loved ones with friendly good humour, please spare this guy for you may hurt him a thousand different ways in a day.

His ambition is his driving force and you have to share him with it. He can drive himself hard, wanting you to carry out the more conventional duties of the house. He is the more controlling of the two. Authority flows from him and he does not like to

---

[14] http://www.harpersbazaar.com/magazine/cover/scarlett-johansson-cover-story-0209
[15] http://en.wikipedia.org/wiki/Scarlett_Johansson

be answered back. You need to be the softer one in order to keep the relationship in balance. If you ever want to do something against his wishes, ask respectfully. Never try and deceive him for he knows you too well to be fooled. Jealousy is very strong in him and he just hates to see others stare at you.

He is a controlling father and wants his children to listen to him yet he will also know their dreams and will do everything possible to fulfil them. There is always a reserve in him that intimidates his children despite his love for them. He demands their respect.

Love and Marriage for Her
This lady is strong, ambitious and ready for anything in life. You have to love her to be near her. She cannot accept a man who flirts (even harmlessly) or even thinks of complimenting another woman. You have to love only her, think only of her and be only with her to make her love you. Absolute loyalty means a lot to her.

Be extremely careful of what you say to her for forgiveness does not come naturally to her and she could be planning revenge. No problem or burden can ever stop her from working towards her dreams. This lady works with or without your help, but it is better to extend your support to her, for, in return, she gives herself wholeheartedly to the relationship.

Be under no misconceptions for even when this lady uses her charms, she dominates. Though she likes a man who is in control, she has her own individuality and does not allow anyone to ride roughshod over her. She is extremely protective of her family and anyone who dares harm them had better watch out.

She is a loving yet controlling mother. She commands respect from her children and knows their deepest secrets without them uttering a word.

At the Workplace
Profound perceptions and unorthodox ideas characterise Scorpios. Scorpios bring in intuition, aggression and competitiveness to anything they do. Scorpios want a profession in which they can delve for the deepest truths. With their penchant for uncovering mysteries, they can become great researchers, detectives or scientists. They work with passion and integrity and are never content till they use their reasoning and analytical powers to full effect.

The Scorpio sensitivity to emotions also makes them talented actors. Whatever role they perform in their workspace is only temporary. Scorpios have the innate ability to rise from the ashes. They can transcend and transform. They steer clear of convention and tradition to construct something new and extraordinary.

Water endows them with deep emotions and a sensitivity that surpasses all. Scorpios will be deeply passionate and want to live life profoundly. They experience every emotion and penetrate every secret they encounter. If they can discipline themselves and channelise their great inner power in the right direction, then they can master anything in the world.

Famous Scorpio Personalities
Bruno Alves, Chitrashi Rawat, John Terry, J.H. Blackburne, Meenakshi Seshadri, Raghuvaran, Rajkumar Hirani, Ritha Devi, Rock Hudson, Sarfraz Nawaz, Scarlett Johansson, Stephan Andersen, Yousuf Pathan.

9. SAGITTARIUS

The knowledgeable and benevolent Jupiter shines on this exuberant bundle of energy. Sagittarians radiate positivity. Defeats never bother them and you rarely find them down in the dumps.

They love talking with wild gestures. Do not think they are airbags. Sagittarius is probably the most intelligent amongst all zodiac signs, besides Aquarius. They intuitively understand the most arcane subjects and are able to talk about them with such vitality that the topics do not seem uninteresting. They are the professors of the zodiac.

They are frank, honest and opinionated. Sagittarians will tell it as it is. Don't expect them to spare your feelings. They would rather tell the truth and the whole truth.

Adventurous travels excite them as much as new thoughts. They like to go where their fancy takes them. Speed thrills them. They love whooshing around in their thunderous vehicles with not a single thought for safety. The lucky Sagittarians have been blessed in a way – they have the most robust, healthy and athletic bodies amongst all the twelve signs. They are the most fun-loving friends. They enthuse others to go on long treks and see the wild side of life.

Independent and strong, they find it very difficult to do anyone's bidding. They are never submissive. The main problem with them is their lack of understanding. They are able to decode the most complex ideas yet find decoding their loved ones the hardest task of all. They will never read the undercurrents in any conversation and will blunder tactlessly while giving their honest opinions. They expect everyone to be as frank as them and need to be reminded of feelings and emotions.

Love will not find them easy nuts to crack. Sagittarians are too engrossed in their wild ideas to actually think of love. They are friendly creatures and have hordes of friends of either sex but rarely think of them as more than friends. Actually Sagittarians are quite apt to make the wrong decisions about the kind of partner they need, for they lack sensitivity and empathy. They don't like being tied down to a domestic existence and will always rebel against strong bonds. They can have a lot of relationships without giving love much thought and might start thinking of settling down quite late in life. But a true Sagittarian is so brutally honest that he will be quite open about past relationships.

Sagittarians have a spiritual streak in them. They believe that there is a higher power at work in their lives. Their desire for spiritual knowledge can lead them to search for higher truths. They can also become quite ritualistic in their beliefs.

Money does not mean much to them. They prefer glory and applause to cash. Their instinct is to gamble on money rather than stock up on it. They also like fighting for the underprivileged. They are strong and resilient fighters who stand up for their beliefs.

Anger management is a key issue with them for they can really let their anger flare. Their temper is a sight to behold for they can rip their opponent apart with their strong words and aggressive stance. Run for cover when the archer unslings his bow and arrow!

There is a slight clumsiness about them. They drop things, splatter food and litter their rooms. Food is their weakness for sure. But their extreme enthusiasm and love for sports help to keep their calories in check. They are also the biggest pranksters of the zodiac. They are goofballs, really, and love practical jokes and slapstick comedy.

Volatile and wild, Sagittarians will definitely dream big dreams and not be bothered by narrow-minded beliefs. The archer's arrows may be scattered at the beginning, but when he starts aiming them right, you know he will be a winner. They love the arc lights, and feel immense joy on stage. They are extraordinarily good at the physical expressions of art, like dance. They are natural masters at practising sports as an art as well.

Sagittarius is ruled by the planet of knowledge – Jupiter. The largest planet in the solar system, the 'Guru' makes Sagittarians the teachers of the zodiac. Sagittarius is symbolised by the half-human, half-animal Centaur, the Archer – which depicts the ambition, energy, dynamism, restlessness and candour of the zodiac sign. Sagittarius corresponds to the ninth house of spirituality, philosophy, travel, law, education and writing – the natural areas of interest for the archers.

Sagittarius – Brad Pitt
Brad Pitt's life or his path was never charted out with great detail.

In his last semester at university he realised, 'I can leave.' He dropped out of college, packed his bags and headed west to pursue an acting career in Los Angeles.[16]

'I do have a kind of knee-jerk reaction to go the other way than I'm supposed to.'

'If you look at where Brad came from and the transformations he has realised, you see a person who's staged multiple revolutions in his life and career,' says *Moneyball* director, Bennett Miller. 'There's a revolutionary spirit there.'[17]

Pitt exemplifies Sagittarian thought, honesty, generosity and unpredictability in his actions and words.

Love and Marriage for Him
He is your best friend. He pushes you to achieve your dreams just like he motivates himself, but do not expect him to stay at home for long. He loves travelling to different places and meeting lots of new people. Be ready for adventure and keep your bags packed! You have to prefer the adventurous ways of travel rather than luxury, for he prefers the wild. Household duties rarely interest him.

Only a strong, independent lady may apply. He gives you enough space in the relationship but absconds at the first sign of emotions. The best way to keep him is to let him live his life on his own terms and not bother him with household rules.

You need to be financially independent for this guy's money is always out for a gamble. His ideas might sound great and might actually be great too, but you will be better off saving and investing on your own.

If you have views, express them. This guy will definitely not understand moods or sighs. He will be your buddy whom you feel free to talk about any subject. He is the right guy for a woman who has her own views and does not need a man for sustenance. He loves showering you with gifts whenever it fancies him.

---
[16] http://www.biography.com/people/brad-pitt-9441989x
[17] http://www.hollywoodreporter.com/news/brad-pitt-oscar-nomination-moneyball-tree-life-angelina-olie-284635

His anger will be bad and he can be really loud in his angry moments; but he will never hold a grudge and be calm after the stormy weather.

As a father, he may not be comfortable with his kids till they start talking intelligently. Then on, he loves to explain concepts to them and wants to see them grow as strong individuals.

Love and Marriage for Her
Independent and honest, she is the antithesis of a conventional bride. Do not expect her to simper and blush or take on a submissive role. She is loud, optimistic and highly volatile.

She will be a strong lady and I am not talking brute strength here. She will never lie low in any situation and will rarely run for cover. Her tactlessness can get her into many problems but her friends know her true worth as an honest person. She is not always callous. There is a sentimental side to her too, which can come as a surprise to many. You need to leave all your conservative ideas behind when you take her on.

The best way to bring a smile on her face is travel. She loves exploring new places and going off the beaten track. She enjoys partying and eating out. She admires a strong man who is secure in his love for her and does not stop her from doing her own thing. Jealousy and possessiveness are traits she hates.

This girl is the perfect friend and she will expect you to behave as her friend too. Money can be an issue with her for she rarely listens to advice or maintains budgets. She may take time to understand the duties of a wife, but once she does, she cheerfully accepts the responsibilities.

As a mother, she fills her children with optimism and enthusiasm. They learn to live their dreams and never think of giving up their ambitions.

At the Workplace
Sagittarians are enthusiastic, highly ambitious and optimistic. They seem to carry forward with the sheer force of their determination. It takes them time to realise what they want, but once they do, there is no stopping them.

Routine and monotony do not work for them. They need to think, travel and relax in between their bursts of energy. They can be professors who explain complex theories, or researchers excited by new possibilities. They can also be adventure travellers who host shows on their wild experiences or powerful sportsmen who reduce their opponents to pulp. They can be highly creative too and love professions that allow them to think out of the box.

They need lots of applause and work very hard for praise, so never be stingy in your admiration. Honour their achievements publicly.

Fire gives them volatility and enthusiasm. Honest, excited and aggressive, Sagittarians are fighters and never give up on their dreams.

Famous Sagittarius Personalities
Anthony Hopkins, A.K. Antony, Brad Pitt, Johannes Kepler, Loretta Young, Sajid Khan, Marlon Samuels, Uday Chopra, Shakti Samanta.

10. CAPRICORN

Saturn, the wise old man, watches over this sign. It imparts wisdom and responsibility along with a certain melancholy.

Capricorns are extremely responsible and aware of their duties. Even if they happen to be the youngest of all the siblings, they carry the weight of their families on their slim shoulders. Family is extremely important to Capricorns. They are capable of sacrificing their happiness for the good of their family.

They desire status and respect in society and are quietly ambitious. They diligently persevere in their dreams and work patiently towards their success. They rarely confess in you their plans of world dominance, which is what they actually want. Failure will just be another obstacle on their path and they will never give up.

Tradition is important to them, as is keeping up appearances. The Capricornian mood is not generally light and sunny and they find it hard to loosen up. Their sense of humour will be quite wry and dry. Only family and a few friends will see their lighter side.

The paradox with Capricorns is that they grow younger as they age. It is almost like the *Curious Case of Benjamin Button*! They laugh more and are more cheerful as they cross their thirties. Some of them may even philander once they become more successful and/or have fewer responsibilities.

Capricorns have a creative side to them too. They might keep it hidden and not boast about it but you can expect them to know its worth and they will know how to work their talent.

They always dress the part. They also talk well. Erudite and intelligent, their talk will never seem out of place in the glitziest of places though they might have come from humbler backgrounds.

Anger is non-existent in Capricorns. They find ways to get what they want without giving way to unnecessary negative emotions. They rarely think emotionally and never let emotions detract them from their ambitions. When they are young it will be a blessing, for you will rarely find anyone so young and so purposeful.

Love will not find them being wild-eyed or rebellious. Capricorns choose their partner with care and are not happy flouting society's rules. They want a partner who adds to their status and expect one who cares for repute and respect as much as them. Capricorns find it very hard to indulge in public displays of affections or even mouth sweet nothings. If you prefer a more expressive love then please move away, for you will find it impossible to change their habits.

With their intense desire to succeed, and their inability to get distracted, they tend to get quite melancholic if things do not go according to plan. They are normally grim and always seem chained up to their duties. Dark mood swings and deep depression can haunt them if they are not close to the material and emotional security that they aspire to. Money is very important to them. They love to conserve it and find it very difficult to part with it. Impulsiveness is not part of their DNA and they are savers by nature.

They are very logical. They do not think of wild, innovative ideas but are content implementing tried and tested methods on a larger scale. You can expect reason and sense from their decisions and they can be relied upon in times of stress. They know just how to manipulate situations to their own advantage. They lack the sensitivity of a Water sign, so their ways might not be that subtle but they know which strings to pull in order to reach their goals and they do not mind pulling them.

They have this cold practicality in them. They can even seem self-centred for their lack of empathy for people who don't matter to them. But Capricorns don't get flustered or distracted by emotions by this and continue with their relentless climb to the top.

Capricorn is ruled by the restrictive Saturn, which ties them up to tradition and customs and makes them very self-sufficient. Capricorn is symbolised by the mountain Goat, which shows their steady sense of purpose and secret ambition to reach the top. Capricorn rules the tenth house of career and fatherhood. They are really father figures to the family and are single-minded in their search for enduring power and legacy.

Capricorn – Sarah Palin

Sarah Palin could be the cover girl for a true-blue Capricornian woman. She has a conservative streak and loves being mom to her five children, but that does not dissuade her from being ambitious too. Politics is the natural arena for Capricorn and she plays it well, being an astute politician while managing five children. You can see her Capricornian attitude in the way she dresses too. She always puts her best foot forward and is rarely seen in mismatched attire. She is the quintessential Capricornian woman.

Love and Marriage for Him

He cares for you and is the most reliable and responsible person in your life. You can trust him to do what is right for the family. A Capricornian man does not mind marrying a woman older than him if she represents success and can be a catalyst to his growth.

He prefers a more conservative attitude in you and does not fall for tattoos or highlighted hair. He also wants you to love his family and not sever ties with them. There are only two things that count in his life – family and ambitions. His ambition is extremely important to him and, though he does not state his desires, he expects you to understand. While he works hard at his office he wants you to hold the fort at home.

Despite his stern and often despondent air, he loves compliments. He is a little stuffy and you will need to teach him the nuances of expressing love. Don't foresee a grim future with him for though he acts sombre and responsible he will have a wry sense of humour – and he will be more expressive of his love and even become more romantic, with age. Remember, he finds it extremely difficult to understand your emotions if you do not spell them out for him.

Capricorn rules fatherhood and they make the best father amongst all zodiac signs with the exception of Cancer. They love to nurture their offspring and watch them grow and make them proud. They preside over family get together and systematically plan for budgeted family holidays. At the same time, they know when to be strict.

Love and Marriage for Her

She is the ideal wife. You can easily take her to meet your parents. Her ideals are quite conservative and she loves family. This lady will be capable of great sacrifices for her family and will want to be there for them every time.

She carries herself with conviction and is very consistent in carrying out the duties and responsibilities expected of her. This is one lady who never cribs when you send money to your family. She may seem boring at times, because of her ideas of sober respectability and status. Give her some time and she can surprise you with her ability to laugh and have fun, especially when she reaches her thirties.

This lady values ambition and status above everything else. If you are ambitious and fulfil her dreams of status then she will be content to sit back and enjoy the life of a homemaker. But if you lack the burning drive to do something outstanding, hand the baton to her and she will be happy to chip in and steady the boat. She has an artistic side too. Please praise her talent even if she dismisses it as unworthy.

She loves being a mother and knows just how to blend authority with fun. She is very happy with her children and understands how to enjoy their childhood without letting them run all over her.

At the Workplace

Ambition and status rank high on their list. Capricornians want to make a name for themselves and leave a legacy behind for their children. They work extremely hard and soon make themselves indispensible.

They have the ability to be in the right place at the right time. You rarely find them in professions or careers that do not seem to be going anywhere. They can do anything, from finance to acting, and are always in careers that promise growth. Capricorns will have formidable organisational powers, the ability to ideate and manage larger realms with the knack of networking with people across boundaries to get their work done.

They can take a small idea and build on it with attention and detail, and still manage to keep the costs low. Capricorns also know the value of everything and everybody and you will find it hard to convince them with vague statements. Capricornian bosses get a lot of work done and are quite controlling too.

They manage to keep their emotions at check and are amazingly rational in the workspace. They definitely are caring bosses, almost father figures, but they are not the bosses who keep their doors open.

Earth adds stability and perseverance to Capricorns. They want to grow in stature and respect, are intimidating in their ambitions, and loving with their family.

Famous Capricorn Personalities

A.R. Antulay, Ashton Kutcher, Bhuvneshwar Kumar, Cary Grant, Mayawati, Megan McCafferty, Rafael Van Der Vaart, Ramesh Sippy, Robert Green, Manish Malhotra, Mohammad Ali, Sarah Palin, Shobhan Babu.

11. AQUARIUS

This exquisitely eccentric sign is ruled by the highly inventive and unconventional planet, Uranus. People of this sign never bow to conventions, neither in looks nor in thoughts. You can make out an Aquarian from miles away as they always stand out. From tattoos, wildly mismatched clothes and body piercings to new hairstyles and different hair colours every year, they love to experiment with their looks. They change drastically over the years.

Aquarians are always ahead of their times, they almost live in the future. Rigid ideas and unflinching beliefs are not their domain. Their ideas are more flexible, their views more humanitarian and their actions more free than the run-of-the-mill person. Uranus also rules science and invention and gives them a scientific bent of mind. This total disregard for conventions can also make them highly rebellious, especially in their youth. They love flouting rules and lock horns with rigid elders over the right way to live their lives.

An Aquarian can think so many thoughts in a moment that it will be very hard for them to be centred on one idea. They seem uninterested in the real world for they easily get bored with long conversations. They may seem spaced out at times and detached from the real world; it is at these times that their brilliant ideas and wild dreams will come to them. So let them be at those times. Everything from their clothes to their laughter will be wacky and startling. They love playing practical jokes but you can be sure that their idea of fun will never cause any harm to anyone.

They are intensely curious about people and emotions, and love to mentally dissect every one they meet. You can expect them to be empathetic for they understand how you feel. They are the friendliest people around and make reliable friends. They are very friendly and approachable, but they do not desire company for happiness. They give honest opinions and know when you respond with lies.

They also have a deep interest in spirituality and are psychic to some degree. Their sense of religion is not mired in rituals or traditions. They are more spiritual than religious. Humanity is their religion. Humanitarian and extremely broadminded, they can never be motivated by money. They prefer doing things that benefit the world. They are extremely non-materialistic and work for ideals and ideas rather than cash. Despite their predilection for non-monetary thoughts, they save for the future. Old age is their one concern and they battle it by saving for it.

Reform and revolution are the basis of their dreams. Their thoughts are not merely centred on their lives but about the greater good. However, they are not known for their love of cleanliness or orderly rooms; do not expect them to change, either. They can change the whole world but not themselves. Their anger is sudden and extremely volatile. They do not hold grudges but say what they think even if they know the consequences.

There is a clumsiness about Aquarians that makes them seem like accident-prone moving bodies. This is because they are constantly in the future, which makes them indifferent to the present and they do not always see what they do.

Their love lives are quite unique. They will rarely be love-struck for they simply cannot stay with one idea or person for long. They need a purpose in life and if they don't have a purpose they can drift from one relationship to another, innately curious about each person they meet no matter their looks or imperfections, and leave when they have deciphered all. Aquarians also find the idea of loving one person very weird, for they love everybody. They will often get confused between love and friendship and will take time to realise that their friendship counted more.

Aquarius is ruled by the rebellious planet of invention and change, Uranus. Aquarians never confirm to rules and are known to be progressive, original and resourceful. Aquarius is symbolised by the Water Bearer who brings new ideas and a trailblazing vision to the world. Aquarius rules the eleventh house that indicates the social circle and the second half of life; no wonder they make great friends, want to change the world and are always situated a little in the future.

Aquarius – Sabyasachi
Sabyasachi clothes are never out of fashion. He combines a unique blend of tradition and modernity in his designs that make him stand out as an original – the mark of a true Aquarian mind. Janice Blackburn shared her verdict on Sabyasachi, 'He is to my mind the finest and most original of the Indian dress and accessory designers… His work is very Indian but in a way that we in the West understand and appreciate and value.'[18]

Like a true Aquarian, he too found his own path after rebelling against his parents' wishes. He is the quintessential Aquarian with his creative force and conviction to think differently.

Love and Marriage for Him
If you have an Aquarian husband, you must be one interesting person to get him to stick around, for he doesn't go for looks but delves deeper into personality to find someone suited to his intellect and ideas.

This guy is empathetic. He understands you well and does not judge you based on your past. But don't expect him to be too considerate or sensitive – he will know how you feel but he might not give you the responses that you desire and crying will definitely turn him away. Your best bet with him is to let him be. He will surely respond though the response may be delayed. His attitude of knowing yet remaining unaffected is the greatest strength and the biggest flaw in his character.

Change, controversy and untested ideas are his motto in life. If you are traditional, he introduces you to a broader way of thinking. But if change frightens you then don't take him on, for change will be essential to him. He might try his hand at different careers and will not think about the bank balance while deciding on his shift. You also have to be the one to keep an eye on the finances and ensure that the bills are paid on time. He loves to travel, learn new skills, and take you to exotic places.

As a father, he is really fun to be with. He loves to talk to his children and explain different concepts. He is their friend and lets them live their lives the way they want. He will wait for them to start understanding him before taking an active interest in them.

---
[18] http://articles.timesofindia.indiatimes.com/2012-04-19/designers/31074753_1_designers-guild-sothebys-indian-fashion-designer

Love and Marriage for Her

She has a colourful personality and an independent mind. This girl loves shocking her in-laws just to see the look on their faces. If she chooses you, you are able to hold her attention, and that means something to an Aquarian.

She needs complete freedom to try out her ideas. Her extremely logical mind works quite illogically too. She will talk of bills when you talk romance and build castles in the air when you want to be practical. Don't expect her to be on your wavelength for her mind can wander off into too many interesting things.

She lets you do your thing and does not sulk if you forget important dates. Once you get her you can be sure that she will be absolutely honest with you. Don't expect feminine wiles or coy glances from her just because you happen to be a man. She believes in equality and expects you to do your share. Her love is more detached; she finds it hard to express her emotions. Jealousy and possessiveness only drive her away and she flies at the first sign of ultra-conservative behaviour. She can easily cut all ties and walk away without another glance if the relationship goes into a downward spiral. She also understands if you do so and is one of those rare women who can be friends with her ex.

As a mother, she needs lots of help in the initial years. She gets into the groove once her children grow older and learn to communicate with her. She is their friend who loves to amuse them with wild ideas and pranks. She teaches them the values of honesty and imagination and is never shocked by anything they say or do.

At the Workplace

Aquarians never settle down in monotonous jobs. They need change. They also take time to settle down as an Aquarian finds out quickly that what he is doing currently may not appeal to the world later and he needs to switch now. They need challenges to be motivated and money can be scarce so long as they are happy.

Humanitarian causes, spirituality and paranormal sciences find able contenders in them. They are also at home with technology. They are the innovators, pioneers, scientists and researchers who will present unique ideas to the world. Aquarius always wants to change the world for the better. Even if they do not do these things professionally, they do so on a personal level.

Aquarius is the thinker of the zodiac. It is the sign that venerates change and looks down upon tried and tested paths. This gentle innovator can lead many a rebellion with far-reaching consequences.

Famous Aquarius Personalities

Cindy Crawford, Sabyasachi Mukherjee, Herschelle Gibbs, Pran, Sahir Ludhianvi, Ramakrishna Paramhansa, Sushma Swaraj, Rachel Weisz.

12. PISCES

Neptune, the mysterious lord of the seas, rules over this seemingly docile and extremely affable sign. Pisceans have depths that even they are unaware of. Pisces is the last sign of the zodiac and holds within itself the attributes of each of its 11 preceding signs. Pisces can be anything as it has the vitality of a Fire sign, the inquisitiveness of Air and the sensitivity of Water.

Decoding Pisceans is no easy task. A natural Piscean hates numbers, but when young, if taught by an empathetic parent who excels in maths, then the Piscean would not just be at ease with number crunching but may even master it. They can be peaceloving, as is their wont, or be aggressive, especially if they are brought up by aggressive parents. They retain the essence of early learning, good or bad, more than any other zodiac sign. They mop up lessons learnt, feelings and emotions and reflect them back to the world.

Their affable nature makes them get along with almost anybody. They can see the reasons behind unreasonable behaviour and find it in their hearts to forgive even the most dastardly of acts. They never display signs of ego and are willing to act submissive if that is what makes you happy.

There is a happiness about Pisceans that is quite enchanting. They are contented with life and not ambitious. They understand the temporary nature of success and wealth and do not kill themselves to reach anywhere. This stress-free nature often hampers them. It makes them rarely want to move up in life.

They can be your shoulder to cry on and be the friends whom you can count on for help when everyone else deserts you. They can make you laugh, are soft-spoken and are patient listeners as well. They are the friends to keep for life.

Pisceans are fabulously creative and have an artistic temperament. Arts, music and drama are natural abodes for Pisceans. They love make-believe and would be quite good at creating a parallel reality. You won't be able to push them into a nine-to-five routine.

They fear confrontation and try to do everything to avoid conflict. Anger is not a Piscean trait, but do not think that they are pushovers. Slow to anger, they start with depression and go on to stony silence. If their present reality becomes too harsh, they resort to daydreams to feel good. They need to be pushed into action. Despite their love for dreams, they often surprise you with their grasp over reality. They realise the undercurrents of any situation, but try and keep themselves aloof to save themselves from hurt.

Other than the environment, life, too, is a big teacher for Pisceans. If they see a lot of sadness around them then they can change from a small timid fish to a dangerous whale. No one can deceive as artfully as Pisceans for their power of empathy lets them don any role with ease. Flexibility is their greatest strength. By flexibility, I mean letting go of rigid ideas and allowing themselves to learn from different situations. They are the masters of learning and, thus, earn the epithet of the 'wise Piscean'.

They are very talented but feel unequal to the task. They need to be made to feel confident fo their abilities and will need a lot of care and encouragement to shine. They are subject to phobias and fears. There is an inner insecurity in them that pulls them down in their moments of triumph. Pisceans are very sensitive and you have to tread carefully around them for they get hurt very deeply. Compassion is their virtue and Pisces also feel the pain that you suffer from.

Love is very important to Pisceans. They need to be in love. A Pisces looks for spiritual and emotional bonding. When a Pisces doesn't find its soul mate they suffer without letting anyone know. Love is the only thing they want in life.

Money holds no value for them yet they need it for they wither in a sparse environment. They do not know how to save and are very bad at earning as well. Addiction is the worst Piscean trait. They can get addicted to anything, from food to cocaine. These easy-flowing creatures can give in to vices to keep themselves from thinking about harsh realities. The biggest pitfall for a Piscean would be *self-undoing* and *self-denial*. They can get into a trap where they feel that nothing can change, no one can help them and develop a defeatist attitude.

Neptune blesses Pisceans with compassion and sensitivity, and makes them rise above worldliness. Pisces is symbolised by two fishes swimming in opposite directions, indicating the choices that the Fish has, to be a highly evolved dolphin/whale type or the introvert Fish that wanders aimlessly deep in the abyss. Pisces rules the twelfth house, of self-sacrifice and service to others, encapsulating the philosophy of Pisceans.

Pisces – Jaya Bachchan

'My children are more important to me than even my husband. I come from a home where my mother was always around. Just her presence gave me a lot of strength. I became the person that I am because of her. I'm very duty-conscious. And I've become even more so now after marriage because Amitji is very conscious of his duties towards his parents.'

'The name, fame, glamour... it all vanishes. What survives is goodness.'[19]

A Pisces is affected by its environment and Jaya Bachchan clearly was influenced by her mother and later by her husband. She is also creative, sensitive and quite philosophical in her approach to life. A Piscean to the core!

Love and Marriage for Him

Please take a word of advice, if this wonderful man is around twenty-five and has no idea where he is going, kindly give him a miss. It is very easy for Pisceans waste their talents in a pathetic manner. Look at him with clarity and decide if he is worth the effort. If he is, you are in luck for he is the kindest and sweetest guy you can ever meet. He is extremely caring and is able to decipher even your sighs. Plus, he is a wonderful listener.

He needs a strong, positive woman to push him out of his laziness and self-misery. But, if you push him too hard, you find yourself left alone. He needs a person who is strong, yet emotionally sensitive to understand the delicate beauty of his inner world. He can go into depression or fall for addictions. Nurturing is

---

[19] http://www.glamsham.com/movies/interviews/jaya_bachchan.asp

what he needs.

As a father, he is extremely caring. He understands his children's wishes and never forces them to do anything. He knows how to have fun with his children and they surely love his deep sensitivity.

Love and Marriage for Her
She is the softest and sweetest woman you have ever met. Completely feminine and extremely loving, she fills your life and home with a soothing softness. When you come home to her, you are able to leave your worries behind for you find it hard to worry when your surroundings are so calm and peaceful.

But you have to care for her. This lady needs a man who can talk to her at a deep emotional level. She needs lots of love and care to make her feel special for she easily surrenders to self-pity. Do not grumble at her or raise your voice for she catches the smallest inflection in your tone and her delicate heart breaks in two. She can cry buckets. You have to understand her moods to deal with her.

She allows you to be the man of the house. This lady does not need to be independent nor desires to assert herself. Be very loving to her for if she is not treated well, she disappears. She does not walk away or create a scene. She just creates another reality for herself in which you don't exist.

Encourage her to pursue her talents. She is extremely talented but has an inclination to push herself down. She gives importance to everybody and everything, her friends' midnight calls, her child's need for emotional care and your desires for a calm house, to her own disadvantage. Tell her to take time out for herself, and praise her efforts.

She is an extremely loving mother. She cares for her children and is their best friend. They tell her all their secrets for they know that nothing they do can ever upset her. You will have to provide the discipline as she secretly hates discipline, routine and homework herself.

At the Workplace
Artistic and creative, Pisceans work well in jobs that are not restrained by time or stifled by routine. They need to be encouraged to achieve their dreams for they can deny their talents if they are faced with indifference.

They are very spiritual and find it easy to understand the occult sciences, philosophy and astrology. They can be very good practitioners of alternative sciences. The Piscean ability to replicate emotions and understand the sentiments of people make them excellent actors as well. They are poetic and know how to express themselves with emotion. Money or glory does not matter to them as much as enjoying what they do.

Water gives immense depth and emotion to Pisces. They are sensitive, compassionate, loving and friendly souls who value people and understand the impermanence of life.

Famous Pisces Personalities
Jaya Bachchan, Kasturba Gandhi, Gayatri Joshi, Terence Lewis, Jennifer Capriati, Ehsaan Qureshi, Alessandro Stradella.

13. ARIES–TAURUS

The fearlessness of Aries and the stability of Taurus bring a formidable force to this combination. Mars, the violent god of war, rules Aries and makes it dominating in will and pioneering in desire. Added to it is the solidity of Taurus, the bull, and it makes AriTau a forceful and strong combination of daredevil achievers.

A fierce Ram and a snorting Bull combined together in one person. Astonishing! They have unbelievable power, force, energy and strength –both physical and emotional. These people are blessed in a way. Aries gives them extreme fearlessness and Taurus is the sign with the highest emotional stability. Since there is no Water or Air in it, there is no vacillation, no tears, no flightiness, nor distraction – a mind and heart that knows exactly where to go with the immense inner strength to actually get there.

Power and money rate high in their life. They need to win and that need overshadows everything else. AriTaus always want to succeed. After every defeat they bounce back with a stronger will to succeed. The Arian adventurous streak in them loves to conquer ideas and territories; the more difficult the task, the more excited they are, and they succeed because they do not understand the meaning of defeat. The Arian innovator will come up with something unique while the stubborn Taurean streak can make them attempt untried ventures and stay put despite troubles. If the problems happen to be man-made, then the people who made them need to look for a hidey-hole, because they will come and get them.

They are forceful and matter of fact and they believe that whatever they say or do is absolutely correct so they don't feel the need to ask anyone else for an opinion. Extreme focus on their tasks and the basic need for success can make them seem totally heartless to the needs of others. They can be perceived as extremely selfish. But don't be in a hurry to form an opinion yet. Though they are tough taskmasters and want 'their' stuff done as quickly as possible, if you get into their good books you will be surprised by their generosity. The apparent lack of sensitivity mostly affects colleagues and subordinates – they are always there for their families. The sentimental streak seems missing, but it is there.

There is also an insecurity that hides deep in their hearts All Fire signs add bluster to their talk to hide the niggling fear deep within. They fear failure too much to allow it to happen. Any failure means that they were wrong in their judgment, and they can't bear that. Family and friends must never criticise them at such a point. They need gentle consolation to bounce back. In no way should the AriTau pride be hurt.

The AriTau has a creative side too and loves music and earthy colours. Music helps them de-stress. They will work hard and party harder. Fun is as important to them as work and they have a loud resounding laugh. Family will be everything for them and most of their ambitions will be directed towards making their family a success. They are fiercely protective of their family and unconditionally love and support them.

Fashion can be a bit of a problem with them for they refuse to listen to others' views and wear what they like. They are too thick-skinned to bow to criticism. In fact any criticism only makes them more stubborn about what they do and believe. They are also very spiritual. They are traditionalists at the core and veer towards anything that is conventional and cultural. They are an interesting mix: forward thinking in their goals and ideals and traditional in their belief system and approach.

If you thought that these absolutely strong, menacing and domineering people would shun romance think again. Aries needs idealistic love, while Taureans are real goofballs in love. They are wonderfully romantic and become extremely sentimental and soppy when in love. They believe that they are destined to have a wonderful mate and keep their eyes wide open for them. You can expect them to be as bold and forthright in their love as they are in their life. If they are in love they will declare it without any fear of rejection. If you ever love an AriTau you must love their ego, too, for it comes with the package.

Money is very important and they look upon it not only as a source of investment but also as power. They are not stingy and can be very generous with friends, but at the same time, do not spend needlessly on trivial expenses. The AriTau loves food and loves feeding others even more. It makes them feel really good to spread their largesse around.

Be wary of their temper for they can really blow their tops. They usually attack with such ferocious force that people give way to them. Funnily enough, when things are really stacked against them, they are calm.

It is truly a learning experience to watch them work under pressure. If you have watched sports-people of this combination, you will know what it means to perform under pressure. If there are any doubts about their ability, they will do it with even more passion and single-mindedness to prove you wrong. They will always find a way to bulldoze their way through any problem.

Aries–Taurus – Ekta Kapoor
'I wear my brands, I have my style and I really don't care what people think. I have never followed the beaten path. I clearly wear my attitude; it can be a point of ridicule or discussion.'

'As a child I always believed that I had slightly different opinions about everything, and I prided myself on that.'[20]

'People find it hard to believe this, but I'm a die-hard romantic. My favourite film is Yash Chopra's *Dil To Pagal Hai*.'[21]

In-your-face, frank, opinionated, ambitious and full of visionary ideas, Ekta Kapoor defines AriTau. She understands the need for power yet is romantic enough to desire an ideal love.

Love and Marriage for Him
He needs to be the boss at home. Once you understand and comply with this basic fact, he allows you to do what you want. Actually, he sets boundaries for you and you can do whatever you like within those restrictions.

Home and children become your responsibility for he concentrates only on his career. Of course, he is always there when you need help, but if you expect help

---
[20] *Hi! Blitz*, June 2011
[21] *People*, July 30, 2010

in nappy changing or grocery shopping, you have picked the wrong guy. He needs to be pampered and loved at home. It is essential for his ego.

This guy loves food too. He can have a terrible temper but it cools down quite fast. It mellows down as he ages too.

He is strict and controlling as a father. He is a little old-fashioned but listens to new ideas if he thinks they have merit.

Love and Marriage for Her
She is always in command and takes the initiative in most matters. All that forceful energy and need for success make her want only one thing in her relationship – she needs to feel that she is the centre of your universe. Shower her with praises, load her with gifts, pamper her every wish and she is happy. She works hard for her family's success but hates interference from family members, especially in-laws.

She is made for things beyond household tasks. You need to delegate those duties to someone else. Though she loves food, and even likes cooking, she is not a domestic goddess. She needs adventure and ambition to spur her forward. Exotic massages, body and hair treatments will keep her happy and contented.

She is extremely proud of the smallest of achievements of her children and loses no time in announcing it to the rest of the world. In her eyes, they are perfect.

At the Workplace
At work, they are the leaders. They are great at execution and planning. They are go-getters and no power in the world can withstand their force. If they work for you then ensure that you provide them two things – money and position. They need to hear the applause and the counting machines working nonstop.

They are the bosses everyone runs from. They will be extremely generous if you are valuable and throw you out if you are not. They will have no qualms in calling you at 3 a.m. to find out if you are on target to meet their goals.

They will be the model of impassivity in troubled times. Rock-steady and serene in the middle of a hurricane, they can withstand tragedy and are good at calming unsteady nerves. They have the capability to scale up things phenomenally and are extremely good at controlling expenses. Their belief in their strength leads them to create magic and achieve impossible results in undreamed-of ways.

Fire and Earth meet in this powerhouse combination to give it volatility with stability.

Famous AriTau Personalities
Anil Ambani, Bjorn Borg, Bob Dylan, Katharine Hepburn, Chandrababu Naidu, Karl Marx, Dadasaheb Phalke, Ekta Kapoor, Pope John Paul II, Karunanidhi, Sukhdev, Rohit Sharma, Krishna Ghattamaneni, Laxmi Ratan Shukla, Paul Collingwood, Shane Bond, R. Madhavan, Mark Van Bommel, Michael Bevan, Miguel Veloso, Pendyala Harikrishna, Ramnath Goenka, Rory McIlroy, Rosalind Russell, Sigmund Freud, Steven Smith, Sir Thomas Lipton, Queen Victoria, Omar Khayyam, Fred Astaire, Balu Mahendra, Mohan.

14. ARIES–GEMINI

Aries is ruled by Mars, which displays forceful aggression and energy. When that combines with the bubbly energy of mercurial Gemini, it makes for a person full of passion and enthusiasm. This is a very difficult person to ignore with his talking, gesticulating and overall excitement.

Aries is called the baby of the zodiac, while Gemini is known as the teenager of the zodiac. The combination ensures that they remain young in their heart, mind and spirit – forever. The AriGem is a powerhouse of ideas. While Aries are pioneers, innovators and ideators who want to gift the world with a path breaking invention or two, Geminis are full of inexhaustible, breathtakingly new ideas and expressions that they keep churning day in and day out.

AriGems make friends easily. They attract people with their joy and enthusiasm. AriGems make fabulous first impressions and people think of them as forceful, charged and optimistic. Their extraordinary communication skills and gift of languages along with funny impersonations and anecdotes add pizzazz to their conversations.

This is a double masculine sign, so expect a lot of energy and brashness. Their behaviour is often rash and impulsive. They like speed and revel in adrenaline rushes. They also have varied interests from bungee jumping to kabala meditation. They are also spiritually inclined and believe that all things happen for the good with them.

The Aries drive, combined with the multitasking ability of Gemini, helps them work tirelessly for their dreams. Neither Gemini nor Aries are driven by money. The Arian optimism keeps them smiling in the face of adversity. They possess supreme will power and the eagerness to shine and showcase their multitude of talents.

They want the best of everything; from career to spouse and house – they want them to be outstanding. They love the limelight too. They are extremely inquisitive about everything in life. Despite their bubbly personality there is a strange naïveté about them, which makes them endearing.

They can be fearless flirts too and not care about what society thinks of their on-and-off relationships. In relationships, they can be very demanding – from wanting partners who stand out to always looking for something better. These guys will have a tough time settling down. The Gemini love for experimentation expresses itself strongly in their relationships.

Expect them to tell you some tall tales – some of them will be coloured with their imagination. You will know with experience what to believe and what not. Sometimes they can be brutally honest and tactless as well. They keep you guessing with their changeable behaviour.

When Arian selfishness meets Gemini cunning, it can sometimes create crooks. They can sometimes do outrageous things just for the excitement of being 'different' or interesting. The Gemini love for playing pranks is also very evident in them. Their attention span can be very limited at times. The initial excitement of being around these extraordinarily talented, fabulous communicators wears off once you feel that their dreams don't seem to have a sound footing.

AriGem does not have the elements of either Earth or Water in their makeup. Hence they will have ideas but might lack the stability and cool-headedness to see the ideas through to completion. They are also quite insensitive to what's happening around them and can't decipher feelings till they are decoded and explained. They can also be pretty spaced out and aloof at times. They cannot relate too much with emotions and cannot empathise at the depth that you may desire. They are also a little thoughtless of the people around them.

The Arian anger and the Gemini sarcasm both are facets of their temper. They can totally lose it or be absolutely arrogant and rude – either way it can be tough to deal with their temper. When used positively, their temper can make them champions of various causes. They are those forceful, idealistic communicators who use words or violence and sometimes both for a just cause.

They get bored with things very quickly and need constant excitement in life. They run the risk of running around chasing impossible dreams, only to find a mirage at the end. Then they re-start the process. Till they find some ideal that they can live and die for, they feel empty within. They want to do something big and important but don't know what. The problem is that they are good at many things but still run around in circles. Their biggest issue is in deciding what is best for them. But once they decide on it – they will be unstoppable.

Aries–Gemini – Manoj Bajpai
'I am serious, but only about my work and the work that I choose. When it comes to saying no to anybody, I am very straightforward.'
   'I speak less but I speak the truth. I say what I feel and in my style, which people take an offence to. They fail to understand me and turn against me. Anyway, I'm not bothered at all.'[22]
   'I get bored if the story is told in the same way all the time.'[23]
   Manoj Bajpai exemplifies the combination with his love for work, his straightforwardness and desire to learn. More than money, it is the challenge of essaying a different character that pushes him forward – a true AriGem.

Love and Marriage for Him
This double masculine sign cries out for attention. This guy wants to be the centre of your universe. He wants you to be at his beck and call. He needs a woman who mothers him, pampers him, feeds him and picks up after him. Sometimes, you may feel you have a grown-up kid at home. He is idealistic and charged-up. To be with him, you need to be realistic and stable.

You cannot expect him to be sensitive and caring. The Arian cry of *'me, me, me'* combines with the Gemini's sense of detachment and he will not know how you feel until you make him aware of it. He does not know how to save. Aries spends from the heart and Gemini buys on impulse. You will have to take control of finances as he has no idea of when to pay the insurance and how to service the EMIs.

His child-rearing skills are evident only after the child has grown up. He finds it easier to talk to a child who understands what he says. Changing diapers and attending parent-teacher meetings are things you will need to do yourself.

---
[22] http://www.filmfare.com/interviews/ive-done-enough-acting-now-i-want-money-manoj-bajpayee-4099.html
[23] http://www.rediff.com/movies/2007/jun/05manoj.htm

Of course, if you want to enforce discipline he is always ready to lend his forceful support; just don't expect him to handle kids or you sensitively.

Love and Marriage for Her
The Arian idealism runs through her and makes her demand romantic ideals in life. She desires a romance that overshadows everyone else's. In spite of this deep-seated need she will portray an uninterested front and act as if she doesn't really need a man in her life.

She is either feminine or tomboyish, but is never a girly girl. She is strong and she knows it. Energy is never in short supply in her and she will never be flustered by the various tasks put before her. Her need for dominance makes her seem overbearing at times. And even if she looks all feminine and soft, she does not have a soft touch. She feels that she cannot make herself understood through words and gestures but needs to shout, scream and yell.

She has lots of friends and loves interacting with them. Her social calendar is packed with activities. Do not expect her to sit at home and spend her time cooking and dusting. She needs to talk and needs an outlet to vent the creative ideas flowing in her. Money is important to her, for spending. She sees no use in saving and lives for the joy of finding new things to spend on.

As a mother, you can expect her to be fully committed to her children. She loves playing games, doing arts and crafts and taking them to shows and movies. What you cannot expect is understanding and sensitivity. She is a very dominating mother who thinks she knows exactly what is right for her child.

At the Workplace
AriGems are great in careers that require them to talk and impress. They can ideate brilliantly and have the drive to put in tons of hard work where required. Gemini is known for its innovative thoughts and Aries loves being a pioneer. So you can expect them to come up with unexpected ideas. They work extremely well in sales, advertising and marketing jobs that require their language skills, impressive behaviour and compelling body language. They hate jobs that involve routine.

Give them a job that keeps evolving and that requires them to move around, talk and ideate. Do not expect them to be sticklers for punctuality. Praise is what they need. Money does not mean anything to them. If they are the bosses, then they need some practical people around to execute their ideas practically. Also, back them up with good accountants as they may go overboard on expenses with their wild ideas.

Fire and Air make them excitable forces of nature. They are whirlwinds of activity and volcanoes ready to erupt with energy, anger or ideas.

Famous AriGem Personalities
Manoj Bajpai, Dr B.R. Ambedkar, Dr Raj Kumar, John Cena, Pamela Anderson, Robert Pattinson, Shirley Temple, Laetitia Casta.

15. ARIES–CANCER

This is a very interesting combination. It has Mars, the powerful god of war, joining the Moon, which depicts emotion and sensitivity. Aries is the first sign of the zodiac and symbolises 'the baby'. Cancer, as a zodiac sign, rules children. When Aries and Cancer combine, it creates a unique person with childlike qualities – sensitive but domineering, emotional but ambitious, caring but ruthless. A contradictory kid indeed… but one who remains a kid all life.

AriCan is a combination where the heart rules the roost. Rams are full of enthusiasm and energy, and are always pumped up for some action. They don't use their cerebral powers but live life as the heart says. The sensitive Crabs also take their hearts seriously. They are extremely vulnerable creatures. When Aries and Cancer combine, it makes an individual who may put up a tough exterior but has a gooey soft interior. The AriCan seems to be telling people, 'I don't give a damn', but they know within that the truth is exactly the opposite.

Family comes first for AriCans. They love their mother, and value her sacrifice, love, care and are convinced that no one can take her place. They would want the best for their family and would die or even kill for their family's happiness. They love their homes and keep them clean and decorated. Every Cancerian has a dream home and pursues that goal till achieved. They have every inch of the home envisaged in their minds and ensure their vision comes true.

Highly expressive, AriCans can articulate myriad expressions through their gestures and eyes. AriCans will be very romantic and sentimental. Arians feel that their love story is the best love story in the world, while Cancerians are so sentimental they can give their life for love. They will be extremely loyal and faithful. The memory of their courtship years will be very dear to them. They seek eternal, everlasting love.

Both Aries and Cancer are cardinal or leadership signs with extremely different behavioural patterns. Aries is totally bossy, dominating, passionate and idealistic; full of vigour and force; while the Cancerian is much more subtle; they may resort to crying, nagging and acting martyred to get their work done. This makes both lose some of their negatives and adopt more positives. The insensitivity of Aries and its absolute selfishness is diluted by Cancer's high emotional intelligence and empathy.

Unlike Aries who get excited at new ideas and rush headlong into another project, AriCans will show more tenacity in holding onto their dreams. The Arian love of speed and adventure will make them love fast cars and exciting escapades. Photography too is a hobby that might attract AriCans. They are also very spiritually inclined and a belief system helps to keep them stay strong in times of distress.

Arians are highly optimistic and act with blustering bravery, and are always hungry for applause. But deep inside they are nervous and jittery. Cancerians never hide their apprehensions and always love sympathy. Hence, expect AriCans to be highly anxious when they start any work. No matter how much experience they may have or how talented they may be, there is this inner insecurity that always asserts itself in them.

The Arian anger combines with the emotional sulks of Cancer. They have a really bad temper that does not abate with ease. Their anger can take the form of unreasonable jealousy. They can be extremely insecure of certain people without any reason. This can be more so in women, who are more emotional and touchy.

Emotions make them think from their hearts. They are also extremely moody. They can be politically incorrect at times. Their passions and emotions dictate their likes and dislikes. Total fearlessness makes them stand up for their beliefs. However, they also show the Cancerian fears, at times, and give in to moments of sheer despondency, but when the time comes to act, they do.

The Aries egocentricity will get a halo due to the Cancerian influence. They are very protective and caring about things and people who affect them. 'My family, my friends, my team' are their concerns. Thus the 'only me' attitude will expand to add more people in their list of 'the ones who need to be cared for'. They will fight for their groups, be nurturing and give love, kindness and advice.

Aries–Cancer – Pooja Bedi

'Despite my bohemian image, I'm quite conservative.' Which is why despite meeting a man who swept her off her feet, she decided to end it when he was unable to commit long term.[24]

'I'm more strict with my kids than my mom was with me. Certain values are important, like respect for elders, food habits and studies.'[25]

A blunt talker and a caring mother, romantic yet aggressive, that is an AriCan, Pooja Bedi, for you.

Love and Marriage for Him

It depends on when you first met him. It is easy to fall for this loving, caring and sensitive soul who is a brave heart and knows to protect his woman. But as time flies, you may wonder if you have truly taken the right decision. He may carry his rash teenage behaviour into his thirties and forties and his sharp anger leaves you gasping for breath. He is deeply sensitive and emotional too, so try not to say things in anger; that makes him sulk for days.

If you are lucky you will be with a deeply emotional, sensitive and caring soul who will love you for life. If you are unlucky, you will end up with an adult who refuses to grow up and has the violent temperament and ruthlessness of a teenager. You have a better chance if you meet him a little late in life. Hope he has learnt all the lessons from his recklessness and has started understanding his 'sensitively aggressive' self and calmed down.

Looking at the positive side, he is full of energy and enthusiasm. He has this burning desire to achieve something in life. The best thing about this guy is that despite all that male machismo, he knows how to be sensitive and caring. He loves his home and family and does not mind showing it in public. He can be really careful with his money. He can be generous, but only to a certain limit. You have to love his mother, for he loves her to bits. His mom is the best! Period. He is softly dominating and states his will softly but firmly. Children love him and he is a very loving and caring father.

---

[24] *People*, April 2011
[25] http://www.cinegoer.com/telugu-cinema/interviews/interview-with-pooja-bedi-230311.html

Love and Marriage for Her

Adventurous yet soft, wary yet rash, sensitive but bold – these are some of the opposites that make up this woman. She is either totally feminine, with an edgy grace, or loud and sensible. It may take you time to decipher her. She thinks with her heart. She loves to mother you and care for you. Share your problems with her for she loves being able to help, and her Arian enthusiasm may make you forget your worries. But expect to give a lot of love in return. She wants to feel emotionally and financially secure all the time.

Just as she encourages you, she needs loads of encouragement in return. Her mother is her hero. The AriCan woman always looks up to her mother for advice and ideals. Her aim is to be like her.

Old memories and pictures will be very dear to her. She will keep her favourite childhood dresses and books as souvenirs and would do the same for her children. She may talk of breaking down due to her insecurities, but whenever problems loom large, she fights them off. She has nerves of steel and an eternally optimistic heart despite her deeply sensitive soul.

Motherhood calms her down and you can expect the wild side to become nurturing and caring in that phase. She adores her children and finds time for them while pursuing her own dreams.

At the Workplace

Never forget that they are born leaders. If given a chance, they like to start right at the top. They can be extremely creative due to Cancer and will gravitate towards the limelight like a typical Aries. Whatever they choose to do, they are known as firebrands and carve a distinct niche for themselves in their selected field.

They treat their colleagues and juniors as their team and like to be there for them. No matter how young they are, they prefer acting like elders. They love dispensing advice and enveloping their team members in a familial embrace.

They fulfil whatever they undertake. Enthusiasm is their hallmark and, when everyone is too drained to think, they come up with brilliant ideas. Encouragement and money are important. They like being told that they are good and want the occasional pat on the back. Give them small increases in salary every year and they will be happy. One day when they feel financially secure they might leave to form their own venture; till then, they will be totally loyal. As bosses, they would be controlling but very caring.

Fire and Water combine to make this combination a palatable mixture of both. They blend energy, passion, drive and sheer power with tenderness, flexibility, imagination and emotions.

Famous AriCan Personalities

Pooja Bedi, Selena Gomez, Penelope Cruz, Himesh Reshammiya, Ravi Kishan, Anu Agha, Jacqueline Kennedy Onassis, Mark Burnett, Tim Tebow, Saint Thyagaraja, J.V. Somayajulu, Mallika Sarabhai, Renée Zellweger, Barbara Streisand, Miranda Kerr, Raja Chaudhary, Suresh Kalmadi, Sulochana, Fran Healy, Benedict Cumberbatch, Lisa Sthalekar, Huma Qureshi, Apara Mehta.

16. ARIES–LEO

This is a double whammy – double Fire, double male – resulting in total aggression, enthusiasm and dominance. There is no question about who is the boss when this super-charged person is around. AriLeos crackle with energy, positivity and confidence. Mars, the powerful god of war, and the Sun, the proud giver of sunshine, reside in this person and make him dazzle everyone with his sheer power.

Look at the two animals that comprise of the combination: the Lion and the Ram. One is the most powerful, the most majestic and the most feared; while the other is goal-oriented, clears obstacles and follows its heart to reach the top. This is a combination of extraordinary dreamers, believers and achievers. They are so full of childlike charm, enthusiasm and positivity that you are swayed by their sheer presence.

Aries is the cardinal sign; and Leo is fixed; which simply means they lead and refuse to be led. The self-confidence of these people is extraordinary. They truly believe that they are the chosen ones. Ambition and drive are part of their DNA. They always look at the big picture and put themselves on top. Matters regarding day-to-day functioning and emotions are beyond them.

They love helping friends. Leo generosity, combined with Arian charity, makes them large-hearted. Are you a part of their inner circle? Oh! You must be somebody yourself! When they make an entrance they just don't walk in, they outshine everybody. They are the quintessential party animals.

They love to spend money lavishly. Saving is not their cup of tea; they prefer using money to fulfil their dreams and enhance their personalities. They love brands, and will sport the most eye-catching clothes.

AriLeos are extremely romantic. You can expect them to woo their chosen partners with flowers, notes, candle-light dinners and exclusive getaways. In this area as in others, they want to shine and overshadow everyone else. Their partner has to have qualities that none other has and their love story should be an example to others. The men might choose a mate who will be a step lower than them so that they are always appreciated and adulated. The women though, want the best.

They are extremely spiritual. They believe in the power above, and feel that they are the chosen ones and have a special relationship with God. Even their spirituality has loud overtones. They donate large sums of money and like wearing all the signs of their beliefs.

But their extreme self-belief holds the seeds of their destruction. They are so full of their plans and achievements that it is difficult for others to warn them of the challenges ahead. They can get so carried away in their enthusiasm and confidence that they can blunder into obstacles that were evident to everyone but them.

The stability of Earth is missing in this inflammable Fire combination. They think big, but at times are not able to give a working dimension to their thoughts. Emotions are their major failing. They cannot understand emotions other than their own. Their life is so full of 'me' that they cannot show any sensitivity. They are not heartless; you just need to tell them how you feel. They will understand and make amends if they like you. The lack of Water in this combination gives them this insensitive nature.

They have terrible anger issues. The worst part of their temper is the amount of harm it does to them. They have to be careful about their blood pressure and can be prone to heart disease due to their high anger levels. Jealousy and a possessive attitude make them even more susceptible to strong rages.

Deep inside they have this insecurity that they may fail, that they are not actually good enough and that everything may come crashing down. This insecurity propels them to put up a façade. What they seek is approval from the world. Give them that hope and you will have a faithful and generous friend for life.

They can be perceived to be arrogant and impulsive by more experienced people. They seem self-obsessed and they live in a world of their own. Their flamboyance, nonchalance and devil-may-care attitude can give rise to hidden enemies who would rejoice at their fall. They need to understand that one needs to give to receive and that giving goes beyond materialistic things.

It is very difficult for people to tell them that they are wrong. It's the perennial problem of 'who will bell the cat'. AriLeos consciously need to ensure that the people around them are not afraid to tell them the truth. The Leo pride and the Arian rashness need to give way to common sense.

Aries–Leo – Siddharth Mallya
'Carrying a burden, yes. But it is not something that should weigh me down. It is something that should actually propel me.'[26]

'I am a very impulsive and impatient person. I want to achieve everything that my father has, immediately. I know that I want to be at the top, as soon as possible. I know exactly where I want to be.'[27]

'I'm self-assured and confident, which some might take to be an arrogance.'[28]

Positive, self-motivating, a go-getter – that is Siddharth Mallya. The double Fire of AriLeo makes him hard to miss, and a head-turner.

Love and Marriage for Him
Pamper his ego – this guy has to be treated like 'the Man' in your life. Even small things matter, like a game of snakes and ladders that you play. Never gloat about your win but try and let him win the second round.

You can save the money you have or try a roundabout way to do it but never tell him what to do with his finances. Like I said earlier, saving is an issue with these guys. He is extremely romantic and likes showering you with gifts and surprises. Public displays of affection are part of his disposition and he loves showing you off to his friends. He wants a partner who looks as good as him, talks well and complements him in every way.

You will be hosting lavish parties and moving around meeting people for he doesn't like enjoying his glory in solitude. This man has style and an attitude – you

---

[26] http://www.moneycontrol.com/news/business/siddhartha-mallyahis-upcoming-roleub-empire_416627.html
[27] *People*, June 17, 2011
[28] *Hello!*, August, 2010

need to keep up. The Leo laziness does not make him much of a handy guy around the house. His dreams are very important to him, so share his excitement and joys.

Love and Marriage for Her
She is a goddess. Recognise it. She needs to be treated well, pampered and adulated. She expects nothing less and is unhappy if she is not given her due. She is a born fighter. Her Leo pride and Arian ego cannot take the slightest of criticisms.

Career is important to her. If she manages the home, do not expect her to cook and clean for you. Those things are to be delegated while she spends her time pampering herself. Romance matters a lot to her. If you want her, you must woo her in style. Get her roses, organise parties in her honour, announce your love for her from the tallest towers, and she will nod her regal head.

Her partner has to stun everybody and make other women sigh. But remember that she is nothing less than a princess and your equal. Nothing she says or does is without a dramatic quotient.

She can be totally generous and her loving care extends to her friends. The only thing she wants from others is to treat her with respect and admiration. It is hard for her to be sensitive. She will tread with hob-nailed shoes on others' egos and misses your worry lines totally. Speak up if you want to be heard.

At the Workplace
They are in a hurry – to reach the top in the quickest time possible as they feel the top position is their birthright. AriLeos have pioneering dreams and drive themselves hard to make them come true. Subservience to others is not in their nature. A piece of advice for them – please realise that you need others to succeed!

They are excellent promoters and, when they talk of their projects, you feel compelled to believe in them. They will have loyal followers and like moving around with a group of listeners; just make sure most of them are practical and realistic. The worst thing AriLeos can do is ignore honest advice. Accountants and people with financial expertise are necessary for them to live royally.

They want and need to be their own bosses. The best part is that they can actually ideate beautifully and their compelling personality will make you agree with their vision. The worst is that they cannot do the minor detailing.

Extremely generous, these guys like to treat their employees well. People who work for them might have to do the dirty work, but AriLeos will never forget to pay them well for their efforts. Flattery works wonders for them but can also be their Achilles' heel.

Two Fire signs combine in AriLeos to give them strength, drive and ambition. They have to be careful in choosing friends, partners and workers to complement their strengths.

Famous AriLeo Personalities
Siddhartha Mallya, Asha Bhonsle, Anand Mahindra, Prince Harry, James Pattinson, Gaganjeet Bhullar, Donatella Versace, Candice Bergen, Bhanumati Ramakrishna, J.P. Morgan, Dmitry Medvedev, Ted Hughes, Ayushmann Khurrana.

17. ARIES–VIRGO

This combination denotes perfection with passion. Virgo, the Maiden, is known as the worker – perfectly diligent, hardworking and even nitpicking, while Aries, the Ram, personifies drive, ambition, idealistic views and high energy. AriVir is a perfectionist who works passionately with a drive to succeed. Mars, the powerful and violent god of war, and 'Planet Y', the god known for his healing powers, rule over this sign. They want to do something path breaking and out of the world. And guess what – they have the perfect plan to do just that. They are rebels with a cause; pioneers who know exactly where they want to go.

Enthusiasm is the AriVir hallmark. With them around, you feel that life is full of possibilities. They are happy souls who are the happiest when they are involved in something. They do not know how to laze. These guys are very intelligent and knowledgeable about their areas of interest. Virgo makes them learn in-depth while Aries loves flaunting the knowledge. They definitely like to sound and act intelligent.

With them, you get what you see. There are no grey shades in them. The Arian blunt talk makes them say just what they think. The Virgo fastidiousness makes them talk with clarity. They are extremely trustworthy. The Arian idealism and Virgo purity combine to make them honest, idealistic and true personalities. The Virgo need to be perfect makes them strict in their views at times. They want a particular thing to be done in a particular way. If things are not done as they desire they will do it again themselves.

Health is the primary issue with them. They like to take care of themselves and watch what they eat. Vanity also is very important to them. The Aries love of getting pampered and the Virgo need to look perfect makes them frequent beauty salons and gyms.

They worry a lot. They plan a lot. You can expect them to plan for everyone in the family. They worry about the well-being of everybody in their inner circle. Money is safe with them. They are perfect when it comes to saving. They use their money wisely and only splurge on designer labels and personal grooming. They are also deeply spiritual. They derive inner strength from the powers above. They study customs very well and know the exact reasons behind every ritual and follow them to the T.

They are not very sensitive. Aries is totally 'me, me, me' while Virgo wants to be giving but lacks a deep understanding of emotions. They are not very good at reading body language or knowing when friends need them around. Don't expect them to look into your eyes and know exactly what you are going through. The Arian anger changes to a calmer buzz. Angry AriVirs will sound more like bees, they will keep on criticising and talking about what they don't like rather than shout. But they will definitely rip you apart with their accurate and brutally honest criticism.

The addition of Virgo reduces the selfishness of Aries. Virgo is a sign that can sacrifice their life for people in need but due to Aries the AriVirs restrict their compassion to their family. They will stand like a rock for their family and be ready to give up anything for them. Expect them be to be rebellious, confrontational and even violent at times during their younger years. They will mellow and learn to express their enormous energy and passionate fervour in a more organised fashion as they mature. They will be patient, less domineering and learn to work with others as they hit their thirties and forties.

They are extremely conscientious; meticulously perfect; painfully focused; and have alarmingly clear thought processes. Despite all of that they manage to retain a childlike charm and amazing purity which is truly heart-warming. They have soft vulnerable hearts that quiver and wonder if they will really be able to do it. Totally uncalled for! They are prepared, well-prepared, for all the vicissitudes of life.

Aries–Virgo – Jack Nicholson
On his rebellious image: 'It's a hard-wired thing in me. I'm not good with being told. I just immediately start resisting the situation.'

On acting and anxiety: 'I worry from the moment I take a job. I worry about how I'm going to do it, if I can do it. I try to work out what I have to do on set and how I do that... I panic. It happens every time, and I get myself into this state, and then I walk on set and the director says, 'Roll', and all of a sudden all of it disappears and it's all happening.'[29]

Jack Nicholson, three times Oscar and seven times Golden Globe winning method actor, has the AriVir ability to shine despite his fears.

Love and Marriage for Him
He is the perfect husband. He worries and frets if he thinks that he is not able to keep up with the image of perfection. He likes strong, independent women. His partner needs to be capable of taking decisions. He criticises but does not like being criticised in return.

He also wants pampering. This guy has very few other demands. He wants everything in the right place and a right place for everything. All you have to do is take care of his health, give him healthy food and a tidy home. You can spend quality time doing yoga or aerobics together.

He is fun too. The Arian enthusiasm and sense of adventure finds him going to places and trying new things. But whatever he does, he will never go overboard in adventure.

If it is romance that you crave, this guy may not light up your life. Virgo dampens the romantic ardour of Aries. Do appreciate that he tries very hard to be a technically superior lover. He will be gentler, but less given to flights of fancy while buying you gifts. If you want to go to a romantic place, book the tickets and take him with you; and remember to leave his smartphone behind. But he is most dependable when you are sick or there is a crisis.

As a father he is a strict disciplinarian. He will research the best colleges his children can go to and plan for it well in advance.

Love and Marriage for Her
She looks perfect. Her hair will always be set perfectly and her clothes will look neat and elegant. A pimple or a rash can totally stress her out and make her snap. She may spend a fortune on her grooming but it is required for her peace of mind.

---
[29] http://www.celebitchy.com/138356/jack_nicholson_im_not_worried_about_wrinkles_in_myself_or_in_women/

In fact, a good head massage/makeover or an adventure trip should be the best antidote for her frazzled nerves.

She has ambitions and it is best if you let her nurture her dreams. Driven, focused and extremely meticulous, she has to succeed in everything. She needs you to be her support. You need not worry about your home; she worries enough for both of you. Her house is always spick and span and she wears herself out trying to maintain order and cleanliness. The Arian in her wants you to be ambitious too. She shares your dreams and works hard for their success. She is a born worrier and is quite capable of nagging. When she has the nagging button on, let her talk and vent her worries.

As a mother, she is caring and nurturing, and loves to play with her children. The only problem is that at times, when they do not tell her their problems, she does not understand, for she lacks sensitivity.

At the Workplace
Aries are pioneers and want to be at the forefront of every situation without dirtying their hands. They like to leave the details to the workers and delegate all the work that is away from the limelight. Virgos are the exact opposite. So the combination packs a punch – a zealous pioneer with great work ethics. Their extraordinary powers of concentration, diligence in working and speed of action is unmatched. AriVirs have passion, enthusiasm and ideals. They are fabulous workers and can drive themselves very hard to achieve their dreams.

Amazingly, they do not let dreams overpower their thoughts. They are fabulous at calculating and tabulating. They are also absolutely comfortable taking major decisions and handling large projects. They will systematically break up their goals into manageable tasks, delegate them to the right people, and supervise every step to ensure completion on time.

Their ambitions are monumental. The high ideals of Aries and Virgo makes them totally unbending on certain points. The fact is that they love perfection and believe that there is only one set way to achieve it. They think and act fabulously, but due to their lack of sensitivity, they may have problems getting their ideas across. For that, it is necessary that they spend some time trying to understand the people around them.

The Virgo strain of criticism makes them very demanding bosses. It is not easy to fool an AriVir boss. Go to them with a foolproof plan. They work extremely hard and expect everyone to do the same.

Earth and Fire come together in this combination. AriVirs have the drive and enthusiasm of Aries with the perfectionism and sensibility of Virgo.

Famous AriVir Personalities
Jack Nicholson, Andres Iniesta, J.P. Duminy, Paolo Rossi, Juan Mata, Ramona Narang, Debabrata Das, Rahul Dev, Rudolph Valentino, Umar Gul, Veena Murthy Poonam Dhillon, Gayatri Reddy (*Deccan Herald*).

18. ARIES–LIBRA

Mars, the powerful and violent god of war, personifying power and determination, joins Venus, which epitomises beauty, grace and luxury. This person is the perfect example of balanced power. Leadership is ingrained in them as both Aries and Libra are cardinal signs. Both are also extremely positive signs; life is exciting for them and they love it.

The first thing you notice about them is their extraordinary power of communication. They speak softly to start with and then the tempo goes up. With controlled aggression and fine body language, they deliver their speech with passion and conviction. Then they finish their oration with their trademark charming smile and you become their fan. Then you realise it was just a normal chat. Libra gives them the power of communication while Aries is all about power, energy and dominance. They can talk convincingly and motivate people. Their enthusiasm makes you want to join their dreams.

Aries is a masculine sign and so is Libra. They are live wires programmed to be ambitious and optimistic. But AriLibs are not as aggressive and ruthlessly dominating as Aries. Venus's charm gives a soft side to Libra's masculinity. They will have a flexible, caring side, yet be totally strong and unshakeable in their beliefs. They love debates – whatever the discussion they will have the final say without trampling your ego. The fact is that they are very hard to resist and they talk incessantly. Idealism is common to both the zodiac signs. Libra has a strong sense of right and wrong while Arians love fighting for their ideals. You can expect AriLibs to be able to tell right from wrong, and stick to their values in the face of adversity. They are very fair in their dealings and hate to hurt anyone.

Grace and power go hand in hand in them. They combine beauty with strength. Their fervour and zeal to succeed make them work hard, but they never lose the indolent streak in them. They like showing off their skills. They love luxury. No matter what they wear, they carry it off with style and elegance.

Their decision-making pattern is quite varied. They react to personal matters very differently from their business dealings. Libra rules the heart and is not known to be a good decision-maker while Aries takes instant decisions. When AriLibs think of matters of the heart, their Libran side will make them ponder and think for days. They painstakingly work through problems and often give in to indecisiveness, while when it comes to matters related to their career they will take instant decisions.

Love is essential in their lives. Librans love to be in love and Arians search for idealistic love. This makes the AriLibs crave love and they will do anything for their loved ones. They will place their partners on a pedestal and be extremely giving. The Arian selfishness is highly diluted due to the partnership-seeking and loving nature of Libra.

They must learn to save. Money just flows out of their hands. This is a combination of Fire and Air. Both are unstable and the stability of Earth is missing in this combination. So you will find that at times their dreams and wishes don't seem rooted. They need people around them to make them aware of the realities surrounding them. Their enthusiasm and charm is infectious, but you need to guide them on the practical side of things. Their anger is quite unpredictable. This keeps you guessing about their reactions.

Music, beauty and ambition are important to them. Beauty and elegance are what they require in their surroundings, both animate and inanimate. In a unique coming together of the opposites they blend courage and beauty, power and grace, style and substance and aggression and balance. They believe in magic, prayers and spirituality.

Aries–Libra – Nita Ambani
'I'm a very easy mother. My children are my soul mates.'

'Whatever I have set out to do, I've gone crazy and passionate over it, dreamt, slept, talked, read about it, done everything to make it happen.'

'Mukesh calls me his electricity, his live wire, because I get so animated whenever I do anything.'

'I like to have everything smiley and happy for my husband, the candles are lit and I don't ever have dinner without him.'[30]

Nita Ambani combines the fire of Aries and the love of Libra in a rare balancing act as a corporate woman, romantic wife and a loving mother. She bears the true stamp of an AriLib.

Love and Marriage for Him
You know why you chose him over the rest – he made you smile and giggle, his positivity made you feel like a queen and his wild-child act made all your maternal instincts gather him in your arms. That is all great. But life together means much more than that, so do not expect him to be that sunny charmer all the time.

Life with him is not without its share of difficulties. He ponders small issues and is totally impractical at times. You need to be the more sensible of the two, and rooted in reality. The Libran charm and Arian impulsiveness make him the best person to have around when a problem stalks and instant decisions are needed but the same thing will not make him very sensible in family matters.

The best part is that this guy will really listen. If you want to tell him your sorrows, go ahead. Emotions do not bother him but he can be totally insensitive at times. Poor guy is not equipped to understand the unsaid things. Tell him what you feel if you want him to be more sensitive to your needs. If you need a partner who talks, he is the one. He can talk for hours on the most uninteresting topics in the most interesting of ways.

Keep financial decisions under your control. This guy is very good at shopping sprees but hopeless in planning for the future. Relationships and family make him think and rethink every decision and he can really be very indecisive. You will have to take decisions regarding family matters on your own or wait till eternity. In urgent matters, I suggest that you decide and at others, let him think that he is deciding.

Ambition and success are important to him. He works really hard to achieve them but, at the same time, he needs you to be on the same wavelength. He needs

---
[30] *Hi! Blitz*, March 2011

harmonious and balanced surroundings to feel calm. Disorderly and untidy rooms affect him negatively. In the same way, keep yourself well groomed too.

Love and Marriage for Her
She gives her hundred and one percent to keep you happy. This woman does not know when to stop giving. She cares for you like you are the only one in her life. Love is the highest ideal in her life.

There is only one demand that she has for you – ambition and ideals. She wants a partner who has dreams and ideals. Romance is very important to her. When you woo her, do it in style. Get that bouquet of roses, reserve that exclusive seat, make her feel like a million dollars. She will do it for you almost every day of your life.

The AriLib woman can make an excellent career woman too. She will beautifully balance her home and office and be most loving and caring despite the work stress and hectic schedules. The best thing about her is that she is so good in both the spheres that no one seeing her as a caring mother could imagine her as a corporate climber or vice versa. She excels on both counts.

It is best to toughen your hide if you are the sensitive sort for her anger can really hurt. She can blast with the Arian fearlessness or cut you into pieces with her Libran arguments. Either way, it is very difficult for you to win an argument. If you want her to do something it is best to spell it out to her, for no matter how much she loves you, your emotions are a mystery to her.

At the Workplace
AriLibs are very good at communicating their ideas. Libran eloquence and Arian enthusiasm make them excel at promoting new ideas and projects. Positive and zealous workers, hard work will never faze them and they do not mind working till the wee hours of the night, provided they get ample recognition. Keep Arian ambition in mind – they are not satisfied with junior roles for long and always aim high.

Approval and adulation are as important to them as annual raises, probably more so. If they do anything good, announce it to the whole team but give constructive feedback only in private. They have the fearlessness of Aries without its tactlessness. They are more politically astute than Aries and know how to speak their minds without hurting anyone. As bosses, they are liberal and democratic. They will take everyone's opinion and then do what they think is right. You can't expect anything more, for they will not be as autocratic as Aries or as indecisive as Libra.

Fire and Air come together in this combustible combination that breathes beauty and thinks ambition.

Famous AriLib Personalities
Nita Ambani, V.V.S. Laxman, Anushka Sharma, Sania Mirza, L.K. Advani, Kumar Sangakkara, Demi Moore, Prince Charles, Bono (U2), Arun Shourie, Dr Dasari Narayana Rao, Jyothika, Arjun Singh, Lalita Pawar, Antara Mali, Ashok Chavan, Princess Mako of Japan, Ellyse Perry, Christopher Hitchens.

19. ARIES–SCORPIO

Mars, the violent god of war, and Pluto, the ruthless and powerful god of the underworld, combine to make this one dynamite combination. AriScorps create their own rules and never look to anyone for leadership.

Rams can clear any obstacles and Scorpions can survive even nuclear bombs. Think what will happen if the two combine – a Ram with horns at one end and a sting at the other? This is power at the extreme – the charisma of these people is throbbing and palpable. Mars endows them with strength, high energy, extreme restlessness and very high endurance while Pluto imbues them with deep mysterious strength and magnetic energy.

Theirs is a journey of ambition and supremacy. In them, you see the force of conviction and the results of sheer focus. They stand out in a crowd and the people around them either hate them or love them. They have admirable strength and passion. Their amazing mental and physical strength help them withstand any crisis. They may look delicate but their inner strength leaves you shocked.

They have the Arian belief in the magic of their dreams. This belief makes them want to give substance to their wild ideas. They are pioneers who show the world what's possible. They are both absolutely aggressive and in control. They have high levels of integrity, yet if they work in a highly manipulative environment they will be ready to use any weapon to succeed.

They are a mix of naïveté and worldliness. In their earlier years, the brash energy of an Arian peeps through, but as they grow older, the Scorpio ability to read minds and souls makes them unearth anyone's innermost secrets and use them to their benefit. Look at the eyes of an AriScorp they will tell you tales full of energy and control. You will never know that under the calm exterior lurks a seething volcano for they learn how to hide their emotions under an impassive gaze. It is extremely hard to deceive them when their Scorpio radar starts working.

They won't care two hoots about upsetting authority or destabilising established powers. It takes time for them to train themselves to remain calm.

The Arian self-centeredness is also quite evident in AriScorp. Arians are like children, for they want what they want without caring about the consequences. AriScorps are very hard to dissuade once their minds are set on their goals. They don't listen to reason or logic but go for it with all that they have. Is it any wonder that they usually get what they want?

They are known for their temper. They have the Arian temper that will erupt like a volcano and cools down equally fast but if they are deeply hurt then they look for a chance to get even and strike without remorse in true Scorpio fashion. If you love them, you will understand that their temper is an aspect of their strength and if you hate them (for there is no third way) you will not be able to withstand their anger nor the damage that it will do.

There is no humility or modesty in AriScorp. They do not mind flaunting their achievements. Hardships do not distress them; on the contrary, they feel energised at the thought of fighting for things. You cannot put them down in any way. AriScorps are like a force of nature and come back with double the fury to fulfil their ambitions.

In spite of their ego, AriScorps are very generous to their friends. They are loyal and steadfast friends who are passionate about the people they like. You call them brash, rude, arrogant and self-centred? Well, ask the people who had been at the receiving end of their generosity.

Scorpio needs to penetrate every mystery whereas the Arian fearlessness makes them super-inquisitive, and they want to try out everything from drugs to rash driving. They scrutinise the deepest mysteries of the world. From sex to death, from life to past life, they are curious about everything and want to unravel all mysteries. They are also deeply spiritual and have their own ideas on spiritually, sin and salvation.

Aries–Scorpio – Lalit Modi
The Arian pioneering spirit and risk-taking ability, coupled with Scorpio passion, made Lalit Modi create the Indian Premier League (IPL).

He says, 'I did things [for starting the IPL] when nobody had done those kind of things…we had hired the best people, we hired the best companies, when you do things for innovating a product or coming out with a pioneering product, if anybody could do it then I wouldn't be needed.'[31]

According to his mother Bina Modi: 'He is brash, even arrogant…he will never curl up and die.'[32]

Lalit Modi personifies an AriScorp.

Love and Marriage for Him
If you are his partner, get ready for an exhilarating time. He shows you the rewards of ambition and power and takes you with him in his quest for dominance. But you must not question him. He needs somebody whom he can control and who is ready to hand the reins over to him. Submission does not mean slavery. He ensures that you enjoy the best of everything: just do not try and guide him.

Totally possessive and loyal, he can never leave you or even think of another. His ambitions and you are all that he wants. Similarly, he wants to be the centre of your existence and needs you to plan your life around him. You must pamper and love him like no one else.

The Arian streak in him makes him impetuous but also brings about an inner fear – something he never shows. When you see that vulnerable side of him, hold his hand and tell him he is right when the whole world doubts him. That's all he wants to hear and that is all that is needed to get him charged up again. He is a fighter and it will be ideal if you play the stable and calm part. After all, the kids will need some soft handling and he will never give them that. You will have to be the more mature and understanding one in the relationship.

As a father, he is extremely dominating and expects his children to follow his orders. Though age mellows him, it does not stop him from controlling. His overpowering influence can either lead them on to leadership or curtail their talents.

---
[31] http://en.wikipedia.org/wiki/Lalit_modi
[32] *Times of India*, 22 May 2010, pg 40

Love and Marriage for Her
She is the strongest woman of the zodiac! This lady possesses extraordinary strength and determination. She is a lioness when angered and is not the person to be disregarded or mistreated. As a girl, she is surely a tomboy – loud, aggressive and unafraid.

You will have to love her wholeheartedly or she will not stand by you. This woman needs a man who loves her for her strength and does not put her down. You will have to be man enough to take her on. She will love deeply and passionately. She can be sensuous, even with her commanding nature. This lady will know you to your smallest faults and can love you despite them.

She has the naïveté of a child at times and you will be surprised by her zest for life. She will never turn cynical and will have a can-do attitude. She has a lot of ambitions and, over time, she hones it down to one. She can walk the road all by her own but will be very happy if you decide to share her passions.

She is full of vivacity and charm and nothing is impossible to her. There may be moments of self-doubt. She needs an understanding friend in a husband.

As a mother, she loves and commands her children. Her love for them is absolute and so is her desire to see them succeed. She motivates them to achieve high dreams. Sometimes, she disregards their dreams in order to control their destinies.

At the Workplace
Pioneering and strong, AriScorps have the ability to develop and create amazing business ideas. With their aggression, dominance and need for control, they love to lead and carve out a niche for themselves. AriScorp can never follow; submission is not in their nature. They are self-motivated. They love contests and enjoy crashing on the finish line. Winning is an aphrodisiac for them and they go all out for it.

Their only flaw is that they do not know when to give up. They can become too brash to succeed at times. With age, the Scorpio ability to read every situation and maintain a steely exterior makes them even more formidable. AriScorps never play for small stakes and need everything – money, power and luxury.

As bosses, they are superb in drawing up a plan and executing it in grand style. The bigger the plan, the more excruciating the path, the more the challenges, the more they are charged up to meet those. But they do falter on the finer points. They need the help of Virgos to tighten up the loose ends.

Fire and Water meet in this astoundingly forceful combination. AriScorps can be saints or sinners; there is no third way for them. This powerful combination can either self-destruct or become the leader with a million followers. Their actions decide their fate and that's the way they like it.

Famous AriScorp Personalities
Lalit Modi, Dharmendra, Sharad Pawar, Jonathan Trott, Pat Cummins, Tipu Sultan, Dia Mirza, Moushumi Chatterjee, Sweta Bhupathy, Ian Healy, Vanderlei Luxemburgo, I.K. Gujral, Divya Spandana, Jamie Foxx, G.V.K. Sanjay Reddy, Bhumibol Adulyadej, Kommareddy Savitri.

20. ARIES–SAGITTARIUS

Extroverted, talkative, full of energy, and optimistic – it is very hard to overlook this combination. The Aries-Sagittarius combination has Mars, the lord of war and courage, and Jupiter, symbolising optimism, valour and wisdom. A Ram and a Centaur – pure power! With these two powerful, fast and furious signs in them, AriSags behave like intelligent warriors. It is also the combination of two of the most idealistic zodiac signs.

AriSags are highly intelligent but not tactful or diplomatic since both the signs are known for their bluntness. They are totally optimistic, though, the kind of people who always see a silver lining. Interestingly, you will notice a strange naïveté in these people despite their go-getter attitude.

Highly ambitious, both men and women in this combination revel in glory and power. Money does not rank high on their list and neither do they excel in managing finances. Their dreams are mightier than that. Of course, they know that once they have power and glory, the rest is sure to follow.

Tradition and convention do not bother them either. They go along with tradition as long as it matches their views. They are pioneers and forge ahead eschewing mediocrity, while lesser mortals wonder how they achieved such stupendous success. They do everything in extremes and you must not expect humility from them. Due to their high intelligence and quick grasping powers, they can seem quite arrogant while dealing with the less talented.

They are adventurous to the extreme. If you see a guy jumping with joy at the thought of falling down a cliff, he must be an AriSag; the more frightening and horrifying an expedition, the more excited he is. Death-defying stunts, adrenalin-pumping rides, sports and bets involving high risk – all these get them totally excited. On the flip side, they cannot tolerate physical pain.

These people can be highly destructive when angry as both the signs are known for their violent tempers. Beware of getting in their bad books: they act impulsively and with deep violence when angry. After the volcano erupts, peace will reign; but you know how destructive volcanoes are, right?

They take calculated risks and have a knack for what others think is gambling. They will be the centre of attraction of any gathering or party and you can't escape their loud jokes and strong backslapping. They are the ones who hit the dance floor first and stay till the wee hours. Their energy levels cannot be matched. Remember they are half-human, half-horse Centaurs, plus the Ram. Raw energy!

Romance features large on their list of things to do on a grand scale. They are not exactly promiscuous but they can go searching for excellence from one relationship to another – leaving them disillusioned. Actually, they want a partner who is intelligent and good-looking, as eye-catching as they are. Sometimes they also get confused between love and friendship. With age, they mellow down and learn to accept that people are not as perfect as they want them to be – so they usually settle down later in life, unless they find their dream partner early.

The Sagittarian dislike of family ties is slightly reduced, but AriSags are definitely independent. They live alone at a shockingly young age but will always be there when the family needs them. They will be the pillars of the family without being glued to them. The Arian tendency of demarcating people into 'mine' and 'others' is quite strong in them too. You are either with them or against them.

Optimism guides their thoughts to success. They might have periods of self-doubt, but those phases rarely last and nor will you know when they occur, for they never even hint at failure. They hide their insecurity in bluster and never admit even to themselves their secret fears.

They are very spiritual. This combination contains the two biggest believers of the zodiac and they believe in the power above. They are absolutely fascinated by abstract and higher knowledge, including astral science, esoteric principles and any form of spirituality. They believe in the goodness of people too. But more often, they end up with people who are unfaithful. They become disillusioned to know that people are not as straightforward or simple as they are. Still they don't lose hope and keep trying with their inborn optimism.

Aries–Sagittarius – Bipasha Basu
'I don't follow rules. I have my own set of rules.'[33]

'My otherwise mundane morning ritual of green tea and small chores is never boring, courtesy my high tempo music.'[34]

Basu, who describes herself as a tomboy, was fondly called 'Lady Don' in her school as everyone was scared of her.[35]

Right from her first movie, *Jism*, where she managed to wow everyone with her acting and sex appeal, Bipasha has never walked the conventional path. She is a fun-loving AriSag who defines herself by her own rules.

Love and Marriage for Him
If an AriSag has chosen you, you are exceptional! He needs an extraordinary mate to keep the flame alive. But no matter how extraordinary you are, treat him as exceptional too. He does not like being criticised in public. Throw him amorous glances during private gatherings and I promise you that he will remain loyal.

Do not nag when you are with him. He prefers an independent girl who can manage herself and the household with elegance and charm. Let him do the manly things and you handle the feminine side of things. He has no problems with you working. Just ensure that your work does not take over the boardroom and your income does not exceed his.

His honesty is his strength and weakness. It is very hard for him to portray things other than as they are and he shows no sensitivity. Never expect him to know how you feel or read your thoughts. If you want him to understand you, tell him how you feel minus the tears and only then will he know. You can expect him to become a little more understanding with age.

He is the most optimistic person around, so do not fill his ears with misery and never say, 'I told you so'. The deep-seated insecurity within him needs comforting.

---

[33] http://getahead.rediff.com/slide-show/2010/jul/19/slide-show-1-glamour-an-interview-with-bipasha-basu.htm
[34] http://www.hindustantimes.com/Entertainment/Music/Music-makes-my-world-go-round-Bipasha/Article1-844516.aspx
[35] http://en.wikipedia.org/wiki/Bipasha_Basu

He loves to travel and takes you along on his adventure trips. He may be a genius with money, but he cannot handle household accounts. His love for eye-catching trinkets will make him quite unreliable in managing savings.

As a father, he emphasises upon his children being open to learning and remaining positive in all situations.

Love and Marriage for Her
With a double male sign, this girl is totally special. Men find her too much to handle and women grudge all the attention she gets. She is a tomboy, a brat – uninhibited, absolutely frank and forthright. She is approachable but has a mind of her own. Respect her ideas and never put her down, for this bubbly and enthusiastic girl demands to be heard with deference. She is not frightened by anything or anyone.

This girl is the happiest if you do something to make her proud. She needs a partner who can be bold and achieve success. If you can't do that, then she will ungrudgingly take up the challenge and work hard to gain respect and power. Do not dampen her spirits by telling her that she is not capable of reaching for the stars. Independent and strong, she is not easily found in the kitchen. She loves her family but cannot be tied down. If you want to live peacefully, I suggest that you live as a nuclear family. Joint families stifle her and kill the joy of relationships. She needs her space.

She may be bossy at times and you often wish that she understood you better. You wish you could make her rooted and tone down her theatrics. But that's ingrained in her and nothing can change her. Accept her for her strengths and enjoy her optimism.

She needs lots of help in the initial years as a mother. She will be very controlling and finds it difficult to understand the innermost needs of her children.

At the Workplace
This combination is a born leader who has to learn to start at the bottom. They are fabulous initiators and promoters. Marketing is part of their DNA and if they agree with a concept, they sell it extremely well. They believe in bold strokes. They leave methodical and meticulous work to others. AriSags are great at delivering results and thinking 'out of the box'. They have a weakness for feeling prized. They work hard but only if you remember to applaud them every day in front of their colleagues and seniors.

They have a thirst for knowledge and love going to seminars and conferences. Beware of their temper, it can give rise to messy issues. They have to be told to be cautious while dealing with seniors and to be tactful. If you are their boss, ensure that their sheer exuberance and positivity is balanced with practicality and proper planning from your end. Mentoring roles also appeal to their sense of worth and they love being looked up to.

Double Fire signs give the fire in the belly, the desire to bully and the never-ending telly of the AriSag!

Famous AriSag Personalities
Bipasha Basu, Mukesh Ambani, Hitler, Dawood Ibrahim, Nagma, Emma Watson, Sabeer Bhatia, Abhinav Mukund, Manoj Prabhakar, Yehudi Menuhin, Gary Cooper, Sofia Coppola, Ryan Seacrest, Howard Stern, Felipe Massa, Stan Lee, Sapna Bhavnani.

21. ARIES–CAPRICORN

The AriCap combines the fiery, powerful and often violent Mars with the wise old man Saturn. Saturn gives the sign an earthy touch along with a scheming practicality.

The signs of Aries and Capricorn are the Ram and the Goat. The Ram of Aries adds its strong legs and fierce horns to the steadiness of the Capricorn mountain Goat. These Goats definitely love the view from the top. The AriCaps climb nimbly over difficulties to reach there.

Both Aries and Capricorn are cardinal signs, so AriCaps are born to lead. The energy, enthusiasm and raw power of Aries combine with the practicality of Capricorn to lead them to sure victory. Due to the Capricornian stability, AriCaps are not given to the impulsive and rash actions that mark Aries, nor do they rush to lead. They prefer a slow and steady rise wherein they learn everything that is required to be learnt in order to succeed and become indispensible. The desire for control is very strong in them. The seriousness of Capricorn reduces the over-enthusiasm of Aries and gives it stability.

This is an amazing combination with the merging of the conservative Capricorn with forward-thinking Aries. They will use tried and tested methodologies and also be open to new ideas. They revere ancient esoteric knowledge, are highly spiritual and pay obeisance to elders and people who have climbed the path before them. But they also possess a brilliant, pioneering mind that can think of path-breaking innovative ideas. AriCaps will use original ideas grounded in reality to achieve their dreams.

They have an extraordinary knack of being in the right place at the right time. They will somehow smell an opportunity and pursue it relentlessly. If you can be a catalyst in their growth, you will be their best friend. They seem to be in the *'me, me, me'* mode sometimes as both Aries and Capricorn are known to be self-absorbed. Call them selfish? It doesn't matter to them as long you get their stuff done. They actually realise their idiosyncrasy and will try and make it appear a win-win for you.

While Aries can think of no obstacle in their path, Capricorn thinks of all the obstacles possible and finds ways to remove them. Therefore, AriCaps are never blindly optimistic, but you can be sure that if they see no problem, there truly is no problem in sight.

They are the most responsible and persevering people you know. They spend money cautiously. They dress conservatively and buy things that are necessary for their careers or families. Family is very important to them. They are very protective of their family members. Capricorn makes Aries very conservative and both love control, so if they are the head of the family, their word is law.

The Arian romanticism and love of public displays of affection take a backseat due to the inherent Capricornian reserve. Emotions are not easy for them. Plus there is no Water element so they will not be good at reading emotional nuances. The lack of Air in this combination makes them more reserved when young. AriCaps are basically late bloomers; the lack of confidence in their earlier years makes them work for security and money. When they achieve some success and feel more secure in their position, then they start looking for love. At those times they can enter fearlessly into unconventional relationships.

Their anger is not violent; they know how to get their way without lashing out. They can keep their cool in the most trying of circumstances. They are master tacticians and politically astute. They need not show anger publicly. They get back at you, but subtly. But don't try to push your luck too far. There is the fiery Aries in them and they can erupt horrifically if seriously wronged.

There is one thing that they do not like you to know – their fear. Arians have a deep-seated insecurity; they just don't want to fail and that makes them fearful. Capricorns, on the other hand, are highly pessimistic, for they can see all the problems that can arise. They will always prepare for the worst. They have a secret inferiority complex too. Their proud poise and external nonchalance are shields to hide this mysterious and sometimes even melancholic interior.

They want to balance out success both in professional and personal lives. They want people to look up to them. They want the applause; they want to hold that trophy proudly when the entire world cheers for them. They work very hard and passionately to leave a legacy. They will.

Aries–Capricorn – George Clooney
'So when you're eighty years old and they ask you what you did, you can go, "When I had the keys to the car, I drove it as fast as I could and as hard as I could. I took it to places that the owner didn't really want me to take it." That's a fun thing to do. Understanding that at some point they're going to come back and repossess the car. I just want to be able to say we gave it a shot when we had the time.'

'There's ten of us, we've been best friends for thirty years. Ten guys. And their wives, and their kids, are all family now.'[36]

Aries and Capricorn meet in George Clooney to give him power, drive and sustainability.

Love and Marriage for Him
He seeks someone who is stable and collected. Arranged marriage is more to his liking than runaway romance. He prefers a partner from a distinguished family. He is totally driven and ambitious. You have to recognise the fact that his career is more important to him. Of course, family too gets his attention, but he shows his caring love through the things he does for his family rather than emotions and words. If you want a guy who will sing praises of your beauty and look at you adoringly while you work, you have come to the wrong guy. Try and teach him how to express his love.

Keep the home environment calm and don't stress him out with small issues. He has a deep-seated need to control. He may not shout or boss his way around, but when he decides, the decision is final. You need to learn that his word is law. He is very sentimental but does not like displaying it. You can be sure, though, that family is the most important thing to him after his career.

Fatherhood suits him to a T. Capricorn rules fatherhood. As a father, respect is integral to his relationship with his children. As long as they follow his dreams, he

---
[36] http://www.esquire.com/features/what-ive-learned/meaning-of-life-2012/george-clooney-quotes-0112-3

is happy. A problem might arise if the children are rebellious or don't believe in his conservative and traditional ways.

Love and Marriage for Her
Ambition is important to her. She can live contentedly as a housewife if you have big dreams. She is the ultimate support in times of need. Aries loves to have a partner who can truly astound everyone around in looks, intelligence and style; whereas the Capricorn girl wants a guy who is well settled. She does not go for a guy who talks poetry and romance but has an empty pocket. Financial stability is extremely important to her. Love does not make her blind to your lineage, stability or prosperity. She wants it all.

She is totally fearless and extremely jealous, so never think that you can get away with a fling on the side. This girl can work extremely hard, support you totally, be there for her family but if she gets the smallest hint of an affair – all her angelic qualities will disappear. All she asks is for you to treat her with respect and love.

As a mother, she is extremely caring. Her children are always well dressed. She takes them for extra classes and works hard to bring them up to be as ambitious and hard working as herself. Her children are never lazy. The only problem is emotional bonding. Their innermost dreams remain unknown to her.

At the Workplace
AriCaps have the ambition to reach the top. The fact that they are far away from the top never deters them, it acts as a spur to motivate them. Their ambition will never be spelled out in words and you might not see a lot of attitude in them. These guys believe in hard work and planning. They work so well that they make themselves indispensible. After that they will rule. The most intelligent thing is to realise that while they are your juniors. Treat them well, mentor them for one day they will achieve the success and you can claim to have recognised their abilities before anyone else.

They are very good at delegating and supervising. They know how to bring out the best in people. Their costing is always accurate. As bosses, they delegate but have total control. Control is the cornerstone of their work triangle that includes effort and strategy.

AriCaps are not fazed by scale: the bigger the scale, the higher their ambition, the harder they work. One day they will want to be their own boss. Aries never wants to report to others while Capricorn is fabulous at business. Politics is also a field that opens naturally to them.

Fire and Earth mix in this double cardinal sign. Leadership is the star that rules over AriCaps; being mere followers is not their destiny.

Famous AriCap Personalities
George Clooney, Andre Agassi, Vladimir Lenin, Xavi Hernandez, Tony Blair, Dr Zakir Hussein (freedom fighter), Uma Thurman, Romario, Taylor Lautner, Vijay Anand, Shoaib Malik, Ashley Judd, Chris Rock, Estelle Lefébure, Ravi Subramanian, Jessica Lange, S. Janaki, Ashwin Sanghi, Orson Welles.

22. ARIES–AQUARIUS

Mars, the violent and powerful lord of war, and Uranus, the eccentric planet of invention and science, come together to make AriAqua a totally rocking combination. Mars of Aries gives this person raw energy and power while the radioactive powers of Aquarius add a totally new dimension. It is forceful energy with the ability to create and/or destroy.

This is again a double male sign. So do not expect the people of this combination to be subdued and ready to listen to suggestions. Both these signs are very outgoing and this makes them total live wires. The Arian energy makes the futuristic Aquarian ideas stand out. Aquarius is one of the most intelligent and unconventional signs of the zodiac. It is also a fixed sign while Aries is a cardinal one. Bubbling with energy and enthusiasm, they love sharing their ideas, which are never ordinary. Both Aries and Aquarius have very high ideals and their thoughts reach for the impossible.

AriAquas are extremely direct and do not give subtle hints. They simply barge in and tell you what they think is right. They are immutable. Once these guys get an idea, no matter how eccentric or out of the world, they will work relentlessly and zealously to make it happen.

Aquarius bestows a fabulous knowledgeable brain and also the ability to read people's minds. Don't try to fool them. AriAquas can see through your innermost secrets and read your devious plans. They are also extremely sensitive to your fears, feelings and failings. But the biggest irony is that despite knowing everything about you they will remain nonchalant and detached. They are not very comfortable showing effusive personal emotions, though they passionately reciprocate high ideals.

They are the most inquisitive and scientific personalities of the zodiac. Expect them to have unlimited interest in everything that is mysterious and deep. If it is a person then they may show deep interest in the person till the mystery is solved. They find it difficult to hold on to any one person for long. They are seekers but unsure of what they are seeking in a person or a possibility. If it is the esoteric, spiritual and divine principles of life that spark their interest, they won't rest till all things are known to them.

AriAquas do not remain the same throughout their lives. The Aquarian love of re-inventing themselves and the Arian desire to show off make them try different hairstyles, looks and clothes. They love being outrageous just to get attention. AriAquas get a high from breaking rules, norms or conventions. They also get bored very quickly. They sometimes seek change just for a change.

They do have a humanitarian streak and like to give to charity or work for the betterment of society, but only after their ambitions are met. The Aquarian dream of an equal society runs through them and their heart is touched by poverty and the maladies which afflict society. Combined with Arian idealism, they become rebels who fight for any cause and against any kind of discrimination. They love changing the rules of the game and bring in a change.

There is one more common thread between the two – speed. Arians love speed while Aquarius's dreaminess makes them think they are flying in a space ship. The Aquarian clumsiness is also to blame for their numerous accidents – glasses will break and stains will blot their clothes. They love adventure. Aquarius always wants to try something new, be it drugs or games, while Arians don't know the meaning of fear. You can expect these guys to have tried their hand at everything at least once.

AriAquas are extremely difficult to control as they scoff at anything that borders on tradition and convention. Aries think they know everything while Aquarius just wants to do things differently. They often quarrel with family elders because of this. There is a silver lining, though – after they hit their thirties expect them to start exhibiting some mature behaviour.

They make fantastic friends. They are people who can even kill for their friends; their extreme anger cannot tolerate people who bad-mouth their friends. They can also be totally possessive, especially of people whom they love.

The people of this combination will take some time in settling down. The Arian ambition drives them to work towards their dreams with little time for anything else while Aquarius works to brings about change. Things beyond their ambition and dreams hold little attraction for them. Despite their desire to change the world they remain unchanged at the core – their personal habits and belief systems.

Aries–Aquarius – Tiger Shroff

'I don't take even a day off. Even when I am not shooting, I go for my martial arts training.'

'I wanted to be an athlete.'

'*Heropanti* gave me an opportunity to showcase my skills as a dancer and an acrobat.'

'Kriti is a very pretty woman but I had to stay focused and not get distracted.'

'I don't have a good track record with girls. None of my relationships have lasted long.'[37]

Tiger Shroff is brutally honest, intensely focused, passionately devoted to work and clear about his long-term goals as befits a typical AriAqua.

Love and Marriage for Him

When you marry him, please understand that you are his second love. His first and undying love is ambition. He spends a lot of time thinking, talking and acting on his dreams. He will adore you if you can fine-tune his ideas.

Routine monotonous work is not his forte, neither are understanding and sensitivity his strong points. Of course, Aquarius gives him an insight into people's behaviour, but he is detached about it. Do not expect him to understand your sighs or expressions. The ground rule for dealing with him is to express yourself verbally. Ask, 'Aren't I looking good?' and he will respond.

He needs a partner who can take care of things while he is out working on his ideas. You must support and believe in him. Never run him down, especially in public: the Arian ego cannot take it and things can get ugly if you do.

---

[37] *Mumbai Mirror*, 7 April 2014

His ideal holiday involves some adventure. He loves adventurous sports. He may be a tad self-centred and selfish. As long as he is happy, he feels everyone else is happy too. If your ambitions clash with his, it is better that you two go your separate ways for he will not compromise.

He may not be around much during the early parenting days. Expect him to team up with his children and be great friends with them when they hit their teens. He will teach them to learn unlimited and live fearless.

Love and Marriage for Her
She is supercharged and ambitious. Do not expect her to nurse you or cook for you. Nothing she does is common. This is a lady whose ideas and views astound everyone.

She may deny it but she is deeply romantic, though she does not indulge in feminine wiles. If she looks at a man at all, her expectations of him are sky-high. She is a very strong personality and expects someone who can measure up to the idealistic standards that she has set for herself. Now you know that you must be someone special for her to agree to be with you. She never comes to you asking for help or protection.

She does not expect compliments. She will open her own doors and never fear authority. She can be quite aggressive and totally unladylike when her will is thwarted. It is not advisable to try and arouse her jealousy. She can erupt like a volcano and leave without ever looking back.

Lack of ambition in a life partner embitters her and she thinks of it as a weakness. If you want a friend, there is no one to match her. She is the most adorable, enthusiastic, fun loving, intelligent and extraordinary friend you can ever have.

She needs a lot of help in the initial years of bringing up her children. She encourages originality in them and fights with everyone for them.

At the Workplace
AriAquas are natural promoters. They can take an idea and make it sound like the eighth wonder of the world. They make fabulous salespeople, but you do not find them behind a sales counter. These guys are made for something bigger. They are good in professions that change continuously and there is plenty of action. They want to give this world something unique, different, pioneering and alluringly amazing.

They resist authority. They have a way of ruffling feathers that can prove disastrous to them if not controlled. They are highly innovative but some of their ideas may be too futuristic. You have to keep your balance and not be swept away by the power of their presentation. It is ideal if they have Virgos, Tauruses or Capricorns as their personal assistants or subordinates. They need some practical people to bring their dreams to the proper conclusion.

As bosses, they will only look at results and wouldn't waste time in knowing the exact processes. They acknowledge smart work and innovation more than hard, mundane work. They love employees who work faster. But remember that in their eyes they are the most intelligent, the smartest and the best. Acknowledge that.

Passion and genius come together in these extraordinary, fearless people who believe in magic and have in them the power to change the world for the better.

Famous AriAqua Personalities
Remo Fernandes, Tiger Shroff, Ross Taylor, Satyajit Ray, Cristina Kirchner, Omar Abdullah, Gopal Krishna Gokhale, Gordon Greenidge, Bobby Fischer, Jessica Alba, Chaitanya Mahaprabhu, Nalini Jaywant, Jerry Seinfeld, Sakshi Shivanand, Anna Magnani.

23. ARIES–PISCES

This is a meeting of the spiritual and the temporal. Mars, the violent and powerful god of war, joins forces with the deep and mysterious lord of the seas, Neptune, to give this combination power, drive and the will to succeed, coupled with compassion and empathy. This is truly a meeting of opposites: the most confident meets the most self-doubting and the most self-centred meets the most worldly. Think of a fish with a horn! Narwhal?

When you meet AriPisces for the first time, they wow you with their energy, positivity and enthusiasm. You go away convinced that you have met the most confident, dynamic and super-smart person ever. Get close to them and they surprise you with their vulnerable, sensitive and under-confident side. This softness serves to emphasise their larger-than-life aura.

AriPisces are intuitive and fearless. These two abilities make them shine through difficulties. They know exactly what people think and can use it to further their own aims without being deceitful. The creative and imaginative ideas of Pisces and the original pioneering thoughts of Aries find a fearless soil to grow in. They take the middle path as it helps them think their way to success. No problem is ever too great for them to handle.

They love adventure. Aries is always a risk-taker while Pisces never dreams of the mundane. You can expect them to try out adventure sports and give in to wild dreams.

They are extremely creative and artistic. Pisceans have a fertile mind with the wildest imagination while Aries powers the shy Pisces to express itself with confidence. These people can express the softest emotions in the most beautiful form either in poetry, the arts, writing or even acting. The Piscean ability to learn and reflect quickly and the childlike Arian enthusiasm can make them the best students and later the masters of any craft or the performing arts.

Pisces is amazingly romantic and their idea of romance goes beyond candle-light dinners to the heart and the soul. Aries believes in the ideal version of love and looks for high ideals in its mate.

Money has no value other than as currency for them. Aries can spend in an unpredictable fashion and Pisces is too unworldly to be concerned with petty matters like saving or investing. These guys believe in increasing their income rather than decreasing their expenditure.

Anger is another Arian fault which is very visible in them, but the calming influence of Pisces tones it down. Hence, their anger is not malicious. Expect them to produce a barrage of verbal volleys or sulk furiously when they feel insulted or undermined. Though they are not vengeful, they never forget.

They long for just two things – love and adulation. They need their daily dose of admiring glances and large doses of love from their loved ones and even people they meet for the first time. The not-so-evolved variety of the AriPisces can resort to absurd tactics to hog the limelight. They may even scheme and control their friends and loved ones and create drama to attract attention and get sympathy.

Piscean mood swings can afflict them at times. They can get cranky and depressed, but the unshakeable optimism of Aries pulls them out. All Fire signs show an outward confidence while deep down they suffer from insecurities, while Pisces is never far from fears. Don't be fooled by their bravado and confidence, they do have fears but will never let you know.

Despite knowing about the temporal world, still they cling to the materialistic aspects of life due to their insecurities. They may also develop an addiction or have issues with weight management or a sweet tooth due to the Piscean in them. They can also be completely deceptive if they choose to. The AriPisces can even be the most self-centred and malicious conman who can get away unnoticed with his fish-like deceptiveness.

The more evolved AriPisces understand the temporal nature of the world and embrace spirituality. They understand the deepest mysteries of the world instinctively and become champions of the underprivileged.

Basic life options for AriPisces – fearless visionary genius with great sensitivity or self-obsessed, self-pitying, extra-sensitive soul with a myopic view.

Aries–Pisces – Chetan Bhagat
'I am not judgemental, my characters in the book are not perfect, and they do falter.'[38]

'Dealing with the lack of writing success — well, I think I will devote myself to spiritual activity more.'

'The 'safety' was the main reason to stay on, as were the middle-class upbringing values that you just don't quit an MNC bank job. I think the final point came when I was able to overcome the lure of money.'[39]

Creative, idealistic, sensitive and philosophical, Chetan Bhagat is a true blend of the fiery Aries and the thoughtful Pisces.

Love and Marriage for Him
He is a very good husband, for Aries is typically all about 'me and my family' and Pisces is very sensitive to its spouse's needs. First things first, you are this guy's ideal so please never do anything that would in any way hurt your ideal status. He may find it difficult to come to terms with the fact that you have your own failings.

Life with him is an adventure trip. He loves travelling and it is great if you share the same love or you may end up feeling lonely. This guy is open to experimentation and does not mind trying out new cuisines or ideas. His ego is quite diluted due to the Piscean effect but he would still mind if you earn more than him. However, he likes you to do your own thing. He loves being pampered, too. You have to be a little thick-skinned around his anger for he can really blow his top.

A word of advice: never speak negatively about his plans and never say 'I told you so'. If you feel that there is certainly something amiss, find a softer way to tell him. This guy needs to keep himself surrounded with positivity.

---

[38] http://zeenews.india.com/entertainment/literature-festival/my-next-novel-is-a-love-story-chetan-bhagat_21936.htm
[39] http://business.in.com/interview/magazine-extra/an-interview-with-chetan-bhagat/8452/1

It is brilliant if you are good at money management for this is one area where he fails. You need to be the one who plans, thinks and saves for the future.

He is a proud father. The Pisces in him instinctively understands his kids' needs and he always motivates them to work towards their dreams without forcing them to do as he says. He is a guide and friend to his children.

Love and Marriage for Her
She is independent, strong, sure and assertive. At times, she is too aggressive to be feminine, but if you love her, you get to see her soft and mushy side. She is extremely intelligent. Take her on if you have deep emotional strength and are not bothered by masculine insecurities. She is highly idealistic and needs a person who fits her version of the 'ideal'. This girl always strives hard to create magic in her world and it is nice if you applaud her success.

She may seem adventurous and even rebellious, but deep inside she is very insecure. The façade of the brave girl she portrays is for the outside world. She craves love and attention, and she depends on you for emotional support. Love her deeply and show her that you care. She cannot manage money but needs a lot of it to live her dreams.

As a mother, she is definitely caring but may take her time deciding to take on that responsibility. When she does, her Piscean instincts guide her beautifully.

At the Workplace
AriPisces ambitions are always sky-high. The Aries in them wants to do something original to astound people. They are totally focused on getting a 'wow' and cannot be tied down to routine jobs. You can expect them to try their hand at many things. They need to travel and move around when they work and are excellent in marketing.

They have the potential to become superstars in the arts. Pisces gives them creative genius and Aries propels them to showcase their talents fearlessly. You can expect these bubbly people to shine in the arts, writing or acting; any profession that takes them away from the beaten track. They shine because they are not chasing money but excellence. They need appreciation and love as much as we need oxygen.

He will be the most jovial, fun-loving and generous boss who makes the environment exciting to work in. They are very flexible and understanding. Yet you can expect to see them charge at you if you let them down. If he is working for you, then you need to give him the flexibility of time.

Fire and Water makes them dream big dreams and breathe originality into common ideas. Fiery yet sensitive, wise yet enthusiastic, AriPisces are a bundle of contradictions that work perfectly together.

Famous AriPisces Personalities
Chetan Bhagat, Marlon Brando, Rabindranath Tagore, Sheila Dikshit, Vincent Van Gogh, B.R. Chopra, Diana Hayden, Murli Vijay, Dev Patel, King Carl XVI Gustaf, Motilal Nehru, Robert Downey Jr., Mandira Bedi, Margaret Alva, Dominique Strauss-Kahn, M.R. Radha, Hans Christian Anderson, Ram Gopal Verma, Norah Jones, David Gower, Doris Day, Gregory Peck, Patricia Woertz, Manal Al-Sharif, Sonja Henie, John Gielgud, Stewart Granger, Uma Bharati, Ludwig Wittgenstein, Dwayne Smith, Jean Paul Gaultier.

24. TAURUS–GEMINI

Taurus means material possessions and practical common sense whereas Gemini displays excellent communication skills and a mind brimming with ideas. TauGems are a combination of opposites. Taurus is known for its common sense and monosyllabic conversational style while Gemini is known for its quicksilver mind, so you can expect this combination to be an interesting mix of the two.

This sign is a combination of extreme intelligence and emotional stability. TauGems give an impression of deep solidity when you meet them, but do not be deceived by it. Their minds are in a constant whirl for they process many things in parallel but they have a method to this madness. All their thoughts are inordinately practical. They can do the weirdest and wildest of things with absolute resolution and nonchalance. Their empathy is restricted only to their loved ones. With others, they can play all manner of mind games to get their way.

Their Taurean side pushes them to achieve material success whereas Gemini makes charming presenters. They understand the power of their words. They know exactly what to say to get the desired results. If annoying you with verbal attacks will get things done, they will do so.

The instinctive Taurean money-management skills are very evident in TauGems. They are excellent negotiators and always look for bargains. They make good investments and know more than one way to multiply money. They are an interesting combination. They love tradition, they are very family oriented, love food, love all the luxuries and are materialistic too. But at the same time they are not bound to any of these for their happiness.

Taurus blesses them with artistic abilities and Gemini makes them multitalented. Expect to find superb creativity and artistic expression in dance, drama, singing and even mimicry. The Gemini wordsmith when combined with the monosyllabic Taurus lets them weave magic with words – both written and verbal. They can express the most in minimum words.

Travel is high on their list of must-do's. TauGems think so much, that at times they need to push their bodies out of routine just to feel alive. They are also very patriotic and love everything about their country.

You can also expect them to have lots of friends. These people spread sunshine wherever they go and are excellent at creating and maintaining relationships. No one can ever be bored in such stimulating company. Of course there will be a small element of moodiness in them and periods when they prefer solitude to laughter, but these will be minimal.

There is no Water element in this combination and that makes it lack sensitivity and empathy. They do not have built-in scanners to read emotions. They want direct, simple communication. TauGems are such intensely pragmatic people that they always find a solution to every problem and can't see anything to be hurt, fearful or guilty about. Their lack of sensitivity also makes them extremely comfortable in their own skin.

The Gemini feeling of not knowing where they want to go, and the desire to always be someplace else, afflicts them. TauGems have a strange conundrum. They are deeply sentimental and extremely sensuous. They quiver at a touch and are mushy about their mates. But they also despise deep emotional bonds, need their own space and may remain detached. They are fine if you are away for some time. They also need a lot of mental stimulation; they seek a companion who matches them on the mental plane as well.

They will never ever be truly content or happy: they will always search for that special dream. This feeling afflicts them in love too. TauGems will never be content with their current love and always look beyond. It can make them try out multiple partners before the calming effect of the Taurus in them makes them understand their complex desires. TauGems are not bothered by infidelity; they will not collapse with guilt at having an affair and treat it with extreme nonchalance.

With their love for talk and a mind that ventures into multiple channels, don't be surprised if you hear TauGems turn away from the views they expressed two hours ago. You can never go by their word for they have a way of rethinking and rewording everything to make it sound different the next time you hear it.

Taurus–Gemini – L.N. Mittal

Excerpts from an interview with Simi Garewal (LNM – Laxmi Niwas Mittal, SG – Simi Garewal):

LNM: I'm an Indian first and I'm very proud of that.
SG: Between the two of you, who talks more and who listens?
LNM: Normally wives should talk a lot but in this case I talk a lot!
SG: So in what way is Aditya's relationship with you different to your relationship with your father?
LNM: I think our relation is very unique. We are very close friends, very close friends.[40]

Mittal is a true TauGem with his love for family and country, entrepreneurial instincts, intelligence, talkative nature and desire for luxury.

Love and Marriage for Him

There are many blessings for you to count although he is not exceptionally emotional. He has an exciting sense of humour. He is able to recount anecdotes, think pragmatically and be a very good companion. If you are prone to worrying, he comforts you with simple solutions.

Family is extremely important to him, though you may not feel it at times when he is really busy with his myriad projects and distractions. He is also a hit with relatives. This is one guy who loves his mother-in-law and does not run at the sight of her. He treats your family as his own.

He ensures that you have everything you need though he likes to spend wisely not lavishly. Monetary possessions are a big factor to him and, sometimes, you may have to play the moderator to stop him from trying out shortcuts to success.

---

[40] http://www.rediff.com/money/2006/may/06mittal.htm

He likes to travel a lot. It not only excites, but also rejuvenates him. He needs to see new places and new faces.

As a father, he is fun and educative. He broadens their minds and helps them look at life logically. He may not be around sometimes but he makes it up with his sane advice and long chats.

Love and Marriage for Her

Although she seems stable and grounded, her mind is in a whirl. It runs helter-skelter. This lady just does not relax. She is always doing things but with practical, commonsensical logic. She loves to multi-task and does so efficiently.

She is definitely not clingy or possessive and finds it very strange if you resort to such methods. She is your friend – independent, opinionated and fun. She is sensuous and also needs a companion who can keep her challenged mentally. She doesn't drain you emotionally despite being very sentimental. She loves being part of a family or group and is the force that binds.

She needs intelligent conversations besides the cuddles. She can wander off if either of her needs are not met. If she has settled down to marital bliss with you then you can be sure that she has reached some agreement with her mercurial nature. You just need to talk to her. Speech is very important to her and she can regale you for hours with her anecdotes.

Material possessions rank high with her. She is great at budgeting. This girl is ambitious and wants to achieve a sense of stability in her life by owning materially. She can tackle boardrooms with ease and should do that or would get restless. She can be highly productive if allowed to pursue her career or hobbies.

As a mother, she is sensible and practical. She introduces her children to the possibilities of life and does not force them into choosing only one direction. She understands them well and is a mother who is fun, inventive and playful.

At the Workplace

TauGems are wonderful as marketers, sportspeople, business people and excel even in creative fields. Their solid practicality and exceptional thought-process make them excel in the corporate world too. No one can think faster on their feet or as imaginatively as them; and absolutely no one can communicate their ideas so well and as logically as them. They are excellent writers with great common sense, satire and wit. They can also be good creative artists excelling in dance, music, etc.

TauGems excel as negotiators and deal makers, their deals will be finalised before the parties meet and you can be sure that they will arrange to get their way. Money, and the promise of more, prompts them to give their best shot. They also love it if their jobs offer the scope of travel. They know how to have fun while working.

They can play mind games very well, use sharp, snide remarks to great effect and mentally disintegrate their opponents. They themselves remain nonchalant and insulated to anything that happens around them.

Earth and Air meet to impart practical ideas to airy thoughts. TauGems are vivacious yet full of common sense, calm but mentally agitated, unemotional yet understanding, with a deep laugh and a solid tread.

Famous TauGem Personalities
Lionel Messi, Steve Waugh, L.N. Mittal, Mark Waugh, Prince William, Khloé Kardashian, Mithun Chakraborty, Suresh Gopi, Franz Kafka, Vikram Seth, Jean Alesi, Heidi Klum, Michael Platini, Kylie Minogue, Boris Gelfand, Toby Keith, Shantanu Kirloskar, Shweta Gulati, Vir Sanghvi, Prince Frederik, Eric Contana, Pierre Cornoy, Aiden Blizzard, Bimal Roy, Christopher Leigh, Errol Flynn, 50 Cent, Phyllis George, Mary Schapiro, Jim Walton.

25. TAURUS–CANCER

The calm and stable Bull meets the deeply emotional Crab in TauCans. It is a match made in heaven for the emotional and often cranky Cancer gets a stable head on its shoulders while the practical and extremely commonsensical Taurus finds a more sensitive outlook.

They may look frail, but that delicate frame hides within itself immense strength. TauCans are shy and reserved in company. They do not feel the need to communicate every idea they get. They do not give in to impulsive desires and wild schemes – every step taken is deliberate. The Taurean mind is inflexible while Cancer is not bold enough to walk the untested path. So, change is one thing that worries them. They are traditionalists at heart. New ideas and philosophies do not attract them.

They are creative and imaginative though. The Taurus in them makes them connect with music and art at a soul level, while their Cancerian side makes them imaginative. They would be hesitant to showcase their talents initially but you will be stunned by the depth of their artistic side. They also have a fabulous sense of humour derived from everyday observations of life. The TauCan humour resides in subtle and witty statements that have people rolling on the floor.

They are deeply attached to memories as the past comforts them. They have elephantine memories, which can be a boon or a bane. While it helps them in memorising complex theorems, rewinding good memories and being nostalgic, this can also make them nurse past hurts. They are also extremely emotional and sensitive. They can be sensitive to even things uttered unintentionally. They can sulk for hours and cry buckets if hurt.

Money is extremely important to them. The Taurus in them desires material possessions while the extremely insecure Cancer has an overpowering need to conserve and create wealth in order to feel secure. They work very hard to gain financial stability for themselves and their families. They are preservers by nature and have a deep-seated need to build upon their wealth and relationships. They are extremely protective, sensitive and nurturing towards their families.

As in work so in love, they will opt for the basics. They are softies in love. Loyal and steadfast, they will never opt out of a relationship when it gets tough. Family, especially their mother, will be of prime importance to them and they always take their mother's advice. Food is another common thread after love and money in TauCans. They love to eat and cook. Both Taurus and Cancer are experts at cooking. They love to watch their friends eat and frequently invite people over for lavish meals.

You rarely see a spark of temper in them. Only extreme circumstances make them lose their cool. Caring, protective and extremely basic in their approach to life, they are easy people to deal with. They need a lot of love for they give a lot. And yes, if I have forgotten to tell you, they are STUBBORN! Once a TauCan has made up his mind he finds it extremely difficult to change.

Nothing shakes their outer composure. They can act calm but, inside, they are full of untold fears. Cancer is a very insecure sign and it makes them fear everything. Taurus, too, is not a very optimistic sign. They act strong but their families and loved ones are familiar with their dark moods. These mood swings can be terrible. They are also prone to depression.

TauCans can over-think their problems. Their rock-steady façade doesn't help, for they mask their fears but kill themselves over it. Remember; there is a softie inside that inflexible exterior they put up to protect themselves from hurt.

Taurus–Cancer – Sanjay Dutt
'My mom was a fantastic person… I miss my mother one hell of a lot. She was the life of our home and since she died, it feels like the light has gone. God! How I miss her.'[41]

Suniel Shetty: 'I will not call him a man…I will call him a boy…that's why they call him 'baba'…the man with the golden heart. The biggest child.'[42]

The Cancerian love for the mother is very evident in the words of Sanjay Dutt. He is as emotional as a Cancerian yet as strong as a Taurean. The persevering Cancer just adds to his resilience. Sanjay has done it all – tasted success and then gone down the depths of life to come out and succeed again. He is a true survivor in the TauCan mode.

Love and Marriage for Him
Here is a guy who will never stray and is committed to you forever. He also works extremely hard to create a safe and secure abode for his family. He lets you work and do whatever you want as long as you take care of the house. He is not chauvinistic but neither is he in favour of modern women. Traditions and values bind him to his family. Don't pester him, make a joke at his expense, ridicule his mother or call him lazy, and he will be a great husband.

His family is his priority and he loves to spend a lot of time with them. Family holidays, outings, get-togethers, are all very precious to him. He does not like to spend money easily except on food. He is a fabulous mate for he has no problem understanding your views. If you want a sensitive partner, this is the right guy, for not only is he considerate to your moods, but also gives you tangible solutions to your problems.

This guy may not tell you everything he feels, though. Be as understanding as him and let him relax peacefully and sleep off his worries. He can be stubborn at times and may withdraw into a shell or bellow at you. Give him time till his temper cools.

He is a loving and protective father. He understands his children but may find it difficult to comprehend their varied desires. You need to make him let go of some of his traditional notions if they hamper his relationship with them.

Love and Marriage for Her
Don't be fooled by her corporate poise and modern outfits, she is very traditional. She wants to work as she needs financial independence; at the same time, her family is the centre of her universe. There is nothing that she would not do for them. She is fun-loving and cheerful with her family.

---
[41] *Showtime*, June 1988. 'Straight talking…!'
[42] https://www.youtube.com/watch?v=TyU9wfHzC6s

A piece of advice – even if she does not work, please open an account in her name and let her invest. She will manage your home well, save every possible penny and build savings that will help on a rainy day.

Ultra-loyal and strong, this girl not only withstands the storms you face but also helps you deal with them. She does everything and more to keep the relationship alive and keep you from any harm. Her heroic acts are covered with such lady-like grace that she never seems stronger than you. She is not aggressive, either. Her conservative and traditional nature does not allow her to walk away from a bad marriage but makes her work at it wholeheartedly. She is extremely emotional and needs your understanding to overcome her insecurities.

Children are her weakness; nothing is too good for them. That does not mean she spoils them. She finds it very hard to let go of them once they grow up and, in her eyes, nobody is ever good enough for her darlings.

At the Workplace
TauCan sees the coming together of a fixed and a cardinal sign. You can expect them to dream practical dreams and bring them to reality. If TauCans work for you, you can motivate them with timely holidays and good packages. Designations and titles do not excite them. Steady growth and rise in income is what they need.

They are also cravers of 'security'. If your job provides that they will not leave. Besides, they are also extremely loyal and need more than ample reasons to quit. They may probably leave you only to pursue their dream to become their own boss. They can excel in corporate careers or even artistic ones, but you can be sure that they will create wealth.

As bosses, they are extremely good, though they can make you restless with their slow decision-making. They put their trust in tried and tested methods. They are considerate and treat their subordinates as family. They realise the simple fact that they need all sorts of characters to run an organisation and arm themselves with people of different skill sets, especially those skills that they lack themselves.

They are excellent at motivating people, especially with their unique brand of humour, laced with funny anecdotes. They don't mind you taking some time to understand their pattern of work. But if you continue to fail to be 'productive', then you will be shown the door. They are good at budgeting and can nurture and grow an organisation while keeping a tight control on finances.

Earth and Water meet in this wonderful combination to give it mental strength and creative talent. TauCans will be patient yet emotional, stingy yet sensual and loving yet practical.

Famous TauCan Personalities
Sanjay Dutt, Madhuri Dixit, Barack Obama, S.P. Balasubrahmanyam, Miroslav Klose, Clint Eastwood, David Hasselhoff, Kate Beckinsale, Mick Jagger, Ambareesh, Anand Bakshi, Benito Mussolini, Margaret Court, Yogeeta Bali, Vyjayantimala Sharada, Kanchi Paramacharya, Alfred Tennyson, Ruskin Bond, Vir Das, Sukhwinder Singh.

26. TAURUS–LEO

Taurus is ruled by a yet to be re-discovered planet, which I call 'Planet X' for the sake of convenience. This strong but silent planet bestows peace and maturity on Taureans, while Leo is ruled by the generous and shimmering Sun. But more than the planets, we can use their animals to envisage just how this combination works. Look at the Bull and the Lion, the first thing that strikes you is their extreme immobility. They can lie still for hours although you cannot miss the sense of stability and strength in them.

TauLeos act like the laziest people ever, but that is only an illusion. They are capable of real, hard work. But the Lion's regal bearing and the Bull's deep reserve of patience are very evident in them. They mind their own business, keep to themselves and do not bother people unnecessarily. But Taureans hate being teased and if you hurt the Leo pride, you will be doing a big disservice to yourself. The shy charming smile of the TauLeo hides the growl of the Lion and the bellow of the Bull. Be warned.

They have great reserves of strength, both emotional and physical. The environment around them reflects their serenity. They do not like flashing lights or bright colours, their style is subtle and light. Luxury is another common point between the two. Taureans love all the good things that money can buy. They spend a fortune on cosmetics and perfumes for they love smelling good. Leos have a lot of vanity and love looking good. They are also very sensual and earthy.

They talk little and in monosyllables most of the time, but are impressive orators when in the mood. They talk plain common sense with hard-hitting reality. They are big-hearted. If you are really in trouble, they are the ones to turn to. Taurean faithfulness for their motherland makes them love their country and they are naturally aghast with injustice to their country or countrymen. The Lion loves being leaned upon and this makes them natural protectors and champions of the less fortunate.

The Taurean love for music and the creative arts, combined with the Leonine desire to be the centre of attraction, will make them fabulous performers. They might hesitate and display the Taurean shyness initially, but some encouragement will help get over the fear. The transformation from a shy introvert to a mass-entertaining rock star is a distinct possibility. They love slapstick comedy and have a pronounced funny bone.

Money will be important to them. TauLeos dream of lazing in luxury. Among other things they want to own a house near a water body or in the hills, which offers relaxation with serenity. These guys want to make their money fast and retire to enjoy it. They are not ready to spend their whole life working the grind.

You can expect Leo sentiments and need for adoration in romance, with soft Taurean sentimentality. There are only two things that drive a Taurean – money and love. When TauLeos are in love you will not find them lazing. TauLeos are everything you would wish for in a romantic partner – warm, emotional, generous and dependable. They will not jump wildly into love, but take their time, decide and then commit. Their love is for keeps.

They are excellent hosts. Taureans love feeding people while the generous Leo's love to put on a great show. They treat you with individual attention and care in such a way that you feel honoured at their parties. They are also very spiritual. The Taurus is traditional while the Leo is a natural believer. Expect them to follow customs with diligence.

They are stubborn people. Once their mind is made up, nothing can change it. There is one saving grace: they take a lot of time to decide. No decision is ever taken in a hurry and that gives you a window to make them rethink. Remember; bear hugs and loving praise are the magical weapons you have to overcome their stiff pout and stubborn resistance.

Deep inside, every Leo is insecure and feels that they are not equipped for life. But Taurus tones down the insecurity. When grave situations actually arise, TauLeo rise to the occasion bravely. They are extraordinary at handling emergencies.

TauLeos never think small. They need fat bank balances, huge careers, big cars, luxurious homes and want to have a huge impact on people. Their canvas is large in every sphere of life.

Taurus–Leo – Arvind Kejriwal
'I think the government has no business to be in business. The government should leave business to the businesspeople and ensure that they play by the rules.'

'We are not ideological animals, either blindly opposing reforms or blindly supporting it.'[43]

'No action has been taken against those identified because the people against whom action is proposed to be taken are either those who themselves have to decide whether to take action or not, or can influence decision-making.'[44]

'I don't have aspirations to become the Prime Minister or Chief Minister. I'm a common man of this country, which is burdened by corruption and inflation.'[45]

Calm, courageous and full of common sense, Arvind Kejriwal is a true TauLeo.

Love and Marriage for Him
He is the most generous and kindest of husbands, but you need to be smart enough to keep him that way. Treat him like the boss, let his decisions be viewed with respect and allow him to rest majestically in the house. He wants his wife to behave like a lady. Do not wash your dirty linen in public or crack jokes at his expense. This guy is very conservative. Clingy possessiveness and foolish beauty do not impress him. He can be totally easy-going and does not expect you to be tied down to him. A strong, independent and beautiful woman, who behaves appropriately in public, is the one for him.

He loves food and music. Pamper him with good food and music, and keep him in soothing surroundings. He is the shoulder you can cry on. No matter how bad the situation, this guy never gets flustered, rather he is a support for everyone. He knows how money works and is a great provider. His home is a beautiful and luxurious abode.

He is stubborn. Make sure he never gets into that mood. If he does, gently cajole him back to normalcy with love. Crying, nagging and yelling will only worsen things. He has an amazing knack for fixing things; you somehow feel that gadgets speak to him.

---

[43] http://articles.economictimes.indiatimes.com/2013-04-12/news/38491458_1_aap-members-aam-aadmi-party-existing-unorganised-colonies
[44] http://www.outlookindia.com/article.aspx?267215
[45] http://www.ndtv.com/video/player/news/ndtv-exclusive-don-t-need-character-certificate-from-rahul gandhi-says-arvind-kejriwal/300710?ndtv_rhs

As a father, he is quite easy-going but insists on respect from his children. He wants them to excel in some field so that he can brag about it to his friends. He will actively advise them on career moves. He prefers practical experience over bookish knowledge and insists that they experience life to learn from it.

Love and Marriage for Her
She is extremely romantic and retains her romanticism even in the twilight of her life. Loving, kind and generous as she is, do not forget she has a will of steel. No challenge or emergency can derail her calm composure. There is such warm optimism in her that all fears seem imaginary.

Respect and love are what she craves. She is regal and has a shy, engaging smile. Her need to be loved is quite high and she likes being courted. This romanticism hides her practical nature at times, but underneath the sentimentality, she is extremely practical. The lady loves luxury and would spend wisely and look for the best bargains on brands. She is also prudent enough to save, invest and grow money carefully.

She can be extremely stubborn at times and will not heed any suggestions or instructions. Trying to command her or teasing her will only worsen matters. You can't dictate terms to her or try and control her. She is a fabulous cook and knows that the way to anyone's heart is through the stomach. She is truly happy when you invite your band of friends over to an impromptu dinner.

As she grows older, she is the grandmother everyone loves: full of stories, wise anecdotes and a calm command over every situation.

At the Workplace
TauLeos dream big: *huge*! They are extremely good at starting small and scaling up things to something grander and greater. They are never impulsive and prefer taking small steps to giant leaps.

TauLeos need a job where they can command without moving around too much. Ideally, they love jobs that have less work and more money. In time, they settle for work that involves hectic hours interspersed with idle periods. Their undeniable creative leanings and the Leonine love for the arc lights make them lean towards the creative arts.

If you want to keep them, you have to offer money and learning. They like positions where they can learn and also command. Fancy designations hold no charm for them if they feel that the work offers no opportunity to grow. They hate selling but can teach you how to sell sensibly.

Their mental strength and unruffled composure make them ideal in handling high-pressure jobs. Owning their business is a dream that is eventually fulfilled.

Earth and Fire come together in this adorable mish-mash of stubbornness and elegance, strength and common sense; practicality and romanticism. TauLeos deserve a hug for being so sure and secure.

Famous TauLeo Personalities
Arvind Kejriwal, Fatima Bhutto, Sameer Kochhar, Judith Rodin, George Fernandes, Peter Sellers, Sir Lawrence Olivier, Sir Arthur Conan Doyle, Mikhail Botvinnik, Bernard Baruch, Govind Ballabh Pant, Sangeeta Ghosh, Gauhar Khan.

27. TAURUS–VIRGO

This is a combination of double Earth. The calm and powerful 'Planet X', the god of wealth for Taurus, and 'Planet Y', the god of healing for Virgo, combine to form the most rooted and stable of all signs. TauVirs put on no artificial airs. They know exactly what they want and who they are. Their wishes are simple and they never dream bigger than they can achieve. They think, act and believe in practically achievable dreams. No matter if they are born to a farmer or to a president, they are contented and only desire to increase their monetary worth.

When these guys talk, it's good to listen. They talk about simple, common-sense stuff, deeply immersed in practical knowledge. They have an unusual calm about them but you can be sure that their mind is ticking. The immense inner strength is visible to all. They are very dependable.

They are the perfect doers. They just don't plan meticulously but also go ahead and complete a task. There is an industriousness and seriousness about them. They are conscientious about everything. They may be thin and frail but they have great stamina and are geared to tremendous amounts of physical and mental work.

Both Virgo and Taurus are loners. They do not need people around them to feel happy. Contentment is always within their reach. Their friends are few and they do not desire a social circle. They prefer to sit alone, spend time with family, probably even laze around the home or read books on health, medicine or art. 'Sitting alone' is essential to them.

Taureans obsess over material stability while Virgos have an analytical mind. They are also conservative, with clarity of thought. They are definitely materialistic, they want comforts and luxury; but they are not greedy. Rather than volatile options, they go for tried and tested secure methods of investment. They create wealth through proper financial planning and wisely use their disposable incomes.

Health is a very important issue. Most of them drink boiled water, eat non-oily food and exercise daily to keep themselves fit. When you are sick, these are the guys to call. Healing and nursing come naturally to them. They know what traditional medicines and kitchen herbs can help you.

They are deadly in critical mode. They will be so spot-on with their criticism and analysis that you will have to agree with them. They are also very stubborn. Once they decide on something, they stick to it. It is because they have already thought out everything. Interestingly, there is a strange kind of a purity that emanates from them. It is probably the combination of the Virgin Virgo and the simple and earthy Taurus. That's really cute and lovable.

TauVirs have a fun side as well. The Taurean love for slapstick comedy and the acting ability of the Virgo sees them act innocent while playing the devil. Watch out for this when they are in those rare light-hearted moments. They are also very artistic. Taurus blesses them with great musical sense and all things creative while Virgo gives them perfectionism. This is an extraordinary combination for the most perfect artist.

Family equates duty for them. They are very loving and warm to their families; yet, you feel that they do it more out of a sense of duty. They seem unemotional but are never insensitive. Despite having no water, double earth ensures every thought and action of theirs is based on such common sense and practicality that they know exactly what to do in any circumstance and this makes them appear sensitive. Virgos can sacrifice everything for their family and are extremely duty-conscious while Taurus has an earthy endurance that can tolerate any mental or physical anguish. This makes them rock solid in their support.

They are very sentimental and loving, yet they might not be able to express their love. TauVirs are capable of loving deeply and silently. But don't expect any wild declarations of love from them. You can be sure, though, that their love is true. In fact they remain calm, unperturbed and tongue-tied in almost all situations in life. They hate drama and are not comfortable talking about their feelings.

Don't forget that TauVir is a complete Earth combination. They are very earthy and physical. There is this deep sensuality in every Taurean and they love touch, hugs and cuddles. Besides, the Virgo in them will make them try very hard to be perfect lovers, at least technically. So please cut them some slack and don't expect the impossible from them.

Taurus–Virgo – Anil Kumble
Kumble resembles Glenn McGrath because he does not so much baffle batsmen as torture them with precisely-pitched deliveries. Like the Australian, he does not tear opponents apart, just works away methodically till the deed has been done.[46]

'Cricket should talk. I have always believed that, no matter what, cricket should talk.'[47]

'Even when I was announced the captain, and also after I got 10 wickets, people wanted me to show emotions. But that doesn't come.'[48]

Anil Kumble is one of the increasingly rare breed of performers who let their work talk for itself. He is not given to histrionics and is always working to perfect his killer bowling – a true TauVir.

Love and Marriage for Him
He is the perfect husband – responsible, duty-bound, warm and caring. He neither gives you sleepless nights nor does he expect you to centre your universe around him. He does his duty and expects the same from you.

Family is extremely important to him. His idea of an ideal holiday is to visit his parents in their hometown. If you love parties, enjoy surprises and want a romance that is passionate and exciting, please give this poor guy a miss. His love is reflected in the way he pays bills before the due date, budgets your expenses and trips, works hard to provide financial security, plans family time and nurses you when you are sick. Love with him is not adventurous and exciting but safe and secure. If you want to feel warm and protected, choose him.

He is stubborn on certain points. When stubbornness catches up with him, you can only use charm to try and change his mind. He needs a clean house, space for himself and healthy food. If he gets all this, he is the happiest person on earth who, in turn, works hard to ensure your happiness.

---

[46] http://en.wikipedia.org/wiki/Anil_Kumble
[47] http://www.espncricinfo.com/magazine/content/story/336601.html
[48] http://www.hindustantimes.com/Cricket/InterviewsCricket/Exclusive-interview-with-Kumble/Article1-264227.aspx

He is the most responsible father; he will be around when they are tiny tots and even later when they need to solve complex maths problems. But his stubborn and traditional views on their modern relationships can affect him a lot.

Love and Marriage for Her
She is the true *Bharatiya nari*. She is the cement that binds the family together and an angel who works tirelessly for her loved ones. She is extremely self-sacrificing. She rarely thinks of herself while giving up everything dear to her for the family's well-being.

Shopping with her is a delight. She is one of those rare women who know exactly what they want and at what price. Money is very important to her and she makes sure she gets value from whatever she buys. Her style is simple and elegant. She does not desire the limelight but prefers solitude to the excitement of parties. Gardening, reading and cooking are her favourite activities.

She may look frail and thin but has endurance levels that can put a giant to shame. Despite her mental strength there is a soft femininity in her that you will find irresistible. Virgo purity of thought, combined with Taurean sensibility, endow her with outstanding values. And she is double Earth and very sensuous.

She will sacrifice anything for her children and will be a perfect mother who will be there at all the difficult times of their lives.

At the Workplace
TauVirs are extreme workaholics. Taurus has great stamina and Virgo has extreme work ethics. They are the most efficient and rigorous workers you will find. Their eye for detail will make them go into the nitty-gritty of every document and project. They can sit in one place for hours, working and concentrating on the problem at hand. Routine is very important to them and they will like doing things by the clock. They can keep on doing the same thing again and again meticulously, tirelessly, with the same perfection, every time.

TauVirs want a clutter-free work environment and clear instructions. They will offer constructive advice and not just talk to impress you. Planning, detailing, clarity, razor-sharp analysis, common sense, practicality and excessive hard work are what they bring to any job. If you want to keep them, ensure that you keep giving steady increases in their incomes.

They make brilliant presentations and create deeply analytical reports. But their speech can be too precise and too dry to motivate or excite. Sales and marketing are not for them. Instead, they are excellent in accounts, law, medicine, wealth management, research, and even manufacturing. As bosses, they can be extremely demanding. You need to be totally updated on facts, figures, plans and percentages to be able to face their rigorous questioning.

Double Earth makes this person the most stable and dependable in any sphere of life. Give them their due for they will never ask for it themselves.

Famous TauVir Personalities
Anil Kumble, Dimple Kapadia, Bhagat Singh, Vijay Merchant, Meiyang Chang, Mata Amritananda Mayi, Anastacia, Chris Cairns, Henry Kissinger, Ishwar Chandra Vidyasagar, Maria Canins, Jermain Defoe, Zara Philips, Wesley Sneijder, Justine Henin, E. Sreedharan.

28. TAURUS–LIBRA

The slow and steady Taurus meets Venus, the lover of beauty and luxury, to give this sign a desire for the good things in life. When the most practical of all signs, Taurus, combines with Libra, the sign that seeks balance – you get a person who is the most level-headed and rational being around. TauLibs may take time reaching a decision, but once they do, their decisions are rational and logical.

Slow and sedate, they are not easy to agitate and exude calm confidence rather than excited activity. They are never in a hurry to do anything. Even when they talk they take their own time to explain and listen. They make interesting conversationalists with the Libran love for talking and the simple earthy common sense of Taurus. They are practical, live in today and let bygones be bygones.

Both Libra and Taurus are signs that love music and all things artistic. So you can be sure of one thing, no matter what TauLibs do, they crave a fabulous music system and hours to spend listening to it. Music speaks to them at a deeper level and helps them relax. Food is another common denominator – they love eating, and feeding others, which ensures that they are never lean or thin.

There is great hidden strength behind their calm exterior, but they are not aggressive. They are the most peace-loving people around and hate to be drawn into an argument. Their philosophy in life is to live and let live. But you can sense their deep strength and endurance. They can endure massive physical and emotional stress without breaking down or opting for counselling. This strength is their biggest weakness too, for they take so much on themselves that people may pile more onto them.

TauLibs have a lot of stamina and this will be evident if they take to sports. You can expect them to choose a sport where they have to stand and attack and not run around. Fancy legwork and excited aggression will not be their style. The Libran gift of talking lends a voice to the strong and silent Taurean in them. They are able to talk charmingly and convert even enemies to friends.

Family oriented, their life is centred on their family and its needs. The Libran love of the idea of eternally being in love and the Taurean love of their family is reflected in them. They long to be in love and be very willing to settle down. TauLibs can also become confused between love and friendship and Taurean common sense might not help them much in matters of love. But they will be good friends with an adorable sense of humour that is more earthy than witty. They are trustworthy and reliable.

They have a keen sense of smell and love perfumes. It goes without saying, they want their house and environment to smell clean and prefer soft fabrics and earthy colours. They are also very sensuous and love revelling in the aesthetic and physical pleasures of life. Food, art and love in all their forms are the weaknesses of the TauLib. They love money but do not let it become their sole passion.

TauLibs can be extremely lazy. They just won't be able to help their lazy spells for both Libra and Taurus are deeply lazy and it just gets magnified in this combination. They simply lounge around the house, eating good food and listening to music. That's their idea of heaven. Libran indecisiveness can also afflict them at times. They find it very difficult to take decisions quickly, especially those involving family matters. The need to be fair can push them into procrastinating and postponing their decisions.

You definitely need to know an important set of contradictions in them: they are sentimental but not emotional, they are sensible but not sensitive, they are considerate but not empathetic. Talking is the only form of communication they understand other than those physical ones of course. If you need to be heard – speak up.

They have one major fault – a very irritating problem – they can be very, very stubborn! Most of the time they may not slip into that mode but for some reason if they are convinced that they are right, then you can just forget it!

Taurus–Libra – Virender Sehwag
'I want my mind to be absolutely free while facing up to a bowler. I try to hum songs, Sai Baba *bhajans* and Kishore Kumar songs, especially those pictured on Amitabh Bachchan, till the bowler is about to deliver.' 'I never look back. I have never looked back on that innings. What is gone is gone, it's over.'

'It would surprise most to know that I never look at the wicket. Never. I don't worry about whether the pitch has grass or moisture or is flat.'[49]

Virender Sehwag keeps it simple, has the calm strength, practical common sense and insight of a TauLib.

Love and Marriage for Him
He wants to be the provider and works very hard at getting the dough. You may not believe this for you see him lying around most of the time. He will find the slightest excuse to laze in the house. He lets you take the centre-stage at home and will not be aggressively egoistic but you will soon realise that he usually gets his way without fighting for it. He will be able to charm a 'yes' out of you when he wants!

One thing is certain, he easily settles down in matrimony. He is the most considerate of husbands. Just feed him well and let him listen to his favourite tracks, and he will listen to you. There is just one more thing: if you want to go on a cruise or a holiday, you have to plan it. And then you will have to plot and plan to get him out of the house.

He will be a little conservative about money and have a strange way of feeling secure because of it. Just make sure that he feels you are not spending excessively on household expenses. And yes… make sure you don't tease him or nag him. Also avoid anything that pushes him into stubborn mode and life will be hunky-dory. He understands your point of view if you express it to him. He cannot read your dreams or sighs.

His calm and easy exterior makes him an expert in dealing with kids. He has the right amount of reserve and fun to make him a good parent. He can soothe a frightened or hurt child with his humour.

---
[49] http://sports-sportsnewslive.blogspot.in/2009/02/virender-sehwag-interview.html

Love and Marriage for Her
She has grace and wit and also a soft heart. What more can you ask for in a wife? She is the softest, cutest wife but don't take her softness lightly. She will be the rock of her family. Her decisions may be expressed in soft tones but are etched in stone. It is very hard to negate her views.

She likes to keep the house neat and clean with soft billowy curtains and pastel shades. Unorganised drawers and messy cupboards make her extremely irritated. She is a good housewife but can get lazy about things other than cleanliness. If you want your bills paid on time, pay them yourself for she may forget despite her good intentions.

She could be extremely interested in an art form. Encourage her to pursue it for it keeps her occupied and happy. It is her romantic fantasy for you to join her in some form of art, be it salsa or singing lessons. She has fairly traditional views and will not find it easy to change her stance on them. She is stubborn at times but cannot remain without your company for long. She likes to spend on luxuries. Branded clothing, charming decorations, silken bed sheets and flowery perfumes all entice her.

As a mother, she is exemplary. She loves to spend time with her children and is not hassled by their demands. She is fair and reasonable.

At the Workplace
TauLibs are extremely loyal workers. They will work very hard but their agile mind and talent for communicating their thoughts and ideas will enable them to find a way of working in one location. They prefer their home comforts and do not like to be away for long except when required. Working from home will be a great idea for them.

They excel in artistic careers. They can be great singers, dancers, interior decorators, painters, etc. They must not go into careers or businesses that require them to work endlessly for they have a deep-seated need to relax in between hectic bouts of work.

The Libran ability to talk logically, along with the practicality of Taurus, makes them good at business, as sales people and as negotiators. They believe in and seriously practise a win-win philosophy.

As bosses, they are extremely liberal and democratic. But they take their own decisions and are stubborn once they take them. TauLibs dream of making their money fast and retiring early to a life of luxury.

Earth and Air combine to give grace and common sense to TauLibs. They will be indolent but hard working, creative yet temporally astute with unhampered strength and stamina.

Famous TauLib Personalities
Virendra Sehwag, NTR, Brett Lee, Rahul Bajaj, Liz Hurley, Dinesh Karthik, Aurangzeb, Tony Curtis, Kitu Gidwani, Jaami Nooruddin Abdurrehman, P. Susheela, Abhijeet, Anbhazhagan, Terrel Davis, Amala Paul, Lindsay Davenport, Roshan Mahanama.

29. TAURUS–SCORPIO

This is a very powerful combination of double fixed signs. Water and Earth combine in TauScorps and they have the Scorpio intensity, passion, ruthlessness and deep-seated desire to win, combined with Taurean patience, silent power and steely resolve. The bellowing Bull with a sting in its tail. Deadly!

They are usually not bubbly or talkative, but behind that subdued voice and steady gaze, is a person you should never underestimate. Stubborn and obstinate, it is very hard to move them once they make a decision.

Reason and passion go hand in hand with them. They have the ability to make the most complex things sound simple. They can amaze you with their logic and commonsense, and use them to correctly guess at outcomes. The Scorpio ability to unravel the deepest mysteries combined with Taurean will and patience ensure that they give their full passion and energy to whatever they do. There is something extraordinary about them and their inherent magnetism is vitally palpable.

The Taurean love for material possessions makes them very focused in their work. The Scorpio ability to penetrate the secrets of the universe makes them near-invincible. They can easily read people and know exactly what makes others tick. They do have short bursts of laziness, which is necessary for them to reduce the stress under which they invariably put themselves.

The Taurean love of home and the deep-seated loyalty of Scorpio find them firmly rooted to their families. They are capable of the greatest sacrifices for their families.

The Taurean flair for music and arts can turn into an obsession for TauScorps as well. In fact, they bring in the sublime art of controlled aggression to everything they touch – be it arts, sports, career or even love. The advantage of the calming effect of Taurus is that all that passion and energy churning within them can be effectively channelled, when required, into an important task and also can relax into complete tranquillity when it is completed. They remain calm and quiet most of the time, which belies their inner strength that can come to the fore when faced with emergencies. You will be awed with the power, almost 'super powers' they exhibit in times of calamity.

People of this combination are most probably born on a full moon day and that adds to their power and personality. When Scorpio energy levels and mystical powers combine with the steely resolve of Taurus, success is a foregone conclusion. No circumstances can keep this person down, once he decides to win. Their inner strength and determination make them stand out in a crowd.

Extremely good friends, they are loyal and courageous. They have few friends for they need to be sure of the people around them and their Scorpio characteristic of utterly knowing a person at a glance makes them choose wisely. Once you are their friend, they never hesitate to help and stand by you through thick and thin.

They are extremely sensitive. They can get hurt at the simplest things that you said. The Taurus in them can brush it off but they find it difficult to forget. Be careful about what you say to them. They are not known to be extremely eloquent themselves. They communicate more though their eyes and, of course, with their bear hugs and amazing body language.

They have high levels of endurance. Circumstances that seem back-breaking to many never manage to hurt them. Even the frailest people in this combination can withstand the most severe problems. Do not ever make an enemy of such a strong person. They are quite vengeful but think through their revenge and attack only when they are sure of victory. They have an elephant's memory, so if you have ever done them any harm, please be wary.

This combination perhaps has the strongest will power in the entire zodiac. They can achieve anything they want just by stubbornly being there. This combination would also be the most physically robust amongst all the zodiac signs. TauScorp exemplifies the culmination of extreme mental, physical and emotional strength. They are literally the powerhouses of the zodiac.

Taurus–Scorpio – Wasim Akram
'I discovered that I had diabetes when my father forced me to consult a doctor as I had been feeling uncharacteristically tired for quite a few days,' he explains. 'It was a huge shock because at that age you think you're invincible!'

'Once I'd made up my mind that I wanted to continue playing cricket, I just did what I was advised to by my doctors and went back to play for Pakistan,' he says. 'I played for another nine years before I retired.'[50]

Wasim Akram, world-renowned, most accomplished all-rounder, has the passion, the intensity and the dependability of a TauScorp.

Love and Marriage for Him
He is the most practical person you have ever met. But under all that reason and logic hides a passionate and sensitive soul. Once he is with you, he is yours. When he loves, he loves truly and deeply.

Ambitious and deeply driven, he strives to achieve his goals. You have to understand that the Taurean desire for material success and the Scorpio intensity make it very difficult for him to rest. He needs a calm environment to de-stress. Do not be clingy or possessive.

You can expect him to love music. He also enjoys cooking and likes surprising you with his talent in the kitchen. The Taurean love of eating and feeding others will be evident in him.

Flattery and compliments don't come easily to him. If you can understand the sentiment behind an intense gaze or can be satisfied with an 'ok' when you ask him how you are looking then you will truly know him. He is extremely understated and intense. His unabated passion between the sheets should convince you anyway. Don't try and arouse his jealousy though: then he can be totally deadly.

As a father, he is high-handed and authoritative at times, and his fixed views can make it difficult for him to understand the ways of the young.

Love and Marriage for Her
This woman is pure steel. No adversity can break her. Totally loyal, she will never break your heart; but do not lie to her. Her Scorpio skills at intuiting the deepest secrets make it very hard to keep her off-track. Flirting is not allowed if you really

---
[50] http://gulfnews.com/life-style/health/wasim-akram-i-won-t-let-diabetes-bowl-me-out-1.935660

want her. Do not treat her as one of your conquests. The lady has deep self-respect and it does you no good if you try and shatter it.

In her youth, she may have been a tomboy, but this girl has the Scorpio ability to transform herself into anything. She can be a diva or a homemaker, depending on her circumstances and ambition.

The Taurean love for home and earthy colours are evident in her. She loves her home and likes to decorate it in soft hues. Nothing flashy works for her. Of course, she has respect for money and the luxuries it can bring. Expect her to indulge in the best, but be sure that she does not spend needlessly.

She does not expect compliments and flattery. She places more value on common sense than high-sounding degrees. However, expect her to be extremely passionate and sensitive. She will try to hide that side of hers under practical common sense. But if you try to say anything unkind to her under the garb of joke, she will never forgive you. Be warned that her calm and composed exterior can suddenly burst into anger.

Money and security are important to her. She is highly ambitious and can transfer those ambitions to you. If you are not as driven as her, then let her reach for her goals.

She urges her children to have a passion and go for it. She takes the tough route herself, to teach her children practically how it can be done.

At the Workplace
They are extremely passionate and driven about their work. They are strong, silent workers and the most dependable of your staff. They need to be treated with respect. Money and respect are very important to them. Those are the only incentives that work for them. Family is very important to them, so be sure to give them family time. They never take their work home.

This is a fabulous combination for sportsmen. They display raw power and passion for their game. They are very good at sizing up their opponents and instinctively going for their weaknesses. They can be in any field from sports to arts, politics to business, or even just be a mechanic. Whatever they do, they do with a dedication, passion and commitment that is hard to match. They work towards being the best in the arena and they want it all – power, material possessions and comforts.

Their one aim in life is to be their own boss. While they work for you, you can be sure of their loyalty but once they leave, they never look back. Is he your boss? Well you have the privilege of knowing what it is to work under intense pressure while soaking it all up with a smile. He knows exactly what you are up to; never try to deceive him.

Water and Earth give this combination power and deep sensitivity, tempered by a realistic attitude. They achieve whatever they dream of.

Famous TauScorp Personalities
Wasim Akram, Arjuna Ranatunga, Iker Casillas, Romesh Kaluwitharana, Javed Miandad, Andy Murray, Tina Turner, Brendan Fraser, Julianne Moore, Karl Benz, Daryl Hannah, John Wayne, Jacqueline Fernandez, Nutan, Ghantasala, Al Bano, Douglas Fairbanks, Esha Gupta.

30. TAURUS–SAGITTARIUS

The calm and extremely powerful Taurus meets the highly intelligent Jupiter in this combination of opposites. While Taurus is solid, earthy, grounded and practical, Sagittarius is an excited scatterbrain and an intelligent nomadic wanderer with a carefree attitude. TauSags can be quite grounded as well as quite wild in their ways.

There is extreme honesty in this combination. Sagittarian bluntness meets Taurean straightforwardness. They do not manipulate or play games. You hear common sense from them but be ready to hear the truth as well. They are not encumbered by the past or misty-eyed about the future. They are practical people who live in the present. They have oodles of self-confidence and tremendous staying power. They can move mountains with their inner confidence and they just do not know how to give up.

Friendly and adventurous, TauSags are relaxed and happy people. These guys are very comfortable being themselves. It is quite easy to talk to them for they are quite grounded. Taureans love slapstick comedy and practical jokes. Sagittarians are fun loving and happy-go-lucky. They can be the funniest people you know. They do not mind even if the joke is on them.

Basically, they are simple folks. What they think and feel is evident. There is a certain naivïté about them for they do not realise the undercurrents of a conversation. They expect the same frank outspokenness from others and are quite surprised when they learn that most people don't speak the same way as them. Emotions and sensitivity will be absent in them and they will not know what their dearest friends think or feel till they hear them say it. Frankly, they will not be interested in knowing your deepest wishes either.

TauSags are the easiest people to understand. Frank, blunt and emotionally stable, they are large-hearted and loving. Bad moods do not mar their happiness for long and they know how to enjoy their lives. They love their families and are pillars of strength and support for them. They make up for the lack of emotional sensitivity with their dependability and solidity. While their extraordinarily intelligent mind can grasp the most abstract subjects they also possess that rare, practical and earthy common sense. They have crystal-clear minds and astonishingly strong hearts that can withstand any catastrophe.

Taurean bullheadedness sometimes makes them extremely uncaring of others' views, especially when they clash with their own. TauSags do not easily take to new ideas just because they sound interesting. It will take more than mere innovation to convince them that a path is viable.

They can also be fighters, especially when they believe in a cause. They love their motherland and its customs. They are extremely conservative and traditional in their views. Sometimes, though, they start thinking differently and set out to create a new world with realistic aims. If they believe they are right they will put up a strong front. They can get very angry and when they do, it is better to hide. The best and worst thing about them is that they never keep their resentment bottled inside.

Sagittarius also makes TauSags likely to be confused between love and friendship. When TauSags fall in love, everyone will know for with their characteristic honesty they will be unable to hide their emotions. They will definitely be quite unable to read their love's desires so be sure to spell out what you think and want. While Sagittarians have the devil-may-care streak and can rebel against authority, Taureans will be much more conservative and traditional. Hence, TauSags behaviour can range over the two extremes but one thing will be certain, they will take their time settling down and will not be in a hurry to tie the knot with the first person they fall for nor will they hold any grudges against their exes. TauSags will know how to break up and still be friends. They will never give up being friends.

Food is a common love of the two signs. You can expect TauSags to be solidly built. They really like food and are good at cooking too. Money is important to them. They definitely are ambitious, especially about the materialistic aspects of life. Music is one of their passions. Taureans love anything artistic and music touches their soul and relaxes them. The uninhibited nature of Sagittarius can make them fabulous dancers too. They love to put up a show and are naturals at showbiz.

Sagittarians and spirituality have a strange connection. Sagittarians can move from being atheists to believers and vice versa over their lifetime. Taureans are bound by customs and tradition and believe in anything that is a product of their land. They will love talking about the subject, too.

Taurus–Sagittarius – Johnny Depp
'I experimented with drugs and stuff, but I got out of it by the time I was 14 or 15. I saw the kids around me, not doing anything, not wanting to change their lives. I didn't want to be like that. I wanted to continue with my music, and I knew the drugs were holding me back.'[51]

When his child was born: 'Ah, that's what it's for. That's why you care about integrity or doing things without compromise. It's for that. It's for her.'[52]

Johnny Depp knows what he wants and, though the Sagittarian wildness afflicts him, he is Taurean enough to hold himself firm.

Love and Marriage for Him
Rock solid and unwavering, he rarely falters in times of crisis. This guy wants to be the guy in the relationship and though he is never aggressive or commanding, it is impossible to dictate terms to him. Be ready to play a traditionally feminine role when you marry him.

It is easy to know what you need to do in the relationship for he tells you what he wants. He is a simple guy to handle. Let him relax at home and do not burden him with your problems. You have to love food or at least feed him well, for food is his weakness. He is not wired with the ability to read your mind or understand sighs or looks, so state exactly what you want and he will respond beautifully.

This guy definitely has ambitions in life and he works extremely hard for them. He also holds certain causes dear, for which he is ready to fight. There is also a deep niggling insecurity within him that few know of. Stand by him and watch his confidence double. He may sometimes appear old school or traditional. Understand why he doggedly believes in those customs before forming your

---
[51] http://interview.johnnydepp-zone2.com/1988_09Splice.html
[52] http://interview.johnnydepp-zone2.com/1999_10TalkMagazine.html

opinion. He has a fun-loving side; exploit it to the fullest. He loves escapades and practical jokes – indulge him.

Fatherhood makes him more peaceful. He loves playing the protective role and is a father who enjoys his children's childhood. He loves travelling with them and shows them a world full of adventure.

Love and Marriage for Her
She is definitely a strong lady. There is an honesty in her that surprises you for she is one of those rare women who say exactly what they think. Do not expect her to last long in a joint family. This lady is rarely subservient.

Adventurous and fun loving, she loves travelling. Shopping does not excite her. She would rather be working on her causes. She holds strong views on certain subjects, which you may find very hard to change. The more you try to make her see an alternative, the more stubbornly she sticks to them.

She loves cooking. Food and music are the two calming forces in her life. Do not be egoistic when she is angry, wait for her anger to subside. She is not a docile wife – that is for sure. She may not be sensitive to your every emotion but count your blessings too – she isn't clingy, nagging or controlling and is a pillar of strength. There is an indomitable strength in her and she can withstand any emergency by standing tall for you and the family.

As a mother, she is caring and protective. She likes telling her children what to do and loves cooking for them too. She never clings to them but trains them to be responsible adults.

At the Workplace
Hard working, sincere and highly opinionated, TauSags are workers you find hard to ignore. They work to achieve their ambitions of money and luxury and want to take their ideas to the next level. Routine work does not appeal to them and their indomitable enthusiasm is wasted in drudgery. They can fight for any cause. Give them roles that suit their exuberant and steady minds. From singing to fire-fighting, they can do anything except jobs that require communication.

If they are forced into selling, they will find it hard to hide the truth or may blurt out classified information. They have no trouble grasping complex theories and also have creative abilities. The only thing that you need to watch out for is their unruly temper. They are capable of stepping on a few egos. As bosses, they will be fun loving but point out subordinates' flaws outright. You will be amazed at their energy levels and the way they keep things simple.

Earth and Fire meet in this highly outspoken and often rash combination that exudes power, determination and a will to succeed.

Famous TauSag Personalities
Johnny Depp, Mamata Banerjee, Michael Hussey, Alex Ferguson, Abigail Johnson, D. Rama Naidu, Bobby Piyush Jindal, Rowan Atkinson, Chandra Mohan, Joan Baez, Pt. Shivkumar Sharma, Louis Pasteur, Bar Refaeli, Kerry Packer, Badriprasad Poddar, Dion Boucicault, Milla Jovovich, Joe Root, AbRam Khan.

31. TAURUS–CAPRICORN

The calm and powerful 'Planet X' rules Taurus while the sombre and wise planet, Saturn, lays claim over Capricorn. This combination of double Earth ensures that TauCaps are totally practical and down to earth. There is nothing showy or flashy about them. Every action is well planned.

Look at the two animals that represent them – the Bull and the Goat. Both are solid, steady, calm and dependable. The Goat gets the extraordinary stamina and staying power of the Bull to supercharge its quest to reach the topmost mountain. Family is common to both. TauCaps are total home-birds and even include extended families in their warm embrace.

The Taurean warmth is displayed every time they meet friends. It makes them very easy to get along with despite the saturnine nature of Capricorn. TauCaps can get their work done with shrewd Capricornian tactics and the sunny charm of the Taurus.

They have a maturity beyond their years. Young TauCaps can act melancholic and treat life too seriously; the poor guys will kill themselves under responsibility! Of course, Taurus adds its love for fun to them and they do have a wry sense of humour. But they limit their fun side to only people who are very close. They are very balanced till they are in their thirties and can display symptoms of youth in their forties and fifties. They may become less responsible and more fun loving as they grow older.

Money is extremely important to Taureans while Capricorns are very ambitious and career-oriented. Money, power, material possessions, career and family are a TauCap's touchstones. Their ambitions are built on a solid base. You can expect them to think on a grand scale without being flashy. The laziness of Taurus will be diluted due to the extreme work ethics of Capricorn. TauCaps will be very hard working and work diligently to improve two things – money and prospects.

They do not spend money unnecessarily. Every penny is accounted for and they find ways to stretch an amount of money to its maximum. Do not expect them to invest in new economy shares or to think of highly innovative businesses. They stick to traditions and conventions. This is reflected in everything they do. They dress conservatively, have strong family values and shun new thoughts and ideas. They often act like people who resist change. Their love for the tried and tested makes them ignore the positive possibilities of change.

Music is their soft spot. Their love for music, like everything else, is rooted in tradition. Music is a Taurean love while Capricorns have a secret creative side. They will be good at singing, dancing, drawing or even painting. It will not be something that everyone will know of, they would prefer to keep it to a very limited circle. They are very shy in this respect. But if they do have a talent that can take them places, they will showcase it to the right people who will help them get there.

Obstinacy is their greatest weakness as well as supreme strength. They shut their minds and ears once they decide on a course of action and nothing can change it. But they are also careful not to take hasty decisions. The only window of influence you have is *before* they take a decision. They can also be possessive, controlling and over-concerned with security, comforts and societal acceptance.

Their biggest pitfall is materialism. They court materialistic success and will do anything for that. They can be scheming and conniving and planning their every move to go up in life. They may even consider marriage as on opportunity of growth. Greed is their biggest enemy and if they do not achieve the success they desire they can turn solitary and melancholic.

They are predictable and, sometimes, insensitive. The two things that can make them soft and mushy are arts and love. They are not swayed by emotions and can remain extremely cold and practical. There is a grim solitude that hangs about them. As there is no Air element in them they are also not given to shows of energy or artificial excitement. If you do meet any excitable TauCap characters that seem fun loving and jovial – look deep into them. They are probably doing it to get attention, to salvage their career or simply for their family. They will do anything for their family.

Taurus–Capricorn – Jim Carrey
At the age of 15, Carrey began performing at Yuk Yuk's, a famous Toronto comedy club.

His life was going well until his father was fired from his accounting job. All of Jim's family had to get a job at a factory as janitors and security guards. Jim dropped out of high school to try and help support his family. It was one of the lowest times in his life. The only way the family kept their sanity was Jim's jokes. Jim, no matter what the situation, would cheer the family up.[53]

The Taurean endurance and funny bone, along with his Capricornian diligence and love for family, make him a true TauCap.

Love and Marriage for Him
He is the most responsible and dependable person. This makes him command respect at home and in society. The house will be his place of rest and relaxation and you will have to keep it that way. Tradition will be the watchword of his life.

Emotions and deep insecurities are things he can't understand. You will have to express yourself in simple, clear language if you want to be understood. He has a cold practicality about most things in life. You need to work towards making things exciting for you and him. The soft Taurean warmth will make him the best companion to spend the day with and as you know, despite his dry talk he has a funny bone. Help him relax and take life easy.

If you love him you will have to love his family too. Be ready to play host to your in-laws and the extended family. Career is very important to him and he spends a considerable time worrying and planning. Do not nag him about the time he spends in networking with the right people. Do watch out for him when he hits the forties, he may turn truly naughty then.

He is the most exemplary of fathers. He is your daughter's favourite parent and your son's role model. If they have problems, they know they can turn to him for support. He brings discipline into their lives without rigorous control. His attachment to his family's 'status' may create issues with them.

---

[53] http://www.jimcarreyworld.com/jim-carrey-bio.php

Love and Marriage for Her
She is the ultimate home-bird, the kind of girl your mother loves to have in the family. She is soft-spoken, well educated, cultured, conventional and traditional. Beneath her apparent stuffiness is a sensuous earthy woman who needs lots of love. She definitely understands physical expressions of love very well. Don't let her be deprived of that. Those cuddles will go a long way in solving many issues.

She is capable of great warmth and love. There is nothing she does not sacrifice for her family. She is content to stay at home provided you have high ambitions because status means a lot to her. But if that spark of ambition is missing in you, she takes it upon herself to provide for her family and manages home and career with equal flair.

The fact is that she is as stable as a rock despite her apparent softness. She is never distraught or flustered in front of people. Many of her decisions are taken keeping society in mind.

Motherhood is very easy for her. She knows exactly how to bring up her children with fun and pleasure without losing out on discipline.

At the Workplace
Career is the love of Capricorn and the way to financial stability for Taurus, so you can be sure that TauCaps give a lot to their careers. They reach the top in whatever they undertake. They do not mind starting at the bottom as long as they see opportunities. You can expect them to work very hard, be well informed, speak sensibly and take calculated steps. Money and status are what they desire.

They normally are only at places where they can grow, reach the top and also achieve material success. They know the right people, the right place and the right price to exhibit their latent talents. They can catch on to the political repercussions of any conversation and will know just how to get their work done.

This combination makes a wonderful politician. It combines the shrewdness of the Capricorn with the genial charm of the Taurus. They rarely make enemies and get their work done with their well-laid-out plans. As bosses, they delegate superbly and build a team of people who know their jobs well. They have great managerial capabilities and people skills. They can lead and motivate people brilliantly and are father figures to their employees. The only problem is that they are slow to understand change.

Double Earth makes this sign stand out with its practical, common-sense approach to any problem. TauCaps are people who plan big and make things happen with their endurance and will.

Famous TauCap Personalities
Jim Carrey, Aditya Thackeray, Bikram Choudhury, Marilyn Monroe, Sushant Singh Rajput, Shirish Kunder, Christophe Lemaitre, Vikram Bhatt, Vinay Kumar, Daniel Balavoine, Dante, Ravinder Singh, James Stewart.

32. TAURUS–AQUARIUS

The calm and powerful Taurus meets Uranus, the highly eccentric planet of inventions. TauAquas have the rebelliousness of Aquarius and the strength of Taurus – a formidable combination indeed! They have the ability to envisage unique, revolutionary ideas and the relentlessness to implement them too.

This is a strange fusion of opposites. The rooted, grounded, practical and materialistic Taurus combines with the revolutionary, outgoing, idealistic and humanitarian Aquarius. There is a clear-headed rationality in TauAquas. They are definitely for change and original thinking but would do it without foolish, destructive attacks on tradition.

There is an assured tranquility about them that baffles you. Actually, they are quite unpredictable. There are times when they talk a lot and times when they do not. They seamlessly combine the peace and calm of Taurus with the eccentricities and wildness of Aquarius. Never take a silent TauAqua at face value for he may just be thinking of something novel. They are not shy but like to sit and observe silently!

Both Taurus and Aquarius are fixed signs and it makes TauAqua a double fixed sign. It means that once they make up their minds, it is very difficult to make them change it. Don't argue, just tell them your views and give them time to think.

The calmness about them is surprising because their thoughts are not calm. The Aquarian mind is boundless and moves in many directions. The Aquarian in them loves change while Taurus does not. They therefore have the extraordinary knack of doing old things in a new way and new things in a practical fashion. The old and the new seamlessly meet in them. A confusing situation indeed, for you never know what they are actually thinking about: it could be a futuristic dream or a thought for tradition. They can go either way and once they make up their minds no power on earth will make them change it – till a new brainwave hits them again.

The love of fun is evident in TauAquas as both the signs like to enjoy themselves. The Taurean in them loves slapstick comedy and you find them laughing at obvious jests and even enjoying cartoons. The Aquarian element of fun makes them love wisecracking and playing pranks on friends.

They also read people well, thanks to the Aquarian trait of wanting to know what makes people tick. They have this innate ability to look at complete strangers and know how they think and why. They are extremely broad-minded and non-judgemental. They may prefer traditions but do not try to influence anyone by their views. They are totally humane in their approach to people.

At times, the peculiar detachment of Aquarius may take over and they suddenly seem very distant. Don't worry; TauAquas will come back, maybe with a new idea or innovative thought. The Taurean indolence and patience makes TauAquas relax and take it easy. They are never in a hurry to do anything. They take things slowly, one by one, even if their mind is extremely restless and active.

You rarely see them losing their temper. But once they do, they can be extremely violent. Inequality, discrimination, poverty, humanitarian ideals, dangers to their motherland, etc. can incite the revolutionary in them and they can go to any extremes to protect the weak or their country and its traditions. They would have been warriors if born a few centuries ago; they are silent change agents in the modern era.

Aquarians worry about their old age and Taureans have an extraordinary sense of money. They would like to earn a lot very early and then retire soon into a life of dreams and thoughts. They are blessed with superb creativity. They can use their extraordinary sense of fashion, music, arts and creativity to set up innovative and interesting money-spinning ventures.

They have this amazing ability to be path breaking and innovative. They are pioneering and have a far-sightedness without being dominating and controlling. They bring in the changes slowly but steadily. Despite all the winds of change they bring, they remain what they are – rooted, practical, stoic, unflustered and even stubborn. Quite a contrast, isn't it?

Taurus–Aquarius – Mani Ratnam
What made this man who was born in a conventional Brahmin family break the mould, set new trends and create something that borders on blasphemy? 'You grow up as a normal child, but, in the process, you also agree with your parents, or you disagree; you form your own opinions, whatever,' he says. 'I think it is part of growing up.'[54]

The Aquarian desire to do something different and an enduring Taurean belief make themselves evident in Mani Ratnam.

Love and Marriage for Him
He loves his family, but holds you dear. His care and concern speak more than his words. Even if he seems lost in his own world at times, remember that he will never let you down. This guy is very intelligent but it is hard, at times, to make his mind settle on one thing. His obstinacy lends strength to his character and you do not find him giving up easily. It may also make him refuse to see your point of view. He can be extremely stubborn.

He is totally chilled out and fun loving. He loves to amuse and amaze you with his thoughts and ideas, and his sense of humour keeps you in splits. He is lazy too, and likes to lie around the house just listening to music. Of course, there are times when he is totally lost to the world. Let him have his moments. He is not a dominating husband who thinks only of his needs. He is liberal and modern.

He doesn't lose his calm and is the serene and solid support you need. He may not be extraordinarily profuse with words or charm you with romantic gestures. But when he does speak in his buttery-soft voice he makes you go weak in the knees with his phenomenal common sense and extraordinary genius. His soft and kind heart and natural goodness are truly endearing.

He is an excellent father, totally relaxed and cool. He loves and enjoys his children. They love, respect and admire him.

Love and Marriage for Her
She is the perfect wife with her traditional views and modern outlook and loves mothering her family. She loves you but she is more than a wife or a mother. She cannot be tied down to household duties alone for her mind compels her to think of different things. She needs space to be herself.

---

[54] http://satyamshot.wordpress.com/2010/07/03/post-raavan-mani-ratnam-is-working-on-his-next-movie/

Caring for family comes naturally to her. She loves cooking, especially different cuisines. But she may not like cooking all the time. This lady has a very different streak in her... a practical whimsicality that keeps you engaged. She thinks of doing things that other people never do. Let her be herself. She needs a little help in the communication department. Although she thinks a lot, she is unable to express her feelings all the time. Whenever she does, she talks sense and it can be a shock to hear her unconventional and frank opinions. Honesty is her biggest virtue.

There is also a streak of obstinacy in her that can confound you. Anger has no effect whatsoever on her. At such times, learn to give in with dignity. She is very creative and needs an outlet for her creativity. She will find her own way, you just need to sit back and let her do what she wants. She is a great mixture of femininity and intelligence. She has an extraordinary and unique fashion sense with her ability to mix innovation and wildness with aesthetics, style and sensuality.

Her children are her friends and she enjoys spending time with them. She will never be shocked by what they do and will learn and grow with them. She can balance being a career woman without compromising on family time.

At the Workplace

They are the modern mercenaries and revolutionaries without holding a sword or a dagger. The sword is replaced with a movie camera, pen, ball or a musical instrument. Their far-fetched ideas can definitely startle you. They are the quiet change agents. They revolutionise but silently; they bring in freshness to everything they do.

In their youth, TauAquas may take time to decide what they want in life. They will try many things, usually a mixture of creativity and finance. It takes them some time to find out what they really want to do. Routine and repetitive work is definitely not for them. They enjoy enterprises that make use of their creativity and talents. The Aquarian love for innovation and the Taurean eye on finances will surely create something novel yet productive. They can create poetry on celluloid, create magic with words as authors or be futuristic investment bankers.

The only fear is that they may get bogged down by too many ideas and lose themselves in the sea of thoughts. They are great taskmasters as bosses, who have an eye for innovation while keeping a tight rein on the budget. But the best thing about them is their ability to discover, unleash and nourish rare talents.

TauAquas have the Taurean steadiness of heart and the inventive mind of an Aquarius. They are earthy with an element of airy surprise in them.

Famous TauAqua Personalities

Mani Ratnam, Shivaji Maharaj, Veer Savarkar, Jagmohan Dalmiya, Maharana Pratap Singh, Che Guevara, Ravi Shastry, Sonam Kapoor, Samir Jain (*TOI*), Ban Ki-Moon, Nargis, John McEnroe, Manorama, Mark Knowles, Roberto Baggio, Tim Bresnan, Florian Kunz, Prince Joachim of Denmark, Pritam, Tony Parker, Yannick Noah, Laura Pausini, Olivia Wilde, Kanye West.

33. TAURUS–PISCES

Taurus is guided by 'Planet X', a calm and powerful planet, while Pisces is ruled by Neptune, the deep and mysterious lord of the seas. This combination ensures that TauPisces face every situation in life with fortitude. Earth and Water combine to make them rooted and calm while displaying deep sensitivity. They are also very good at adapting themselves to situations.

Pisces is symbolised by a Fish and that Fish can be a sweet angelfish, a playful dolphin or a big shark – it can turn into anything, anytime – depending on the situation and the environment. Taurus is the most emotionally stable amongst the zodiac signs and are peaceful souls. When combined together, they can be harmless water buffalos or even transform into the bull variety of whales. TauPisces allow you your ego; they submerge their own, to make you happy. But it is not wise to underestimate them. They are stronger and deeper than you perceive.

The first thing that strikes you about this sign is their assured calmness. They are unhurried and glide rather than walk. Their presence puts you at ease immediately. There is a down-to-earth Taurean simplicity and warmth in them, along with Piscean compassion.

These seemingly soft creatures can handle a lot of situations that can break stronger signs. They have adaptability and patience. The Taurean softness and sensitivity in matters of the heart gets enhanced by the Piscean understanding of their environment. This makes it very difficult for them to fight as they very easily understand the other person's point of view and also sympathise with it to an extent. But don't expect them to calmly accept whatever life dishes out to them. Taurus makes them quite stubborn in some of their views and they can stand firm on certain decisions despite their smile.

They are extremely attached to their roots and are slow to change. You could call them conservative but they are happy with the familiar. They are slow to anger, but when roused, fight for their rights. The Taurean love for materialistic things makes TauPisces desire the good things in life. They want everything but do not like to work too hard for them. The Taurean laziness and desire to conserve energy will also afflict them. They can work very hard at their jobs and be total slobs at home.

The cool and collected image of TauPisces goes for a six in matters of the heart. Taurus is very sensitive to its loved ones and Pisces needs a soul mate to feel complete. Taurean sensuousness and Piscean spiritual love will make them perfect partners. They sometimes submerge themselves in the pleasures of love just to escape the harsh realities of life. They are very spiritual and have a great commonsense understanding of the mysterious aspects of life. They find peace and hope in the divine and surrender themselves completely to the power above. Kindness and charity are also virtues that are ingrained in them.

They are popular amongst their friends for the simple reason that they are quite non-judgemental. Their sense of humour is very well developed and they have the ability to laugh at themselves. They are very family oriented and love being in the midst of the affection, warmth and happiness of large joint families.

TauPisces are fabulously artistic. They are known for their originality and creativity. Their extraordinary Taurean memory and sponge-like Piscean sensitivity makes them great students of the arts. They are artists who can learn a new art, pick up a culture or accent with alacrity and perform exactly as the original. In fact, they learn every day from life and people around them. They can mimic you even if you have met them just twice.

The Taurean pleasure-seeking nature when combined with the escapist tendencies of Pisces can be the disastrous recipe for a lazy and irresponsible reveller. The Piscean need to find solace in some kind of a mild addiction and Taurean love for food is the pathway for them to self-induced health afflictions: a path that the TauPisces should carefully avoid. They need to practise immense discipline and more self-control than others or they may lose their way. However, they are ideally suited to learn these qualities better.

Taurus–Pisces – Novak Djokovic

'I didn't have great conditions and facilities to practise and develop but look, I dared to dream, and to dream about becoming the world's best tennis player and world's best athlete.'

'My religion and my family play a huge part in my life. My family and team should have the same credit as I have because they really supported me, they allowed me to develop myself, develop my character.'[55]

Novak Djokovic is known as the Djoker by friends for his ability to impersonate others and make dull moments sparkle. He has the endurance and capacity to learn, plus the humility of a TauPisces.

Love and Marriage for Him

He is charmingly soft. This is a guy who never stops you from doing what you want. He loves peace and likes to laze around at home and spend his off hours in artistic pursuits. He can be quite trying at times, lazing away while important household chores wait. An energetic and zesty partner complements him. He sticks to his comfort zone, resisting new things, which an adventurous partner can rectify.

Romantic and loving, he loves you and even understands you: something rare in a man. The best part is that he is always ready to listen and you can reach him through emotions or logic – both work for him. You need to overlook his indolence and stop him from giving in to his addictions. Pisces makes him very susceptible to addiction, especially that of alcohol.

Money is an area of concern. The Taurus in him ensures that he realises its worth, yet he has problems conserving it. It's a possibility that Piscean deceptive behaviour and the Taurean desire for indolence would make him resort to unfair means of earning money.

As a father, he is deeply involved with his children's daily activities. He is the one they confess to for he understands. There is nothing that he will not do for his children. He is not one of those parents who want their children to listen to them. He is happy being their friend.

---

[55] http://www.tennisworldusa.org/TWI-EXCLUSIVE-Novak-Djokovic-I-dared-to-dream-articolo4573.html

Love and Marriage for Her

This combination makes a girl totally feminine, as both Taurus and Pisces are feminine signs. She is totally practical and down to earth with oodles of common sense yet deliciously feminine in her own way. But don't go by appearances – this girl is totally capable of looking after herself.

The Piscean tendency to copy others and to absorb and reflect the environment around her makes her fit easily into any situation and she looks more a part of your family than her own. She is a loving and caring wife and her family is her first love. More than anything else in the world, she desires to belong to somebody. She does not dominate. The relationship is everything for her.

Her adaptability makes her very good at dealing with family disputes and she is always the one who looks for a solution. Her emotional strength is far more than the average person's and she is able to deal with problems with a smile. She will be accommodating and adaptable, plus she will be an excellent cook and hostess.

Of course, this lovely package does come with a few faults. She is very laid back. Taurean laziness and the Piscean tendency of slipping into daydreams make her find the easy way out of things. She refuses to be hassled by things around her. The Taurean stubbornness sometimes rears its head in her. Mood swings afflict her and it is impossible to get her to smile at such times.

As a mother, she is what every child wants. Nurturing and caring, she does what is best for her children. They are like her friends and share everything with her because they know that she stands by them always.

At the Workplace

Taurus has artistic sensibilities and Pisces is creative as well, so TauPisces do very well in streams related to art, music or anything creative. Pisces are also fabulous actors, given their gift for emulation and their empathetic nature. Besides acting, writing is their forte too.

Deep, sensible and sensitive, they can write soulful lyrics and tearjerker tales. Pisceans are very good at adapting, so if their family environment is motivated towards another profession like accounts or even the army, they can easily tune in to that, too. Pisces gives them the ability to be anybody.

If the Taurean effect is stronger in them, they will have the Taurean shrewdness and excel in business. Calm and collected, they portray a stable image and never get flustered. As bosses, you just cannot fool them, though they are very tolerant towards most of your faults.

Earth and Water combine to give this sign stability and a deep understanding of human nature. Sensitive yet strong, TauPisces know the best way to move ahead is not by dominating but by understanding and caring.

Famous TauPisces Personalities

Novak Djokovic, Angelina Jolie, Mohanlal, Parveen Babi, Simran, Ram Charan Teja, Prahlad Kakkar, Stanislas Wawrinka, Amancio Ortega Gaona, Amy Pascal, Uday Kotak, Sendhil Ramamurthy, Helmut Kohl, Keira Knightley, Elle Macpherson, Sonia Braga, Omar Sharif, St Francis Xavier, Nawazuddin Siddiqui, Mika Singh.

34. GEMINI–CANCER

The emotional and extremely imaginative Moon meets the highly active and intelligent Mercury in GemCans. The first thing you notice about them is the twinkle in their eyes. They are fun loving and their mischief lightens boring lectures. GemCans are always ready to think differently, which keeps them alive and young.

There is an emotional side to them too, but that is only visible to their families. No matter how fickle and flirtatious they seem, they will always be true to their home and family. It's as if GemCans are two people. They idolise their mothers and share a strong bond with her.

They will be emotional, extremely sensitive, touchy and moody. But their Geminian side will make sure that it's covered up most of the time. They burst with creative energy. Highly imaginative and artistic, they bring their creative sensibilities to everything they do. They collect beautiful and highly original artefacts. The flip side is that they easily lose interest in things. They need constant change or get bored.

They are great communicators. They always have the right words or an amusing story to befit the situation. They have such expressive faces and they speak so well that it is easy to get swayed by it. They love adding spice to their stories. Look at it from their perspective; they are just adding some more zing to your boring existence, so what if some of the facts are actually not true! Their imagination can run wild. They are also extraordinary at picking up new languages. They are often gifted linguists.

Anger is rarely visible in them. They are not aggressive; they prefer using charming diplomacy to get their way. They sulk and get into a brooding silence if they are angered. Multitasking comes naturally to GemCans and is also a source of exhaustion. These guys enjoy thinking hugely divergent thoughts while also pursuing the task at hand. They are also harmless pranksters. Their sense of humour is extraordinary and sure to keep you entertained. They specialise in smart one-liners and quick rejoinders.

They love to travel to faraway places. Water holds a special charm for them. They do not mind backpacking around the world for it serves the twin purpose of saving money and travelling. They like to save and are very good at bargaining. They will be able to cajole and make their point with such tactfulness and perseverance that they will wear down any resistance and get good prices. They dream of a house and a car. These two assets are a must for them.

They might take their time finding the right life partner. Gemini will confuse and confound them with its ever-optimistic desire of finding someone better. Yet when they truly find their partner and decide so, then they will stop looking. They will be very emotional and sentimental in love. If you have married someone with Cancer strong in them, you should know that you have married their family too.

Often they are plagued by insecurities and feel overawed by their goals. They live life believing that it is full of possibilities yet fear the worst. Sometimes their optimism fails and they will be given to terrible mood swings and melancholy. They are also extra-sensitive; they read between the lines and nurse imaginary hurts. Still, the exuberant Gemini in them will revive the GemCans – just give them some time to sort themselves out.

The biggest flaw which can actually be a blessing in disguise would be their Geminian duality. If they use this inherent ability well, they can become truly versatile. If they use this negatively then they will develop multiple personalities living varied lives to escape boredom, deriving a strange comfort and secret pleasure in the ensuing deception.

Gemini–Cancer – Sonu Nigam
'Versatility is my strongest point. All my songs are radically different from each other. But I am at ease singing all of them.'

'My biggest gift is my 'shamelessness'; I am 'shameless' enough to explore every possibility open. I hated dancing, but still learnt it.'[56]

Sonu Nigam is always ready to try out new thoughts, ideas and looks. He is also versatile. Many times, he has brought the house down with his extraordinary impersonations of various singers. He is also a proud father who has initiated his son into music at a very young age. Like a true GemCan, his contentment lies in his search.

Love and Marriage for Him
Caring, sensitive and nurturing, this man is a good catch. He knows your deepest fears and understands your unspoken needs. He also knows how to charm you out of a bad mood. He is a great partner who needs a person who is stable and sensitive. Independent women do not put him off and he never grudges you your place in the sun. He has no ego hassles and likes a woman who can make up her own mind. He also wants to be understood. He is sensitive; do not be aggressive with him.

There is something about him that is mysterious. He has the ability to surprise you with novel sentiments, thoughts and views. He is a fun-loving partner and is always game to try something new. But he is also a victim of dark moods, which make him insecure.

His one big flaw is his inability to spend without thinking. He is never able to laugh away bills. He wants to save and provide for his family's future, though. He has a special place in his life for his mother. He is the happiest if he sees you being friends with her.

As a father, he is truly wonderful. He loves telling his children stories and is never too tired to play with them. His family is definitely his love and he personally sees to his children's growth and well-being.

Love and Marriage for Her
She always seems young, even when she is 70, because of her youthful attitude, and charms everyone. Aggressive commanding is not her style. Why does she need to be loud when she can get her work done with her femininity and charm?

She gets bored with routine. To escape that, she loves learning new things. You will find her taking pottery classes, giving aerobic lessons, immersed in cake decorating and more. She likes being busy because lethargy and idleness do not appeal to her. Sometimes this constant running around will get her down and she is prone to mental exhaustion at such times.

---

[56] http://www.indiantelevision.com/interviews/y2k3/actor/sonunigam.htm

She will be full of excitement and fun. But don't think her shallow – her emotions run deep, and behind that giggle hides a sensitive lady whose heart beats only for her loved ones. She might flirt with all the boys around, but that's just her way of expressing her Gemini chirpiness and it will be harmless.

She loves partying and her delighted laugh adds zing to any gathering. She is the perfect hostess. She conjures up delicacies while you chatter the night away. Although she seems happy with people, somewhere inside lurks loneliness. Keep her busy, inactivity is what she hates, but also give her space to be herself. She surely needs your attention. Shower her with it, and with love, for she can become insecure otherwise. Insecurity is her way of seeking attention.

An ideal mother, she nurtures her children. She is more a friend to them and plays games with them, acts out stories and takes part in all the Parent Teacher Association activities. Her only problem is that she does not know how to let go and may want to treat them as children even when they reach adulthood.

At the Workplace
Routine and monotonous tasks pull them down. They love doing a variety of things at the same time. The more energy-draining and exciting the work, the more they are pumped up to do it. Professions that have constant interactions with people appeal to them. Professions that require playing with words will find them at home too. They are fabulous in sales and can sell anything to anybody. Challenge them with diverse ideas and they are happy.

They are good at delegating and getting their work done. GemCans will take time to find their true calling and might change a few professions before zeroing in on one. They value the 'security' factor, so once they find their calling they will persevere and work on it unflinchingly.

They will want money from their work and to be challenged by new thought and ideas. Creative and innovative fields will find them working with enthusiasm. As bosses, they have the knack to innovate while managing costs diligently.

Air and Water meet in this ever-changing and evolving combination. Creative, sensitive and fun loving, GemCans will do a lot for their family and loved ones.

Famous GemCan Personalities
Sonu Nigam, Vijay Joseph, Sanjeev Kumar, Sonu Sood, Vairamuthu, Kishore Biyani, Tom Hanks, Arbaaz Khan, Harshad Mehta, Geri Halliwell, Victoria Azarenka, Micky Jagtiani, Wayne Parnell, David Hussey, Semmangudi Srinivasa Iyer, William Thackeray, Courtney Love, Babe Didrikson Zaharias, David Hemery, Yusuf Garibaldi, Camilla Parker-Bowles, Chandrakant Borde, Princess Beatrice of York, Harshavardhan Nawathe, Akhilesh Yadav, Emily Brontë, Annie Oakley, Arianna Huffington, Roger Binny, Devayani, Alok Nath, Anne Lauvergeon, Sofia Vergara, Kalyanji (Anandji), Geoffrey Rush.

35. GEMINI–LEO

Royalty joins intelligence and sparkling wit meets indolent grace in this combination. GemLeos are ruled by the maverick planet Mercury that gives them superlative communication skills and superfast minds, along with the generous and magnificent Sun.

Fun loving and gregarious, they are very popular and know how to make a grand entrance. They are the friends who excite the rest of the gang; the ones who make dull classes enjoyable; and the ones with a string of love interests.

They are naturally curious and always seek improvement. They do not know what they want, so they look around till they find something. They are not traditional in their ways. Talking is their birthright, especially if the topic is them. No one can stop them from talking, boasting, exaggerating, dramatising and going on and on about everything. Wit and resourcefulness mark them out as excellent communicators and adept multi-taskers. Everything interests them; they are born curious and are interested in new ideas and thoughts.

They know how to look good. Their royal grace oozes out no matter what they wear (and what they wear is always the best). Whether early in the morning or late at night, their natural grace and elegance always assert themselves. This obviously also incurs a lot of bills. The Leo generosity will make itself evident in GemLeos and you will be surprised that a person who seems so flighty actually helps when the need arises. They are protective of their families and the ones they love.

They are natural thought leaders. When they speak, people listen. Their intelligence sparkles bright when they elaborate upon their plans. They are extremely solution-oriented. They can think of ten different ways of dealing with one situation. From changing car tyres to disintegrating enemies at war – a GemLeo will have solutions for it all.

They love flirting and all the attention it gets them. Attention is what they crave, which is due to their deep-rooted feelings of insecurity. This is common to all Fire signs but most prominent in Leos. Of course, it is well hidden under their natural confidence.

There is no stability in this combination due to the lack of Earth, which makes them less practical at times. Their enthusiasm for life and thirst for adventure make them seem young forever. The inquisitive Gemini in them gets bored by the usual routine and needs new things and different perspectives to make them feel alive. But don't expect sensitivity from them, this combination lacks Water and that makes them quite insensitive to the needs of others. Ask for what you want from them and most of the time you will get it.

Love will not be a burning passion with GemLeos though they dream of that one person. They usually find so many good qualities in so many people that it makes it hard for them to settle down. They need a mate who is as classy as them and as wild as their dreams. The dream guy/girl needs to be a bit of a mystery to keep the ever-changing Gemini in them interested. Besides which, good looks, wit and charm would be a plus.

It is not just in love, they are easily distracted in all matters; it is very difficult to pin them down to one thought for long. It takes them time to settle down. When they are angry or upset, the Leo in them sulks. Thankfully, they do not stick to that mood for long; you just have to pamper them a bit to make them smile again.

They know the art of making things seem more important than they are simply by their showmanship. They are glorious orators who can mesmerise you with their knowledge, diction and foresight. They seem braver and more confident than they really are. Despite all the buzz in their heads they maintain their poise with grace and seem to be in total control: an art, actually.

Gemini–Leo – Mahendra Singh Dhoni
'I love to analyse things a bit. It is important to realise what went wrong, not only when you are losing a series or a game, but also when you are winning; to realise which are the areas you need to work on.'[57]

Like a true Gemini, Dhoni tried his hand at various sports before deciding on cricket.

'Self-confidence has always been one of my good qualities. I am always very confident. It is in my nature to be confident, to be aggressive. And it applies to my batting as well as wicketkeeping.'[58]

Cool, suave, articulate and a fabulous leader, Dhoni makes his mark as a GemLeo.

Love and Marriage for Him
He is a charming companion, a fun-loving friend, a witty escort and an elegant partner. He is always nattily dressed. There is fun and laughter wherever he goes. He likes being pampered at home but asks for attention in such a charming manner that you have to give in. His Leo ego looks for a life partner who does not overpower or outshine him, while the Gemini in him wants a girl who can keep him enchanted.

Money and time are irrelevant to him, so you have to be the one in charge of the two. It is slightly tricky, for you have to manage being in control without actually showing it. Actually, you will have to manage the house and even your career, for this guy will be too involved in his myriad projects to be seriously responsible around the house. He will not mind you taking charge if you do it with tact.

He always has a travel bag ready because he loves to travel. He travels to far-off places and feels at home anywhere, quickly learning the language and adapting to new cultures. Anything new is definitely more exciting to him than the known.

As a father, he is there for his children and is very proud of them. But he may end up missing important school days and functions. He loves to talk to them as they grow older. He has a few fixed views in his mind and expects a certain kind of behaviour from them. Beyond that, he is just happy to show them off.

Love and Marriage for Her
'Girl' is what you call her, whether she is 16 or 60. Age does not make her stolid and the same youthful impulsiveness guides her to her walking stick. This girl makes heads turn wherever she goes.

---
[57] http://www.espncricinfo.com/magazine/content/story/545762.html
[58] http://www.rediff.com/cricket/2005/apr/06cinter2.htm

Her multitasking abilities enable her to handle many responsibilities. She easily manages home and work. Do not expect her to be content doing housework alone, she needs more things to do or she is soon tired and bored of routine. Also, never forget to compliment and pamper her. Give her your undivided attention, without giving total access to your bank account! You have to manage the finances.

She loves excitement, drama and socialising. She is not content to sit at home waiting for you all day. Party lights and nights out with friends keep her ticking. Nothing excites her more than being the centre of attraction. She can be elegant and charming when she wants; she can also be the siren. It all depends on her mood. This changeable nature will make her seem mysterious and she loves it. She is easily hurt too, if you step on her ego. Have lots of pampering ideas ready to make it up to her.

As a mother, she pampers her children. She expects them to excel academically. She wants them to be as smart as her. She is not the regular mom, staying at home and making them do their homework. Independence is what she teaches them.

At the Workplace

GemLeos' agile minds and unconventionality make them choose uncommon roles and jobs. They have it in them to be brilliant actors, sports persons and even writers. They can be gifted linguists too. The only problem is that you never get to know what goes on in their minds.

Their career choices are different and they may change their careers many times to suit their changing interests. For the more grounded, they can seem lost in their own world, but their wild imagination and unpredictable nature is the essence of their being.

In the corporate world, their charm, persuasiveness and excellent communication skills can make them ideal in sales-oriented jobs. They are extremely good at multitasking too. Remember that they need a lot of appreciation. Giving them an important-sounding title can compensate for some cash. Routine and monotony are not for them. They need jobs that offer change and even a chance to see the world. Properly channelled, their communication skills and creativity can make their career a brilliant journey.

As bosses, they are ingenious and commanding but not aggressive. They revel in roles that require planning and leading from the front. Remember that they think of more things than anyone you know, so don't be surprised if they change their plans without a moment's hesitation and leave you to clear the mess.

Fire and Air meet to make them driven yet unfocused, regal and multi-talented. This combination needs a purpose to grow and once they find their niche they will be unstoppable.

Famous GemLeo Personalities

M.S. Dhoni, Dalai Lama, Karishma Kapoor, Keanu Reaves, Venus Williams, Sachin Pilot, John Wright, Jhumpa Lahiri, Kamya Punjabi, Adam Sandler, Alluri Sita Rama Raju, Jennie Finch, Fabien Barthez, Carol Bartz, Mika Boorem, Amitav Ghosh, Pt. Hariprasad Chaurasia.

36. GEMINI–VIRGO

The fickle and maverick Mercury and 'Planet Y', the healer, rule this combination. A mercurial intelligence combined with love for detail and perfection mark this person. Gemini and Virgo are mutable signs, so GemVirs do not desire leadership nor do they hold fixed opinions. There is one more similarity in the two signs – both are known for their leanness.

GemVirs are extremely powerful thinkers. They are intelligent as well as street-smart. Virgo intelligence and clarity of thought combined with Gemini's inquisitiveness makes them grasp different ideas with ease. They have high foreheads indicating their love for thinking. The fabulous communication skills of Gemini combined with the hard-working and workaholic nature of Virgo makes them extremely sensible people. When the Gemini habit of wanting to know something about everything meets the Virgo's eye for detail and analytical skills you have a person who can talk well and in depth.

Virgo adds a deeper facet to the mercurial charm of Gemini. While Gemini is good at multitasking and has varied interests, Virgo gets into the nitty-gritty of things. Actually, this problem of too many interests will have them try out a variety of professions in their youth. Like true Virgos they will go deep into each and then with Geminian fickleness leave for another. This fickleness can be extended to any aspect of life, be it work, interests, hobbies, or even love.

You can also expect the deceptiveness of Gemini in them. They like adding colour to their imagination. They add spice to events and have convincing acting skills that make people believe them. If they want to be bad, they can turn into perfect con artists with Gemini dexterity and Virgo attention to detail.

They are athletic and fit. The Gemini constitution combined with the health-conscious Virgo makes them opt for healthy food. They like taking multivitamins, prefer vegetarian food and are teetotallers. They also cannot stay in one place and like to move around constantly.

On the flip side, this combination doesn't have Water or Fire elements; hence they often lack sensitivity and drive. While this blesses them with no emotional baggage and less dependency on people, the same thing can also make them insensitive. Emotions will not speak to them and they cannot perceive the inner workings of anyone's mind. You need to spell out clearly what you expect of them.

Violent, destructive anger is not for them. They use their smartness to get their way. They mind their own business too. When irritated, they use their language skills to flay you with criticism. This brings us to their biggest flaw – love for criticism! Their intention, however, is not to make you feel bad but they just cannot stand anything sloppy or half-done.

The Virgo tendency of living alone and Gemini detachment make GemVirs self-sufficient. This, combined with their habit of worrying, make them over-think what it would be like living with someone. They are also afraid of the added tensions and responsibility that marriage brings. So you might find them living quite happily single, and amused at people who think that they are missing out on something great. They are content in their space, working and living by themselves.

Geminis are born flirts while Virgos are pure at heart. They can be either but most of them will be harmless flirts. Gemini adds gregariousness to Virgo's puritan streak. There are also some GemVirs who go from relationship to relationship, not knowing exactly what they want, sometimes just for fun, to seek a change or for the thrill of playing mind games.

They are the thinkers and talkers of the zodiac. They are forever seeking clarity in the anarchy around them. They are detached, yes, but they need that solitude to replenish their thought and ideas. When they do prefer to speak... well, no one can match them.

Gemini–Virgo – Ashok Kumar
Ashok Kumar was a legendary Indian film actor, but he was much more than that. The Gemini curiosity made him enjoy learning new languages and he was a talented painter too. He had learnt astrology and the Virgo gift of numbers surely helped him there.

'Ashok was a complete believer in astrology as long as the calculations were accurate.'

'He would take great pains over even the smallest scene. A day before the scene was to be shot, he would go over the screenplay—and spend hours in the loo ruminating over it.'[59]

Curious, creative and extremely intelligent, Ashok Kumar embodied a GemVir.

Love and Marriage for Him
Remember one thing about him – he is a worrier. He worries about his job, looks, food, clothes and, most of all, about you. He can neither sweep you off your feet nor exhibit macho-man tactics. His only way of showing his love is to think of ways to please you. Duty is his prime concern. He always does what is required of him and expects the same from you. You have to love work, or at least act like that, with this guy around. Hard working and a multitasking genius himself, he cannot bear laziness.

He is very finicky. This can get to you at times, but remember that it is hard for him, so please try and reassure him whenever you can that he is doing the right things and living the right way. He can be morose at times and needs you to cheer him up. The need to be perfect makes him very conscious of what he eats. He has a lot of interests and is equally involved in all of them, which he would love you to share.

Criticism is his fiercest weapon and he uses it with lethal accuracy when angry. Do not say anything at that time. Life is not all duty, though. He is a fabulous companion to match your wits with and can be expansive, like a Gemini. His wisecracks will keep you and your friends in splits.

As a father, he will be responsible from day one and will be an intelligent friend to them. He will focus on high-quality education and help them in their homework enthusiastically.

Love and Marriage for Her
She is a very good companion. Intelligent talk personifies her and she knows so much about so many things that you are amazed. As a plus, she is neither extra sensitive nor does she have a strong ego. Virgo makes her extremely feminine. However, the Gemini detachment makes her seem a little aloof at times.

---
[59] http://www.openthemagazine.com/article/arts-letters/ashok-kumar-the-evergreen-hero

She is quite capable of taking care of herself and her family. Her way of taking care of everyone is by worrying for them. She worries about your health, her children's education and her friends' relationships. It is just her way, so do not get involved. She is also a fun-loving girl who loves cracking jokes and displays inventive wit.

As a mother, she enforces discipline but not at the expense of fun. Her children are always well-dressed and taken care of.

Remember a Virgo is perfectly capable of cutting off all ties and Geminis can wander off in search of that elusive rainbow. She has loads of patience and if you are still not being the dutiful and responsible man in her life – she will walk away never to come back again.

At the Workplace

Work is their passion. The Virgo desire for excellence forces them to prepare for every question and look into each detail. When combined with Gemini quick thinking and multiple talents, you have an intelligent and versatile live wire. They have amazingly creative and original ideas, which they communicate beautifully and sell very well. They don't just ideate; they are the guys who can follow through with perfection. They will detail the plans you made and create back-up plans, communicate perfectly and ensure that your idea is workable in every way.

Virgo's eye for detail in picking up the nuances of characters and Gemini versatility makes them good actors, too. They can be in the media and charm you with their intelligent words and knowledge. They make excellent writers, as Gemini loves words and Virgo knows how to write. Their excellent written and verbal communication skills make them excel at any profession that relies on words.

Highly analytical, they speak with clarity and can also throw in jargon to impress. Excellent communication skills with a strong foundation in technical details make them star performers. As bosses, they are extremely critical. Their intention is never to put you down but to create perfection. They will lead by example and lazy workers will find it difficult to maintain their charades under the reign of GemVirs.

Hard and smart work will get them almost all they want, but sometimes they should take the help of the Arians, Sagittarians and Scorpios to carry out their plans as they don't have a Fire or Water sign and hence they lack speed and passion.

Air and Earth make this a delectable combination of wit, charm, perseverance and intelligence. Earth makes the Air more grounded while Air adds communication skills to the steadfast Earth.

Famous GemVir Personalities

Ashok Kumar, Cyrus Mistry, Jean Dujardin, Ronaldo, Sebastian Vettel, Shaan, Radhika Sarathkumar, Tillakaratne Dilshan, Hashan Tillakaratne, Martin Crowe, Gautami, Annie Besant, M.S. Vishwanathan, Adoor Gopalakrishnan, Rahul Khanna, Mira Nair, Julio Iglesias, William Hesketh Lever, Nikola Tesla, Eleanor Roosevelt, Marc Anthony, Gwen Stefani, Lisa Haydon.

37. GEMINI–LIBRA

This is a combination of two Air signs. Gemini is extremely intelligent and the best communicator of the zodiac while Libra is the sign of beauty and grace. Libra is also the second-best conversationalist in the zodiac. Just imagine the amount of talk, intelligence and wit that can flow! This person is a communicator par excellence and you cannot win a verbal duel with him. GemLibs can argue and counter-argue each and every point without showing the least sign of fatigue.

Gemini is ruled by the maverick messenger god, Mercury, while Venus, the planet that rules relationships and love, represents Libra. Librans love companionship and hate being lonely. The Geminian too likes to surround himself with people. So expect them to be warm and friendly people with charming smiles.

The double Air can make their thought processes wander a lot. The Libran desire for cleanliness might see them pick up a dusting cloth but by the time they pick it up, their over-active mind will list five other tasks for them and they will not know where to begin. Libra will also give them laziness; it will take them a lot of effort to convert their tasks from mind and paper into actual work.

Romance comes early to Librans. With their soft hearts and need for companionship, the Libran is in love with the concept called love. Here, Gemini plays the spoilsport. Gemini's flirtatious nature and aversion to commitment make GemLibs think and debate a lot before signing on the dotted line. Actually, it is foolish to expect total commitment from them when they are young. GemLibs are people who can be in love with two or three people at the same time. The poor dears are so caught up in their own brilliance they can't resist charming others. They also find so many positives in everyone, one guy might be charismatic, the other might have soulful eyes while the third's passion might make them breathless. You never know how difficult it is for them to decide. You might have to fool them into making a commitment or wait for the Libran desire for a steady relationship to take over.

They will be multi-talented. One of the reasons for their numerous talents is their curiosity and willingness to learn. They also cannot keep doing the same thing every day. They either outgrow things or get bored. This habit of getting into something and then getting bored and leaving it for something more interesting can afflict them in all spheres of life. ALL!

All that talk and grace also means that you cannot pin GemLibs down to a decision. It's also hard to take a decision when you want to be scrupulously fair and that's the Libran's whole dilemma. On the other hand Geminis are known for their wavering minds. GemLib are always indecisive and take ages to reach a conclusion.

They also have a tendency to exaggerate or add their colourful imaginations to the truth. They love having fun with words and can easily dream up fictitious versions of events. Just ensure that whatever you hear from them has the backing of facts from someone else too.

Their fabulous chatter does not have sensitivity or emotional content. These guys cannot feel the pain of others and can be quite insensitive without realising it. A GemLib is never able to understand exactly what you are going through. But they somehow seem to compensate with the empathy of the Librans.

Fabulous ideators and thinkers, you can expect these people to express their ideas beautifully and to talk astoundingly well. What you should not expect them to do is carry the idea through to execution – they lack the force, drive and conviction to do so. Also, the fabulous master communicator and thinker runs the risk of frittering away energy with too many distractions.

They don't have the realistic and practical streak of Earth signs like Taurus and Virgo and are easily excited by new ideas without really checking their feasibility. Fire signs like Aries, Leo and Sagittarius are known for their drive, ambition and faith, and their sheer passion keeps them glued to the goal; not so with GemLibs. They need to learn how to persevere and see things through to their logical conclusion.

Gemini–Libra – Sonali Kulkarni
Sonali Kulkarni is a two-time National Award winning actor. She was also an editor with *Viva*, a supplement of Marathi daily *Loksatta*. She displayed her dancing skills in the popular celebrity dance competition show, *Jhalak Dikhhla Jaa*.

'Since my theatre days, I have always wanted to do things that excite me as an artist. For me, it has always been very important not to restrict myself as an actor and I am lucky that in every film of mine, I have had a very different look. In real life, I am a fun-loving person who always makes others laugh.'[60]

Sonali is a true GemLib with her ability to think and act as multiple people!

Love and Marriage for Him
If this guy has chosen you, you must be extremely intelligent. Expect him to be wildly amusing and great company. Just do not expect him to change the light bulbs or carry groceries. He is great to talk to, but if you want someone who knows how you feel from the look in your eyes, you should have looked for someone with Cancer, Pisces or Scorpio in them. This does not mean he is unromantic. On the contrary, he is highly romantic and knows just the right words to make you smile. He brings flowers, writes love notes and takes you out to candle-light dinners.

Getting him to commit is difficult. He loves flirting, and most of the time it is harmless... yes, most of the time! Learn to turn a blind eye to it or take it in your stride. Jealousy and possessiveness turn him off. He does not understand why you worry, when he is with you.

He is extremely sensitive to one thing – his surroundings. The Libran in him simply hates mess and disorder. No matter how long you stay with him, you always find something new in him. This guy loves being an enigma. He is not secretive, it is just that he has so many interests that even after ten years, you will find something amazingly new about him. Money matters are not understood by him, so it is better you handle the finances and let him enjoy the privileges.

He will love talking to his children and having fun with them. Ensuring they do their homework on time should be your duty.

---

[60] http://www.sify.com/movies/bollywood/interview.php?id=6006579&cid=2398

Love and Marriage for Her
Talkative and cheerful, she is the quintessential chatterbox. Her intelligence and ready wit make her a great party companion. She is totally girlish, both at 15 and 50. Her youthful looks and ready smile make many hearts beat faster. Be happy that she chose you; it was not easy, considering the fact that decisions are difficult for her. But be ready to lose every argument. It is not that she is right every time. It is just hard to find answers to her arguments.

She is extremely loving and caring, but sometimes she just does not understand how you feel. Talk to her and let her know your point of view. She needs to be guided on emotions as double Air makes her quite frivolous at times. This girl is highly romantic. You have to shower her with flowers, hold her hand while walking and surprise her with love notes.

Do not expect her to save. She is playful and has a youthful heart and she can fall in love at any age; hope you can keep this girl all to yourself. Do not neglect her and forget to cater to her extraordinary mind.

She is a fabulous mother and loves multitasking for her kids. Of course, when she does that, she thinks and delegates all the work to you. That is why she chose you, for your organising skills. Scrupulously fair and just, all the children will come to her for final decisions in their quarrels.

At the Workplace
Choosing a career is difficult for them – as hard as choosing anything in life. Decisions are not their forte. With their excellent communication skills and selling prowess, there is no one better than them to present ideas or communicate designs. They are masters of the spoken word and make the most ordinary ideas seem brilliant by their glib talk.

The Libran excellence at artistic ventures and Geminian multitalented skills will ensure that they have at least one artistic talent. No matter what they do in life, they ensure that they are adept at more things. They make an excellent impression as they walk into a room, but need juniors who can carry out their ideas.

They are very good at talking themselves out of situations and can lie or colour the truth, and use their charm to get away from disasters. If a GemLib boss has told you to respond in negative to your superior boss, be sure to take that in writing; for in front of the superior he/she can totally change their stance.

Famous GemLib Personalities
Sonali Kulkarni, Raul, Aravinda De Silva, V.P. Singh, Dr Balamuralikrishna, Condoleezza Rice, Theodore Roosevelt, Nelson Rockefeller, Mohd. Ali Jinnah, Laxmanrao Kirloskar, Owais Shah, Karan Thapar, Dr Rajasekhar, Shivrajkumar, Geoffrey Boycott.

38. GEMINI–SCORPIO

The irrepressibly maverick Mercury meets Pluto, the ruthless lord of the underworld, in this mix of light and darkness. The outgoing nature of Gemini combined with the deep passions of Scorpio endows GemScorps with the passion, energy and intensity of Scorpio and the speaking skills and multitasking abilities of Gemini.

GemScorps are forceful communicators. They not only talk but feel too, and those deep emotions come across strongly every time they say something. This combination gives the airy Gemini a heart and makes it feel deeply and intensely.

This is a very intelligent combination. Gemini makes them very quick at understanding new and abstract concepts while Scorpio makes them instinctively read into the depths of any subject. GemScorps are never befuddled and are always ready to think new thoughts. Intelligence and wit are their hallmark. Their dynamic style is as hard to hide as their wit. They can readily understand, converse and even opine on any subject; a difficult combination to get into an argument with.

The Gemini tendency of not saying exactly what they think and the Scorpio nature for secrecy have them thinking deeply and deciding at the last moment. You never know what they will eventually decide to do. They usually have the upper hand in dealing with others.

GemScorps will have the Gemini mind and be interested in many things but unlike the airy Gemini they will also be passionate about their varied interests. Though lack of focus can mar their obvious talents at the beginning, the intensity of Scorpio can reduce the distraction to some extent. However, till GemScorps learn about their weakness they won't be able to sustain their interest for long. Thankfully, they will be wise enough to understand their fickleness and as they grow older they will learn to come to terms with it and also control (to an extent) their ever-distracted mind.

The vindictiveness of Scorpio makes them dangerous people to incite. They not only have the revenge syndrome but are also able to think of ten different ways to get back at you. They rarely forgive, so it is not advisable to hurt them. Aggression is not the only weapon in their arsenal – their amazing language skills come in handy here and they can use jokes, pranks, snide sarcastic remarks – anything to get back at you and then forget all about you!

Fun-loving and born pranksters, they create a buzz wherever they go. Sometimes parties can become a habit and lead them astray. Yet their alert mind will always guide them to wherever they want to go. This lethal combination can make them saints or sinners; they can channel their undoubted skills either way. Geminis love trying out everything, be it good or bad, and the Scorpio focus, plus its desire to know the deepest, darkest secrets, can become a trap. They can use their brilliant minds to work at negative things. They do not mind taking shortcuts and, if those shortcuts happen to be wrong, they can turn all bad. Whatever path they walk it will be difficult to put them down.

The need to try out everything and many easy distractions will make them change many partners in love, but don't think they are immune to love. Once GemScorps understand and come to terms with their natures they will learn to focus their energies and they can settle down as well. They need a partner who is intelligent enough to talk to them on diverse topics and sensitive enough to realise their vulnerabilities. They can love with the intensity and passion of Scorpio if they find a partner whom they trust and talk to without misgivings.

The tendency to get bored with things quickly and move on to something new and interesting after the novelty factor wears off is something that they need to be consciously aware of, as it can make or break them.

Gemini–Scorpio – Shane Watson

To conquer international cricket, Shane Watson first had to beat his fragile body. Watson's frame was so brittle it threatened to break him. He refused to give up. Not through recurrences of back-stress fractures, hamstring strains, calf problems, hip complaints or a dislocated shoulder.[61]

'Watson screamed maniacally and aggressively in Gayle's direction after dismissing him. While Gayle was somewhat critical of Watson, he was also understanding. 'He's a passionate person,' Gayle said. 'That's how he expresses himself but maybe he just overdid it a bit, but that's Shane.'[62]

Passionate yet flexible, Shane Watson has the sting and resilience of the Scorpio and the mercurial aspect of Gemini.

Love and Marriage for Him

He is the best thing that can ever happen to you. This guy creates glamour and love in his life. But he needs a stabilising and calming force to take him on. If you are as footloose and wild as him, life can go a little out of hand. There is no dull moment with him around. You need to be a little less possessive about him for he really desires to do many things and needs space to do them. He can be possessive about you, though. Please do not complain.

Despite his evident fun side, he has deep emotions running through him. His ego is very prominent and it does you no good if you decide to get back at him with sarcasm. There is no one better than him at ripping people apart. Be careful.

On the other hand, he can be a total fun addict, full of jokes and stories. He loves partying and can be a harmless flirt too. You must have the confidence in him to let him be himself, for tears and suspicions drive him away. Only an intelligent and calm woman can hold him down. He is content to sit and talk to one who matches his mental strengths.

With his children, he is fun loving and chilled out. He knows exactly what they are up to and is not easily fooled. Though he is not controlling, he needs respect. He may be guilty of expecting more from them, especially the traits that he lacks, like stability and an even temperament!

Love and Marriage for Her

She is extremely good at doing things. This lady is not only intelligent but active too. She does not have a lazy bone in her body and works on ten different demands from ten different family members all at once. Energetic and imaginative, she is a delight to have around. She can talk, be opinionated and even debate while doing her chores.

---

[61] http://www.espncricinfo.com/India/content/player/8180.html
[62] http://www.smh.com.au/sport/watson-slapped-on-wrist-for-unsightly-celebration-20091220-l77h.html

Expect lots of chatter for she has too many views to keep to herself. You have to be receptive as well, for she needs a companion with whom she can share her ideas and laugh at jokes. You need to be as mentally alert as her.

Tradition is not very important to her and she is more a rebel than a conformist. You find her radically different at different stages of her life. Whatever she does, you can be sure that she displays sparkling intelligence. She is deeply emotional and sensitive as well. There are innumerable things that can hurt her and you must be careful when you discuss her problems. Never discuss the things you feel are wrong with her for she does not know how to deal with it except by trying to get back at you.

She needs a guy she can look up to. She desires intelligence, above everything else in you and loyalty. She can act flirtatious or be the femme fatale at parties but, from you, she wants nothing less than a declaration of absolute allegiance.

As a mother, she is loving and understanding. She is rarely shocked by new ideas and encourages her children to be multitalented. She needs respect too but is quite chilled out otherwise. She is never imposing, but they find it hard to ignore her valid ideas.

At the Workplace

GemScorps have the energy, passion and magnetism of a Scorpio and they are so good with their words, and so street-smart, that they excel at convincing people. This is a very good combination for people-related careers. They are outgoing and fun loving with excellent social skills.

The Scorpio ability to penetrate the deepest mysteries of the world when combined with the lucidity of expression of Gemini can make for fascinating writers. Sports, too, are a distinct possibility for them; they are bundles of nervous energy with the ability to think on their feet and the passion to overcome all obstacles and win.

As bosses they can be demanding and controlling, but when they put forth their ideas in a spine-tingling, mesmerising and persuasive presentation, you are motivated to follow their ideals. They bring that rare combination of passion and dexterity to the table. The danger that lurks is that they can use that Scorpio passion in doing five different things at one time and scatter their energy wildly. If they channel all their inexhaustible energy and indisputable intelligence into ONE field – they will be invincible.

Air and Water combine in GemScorps to make them intelligent yet emotional, fickle yet focused, and passionate with a love for being with people and learning new things every day.

Famous GemScorp Personalities

Shane Watson, Sonia Gandhi, Zinedine Zidane, Dan Brown, Pranab Mukherjee, Sathya Sai Baba, Udit Narayan, Nicole Kidman, Mithali Raj, Sylvester Clarke, Jayaram, Bo Derek, Radhika Roy, Padmini, M.F. Dostoevsky, Goldie Hawn, Sarah Jane Dias, Yingluck Shinawatra, Kaley Cuoco-Sweeting, Sarika.

39. GEMINI–SAGITTARIUS

Mercury, the maverick messenger god, and Jupiter, the benevolent and knowledgeable, join in this combination and give it energy and power. GemSags cannot be chained to one place or one idea, and their minds are always open to multiple possibilities and ventures. Inquisitive and curious, they love knowing everything about everything around them and effortlessly manage two or three tasks together. Gemini gives them extremely agile minds and Sagittarius adds its extreme intelligence to enable them to easily tackle topics as varied as abstract sciences and languages. Languages are their gift.

They are full of energy and have an optimistic aura around them. They love to play pranks and have fun. They light up parties and get-togethers with their humour. The excellent communication skills of Gemini make them witty, with a penchant for punning. The theatrical quotient of Sagittarius makes them riveting speakers with their expansive gestures and loud exclamations. People invariably crack up when GemSags mimic others or re-tell incidents, in their own inimitable way.

GemSags cannot sit still doing nothing or not talking. They need to do more than one thing at a time or they become bored. They fear stagnation and hate routine. They may find it hard to keep their interest in anything for long.

They are a double mutable sign, which rules out aggression. They will never force or bully anybody to do what they want, yet they will use astute tactics to get their way. Their anger may erupt like a volcano before cooling down faster than a cucumber in a fridge. They become their sunny selves after telling you exactly how they feel. Thankfully, they are not malicious or vindictive, so it is better to have them express their irritations and move on.

They are great friends who are never mean. They are essentially party animals and they never shy away from jiving on the floor. They are eternal seekers – they seek knowledge and are always ready to learn. They are also thrill-seekers – they love adventure, travel, sports and entertainment. They are die-hard foodies – they love travel partly just to taste the exquisite cuisines of different cultures.

Deeply independent and curious, they hate being tied down. The Sagittarian need for freedom and the Gemini's desire for change, make them unreliable at maintaining relationships. They need excitement; and sadly, both Gemini and Sagittarius are not known for their love of commitment. The best thing about them is that they do not pretend in love. They will tell you clearly if they have grown out of a relationship.

There is this very interesting paradox about them. They have a dilemma – while they have the Sagittarian tendency to be blunt and tactless, they also possess the Gemini's love for deception. So it might be pretty confusing dealing with them at times. During fun moments, they might enjoy leaving out important bits of information or add zing to a story for their own private amusement. But during serious conversations they can rip you apart with the point-blank truth. You never know what to expect from them.

Their Sagittarian streak makes them highly ambitious but the Gemini in them can scatter that ambition into various fields. They also have a tendency to get bored very quickly and so the need for continuous excitement. Gemini makes them talented in so many fields, and keeps them brimming with so many ideas, they find it difficult to do just one thing. If they find that ONE thing that they want to do the rest of their lives, they will go all guns blazing with Sagittarian enthusiasm. But that may never happen. They may end up juggling various options throughout their lives.

Despite all their unpredictability, there is one thing that is predictable in them, though. They will be deeply spiritual. They believe in a higher power and derive strength from that invisible force. Their invincibility and extreme positivity probably emanates from that deep spiritual belief. They remain timeless and retain that naïve enthusiasm and zest for life well into their nineties.

Gemini–Sagittarius – Leander Paes

'Put me in a situation where most people will crumble, and I seem to thrive.' While undergoing treatment for a parasitic brain infection, the ever-optimistic Paes says, 'It gave me a lot of time to think, ponder and look at my life in its totality, not just be single-minded about tennis.'

Now, he wants to start his own clothing company, get into films and entertainment, release his first graphic novel and expand his orphanage; plus he is a trained dancer and even has a company called Leander Design that enhances the sports design of a company.[63]

There may be a hundred different ideas of the Gemini but Leander brings in Sagittarian vitality to every one of them He has also astonishingly reversed the clock to be victorious at forty-plus!

Love and Marriage for Him

He is the irresponsible husband to your responsible wife. Only strong independent ladies may apply, for the one thing that turns him off are soft, clingy women.

Let me talk about the good things first. You can enjoy life with him. He knows how to make you laugh and is the most charming guy you have ever met. You are able to talk about anything with him. He absorbs knowledge wherever he goes. He does not let you rot in routine but zings up your life with travel, adventure and thoughts.

Now, about the things not to expect from him: emotions do not speak with him, only words do. He cannot understand sighs and moods. He is also not interested in household duties. He loves going to parties but hates organising them. Detail is not what he is known for; it will be your department. He needs a partner who effortlessly takes care of the house while not getting bogged down in finicky details. He might call a few friends to a party but don't panic; he doesn't want you to slog in the kitchen, just arrange for everything and have fun with him. You need to provide the stability and steadiness that he lacks. He loves change, so keep on changing the décor, create new fun things to do together, solve problems, if any, and basically enjoy life with him.

As a father, he is good at communicating with his children. They learn a lot from him for he broadens their horizons and makes them see the world as an exciting adventure rather than a dull, boring place. He is their friend and confidante.

---

[63] *Hi! Blitz*, September 2013

Love and Marriage for Her
She is an exciting companion and there are no dull moments when she is around. This girl is the life of any family. One thing that you can always expect from her is truth – honest, point-blank, bitter truth. If she is in love with you she will not be able to hide it; the same goes if she falls out of it.

The kitchen is not her domain and it is unreasonable to suppose that she would spend her life there. She needs travel, excitement and adventure in her romantic relationship. This girl needs to breathe new thoughts and ideas.

She is a colourful personality with a loud laugh. Her appetite for life is as large as her friends' circle. You can expect impromptu parties and get-togethers at your place. Her menu might be simple but her friends won't mind as long as she keeps them in splits. She likes impromptu treks, camping and adventure sports. She doesn't believe in being faint-hearted.

She can manage home and career together so efficiently that you are amazed. Actually, she must have a career for it keeps her abundant energies balanced. Her multitasking talents make her inexhaustible.

As a mother, she is everywhere doing everything with her baby, and with her smile intact. Her children have a friend in her for she never bosses them around. She knows how to have fun with them.

At the Workplace
The excellent communication skills of Gemini and the intelligence of Sagittarius see GemSags excel in any field. Their only criterion is that the work must not be repetitive and they must not be bound by monotonous routine. They can be good in fields as diverse as writing, showbiz and sales. Any field that has anything to do with communicating ideas and thoughts, sees them shine.

With the dexterity and quick impulses of Gemini and the boundless enthusiasm and vigour of Sagittarius, GemSag is a great combination for a sports person too. This is a combination of physically the most robust (Sagittarius) and mentally the most agile (Gemini). They will be ageless while playing, due to their energy levels, which are as high as a child's.

They need money but more than that, they want a WOW. They love adulation and want to be recognised for their feats. Their ability to multitask and think on their feet make them overcome challenges with ease. As bosses, expect them to be very outgoing, energetic and in your face. You need to develop a thick skin for their sarcastic remarks. Also don't be surprised if they change their opinions and plans too quickly. Polish your presentation skills before facing them.

Extremely energetic, GemSags are blessed with the gift of the gab; accentuated by their adventure-loving nature and a mind that can think of ten different things in one moment.

Famous GemSag Personalities
Leander Paes, Sunil Gavaskar, Frank Lampard, Lewis Hamilton, Brad Hodge, Veerapaandiya Kattabomman, Salim Durrani, Liv Tyler, Darren Sammy, Twinkle Khanna, Isaac Newton, Ramanand Sagar, K. Balachandar, Rakeysh Omprakash Mehra, Bidhan Chandra Roy, R. Sarath Kumar, Manolete, Manjari Phadnis, Elin Nordegren, Lara Stone, Mahie Gill, Tuba Büyüküstün, Prince Bernhard of Orange.

40. GEMINI–CAPRICORN

The mercurial Gemini and saturnine Capricorn come together in GemCaps. Gemini is the most versatile, wily and intelligent sign of the zodiac while Capricorn is endowed with practicality and shrewdness. Both these signs complement each other beautifully. The airiness of Gemini is its greatest strength and biggest weakness. But with Capricorn's practical and grounded approach, those airy thoughts find a solid foundation. GemCaps are capable of thinking of out-of-the-box ideas that can be implemented.

The Capricornian love for scale gives Geminian thought a big canvas. Capricorns dream big, are always well turned out and aristocratic, with an air of seriousness about them. They speak in a measured manner with a lot of maturity. Geminians are master wordsmiths, extremely intelligent, full of ideas and very chirpy. The common thread is that their minds are always ticking. Both are very intelligent. In GemCaps you get a master strategist who knows the power of words – both written and verbal.

GemCaps find a way to do anything. They get exactly what they want by coaxing, cajoling and manipulating people and situations and they can talk anyone into doing anything they want. They dabble in many things. They take on hobbies and creative ideas from fields other than their work. They can smartly turn their hobbies and other interests into money-making ventures. They will usually have a job and a side business going for them. They are not lazy and always find time to do other things.

They are also extremely close to their family members and are their pillars of strength. The family's wish is their command. They always think of how to increase their position and wealth in society. They forever hunt for ways to make money along with status and respect.

Romance is more sedate for them due to the inhibitive Capricorn. The Gemini expressiveness is limited in love for GemCaps due to the old values of Capricorn. They will display their love by practical things like taking care of your needs and making sure you never want for anything.

The Gemini restlessness finds expression in an inherent agitation within them. Gemini needs continuous change while Capricorn strives for stability and this is the eternal conflict they struggle with. They have a habit of colouring everything with their vivid imagination. They love expressing themselves and make the most mundane and ordinary happenings sound exciting with their embellishments. Do not assume that everything they say is the truth. They also have a sharp tongue; think twice before criticising them.

Capricorns are extremely self-centred. They include only themselves and their family in their core care group and don't think about any others if things turn bad. When combined with the cunning of Gemini, GemCaps hide their true motives with smooth words and charisma, and never attack directly. Their methods are subtle but deadly. If you don't mean them well, it is advisable to be a little wary around them.

As with other combinations, GemCaps have their own set of shortcomings. To start with, the Geminian fickle-mindedness and not knowing where exactly they are headed. The Geminian duality and the need to always have various options for everything in life can be a dizzying experience. Added to this, both Gemini and Capricorn look for short cuts in life and have a compulsive need to become successful by any means at their disposal. If GemCaps can overcome these particular pitfalls, half the battle is won. If they can also defeat melancholy and a tendency to slide into depression when things don't go well – then they can soar high with the superb intelligence and tremendous wisdom of Capricorn.

Gemini–Capricorn – Carl Lewis
'I want to be a millionaire and I don't ever want a real job.'[64]

'There is no such thing as a piece of pie. You raise the pie. If Carl Lewis comes in and gets more money, I'm not taking money out of the pie, the pie gets bigger.'[65]

When he was a runner, Lewis had a reputation for being aloof. It was also a legacy of childhood shyness allied to a single-minded determination to be the best.

The legendary Carl Lewis displays the GemCap need for money and respect.

Love and Marriage for Him
The perfect husband and father, he is an excellent family man. You find him relaxed and cheerful in the family setting. There is no place that he loves as much as his home. Actually there is: the airy Gemini makes him want to fly to different places but the stable Capricorn holds him down. It may make him restless at times, but do not worry, for he does not fly away. He is lost without his home.

When angry, he can sulk and spout sarcastic comments. He can be very sardonic and his words can cut deep. He wants to be the man of the house and deferred to in times of crisis. Yet, he wants you to manage the home responsibly. He wants a woman who can take charge of situations without being aggressive. The Capricornian love for conventions and traditions will make him opt for an arranged marriage. But if he falls in love, (and yes, that is a possibility due to Gemini) he makes sure that he gets his parents to agree too. Therefore, the extremely smart Indian option of love-cum-arranged marriage is his choice! If he chooses you, you can be sure that you match his concepts of status and lineage.

Capricorn rules fatherhood and it makes him a fabulous father. He involves himself in every facet of his children's lives. He is the one father who attends all the school meetings and Sports Days. Despite the sternness of Capricorn, he is a fun-loving father who loves taking his children out on holidays.

Well, I need to say this… this is a well-guarded secret of the GemCap males. They *are* philanderers. It can start with them when young, *à la* Gemini or may develop late in their forties when they become successful (the reverse aging syndrome in Capricorn) but a GemCap without an extra-/pre-/post-marital affair is rare.

Love and Marriage for Her
She is an excellent home-maker. Actually, that is her confusion. She loves being at home and taking on everybody's problems. She is also good at her career. She cannot decide which is more important to her. During such times, she needs your support and understanding.

---
[64] http://en.wikipedia.org/wiki/Carl_Lewis
[65] http://www.guardian.co.uk/sport/2007/sep/30/athletics.features

She is the kind of girl you can take to meet your mother for she is a traditional girl. She seeks loving in-laws and is worried about getting the wrong ones. If, despite her efforts, there are still some family members who refuse to acknowledge her worth, then her sarcastic tongue will be totally justified in running free. She is a good person but is assertive as well.

There is only one warning though – do not believe everything she says. The Gemini habit of adding spice to most conversations is inherent in her.

She has a creative side to her. Support her in exploring it fully. Ambition is extremely important to her and if you can't deliver on that count, let her try her hand at it. She is quite capable of working double shifts as a mom and a career woman.

She is an excellent mother who plays games with her children and inculcates good habits in them. She is the one who solves every problem with amazing ease and is friend, philosopher and guide to them.

If you cannot not be the husband she can look up to then she could seek solace in a relationship outside marriage and you will never ever know. But remember, she gave you every chance, bore all your faults before she decided enough is enough. And what did she ask from you? Some understanding, some heart-to-heart talk, some responsibility from you, and to occasionally go wild, get some fresh air – out of that boring rut.

At the Workplace
They are people who can work and lead with ease. GemCaps excel at every level. Their innate intelligence makes them quick learners. They are extremely good at multitasking too. They know how to lead by making the right noises and the right moves.

The Gemini flair for writing sees them excel in written and verbal communication. They are extremely smart, so whatever they say is sensible and logical. They make extraordinary facilitators, teachers and mentors. This is a combination par excellence for a shrewd businessman, a clever politician or a consulting strategist for any business. They are also open to unusual careers where they can reach the top. They are hard-working but along with that positive trait, they are also capable of scheming and planning their way to success while acting affable. Always ensure that any deal you do with them benefits *you* too.

As bosses, they are masterminds; expect them to come out with extraordinary planning and solutions even during the toughest times. Do not expect sympathy or sensitivity from them. They are family-oriented and definitely understand if you have family commitments but they are also shrewd enough to know where to draw the line.

Air and Earth combine to give the strength of each and dilute many of the negative traits of both. Family and status are the two loves of a GemCap and they will do everything they can to achieve those two aims.

Famous GemCap Personalities
Carl Lewis, Raj Thackeray, Amrish Puri, Kalpana Chawla, Fabio Capello, Tina Munim Ambani, Ali Ferzat, Janis Joplin, Gulzarilal Nanda, Yashodhara Raje Scindia, Mischa Barton, Brad Hogg, Liona Boyd, Rakesh Sharma, Yasmine Bleeth, Pierre Samuel du Pont, Angela Braly.

41. GEMINI–AQUARIUS

The changeable Mercury and the highly eccentric Uranus mark this extremely unpredictable and intelligent combination. GemAquas are an effervescent double Air combination. They are full of so many ideas, opinions and thoughts that, after a conversation with them, you may lose track of exactly what you were discussing. But they are never boring. There are just too many things they are curious and knowledgeable about.

Intelligence is their trademark. Their minds are ever active: forever questioning, learning and visualising. Every time you meet them, they seem different. Air signs always change and this is a double Air sign; they will always be changing and evolving – for the better. Adaptability and malleability are inherent in them.

Languages and cultures hold no barriers for them. This unique flexibility makes them very people-friendly too. They are able to emote, connect and empathise exceedingly well. As an added plus, they can easily look at situations from another point of view. They always seem young. No matter how old they are, they look younger and brighter than their contemporaries.

They can act serious and sombre one minute and become giggling teenagers the next. The only way to handle them is not to try and label them. They hate boundaries, and anger, jealousy and orthodox views turn them off completely. These guys are shockproof. Nothing in this world can shock them. Customs, traditions and lineage make no impression on them. They can live utterly shocking lives too – shocking to you that is.

They are not extremely passionate or emotional. They are so well tuned to everything around them that they cannot possibly be held by one emotion for long. They desperately need to join meditation classes to find some focus. Though they may mellow down with time, they never conform to ideas that they feel are not right. They do not care about society at all.

You never find them drooling over money but they are never short of money either. They use their able minds to get what they want without hassles. They can live happily in modest surroundings as long as they have friends around them.

In romance they will take a little time. They treat every new person as a curiosity. They want so much, are excited by so many, that they have a tough time deciding what they actually want. Till they decide, GemAquas can easily have a string of romances. Each relationship may seem like true love to them. They will need time to figure out their desires. Once they manage to decode themselves they will calmly settle down.

It is the mental union that they look for and keep trying till they find someone as out-of-the-world as themselves. Their ability to dissect and scrutinise each individual they meet also makes them *know* people much earlier than others and hence they *seem* to change partners so often. Oh yes – they do get bored with 'normal' people easily; so can't blame them either.

They love being enigmatic and can be somewhat manipulative. They love mystery and always leave you thinking that you have cracked the code only to discover that you never knew the key in the first place. The mystery is never solved! This leaves many suspicious of their true motives. It is very hard to know what actually goes on in their minds and hearts.

They can be eccentric geniuses or waste their mental powers on varied thoughts. They get into something with a bang only to fizzle out later, till something new catches their eye. This lack of focus will make them achieve less than their more focused but less intelligent colleagues. Once they know what they want, their great communication skills and extremely agile mind will push them to success.

The danger is – the brilliant mind can become a scatterbrain and the potential genius can become wayward. They need to understand that Mercury and Uranus makes them go through a rollercoaster of experiences but that makes it difficult to select one that suits them the best and stick to it. This applies to everything in their life – be it love, career or anything else they go into. If they understand this basic nature of theirs and come to terms with their idiosyncrasy they will be able to settle down in their minds and hearts, and rein in that wavering soul. Till then… it's a circus!

Gemini–Aquarius – Pooja Bhatt

'If there is no growth, then you are in the wrong profession. I have made mistakes and learned through experience.'

'And I am not outspoken, just honest… It's just the way I am. It has not affected me, if it has, then I don't know.'[66]

Pooja Bhatt shocked one and all when she kissed her father, filmmaker Mahesh Bhatt, for a magazine cover. She also shocked us when she appeared only covered in paint on another magazine cover.[67] Controversial and unapologetic, Pooja Bhatt has her own views about her life. Like a true GemAqua, she has changed with time, but every time she has been herself!

Love and Marriage for Him

You need to be extremely stable and grounded to balance out the airy nature of this guy. Emotional and possessive women are not for him as, though he understands them, he is not affected by their tears or need for sensitivity. You also need to be the one in charge of your lives and the household. If you decide to wait for him to do his part, you may keep waiting for he can easily get distracted.

He never tires of surprising you. He is super-duper intelligent and it rubs off on you. He teaches you to take life easy and not be bound by conventions. You can help him discover what he actually wants in life. Help him in settling down his mind and finding that one passion that he wants to, and needs to, pursue in life – other than you that is. Many times he may be aloof and lost in his own thoughts; give him some 'me' time – he will be back soon.

This guy loves to travel and shows you sights you have never even dreamt of. You may have to plan the trip, if you care about the details, or let him do it his way, when you can expect the unexpected.

---

[66] http://www.rediff.com/movies/apr/04puj.htm
[67] http://www.indiatarget.com/cgi-bin/slide_shows.cgi?1066:5

As a father, he is exciting. He is always there to share his views. He helps his children to be independent. He is their friend and philosopher who tells them which path to avoid from his own experiences.

Love and Marriage for Her

She talks, communicates, extrapolates and is so clever about whatever she says that you just have to agree in admiration. Her communication needs are very high, so you must talk to her. She likes multitasking and juggling her family and career but somewhere along the way she gets distracted. If you can handle this bundle of intelligent energy and channel it into the right path – she will be eternally grateful to you.

She has a unique style. She is never dictated by society on fashion trends but with unusual creativity, makes her own fashion statement. She thrives on being different from others.

Do not look to her for emotional care. Her way to deal with situations is to think of better things, ignoring the dreary problems. She does not spend time crying over mistakes, but marches out in another direction. The girl in her will never truly grow up.

As a mother, she sets high academic standards for her children and that is not limited to studies alone. She values extracurricular activities and is a lively and fun-loving parent who neither stresses on conventions nor looks to their friends for comparison. She can be a bit careless about maintaining routine and ensuring discipline, though.

At the Workplace

The watchword of their lives is change and they revel in it. Not for them the stability of a plain old job that requires them to sit at a table all day staring into the computer! It is far better that they utilise their gift of communication and make it a part of their careers. Jobs that excite, challenge and require new thoughts and ideas on a daily basis are ideal. Their skills at empathising and understanding those around them make them great at handling people too.

This combination also makes good writers and thinkers who have original thought processes. They can revolutionise with their visionary views. Their fabulous communication skills can help them further expound on their views. But they will take some time to discover what they want out of their lives.

They are very adaptable and flexible, and those are their best traits for they are always willing to learn and improve themselves. They cannot be motivated by money. If they are your bosses, you will have the most memorable fun and learning moments; but don't try politics with them – they will weed you out if you do.

GemAquas will truly want to create something unique yet their love for ideas and thoughts can also impair their practical views. They need the help of Earth signs like Capricorn, Taurus or Virgo to help them bring their ideas to fruition.

Double Air makes them truly intelligent. Forever evolving and highly interactive, GemAquas desire nothing less than to create a life far removed from conventionality.

Famous GemAqua Personalities

Pooja Bhatt, Princess Diana, Ivan Lendl, Satish Shah, K. Kamaraj, Cheryl Cole, Kurt Cobain, Kavita Kaushik, Charles Lamb, Abby Elliot.

42. GEMINI–PISCES

GemPisces is a double mutable combination. The Piscean Neptune is the most mysterious amongst all planets while the Geminian Mercury is the most elusive. This makes it very difficult to pin these people down to specifics. Both Gemini and Pisces depict duality in their signs. The symbol of Pisces is two Fish swimming in opposite directions while that of Gemini is of Twins. This duality is an abiding aspect in GemPisces.

In order to understand this elusive combination more I would like to talk a little bit about the signs that make them up. First, there is Gemini – communicators par excellence, brilliant with words, brimming with ideas and funny one-liners. They are supremely talented, mercurial, live wires, and fun-to-be-with people. But beneath the surface, you would see that they are usually torn between two things. This feeling of indecisiveness, of always wondering whether they are on the right path or not, makes Geminis lack conviction. A tendency to get bored with things quickly is another such trait.

Now we come to Pisces. It is the most evolved sign of the zodiac. Pisceans are full of wisdom, understanding, tolerance and empathy. They are truly spiritual beings who treat material success and possessions as non-essentials. The two fish going in opposite directions signify the eternal fight – to swim up or down – within Pisces. The fact is Pisces know life and emotions so well that they can see the pitfalls in each path; this makes it very difficult for them to see a clear path for themselves.

The life of a GemPisces is not easy. They are always pulled in four different directions! The Twins have two paths and the two Fish have a path each. A corporate life or chuck it up for a dream that may not be materially rewarding? To follow conventions or to live a hippie's life? Well, it's a constant fight. Their bent of mind is creative and if you want them to find stability in their work, you have to inculcate the habits of discipline in them from a young age. If you try and force them to behave a certain way, they slip away. You have to be convincing and lead by example. The best thing about Pisces is that it easily imbibes the atmosphere it lives in.

They have absolutely no ego and do not mind changing or aligning themselves to any philosophy. You will never find people who are more positive or soft. They are easily affected if they see pain or suffering. Being such softies, they are very good at relationships. Gemini communication skills and Piscean empathy give them an uncanny ability to say exactly what you wish to hear. They are extremely talkative and love telling stories and tales of things that happened and people they met.

They have to be cautious of escapism and addictions. Geminis create an imaginary world when things go bad and refuse to look at reality while Pisces is attracted to addiction, be it coffee or marijuana. The airy Gemini doesn't like to stay in one place for long and the Fish can just disappear! GemPisces despise routine and mundane life, hate responsibilities and lack dependability. If incensed, they can turn depressive or sarcastic. Actually, they are quite moody and the Gemini tongue can lash out if you keep on pestering them.

Money is not their priority. They neither worship nor desire it but, of course, they love the life it provides. If they are born into rich families, they do not strive to increase it but rather use it to fulfil their desires to see the world or indulge in their favourite hobbies. If they are not born into privileged circumstances, they still do not work for it.

The biggest gifts of this combination are the innate high spiritual quotient and the extraordinary ability to express those ideologies beautifully. Their biggest threat is in becoming clueless, aimless, perpetual wanderers.

Gemini–Pisces – Bill Cosby

Bill Cosby is an American comedian, actor, author, television producer, educator, musician and activist.[68]

One of his teachers once noted, 'William should become either a lawyer or an actor because he lies so well."

After leaving the Navy, he went to Temple University where he had been given a track scholarship. In the middle of his junior year of college, Cosby decided to drop out to pursue a career in stand-up comedy.

Cosby achieved another career milestone – becoming a bestselling author.[69]

Bill Cosby is innately gifted like a true GemPisces along with the ability to learn and change.

Love and Marriage for Him

He is the most caring and loving guy ever, but you have to be strong to marry him. He needs a woman who is everything he is not – decisive, organised, grounded and sensible. An aggressive, ambitious or extremely vocal woman could ruin her chances of happiness and drive him to seek solace in his dreams or elsewhere. If you married him for his talents (for creativity flows from him), do not relentlessly force him to achieve your desire for success.

He shows you things that you may never have realised with another person. His view of life is so selfless and different from the rest of the world that it amazes you. When GemPisces fall in love, it is at a spiritual and deep level. He is not averse to expressing his love in words. He is the perfect guy in love – sensitive, caring and emotional. He takes care of all your emotional needs and never questions you. There is nothing that you tell him that shocks him. He is the exact opposite of conservative and does not believe in society's rules.

He has neither any idea about money management nor does he bother. You are his link to the real world, so be sure that you handle day-to-day activities. He may also seem detached. Take it in your stride and do not pay much heed to it. He bounces back soon enough.

As a father, he is very loving and caring but discipline will be your department.

Love and Marriage for Her

She is a fantastic wife – loving and caring and, yes, she does not ever harbour feminist thoughts. She never judges you harshly and looks at you through rose-coloured glasses. Pisceans want to love and be loved while Geminis love romance

---

[68] http://en.wikipedia.org/wiki/Bill_Cosby
[69] http://www.biography.com/people/bill-cosby-9258468?page=1

and can talk love for hours. She needs a partner in life and is not happy being on her own.

She does not stay in one place for long and likes going through new and varied experiences. She has artistic and creative talents, let her explore them. The one thing that she hates doing is housework. If you do not treat her well, she is sure to find love somewhere else. She is not bound by restrictive societal values and places no importance on a relationship sans love.

She wants a man who has the conviction she lacks. Ambition does not rank high in her list of needs. She wants faith, love and respect. Her environment needs to be happy. If she is in a place where anger and distrust predominate, she is very unhappy and does not know any other way than diving into her imaginary world to defend herself. Take her out often, pamper her and give her some time by herself. That is all she needs to be happy.

As a mother, she is fun and loves telling stories to her children. Do not expect her to set rules. She does not ask them to abide by conventions just because society does.

At the Workplace
They need to work in environments that promise constant change. Routine and logic are two things that must not be forced on them. They are so good at knowing what makes you tick just by talking to you that any field that puts them in contact with people is good for them. They can talk and emote beautifully. They are great at support roles and do not demand recognition. They are contented in being background men/women. Careers in human resources, mentoring or coaching are very good for them.

Writing is an obvious choice with the Gemini flair for words and the Piscean love of poetry. They are those extraordinarily creative artists who revel in the pure pleasure of creating mesmerising, ethereal work that is unscathed by materialism. Acting, dancing and music too are fields that excite these extremely creative people.

You cannot tempt them with money, power or job titles. The biggest flaw in their work life is their irresponsibility. Here, again, the Piscean mutability comes into play. If they are trained by a fabulous boss, they inculcate his values.

If you have a GemPisces boss, you can be sure that he is the easiest person to work for. But beware – do not try any excuses with him: for all his good nature, he is very hard to fool. He can easily see through your lies and excuses. He duly rewards you for your work and does not steal your thunder.

Air and Water meet in this dreamy combination that lives in an idealistic world. Respect that and never force them to become what they aren't.

Famous GemPisces Personalities
Bill Cosby, Mariah Carey, Carles Puyol, Kiran Mazumdar Shaw, P.V. Narasimha Rao, Manav Gohil, Paris Jackson, Shubhangi Atre Poorey, Spencer Tracy, Charles VIII of France, Mumtaj (Tamil actress), Isabeli Fontana, Irene Cara, Margaret Hamburg, Heath Ledger.

43. CANCER–LEO

Moon, the ruler of emotions, and Apollo, the generous and life-giving king of the gods, rule this emotional and proud combination. Creative and imaginative, CanLeos can think of anything. Their minds are reservoirs of creativity. They always dream big. They have the audacity to think of extremely imaginative ideas and then think of ways of making those ideas generate a 'Wow!'

They project a tough exterior and give the impression of being complicated, but they are easy to understand. This is the coming together of the royal, majestic Lion and the sensitive and touchy Crab. Can we call it crabby lion? Probably. Sensitive lion? Definitely. While Cancer needs love, Leos cannot live without respect. While Cancer wants to amass wealth to overcome an inherent insecurity; Leos want to make it big to gain power and esteem. While Cancer is extremely sensitive about what you think about them; Leos want you to think only highly about them. Put simply – CanLeos are touch-me-nots with fragile hearts. They want people to look up to them, love them, respect them and adore them. But they seem nonchalant about the whole thing.

They are those extremely high-strung people who get offended by trifles and swell with pride at small praises. They get hurt pretty quickly and if you hurt them they will remember it for a lifetime. If you honour them, they will remember that, too, till eternity. Choose your words with care while talking to them, as you don't know what exactly can create the hurt.

Leos are natural leaders who love the spotlight. Cancerians like to build a solid foundation and then create a permanent structure. The CanLeo approach to every aspect of life is spurred by the twin parameters of achievement and permanence. Leos do it for the applause but Cancerians stretch themselves to assuage their secret fear of failure.

CanLeos are emotional, sensitive and incurable romantics. They are generous and fun as friends – full of funny anecdotes. They are great hosts and love to cook. There are very few things that agitate them. Their stride is one of lazy grace and they always look up and walk. You never find hunched shoulders in them.

Family is extremely important to them and they dote on their mothers. Cancer gives them the mother orientation while Leo loves family. They would love to be leaned on and work very hard to see that the family is happy and secure – financially and emotionally. They also take immense pride in the achievements of every family member. They can be strong and arrogant for the world but to their families, they are eternal softies. They are also ready to sacrifice everything for them.

Dramatics is their specialty. They can bring drama to the most inane conversations. They are also so emotional and sensitive that they bestow undue significance upon even everyday events. Respect and unconditional love are extremely important to them. Undermine their importance or rub them the wrong way and watch them sulk mightily or erupt in temper.

Insecurity is their curse. They look confident and talk with easy command, yet, deep in their hearts, insecurity rules. They try very hard to overcome it and either take to extreme shows of arrogance or build a wall around themselves. They find a way to rise above their insecurities for the Leonine sunshine does not wallow in darkness for long. They need a lot of pampering, care and flattery to help them move on. The Cancer sensitivity can make them sense untruthful words and they do not like being lied to. So make sure your praises are genuine.

Money is another tug-of-war with CanLeos. They want to save desperately but also need to show off a bit. They have periods of saving followed by binges at the malls. But their generosity and the kind of money and love they splurge on the family and friends is unlimited and truly unbelievable.

Cancer–Leo – J.K. Rowling
From her commencement address at Harvard – 'What I feared most for myself at your age was not poverty, but failure.'

'I had been writing the Harry Potter series...[when] my mother died. I really think from that one moment on, death became a central...theme of the seven books.'

'I would really have to be very stupid [to not be wealthy forever], but, yeah, I do still worry. Not all the time, most of the time I think things are great.'[70]

J.K. Rowling has the idealism of Leo and the stunning imagination, love for her mother and the insecurities of a Cancer, to make her a true CanLeo.

Love and Marriage for Him
He wants to be your most loved, respected and adored person. He chooses his life partner carefully. He is likely to select a woman who is a notch below him in social status. This way he can ensure that his wife toes the line, pampers him and is grateful to live in his kingdom. You have to watch what you say to him. It is very easy to let the air out of his ideas. Please do not use your wit against him.

Home means a great deal to him and he likes to spend his holidays in a family reunion. He is one of those few guys who is glad to see his in-laws, especially if they invite him as the chief guest. He does not mind paying the bills if he is respected and adored as a great son-in-law. Be ready to cook for friends and family on short notice. Of course, he helps you a lot here. He is extremely good at whipping up home-made economic alternatives and repairing gadgets too. This is one husband who helps in all the household activities.

You will also need to have a perfectly cordial relationship with his mother. Actually, he will always be thinking of ways to make his mama happy and it would be good if you can take that department on.

As a father, he is wonderful. His children always seem the most brilliant and the most talented to him and he loves pampering them. There is nothing that he does not give them. In return, he only demands respect. He also finds it hard to let go when they grow older.

Love and Marriage for Her
She does not have to try too hard to attract. Grace comes naturally to her. Heads turn and necks crane when she enters the room. This does not mean that the girl lacks heart. Vanity and concern are the opposite ends of her soul; it is amazing

---

[70] http://today.msnbc.msn.com/id/19991430/ns/today-wild_about_harry/t/rowling-regret-never-told-mom-about-potter/

how both work in tandem to create her unique persona. Understand one fact about her though: she is a drama queen. You need to be her stable anchor and are also required to attend to her dramatic expressions with concern.

She needs tons and tons of attention. Praise her, be attentive to her needs and be romantic. She loves romantic outings. Take her out, especially to places near water; they hold a special attraction for her. Be sure not to look at any other woman when she is around for she easily detects the vibes. The end result of the wandering attention will not be good for your health.

She likes to be self-sufficient and have a career. The lioness in her loves her independence. Mood swings afflict her. The sunny smile can soon turn to gloomy despair. What saddens her may be hard to detect, but let her battle it out alone and pamper the moods out of her. The sunny smile soon returns.

She is an ideal mother, ready with a handkerchief and a kiss to wipe away tears, bruises and hurt egos. Her kids love her for she not only plays games but also adds a touch of glamour. She loves to spend on them. They get away with anything if they praise her.

At the Workplace
This is an amazingly creative combination. CanLeos can take creativity to new levels and add zing to it. Not only are their thoughts creative, but their faces mirror their emotions beautifully. Putting such gifted people in monotonous jobs just kills their talent. They need applause and space to build on their creative thoughts.

They are extremely loyal and tenacious in their chosen fields. They never leave their jobs on flimsy grounds but prove their loyalty by staying put. They have three basic needs – respect, appreciation and money. Give them all three and they never let you down.

As leaders, they command and also know how to cajole. They make their subordinates a part of their lives and, if you are on their team, you are likely to be invited for numerous dinners and lunches with their families. They like to adopt a parental role and make everyone welcome with their warm smile and genuine concern.

Water and Fire mix in CanLeos to give them drive tempered with insecurity. They are creative and loving yet dramatic and egoistic.

Famous CanLeo Personalities
J.K. Rowling, Larry Ellison, Richard Branson, Prasoon Joshi, S. Shankar, Dhyanchand, Greg Chappell, Meena Kumari, Mumtaz, Princess Akishino, Zhang Xin, Nathan Astle, Chandra Shekhar Azad, Shivaram Rajguru, Dustin Hoffman, M.S. Oberoi, Sir Dorabji Tata, Sir Pherozeshah Mehta, Freeman A. Hrabowski III, Arjun (Tamil actor), Sir Frank Worrell, Aruna Irani, Mahesh Manjrekar, Peter O'Toole, Hansika Motwani, Bansi Lal, Paul Wesley, Sana Khan, Manish Paul.

44. CANCER–VIRGO

CanVirs are a perfect blend of emotions, commitment and attachment. Cancer is ruled by the Moon that waxes and wanes and Virgo denotes perfection and duty. CanVirs never shirk their duty and are extremely loving. They are prone to mood swings and are absolutely finicky about neatness. They are a complicated mix of practicality and sentimentality.

Loving, caring and nurturing come easily to them. They have an innate ability to care for the wounded and depressed, and everyone around them senses their care and selflessness. The Virgo in them gives them a keen eye for detail and, despite their sentimental nature, they have an in-built sensor for detecting lies; a facility that makes them formidable parents and strict teachers.

Loyalty is their trademark. They are extremely loyal and expect the same. Family is everything to them. They adore their mothers, love their children and belong heart and soul to their spouses. You can always spot them with their big smiles at family gatherings. They are extremely happy if they live in joint families. No sacrifice is enough when their family's happiness is in question. Yet, there is a small contradiction. If they feel that the love around them is not enough, and if they find true love outside, they leave without a second thought. Just two conditions need to be met – one, they feel that their family will not be in disarray and their children will be well looked after, and second, if they feel there is financial security, besides the emotional.

There is only one fault in CanVirs. They are very emotional. It makes them very insecure too. They can take even friendly advice as criticism and be very hurt. Anything can cause their emotions to break out. Their mood swings also give grief to their families. Their moods change with the phases of the moon. The full moon can make them highly sensitive and moonless nights can see them at their irritable worst. They need a lot of reassurance and love once they get into the Cancerian shell. Saving money is their religion. They spend hours worrying over their financial status if they are not saving enough. They never really feel financially secure.

Worry comes naturally to them. They can worry about their friends' careers, their mother's health, their spouse's decisions, their children's education; all of them receive their undivided attention and care. This constant worrying can make them nag or be extremely critical. They are also loners and do not mind solitude. It can make them depressive if they are left alone during their worry periods. Keep them involved and don't let their worry create a wall.

In all their relationships they consciously try to do their duty. Duty and responsibility define their relationships. This is their strength and also their weakness, for they will strain themselves to the limit to fulfil their duties and responsibilities.

They love food and enjoy feeding people. They are extremely fussy about eating out, and try and avoid it altogether. They also take good care of their health. They know what works for their bodies and what doesn't. They are extremely meticulous and conscientious about everything in life.

Most of their troubles are self-induced. Most often they do not express their opinions and suffer silently, while slogging away at their responsibilities. If they learn to overcome their unnecessary insecurities, their habit of getting into a shell every time or getting depressed over petty things, if they learn to fight for their rights forcefully – then they would be truly liberated and ready to take on the world. They also need to learn to not be too paranoid, not magnify and worry about every small thing in life. Tough task, though!

Cancer–Virgo – Yash Chopra

Yash Chopra epitomised love in Bollywood movies. It may be surprising to many that he is not a romantic Leo or a lovey-dovey Libran, not even a passionate Scorpio or an idealistic-in-love Arian. Yash Chopra brought out the essence of the CanVir type of love, the highest octave of love – sacrifice! Sacrificing love itself for the sake of the happiness and well-being of someone you love! Sridevi does that in *Chandni*, Karishma Kapoor does that in *Dil To Pagal Hai*, Anil Kapoor does that in *Lamhe*, SRK does that in *Veer Zaara*... just to name a few.

His wife Pamela Chopra said at the 58th Filmfare awards that the three most important things in his life are films, food and family.

Love and Marriage for Him

He is extremely loving and caring: the perfect husband. Devoted and diligent and forever loyal, he takes care of your every need. He does not go for wild displays of emotions or passionate declarations of love. You can expect him to pay bills on time, buy groceries whenever you need them, tenderly care for you when you are sick and even cook tasty meals for the family. He may even surprise you some days with poetry, for the fertile imagination of Cancer can move him to express his love in various wonderful ways.

He has two passions – his career and family – and always worries about both. He knows how to perfectly balance his work and home. He is content limiting his life to work and family and being extremely duty-conscious to both. You will need to be his support system and try to resolve as many issues without letting his fears get the better of him.

He may not be very communicative at times or go into a lonely shell. You need to be aware of his moods and draw him out of them. His views may be more traditional, yet you cannot find a reason to blame his ego for he never stops you from pursuing your own dreams. Actually it will be better if you are a little more outgoing and aggressive than him.

As a father, he is exceptional. Caring, nurturing and self-sacrificing, he ensures that his children never want for love or attention. Plus, he makes sure that their academics are up to the mark. He is one of those rare fathers who come home and teach their children.

Love and Marriage for Her

Ladylike to the core, do not expect any crude or aggressive behaviour from her. She is a loner at heart and does not like to party. The place to look for her is her home. She loves her home and family, and is very sensitive to their needs. Her career, friends and social life are all secondary.

A warning – realise that you are dealing with someone who is not only extremely emotional but also highly loyal. So please do not venture near her if you are not looking for someone to mother you and pamper you. She will love staying at home, arranging the flowers, budgeting the household accounts, looking after your mother, making your kids finish their home work and doing everything to make her home perfect. If you want something else, don't bother her.

Her emotional needs are like a bottomless pit. She needs to be reassured all the time that she is a good cook, great daughter, fabulous wife and exceptional mother. Just do it. Her insecurity is too strong to let her believe in herself. It can make her clingy, too.

She is the perfect helpmate. Flirting is not her idea of fun. She believes in intelligent conversations and nurses you through your illnesses. At times, she is a nag and that is only because she knows the right way to do everything. Just do not criticise her.

As a mother, she is unbeatable. Caring and strict, she imparts good values to her children and points them on to the path of hard work and truth.

At the Workplace

CanVirs are extremely focused and committed. You can be sure they will give their hundred percent to any project or work they undertake. Job-hopping is not their style. The only reason for them to leave a job is either family or a substantially better pay. Fastidious, honest, focused and ultra-loyal, they are any employer's dream.

They are extremely creative and meticulous. You can expect them to work in creative fields or even desk jobs. They are perfect at routine jobs too, and make fabulous number crunchers and planners. They also excel at being the devil's advocate and check all the loopholes in a project.

Their work will be meticulously prepared and their projects will be well researched. No one can accuse them of unpolished work or not meeting deadlines. Lying and evading responsibility are not in their nature. One important thing to note is that their family comes first for them, always. Apart from compensating them monetarily, you need to give them time off for family holidays too.

Cancer is a cardinal sign and this makes CanVirs good leaders who know how to command without aggression. Subtle orders are more their way than loud demands. Most CanVir bosses treat their subordinates as family. But there are a few who can be cranky and extremely critical about your every move and a few others who pass on all their insecurities, mood swings and anxieties to the poor subordinates.

Water and Earth combine and make this sign stable yet sensitive, duty conscious yet imaginative, docile yet firm. You can always expect the best from them and not be disappointed.

Famous CanVir Personalities

Naseeruddin Shah, Lata Mangeshkar, Dr Manmohan Singh, Yash Chopra, K.S. Chithra , Paul Muni, Charlton Heston, Fidel Castro, Monica Bellucci, Shama Sikander, Britt Ekland, Kapil Sibal, Ehsaan Noorani, Crazy Mohan, Isha Koppikar.

45. CANCER–LIBRA

The Moon, which rules emotions, and Venus, the planet of beauty, grace and luxury, merge in CanLibs. CanLibs are emotional and sensitive with an innate sense of grace. Tactful and diplomatic, they know how to use their words for maximum effect. They desire a balanced view and hold justice above everything else. Arguments with them can get tiring because they love every point and communicate each idea so well that you have to bow to their logic. They are also very good at using emotional tactics to get their way.

Artistic and creative, CanLibs love music, especially old-time, soft music. They have the superb Cancerian imagination with the Libran gift of arts, beauty and the extraordinary way of communicating their thoughts. All the creative arts have a special place in their hearts. From acting to painting or music you can expect them to excel in one or all.

They are extremely sentimental. They love their memories and like keeping souvenirs of the past. Learning to let go of old things is a very important lesson for them, which they take years to master. They are extremely emotional and sensitive. They are very loving towards their families and are especially close to their mothers. They know how to show their love in caring ways and are there for everyone in their time of need.

Love will be a deep emotion for them. The Libran in them will be in love with love while Cancer is naturally nurturing and caring. The Cancerian longs for eternal love while the Libran feels life is incomplete without a partner. Soft and sensitive, with a longing for love, they might take their time choosing, for they get confused between friendship and love. They are such loving people, they live and die for their love. When there is no love they do not listen to logic or be analytical, they just go deep in a protective shell and refuse to come out.

After love, it is food that gets their undivided attention. Their love for food can find them binging on it during times of stress. They never shy away from the kitchen and are always ready to cook up a meal for their loved ones. They also want to dress up in the most fashionable manner. They have fantastic style and a great sense of aesthetics. You can expect them to look good at the least cost. They are the most sociable creatures. They have this velvety soft voice and alluring charm. They have many friends and are very talkative. They always want companionship and do not like being alone.

Despite their emotional ways and teary eyes, they are a double cardinal sign. Tough situations always see them work their way out. They win over rough weather just by hanging in there. They work harder and stay put. In the truly balanced Libran way, the men are softer than the women. CanLibs can cry, howl and break down, yet they know how to get up and take charge afterwards. You will not get any bossy attitude from them nor hear dictatorial commands. They have a very effective smile and use it to get their way. They can smile their way through an argument and win without ever letting you know that you have lost.

Cancerian insecurities and fears can attack them. They can also be extremely moody and be plagued by imaginary fears. They need a lot of love, care and attention in such moments. Don't brush their fears away but reason with them – logic always works with them. The Cancer in them makes them stingy with money and the Cancerian insecurity makes them fear the future. But their biggest challenge is Libran indecisiveness and quest for fairness. They find it tough to take decisions, especially in personal situations.

They act as peacemakers and agony aunts for all their friends. Their soft heart and protective nature will make them adopt many issues and they will hotly debate for the rights of the underprivileged. Injustice and inequality makes their argumentative side surface. They will seem timid, but the truth is – they will be exactly what the situation demands. They are the softest yet the firmest of people – this is the extraordinary contradiction that defines CanLibs.

Cancer–Libra – Nelson Mandela

'If people can learn to hate, they can be taught to love.'[71]

'For to be free is not merely to cast off one's chains, but to live in a way that respects and enhances the freedom of others.'[72]

'If there are dreams about a beautiful South Africa, there are also roads that lead to their goal. Two of these roads could be named Goodness and Forgiveness.'

'Lead from the back and let others believe they are in front.'[73]

Nelson Mandela displays the CanLib perseverance, its desire for equality, and ability to lead without aggression. If you have not noticed yet – Gandhi*ji* was a CanVirLib and the South African Gandhi was a CanLib!

Love and Marriage for Him

He is wonderfully soft and deeply understanding. Do not take his softness for meekness and do not try and boss over him. Family is very important to him. He is caring, protective, nurturing and all the other good adjectives you can think of. He never shirks his duties and is there whenever you need him. Please remember that his family also means his mother. It does no good to declare war on her for he cannot choose one over the other.

There is a deeply sensitive side to him and he can cry as easily as you at a happy ending. The fact is that this guy is so caring that he can even give up his dreams if you desire. It is best if you help him overcome his insecurities rather than adding to his emotional stress.

He likes his surroundings to be unaltered and prefers an orderly room to a messy one. It helps him think more logically if he sits in an aesthetically done up room. However, you have to be economical as he does not enjoy paying hefty bills.

As a father, he is just what parenting books teach. He helps out by burping the baby and does not get fazed by nappy-changing either. You can easily leave him with the children and go for a girls' night out. The only hitch comes when

---

[71] http://www.nelsonmandelamuseum.org.za/about-us/about-the-nelson-mandela-museum
[72] www.brainyquote.com/quotes/authors/n/nelson_mandela.html
[73] http://www.foxnews.com/politics/2013/12/06/lead-from-back-and-let-others-believe-are-in-front/

they grow up. He does not know when to let go. He can be over-protective and deeply scared for his children.

Love and Marriage for Her

The eternal girl! She is feminine even when she is heading a corporation. This lady knows how to be firm without looking it. She knows how to run your life and if you think that all the decisions are yours, think again. Did her smile not charm a decision out of you? She looks up to you even when she takes the decisions. She needs love and protection. She does not look for status in a relationship. She just needs to feel cared for.

She is caring and nurturing. She loves doing things for you and stuffs you with so much love that you are in bliss! She is excellent at managing the house and also looking after her career. Of course, she is moody and cranky at times. The phases of the moon affect her and you find her feeling low for no apparent reason. Just listen to her woes and remember not to laugh at them. She desires the best brands and accessories while wanting to save.

As a mother, she is remarkable. She is everything that her children desire. They never defy her for she is never domineering or authoritative. She makes them obey without raising her voice and they never once feel that she has decided for them!

At the Workplace

Being a double cardinal sign, CanLibs are great at leading. They communicate their ideas beautifully. Plus, they know how to get their work done by being charming. The only thing that stops them from reaching for leading roles is their fear of 'not being good enough'. They need a lot of appreciation to feel secure. They do not mind starting at the bottom but you can be sure of their tenacity and leadership skills.

They can do anything from jobs demanding people-skills to creative professions. They can be good lawyers and negotiators too with their analytical skills and innate sense of justice. They can handle their own business with Cancerian shrewdness and careful use of money combined with Libran smooth talk. They know how to create aesthetics at least cost and can excel at creating economical interiors too. The whole world of possibilities is open to them if only they overcome their insecurities and climb out of their shell.

Money is important to them and so is family. They can be motivated by pay packages and the lure of family holidays. They will definitely ask for more leave than their colleagues and will prefer working from home. As bosses, they are very considerate, especially in matters regarding your family. They would treat you just as family. Just ensure you don't take them for granted.

Water and Air combine in this double cardinal combination to endow CanLibs with sweetness without reducing their abilities. They will be tenacious yet gracious, sensitive yet strong, insecure yet leaders.

Famous CanLib Personalities

Nelson Mandela, Roger Federer, Mukesh, Freida Pinto, Francesco Petrarch, Oscar Wilde, J.P. Chandrababu, Andy Abad, R.K. Laxman, James Cagney.

46. CANCER–SCORPIO

The hermit Crab has an amazing defence mechanism. Their legs have break points and it can choose to cast off a limb and escape to safety. Now what happens if the Crab grows a poisonous sting, together with its claws and defence mechanism? It becomes a master of defence or attack. The Moon, ruler of emotions, and Pluto, the secretive and ruthless lord of the underworld, rule over this combination.

Emotional sensitivity is the trademark of Water signs. CanScorps are dual Water signs. So you can expect an abundance of emotions in them. They are deeply sensitive with the most expressive faces. This expressive behaviour can be seen even when you tell them your experiences. The fact is that they can instinctively feel love, hurt, pain or desire.

Family is their love and life. CanScorps are exceedingly loyal to their families and adore their mothers. They can sacrifice all that they have for the honour and upliftment of their families and literally put their mothers up on pedestals.

Cancer is always insecure; they fear the worst and require security in the material and emotional aspects of life. They are extremely cautious about money. They need a lot of money for they fear poverty. So they earn, invest and save. The only ones they spend freely on are their families. The positive aspect of all this apprehension is that they hang in there and get things done. They have so much patience and persistence that they can slowly and steadily achieve anything, just anything.

Once they are committed to anything – be it a marriage or a job, they will not think of leaving even when circumstances are tough; their first and last reaction is to stick it out and fight. Sentimental and emotional, they always see their past through glowing sepia-tinted glasses. They store the memorabilia of their past. Absolute and complete loyalty is what they give.

Love is very important to CanScorps. They don't need flowers, words or gifts to express and understand love. They will express love through their eyes and expect you to understand that. If they feel that your 'love you' was a little lacking in passion or you didn't look at them with the same degree of tenderness, then they will feel very hurt.

All said and done, never forget that the other half of this combination is Scorpio – the secretive, mean, ruthless and powerful Scorpio. Making them into enemies is inviting much more than trouble. They never forget an insult or a favour. They give back both in double doses.

There are three ways that CanScorps react when hurt – the flight mode, the shell mode or the attack mode. Which way they choose to react depends on how close you are to them. If you are a family member or a friend, you are in for the mild treatments of flight and shell. In flight, they cry and move away from you and you have to use all your powers of conviction to get them back. The shell mode again starts with tears and ends with them acting out of false bravado or sulking. The third and vindictive Scorpio tendency comes in when you hurt them a lot or they feel that they can easily get even with you. They can hide their emotions under a sweet smile or cold shoulder you, but they get even – definitely.

The deep insecurities of Cancer, when combined with ruthless Scorpio, can create some downbeat tendencies in CanScorps. They can be extremely possessive and jealous. They may also develop the attitude of wanting to win at all costs. If they cannot achieve their aim by crying or nagging, they will get it done by intimidation or even emotional blackmail.

When they are stupefied with emotions, they don't say much but you can feel the depth of their feelings. A look into their deep eyes and you feel pity or it can send a chill down your spine with fear. Handle them with care and at your own risk. Due to their moods and emotions, people view them as moody, grumpy or snobbish, but they are none of these. They are the softest people. You just need to understand their deep rooted insecurities and deal with them sensibly. If you are good to them they will reward you doubly.

Cancer–Scorpio – Arjun Rampal

'Now off to make some caramel custard with my daughter,' tweets Arjun Rampal. He has both his daughters' names inked on his forearms. This shows two things – he loves cooking and is a fabulous father. Obvious traits of a Cancerian. He also owns a restobar – food being the Cancerian idea of the best business in the world.

None can contest the perseverance and hard work of Arjun. He went through unsuccessful times, but waited patiently with the tenacity of Cancer and fought bravely like a Scorpio – a true CanScorp indeed.

Love and Marriage for Him

He is extremely dependable. He is physically, emotionally and even spiritually there for you. His love overflows and if you are not one of those who really desire to be 'loved', you may feel suffocated with the sheer abundance of it. Of course, he expects the same from you. He is highly loyal and deeply possessive. When you go out with him, it is like you are out with a bodyguard. He guards you even against stares and glances.

He is very sentimental. You can expect him to remember the day he first looked at you, your first date and all those moments that he shared with you. Sometimes, you may find his emotions very controlling for he is a mix of a cardinal (Cancer) and a fixed (Scorpio) sign. He wants things done his way and does not listen to opposing views, at times. He needs a partner who understands his deep emotional needs. Only a Water sign can understand that. His partner must have a combination of a Water sign or he is sure to be heartbroken by the lack of emotional understanding.

He is money wise and wants everyone around him to realise the importance of it. Do not spend and splurge on luxuries. He is incapable of spending freely and spending without worrying.

And one last thing, my dear girl – remember – his mother is the first woman in his life. You will always be second to her. And yes, also don't forget to remember that *he* is the boss.

He will be a proud and embarrassingly emotional father when his child wins any trophy and will always be there for his children.

Love and Marriage for Her
She is one of the most committed and passionate in the zodiac. If she is with you, she takes care of every need. She will be your mother, friend and soul mate all rolled into one. The problem is that she expects the same in return. You need to be totally responsive to her emotions or you are in for a bad day. She can sulk and cry. This girl is tenacious and persevering like a Crab and has a deadly sting if provoked. She can read your thoughts, so never even think of going around with your hot office mate, for the frail-looking CanScorp can shoot you down. She is extremely possessive. Very importantly, never venture near her if you are not thinking of the long term. She looks for permanency in everything in life.

She is riddled with insecurities and you need to soothe them. Myriad terrors plague her. She needs to be reassured that all is well. Compliment her sincerely (for she can easily sniff out lies), give her a separate bank account where she can save and feel happy, and call her mom over as many times as she wants! This girl will be happiest decorating her own home where she can shape each corner the way she wants.

As a mom, she is wonderful. There is nothing that she does not do for her children and despite that, she never spoils them. They are well behaved and beautifully turned out.

At the Workplace
If you have a CanScorp in your team, you can be sure that they never leave you in the lurch. Their office is their second home and they treat it as family, with unswerving loyalty and love. They need money, so make sure you reward them well and give them sufficient raises at regular intervals. They are not in a hurry to move ahead and prefer a job that offers growth, even if at a slow pace.

Even if they don't seem to ask for it, always give them a pat on the back. Their inner insecurities will be quelled by these appreciations. Give them family outings as incentives and they will work even harder. They love working in teams and are very good at understanding the motives and inner desires of their teammates. They lead by example and are bosses whose doors are always open to their juniors whom they treat as family. They read between the lines and can be very snoopy. Keep your house in order. Never try to hide facts from them or top them in an argument.

This dual Water sign is full of emotions and needs to be handled with care. Nothing deflates them more than unresponsive behaviour.

Famous CanScorp Personalities
Jennifer Lopez, Arjun Rampal, Zeenat Aman, Sir Garfield Sobers, Subhash Chandra, Gautam Thapar, Jimi Hendrix, Genelia D'Souza, Taufik Hidayat, James Anderson, Deepak Chahar, Dinesh Chandimal, V.V. Giri, Lisa Kudrow, Lauren Hutton, Zarina Wahab, Gonzalo Higuain, Jhulan Goswami, Mary Callahan Erdoes.

47. CANCER–SAGITTARIUS

Emotions and intelligence churn in this combination. Cancer is deeply emotional and sensitive, while Sagittarius, the Archer, is known for its intelligence and ambition. Their visage is free of guile and shows an integrity that instinctively makes you feel that here stands a person whose heart is pure. CanSags never try to dominate, control, or make you feel inferior in any way. You relax in their presence.

These guys are nice but not soft in the head – never try to manipulate them. Jupiter is an extremely intelligent planet and endows its people with an understanding of even the most abstract of sciences. There is a zing about them that is hard to miss. They love to poke fun at others and at themselves. But they get hurt when other people laugh at them. It is difficult to get them to forget their hurts easily.

They are quite moody at times. The effect of Sagittarius will reduce the moody nature of Cancer to some extent but they are still sensitive to the phases of the moon. Insecurities will beset their every move. They are a complex mix of dark moods, intense insecurities, driving ambition and amazing creativity.

Ambition is a major factor in their lives. The Sagittarius side of them makes them dream big but it may take them time to realise their path. They will not admit it, but they love to be the centre of attraction. They are enthusiastic students of the arts. They love showbiz and can enthral everyone with their acting, singing or dancing skills.

Their mother is an important part of their lives. For CanSags, mom is synonymous with home and they love both deeply. These guys can take on the responsibility of their families from a young age and work and worry about them. They show the same love and care for their myriad friends too. They are the best friends to have, for they are sensitive and know how to maintain their friendships.

Nostalgia and old memories hold a special place in their hearts. They have extraordinarily photographic memories and love looking back at their good old days and reminiscing. They are prudent with money, unlike the typical Sagittarians, but they are generous to family, friends and loved ones.

Fashion does not come easily to them. They may end up as fashion victims at times although they sail through with a devil-may-care attitude. They are extremely athletic. Sagittarians have a natural athleticism and are sports freaks. They love climbing mountains, bungee jumping and any activity that sets their adrenaline soaring. They can develop a fantastic exercise regimen and shape beautiful bodies – which they love to flaunt!

Food, too, is their particular delight. Cancerians dream of food and Sagittarians are adventurous by nature, so CanSags love trying out different dishes and are good at creating them too. Food is one thing that they do not mind spending on; they also hate food being wasted. They love travel. They love visiting far-off lands, exploring new cultures and learning about people.

They love deeply, truly and completely and they want the same. The Cancer in them wants to be cocooned in love and in a stunning contradiction, their Sagittarius side pines for freedom. This will be their inner turmoil – to be wrapped up or run loose – and they will alternate between the two before they realise what they want. They might feel that marriage with its responsibilities is a difficult proposition and thus defer it.

Another important thing is that Sagittarians love their freedom and though the Cancerian in them would love to take up the responsibility of the family and being there when needed, the Sagittarian would leave if the family tends to make him claustrophobic with excessive demands on his freedom and liberty. CanSags change a lot after they marry and become parents themselves. The Cancerian in them is very nurturing. Their love and care for their own parents goes up several notches after that.

Spirituality is their biggest strength. These honest souls submit themselves to the almighty and believe in creating only good karma. When hurt they yell and vent out or carry the hurt and sulk deeply for days. They never forget but they do forgive. Their inherent goodness probably helps them sail through most of the tough times in life.

Cancer–Sagittarius – Hrithik Roshan

'I was very introverted. Shy. I still am.'

'I did everything that I thought will help. I used to live with a video camera – shoot myself, act out scenes, how I look, how I walk. If I failed it would be because I was not good enough.'

'I romanticise everything in my life. Everything goes down as memory.'[74]

On his mom: 'I have seen how much she loves her family, seen her make too many sacrifices, and sometimes I just want to shake her up, tell her to just go and have fun... she's always put us first.'[75]

Hrithik Roshan – actor, superstar and a true blend of the emotional, insecure Cancerian and the showbiz-loving Sagittarian.

Love and Marriage for Him

He is amazing. You surely get jealous looks from your friends for having this guy who is loving, sensitive and understanding, in your life. He does various things to make you happy and even cooks for you. What more can you ask for? He is also very good at reading signs and knows when you are feeling low or uncomfortable and you can be sure of a big hug to help you cheer up. He is not domineering or egoistic, but do not try and dominate. This guy is not a pushover though he may give the reins into your hands.

Only strong, independent women need apply for he is quite emotionally demanding himself. You need to be sensitive and strong, as insensitivity can make him difficult to manage. His family, especially his mother, is extremely important to him and you have to love her as your own. He needs lots and lots of pampering. You really need to show him that you love him. Do that and he is relaxed. Travel is high on his agenda and he likes to take the whole family to new and exciting places. He is very loyal, overall. In those rare instances where he gives in to those Sagittarian instincts, he would be intensely remorseful and confess to you. But he wouldn't be the one to break the family under any circumstances.

---

[74] http://www.youtube.com/watch?v=QRJhcN7u2YY
[75] *Hello!*, May 2010

As a father, he is amazing. His life revolves around his children and he is very loving and caring towards them. He is also aggressive about their success. He wants them to have big ambitions and work towards them unflinchingly without any insecurity.

Love and Marriage for Her
She is all woman – sensitive, emotional, loving and caring. Her touchy side is a little more pronounced and she cries easily. The fact is that you have to be her support system. This girl loves you so much, yet is so insecure, that it is up to you to dispel her fears about everything. Be sensitive and be empathetic to her various moods. Her face reflects all her emotions. You just have to look in her eyes to know how she feels.

She loves pampering you and makes you feel the king of the castle. But do not forget that she is a cardinal sign too. Her ambitions move beyond home. Set her free and see her succeed. This girl will carve a place for her ambitions but never leave her family behind. A good blend of the traditional and new, there is a balance in this girl that makes her an ideal companion. Her cooking skills are outstanding but do not let her make the kitchen her realm, for there is so much more to her. She loves travelling and has an adventurous side. The adrenaline rush of daredevil acts liberates her soul. Give her those breaks.

She is a wonderful mother who hesitates for a long time to be one, out of many fears. Whatever the reasons, they all disappear when she becomes one. She will suddenly transform into an ideal mother and you will be amazed at how this naysayer learnt the skills. She tries and makes her children work towards their dreams.

At the Workplace
CanSags are extremely creative and utterly original. Their fertile minds find different ways to succeed, for ambition is a strong part of their makeup. They use their imagination and intelligence to reach for their dreams. While they are a natural at arts and showbiz, their enthusiasm, athleticism and doggedness make them good sportspeople too.

Money is extremely important to them. Be sure to pay them well for their efforts and also make them believe in themselves when they are feeling low. These guys need to be told that they are assets to the company. If you handhold them and allay their fears and inner insecurities, they will be loyal to you forever. They stick on when others give up in defeat. They are excellent team workers and treat their office mates as extended family. As seniors, they act in a fatherly fashion to their subordinates.

Fire and Water combine to make them fun loving yet caring, adventurous yet mama's babies, emotional yet free birds.

Famous CanSag Personalities
Hrithik Roshan, Farhan Akhtar, Yves Saint Laurent, Francois Hollande, Vaibhavi Merchant, Sonali Bendre, Jonty Rhodes, Magic Johnson, Hanif Mohammad, Aditya Narayan, Yashpal Sharma, Jane Fonda, Joe Frazier, Filippo Inzaghi, Terry Bozzio, Helder Postiga, David Bowie.

48. CANCER–CAPRICORN

Okay, so these are the serious, intelligent-looking people who have that extraordinary maturity. You almost feel juvenile when they are around. Even when they laugh, there is some elegance and they don't let their guard down completely. They seem in total control – well, almost!

Wise old man Capricorn combines forces with the family-loving, sensitive and ultra-emotional Cancer. CanCaps have the sensitivity, imagination and perseverance of Cancer with the down-to-earth practicality and planning abilities of Capricorn. Both are cardinal signs. They are amazingly strong personalities.

Family is their love while ambition is sandwiched in between its layers. CanCaps are the most responsible children who take care of their siblings, and help their parents, and may even start working at a young age. You find it strange that a child so young thinks so much and behaves with such maturity. That is the effect of Capricorn's Saturn. It makes them think and act much older and wiser than their age.

Money is extremely important to them; it is not poverty that drives them but the fear of it. They become more chilled out after their thirties or maybe forties. As their peers start acting responsible, these guys can go the opposite way and start shedding their inhibitions late in life. Of course, they are not totally humourless before that. Their funny side is reserved for their families and close friends. Their humour, however, is subtle and wry and compels you to think.

CanCaps know what they want and they know how to get it. They take each problem one by one, and, in well-planned manoeuvres, overcome them. Their aim is simple, they have to grow, build a solid foundation, bring in stability and become the *numero uno* to take care of their family.

Whenever they fall in love it will be for life. Their romance is deep and emotional. The Cancerian need for security makes them go for partners who can support them emotionally and materially. CanCaps will be shy in love and never make the first move, actually they will intelligently plan it in such a way that you end up proposing to them!

After the extreme hard work of the initial years and the numerous sacrifices for their family bear fruit, you can expect them to turn a little naughty. The reverse aging syndrome of Capricorn may catch up with them, but even if they stray due to the urge to compensate for their youth, they will regret it and come back when they realise that they are hurting their family.

They love cars. Cars hold value as it gives social prestige. They also spend on their families. They make traditional and conventional investments and, more than that, they love tips on moneymaking. Their values are based on tradition and conventional ideas.

Cooking is a natural ability for them, even the men. They know how to cook and make delicious meals out of everyday ingredients. Actually, cooking saves restaurant bills, so they prefer to cook at home and invite friends over for a meal! Cost saving and effective!

Despite their high sensitivity due to Cancer, they never display their emotions. Anger and tears are hidden till they are certain that displaying them helps them score a point. They know the score and desire success too much to be fooled into displaying weakness. You find them sulking or silent when they are hurt. The emotional sensitivity of Water makes them realise how people feel. Thus, Capricornian shrewdness gets sharpened due to the amazing intuitiveness of Water.

One thing that you can be sure of is that man or a woman – a CanCap would be the ideal child. They would sacrifice anything for the happiness of the family and their parents.

Cancer–Capricorn – Cristiano Ronaldo
'My family comes first – my son is the most important thing in my life,' Ronaldo says. 'After that, it's the football that matters most to me. Money comes after that.'

'I bought my mother a house in Portugal, she lives there with her partner and my son. I bought my sisters houses as well.'

'My brother runs my nightclubs and various bars. I also own a hotel. But money hasn't changed me – I'm still the same person.'[76]

Ronaldo works hard, invests wisely and has his family take care of his business. Hugely successful, he has the CanCap love for family and its desire for success.

Love and Marriage for Him
He is responsible, caring and, above all, stable. There is one problem though: his deep-rooted insecurities and fears. The mood swings that he hides from the rest of the world are not hidden from you. He can get into a shell or cry in private. These are times when he needs you to stand like a rock beside him. He needs constant reassurance and emotional support.

Romance is something you have to create. This guy is romantic yet very diffident in displaying it. With middle age come some problems for the Capricornian as sternness gives way to teenage romanticism and he can even stray. But remember, he never does anything that hurts the family. He would also be an ideal son with strong bonds with his family. Only if you do not get claustrophobic with family ties and can give yourself over to the secure love of strong relationships should you consider a relationship with this guy.

He spends only in areas that promise returns and for his children. He needs to see value for money. He is the personification of the ideal father. Capricorn rules fatherhood while Cancer is deeply nurturing. He is always there for his children and plans holidays and outings around them. However, he does not spoil them and teaches them to value money and ideals.

Love and Marriage for Her
She is a gem of a wife. She is her mother-in-law's favourite. Family comes foremost for her and she does everything in her power to keep her family happy. She is

---

[76] http://www.mirrorfootball.co.uk/news/Exclusive-interview-The-real-Cristiano-Ronaldo-My-priorities-are-family-football-and-money-says-Real-Madrid-star-article755771.html

thrifty, traditional and carries herself with dignity and talks sense even if she is not well educated.

The best part about her is that she acts like a total '80s movie heroine. The one who looks after your ailing mother, teaches and loves your younger brother and sister, and is the perfect foil for the meddlesome aunt.

It is security that she needs. A bank balance and the feeling that things will only get better are essential for her. She works hard in every sphere of her life for she always fears the worst and strives to avert that. Be her support system, reassure her and make her feel that everything is going as planned and she will relax.

If she chooses you, it is because she sees you as a safe bet. She needs her partner to show stability, have a secure job and a good house. The Capricornian in her can judge people well and know whether they are worthy. She is very good at managing her life and just needs you for emotional support. Yes, her emotional needs are very deep and you have to take care of them or she can spend an inordinate amount of time worrying and sulking.

She wants you to have ambition and strive for it. She will be a great hostess and not mind if you invite your boss for an impromptu dinner. If cooking helps in clinching the promotion then she will be more than happy to pitch in! Remember, she has the capacity to be a great career woman. However, her first priority in life is to find a man who is financially well-off to take care of her and her children. Then comes emotional security. If these two are taken care of, then she may even skip a career entirely as she doesn't need a career for her emotional fulfilment.

Motherhood suits her wonderfully. She is a mother who combines a stern glance with a soft smile. She can be the most loving of mothers yet her children know that there is an invisible line that they cannot cross.

At the Workplace
Ambition is the hallmark of Capricorns, and Cancer, too, is a cardinal sign. Leadership is what they aim for. When you have a CanCap in your organisation, you can expect them to succeed. If they feel that the company has opportunities for them, they stay while other more adventurous souls walk out, lured by better offers.

CanCaps are born businessmen with Cancer's tight-fistedness and Capricorn's shrewd calculations. Even if they work for someone, they look at their value addition to the organisation purely from a return-on-investment perspective. There is such an amazing maturity about these guys that leadership roles are automatically diverted to them.

They somehow talk sense, are logical and responsible. They display these qualities in the most understated fashion and probably that is exactly what works in their favour. But remember: no one plays politics better than Capricorn. They assert themselves through schemes and manipulations.

CanCaps can shine in any field. They can be the most creative artists or logical businessmen. Whatever they do, they do it with a will to reach the top. Yet, these guys can actually shelve their projects or take a temporary break from their job just to take care of their ailing parents.

Water and Earth come together in CanCaps to endow them with imagination and sensitivity that are rooted in firmness and determination, with a strong love for family, values and tradition.

Famous CanCap Personalities
Cristiano Ronaldo, Siddharth Roy Kapur, Mohd. Azharuddin, Manoj Kumar, Amar Singh, Shaun Pollock, Henry Ford, Clark Gable, Yani Tseng, W.G. Grace, Renuka Chowdhury, Ayaz Memon, Faye Dunaway, Shobha Gurtu, Princess Mathilde, Jesus Luz, Kelly Kelly.

49. CANCER–AQUARIUS

The emotionally abundant and imaginative Moon joins the highly innovative and futuristic Uranus in CanAqua. Cancer is one of the most nostalgic zodiac signs, it loves reliving the past; while Aquarius is one of the most detached signs and thinks only of the future. The past and the future mark the two extremes of CanAquas. They never forget their old friends and teachers, the taste of their mum's food or their first kiss. Every memory is dear to them and they love going through old photos. They plan for the future, as much as twenty years ahead. This is their eternal problem for they spend their time thinking of their past or planning for the future while the present passes them by.

The detached Aquarius outlook is diluted by extreme Cancer devotion for family. Cancer steadfastness is part of their nature. They are tenacious about their likes and don't give up easily. Cancer stabilises the potential genius of Aquarius and adds a bit of maturity to Aquarian eccentricities. True-blue Aquarians are too detached to bother about human relationships and live only for their ideas, but CanAquas try to build support from people around their ideas and do not treat relationships as secondary.

Emotions play an important role in their life. They are people-centric and very good at discerning the true feelings of a person. Cancer is extremely sensitive and perceptive while Aquarius is always curious about what makes people tick. CanAquas can sense exactly how a person is feeling. They are fabulous friends – non-judgmental and unorthodox. So, if you are their friend, they never judge you by society's standards but accept you as you are. Imagination is something they have in truckloads, right from the extremely creative ideas of Cancer to the highly innovative thoughts of Aquarius. They are adept at donning different roles as required. They can be wild party animals at night and completely change over to responsible corporate warriors in the morning.

They can be quite temperamental with the trademark Aquarian detachment and Cancerian moodiness. It is difficult to predict how they will react to a particular situation. The *extra* perception due to Cancer and Aquarius can sometimes make them read too much between the lines and they can nurse a few imaginary hurts too. Cancerian insecurities can sometimes be manifested, but usually they are the most happy-go-lucky of people. They also have the Aquarian clumsiness and forgetfulness.

Money is of concern to them for their future. Cancer and Aquarius think of the future in different ways – while Cancer is scared of it, Aquarius dreams about it. They think of saving for the future in order to have an enjoyable life with their families. Aquarius is a humanitarian sign and Cancer feels for children. A CanAqua would definitely want to give back to society. They are deeply moved by poverty, hunger, disease and would love to work for causes related to children and the elderly.

CanAqua are very sentimental in love. The clumsiness of the Aquarius makes them act in weird ways when they fall for someone. They are truly lost in love. It is fun to see them behaving as if the world has changed ever since they sighted the ONE. They are not bothered by traditions and conventions in their quest for love. CanAqua will fight the world to live happily ever after.

They metamorphose as they grow older. In their twenties, they exhibit the unorthodox or geeky eccentric look of Aquarius. They love doing wild things and are totally indifferent to what people say. Despite all that, CanAquas obey their parents, especially their mothers. As they grow older, and the phase of parenthood strikes them, you find them totally transformed. The Cancerian love for the home will emanate from them and they will display their nurturing and caring side. You can actually divide their life into two parts – before their child and after. When they become parents, they learn to appreciate their parents even more. They adore their children and relive their childhood through them. CanAqua can sacrifice everything for their children's happiness.

Cancer–Aquarius – Kajol

Close friend Karan Johar on Kajol: 'Kajol will definitely seek her mother's advice but will eventually do what her heart tells her.'[77]

'I was born to be a mother because I consider motherhood my exclusive niche in life. Nysa is my top priority. I can give up everything and anything for her. Why Nysa alone? I am at the beck and call of my family at all times. I think the family is and should be the first priority in any woman's life.'

'I definitely want to open an orphanage in the near future.'[78]

Family loving, highly individualistic and caring, Kajol comes across as a brilliant combination of a CanAqua.

Love and Marriage for Him

Unconventional and considerate, this guy is never judgmental. He does not expect you to behave in a certain way just because you are a woman. Aquarius believes in equality and he is the best husband to have if you want to take on the world.

The futuristic Aquarius makes him a little lost in the present. He loses his keys, misplaces pens and is very careless about his appearance. This guy is a bit stingy. It is very frustrating to go shopping with him. He looks for bargains and wants value with every purchase.

There is one golden rule you must remember – his mother is never wrong. Never ask him to take sides, for he loves his mother too much. Please accept that. He can also get very moody and be detached at times. Those are the times when he needs to be left alone. Cancerian insecurities can also pull him down. Reassure him and give him time to mend.

Fatherhood is life changing for him. You'll be amazed at how quickly he changes to a fun-loving family guy. He dotes on his children and never forces his views on them.

Love and Marriage for Her

She has a sensitive nurturing side and a highly independent one. She mothers you and cares for you like a typical Cancerian but she has a mind of her own. This girl takes on jobs that very few people can manage.

She is a Moon-maiden with the eccentric streak of Uranus, so it is very hard to decipher her. Her views are her own and she is not bound by conventions. She has

---

[77] *Hello!*, May 2010

[78] http://www.glamsham.com/movies/interviews/07-kajol-interview-040813.asp

a clumsy streak in her that increases when she is upset or angry. The Cancer in her makes her very emotional and sensitive, but she can often surprise you with her complete nonchalance and non-possessive attitude. The paradox in this girl is that though she is emotional, she finds it difficult to express her emotions. This is the reason that she comes across as reserved and snobbish to others. But she genuinely likes being left alone at times to pursue her off-beat interests.

The Cancerian in her will equip her for any sacrifice required for the family – yours and hers. But don't take her for granted, as she is uniquely talented and can doggedly pursue a dream. Her memories are very dear to her. She loves to save money and goes for long-term investments. Her fashion sense is strongly individualistic and she wears what she likes, in her own style.

Motherhood brings about a massive change in her. She becomes more caring and nurturing. Despite her sense of detachment and initial wild years, she makes an amazingly sensitive mother. She grows with her children. She has great dreams for them and guides her children to turn them into reality.

At the Workplace

Cancer makes them persevering and CanAquas do not give up easily. They are very tenacious. They have a unique ability of loving the past and thinking of the future. When they use their tremendous imaginative skills, they think of ways to combine the past and the future, for example, using stories from Indian mythology to solve present challenges.

They do conventional things in an unconventional manner and vice versa. They can be interested in parasciences and alternative methods of healing. They are also extremely people-oriented and do well in careers related to people and creativity. They are not commanding or controlling as bosses and prefer to treat their teams as family.

They do not know what they really want when they start out. Aquarius makes them have varied interests but the Cancerian need for security makes them stick to a profession. The revolutionary genius of Aquarius when combined with the creative visualisation of Cancer can create extraordinary thinkers, scientists, writers or even poets. The work they are doing now is only temporary, they will someday go after that bright, avant-garde idea to change the world, but only after they have taken their family to the shores of safety.

Water and Air combine to give CanAqua their unique vision that mixes the past and the future. Unorthodox and emotional, they live for their family and their ideals.

Famous CanAqua Personalities

Kajol, Dhanush, James Cameron, Robin Williams, Eva Mendes, Shabbir Ahluwalia, Andrew Strauss, Petra Kvitova, Mikhail Gorbachev, Adnan Sami, Paris Hilton, Gillian Anderson, Skylar Grey, Anup Jalota, Stieg Larsson, Mukesh Khanna, Hiten Tejwani, C.K. Prahalad, Elinor Ostrom, Charlotte Church, Chelsea Clinton, Michael Holding, Purushottam Das Tandon, Mehdi Hassan.

50. CANCER–PISCES

Emotions – overpowering and strong – define this combination. This is a complete Water sign and is ruled by the Moon and Neptune. Both the Crab and Fish are defensive types. The Crab gets into its shell quickly or hides in holes, while the Fish disappears when it sees danger. It is also a combination of two feminine signs, so be it a man or a woman, you can expect 'feminine' traits of being nurturing, caring, highly-strung and sensitive. CanPisces is the most sensitive and emotional amongst all the zodiac signs.

While Cancer makes them deeply emotional and responsive, Pisces makes them absorb and reflect the emotions around them. Highly empathetic beings, these people can easily feel the pain of another. It is a soul-scorching experience to live the life of a CanPisces. They are the nicest, noblest and most down-to-earth souls you can imagine.

Extremely complex and sensitive, it is hard not to pity them. This is a person who is there for everyone, and seeks nothing but acceptance and love. These guys are nearly saints and that is a difficult cross to bear. So give them your whole-hearted support.

Cancerian insecurity is heightened by Piscean fears. They feel they are not good enough, strong enough, clever enough, etc. They are painfully shy and cannot assert themselves in public. Their active imaginations make them exaggerate and amplify the smallest gesture and feel bad at imagined hurts. Whenever they are hurt, feel inadequate or have imaginary fingers pointed at them, they go into a shell. They need lots of unconditional love, understanding and encouragement to face the world again.

The Moon's mysterious phases affect them. Their moods vary and range from joyful on full-moon nights to cranky and sensitive on moonless ones. Despite all their doubts and worries, they are quite capable of taking care of themselves. After all, Cancer is a cardinal sign and they lead – albeit unobtrusively. Their softness belies their inner strength. Their biggest strength is that they just stay put till they achieve their aims. They persevere with the tenacity of the Crab and the optimism of the Fish.

Cancer makes them very worried and insecure about money matters. They could be born into the richest families and live a life of luxury, but the fear of poverty seems to motivate them to achieve more. The Piscean habit of foolish spending is replaced by a more sensible approach to buying and CanPiscess will make sure that their finances are in place. Thankfully, the stinginess and safeguarding streak of Cancer is mitigated by the giving tendency of Pisces. For Cancerians, self-preservation comes first, while Pisceans think of others, so people in this combination work first for financial stability and help others along the way.

They are made for love. Love is the only thing that makes their world go round. They want acceptance, peace and love from all. Their love is all-encompassing, deep, and has a soul-to-soul connect. They can understand every sigh and even the twitch of an eyebrow of their loved ones. Their love has no parallels. There is total acceptance and total surrender in their love.

They are natural mothers. Man or woman, under this combination, both are great with children. The Piscean regard for the old and wise makes them great at handling the elderly. They are extremely attached to their parents. Their upbringing has a big role to play in whatever they do later in life. They hold on to values and habits they learn in their formative years. They are very traditional and hold the institution of family in high regard.

There is one thing to be wary of. The Piscean's escapist nature and the Cancerian's indulgence in self-pity can put this combination on the rocky path of delusions and addictions. This double Water sign should not indulge in alcohol and substances that give them a temporary high for they may lose themselves in it.

Remember one thing about this people though. Both are Water creatures. A Fish can be a goldfish, an intelligent dolphin or probably the largest and most dangerous shark you have ever known. Similarly, the Crab could be the sturdiest and the fiercest ever. So CanPisces definitely have it in them to overcome all their emotional baggage and evolve into mighty creatures.

They can easily mirror and live the emotions of others. This ability can aid them in fooling people in case they decide to use their talent to con others. Just like a whale can engulf everything in its path and cause destruction or a crab can eat away your toe, they can rise from the abyss to capture the limelight. Just with their ability to 'see through' everything and 'feel' just what others feel, and 'say' what others want to hear, they suddenly develop this wisdom to overcome anything. Then they can be more in control and more dangerous than all the Scorpios, Aries and Leos put together – be aware!

Cancer–Pisces – Mahesh Babu

Wife Namrata: 'Mahesh Babu is not at all a 'star'. He's very, very loving, caring and understanding. He believes in family values. He's very shy.'[79]

Mahesh Babu: 'There have been times when I didn't come out of my house because my films didn't do well.'

'Even in school, I never used to tell anyone that my dad was an actor. Our upbringing reflects in our lives today. We are all very grounded people.'

'There are no controversies because when I am not working, I am home. Home is where my strength is.'[80]

Like a true CanPisces, Mahesh Babu is shy, reserved, extra-sensitive; he is grounded and prioritises relationships above fame.

Love and Marriage for Him

He is the perfect gentleman – loving and kind. He truly looks after you. Respect for women and the elderly is part of his DNA and he is never aggressive or dominating. This guy can cook as well. He is too evolved to have an ego. There is only one thing I ask of you – do not take advantage of this soft soul.

He is highly romantic, so be ready to be charmed off your feet. This guy knows exactly what makes you happy. His emotional needs are high. He may not always be very eloquent about his feelings and may turn to you for confidence occasionally. Straight talking or criticism is not what he needs. This guy takes on too many emotions so don't put added pressure on him. He needs your support. Do not let him down.

---

[79] http://www.indiaglitz.com/channels/hindi/interview/6267.html
[80] *Hyderabad Times (Times Of India)*, 22 July 2012

He needs a calm environment to soothe his high emotions. Let him be peaceful and happy, and he rewards you by being the most understanding of husbands. His need for financial security makes him work towards his goals. Do not impose your high ambitions on him.

He is a sensitive and nurturing father. Children who are sickly or weak will have a special place in his heart.

Love and Marriage for Her
She is a hundred-per-cent girl – one your mother loves and your father dotes on. She has a special way with the elderly and no family function is considered complete without her charming presence. She is totally home-loving and gives motherly care to all relatives. She has fabulous cooking skills too. She loves nurturing and caring for you. But be aware that she is highly sensitive. Keep telling her how much you love her for it is never enough for her and be patient when she clings to you. The poor darling is just too full of insecurities and looks to you for support. She needs a person who is patient and strong, who can take her nagging and yet not tell her that she nags.

She is financially insecure too, and would love it if you have enough money, or the street-smartness to get it. You can reduce her fear of becoming poor by opening a bank account in her name. Rest assured she will never spend the money, but invest it safely.

Her mothering capabilities make her the favourite aunty to all her nephews and nieces. Her children find her the most malleable of mothers till they ask her for extra pocket money. It is then that she tells them of the importance of saving and the need for hard work.

At the Workplace
CanPisces are highly artistic and do not gravitate easily to the corporate space. You can mostly spot them in creative situations. The Cancerian's imagination and the Piscean's empathy make them fabulous actors.

They are not very ambitious souls and are not bothered about fancy-sounding titles. They are great at handling people. Human resources and customer management are also good for them. Teaching and mentoring are the natural abodes of this combination. Piscean wisdom, coupled with Cancerian sensitivity and skill, help them excel as life coaches.

The science of looking into the minds of people, like psychiatry, might claim them. Their instinctive understanding of people aids them in this field. It is also important to know that this wonderful combination has a dark side. The Cancerian need for financial security and the Piscean impressionability can make some people of this combination take shortcuts to success.

This double Water sign is highly malleable yet it retains its own flavour as a deeply sensitive and evolved soul. It is hard not to love them.

Famous CanPisces Personalities
Mahesh Babu, Rani Mukherjee, Daniel Radcliffe, Mugdha Godse, Lenin, Charles Baudelaire, Antonio Banderas, Sheela, Soundarya, Balan K. Nair, V. Naagaiyya, Jayant Narlikar, Cecil B. DeMille, Ilie Nastase, Crown Prince Haakon of Norway, Marcos Senna, Cobie Smulders, G.V. Krishna Reddy, Paul Verlaine, Hariharan.

51. LEO–VIRGO

The generous and life-giving Sun combines with the meticulous and almost perfect Virgo. LeoVirs have the generosity and majestic charm of a Leo and, of course, the need to be the main attraction. The superb perfectionism of a Virgo makes them dignified and royal.

They are extremely positive and vibrant personalities who crackle with energy. Deep ambition meets excruciating hard work in them – they know the true secret of success. They come out dressed to perfection for they put in a lot of effort in their grooming. They need to be admired and respected. The Leonine trait of basking in the limelight is totally them, so don't expect them to work silently like true Virgos. Every time they work hard and do something smart and productive, everyone from their bosses to their neighbours will know about it.

The generous Leo makes them fabulous friends. Thankfully, the analytical thoughts of Virgo stop them from being ripped off by 'friends' who are always in need. They can see through any subterfuge. LeoVirs will be total fun when the time is right. At parties, they will be excellent guests – full of good cheer and conversation. They love to be the centre of attention, but don't expect goofiness from them. Regal and dignified, they will stand out in the celebrations.

LeoVirs not only *act* confident, they can also be *truly* confident for they think of everything. They are masters of planning and go through every detail before they attack. They are not pompous without a reason. But beware, with their love for perfection and keen eye – they can be harsh and vocal critics, whether you can take it or not. The lack of Water in this sign makes them insensitive at times. However, you cannot criticise them if you want to be their friend because if you do so, they sulk for days till you apologise.

They are always there for the family. They act as the elder siblings even if they are the youngest. They love being leaned upon and are very responsible. Their generosity and sacrifices for the family and their commitment to all their duties is truly heart warming.

They are absolutely romantic and when they fall in love there is bound to be drama and excitement all round. They meticulously plan every move and bring classy glamour and style to all their rendezvous. They love to impress with their charisma, knowledge and personality.

But their critical eye is evident when they fall in love, too. Though romantic, they will look for perfection in a partner. For them their chosen one must be exactly what they want, perfect in every detail. They will have extremely high standards while choosing and if you are chosen then treat yourself to a royal celebration for you have been named king/queen.

There are obviously some problems in this excellent package. For starters, they have very fragile egos. All Fire signs have a fear within them which they try and mask with sheer confidence and bravado. Respect is very important for them in every relationship but to people who do not know them well, they seem exceedingly arrogant. They are also very hard to please. Their need for perfection, along with their extremely critical eye, adds to their stress levels. Sometimes, it may get hard to work with them.

They are extremely finicky about everything, from the things they eat to the clothes they wear; they will want certain particulars to be met. Virgo also makes the lazy Leo in them abide to routines. The point is that LeoVirs will make everyone around them also abide to the same routines. They do not like doing things halfway and will be insistent on sharing their knowledge with others. They would also be very spiritual and sometimes even ritualistic and follow all customs diligently.

Generous and caring, LeoVirs act like kings even when they are paupers. It is hard to fault them, but they have their idiosyncrasies and it is best to be aware while dealing with them. Their boastfulness and love for attention, seems a bit too much at times, but give them respect and adulation and you have a friend who is generous, sincere and will never shirk his/her responsibilities, ever.

Leo–Virgo – Sean Connery
Sean joined the Royal Navy when only 15, signed up for seven years but was through after three. 'I was temperamentally unsuited for the service,' Sean admitted. 'I disliked the authority to the extent that I got ulcers.'

Sean's independence was evident when he refused to accept the lead in *Marnie* until he had read the script. 'Even Cary Grant doesn't ask to read a Hitchcock script,' he was told. 'Well, I'm not Cary Grant,' Connery snapped back. 'If you want me in the movie, send me a script.' They did.[81]

The Leo desire to shine and its inability to be subservient to others are as evident in Sean Connery as is the Virgo earthiness and its perfection-seeking attitude.

Love and Marriage for Him
Congratulations! You have caught his attention. Now begins the difficult part. You have to be perfect all the time! This man loves a girl who looks good in his arms. Independent and aggressive women are not for him and he usually prefers a mate who is stable and well dressed. He can be quite fussy. He will be extremely punctual and if you keep him waiting for even five minutes, he may walk out. Look out for his trigger points and if you want him for keeps, act with caution!

This guy makes a great partner once he has decided on you for he has the Leo generosity and a non-interfering nature. He loves his home and never shirks his responsibilities. You have a king, albeit a king who does not mind working. Do not wash your dirty linen in public or treat him with disrespect. He gives you the best life he possibly can. What he wants is absolute loyalty and appreciation from you.

As a father, he is full of fun and discipline, though he takes time in deciding to become a father. The thought of the responsibility of fatherhood is the cause of this but once he does, he happily shoulders his responsibilities. He has to learn to let go when children grow up and let them live their lives as he lived his.

Love and Marriage for Her
She is stunning whether she is watering the garden or greeting you with a smile. This girl knows how to look like a woman without overdoing it. The other shocker

---
[81] http://jeremyduns.blogspot.in/2010/08/007-in-depth-sean-connery-interviews.html

will be that she understands perfectly when either the accountant or the lawyer speaks. This girl has beauty and brains and she doesn't mind using either.

She will be independent and strong. There is deep ambition within her and she really wants to do something big. The Leonine desire to shine and the Virgo effort makes her unstoppable. Ambition is everything for her. She has it in bundles within her and she expects her partner to have it too. This girl needs a man who dreams as big as her.

You must appreciate her every day in every way. Delight her with flowers, cards, gifts and small tokens of appreciation. She can nag a bit and tell you how to do things. Do not ever try the same on her; she thinks she is perfect – isn't she?

As a mother, she tries and does everything for her children. They are her prized possessions and she can take on anyone for them. This is not a mother who takes kindly to teachers' negative views on her darling children.

At the Workplace

Optimistic, ambitious, hard working and extremely courageous, LeoVirs are crafted for success. Give them the toughest roles, the hardest assignments and applaud them. They need tons of appreciation. But you can be sure that they will deliver brilliantly. They need money along with the applause. They know their worth. It is not easy to negotiate a lower pay with them.

They can do everything from planning to executing dreams. They will think up the details and scale up the plans for they don't do anything on a small scale. Their projects are as big as their dreams. They seem to have that charismatic personality that makes their subordinates love to work for them. They lead from the front, take up the onus and put their necks on the block. Their generosity in appreciation and help in perfecting skills make them popular bosses. But there is no doubt about who the boss is.

Virgos have great acting talents. With their hard work and attention to detail, they can bring diverse characters to life. Add to this the Leo's love of bright lights and an audience, and you have great star potential.

Fire and Earth meet in LeoVirs to add dazzle to earthy sentiments. Optimistic yet diligent, proud yet delvers of detail, planners with the flair for execution – their desire to succeed and their will to achieve perfection are brilliantly evident.

Famous LeoVirgo Personalities

Sean Connery, Shane Warne, Chiranjeevi, C.N. Annadurai, Cher, Ian Chappell, Lance Armstrong, Thierry Henry, Ian Thorpe, Madhur Bhandarkar, V.O. Chidambaram Pillai, Pippa Middleton, Michelle Bachelet, Vidhu Vinod Chopra, Romy Schneider, Anurag Kashyap, Tyler Perry, Kumar Sanu, Prachi Desai, Dr S. Radhakrishnan, Mehmood, Priya Raman, Padma Lakshmi, Bhupen Hazarika, Agatha Christie, Chunky Pandey, V. Bhaskaran, Jwala Gutta, Pragyan Ojha, Eleonora Duse, Bill and Tom Kaulitz, Adriana Karembeu, Mylène Farmer, Delnaaz Paul.

52. LEO–LIBRA

The sunny, radiant and kingly Apollo joins the luxury-loving, beautiful and artistic Libra. This is the most regal and radiant combination and the actual sign of a true king. LeoLibras have all the royal qualities. They protect the weak, are fair and just, majestic and controlling, like delegating, love to laze, patronise the arts and are very romantic.

Laziness is common to both the zodiac signs. LeoLibras love to lie around but, even when they do, they look regal. There is a natural grace in their movements and they never look out of place or awkward. They love food, luxury and all the nice things of life. They like to splurge on clothes, perfumes, lotions and spas.

LeoLibras are extraordinary communicators. Words flow naturally from a Libran and Leos know to communicate beautifully with an imperial stance, the right punctuation, elegance, glamour, animation and wit. They love talking and giving advice, and are excellent peacemakers. They are never perturbed or flustered when things get tough. They display amazing balance in all situations.

They need to be adored. This is their basic need. They have enormous egos and a highly inflated sense of self, which needs to be catered to. Generosity, too, lives in their regal hearts. Librans are very good at putting themselves in others' shoes. They want to see happiness around them and desire love from others. They believe in the concept of *noblesse oblige*, which means that with wealth, power and prestige, come responsibilities.

LeoLibras are highly romantic. When they love they want everything to be perfect – from their date to their clothes and the flowers – it should all be as magnificent as them! The best part is that when they are in love, they are totally in love and the worst is that they expect the same from you. They want looks, charm and style in the one they love – but remember, that style should never overshadow their own.

They are amazingly artistic. They have an extraordinary sense of beauty, arts and creativity. They are naturally endowed with a sense of music, drama, dance, etc. The creative leanings of Libra meet the showmanship of Leo, which makes LeoLibras extremely confident performers who live for applause. Unlike Librans who will not step on the stage if they are not prepared, LeoLibras love attention from a young age and like to show off their skills to an admiring crowd and it comes naturally to them.

They know how to dress. You will never find them looking awkward or out of place, they instinctively own the place they walk into. They have an extraordinary sense of colour coordination and a great sense of fashion. Money is extremely important to them. They need pots of it for there is always something that they desire. The problem is that money does not stick to them. They just cannot save and investments are beyond them.

They have an amazing sense of humour and love cracking jokes and playing pranks. They can be very good mimics and play to the gallery while making fun of you, but don't play the same trick on them. They have the explosive anger of Leos that turns fiery if not shown proper respect. Librans believe in non-cooperation when they are angry. The Leo in them will sulk for hours in case of any disrespect or due credit not given.

Despite the controlling nature of Leos, the indecisiveness of Librans affects LeoLibras. They also hate being wrong and ponder for hours, days, weeks and months before arriving at major decisions. They appear confident but are racked by insecurities. Fire signs, especially Leo, have an inner fragility that they will never admit to but which they camouflage with a bustling bravado, while Librans want perfection. This makes them drive themselves towards achieving illusory glory. Though they never ask it, they need reassurance and support.

There is no Earth or Water in this combination. Hence, they may not be very practical or emotional. They lack the sensitivity and deep understanding of Water signs. The Libran ability to put themselves into other people's shoes will make them *appear* to be empathetic but they are not truly so. They cannot read your mind nor do they understand what you feel. They also lack the organisational skills of an Earth sign though they make up for it with their ability to think and mitigate risk. They become more chilled out and mellowed later in life, mainly due to the Leonine inclination towards spirituality. Their innermost needs are peace, harmony and companionship and they find that only in love and spirituality.

Leo–Libra – Julia Roberts
'Of course my life has changed and I work less (after becoming a mother), but I was never really one to work too much,' Julia says. 'I never really did years of movie-after-movie-after-movie…'[82]

The entire Roberts–Moder family, she reveals, goes to the temple together to 'chant and pray and celebrate. I'm definitely a practising Hindu,' says Roberts, who grew up with a Catholic mother and Baptist father.[83]

Julia Roberts can be lazy, creative or melodramatic but she eventually balances out her need for glamour and family like a true LeoLibra.

Love and Marriage for Him
He is an absolutely fabulous husband. You just need to know how to handle him. Give him all the attention he desires, adore him, tell him that he is the best, and he will stay happy – so will you be. He showers you with love and fulfils every wish of yours. Do not expect him to help around in the house, though. It is beneath his dignity to help in 'menial' chores.

He wants a mate who looks up to him. She must also have a royal style. He needs lots of rest and he loves to laze. Feed him well, play his favourite music and allow him to relax and he will adore you. He is very generous with his money so you need to care for it and see that it is not blown away in extravagance. He is that one husband who will always be game for breaks and holidays.

As a father, he is very permissive as long as his children listen to him. He loves giving long lectures and advising them on exactly how to behave. He loves to show off their abilities and also expects academic excellence.

---
[82] http://www.telegraph.co.uk/culture/film/starsandstories/4944250/Duplicity-Julia-Roberts-interview.html
[83] http://www.people.com/people/article/0,,20407807,00.html

Love and Marriage for Her
She is a queen and don't you forget it. She needs love and adoration in equal measure. She needs a mate to share all things of life with. She needs someone to talk to. Someone who will be her king, whom she can adore. She is always ready to pitch in with her part of leading a happy and successful life. If that involves taking up a career or giving it all up, she will do what is right for the family and partner. She will be your pillar of strength when you need to grow in your career.

She is the most generous of souls and is a great hostess. She loves being with people, and her smile and charm light up gatherings. The best part about her is that she always has a sunny smile on her lips. You will know exactly where you are with her. If your house is spick and span and looks ready for royalty, then she is happy. But if things are messy and the house looks as if a tornado has hit it, then it's time to duck for cover. She is extremely romantic too. You have to remember the important dates, give her flowers, take her out for dinner and treat her as The One.

As a mother, she is fun, gregarious, generous and exciting. She is the kind of mother whom her children's friends adore for her style and wit. She wants her children to succeed and insists on academic excellence. But she lacks sensitivity and this may cause her to overlook some of their dreams and fears.

At the Workplace
LeoLibras are very artistic and love showing off their talents. They choose careers that include their creativity. Careers that involve music, dance, arts, crafts, aesthetics, fine arts, architecture, design, fashion, etc. find them at home and work would then be play for them. They are also good at those jobs that involve meeting and communicating with people.

These guys do not like starting at lower positions and are such positive and radiant personalities that nobody would ever think of placing them in menial jobs. They need money and fancy titles, and work with a magnificent show of power.

They are fabulous at delegating; they instinctively know who does the job well and leave the details to them while they relax and oversee in style. They are born bosses – creative, controlling, stylish, commanding and extremely generous to people who do their jobs well. They never stint on money but their subordinates need to remember that they need respect. Flatter their ego, ask for their advice, listen to their long-winded speeches and of course do some work – they will be happy and so will you.

Fire and Air meet in this personality to lend warmth and sunshine with a nature that loves to smile at the beautiful things in life. A true kingly disposition resides in this combination.

Famous LeoLibra Personalities
Julia Roberts, Suzanne Roshan, Sean 'Diddy' Combs, Amy Fisher, Franz Beckenbauer, Ram Kapoor, Raquel Welch, Roshni Chopra, Shazahn Padamsee, Sir Walter Scott, Bhakti Barve, Ambika Soni, Subramanian Swamy, Gauri Pradhan Tejwani, Kamalapati Tripathi, Usha Uthup, Arun Sarin, João Moutinho, Parupalli Kashyap, Edward Norton.

53. LEO–SCORPIO

Whoa! This combination sees the coming together of two fixed and extremely strong signs. There is no way this person can ever be average. He commands respect. The Sun, the energy-giver, life-sustainer, and the most powerful planet in the solar system, combines with Pluto, the most powerful planet in the zodiac. The roaring Lion now also has a sting in its tail! You can expect extreme passion, power, pride, revenge and ego in LeoScorps.

They are driven by extremely high values. They always think big and desire to do something that leaves people gasping. They are not content living an ordinary life. Due to Scorpio's secretive nature, they will not brag about their desires but you can discern their need to be powerful and different from the look in their eyes and their swagger. The Leo desire for excellence and the Scorpio need for supremacy make them work hard relentlessly to achieve their dreams.

It is very difficult to recognise a typical Scorpio as they work silently and don't display their passion, intensity or vindictiveness. There are also many kinds of Leos; there are some who act like sweet pussycats with a purr instead of a roar, while others behave like lions. Due to Leo's sunny personality, the LeoScorps appear cool and relaxed, but don't take that at face value. Don't play around with their ego or joke about them, either.

Scorpios give everything to those whom they love while Leos are extremely generous. They are big-hearted to those who are important to them and who treat them with love and respect. But both are also fixed signs, thus, once they make up their minds, it is very difficult to change them. They never accept a view if it is forced on them.

Passion is their trademark. LeoScorps endow every facet of their life with passion. Unlike Geminis who can do ten things at a time, LeoScorps do only one thing at a time. They can actually divide their life according to their passions. They have an extremely romantic phase when they passionately woo and love and they have a career-oriented phase when they give their all to their work.

Romance is extremely intense with these guys. While Leos want the best of mates and seek perfect settings to showcase their love, Scorpios are intensely passionate. If they fall for you then they will pursue you with such passion and commitment that you will be forced to say, 'I do'.

Style is another factor in their life. There is a unique majesty, supreme confidence and self-assuredness in the way they look or talk. They will do not ask for compliments but they definitely glow at them. But remember, the compliments have to be genuine or the sensitive Scorpio will discern the hidden truth.

Most LeoScorps talk little; their intense, confident eyes speak volumes to you. Whenever they do open up and talk, you will be spellbound. There are those less evolved LeoScorps who love to be the centre of attraction and talk about themselves till people's ears ache, but they are very few. Friends are their lifeblood. They treat friendship with religious intensity. Their word is their law and once they promise their friends anything they will overcome every problem to find a solution. Friendship, pride and excellence are the nuclei of their life.

They are very emotional and touchy and the worst part is that you might never know that they have got hurt for they never show it. You have to be very careful around this combination, for not only are they sensitive, but also dangerous.

There is an interesting irony to them. Leos are secretly under-confident and put up a façade of bravado. Contrarily, Scorpios fear nothing in this world and can face the most dangerous danger head on. The combination of the two makes an individual who may be not-so-confident to start with but who gains confidence with each success he achieves. But the need to portray a strong exterior in whatever situation they are in is a compulsion on them. The point at which their portrayed confidence merges with the real confidence is the moment of truth for a LeoScorp. They become most dangerous when they realise that they are really stronger than when they started.

The Scorpio in them can read your innermost secrets and any devious plans against them. It is a dangerous ploy as they have an explosive temper. The Scorpio intensity and the Leo's roar is not something to toy with. They also hate people who undermine their importance or try to overshadow them. Think twice about messing with them.

Leos are highly spiritual and Scorpios penetrate the deepest mysteries and secrets of the universe. Expect them to talk passionately and have strong opinions on rituals, religion, sex, birth, death, etc. LeoScorps pursue money, control and fame. Love and lust are also important in their life. They desire to rule and reach the top echelons of power.

Leo–Scorpio – Dilip Kumar
Dilip Kumar, perhaps subconsciously, revolutionised modern acting, and is referred to as 'the tragedy king'. The legendary filmmaker, Satyajit Ray, dubbed him 'the ultimate method actor'.[84]

Dilip Kumar is the first star of the Indian silver screen.

The flamboyant hand movements of a Leo and the intensity of a Scorpio personify him. He is known for the way he brings his characters to life. He was awarded the Nishan-e-Imtiaz, the highest civilian award conferred by Pakistan, for his efforts to bring the people of India and Pakistan closer. Dilip Kumar *saab* personifies the zeal and zest of a LeoScorp.

Love and Marriage for Him
He is the most responsible of husbands and loves being leaned upon. He needs to be the man of the house. This guy also comes in a package marked 'Fragile. Handle with care'. For all his bustling energy and intensity, he has a very soft heart that is easily bruised. Be careful of making unkind and insensitive remarks for he will never forget and most likely get even. He is the guy for you if you are independent but not aggressive, romantic but not clingy and, most of all, an adoring wife.

He is extremely ambitious. He needs to achieve success to feel proud of himself and also to overcome his hidden fears. So let him strive. Be his support system without being too obvious about it. Always look at him with admiring eyes and he will never stray.

---
[84] http://bollyspice.com/52575/dilip-kumar-the-greatest-of-the-actors

As a father, he is tough, controlling and demanding. He wants his children to succeed and does not tolerate ideas different from his own. Please don't expect any help in the initial years; he will come into the picture once they are able to have a conversation with him.

Love and Marriage for Her
She is an extremely strong person and to complement her you have to be calm but commanding in your own way. This girl needs to be handled carefully for her fragile ego must never be harmed.

She is brilliant at her work and at home. Whatever she does, she does it wholeheartedly. She is an extremely generous and loving person and, in order for her to remain so, you have to adore and appreciate her. There is a burning fire within her always. She wants to achieve so much. She can be the woman who pushes you to achieve impossible results.

She is a head-turner with the Leo love of style and intense looks. Look at that adoring audience wherever she goes. She does work her charm. She also evokes reactions of fear or respect. It may get on your nerves sometimes but you did get married to her because she is mysterious, sexy and confident… right?

As a mother, she sets the rules, yet is good fun. Her generous streak sees her spoiling her children and giving in to most of their demands till they stop respecting her. She demands excellence from them and it may be difficult for them to keep up to her high standards at times.

At the Workplace
Passion and ambition reside in LeoScorps. When they work for you, you can expect them to sweat and toil to achieve results. They go all out to achieve what they desire. These guys don't like menial jobs, and after seeing them, you won't offer those to LeoScorps. Their canvas is large and their dreams never ordinary. They covet the top position and they have the charisma, command and natural leadership abilities to reach the top. They have style and that comes in handy during presentations. They are masters at expressing themselves impressively and bring power, energy and passion to whatever they do.

They are totally blunt and do not play politics. But they have a sixth sense for negative undercurrents. It is dangerous to play politics with them. If a LeoScorp is your boss, be sure to work well, for they don't like pretenders. They like flattery but only if it is genuine. Go to them for advice, listen to their views and treat them with respect. They are very protective of their teams and fight for them. If you make them look good before senior management, they will reward you generously.

Fire and Water meet in this amazing combination that is strong, powerful and almost invincible. The most deadly and the most generous, mixed with equal doses of passion and power, make the LeoScorp.

Famous LeoScorp Personalities
Dilip Kumar, Mammootty, Paulo Coelho, Sanjay Gandhi, Rana Daggubati, Jodie Foster, Eoin Morgan, Yuvan Shankar Raja, Antoine Lavoisier, Shikhar Dhawan, K.S. Ranjit Singhji, Percy Chapman, Letizia Ortiz, Sofia Hayat, Dutta Samant.

54. LEO–SAGITTARIUS

Double Fire, double male! Volatile, expressive, talkative, this person is a performer in every sphere of his life. LeoSags have the benevolent Sun, the life force, combined in them with the knowledgeable, frank and intelligent Jupiter. The double male sign makes them extremely outgoing. They never bottle up their emotions. This is the Lion simply 'horsing' around with intermittent roars! They are born party animals; with their exuberance and a loud booming laughter. They need to talk and assert themselves. They love to feel that they are affecting your life positively and want to make a difference to those around them.

LeoSags have style in abundance. Their walk, talk, and look will be so 'them' that you will never mistake them for somebody else. They are true warrior kings – royal and brave. Leo makes them extremely majestic; whenever they stride into a room you feel that you are in the presence of SOMEBODY. They love to showcase themselves. If a LeoSag can strum only one tune on the guitar, he/she will walk confidently to the centre stage and belt it out like a rock star.

In spite of being chatterboxes, they are extremely intelligent. Sagittarius is the most intelligent amongst all zodiac signs and a LeoSag is not just intelligent but knows how to package it well. Ambition is a driving force within them. Leos demand to rule while Sagittarians need to reach the top. They will do everything to succeed.

They have an amazing sense of humour and can keep you in splits. They love slapstick comedy and pulling pranks on people. Just don't try that on them; remember the Leo pride and ego. They never mince words and are totally fearless in their opinions. On the flip side, they cannot keep secrets for it is as bad as asking them to keep quiet! Adventure courses through their veins. LeoSags are not afraid of bungee jumping or mountain climbing. They take each adventure by its horns and turn it into a breathtaking performance.

They thirst for attention and adulation. While some sober LeoSags visit salons and sweat it out in the gym, some of them try many outrageous things to get the maximum eyeballs. This is so apparent that everyone around them knows flattery is their Achilles' heel and panders to it for their own motives. The lack of Water in them doesn't let them see beyond their own glory when they are being used.

Money is a means to an end for them but they can never save it. The concept of saving seems bizarre to them. They use money for reasons beyond investing. They are the most generous people on earth. If you flatter them, they grant you anything in their power.

Romance for them is another avenue to showcase themselves and indulge in some narcissism. However, they are most dignified during courtship. When LeoSags are in love you can expect drama and action but they are very difficult to pin down. They will take some time in settling down due to Sagittarius's need for independence and fear of family ties. Sagittarian forward thinking and Leonine romanticism make them fall in and out of relationships.

All this pomp and show hides an important aspect of their personality. Leos have deep-seated uncertainties that they will never admit to. It is the cause of all their posturing and bravado. Sagittarians, too, are scared inside. Thus, LeoSags come across as truly fearless for they suppress their fear to go out and conquer. It takes some time for them to overcome their inner fears but once they see initial successes their confidence rises. This supreme confidence is their greatest strength and worst weakness.

When they are angry, they are extremely volatile and caustic. But they cool down quickly and then they will not hold any grudges. Expect them to staunchly believe in certain ideologies for which they will fight anyone. Their blind belief in their own invincibility, their supreme ego and anger are the three traits that can bring their downfall.

They do not have any Water or Earth element. This will make them extremely insensitive to people around them. They will walk all over people's egos and hearts and will be totally oblivious to the fact. They will never ever realise the damage they have done to people's emotions. They will also have ideas that may be farfetched, have no firm grounding and would remain castles in the air if not implemented with proper planning.

Fire signs believe in the power above and are extremely spiritual. Expect LeoSags to explore spirituality in their own way and come up with their own interesting interpretations. They will be extremely proud to exhibit their spiritual leanings. And spirituality definitely is the secret to their strong values, clean minds and immense self confidence.

Leo–Sagittarius – Rajesh Khanna
Rajesh Khanna was Indian cinema's first superstar.
He was a megalomaniac. It was his absolute refusal to face reality once the decline in his career set in that led to his eventual isolation from the film industry.
A young actress spoke candidly about this insecure, uptight, self-conscious superstar. Were they truly in love? She smiled and shook her head, 'Kaka was incapable of loving anyone. He was only ever in love with himself!'[85]
For the one thing nobody can ever deny Kaka is this – everything that Rajesh Khanna did, he did it his way. A true LeoSag indeed.

Love and Marriage for Him
He will remain a starry-eyed, slipshod teenybopper throughout his life. You need maturity and understanding to live with him. Appreciate and praise him, and he is your man. If you nag, dominate or even try being clingy or possessive, he is sure to walk out. He cannot handle emotions and has no sensitivity. Do not expect him to understand your sighs and reassure you. What he can give you is adventure, independence and a life that is far from ordinary. If you want a home-loving, caring and deeply understanding man in life, you should look elsewhere.

He will party hard, throw money around, and have a whole lot of friends who will turn up at a moment's notice. If you want to save, you have to make the extra effort. All he wants from you is his freedom. You can have whatever you want if you only allow him to be himself. Please do not forget to praise him too. He needs

---
[85] http://articles.timesofindia.indiatimes.com/2012-07-19/news-interviews/32746221_1_rajesh-khanna-film-industry-isolation Shobhaa De on Rajesh Khanna, *Mumbai Mirror*, 19 July 2012, Pg 15

a partner who is independent, self-sufficient, a queen in her own right and a person who never points out his flaws.

As a father, he is most permissive as long as his children know how to handle him. They have to listen to his long-winded talks, nod in agreement to his views and praise his abilities.

Love and Marriage for Her
She is a social butterfly and parties are her domain. She needs to surround herself with people or she feels stifled. She is totally ambitious. It does not matter whether it is her office life or social life, she wants to dominate both. She needs appreciation and independence. It would be a mistake to stifle her with excessive emotions and family bonds.

Do not expect her to be a conventional wife and spend her time cleaning the house. Maids are a necessity for her; ensure that she has at least two. She is totally independent and blunt. She will not nod her head to your ideas if she finds them silly and will not bow down to family pressure. Her life and thoughts are her own and she can't understand why people have such a hard time realising that.

As a mother, she expects the world from her children and also gives it to them. She is so generous that she spoils them with extravagance if they learn to flatter her ego.

At the Workplace
Ambition and drive make up LeoSags. They promise a lot and always deliver. Then they go and expound their achievements to their bosses for a raise. They think big, motivate and delegate. You cannot put them in menial positions. These guys are meant to lead. You need to ensure that you tie the loose ends in the plans of these over-exuberant people. Their plans may be too ambitious or too far-fetched. Just don't get carried away by their charisma and flair. Always listen to their promising and interesting spiels but have them validated by some Earth sign people.

If a LeoSag is your boss, flatter him immensely and work to achieve his dreams. If you do that, he looks after you. They are extremely generous to the people who help them achieve results. They are naturals as bosses and appear as if the corner office was just made for them. However, they definitely need help in managing their finances.

Fire and Fire – what a blazing combination this is! There is no Earth for stability, no Water for sensitivity and no Air for communication. It's just sheer power, but this power can be benevolent and warm if you know how to fan it. They are what they seem; there is no duplicity or meanness in them – that is the beauty and paradox of a LeoSag.

Famous LeoSag Personalities
Rajesh Khanna, Charlie Sheen, Carla Bruni, Jeremy Lin, Murli Manohar Joshi, Sandeep Patil, Marlene Dietrich, J.P. Morgan Jr., Benjamin Disraeli, Aurobindo Ghosh, Saira Banu, Freddie Mercury, Amy Winehouse, Gene Kelly.

55. LEO–CAPRICORN

Have you watched a goat climb the mountain slowly but steadily? It brooks no distractions, but silently goes about its work. Now infuse the power, vitality and forcefulness of a Lion into the Goat. The Lion-Goat desires nothing less than being the king of the jungle with a view from the top.

Fire and Earth, the Sun and Saturn, meet in this combination. It has the radiance of the sun and the shrewd aspirations of Capricorn. First things first, ambition rules this combination. No one wants or desires as much success and plans as much for glory as LeoCaps. They want to rule the world, they want everyone to sit up and applaud. They want to live with pride and honour and leave a huge legacy behind.

According to them, the world is divided into two watertight compartments – their families and the others. Capricorns can sacrifice themselves for their family while the Leo generosity overflows with family. Their duty, love and selflessness are reserved for the family while others get a taste of their cold and calculating ambition.

They are extremely mature from a very young age. You rarely see them going through the awkward pains of adolescence. They act and talk like mini-adults from the time they are three. The reverse aging of Capricorns plays its role in them and as they grow older they might become more irresponsible. When in their forties and fifties they achieve the power, status and money they craved, they give vent to their romantic desires. You might find them even straying at that age.

The Leo need for adoration and appreciation is extremely evident in LeoCaps. They may act least interested but you will see their eyes light up when appreciated. Deny them importance and you will see them sulk. They are extremely conscious of their appearance. They are prestige and society conscious and love to buy things and power dress to impress. Thankfully, their spending is a little limited due to Capricorn, which is penny-wise.

Money is extremely important to them and they need it along with power, status and fame. They spend wisely. They can also be stingy when others are not looking. Their generosity and benevolence are only for their families. There is also a deeply spiritual side to them. Fire signs are usually spiritual while Capricorn goes for old and traditional values. They fear only God.

Leos always dream big and Capricorns want to create empires. LeoCaps always have grand visions. They have intense powers of concentration. They are never worried about the enormity of any task. They are not stifled by obstacles or affected by the feelings of others in their quest for greatness. They are fantastic in self-promotion and know how to bond with people who matter. They want to reach the summit!

These guys can talk, lecture, advise and counsel for hours. They just love to hear themselves talk and expound on topics. Every LeoCap will have some serious artistic talent. But they would initially be shy to express themselves. But encourage them and you will see them morph into stylish entertainers. You will be stunned by the depth of their performance.

They can be loving friends. But their friends need to have thick skins for they are totally self-obsessed creatures. It is not that they do not like to appreciate; they do, but only after letting everyone know that they are the best. There is a lack of sensitivity in them that is evident despite their knowledge and maturity. These guys really cannot put themselves in others' shoes. They find it difficult to understand what goes on in people's hearts.

They show their anger through deep sulks. The explosive anger of Leos is reduced as Capricorn's more prudent method is to show annoyance, especially if people are not listening to them or respecting them. Shower them with respect, lean on them, ask for their advice, admire their talents and they will be on their best behaviour and become the most generous of souls.

Both Leo and Capricorn have deep-seated insecurities and that's the reason for their false bravado. They love the limelight and applause and if they can overcome their inner diffidence, they can showcase their talents. That is what their heart deeply desires. The Capricorn in them always wants to entertain crowds and lead a carefree life but Saturn orders them to focus on goals and to lead a Spartan life. But the Leo in them manages to release them of this self-induced reticence and soar high. If you are in their close circle you know that they have a golden heart. It's only that they ask for some recognition of the obvious talents that they have. That's fair, isn't it?

Leo–Capricorn – Clive Lloyd
The biggest factor in Clive Lloyd's success as a leader was his ability to inspire something not far short of love. Clive looked Kerry Packer in the eye, counted him as a man he could trust and was rewarded with Kerry's lifelong friendship. Most importantly, he gained the love of the disparate group of men who represented the West Indies in his time. Andy Roberts, Michael Holding and Gordon Greenidge speak of him as 'Cappy' and he speaks of them like a proud father.[86]

Clive Lloyd has the natural leadership qualities of a LeoCap. He was a father figure to his teammates and knew how to extract the best from each one of them.

Love and Marriage for Him
LeoCaps are total family men. He ensures that no problem ever hits his family. He needs a wife who adores him and looks up to him. He looks for stability and status in marriage, and may prefer a traditional arranged marriage. Even if it is a love match, it has to be ratified by the whole family, for Capricorns need the love and respect of their family.

Do not expect him to express his love in romantic ways. His life is more practical than that and, if he takes care of you, take it as his love song. There would be times when he goes through one of those melancholic, unsure moments. Understand him and support him without being domineering. There is a possibility of him straying once he achieves his ambitions and there is not much that you can do about it. But he will never wreck his home, whatever the situation.

Capricorn rules fatherhood. This makes LeoCaps fabulous fathers and loving sons. He dotes on his children yet ensures that they love and respect him. They

---
[86] http://www.britannica.com/EBchecked/topic/973117/Clive-Lloyd

learn their values from him. He will work very hard and scheme and plan to make his children a success.

Love and Marriage for Her
She is traditional and prefers solid conventions to modernity. The Leo in her makes her want to appear impressive and stylish. She can come across as a little snobbish due to the Capricorn influence. Her appearance and behaviour will be classy and will inspire awe or hatred in other women.

The Capricorn girl wants to marry and settle down with the most powerful man while the Leo girl wants a guy who catches everyone's attention. If she is married to you, you have to be quite notable to have impressed her. She loves being of help to her family and is the soul of generosity to them. But she needs a lot of praise to keep her going. She loves talking and advising.

Her pride and ego are very fragile; she doesn't like being taken lightly so treat her with respect. She is very ambitious. You have to either live up to her ambitions or let her act on them. She cannot live ordinarily.

Motherhood comes naturally to her. She is protective and loving towards her children. They see the soft and gentle side of her. She insists on academic success and ensures that they achieve success.

At the Workplace
When you meet them for the first time, you can be blown away by their style, panache and regal bearing. They look dapper and dressed for success. Leos desire the symbols of status while Capricorns want power and money. LeoCaps do not mind working hard as long as it ensures success. Menial jobs do not interest them. Capricorns have this innate ability to sense opportunities and you will always find them in the right place at the right time.

They want to be appreciated and can make a show of their work to get praised. The Capricornian shrewdness and Leonine inherent leadership makes them fabulous delegators. They know what to delegate and to whom. LeoCap bosses are the mentors you look up to in your workspace. They love to advise and would be mighty pleased if you follow their example. But they can be highly unemotional and not listen to family woes when there is work to be done.

LeoCaps always look to the next position and need promotions. He may not necessarily steal your work or rob you of credit, but a LeoCap naturally believes that the best ideas that win the company the biggest contracts are actually his. Yes… you were there too… but *he* was the reason you thought of that idea… isn't it?

Fire and Earth combine in this stable combination, whose flashiness is expressed in the Leo talk and style. LeoCaps are naturally upwardly mobile; they move up in life and are never satisfied with the status quo.

Famous LeoCap Personalities
Clive Lloyd, Subhash Ghai, Pawan Kalyan, Kiran Desai, Chembai Vaidyanatha Bhagavatar, Shruti Haasan, Bobby Deol, Sadhana, Rajeev Shukla, Riya Sen, Bobby Brown.

56. LEO–AQUARIUS

The proud, generous and benevolent Sun adds its lustre to the wild ways of the intelligent Uranus. LeoAquas are flamboyant, large-hearted, uninhibited and extremely unconventional. They are stylishly different. They like doing things on a grand scale. Style and attitude are inherent in them. Behind all that charm and sparkle, lies a very intelligent and sharp mind. The creative brilliance of Aquarius sparkles in them. Uranus is known for its eccentric genius, and it endows its people with the ability to march out on their own. LeoAquas are not bound by traditions, conventions or rules.

They can talk intelligently on diverse subjects with ease. More than academics, their brilliance is noticed in extracurricular activities like drama. They love an audience! They do not mind being melodramatic just to get attention. Film heroes can learn a trick or two about making a grand entrance from them.

LeoAquas can be extremely funny, but with dignity, due to their innate Leonine style and elegance. They can have very plain features, but their boundless energy, romantic sizzle and uninhibited charm will always appeal. They know how to attract the opposite sex and will be well versed in the conventions of romance.

The Aquarius in them hates routine and wants constant change. They love surprises and are ever ready for adventure. They take decisions at the spur of the moment and rarely listen to reason when their minds are made up. They do not have control over their expenses and may splurge lavishly on people whom they love or want to impress.

Generous to the extreme, they are excellent friends. They are quite capable of fighting for their friends. They can read people. Aquarians love to scrutinise people and ferret out their secrets. They are also into unravelling the various mysteries of life and learning the alternative sciences. Leos are highly spiritual. Expect them to go on grand expeditions or exotic adventures in the quest for spiritual enlightenment. Even this they do in style.

LeoAquas are born flirts; with Uranus's need for change and Apollo's desire for romance, what else could they be? They want a fabulous romance but they just won't be able to stop thinking 'What if...' It will take them some time to know their hearts but this can't be helped. The best part is that they will be very attractive to the opposite sex despite being loud and wearing their heart on their sleeve. They will always be confused between love, romance and friendship.

They are such positive people that you never guess their inherent fears. Leo knows how to dazzle despite its fears and insecurities. Whatever you do, do not express any doubts about their success for their confidence is not as strong as they portray. Self-respect is very important for them. Never insult them or undermine their importance. You will make bitter enemies of them. They sulk and brood when their importance is denied. Look at them beaming with pride and happiness, when they are appreciated. Their self-indulgence and self-praise can be annoying at times, but flattery is the best way to keep them happy and it's the best way to keep your sanity and peace of mind too.

LeoAquas dazzle you with their boundless exuberant energy, but many times, they will also indulge in laziness. Hard work and diligence are not their strong points, they prefer shining with spontaneous brilliance than spend hours practising. This lack of focus can affect their work. The Leo in them wants to be the best but Aquarius is attracted to something that is path-breaking or just plain *new*; and here's where the troubles start. The need for change affects everything from their love life to their career till they realise the need for stability.

The far-thinking, futuristic and wacky Aquarian, when combined with the bedazzling Leo, would want to bring something novel to the world. Chances are they can. Aquarius is a humanitarian zodiac sign and deep inside, every Aquarian wants to change society for the better and help the underprivileged. Leos have generous hearts that bleed when they see poverty. LeoAquas will take up social causes or at least donate to good causes.

Leo–Aquarius – Michael Jackson
Michael did selfless things – contributed to children's charities, started his own 'Heal the World Foundation' – he was everywhere, giving as much as he got.[87]

'When I hit the stage, it's like all of a sudden a magic from somewhere just comes and the spirit just hits you and you just lose control of yourself.'[88]

Despite his No. 1 hits (13), albums sold (some 750 million worldwide) and partial ownership of a music catalogue valued at close to $2 billion, Jackson was reportedly in debt to the tune of $500 million because of his outrageous spending sprees.[89]

Intelligent, creative, a tad eccentric, generous and loving, Michael Jackson was a truly original LeoAqua.

Love and Marriage for Him
As a partner, he is quite difficult to pin down but, if you managed to get him to commit, you have more or less got him. Once committed, he usually stays that way, but you might have to make allowances for his roving eye. The most exciting thing about him as a partner is his romantic nature. He is one of those guys who remembers to get flowers and trinkets, and may even attach a romantic note to them. He loves being adored by you and it is essential for his well-being to be shown respect and adoration.

He has his moments of aloofness. There are times when he seems lost to the real world. Those are his most creative moments. He needs your common sense to help him get through certain facts for he is capable of thinking a lot. Money, too, is not his domain although he may not like to give over the reins to you. Respect and tact should help you get your way with him.

He is romantic, yes, but not sensitive. It can become a little tiring after some time, to have to keep admiring him; and make him the centre of your world while he remains oblivious to *your* needs. Tell him your deepest needs gently and he will make every effort to please you.

Fatherhood is totally his thing. He loves being adored and respected by his children and loves to be listened to. He also loves being friends with them (of

---
[87] *Hello!*, July 2009
[88] http://www.interviewmagazine.com/music/michael-jackson/
[89] *People*, July 17, 2009

course, they still need to respect him). A doting father, he loves surprising them and throwing grand parties for them.

Love and Marriage for Her

She is stylish, unconventional and extremely independent. She will definitely be a prize catch. Her ways can be a little flirtatious and you have to be a little less possessive about her. You cannot tell her how to behave and she expects you to look at her with an indulgent gaze. She loves being an enigma and does not settle down easily into marital bliss.

She requires an intelligent mate to match her – a guy who is better than her. It goes without saying that household work is definitely not for her. She needs a battalion to help her out in that department. Take her bungee jumping, promise her a ride through the stars and she will be happy. Never ever forget important dates. In short, she is a bit high maintenance.

You cannot doubt her generosity. She unselfishly goes out of her way to help people in need. Her ways will be unpredictable and so will her temper. She will need your stability and cool head. She needs respect and adoration in equal measures to feel comfortable.

As a mother, she rules. Her ways are friendly yet commanding. Her children look up to her. She teaches them to be unafraid and follow their hearts. She makes them independent and strong and does not cling to them longer than necessary.

At the Workplace

The world of glamour holds a special place in their hearts and they may end up in showbiz. The spotlights and the joy of impressing millions call to them.

The Leo in them loves to dream big while Aquarius thinks of such futuristic plans that they may seem impossible. They are visionaries in the corporate world but need to be ably assisted by people who can fill in the details. Expect them to come out with extraordinary, out-of-the-box, mind-boggling solutions to the biggest maladies that afflict the field they work in. You find it hard to keep them down; they are born for the big leagues.

The best way to handle them is to shower them with praise in front of everyone and tell them the uncomfortable truths in private. They are motivated to perform for a big idea and glory rather than money. But don't forget to compensate them well, for looking good costs money. If you work for a LeoAqua, buy those glares. You will see a lot of sunshine. Keep your ego away and learn different ways to compliment him. He will be extremely generous if he likes you.

The regal Leo and the eccentric Aquarius create a combination that is hard to match. Their path will never be guided by conventional logic, but they will create their own kingdom and live life king size and footloose.

Famous LeoAqua Personalities

Michael Jackson, Rishi Kapoor, Gautam Singhania, Robert De Niro, John Travolta, Jayalalitha, Coco Chanel, Michael Bay, Danny Denzongpa, Fardeen Khan, Atul Kulkarni, Neha Dhupia, Sophie Choudry, Johann von Goethe, Jesse Owens, Dick Fosbury, Charles Goren, Vida Samadzai.

57. LEO–PISCES

Often a popular attraction at zoos and aquariums, sea lions are considered very intelligent animals. They are trainable, friendly and harmless. Though they love putting on dazzling performances, they can also be pleasure seeking and quite lazy. These characteristics almost explain the LeoPisces combination. The generous and luminous Sun meets the highly mysterious and sensitive Pisces in this overwhelmingly creative sign. The exuberance of Leo makes them glow with confidence. The normally reticent and self-effacing Pisces becomes more ready to show off its evident talents in this combination.

Pisces makes them very good at absorbing new ideas and concepts. They are open-minded and always ready for change. Routine does not appeal to them. Leos love surrounding themselves with an admiring crowd and Pisces are the most affable people. They like having fun and are genial and generous.

They are especially generous with money. They are able to discern a genuine need and go out of their way to help their friends. Loving and caring come naturally to them. They know how to stun with their talents and not waste their energies with negative thoughts.

They are dazzlingly talented. Pisces blesses them with originality and creativity, while Leo is a reservoir of artistic expression. The combination works brilliantly as there is an extraordinary synergy between the two. While Leo becomes more perceptive, Pisces becomes more expressive.

Romance and expressing love will be instinctive in LeoPisces. Leos are well-versed in the art of expressing love and Pisces understand all facets of love and are generally very mushy. They need to belong to someone and immerse themselves in the soft cocoon of love. A LeoPisces wants to be pampered and loved. Romance and everything that comes with it also helps them get out of stultifying routine. If they can attract love, the confidence rubs off in other aspects of life too. It works very strangely with LeoPisces.

They are very good at listening to and understanding people. They can internalise others' emotions. They don't just understand you but also will help you overcome your issues, like guardian angels. They also like giving a lot of advice. These people are always there for their family and friends. Money is for spending, according to them. They rarely have the concept of saving. They love luxury and are heartbroken if they have to live in penury.

Their anger is not scary. They sulk but soon smile when appreciated. No cloud is ever too dark to dampen their natural joy. Lazy and often laid back, LeoPisces like to sit in one place and look regal while doing their work. They also like to take lots of breaks. They are definitely talented and quick learners but need to be pushed to work hard. You can obviously push them to work for they will really want the glory and the admiration that comes with success.

There is also a strong and instinctive spiritual side to them. You can expect them to conduct prayers wearing appropriate clothes and chanting the right mantras. They have a child-like quality of limpid belief. They believe that everything happens for good and only good things will happen to them. They definitely believe in magic.

The Piscean desire to see the world through coloured lenses and the Leo ego can stop them from taking corrective steps when problems arise. This combination makes the escapism of Pisces rise to its peak – they act like kings with no responsibilities.

They can also give in to addictions. From substances to love, they can be addicted to anything. The Piscean fondness for illusions and Leonine theatrics will sometimes make them spin stories. Take some of them with a pinch of salt. Vanity is quite high in them and they like to make heads turn. You can expect them to be stylishly, and even differently, attired to get attention. They also spend money thoughtlessly on partying.

They have many fears and phobias. Leos show external bravery but are deeply scared inside. Pisces have extraordinary perceptiveness. They can *see* things that people usually don't see. They can have premonitions and ESP too. They also instinctively understand the various esoteric principles of life.

One thing that you need to know is that both Leo and Pisces are insecure deep inside. While Leos purr and roar their way to show they are not, Pisceans waste time in self-pity. The constant struggle for a LeoPisces is to overcome this weakness and rise above.

The transformation from a shy pussycat to a confident lion is fascinating. So is the possibility of the timid fish morphing into a playful sea lion or an all-engulfing whale. Deep inside, both Lion and Fish have that power of transformation. They just need to have faith, refurbish their belief in magic and shrug off laziness and the make-believe world that they created for themselves. If that happens, they could be the most dangerous if required. But they will be their sweetest best, knowing that no one can vanquish them in this avatar. The makeover will require a magic and with LeoPisces – their middle name is *magic*.

Leo–Pisces – Salma Hayek
'When you're making money, they're never going to tell you whether you're good or bad. I never wanted to be a famous bad actress! I had a panic that people would think, she's good only because everyone knows her.'[90]

'I'm concerned about my daughter because she will not believe in Santa Claus. I'm hoping she'll believe in fairies because I want her to have some kind of make-believe characters in her life.'[91]

Salma Hayek has the Piscean ability to see beyond the obvious and the Leo positivity. She knows how to dream the impossible and doesn't lack the courage to make them come true like a true LeoPisces.

Love and Marriage for Him
He is the lord of the house as far as pampering is concerned. You have to care for him, love him and be there with him. But he does the vanishing act when there is work to be done! Be ready to be the one in charge, but do not shout or scream at him, for his ego gets hurt very fast. He is very romantic and knows how to please you with flowers and love notes. He understands you very well and you are able

---

[90] http://www.oprah.com/omagazine/Oprah-Interviews-Actress-and-Producer-Salma-Hayek
[91] http://collider.com/salma-hayek-interview-grown-ups/33684/

to talk about your deepest desires to him. He will be your support in times of crisis and will stand tall when the going is tough; but don't expect him to look into domestic details.

His career is important to him and he will want to make a big splash and that's the one area where he will work. You will have to save the money and set the budget; for investing and budgeting are words beyond his ken, and he loves going on shopping sprees. You have to keep a keen eye on his friends for this guy can easily falter if the company is bad. He needs steady, stable people around him.

As a father, he is protective and loving. He knows how to enjoy his children's childhood and never burdens them with expectations beyond their abilities. He loves advising and pampering them.

Love and Marriage for Her
She loves romance and expects you to woo her in style. You have to admire and understand her for this girl wants a man who knows, loves and respects her. She wants a soul mate and can break conventions for her love. She has a refined dressing sense, a majestic glide and the elegance and grace of a queen. She will also want some kingly qualities in you – you will have to be worthy of her.

Creative and artistic, she takes pleasure in pursuing her talents. Encourage her talents and be her biggest admirer and *you* will have a fan for life. She is very affectionate and loving. Her family and friends find her willing to listen and help. Cheerful and smiling, she faces difficulties with inimitable grace. But don't think she is unbreakable, she will hide her fears but they will be lurking under her smile – just never let her know that you see it.

As a mother, she adores her children and pampers them with love and care. Nothing is ever good enough for her darlings. She understands their deepest fears.

At the Workplace
The corporate life, full of work and menial jobs, holds no interest for LeoPisces. They want to be their own bosses and do what they enjoy. They are made for a career in the artistic fields. They also do very well in people-related fields. They think big and want their careers to provide them the platform to dazzle. They can be very good as directors and trainers. They do well in any career that requires charm, understanding and style.

You need to praise them and applaud their efforts publicly. They will work for glory and joy rather than money but they would need the money too for they have expensive tastes. They are also very good at delegating. They learn quickly and teach others beautifully. If they are your bosses, you will fall in love with their charisma and easygoing nature. But they definitely can read you and see your weaknesses.

Fire and Water combine in LeoPisces to make them sensitive yet strong, creative yet proud, and shine radiantly.

Famous LeoPisces Personalities
Salma Hayek, Lil Romeo, Aamir Ali, Kevin Federline, Ingrid Bergman, Aditya Pancholi, Thilakan, Pink, Amit Trivedi, Ustad Bismillah Khan.

58. VIRGO–LIBRA

Virgo, meticulous and diligent, meets Libra, the lover of beauty, grace and luxury. Earth and Air meet in this combination and bring about a positive transformation in each. Creative and talented, VirLibs exhibit an artistic bent of mind from a young age. You may have to cajole them into the limelight for they prefer to hide; yet, when they perform, they can amaze you with their talents. This combination can turn an art into a science, researching and practising myriad ways to perfect astounding effects.

Libran excellence in communication and Virgo sophistication makes them extraordinary speakers. They can sense the atmosphere and say just the right words at the right time. You will never get to know about the hundred-odd hours they spent in meticulously rehearsing those lines. Their communication style is dialogue-oriented and contains perfect articulation and intonation. They are graceful, charming, well mannered, cultured and humble, whatever their social status may be.

They like routine and duty. They get up at a specific time every day, and let their set pattern take over. Virgo is a loner with an obsession for perfection but Libra adds a sense of balance to the mix. VirLibs have a process for everything they do. They worry incessantly and only if things are A-OK do they relax.

Life may not always be easy for them for they desperately want everything to be in harmony and balance. Decision-making is a long-drawn-out process as each fact is minutely checked and diligently investigated. Cleanliness is almost their religion – they are fastidious about it. Good health, too, is of prime importance and they diet, exercise, and meditate to maintain it. They are well read on various ailments, and the associated medical procedures.

VirLibs prefer solitude and seek silence. They love gathering knowledge through books and can speak intelligently on various topics. Their literary tastes, combined with an excellent sense of humour and love for music, make them wonderful companions. They might even surprise you with their singing/dancing abilities, after they overcome their initial shyness.

For them love goes beyond physical attraction. Librans are tender-hearted and melt when in love, while Virgos are pure at heart. VirLibs love with rare honesty and commitment. But the sticking point is: who will be the first to declare their love? They never take the first step and it will be even worse if they are 'good friends'. VirLibs can be quite insecure in such a situation with their minds in a tizzy. They will always underestimate their own worth and will kill themselves thinking that he/she will find a better mate in someone else. Their biggest virtue is self-sacrifice. They can give up anything for true love – even love itself. Conversely, they can also cut off relationships without any remorse if it is an unhealthy one.

Anger is nearly non-existent in them; what they do get is critical or silent. They can absolutely rip a person apart with their frank and critical analyses. Their silent treatment can be scary and worse than their criticism and they use it as a final weapon. Money, thankfully, is saved despite the Libran love for brands and luxury. This is their most valuable trait for they know how to spend money to get the highest benefit.

You would find it hard to argue with them as they invariably find the right way of doing things after trying and testing every other way possible and wouldn't prefer any other. They can be extremely particular and will not compromise on certain things. However, the Libran ability to see every facet of a situation and sensitivity to others' problems compounds the situation at times.

It is rare for VirLibs to be totally judgemental. They can also get into over-analysis mode, in which case they keep postponing important decisions. Extreme vacillation of the mind is one of their biggest pitfalls.

Virgo–Libra – Amitabh Bachchan

'There is a slip on every newspaper… after you read the magazine or paper, you tick your name, so that others know that you have read it. There is a process for everything at home. Papa is the most organised person on the planet. He has a pair of glasses for the bed, one for the car, inhaler for the bedroom, inhaler for the car, for the bathroom. It's sort of obsessive.'[92] 'Going through my scene and my lines repeatedly… sitting and saying them, standing, walking around… while having a meal, dressing up, idling, or as of now, even when posting the blog! It's the thing to do. I do it all the time. Obsessive? No, I do not think so. I believe repeating the lines fetches one a degree of comfort as far as memorising them is concerned'[93]

Amitabh Bachchan is the most well-known and beloved face of Indian cinema. You find no blatant swagger in his walk nor hear any undiplomatic retorts from him. He marks the confluence of a balanced Libra and a meticulous Virgo in his words and actions.

Love and Marriage for Him

You are truly blessed to have him for a partner for this one rarely strays. He loves with a purity that touches the soul. There is no responsibility too much for him and no duty that he shirks. Even if he is a bachelor, his house is never messy. He can give a girl a complex, especially seeing how he grooms himself. He is the perfect metrosexual!

He has certain exacting standards: his clothes should be done in a particular way and the spices in his food should be in a certain proportion. Ensure you know all those details and work them into your schedule, for his peace of mind.

For him love is duty. Though circumspect in public, he showers love, attention and care on you. There is a shy, romantic poet hidden in him that is revealed in special moments. However, he is not very sentimental or emotional. He can't look into your eyes and know exactly what you need and want. He is a good lover but don't expect too much mushiness from him. He is always there for you but will still seem a little distant as well.

He loves his children and he is at his most relaxed with them and loosens up for some serious fun. He also focuses on giving them a good education, fulfils their needs, and sometimes their extravagances.

---

[92] Shweta Bachchan in 'Koffee with Karan', Season 3, Star World India
[93] http://srbachchan.tumblr.com/post/25022479479

Love and Marriage for Her
She is beautiful and responsible, and the epitome of a good daughter-in-law. Duty and responsibility suit her and she truly enjoys these aspects of domestic life.

She loves you to bits. She will take care of your diet, feed you nutritious food, and she will also worry about you. She knows how to get her way and does it with such grace and charm that it is impossible to refuse her. She has the innate ability to sort things out in just the way she wants while ensuring that everyone else is OK with it.

She loves to be with the family and enjoys family holidays. Take her to places that offer historical tours or cultural interactions, as her bright mind is always ready to pick up new facts. She can get critical at times, and even nag a little, but that is a small price to pay for such a loving wife. You can woo her with romantic dinners for she is absolutely enamoured of the notion of love, despite her declarations to the contrary.

As a mother, she is firm yet loving. She disciplines her children with fairness. She is a model mother with her caring ways, unconditional love and adherence to duty.

At the Workplace
VirLibs can do anything – from art to accounts. They have diligent, meticulous minds and a thirst to learn. Libra makes them excellent communicators and they can explain things precisely and beautifully. They can be very good teachers, writers and even poets. From routine jobs to the creative field, nothing seems out of reach for them.

They can be extraordinary actors with the Virgo perfection of pitch and nuance and the Libra command over diction and language, sense of beauty and the ability to think from another's perspective. They have a great talent for research and their findings are not just accurate but unbiased as well.

They are apolitical creatures, who prefer to let their work talk for itself, yet they never truly blend into the background, for the cardinal aspect of Libra makes them lead with subtlety and grace. They have very strict moral values and a personal code of conduct, which they will never breach.

As bosses, they are extremely focused and meticulous and demand the same from their subordinates. They are good micro-managers and number crunchers. They can decipher the most complex of accounting issues and have in-depth product and sales knowledge. You should be well prepared for any discussion with them and never dissemble with them.

Earth and Air meet to give this combination clarity with a sense of beauty. VirLibs are duty-minded but charming, intelligent and humorous with a true heart and an eye for balance.

Famous VirLib Personalities
Amitabh Bachchan, Smita Patil, Leonardo DiCaprio, Will Smith, Avril Lavigne, Nandita Das, Gwyneth Paltrow, Curtly Ambrose, Sylvia Plath, Jean-Claude Van Damme, Michael Ballack, Deepak Chopra, Nargis Fakhri, Laxmipathy Balaji, Mala Sinha, Sheikh Hasina, Ralph Lauren, Saeed Ajmal, Soha Ali Khan, Julie Andrews, Anne Hathaway, Dwight Eisenhower, Amjad Ali Khan, Persis Khambatta, Ritu Nanda, Kitu Gidwani, Simone Singh, Vinita Bali, Pedro Almodóvar, Lourdes Ciccone-Leon, Drew Gilpin Faust, Emma Stone, Ashton Agar, Deepak Parekh.

59. VIRGO–SCORPIO

Duty and passion are inextricably intertwined in this combination. The duty-conscious Virgo meets the driven and passionate Scorpio. This results in an extraordinary culmination of precision with zeal, diligence with obsession, perfection with perseverance and conscientiousness with determination.

Virgo is ruled by the yet-to-be-named 'Planet Y', which is known for its influence upon knowledge, industriousness and skill, while Pluto the ruthless and dark lord of the underworld rules Scorpio. You find wisdom and perception in VirScorps. They not only do everything in a precise and set manner, they also bring a lot of force to each task. They are very high on energy.

VirScorps carefully divide their life into segments and then further divide and subdivide each segment into tasks. Even after this much thought, they will also set up a plan, a fallback plan, and then a backup plan – each detailing a routine that will be followed relentlessly by them. The best part of all this planning and detailing, coupled with their passion and high energy, is that they find success in whatever they undertake. Actually, details are fun for them.

This single-minded dedication and love for thinking makes them solitary creatures. They do not need people around to make them happy. They are content with their thoughts, work and plans. They prefer being left alone for then they can think with greater clarity. They are not loud or aggressive, nor do they boast of their achievements.

They have one extremely challenging trait – being excessively critical. They criticise, not to put someone down, but because there is something in them that just cannot keep quiet about irregularities. They cannot stand imperfection in anything. Consequently, they are fastidious about their own habits. They like to do things a specific way at a specific time. This shows in their food habits as well. They are very conscious of what they eat. They are equally dedicated to their exercise routine.

Virgos have a slightly conservative attitude while Scorpios too are not known to be flashy. As far as money is concerned, VirScorps are not very generous. They never overindulge in shopping. They don't mind hardship or a Spartan life, they just need a goal and they can endure anything to reach it. They have exacting standards and want their family to behave decorously.

Scorpios instinctively understand human psychology and the dark side of human nature while Virgos have absolute purity of mind and purpose. Despite knowing and recognising the sordid aspects of human beings, most VirScorps retain an endearing innocence. The deep penetration of Scorpio is diluted and they can investigate the darker truths without deriving sadistic pleasure. A few of them though, if they do get into sadism, do so with the perfectionism and clinical precision of a Virgo. Generally, though, there is a seamless culmination of chastity and passion in them.

When VirScorps fall in love, they do so with the passion and intensity that characterises them. Virgo makes the passion pure while Scorpio requires a soul-to-soul connect. VirScorps want and give nothing but the deepest and purest form of love, and they can sacrifice everything for their love. They can even give up their love for love. But they can also be intensely jealous and passionately vengeful, if wronged in love.

They have the perceptiveness of the Scorpio and the eye for detail of the Virgo. You cannot fool them; they have this frightening ability to read your mind and soul. Nothing can be hidden from them; so don't even try. They are deeply knowledgeable, with a natural inclination for research and the hidden mysteries of the world. Once they know the reasons behind a custom, they follow it devotedly. They are deeply religious, even ritualistic; they follow culture and tradition, and are conservative. Conversely, they are also unorthodox and rebellious in a strange way. They can pull down customs and trample on tradition if it helps them achieve their larger goals.

Think before you plan to harm them for they are Scorpios, and revenge comes naturally to a hurt Scorpio. They can plan brilliantly and seamlessly execute a plan for your ruination. They will do it with such attention to detail and lack of emotion that you will never be able to detect their hand in your downfall. Conversely, they never forget a favour and remain thankful for even one act of kindness.

VirScorps have total control. They are ruthless executors of their vision and the greatest survivors. They are extremely restless, with a fire seething within them. They may end up with overworked minds, strained nerves and be highly strung. They need rest, especially for their minds, but that's difficult for them. They just keep going on and on – tirelessly.

Virgo–Scorpio – Narendra Modi
N.R. Narayana Murthy: 'Narendra Modi has been acknowledged as one of the finest administrators in the country.'[94]

'Scale, skill and speed can transform India into a Gujarat.'[95]

'Unpretentiously and ruthlessly ambitious, vindictive, authoritarian, unpredictable and totally impervious to scruples – these are some of the epithets used by political rivals to describe...Narendra Modi.'[96]

'Nobody is perfect. Each of us has some deficiencies. I have every human fault, but my values have taught me to play to my strengths, so that my deficiencies are left behind and the strengths have become my driving force.'[97]

Narendra Modi calls himself the 'prime servant' and not the Prime Minister. The major agenda announced after he became PM was a 'clean India' drive. He urged schools to have separate toilets for women.[98]

Narendra Modi epitomises the essence of VirScorp: the convergence of industriousness, meticulous perfection, passion and complete control.

Love and Marriage for Him
He is a charged battery and his mind is always working. You need to be cool and collected and help him relax. He worries about everything from his mother's knees to his child's sneeze. He looks into every small detail and tries hard to smooth things out for his family.

---

[94] http://www.youtube.com/watch?v=UWnOjqr2AVA
[95] http://www.indianexpress.com/news/narendra-modi-scale-skill-and-speed-can-transform-india-into-a-gujarat/1070749/
[96] http://www.mumbaimirror.com/news/india/The-rise-and-rise-of-Narendra-Modi/articleshow/22567485.cms
[97] http://www.ndtv.com/article/india/narendra-modi-s-address-to-women-entrepreneurs-at-ficci-highlights-351336
[98] *Times of India*, Mumbai, 16 August 2014

The love and romance of the early courtship years becomes a duty for him as the years pass, but he fulfils his duties beautifully. He is very predictable; even a small degree of change in his routine signifies that he is disturbed. His career is very important to him, and also another point of worry. When he comes back from work, create a loving and soft environment in which he can relax for some time.

You will have to mind how you dress as the Virgo in him is conservative and the Scorpio will ensure he is possessive. However, it will work well if you are independent and take your own decisions. That is one set of decisions off his shoulders. If you take the trouble to cook to his rather specific tastes, you will have a much happier, calmer man.

As a father, he is dutiful and caring but a little controlling. He wants his children to behave well. He has plans for their future and wants them to be well educated.

Love and Marriage for Her
She never rests. It is her biggest asset and worst trait for she cannot let things be as they are. This lady takes care of every aspect of your life. All she wants from you, after all the hard work, is love!

However, if you think she can be fooled into becoming your unpaid slave, while you can betray her faith in you then you are very much mistaken. There is no fury like a woman scorned and a scorned VirScorp is worse than a raging tornado. She will move on only after making sure that you are totally destroyed.

She needs passion and a goal in life. It can be her home or work, but there has to be something that occupies her and interests her, otherwise her abundant energy gets wasted. She needs a calming presence when she gets agitated and obsesses about details. This girl needs to rest, so even if she says no, send her to a spa and take her on impromptu holidays. Take care of her as she takes care of you.

As a mother, she is loving, yet duty-minded. She is very conscious of her own health and gives the same care to her family. They get the healthiest foods and a well-balanced diet.

At the Workplace
VirScorps are absolute perfectionists: great as workers but extremely difficult to handle as bosses. They bring passion and detail-orientation to everything they do. The combination of detail and energy, perceptiveness and wisdom makes them excellent researchers, investigators and scientists. If you give them a job, you can relax. They complete it without a glitch. If they ask you to do a job, be aware of every single detail. They can crucify you with critical comments if they find anything amiss.

They deliver against all the odds. They do not commit themselves unless they feel they can succeed. They work systematically, meticulously and with total focus. The position does not matter to them as long as they know that they can grow – their goal is power. They get motivated by completing tasks. This keeps them going. They are designed for work: intense, high-pressure, methodical, exacting work which requires top-notch organisational skills.

Earth and Water combine to give VirScorps depth with stability, integrity with passion and a mind that never stops ticking.

Famous VirScorp Personalities
Billy Jean King, Narendra Modi, Montek Singh Ahluwalia, Zaheer Khan, Nimesh Kampani, Venkatesh Daggubati, Stephen King, Kamal Nath, Mohd. Kaif, Younis Khan, Walt Disney, Laurent Blanc, Tommy Lee, Christopher Reeve, Jay-Z, Mihir Sen, Isha Sharvani, Maarten Stekelenburg, Koel Purie, Sivasankari, Vani Jairam.

60. VIRGO–SAGITTARIUS

The perfection-seeking, dedicated Virgo meets the extremely intelligent and highly adventurous Sagittarius, ruled by Jupiter, in this combination of opposites. These are happy-go-lucky folks with brilliant minds and pure hearts. They live life as it comes, while looking forward to tomorrow with hope and faith.

Both Virgo and Sagittarius are mutable signs. VirSags are fairly uninterested in leadership. They are amiable people who mind their own business and are never arrogant or rude. The Virgo's duty-bound mind adds a touch of responsibility to Sagittarius's natural enthusiasm; while Sagittarian impetuosity inserts outspokenness to the Virgo critical faculty. VirSags know how to speak their mind!

They have certain habits they are particular about while being absolutely careless in other aspects. They hate mess and untidiness, and are always punctual. They love dressing up and presenting their best face to the world. They are very bright and can talk articulately about the most abstract of subjects. Sagittarius is the greatest teacher of the zodiac while Virgo is its best student. With VirSags, learning is a lifelong passion. They work hard and excel in research and investigation as well. They are excellent at explaining concepts with great lucidity.

VirSags love travelling and exploring new places. They live for adventure, enjoying every exhilarating experience. They know how to work hard and play hard too. They are rambunctious and have a phenomenal funny bone, being natural pranksters and masters of slapstick humour. They find it difficult to tell a lie and get caught most times. But the Virgo in them can practise and perfect that art too, if required to survive a challenging situation.

Despite their intelligence, VirSags need someone to explain the subtleties of a situation to them, for they are incapable of realising the undercurrents and emotional aspects of a conversation. They cannot read minds like Water signs. They are not really concerned about knowing exactly what makes you sad. They will do things for you more out of a sense of duty than because they can read your emotions.

There is a certain naïveté about them. They can act inexperienced and immature at times but they are innately capable of looking after themselves. They are excellent friends – fun loving and conscientious. Incurable optimists, they are the most honest, truthful and principled people you will ever meet.

As far as romantic relationships go, VirSags are soft souls. Don't expect them to be emotional or passionate – the duty-consciousness of Virgo and love of adventure of a Sagittarius are present in VirSags but they will never be soulful in love. They take their time deciding on a partner and will always start by being friends. It will take them a lot of time and endless analyses to take a romantic decision. While Sagittarius can make them quite flexible in their morals, the Virgo's purity of heart will also be evident in them.

They have a tendency to nag and criticise. They feel that only they know how to do certain things right. This need to always be absolutely perfect engenders endless stress. Spirituality is very important to them. Sagittarius rules higher knowledge while Virgo makes them bound to custom and duties. They are invariably religious and quite touchy about it too as they are absolute believers in the almighty. They feel certain that most problems can be alleviated by the power above. They find inner peace in being ritualistic.

Health is very important for them. They are choosy about their food and maintain strict control over their diet despite their love for eating. VirSags know how to manage money. They know the cost of everything and are willing to spend on luxuries if it helps their image, but on the whole they are conscientious savers.

Despite their sweet nature, they are definitely not people you should cross. They have a temper and can say very cutting things to people who take them for granted. If they are in a rage, they can simply crucify you or shame you by telling you the raw, unadulterated, infuriating truth to your face.

VirSags have a secret desire to rule the stage. They love applause, and when the mood strikes, they can shed their shyness to dazzle with their performances. Their perfectly practised, energetic dance moves, songs and acts never disappoint. The Sagittarian buffoonery when combined with the Virgo sense of timing can create a riot of laughter. They come well prepared to dazzle and it always seems as if it is a spontaneous act. Clever!

Virgo–Sagittarius – Anil Kapoor
'Well, I don't know if I'm looking twenty years younger but, yes, I definitely feel twenty years younger. I can proudly say that I've preserved myself well. It's a combination of good food habits, regular work-outs, proper sleeping habits and my positive frame of mind.'[99]

Kapoor, like his on-screen avatar, is happy-go-lucky in real life as well. He does not spend too much time chasing success. 'I don't think too much. I move on quickly.'[100]

'I am an actor, not a salesman, that's why you don't see me endorse one brand after another.'[101]

A VirSag, Anil Kapoor works hard, sticks to his principles and follows his own path to success.

Love and Marriage for Him
He is the easiest guy to understand but he has his set routines and you will have to adjust to them. His work consumes him and he will be engrossed in the details. When he works, he will give it his 110 per cent, but after that he will relax. Fun is equally on his agenda and he loves travelling!

He likes to save and money is one of his prime concerns. There are times when he takes on a lot of stress and becomes blunt and aggressive. His critical analyses can be quite painful but it is better to hear him out, as it will help him get it off his chest and clear the air. He might be combative or hold different views from you but he always remembers his duties as a husband or father and carries them out perfectly.

As a father, he is deeply caring. He knows how to look after his children when they are hurt or sick. He is also full of fun and excitement. Educational qualifications mean a lot to him and he wants his children to do well.

---

[99] http://www.filmfare.com/articles/anil-kapoor-im-the-coolest-dad-ever-515html
[100] http://satyamshot.wordpress.com/2010/08/27/anil-kapoor-interview-2/
[101] *DNA*, After hrs, Mumbai, 16 June 2012

Love and Marriage for Her

There is a sweetness and malleability about her that is quite charming. She is loving, kind and, above all, fun to be with. She has no inclination to dominate. She creates her own small, nurturing world and is happy in it. She is very house-proud and loves to keep it sparkling and new. She is happy with a normal life and does not crave more.

When you are with her, please remember that she does not understand your deepest feelings or fears till you spell them out for her. Though she will take perfect care of you, she will never know what goes on in your heart for she will believe what you say and delve no further. But you cannot fool her, for there is nothing deficient about her intelligence. She will easily find the holes in your story.

Virgo will make her quite capable of cutting off relationships. Sagittarius too doesn't like to be bound in relationships. So be careful, for despite her love of duty she will not stand by mutely while you hurt her. She can just pack her bags and leave if she feels unwanted.

The best thing about this lady is that she is one of the easiest people to get along with. She has no ego hassles and is very easygoing. Her deepest desire is to be free and travel. She will gravitate towards adventure trips and here's where you will see the child in her surface.

She is the perfect mom and is great at nursing and caring. She worries for her children and their choices, yet knows how to have fun with them too. She will be the most happening grandma in town in her golden years.

At the Workplace

VirSags have the Sagittarian passion to learn and the Virgo tendency to work hard. They are very ambitious, but may find it difficult, in the beginning, to identify their exact calling. Once they are sure of what they want, they are unstoppable.

At work, VirSags are meticulous, full of energy, and driven. They do not have a burning desire to be leaders but they can follow through perfectly. They execute well and you will never have to go after them to finish their work on time. Details interest them and they can become whistle blowers if they catch any wrongdoing.

The Sagittarius in them loves the spotlight and appreciation. They can definitely make showbiz a profession. They have this childlike enthusiasm for the work they do even in their sixties and maintain a youthful glow. They somehow know the art of having fun while doing stellar work – a difficult balancing act. If they are your bosses, be ready to work hard and to hear honest, point-blank feedback.

Earth and Fire meet in this duty- and fun-loving combination. VirSags will be free spirited yet rule-bound, creative yet conscientious and extremely focused on all the details.

Famous VirSag Personalities

Anil Kapoor, Gauri Khan, Nana Patekar, Lin Dan, M.F. Hussain, Christiane Amanpour, Shah Jahan, Tom Moody, Ambati Rayudu, Shonali Nagrani, Nagesh (Tamil actor), William Gladstone, Madanmohan Malviya, Bhulabhai Desai, Charan Singh, Tycho Brahe, Swami Agnivesh, Amy Jo Johnson, Majrooh Sultanpuri, Rachel Nichols, Katrina Bowden, Goundamani, Shah Jahan.

61. VIRGO–CAPRICORN

The perfection-seeking, meticulous Virgo meets the old and wise Saturn in this highly diligent and focused combination. Imagine being chained to duties and deadlines 24x7. These people bear a cross which ordinary mortals would find hard to carry.

VirCaps have two major concerns – work and family. They work extremely hard, keep quiet about their actual goals and play to win. They can sacrifice anything for their families. Responsible and mature, they act much older than their age. They have clear priorities from a young age and are not prone to rebelliousness. They can take on important responsibilities from a tender age. They are usually the teachers' pets with their respect for authority, ability to work hard and sheer diligence.

Their philosophy is simple: 'There is a time for work and a time for fun.' For them, fun comes only after success. The Capricornian 'reverse aging' phenomenon works perfectly for them. They will be duty-bound, hard working and extremely committed to their work in youth. VirCaps take on more and more responsibility and only when they achieve success do they mellow down and lighten up.

Fussy and finicky, they insist on everything around them being perfect. Extremely health-conscious, they read up on and follow a healthy lifestyle. The Virgo tendency of being fastidious and meticulous will be apparent in their behaviour. They are very conservative about spending. They know the price of everything and never spend a penny more than necessary.

They are sticklers for time and like being well turned out. Their sartorial style is extremely conservative with neat, clean and classy clothing. A mess is something they cannot stand and they have a veritable mania for cleanliness. Routine and discipline are their motto.

VirCaps think everything through meticulously. They dissect each and every point minutely and analyse all the implications of a situation. They can be underhanded while reaching for their final goal. Manipulative thought processes are not beyond them. However, the Virgo and Capricorn trait of love for a clean image nudges them towards sheer hard work.

They will definitely not make the first move in love. VirCaps spend more time in the pursuit of their goals than looking for love. Actually, they would love it if their parents decide on a partner for them; after all they know them best. But if you want to give them the green signal do so subtly and conservatively. They prefer companions who look and act responsible. VirCaps also look for status in a match, they will never choose people who don't have a standing in society.

The double Earth combination makes them steer clear of the flightiness of Air signs, the volatility of Fire and the sensitivity of Water. VirCaps are way too stable and focused to be deterred by anything. They never lose their cool. When they get angry, they simply crib and criticise and their constant nagging can become irritating. The worst thing is they are usually correct in whatever they say!

They seek solitude and are quite happy doing things on their own. Shy and reserved with outsiders, they can be fun-loving too but Saturn's 'old-man ways' make them curb their impulses. They do love compliments, though they will never fish for them, and act nonchalant if given one.

They are not emotional, sentimental or sensitive. They have an effortless, uncomplicated practicality about them, which eschews wild actions or ugly displays of emotion. These gentle and bashful people are chained and married to duty. Understand them. They appear geeky and seem aloof but they crave love and acceptance.

There is a strain of melancholy in VirCaps and they tend to look at the worst side of any situation. They can easily turn into reclusive loners who spend their time working and don't have a social life. They hate losing and fear failure. They find it extremely difficult to share their feelings and inadequacies and can become lonely worrywarts. It will be necessary for their family and friends to balance this negativity with positive vibes and make them smile more often.

Virgo–Capricorn – Abhinav Bindra
'It (shooting) became an absolute obsession and soon I started training about 40 hours per week.'[102]

'I believe there are no short cuts – only sheer hard work, perseverance, and the ability to absorb and react to challenges can ultimately lead to high achievement.'

'I have a tendency to be pessimistic or realistic, whereas my parents are true optimists. They supported me throughout my journey and have played a very important role in my success.'

Abhinav Bindra keeps his family close to his heart and has the focus, determination and deep-seated desire to win of a true VirCap.

Love and Marriage for Him
He will not be able to understand your unstated feelings nor will he bring flowers for every occasion, but he will work hard to provide for you. He always thinks about how to make your life better and he excels at being practical, realistic and rational. Sincere, stable and caring, he does not mind cooking if you need him to and nurses you when you are sick. He is the most stable and caring of partners, with only one glitch – he will not feel free to indulge in public displays of affection. Not only is he shy and reserved in public, he also wants to maintain decorum and dignity.

He likes a life of routine and can be very upset if he has to live a day without discipline. In a partner, he looks for someone he can introduce to his mother. He likes a girl his mother can talk to, and who feels comfortable in his home. He does not let his family down and keeps his commitments. There is one thing I must warn you about though – the 'reverse aging' syndrome. Once he is successful, there is a remote possibility that he may stray!

He is an excellent father – caring, responsible, strict and admirable. Actually, he has been training for those fatherly traits all his life. He insists on academic excellence in his children and ensures that they are well turned out and have good manners.

Love and Marriage for Her
This is the perfect wife. She not only cares for you, and fulfils all her duties; she is also ambitious for you. She worries incessantly for every member of the family. A

---
[102] *Hello!*, July 2009

born lady, she carries herself with grace and class. She is not open to wild ideas. She is quite conservative and expects the same from her family.

Never forget to treat her with respect. This lady is no one's doormat. She can readily sever all ties and walk away without a second glance if she does not get the respect she deserves. Her melancholic moods can make her sound negative and she will need a positive and ebullient approach to situations in a partner and will be glad if you provide it. This girl needs social and financial security. If you don't provide it, she will be quite willing to strike out on her own and work for it.

As a mother, she is perfect. Though she is not very sensitive to emotions, she is able to think through every situation in detail. She plans ahead for her children.

At the Workplace
They dream of nothing less than building an empire and work brick by brick to achieve that goal. Absolutely nothing can come between them and their dreams. They shun distractions, make every sacrifice, work harder and single-mindedly pursue their goal.

They are extremely smart and plan every move. They are politically astute and ensure that they use every resource at their disposal to work in their favour. They know that only hard work will not get you where you need, you need to have other forces working for you as well.

They are naturally shy but if they are in a profession where shyness will be a disadvantage, they fight their inner nature to act cool and outgoing. Remember, the Virgo in them is a perfect actor. However, on the inside, they are always plotting and planning. Of course, the planning is supplemented with extreme, meticulous, rigorous and backbreaking hard work. They are the hardest working employees you will find. If you have five VirCaps working for you, you can relax, and go and play golf. Their plan is simple; they make themselves indispensable and take over the reins! You will gladly anoint them your successors.

Money does matter to them and they know their worth. You have to pay them the right amount. But you will be getting a bargain as they easily take on the work of more than two people. They are quite creative and if they give vent to their artistic side they can become highly disciplined writers, actors and artists. They like working on their own rather than in a team, though they are able to delegate work quite well.

Double Earth gives solidity and stability to VirCaps. They will be responsible, focused, caring and above all ambitious. Earth will give them endurance and also ground them.

Famous VirCap Personalities
Abhinav Bindra, Kareena Kapoor, Ranbir Kapoor, Nolwenn Leroy, Netaji Subhash Chandra Bose, Swami Vivekananda, Matt Damon, Lil Wayne, R.V.S. Rathore, Sophia Loren, Carlos Slim, Sundar C., Neil Nitin Mukesh, Princess Mary of Denmark, Ashutosh Kaushik, Anil Agarwal, Jenna Elfman, Burt Reynolds, Betty White, R.L. Stine, C. Subramaniam, Clara Morgane, Jessica Gomes.

62. VIRGO–AQUARIUS

Virgo is ruled by a planet (yet to be re-discovered), which I have dubbed 'Planet Y' and which should rule healing and orderliness. Aquarius is ruled by the eccentric planet of invention and science, Uranus. This is the amalgamation of two diametrically different zodiac signs. Virgo loves discipline, while Aquarius is a free bird; Virgo has clarity of thought while Aquarius thinks of the wackiest ideas; Virgo is duty-minded whereas Aquarius is rebellious. It makes VirAquas a volatile mix of contradictions.

Surprisingly, there are certain traits that dovetail into each other. Virgos prefer to live on their own, being immersed in their work and are quite self-sufficient. Aquarians have a detached air about them. VirAquas may be physically close to you but they seem miles away. They are quite happy being on their own and do not need people around them.

Both Virgos and Aquarians are thinkers but with one basic difference –Virgos are immersed in the details of the task at hand while Aquarians think of the future. They have a geeky appearance and seem lost in thought. They have a faraway look in their eyes as if searching beyond the present. They are very good at dissecting objects, thoughts, theories and people, and try and gauge what makes them tick.

The Virgo ability to break a job down into activities and tasks will be present in them and they can also think of outrageous and unconventional ways to implement the task at hand. Due to Virgo's practical and logical nature the absentminded and inventive genius of Aquarius will not be wasted. Their minds are always working – solving the tasks at hand and the problems of the future.

This is a fabulous combination for scientific pursuits. In fact, everything they do is with a scientific temper. Virgos seek perfection while Aquarians think of amazingly innovative ideas, with a touch of genius in them. VirAquas will think each and every point through and can execute wild ideas brilliantly. The Virgo meticulousness and eye for detail brings an earthiness to their airy thoughts. VirAquas have the ability to bring every idea to a logical and practical conclusion.

They are very health-conscious. The fastidiousness of Virgos and their fanaticism about health combines with the Aquarian fear of germs to make them extremely conscious about cleanliness, food, exercise and health. They know their body and how to cure it; plus, they love reading up on medications and therapies.

VirAquas are always caught up in a conflict between discipline and freedom. Virgo likes making timetables and sticking to them, while Aquarius revolts at too much structure.

They are very random in their approach to money. They can be careful at times and be totally extravagant at others. Novelty excites them and they want to know what makes things work. The wackier and more outlandish the idea or gadget, the more excited they are to spend on it. They also like to save for the long term due to the Aquarian fear of old age but will be quite erratic in their present-day savings.

You cannot hide anything from them. They can read your mind, know instinctively what you need and can dissect every emotion, displayed or hidden.

Strangely, despite knowing everything, they can be very detached. They are just not good with emotions and words. There is a clumsiness to them, which makes them seem awkward and gauche in social situations.

They do not believe in losing their tempers for they see no benefit to it but, once in a while, when things get difficult, they resort to criticising. The duty-mindedness of Virgos is obvious in VirAquas and they are always there for friends and family. You can go to them with a problem and they will solve it in their own way; just do not expect them to give you conventional responses.

Romance is something they don't instinctively understand and because they like solving mysteries, they gravitate towards it. VirAquas think they can dissect everything and study it to learn from it, and they will do the same with romance. Don't expect sentimentality or mushy behaviour from them, they will find the scientific reasons behind love at first sight and attribute it to raging hormones or chemical imbalances. VirAquas enter relationships out of a sense of curiosity and with a desire to learn every nuance of it. From a look to an orgasm – they will treat each with technical precision and attempt perfection.

Every Aquarian is a humanitarian at heart and every Virgo is a healer. These people truly feel for their fellow humans, especially the poor, hungry, old, diseased and underprivileged, and do whatever they can to make a difference.

Virgo–Aquarius – Ravichandran Ashwin
'I won't say if nerd is the right term, but I'm a big, big cricket fanatic. I do carry notebooks and make notes to look at improving and developing my own game.'[103]

'Personally, I am a strong believer in strategy and planning. It is worth it.'

'I am never shy of trying. Every time I think it would work, I go to these games and try.'[104]

There is a dignified restraint in everything he does, there is a method in his approach. His set of principles and values is complemented by the manner in which he understands or should I say reads the mind of the persons around him. He is profound in his views, intellectual in his mind and intelligent with his words.[105]

R. Ashwin has the Virgo desire for perfection and the Aquarian need to think differently.

Love and Marriage for Him
He is a good partner – caring, responsible and duty-conscious. But you wonder at times whether he is really there. He has an aloof air about him. If you need emotional bonding and deep spiritual understanding, this guy cannot deliver and any criticism will drive him away rather than near. Do not expect mushy declarations of love or possessiveness from him.

He makes sure that he fulfils all his obligations. He earns well, looks after you when you are sick and works for the future. It may be difficult for you to understand the change in him from the wooing days, post marriage. The fact is this guy is innately curious and when he fell in love with you, he was curious about you and wanted to know all about the feeling called love. Now that he has you and the

---
[103] http://www.espncricinfo.com/magazine/content/story/559710.html
[104] http://thecricketcouch.com/couch-talk/transcript-couch-talk-with-ravichandran-ashwin/
[105] http://www.cricketnirvana.com/off-the-pitch/2011/July/off-the-pitch-20110722-5.html

mystery is solved, you will see that he is as curious about people he doesn't know. He is too committed to stray but if you want his attention, keep the mystique alive.

As a father, he is extremely caring and very curious about his children. He would want to witness their births and will notice every small change while they are growing. He is very protective and involved in their progress. He is neither controlling nor demanding; he is a friend to them. He will insist on good habits, discipline and education in each child. His clarity of thought will make him an excellent teacher and he will know exactly how to explain even the most obscure of theorems to them.

Love and Marriage for Her
She is soft and feminine, yet there is a totally individualistic streak in her. She has her own rules and does things in her own subtle way. She is very health-conscious. Her family is served the healthiest of foods, and she likes to enforce a routine. She also gets bored of routine and desires something new while she sets the routine in the first place!

She keeps her house neat and clean and keeps on trying new arrangements, hairstyles, clothes, food, etc. She has beautiful eyes that reflect her soul. There is no meanness in her but she needs space to do her own thing and be herself.

As a mother, she is an absolute angel. She nurses her children with care, is dutiful towards their needs and deeply caring of their griefs. She likes teaching them and insists on clarity of thought. They are also taught punctuality, cleanliness and the right behaviour.

At the Workplace
VirAquas are total workaholics. They are extremely curious and have a scientific bent of mind. They are very good at any work that requires tons of dedication and thought. The perfectionism of the Virgo combined with the inquisitiveness of the Aquarian makes them excellent at solving mysteries. It can range from archaeology to anthropology, religion to the boardroom, sports to arts. They revel in probing the unknown, unearthing mysteries and giving futuristic solutions or making path-breaking inventions.

Scientific fields that deal with research and the future are a great fit for VirAquas. You can find them as astrophysicists, astronauts and futuristic thinkers. They bring practicality and logic to their visionary dreams. They excel in the teaching profession too. They do not require adulation or approval but are happy if their work gives them results.

As bosses, they can be quite demanding. Never go to them without facts and figures. They can also be very unpredictable and you never know how they will react or what they will demand.

Earth and Air meet in VirAquas. Earth gives stability and direction to the unorthodox and futuristic thoughts of Aquarius. Detached yet caring, creative yet practical – this sign embodies innovation, work and dedication.

Famous VirAqua Personalities
Ravichandran Ashwin, Madhubala, Ségolène Royal, Feroz Khan, Jacques Kallis, Jamshedji Tata, Morné Morkel, Kim Novak, Haji Mastan, Richie Benaud, Valentino Rossi, Alicia Silverstone, Rohan Bopanna, Michelle Wie, Joan Cusack, Ahmet Davutoğlu, Arjun Tendulkar, Dr. Dre, Rajeev Khandelwal, Ingrid Chauvin, Kirk Thomas Cameron, J.P. Dutta, Mukul S. Anand.

63. VIRGO–PISCES

When Hans Christian Andersen wrote his popular fairy tale 'The Little Mermaid' a couple of centuries ago, little would he have realised that there existed human beings with those selfsame beautiful qualities. A Virgin and a Fish, in combination, can be the epitome of eternal selfless love, supreme sacrifice and even spiritual emancipation.

Virgo-Pisces is a combination of opposites – the meticulous, perfection-seeking Virgo with the deeply sensitive and mysterious Pisces. Pisceans like places and jobs that are open and free, and never seek perfection. Now pair this with the systematic and routine-loving soul of a Virgo – what a mix-up! But it works wonders in bringing perfection to creative work and sensitivity and feeling to meticulous planning.

Pisces is the most compassionate of all the signs while Virgo is a natural healer. VirPisces have a therapeutic effect on people. They are the guardian angels of the zodiac. They feel for you, love you, care for you, worry for you, sympathise with you, understand you, teach you and forgive you, as no one else will.

VirPisces deserve sympathy. Imagine their plight – they can feel what you feel, they understand what you want, but they cannot do exactly what you want if the Virgo purist in them says it is not the right thing to do. The Piscean forgives your juvenile behaviour and thinks of going ahead just to please you. But Virgo stops it again as it clings to the socially accepted, refined way. Well... this is not like the vacillation of Libra but deeper and more unfathomable than that.

They possess extraordinary creativity and originality. Music, arts, theatre and dance are their natural spaces. They can learn, adapt, mimic and replicate fabulously as a Piscean and perfect it fastidiously as a Virgo. They take art to a scientific level and make science into an artistic activity. Neptune will make them want to delve into the mysterious and esoteric while their Virgo clarity will make them see the logic and truth in the mysterious. They have a deep spiritual and religious side and nurture their mystical leanings.

Both Pisces and Virgo are feminine signs, so VirPisces are soft in their approach. They are gentle, kind, well behaved, pleasant and cultured. They are never violent or abusive. They are very shy and don't open up easily to strangers. Ego is almost absent in them and they will not seek the limelight. They definitely become critical when they are angry. Do not try the same tactic on them for they get hurt easily and become very defensive. They are extremely emotional and sensitive.

Their love for perfection makes them seek solitude in crowds. They prefer to inhabit a world of their own. VirPisces are natural worriers and can strain themselves to the breaking point trying to fulfil all their obligations. Life is hard for them as they are constantly pushing themselves to be good and do not like to display even the smallest negative characteristic. VirPisces hate the strain this creates and constantly battle the stress that pits their Piscean sensibilities and otherworldliness against the Virgoan search for purity and perfection.

Romance will come naturally to them, once they overcome the Virgoan shyness of the opposite sex. The Pisces in them can be very poetic in their expression of love and they will always know what their partner wants. They will be constant and true if they find someone who understands their pensive moods and occasional crankiness.

They are very fussy about how their food is cooked and what they eat. They have their particular likings and do not like them changed. They are also susceptible to addictions. This is very strange, for on one hand they are all for health and on the other, they are prone to addictions that affect their health. It will be the perennial tussle of their lives. The Piscean bane is self-destruction; they might not think twice before destroying what they worked hard at creating. They can also reject the realities of life and live in their own fantasy world if the world seems too harsh. They need a lot of love and understanding to hold on to their positive traits.

The biggest issue with them is non-communication. They carry extreme hurt within them if you are insensitive to them. They will never verbalise their hurt as saying things out loud hurts them even more as they feel *you* should have been sensitive to them in the first place. Many of them put up a façade of being rude or haughty just to escape hurt.

Insecurities loom large in their lives. Both Pisces and Virgo are afflicted by low self-esteem and feel inadequate. Only strong individuals who can put up with their constant mood swings, control their self-destructiveness and constantly motivate them when they are down can bring out the best in these people. VirPisces see the world with all its flaws and imperfections and still accept it as it is. They only slowly learn to look beyond the details and marvel at the abundance and diversity of the Universe.

Virgo–Pisces – Ajay Devgn
'I really don't know how to capitalise on success. I believe that one's work speaks the most…I can't shout from rooftops about the number of hits I have given and all that.'[106]

'I still don't do as much (publicity) as others and I don't think I ever can. I am an introvert. I prefer not to talk about myself.'

Rohit Shetty, director, on Ajay Devgn: 'He understands the logistics of film making brilliantly. The producers trust him because he doesn't put a price tag on his work.'[107]

Ajay Devgn has the strong Virgo code of ethics but is grounded like a Piscean: a true VirPisces indeed.

Love and Marriage for Him
This guy is so committed and sensitive that it is hard for you to emulate him. Do not even try, for he needs you to be different. He fills his life with responsibility and duty and strives to achieve both with perfection.

He needs a partner who does not dominate him. Though he is mild, there are certain things that he insists upon, especially if they affect his health or routine. If you don't understand him, he can be deceptive about certain things. He will say yes to you while doing them on the sly, for he will generally not like to fight.

He is very committed to his work and it plays a prominent role in his life. He never shirks responsibilities. He needs your help in fulfilling his duties.

---
[106] *Stardust*, August 2010
[107] *Hi! Blitz*, September 2011

His criticism is mostly justified. Do understand that he just wants you to be as perfect as possible.

This guy has the ability to talk to anyone with genuine warmth and understanding. As a father, he is caring and loving. He is definitely not controlling or dominating and knows exactly what his children need. His duty-consciousness makes him attend parent-teacher meetings and he knows the names of all his children's teachers and friends!

Love and Marriage for Her
She is the quintessential lady with a dignified manner about her despite her childlike smile. The best thing about her is her ability to get along with and have compassion for anyone. Despite her girlish ways, she is quite capable of managing the home and an entire gang of in-laws. But she becomes stressed-out by the end of the day, after going through her Virgo routine; more so as the Piscean in her is wired to absorb every emotion from people around.

She makes you the centre of her existence. She is tuned to your ways, and knows what you are thinking before you do. She is not bossy and is happy to let you rule. She is very sensitive and gets hurt easily; yet she can hide her pain. She can be a bit of a nag and be critical of certain behaviour. She is also prone to extreme mood swings.

She has a lot of home remedies for medical problems. As a mother, she is loving and nurturing. She instinctively knows her children inside-out and does not need to read parental help books.

At the Workplace
The Virgo eye for detail and the Piscean talent for originality makes VirPisces extremely focused in whatever they do. They work on their ideas without caring about applause or different views.

They can be excellent psychiatrists and counsellors with their compassion and desire to heal. They can also be artists who bring in precision and focus to their art. Their attention to detail and workaholic nature make them good at any profession, but what distinguishes them is their empathy and sheer sensitivity in professional life. This empathy makes them excellent teachers and doctors.

As bosses, they are absolute softies. They know that they can't say 'no' to you, so use strong middlemen to handle you. If VirPisces like their work and get a spiritual 'high' from it, they will not put a price tag to their work.

Earth and Water meet in this extremely sensitive combination. VirPisces will be creatively diligent and meticulously creative – a fabulous mixture of opposites.

Famous VirPisces Personalities
Ajay Devgn, Dev Anand, Shashi Kapoor, Brooklyn Decker, Mahatma Jyotiba Phule, Tommy Hilfiger, Sir Richard Burton, Hansie Cronje, Catherine Zeta-Jones, Allu Arjun, Mouni Roy, Alice Walton, Sharad Kelkar, Polly Umrigar, Rudolph Newreyev, Andrew Jackson, Bhajanlal, Darshan Jariwala, Alagappa Chettiyar, Darby Crash, Asia Argento, Jeremy Irons, Senthil.

64. LIBRA–SCORPIO

LibScorps combine the beauty, grace and smile of Libra with the deep passions and power of Scorpio. It is the coming together of the creative and airy Venus with the dark and ruthless Pluto. LibScorps have a mesmerising smile that may be paired with playful dimples. They talk in the most cultured and sweet manner; do not get swayed by their sweet and innocent ways and think that they are harmless or helpless creatures. They have a spine of steel and are extremely strong.

The Libran love for communication and skill at expressing ideas combined with Scorpio intensity makes them amazing communicators. They love arguing and debating and can spend hours convincing people of their point of view. They can be very talkative or be given to soft ponderous words. Their extremely powerful communication skills make them stand out on the stage to give fabulous, deeply moving and inspiring orations before a mesmerised audience. They can almost touch and feel the pulse of the audience!

They are highly perceptive. They are able to read your mind and know your deepest thoughts. LibScorps are also very good at analysing your approach and their consequent reactions will be thought out to the last detail. It makes them very good as negotiators and diplomats for they can easily mask their thoughts under the Libran smile while taking carefully analysed, determined actions. LibScorps have a well-developed sense of humour and are able to laugh off everyday situations. They also have a streak of sarcasm and dark humour in them.

Love is very important to both Libra and Scorpio. Libras are eternally in love and are incomplete without a mate. Scorpios, on the other hand, display immense passion in love. The natural Scorpio ability to delve into the erotic as fervently as into the esoteric, makes love an enduring passion for them. LibScorps understand love from a very young age and are adept at the spiritual, emotional and physical expressions of love. They can even die for their love and are true romantics when expressing their love.

Libran indecisiveness afflicts them. The Libran in them does not want to be impartial. They go through extreme mental torment before coming to a decision. Yet once they reach a decision, they stick to it. LibScorps can appear very lazy at times. The Libran indolence affects them and they take things easy till the last moment. When deadlines approach, they work in a frenzy and rush to complete the task. They need to learn to divide work into workable parts.

The sweet Libran smile and the Scorpio ability to mask their true feelings makes LibScorps quite devious. They smile even when they are boiling inside and can be very vindictive. It is prudent to be careful about them despite their inherent sweetness. A LibScorp sportsperson will virtually kill you on the field but flash a charming smile after the murder attempt. They do everything to excess – they think too much, talk too much, love too much, eat too much, play too much, laze around too much or work too much.

More than money, they want fame, power and appreciation. They use money to enhance their power, prestige and, of course, comforts. Luxury and beauty attract them. They like to be well groomed and to smell good, given their sensitivity to smells and fragances. They have Libra's elegance and Scorpio's magnetic appeal and instinctively know how to use their strengths effectively. It's a heady mix for sure – the sweet Libran charm and the charismatic alluring depths of the Scorpio.

They have a special interest in unravelling the deepest mysteries of the occult and the supernatural. Love, sensuality, sex and spirituality have deeper meaning for them and they feel that somehow all of these are intertwined.

They have a fabulous aesthetic sense and are glamorously fashionable. They have a highly developed sense of colour, coordination and design. Music, arts and creativity flourish in them. They have an extraordinary understanding and deep-rooted obsession for anything that needs lots of passion and is artistic – it could be music, acting, dancing, martial arts or even pottery.

Libra–Scorpio – Sardar Vallabhbhai Patel
Sardar Vallabhbhai Jhaverbhai Patel is known for helping in integrating India into a united, independent nation. Therefore, he is also regarded as the 'Bismarck of India' and the 'Iron Man of India'.[108]

He coaxed, cajoled and even forced the rulers of forty princely states into joining India after independence. Without the efforts of the 'Strong Man of India' we would not have the Indian map in the shape we know so well.

He reputedly cultivated a stoic character—a popular anecdote recounts how he lanced a painful boil without hesitation, even as the barber who was supposed to do it, trembled.

Sardar Patel knew how to communicate his ideas with zeal and diplomacy, a true LibScorp indeed!

Love and Marriage for Him
This is a one-woman man. He is totally committed and fully in love with you, but you find him changing through the different stages of life. During the courtship period, there is no one as intensely romantic as him. But he finds it difficult to keep up the same intensity when he is married. He will still love, care and worship you but the Scorpio in him will want to achieve something.

There is a way to get him to be more expressive and it's by using tact. Just tell him sweetly that his work comes before you and watch how the Libran love for balance make him express how *you* always come first!

He has the Libran sense of justice and fairness plus the Scorpio perceptiveness, so he can see through any subterfuge. Of course, he has a temper, but I am sure you know how to deal with it and it is not by being aggressive.

As a father, he enforces discipline and believes that his children should behave in a certain way. He wants them to be exposed to the realities of life and does not shelter them from unpleasant facts. He is soft and permissive at times but it is better if they do not cross the line.

Love and Marriage for Her
She has a spine of steel despite her sweet, soft, mesmerising smile. She is extremely strong and determined and nothing can shake her. She will love you to death and

---
[108] Wikipedia

she just needs a passionate reciprocation from you. She is totally dedicated to the relationship. You have to be as involved and as appreciative of her as she is of you, but do not stifle her with over-protectiveness. Let her do things her way and she will not disappoint you.

If she has chosen you, you must be someone special. Do not let go of the trust she has placed in you. She is a one-man woman and can be ruthlessly vindictive if deceived. Handle her with care and love and be absolutely faithful if you value peace and happiness.

She is extremely creative and needs to channelise her abundant passions into a creative pursuit. She can balance work and home well. She is the perfect partner for your business; no one can be as persuasive and determined, without being offensive, as her. She will be proud to be an asset to you.

As a mother, she is disciplined and caring. A bit too loving for sure, she wants her children to be under her nurturing control and finds it difficult to let go. She can understand their points of view as well.

At the Workplace
LibScorps are a great combination of a cardinal and a fixed sign. Hence, they can lead, impress and ensure the work gets done. They deliver results. Extremely passionate and driven, they communicate their ideas beautifully to motivate others with the same fire. They do not run away from hard work, and are ready to start at the bottom. They are very loyal, and will stick on if they see long-term value in your organisation.

You can expect them to have a very democratic approach. They do not have a domineering presence; they like asking for everybody's opinion and then decide on a plan of action. They acknowledge the efforts and ideas of subordinates and colleagues. A LibScorp is a good boss and an excellent team player for sure. However, do not take advantage of their good nature for the Scorpio desire to command still exists.

With their first-rate communication skills, they can excel as coaches and educators. Actually, any field that requires a sense of balance and determination is good for them. They can be in sports or have creative careers as dancers, artists, singers and actors. Whatever they do, they will take it to a new level with a rare blending of zeal and grace.

Air and Water meet in this combination to impart passion and a sense of balance. LibScorps are dedicated yet expansive with brilliant views but open to discussion and possess an energy that is infectious.

Famous LibScorp Personalities
Sardar Vallabhbhai Patel, Bruce Lee, Robin Uthappa, Rahul Sharma, V. Prabhakaran, Waqar Younis, Irfan Pathan, Salim Khan, Miley Cyrus, Tusshar Kapoor, Celina Jaitley, Marie Antoinette, Edwin Booth, Pooja Batra, Manju Warrier, Bjork, Xabi Alanso, Michael Owen, Kelly Osbourne, Seth MacFarlane, Ravindra Jadeja, Hetty Green, Vasantdada Patil, Carl Sagan, Rajpal Yadav, Roja Selvamani, Callum Ferguson, Mamta Mohandas, Nathan Lyon, Anne M. Mulcahy, Yashwant Sinha, Tisca Chopra, Kulbhushan Kharbanda, Chad Taylor, Vanessa Lachey, Archana Vijaya, Arianny Celeste, Masaba Gupta.

65. LIBRA–SAGITTARIUS

Venus, the planet of beauty and love, meets the intelligent and highly ambitious Sagittarius. Air and Fire breathe their power into LibSags and make them light and airy with a burning desire for success. They are characterised by the loudest laughter, the coolest clothes and an air of assured intelligence. Their flamboyance, loud body language and unmistakable style may be misinterpreted for arrogance. Once you get to know them, though, you realise how helpful, honest and gentle they are.

LibSags communicate beautifully and put forth their ideas and dreams with such brilliant words that you will root for their cause. Good orators, they appeal to people on an intellectual and idealistic level. They love the applause too. The forthrightness of the Sagittarius and the diplomacy of the Libran meet seamlessly in them. They always tell the truth but without letting it sound bitter.

Chirpy and fun loving, they are very friendly and can talk for hours upon wild ideas and fun-packed schemes. They have heart-melting smiles and light up any gathering with their charm and exuberance. Jupiter adds a glow to their intelligence and they are very good at grasping abstract theories. Both Sagittarius and Libra are intelligent signs. They have the knack of examining and scrutinising. Interestingly, they are analytical, yet they love the thrill of taking risks in almost every aspect of life.

LibSags dream big – they are path-breakers. Their ambitions are selfless and include all those who matter to them. Their ideas are sometimes vague because of the lack of the Earth element. In the beginning, one thing they are sure of is that they want to make it big but are confused about the how, when and why. They become super-confident once they clearly know what that *big* idea is that they will chase all their lives.

Possessing an independent and adventurous streak, rock climbing and rafting and bungee jumping hold no fears for them. Ideals matter a lot to them. They are ever ready to fight for a cause they believe in. LibSags have a code of morality, which they rarely breach. They care about people in general. Though they have a bit of a rebellious streak, they tend to philosophise and think of the various problems facing the world. They master the art of acting individualistically without hurting anyone.

They are also spiritually highly evolved and can talk interestingly on the subject for hours. They are believers and believe that everything happens for a reason. Prudence in money matters does not come easily to them. They love possessing lots of things, especially expensive branded items.

LibSags might have a hard time finding the right partner and often confuse friendship with love. The Libran in them needs to be in love to feel complete but due to their Sagittarian streak, they will be afraid of settling down and losing their single status and independence. They spend hours analysing and scrutinising their friends to see if they are 'The One'. Their dissections will be deep but will lack emotional knowledge. This inability to read people will make them prone to mistakes. If they realise that they picked the wrong cookie, they will not cling or weep. After all, LibSag is a double masculine sign, charming yet strong. They will not be felled by a broken heart and will not be vindictive, either. It is possible for them to remain friends with their exes. Their hearts are pure, completely free of malice.

Lacking the sensitivity of Water, they take people and events at face value and can often be deceived. They are so open and honest themselves that they do not expect people to be manipulative. It takes them time to learn the ways of the world but they never change into malicious people themselves. They retain their frank and honest ways and fair dealings. However, they do have really fiery tempers that only mellow with age and reason. They get especially angry when they see injustice done to anyone. Their fighting instincts are awakened at those times.

Their concern to take the right decisions and the resulting indeciveness and procrastination can be their common bane. The Sagittarian carefree attitude and Libran exuberance can gift a *joie de vivre* to them, which may annoy the sensitive and serious people around them.

They have an extraordinary instinct for anything artistic and aesthetic. Venus blesses them with a keen musical sense and when combined with the uninhibited enthusiasm of Jupiter, they can be extraordinarily adept at all expressions of art including dancing and composing. They are highly colour-coordinated and always manage to dress well. They are ever ready for three things in life – food, love and art.

Libra–Sagittarius – Deepika Padukone
'I'm a very giving person. I don't expect anything in return. I give my 100 per cent. There is no guard when I'm in the relationship.'

Prakash Padukone: 'She is very determined, very focused. She was always sure of what she wanted in life.'

'My entire persona can be summed up in two words 'gentle tigress'.'[109]

'YES! I am a woman. I have breasts AND a cleavage! You got a problem!!??'[110] (Deepika's Twitter outrage over a *Times of India* article, 'OMG! Deepika's cleavage show!')

'I have spoken out against an ideology that such regressive tactics are still being employed to draw a reader's attention at a time when we are striving for women's equality and empowerment.'

Sportsperson, romantic, honest, a fighter with no grey shades to her personality – Deepika is a true LibSag indeed.

Love and Marriage for Him
He loves to be romantic, but feels stifled with too much emotion and cannot handle tears. If you are looking for a soul-to-soul connect, he is not the guy for it. He expresses his love by surprising you with travel plans and outings. He likes a partner who is strong and independent. Honesty attracts him and he needs a mate who is more practical than him.

His temper is fiery and only reason and logic make him rethink his anger. He loves to talk and explain his views and loves to hear your views. Analysis and argument are his ways of thinking things through. He does not like to hurt you but sometimes he says the wrong thing at the wrong time. The best way to deal with his insensitive remarks is to tell him that you don't like them. He will not utter the same words again.

He likes a house where things are in place and the furniture is well coordinated. Please take care of the money for he can be quite careless in his spending habits. He likes a gamble in life and likes taking risks.

---
[109] https://www.youtube.com/watch?v=bxVGsWkZ0po
[110] https://www.facebook.com/DeepikaPadukone/posts/722345794506193

He becomes more comfortable with fatherhood as his children grow older. He likes talking to them and explaining things. He loves playing with them and bonds over camping trips and treks. He teaches them to live a life of ideals and adventure.

Love and Marriage for Her
She cannot be tied down to home and chores for long. This girl thrives in the outdoors. Take her out often and indulge her fun-loving streak. Then, she stays happy and committed. She is a thinking girl. Also, don't go by her soft demeneour: she has nerves of steel.

Though she may not be excessively emotional, she can get hurt easily. She is deeply sentimental and cannot live without a partner. She puts you on a pedestal and is an ideal mate. She is the epitome of naïve truthfulness but there is no malice in her. The only things she expects from you are companionship and truthfulness. She needs to talk – a lot! It will never be a monologue; you need to participate actively, too.

She has a secret fear of the in-laws and family ties. She will be warm and charming with them; but don't expect her to be a slave to their every word. Ease her worries and help her form smooth relationships with your family.

As a mother, she is total fun. Her ideas are never forced upon her children, but she will lack the ability to understand the emotions behind her children's sulks and silences.

At the Workplace
Ambitious, astute and superb communicators, LibSags excel in careers that require intelligence. They love moving around, talking, expounding and developing ideas. They can be wonderful mediators. They are extremely honest and idealistic and do not like being manipulated. They work for glory and ideals rather than money.

Their ambitions could be scattered in the beginning. Once they are sure of their chosen field they go all out and then no scale is too big for them. They are fabulously artistic and make passionate dancers, extraordinary singers and amazing musicians. Their love for the stage and applause sees them gravitate towards showbiz. The unbridled enthusiasm of Sagittarius and the extraordinary sense of balance of Libra make them phenomenal in sports.

As bosses, they are democratic, liberal and understanding. They are fine with your schedule and way of working as long as you deliver and are loyal. They are idealistic, pioneering and visionary leaders but need support in practical implementation. In finance and meticulous planning, they would be well advised to hire a Virgo or a Capricorn to do the job.

Light as air yet volatile, LibSags are independent and spirited. Driven yet analytical, freedom loving and honest – you get what you see with them.

Famous LibSag Personalities
Ratan Tata, A.R. Rehman, Deepika Padukone, Shahid Afridi, Tabu, Ryan Gosling, M.S. (Vindi) Banga, Nicholas Cage, Orlando Bloom, Nadia Comăneci, Allan Donald, Pravesh Rana,Sanjay Khan, Kunal Kapoor, Swapnil Joshi, Ali Nuri Bahá'u'lláh, Chris Evert, Mehboob Khan, Gerard Butler.

66. LIBRA–CAPRICORN

Venus, the planet of grace and beauty, and Saturn, the old and wise planet of restraints, combine in this wise yet beautiful combination. LibCaps love talking. They talk so well that it is difficult to refute them. The Libran way of looking at both sides of the issue and Capricorn maturity makes them easily view an issue from different perspectives and reach a balanced decision.

Friendly and charming, they find it easy to connect to people who can help them succeed. They can be seen by many as social climbers but the Libran fairness usually stops them from taking advantage of others. Mature and responsible, they act older than their age and can astound you with their wisdom. Though the Capricorn in them makes them shrewd, the Libra in them reduces the self-centredness of Capricorn and makes them accommodative.

They may come from the humblest of backgrounds but they possess an extraordinarily finesse and polished communication skills. When they speak in those velvety-soft voices that exude elegance, poise and maturity, you just listen, utterly impressed. You get swayed not just by their command over the language but also by the depth and breadth of their understanding, which underlines their potential.

Family is extremely important to them. They want their families to be happy and are willing to do anything to ensure this. LibCaps want to see their family status rise. They stay away from anything that can harm their reputation. Their twin commitments in life are family and career and they balance both extraordinarily well.

LibCaps are secretly ambitious. The innate astuteness of a Capricorn makes them very shrewd; they know how to talk to whom in order to get their work done. Libra makes the virtues of Capricorn stand out in a polished manner. The pout is replaced by a cultured smile, solitude is replaced by friendliness and the grim personality is transformed into a suave, multi-talented go-getter.

There is one common thread in Libra and Capricorn and that is love. Librans always have love on their minds. They need a companion and are in love with the concept of love. Capricorns on the other hand want to be with the best person in terms of money, position, family or lineage. So LibCaps look for love and status in the same person. You can't really call them gold diggers because when they are in love they will do anything. LibCaps, with the sacrificing streak of Capricorn and the Libra's desire for love, will not mind sacrificing anything for their family. They do want their love to be approved by society and will be heartbroken if it is not. They can give up all for their love and will not think twice about giving up even their career for it. But you can be sure that they will never choose their partner recklessly.

Money is very important too, not only as an investment but also as a means of spending. They do save but there can be times when the Libran urge to spend overtakes them. LibCaps are definitely not messy creatures. They like clean, colour co-ordinated rooms and feel disoriented in rooms that lack organisation.

LibCaps are extraordinarily talented. Every Libran has a melodious voice and can sing, dance or compose. Every Capricorn has a hidden artistic talent in them that they are too shy to express, but Libra will liberate them. LibCaps are known to even go aggressively after a career in music or the arts.

Anger is almost missing in them. The usual way they show their displeasure is through sarcasm. The Libran smile will hide the melancholy of Capricorn, but it will always be present silently. LibCaps worry about finances and the lack of financial stability can unhinge their smile. The fear of poverty is the biggest fear for LibCaps and they will never let that become an eventuality.

Decision-making could be a problem as they suffer extreme vacillations due to the Libran indecisiveness. The lack of Water in this combination ensures that they are not too sensitive about things; on the flip side they cannot comprehend what goes on in your mind till you spell it out. But they make up for it with their empathy. The Capricornian tendency to age in reverse will be slightly diluted but present in LibCaps. You can expect them to shed some of their earlier maturity as they age and become more fun-loving.

Libra–Capricorn – Eminem
'Even as a kid, I always wanted the most words to rhyme. Say I saw a word like 'transcendalistic tendencies'. I would write – trans-cend-a-lis-tic ten-den-cies – and underneath, I'd line a word up with each syllable: and bend all mystic sentence trees.'[111]

'A lot of it might have to do with moving around so much as a kid, never having stability. My kids are comfortable here – I want them to have the stability I didn't. And it's also nostalgic. Being a few miles from where I grew up, being used to the people, the mentality.'

Eminem has the LibCap way with words and its love of family.

Love and Marriage for Him
He is a fabulous companion and lover. This is one guy to whom you can talk your heart out. He loves to talk, laugh and philosophise with you. He may say 'No' to the world but not to you! Remember; tell him what you feel, for though he will love you, he won't understand your deepest concerns till you tell him. He lacks sensitivity and deep penetrative understanding.

He loves his home and relaxes in its comfort. A messy room makes him start talking about the virtues of cleanliness. He is also quite romantic and you never have to remind him of your special days.

He wants to reach the top and you must realise that, for he will never state the breadth of his ambitions. He is not aggressive and is fine with the idea of you working. His only stipulation would be that you do not neglect the home. When you marry him, you marry his family too, as he is very close to his family. Of course, he includes his in-laws in his family as well.

He is a fantastic and caring father. He lives his childhood through his children and plans meticulously for a stable and secure future for them. He knows just what to say to them and is never over-protective or aggressive.

---

[111] http://www.rollingstone.com/music/news/eminem-on-the-road-back-from-hell-20111017#ixzz293ZT7Rmi

Love and Marriage for Her
She knows how to balance her home and work perfectly. As a partner, she loves being in control but in such a way that you do not mind. Charming and soft-spoken, she is definitely the power behind her man. Both of you can go places if you share your ambitions with her. She will work tirelessly to further your cause and help you in whatever way possible in your career. Even if she does extremely well in her career she will always be there for you.

Family is very important to her and she can sacrifice a lot for it. Remember, when we talk about family, it also includes yours. She is absolutely devoted in love and would do anything for you. She is very good at flirting and knows to use her voice and expressions to convey a whole range of feelings. Though she loves to shop, she knows the best places to get the best bargains without compromising on quality.

As a mother, she blends discipline with fun. Her children know their limits and learn tact and grace from her. She wants them to succeed and loves planning their lives. She ensures that they respect their father as much as her.

At the Workplace
Both Libra and Capricorn are cardinal signs, so they definitely have it in them to rise to the top. They are masters of networking and of being at the right place at the right time. They know how to give the right sound bites and make a situation work in their favour. They beautifully manage their image and portray themselves as the successor-in-waiting. Money and status are what they crave. They will tread a path that leads to leaving behind an extraordinary legacy. They are never content until they reach their goals.

They know what they want and get it with tact and diplomacy. Their skills of organising, delegating and communicating ideas clearly to others makes them very good at handling issues and people. They understand the nuances of power and politics, and are super-smooth operators. They revel in power games in the boardrooms or even national politics. They are good at art too and unlike many artists, they know how to market and sell their wares.

Phenomenal communication skills combined with a shrewd mind for business make LibCaps formidable business leaders. As a boss, they will nurture you and be father figures, but they will know your exact worth and pay accordingly. They are those bosses who will win popularity contests and still deliver results.

Air and Earth combine in LibCaps to make them creative yet stable. They have the ambition to lead and the power to charm the crown right out of your hands.

Famous LibCap Personalities
Eminem, M.G. Ramachandran, James Dean, Matthew Hayden, Kate Moss, Lauren Conrad, Alfred Nobel, Mike Shinoda, Amrita Singh, Bela Lugosi, Theodoros Zagorakis, Kamalika Guha Thakurta, Aravind Adiga, Sandilyan.

67. LIBRA–AQUARIUS

Venus, the planet of love and beauty, meets the most intelligent and wacky planet, Uranus, in this exciting combination. This is a double Air combination and Air signs are the most intelligent.

LibAquas can talk upon any subject with an ease and clarity that denotes high levels of confidence. Their knowledge and their unique take on issues ranging from the mundane to the obscure can perplex you. They are highly individualistic and can communicate their ideas in a lively manner.

Their Aquarian genius will make them think of untried ideas that seem too futuristic for conventional people. The dreaminess in their eyes may not convince you but their minds can think of things that would be common fifty years down the line. When they explain those ideas with the Libran gift of the gab you are transfixed by the brilliance of their minds. Originality is their trademark, be it in thought, word or deed.

They are extraordinarily talented. Their talents can range from mimicking to acting, singing to dancing, acting to directing. They can also be fantastic poets and writers. They can adopt some seriously different, quirky and interesting hobbies. The best thing about their art is that they are always improvising and have ten different way of doing the same thing. They are extremely spontaneous and refreshingly original.

Curious and honest, they make great friends. They are humanitarians, with a deep, penetrative understanding of human minds. There is nothing you can do that will shock them. They are so empathetic that they know what you are going through just by looking at you. But the important thing to note is that as both the signs are Air, they will remain aloof and will not go overboard like a Cancerian or a Piscean to alleviate your pain. They will understand and sympathise, even advise and lecture but will expect you to nurse your problems yourself. Don't expect bear hugs from them when you are sulking. They are a little uncomfortable expressing tender feelings.

They have a hilariously wacky sense of humour. LibAquas seem to pull pranks out of thin air and their witticisms are truly original.

Aquarius gives them a lot of integrity and honesty. Add the Libran desire for justice and you have unshakeably truthful people whom you can rely upon. Humanitarian issues and inequality bother them a lot. They are able to talk and transmit their feelings with such resounding clarity that no one can resist their rallying cry for justice.

Love will find them a bit perplexed. Librans are made for romantic love while Aquarians love humanity and are uncomfortable with the idea of loving only one person. If you are their first love they will cherish you for the rest of their lives, but you can expect them to have more loves than one. Libra can make them marry young but look around later in life due to the innate Aquarian curiosity. They can fall into a trap: of treating love as an experiment. They can spend their lives sweet-talking, meeting new partners to decode new ideas and then moving on. The only way they stay true in a relationship is if they also have a passion, an occupation to still and focus their ever-wandering minds.

They are die-hard romantics but do not expect high levels of emotional caring from them. They will always help you when you are in need but there is a certain aloofness that makes them remain detached.

LibAquas are double Air signs. This makes them build castles in the air despite their intelligence. They need friends and family to infuse practical earthy elements to their inventive thoughts. The passion of the Fire signs is also missing in this combination. This makes it difficult for them to reach their goals – intelligence alone might not help.

Though they speak with clarity, do not expect their minds to be clear or focused. Too many thoughts and ideas keep attracting them. The Libran tendency of over-analysing to reach a balance will make it very difficult for them to take decisions. Also, the lazy Libra can keep postponing decisions and indulge in procrastination.

Their biggest threat is the habit of getting bored with things and moving on too soon. They start every project with enthusiasm but lose interest midway. Their ever-changing nature makes it difficult for them to choose a path in life. Also, LibAquas are so intelligent and talented in so many things that it takes them time to focus on one activity. Their intelligence can even work to their disadvantage at times. They can dissipate their energies and scatter their talents without finding a meaningful vocation. Or they can be those forever-changing and evolving geniuses. Their extreme unpredictability can be a boon or a bane.

Libra–Aquarius – Shammi Kapoor

Naseeruddin Shah: 'The greatest lesson I have learnt from Shammi Kapoor is that a predictable actor is the most boring one. With Shammi, you never knew what he was going to do, even when you saw his performances a second and third time.'[112]

'I discovered Internet before you got Internet in India. I am on Apple and they gave us a website called eWorld in 1994. And by the time Internet came to India in 1995 via VSNL, we were already first-marchers… already *sab kuch dekh liya tha*.'[113]

Shammi's unpredictability, futuristic views, romanticism and *joie de vivre* exemplifies the best of LibAqua.

Love and Marriage for Him

He is your best friend who loves, understands and listens to you patiently. He is not a conventional husband. His views are too futuristic to be traditional. However, he will definitely save for your old age together.

There is one problem, though. Despite his smooth talk and funny banter, he does not always seem to share the same planet with you. There is a certain aloofness in him that makes it seem as if he is a bystander and not a partner in your life.

He will decode your reactions before they occur but he will still lack sensitivity. He is a sweet guy but not the person who can cry and smile with you. He will understand why you feel sad but don't expect flowers or mollycoddling to follow that understanding. Though he never stops you from getting what you want, be careful not to splurge, as he doesn't have it in him to save.

---

[112] *Cine Blitz*, 2011, 'Unforgettable Shammi Kapoor
[113] http://www.santabanta.com/cinema.asp?pid=48755, 'The Shammi Kapoor interview you may have Missed'

He is a wonderful father. His children hear fascinating stories from him and he makes them think beyond their schoolbooks. He is very understanding of their needs and never pushes them in directions they do not choose to go.

Love and Marriage for Her

Libran and Aquarian girls are the most beautiful in the zodiac and a LibAqua girl is truly very pretty, with a luminous smile and soulful eyes. She dresses well and can even wear wild colours and exotic fashion items without looking weird. She can carry off a lot of things that look awkward on others.

She loves to talk! She has so many views, and is so intelligent, that she cannot keep her ideas to herself. From motorcycling to paranormal sciences, everything excites her. She loves doing things that men generally do, like camping, trekking and driving a jeep.

As a mother, she is caring and loving. Her days cannot be bound by routine and she is better at handling her kids when they are over four years old. She needs lots of help before that. She is their best friend and not shocked by any of their views.

At the Workplace

Their biggest challenge is finding where they want to go, because they are too good at too many things. They run the danger of being a jack of all trades and master of none. This highly intelligent combination needs a lot of time to fix upon its interests. They prefer careers that offer them change rather than one that is bound by routine. They need to be interested in what they do. Sales and advertising, and even software development – fields that are dynamic – are the ones that interest them as they provide a platform for them to learn new things every day.

The Libra in them makes them good at expressing their views and convincing people, but their obvious talents should not be wasted on mundane activities. They are better at selling ideas to huge groups or even corporations. Human resources could also be a good space for them; they make excellent mentors, trainers, and teachers. They bring a breath of fresh air to anything that they touch, especially in the creative field. They need ideas, more than money, to stay motivated.

The cardinal Libra in them makes them good leaders when their time comes. Though they will take their time in reaching a decision, once they decide, they will be firm in their beliefs. They will have a democratic style of leadership and will be very inclusive. This is one boss who will support trade unions and has genuine interest in employee welfare.

Double Air makes LibAquas pioneers who try the untested and espouse views that seem improbable and farfetched.

Famous LibAqua Personalities

Shammi Kapoor, Wayne Rooney, Nawaz Sharif, Robbie Williams, Anjali Tendulkar, Raveena Tandon, Grace Kelly, Elizabeth Taylor, Alan Rickman, Brad Haddin, Maulana Azad, Michelangelo, Mark Sanchez, Donald Sadoway, Anushka Shetty, Sohrab Modi, Darsheel Safary, Salim Ali, Winona Ryder, Mitchell Marsh, Eduardo Saverin.

68. LIBRA–PISCES

Venus, the planet of beauty, grace and luxury, teams up with the deep and mysterious planet, Neptune. LibPisces marks the coming together of two extremely artistic signs. Creativity, originality and adaptability are the hallmarks of LibPisces.

LibPisces have an easy charm and exude the radiance of positivity and grace. Even in rare moments of anger, they maintain their poise. The five things that are essential to them are love, peace, the arts, food and change. They are stylish, with a pronounced fashion sense and know how to dress for each occasion.

Balance in life and work is what the Libran in them craves and they strive to surround themselves with peace and harmony. LibPisces are never aggressive, loud or dominating. They like to get their work done with the least possible stress and they will walk away from advantageous situations just to avoid confrontations with aggressive opponents. It takes a lot of courage to do that.

Emotional and sensitive, with well-developed communication skills, they impress with their knowledge. They are good at weighing the pros and cons of anything. The Libran in them will analyse and be fair in their decisions. They will see the good in the bad and the bad in the good. The communicative spirit in them makes LibPisces love to talk and share their views.

They are the epitome of empathy. Librans easily put themselves in the other person's shoes and Pisceans can simply *live* your exact emotions. They understand the fear of a child, are compassionate towards the loneliness of the elderly, and would even give the benefit of the doubt to someone who had tried to kill them. They are spiritually inclined and have a deep understanding of the known, the unknown and the metaphysical realms.

They may love to argue, but they neither give way to anger nor indulge in an egoistic battle of words. They argue to reach an impartial and balanced decision. Anger and aggression are not part of their emotional make up and if they ever act that way, it means that they are still reaching for that balance. This need for balancing and thinking things through makes them keep on postponing decisions and procrastinating.

The Piscean tendency to live in their dreams can see their world coming apart when faced with the harsh realities of life. They like to eat when depressed, a fact that does nothing to alleviate their feelings. Pisces is known for its addictions. When LibPisces turn to addictions in search of balance, it can unravel them. In bad moods, they turn their communication skills to deadly use through sarcastic comments. Lazy Libra and escapist Pisces also make them susceptible to shunning responsibilities.

Smiling and cheerful, they are not inherently pessimistic. So when their dreams don't come true, or problems arise, they don't know what to do. They may even live through disasters pretending they did not happen. They then indulge in food and even drugs or alcohol. This ostrich approach does no good, as they need to realise the gravity of the situation and try to fix it. Despite their tendency to love illusions, they do know right from wrong and can take difficult decisions once roused.

Love finds LibPisces in their element. Librans cannot live without love while Pisces experience love on a deeply spiritual level. LibPisces love with their heart and soul and there is no ego or subterfuge involved in their love. They just want to be cared for. You have to treat them well, for they deserve it with their unending, selfless, unconditional and soul-connecting love.

The Piscean in them has no value for materialistic things. They understand that lasting happiness comes from within. But they still want a little luxury in life. They just need a comfortable home, a car or two to drive them around, electronic gadgets to simplify things and biannual holidays to exhilarate their wandering souls – that's all! It goes a long way in ensuring harmony and serenity for them. Top it with music, dance or some art form as a hobby and life becomes heavenly for a LibPisces.

Libra–Pisces – Kamal Haasan
Kamal Haasan is known for his versatility in playing characters from a dwarf to a middle-aged lady. He is also a renowned Bharatnatyam dancer.

'My father was 50 when I was born. My brothers were like fathers and my father was my grandfather. Thus I made a film like *Hey Ram* because I am stuck in a time warp; I understand the 1940s and 1950s better.'[114]

'I've sung about 50 songs, I learnt classical singing; due to my other pursuits, I couldn't take up singing seriously.'[115]

Extremely creative and highly talented, Kamal Haasan displays the love of art and learning which is the hallmark of a LibPiscean.

Love and Marriage for Him
He is your friend, soul mate and companion. Ego and aggression never enter his conversations and he always listens to you. He is the perfect boyfriend for he talks sweetly, appreciates you, remembers all the important things and is wonderfully caring towards you.

You will need to be his stabilising force. He needs a woman who is independent and strong and a little more realistic than him about the world. He lives a life full of art and fantasy. The Libran indecisiveness in him can be infuriating and if you like a more commanding partner then you will need to look elsewhere. But there is no one who can understand you better, nor anyone who will know just what to say when you feel down. He is the most hassle-free guy you could ever meet.

But there is a catch: if he has not fixed upon a rewarding occupation by the time he reaches his mid-twenties, chances are he never will. The Libran indecisiveness and Piscean impracticality may turn his admirable talents into losing propositions and he can spend his entire life chasing elusive rainbows.

He is a wonderful father, loving, kind and extremely broad-minded. No new idea or philosophy will ever shock him and he is his children's friend.

Love and Marriage for Her
What a delicious combination she is – the mysterious and feminine Neptune and the loving and artistic Venus! She is truly pretty, with an infectious, charming smile and deep, soulful eyes.

She is no aggressive feminist. Her partner is always in charge for she will never ever think of dominating or controlling him. Her entire world revolves around him.

---
[114] From his speech at Avenues '10
[115] http://smaramra.blogspot.in/2006/08/kamal-hassans-interview.html

But treat her well, for there is no other woman who is so intelligent and brilliant herself, yet patient enough to listen to your boasting and gaze admiringly into your eyes. She is good at making a guy feel special.

Her house is always calm and serene. She has no burning desire to get ahead, she only works if it delights her and not as a necessity. As a partner, she endeavours to be in harmony with you. She can live anywhere, if she is loved totally. She can brave any storm – financial instability, pain or challenges – if she feels that you are by her side. The best part of her love is that she never blames you for anything.

She needs to belong to someone, she needs to know that you love her more than anything in this world and she can live with just that love for the rest of her life. She is extremely romantic and loves to feel free, without any cares and responsibilities in the world. Take her out, get her some flowers, light the candles, turn on the music, and keep the romance alive. She doesn't ask for anything more from life.

For her children, she can do anything. They are a big part of her life but she is not a controlling mother. On the contrary, she can be too giving. She is not a disciplinarian and sometimes, they can take advantage of her gentleness.

At the Workplace
Creative, imaginative, and highly communicative, LibPisces make excellent actors, dancers, writers and singers. It is almost as if they have been blessed with the divine spark of creativity. There is something so ethereal about the artistic abilities of a LibPisces! They are born to further the art forms of the world. Even if they work in another area, they should pursue the arts to lessen the burden on their souls.

Other than creative careers, they can also excel as lawyers, human resource personnel, coaches, mentors, doctors, healers and psychiatrists. There are many fields open to them but they need to be decisive to reach out to success. Hesitancy and insecurity are what truly pull them down.

Money does not motivate them; neither does the thought of glory drive them. What moves them is a feeling of doing something that they like and which will help society. If you have them as your boss, don't think you can fool them because they are very sweet; there may be a whale-type Piscean in them and anyway they can see right through all your ploys.

Water and Air combine in this deeply humanitarian sign. LibPisces have the brilliance of mind and intuitiveness of spirit to realise their dreams, yet they need to be loved and moulded to achieve maximum growth.

Famous LibPisces Personalities
Kamal Haasan, Juhi Chawla, Amjad Khan, Kiran Rao, Hillary Clinton, Adi Godrej, Coluche, Kim Kardashian, Anna Wintour, Asin Thottumkal, Michael Vaughan, Vikram Chatwal, Fernando Torres, Hashim Amla, Steven Seagal, Jamnalal Bajaj, C.K. Nayudu, Chittaranjan Das, Rita Hayworth, Pallavi Joshi, Joaquin Phoenix, Alain Delon, Anne Sweeney.

69. SCORPIO–SAGITTARIUS

Pluto, the ruthless lord of the underworld, and the knowledgeable and benevolent Jupiter come together in this powerful blend of Fire and Water. Sagittarius is the most intelligent amongst the zodiac signs; it is powerful and ambitious but with the heart of a child. Scorpio, on the other hand, is one of the most intense, passionate and magnetic zodiac signs. Add these two together and you get an extremely charged-up, intelligent and zealous personality that plays to win.

They have the sheer depth of Scorpio and the exuberance and dynamism of Sagittarius. The powerful half-human, half-horse Centaur, now not only possesses an arrow to shoot at the stars, but also a venomous sting in his tail for anyone who crosses his path. ScorpSags display a wide range of characteristics like passion, power, wit, intelligence, exuberance, etc. These guys are blatantly ambitious, the Scorpio in them brings focus to the wild aspirations of Sagittarius.

The Scorpio side of them is extremely intuitive and they have the inherent (and lethal) ability to read people's hearts and souls. The Archer in them is philosophical and abstract. Sagittarius gathers knowledge on the widest array of subjects imaginable, but not in-depth. However, the intense Scorpio scrutinises anything to the deepest depths possible. ScorpSags are not just intelligent but also among the wisest people in the zodiac.

They make the rules and play the game of life with enthusiasm. Totally unafraid, they are never taken aback by the unexpected turns of life. Whatever comes their way, they either turn it into an advantage or conquer it. They never accept defeat even when it stares them in the face. They have to win at any cost. They hate losing, even in small things.

Fun-loving pranksters, ScorpSags are loyal friends. You can rely on them to light up a party or lend a helping hand. They will be the life of the party and even love getting onto the stage and performing, or telling extremely bad jokes. They have very few grey shades; with them you get what you see. If they are nice to you in front of you, they will never be horrible to you behind your back.

They are inexhaustible. Scorpio is phoenix-like. They can rise from the ashes. Sagittarius is the most athletic amongst all the zodiac signs. This combination is the culmination of the strongest will power and the most robust physical power. They are powerhouses – physically, emotionally and spiritually. They can withstand the toughest and most gruelling situations of life and emerge unscathed.

Scorpios are vindictive and destructive; Sagittarians are extremely volatile. So the most fearsome thing about them is their anger. It blows in like a hurricane and destroys everything in its path. One good thing is that you can expect an open declaration of war when they are angry. They will tell you and then attack. At least you can be prepared!

Excess in everything is one of their faults. They can be foodies and eat or drink to excess, or they can carry the love of excess into their relationships and love life. Extreme fearlessness can make ScorpSags blunt or tactless at times and sometimes the Sagittarian tongue will make them say politically incorrect things. They can also be compulsive punters gambling in every aspect of life. They get a high from taking huge risks. While a victory spurs them to take on bigger risks, a loss only motivates them to give it another go. Just don't expect them to change their ways – they will carry on regardless!

They take their time to find love. If passion enters their lives before love does, it might take longer for them to settle down. They will demand total loyalty from their mate and be extremely possessive though it will be hard for them to promise the same in return. The Sagittarian desire to break free and the Scorpio ability to live a double life can catch up with their good intentions at times.

Travel is important to them. The footloose Sagittarian tendencies make them wander. They want money in life but more than that, they want glory and to have a good time getting to their goals. They simply don't know how to relax. Their mind is continuously on a whirl and they are on permanent alert mode.

ScorpSags have a deep spiritual side. Scorpio will make them interested in the deepest mysteries of life and the Sagittarian 'professor' is always attracted to the spiritual path. They evolve and explore the depths of this side of them as they grow older. Spirituality is probably the key to taming the continuously raging tornado within them.

Scorpio–Sagittarius – Kapil Dev

'He played with pride and passion and always to win. Charismatic, aggressive and headstrong.'

'He had a major injury in his thigh and hamstring, but he played, took five wickets and won the match for India.'

'He played to win. He always thought that till it was lost, it could be won. Before that, a draw was a victory. India dared to win because of him.'

'He was a great motivator. He instilled positive vibes into his players.'

'He was so positive and … [bent on winning] that sometimes India has lost because of his extreme positivity.'[116]

Kapil Dev, the first World Cup-winning Indian great, was the original 'Captain Courageous' who brought bravery and passion to Indian cricket, truly reflective of a ScorpSag.

Love and Marriage for Him

You can be sure of an exciting life with him. He may not be at home that much, and may be lost in his dreams and ambitions most of the time, but, hey, you will never live a boring life, ever! Keep your bags packed; you may need to travel anytime.

Stability and steadfastness are what he requires from his partner while he provides the passion and force. Possessiveness makes him run away. So act self-sufficient and be independent without being aggressive about it. Remember, he is also extremely sensitive and has an ego; don't say anything that can hurt him or you will witness his explosive anger. Also, bear in mind – *he* is the boss – even at home!

As a father, he is totally dominating when required and full of fun at times. He wants his children to excel and is as ambitious for them as he is for himself. He pushes them towards excellence but is also happy to pay their party bills.

---

[116] https://www.youtube.com/watch?v=yijep8_mml0

Love and Marriage for Her

She is definitely not the soft, sweet ideal Indian daughter-in-law. She is the most exciting girl you have ever seen. She is intelligent, fearless and even reckless. Don't expect her to remain cocooned in home and family. She is far too independent and too much her own person to ever bow down to anyone else's conventions. She wants a strong man and secretly wishes to be dominated by an evolved and vital man. She does not expect flowers or flattery and is happy if you take her on adventure trips. She needs and seeks change from routine and will be overjoyed if you can provide that.

She has such an optimistic streak in her that it is very difficult for anyone to be glum around her. She is always ready to work and have fun. She is extremely ambitious and goes about achieving her desires and even providing for the home if required. Her dreams matter a lot to her so never belittle them or say that yours are more important. Beware of her temper; she is very sweet but can blow her top if you insult or hurt her. She can pry open the deepest secrets from you. She only asks for honesty from you. If you are caught telling lies, you will lose her forever.

As a mother, she gets better as her children grow older. She loves talking to them and discussing new ideas. Her shockproof nature makes her their friend as they grow older but she likes to have a measure of control over them.

At the Workplace

Honesty, integrity and passion are the traits that spur ScorpSags. They are workaholics with horsepower; you cannot match their stamina. Whatever they do, they do it extremely well and with amazing confidence. They can succeed as writers, spiritual seekers, sports persons or even mechanics, but they are extremely ambitious and never rest till they reach the topmost echelons of their chosen field.

They have awesome inner strength, which enables them to withstand any calamity. With will and a calm demeanour, they face hazards without flinching. They are superb at handling emergencies. Amazingly intelligent, they will quickly grasp the multitudinous ramifications of a disaster and find one that will make them come out victorious.

As bosses, their decisions are always their own and not influenced by what others say or think. They can go against the tide and even against popular thought, if they think something is right. They never take no for an answer, while aiming for the stars.

Pluto's power and Jupiter's luck – there is nothing more ScorpSags need to achieve their dreams.

Famous ScorpSag Personalities

Dhirubhai Ambani, Kapil Dev, Rajneesh (Osho), Vishwanathan Anand, Shekhar Kapur, Dilma Rousseff, Sharmila Tagore, Mohd. Rafi, Shobhaa De, Priyanka Gandhi, Boman Irani, Peter Siddle, Joel Garner, Barkha Dutt, Atal Bihari Vajpayee, Rati Agnihotri, Beethoven, Jacques Chirac, Subramanya Bharathi, John Milton, Jagathy Sreekumar, Ozzy Osbourne, David Silva, Sayali Bhagat, Frank Sinatra, Dick Wolf, Bixente Lizarazu, Sophie Marceau, Colin Cowdrey, Manohar Joshi, Ramrao Adik, Aranxta Sánchez Vicario, Sanjeeda Sheikh, Kim Bassinger, Sagarika Ghatge, Prince Joachim of Belgium, Nelly Furtado, R. Venkataraman.

70. SCORPIO–CAPRICORN

Pluto, the dark lord of the underworld, and Saturn, the wise old man, meet in this extremely determined and ambitious combination.

ScorpCaps' goals can be summed up in two words – respect and wealth. They want people to look up to them and want pots of money to feel secure. They are savers and need to have a sizable bank balance to feel safe. They also have the secret ambition to soar high in a chosen field and leave behind a huge legacy.

The wily, determined and focused mountain Goat now has a venomous sting, to not just steer clear, but even attack if required. ScorpCaps do not fear hard work or even deprivation to attain what they feel is rightfully theirs. Their single-mindedness in the pursuit of their goals is awe-inspiring and spine chilling. ScorpCaps will never outwardly show that they want your respect or approval, yet they will glow within when they get it and fume with anger when they don't.

The first thing you notice about them is their utter disdain of teenage rebellion. They are unable to understand why people need to act irresponsibly. They prefer older values to new, flighty ones. They are highly conservative in their approach and seem wiser than their years. The only thing that can change their views is age, for they display the Capricorn reverse-aging syndrome. When they cross their thirties or forties you can expect them to become more light-hearted and less fusty in their outlook.

Scorpio's extreme sensitivity is present in them. They can get hurt easily but the Scorpio mask hides this. A typical Scorpio stings after careful planning but a ScorpCap may even swallow his pride, ego and anger if his need for revenge could cause his destruction. He will never forget a slight, though. He will probably get even when the balance has tilted in his favour. Be careful to tread the unmarked line with them.

Family is as important to them as their goals. ScorpCaps can sacrifice anything for the well-being of their families. They are ideal sons and daughters. Their family will also be the only ones who will be privileged to see their relaxed and funny side. The rest of the world will see their reserved or prim and proper side.

Love will find them passionate and intense as always. However, the Capricorn in them will make them want a partner who will stand out amongst others in either quality or family lineage. ScorpCaps want partners who enhance their status and have certain qualities in them. They are extremely careful about choosing their life partners and can be very cold in their calculations before going ahead with the union.

They are often stressed out. The Scorpio's extreme emotional sensitivity and obsessive desire to make something of their lives can engender deep bouts of depression, when things don't go their way. The melancholic nature of Capricorn will further aggravate this tendency for they will always see the potholes on the road to success. They need people around them who can de-stress them.

ScorpCaps know and differentiate between their well-wishers and opponents. They have very few friends and are extremely loyal to them. While they nurture the wellwishers they plan and disintegrate the machinations of their competitors.

Bogged down by insecurities in the beginning, they might not assert their control too much but as they grow in confidence and stature their need for control increases.

They want to know what goes on in your mind. They keep assessing if you are their friend or foe, and they want to know every detail that can be used in a power game. Despite their control over the outward show of emotions, there are stormy seas raging inside. But they are masters of self control and will never let you know their innermost fears or weaknesses. They excel in politics and one-upmanship. There is a cold aloneness about them, and the strange feeling of fear and respect that they evoke in people is palpable.

ScorpCaps also have a deep spiritual side and are interested in all the esoteric sciences, ranging from mysticism to astrology. They instinctively understand the deeper aspects of life and are attuned to religion. Anything old and traditional is sacred for them and they research those aspects that reveal the deepest mysteries of life and help ease or conquer life's challenges.

Scorpio–Capricorn – Oprah Winfrey
'It was so unnatural for me to cover somebody's tragedies and difficulties and to have to not feel anything for it.'

'I left my boss when he didn't give me a raise because I realised he didn't hear or see me. I was not going to get the validation that I was looking for.'

'I decided to myself I'm not going to be used by television but I'm going to use television; use television as a platform to speak to the world.'

'I'm not here just as a talk show host, but to raise people's consciousness.'

'I could keep my feet on the ground. There was no difference between me and the audience.'[117]

Oprah has the emotions, passion, determination and groundedness of a true ScorpCap.

Love and Marriage for Him
His career is his obsession; be ready to share him with his ambition. Family is very important to him and though he has the final say in decisions, he really likes it if you share your views. His views on marriage can be very conservative. He wants a wife who regards her family as sacrosanct. Do not pile emotional baggage on him. It is best if you are independent and cheerful. It is very hard to get him to part with money and you can be sure that he will have the final say in the budget.

The time to watch out for is when he crosses his thirties or forties and achieves some of his ambitions. It is then that he will allow his old values to slide a bit and will not mind a bit of fun. Keep an eye on him if his eyes begin to sparkle and he starts laughing more!

As a father, he is absolutely old school. He is firm with his children and they admire and respect his views. He can be very controlling too, but he is capable of the greatest sacrifices for his children and for you.

Love and Marriage for Her
She is a hundred per cent involved in the relationship. Capricorn makes her the perfect housewife. This lady is ideally suited to be the wife of a business magnate

---
[117] https://www.youtube.com/watch?v=6DlrqeWrczs

or a politician for she easily takes on the added responsibilities and can be of great help. However, if you lack the ambition and drive to make it big then let her take charge, for she will never be content with an average life.

Her emotions are very strong and it would be foolish to discount them. She wants a man who understands her need for security and status. Family problems and irresponsible actions from you will make her very melancholic. This lady is not one who can easily walk out if she sees no future. Tell her jokes, brighten her life with your presence and she will appreciate you. She may not be very expressive in love and needs you to help her loosen her inhibitions a bit.

She is very conscious of society. Mind your public behaviour if you want to live happily with her. Do not expect her to change her views easily; she has very strong beliefs. As she grows older, she surprises you with her light-heartedness. She is quite capable of acting like a giggly teenager in her forties. But beware – if this lady is given a wretched life, and marriage is made a cross for her to bear, eventually she will find solace outside – and you will never know.

As a mother, she is in her element. She knows how to take care of her children without letting them run wild. She can also be a little too controlling but that is one aspect that is hard for her to change.

At the Workplace

ScorpCaps are made to work and succeed. They are the most hardworking, sincere and ambitious workers. They never give up their burning desire to succeed. They have outstanding organising abilities and you can easily leave the whole job, from conceptualisation to execution, to them. They keep an eye on the costs and you can rest assured that they will take the right decisions.

They find ways to make themselves indispensible to the organisation. They know all its secrets and become the power behind the throne, or even the real power. They can be extremely manipulative, and be angels or monsters to get their work done.

Money and status are what they want, need and desire. From politics to the corporate field, and even creative avenues, you find them in positions that promise success. As bosses, they are demanding and ruthless. They expect you to put in the required hard work or ship out. They behave like the head of the family but know where to draw the line. Don't ever try to play politics with them!

Water and Earth imbue ScorpCaps with a sense of purpose. Strong, passionate and extremely intense, they never take life easy and always strive to reach their goals.

Famous ScorpCap Personalities

Indira Gandhi, Shatrughan Sinha, Jennifer Aniston, Kevin Costner, David Villa, Britney Spears, Ramakant Achrekar, Charles Dickens, Voltaire, Mozart, Luis Suárez, Joan Capdevila, Nayanthara, Vishal Karwal, Richard Nixon, Lillian Russell, King Abdullah II, Bárbara Mori, Xavier Doherty, N.S. Krishnan, George Eliot, Mark Spitz, Bob Marley, Ajit Singh, Saqlain Mushtaq, Oprah Winfrey.

71. SCORPIO–AQUARIUS

Pluto, the ruthless lord of the underworld, meets the highly eccentric and inventive Uranus in a combination of power and passion, which generates extraordinarily inventive thoughts. ScorpAquas are mesmerising personalities. You see a penetrating magnetic power in their eyes. They can look into your very soul. They project a feeling of unflappability in even the most trying of situations. There is not much that can displace that look of detachment from them. This combination marks the coming together of the two most volatile planets; the radioactive metals plutonium and uranium are the ruling metals of these planets, which underscores the truly explosive nature of this combination.

Aquarius has a magical quality that cannot be described. They think and act in a way that seems intuitive rather than realistic. Scorpio brings in its desire to penetrate the deepest mysteries of time and space and contributes to the feeling of other-worldliness in them. Scorpio also makes the eccentric genius of Aquarius stand out due to the addition of its passion and intensity.

ScorpAquas may seem a little aloof but it does not mean that they do not notice things. They notice the smallest of inflections in your speech and can fathom your deepest secrets. This combination can make for the greatest detectives in the world, unravelling the deepest mysteries. While Scorpio and Aquarius seem to be totally different signs, when they come together they blend to form a dynamic personality. Scorpio gives focus to the wandering Aquarian mind and makes them revel in challenges. Adding ballast is the stubbornness of Aquarius with its strong beliefs – be it to bring a change in the world or changing the world itself.

The Aquarian in them makes them think too much of the future. It makes them think differently, yet it also makes them think about so many things that they may find it difficult to realise their true destinies in their youth. It takes them time to find their true path and they might wander a bit before focusing on that one passion that will rule their lives forever. The Scorpio in them eventually makes their wildly innovative ideas reach the logical conclusion and helps them realise their dreams through force and passion.

They are deeply spiritual and dabble in the paranormal sciences. Scorpio has an intuitive understanding of the deeper mysteries while Aquarius is inordinately curious. They know how to read body language. From esoterica like Reiki to Ouija boards to past life regression and trances, all of these interest them and they will even master some of these alternative/new-age techniques.

The one thing to beware of is their temper. If you deliberately set roadblocks for them, watch out for the Scorpio sting and Aquarian bursts of anger. Aquarius also makes them highly unpredictable. Mostly, however, they are peace-oriented. In fact, they do have a madcap, intelligent sense of humour; they love shocking people. Conventions and traditions are not important to them. As they grow older, they grow wiser and learn to tone down their brashness.

You cannot find better friends than them. ScorpAquas endear themselves to you with their loyalty, love and insatiable sense of fun. They have more friends than they can keep in touch with daily and as they grow older, their friends become scattered. They might not keep in touch with their friends for long periods of time, yet you can be sure that whenever you call on their help they will always be there for you.

Love calls forth extreme reactions from them. The Aquarian side of them behaves strangely when in love for Aquarians prefer to see people as human beings rather than as special interests and don't like to differentiate between 'them' and 'us'. So when they fall in love they act clumsily and tend not to accept the fact for a long time. They are also intensely interested in people and like to decode everyone they meet. If they are not seriously hit by the lightning bolt of love they will look for variety rather than settling down with one. Scorpio makes them intensely passionate, so they can be extremely committed if they find the right one. Otherwise, they will keep seeking their whole lives. Scorpio and Aquarius combine to make them appreciate the various aspects of love from a young age and they can have early physical relationships due to Scorpio sensuality and Aquarian curiosity.

They are not excited by money. Their wants include more than mere possessions. They want power, prestige, and unassailable positions while espousing ideals inaccessible to mere mortals. ScorpAquas dream more, visualise more and *live* their dreams even before they actually achieve it. That is probably the biggest secret to their success.

Scorpio–Aquarius – Imran Khan
'I have the ability to struggle, to take the falls in my life.'[118]

'Nothing is impossible. Dream big, only then big things will come your way.'

When Imran Khan won the World Cup for Pakistan, his team mates were left red-faced as he did not speak of his team or the victory, but went on to talk about his dream project to build a cancer hospital. Surprised? Well, as a Scorpio, his long cherished passion of winning the Cup was over and an Aquarian always lives in the future, so naturally he started talking about the future, completely ignoring the present.

Scorpio passion, magnetism and Aquarian future-orientation meet seamlessly in him.

Love and Marriage for Him
You have to share him with his passion, which is not easy at times. He gets lost in his own world for long periods of time and does not understand the need to be there for his family. You need to be strong and independent for though he helps you whenever you ask; he prefers not to be clung to. At the same time, never act as if you are the boss; and do not try to change his opinions or views – he can be extremely stubborn.

You can be his sounding board, his devil's advocate; even his muse and hear him out while he fills you in on the details of his latest venture. It would break his heart and push him away if he thinks that his passions bore you to death. If you share his delight in his passions, he feels happy but if you do not, he will go about it alone.But he is broad-minded enough to understand we all have our different interests. If you do have a contrasting passion, he does not stop you; he actually encourages you. So don't stop him from going single-mindedly about *his* passion, however outlandish and futuristic it seems.

---

[118] *Times Life!* Sunday, July 24, 2011.

His flaring temper can be devastating and you need a thick skin and a strong sense of humour to talk away his bad moods.

As a father, he comes into action only when his children begin to talk and comprehend the world. He does not know how to react to a gurgling/crying baby and is no help in the nursery. He understands them when they are older and is not shocked by anything they say or do. He is the father who counsels, philosophises and then lets them decide.

Love and Marriage for Her

She is a strong and independent lady, a powerhouse; and her thoughts are as unique as her. This is a girl who will break every mould; it is not only her volatile temper or unconventional thoughts that set her apart but also her different looks every year. Life for her is an adventure and she likes to experiment and study each facet of it.

As a child, she would have been a rebel and a tomboy and those attributes always describe her. But, she is much more than them. She is unpredictable, knowledgeable, powerful, unconventional, sexy, scientific, adventurous, methodical, spiritual and in a class of her own. Her interests can range from palmistry to acting.

As a mother, she needs some help, especially in her children's younger years. Diapers, wailing children and paediatricians can confuse her. You have to be the more caring and sensitive of the two. She can be a fabulous mother to teenagers and can double as their friend. Nothing they say ever shocks her. She can be a little strict despite her unconventional nature.

At the Workplace

ScorpAquas perform brilliantly in their chosen passions; the problem is to find that passion. They are really blessed if they know what to do from a young age or they while away many years before they find their true path. Once they identify their vocation, nothing can stop them. They work, persevere and think only of their passions and let nothing and no one come in the way.

You can be sure that whatever they do, they will bring an innovative element to it. Their thoughts and ideas may seem too futuristic but they will make it happen. They are also the people who are genuinely moved by the sufferings of the world and gravitate towards higher causes. They are naturally inclined towards revolutionary ideas that can change the world for the better.

They need genuine appreciation for they can see through falsehoods. Money without power means nothing to them and they can strive for it for years. The best thing you can do is direct them on to the right path and be their mentor. They do not forget you in their moments of glory.

Famous ScorpAqua Personalities

Imran Khan, Nitish Kumar, Sooraj Barjatya, Ian Botham, Ben Stiller, Michael Dell, Woody Allen, Amol Palekar, Juhi Parmar, Galileo, Jensen Ackles, Shankar Mahadevan, Dino Morea.

72. SCORPIO–PISCES

This is a truly awesome combination for it combines two extremely unfathomable and mystifying zodiac signs. The extreme passion and amazing strength of Scorpio meets the deep emotions and high imagination of Pisces. Both Scorpio and Pisces hold their destinies in their hands and can decide to be either saint or sinner. They excel as both. Pluto, the secretive and often ruthless god of the underworld, presides over Scorpio, while the deep and mysterious ruler of the seas commands Pisces. If they are good, they are very, *very* good and when they are bad, they are *dreadfully* bad. Do you know a Fish with a sting? Well… a sting ray? A Fish, but with an interesting and dangerous twist.

The deep passions of Scorpio mean ScorPisces hate to lose. Therefore, they do not let events or situations lead them to failure. Scorpio discipline combines beautifully with Piscean creative energies to make them forces to reckon with. Scorpio is all-knowing; it instinctively realises the deeper mysteries of life – from politics to poverty, sex to spirituality, money to theology. Pisces can be anything from a dissolute alcoholic to a singing/acting superstar. This is the power of this sign and also its downfall.

They are dreamers and creators, capable of whiling away time thinking of a world of impossible beauty or dreaming of alternate realities. Despite their tendency to wander into different worlds, they remain grounded due to their passions. In them, you find a blend of the dreamy and the practical, the unworldly and the articulately aware.

Piscean empathy and compassion can be felt in their every action. Yet, for all their powers of understanding and compassion, they can never forgive. The Scorpio in them can make them extremely vindictive and they can use any means, fair or foul, to get even.

They are naturally very sensitive. They might wear the inscrutable mask of the Scorpio and never let you see their feelings, but you can be sure that every unkind word or unsympathetic remark will cut them deeply. They are also subject to mood swings like Pisces; they need love and support, more than any other zodiac combination, for they feel too deeply.

They can sense your deepest secrets, though they will always empathise with you. These guys look fine even after downing ten pegs; their inner core will always be awake and aware to any devious tricks.

There is always a hint of irresponsibility in them. ScorPisces see the world lazily through their penetrating eyes. They recognise injustice and feel bad about it, yet will not take up their duties till pushed. Addictions can be their downfall; the Scorpio in them likes to experiment with the darker side of life while Pisces is always lured by temptation.

Love will define them. The Pisces in them yearns for a soul mate while their Scorpio side makes them intensely passionate. They love with their heart and soul. Their love is their life and they demand the same dedication from their mate. Love and passion goes hand in hand for them, and they become addicted to love and everything that goes with it. Deep, sensuous, passionate, ethereal and supernatural love is what you experience with a ScorPisces.

Their loyalty and love will never give way. ScorPisces have very few but very loyal friends who always stand by them. The Pisces side of ScorPisces makes them extremely socially adept, they can easily communicate with people from all walks of life. They just have to be in the mood for it. Thankfully, the Scorpio in them is prudent when it comes to money. They think before spending and do not splurge on extravagances.

ScorPisces can be extremely spiritual. Both Scorpio and Pisces understand the metaphysical and spiritual side of life and as they age, they delve further into the mystical elements of religion. They have the capability to solve any mystery of science and even of the deeply esoteric aspects of life.

I will summarise with what I started – they can be saints or sinners. They have the capability to be both in the same life time as well. They can choose addiction and be a slave to escapism or soar high as evolved evangelists. Hope you meet the saint.

Scorpio–Pisces – Shyam Benegal

Shyam Benegal epitomises ScorPisces. His films and stories show a deep understanding of human nature. He is credited with the creation of a new genre called 'middle cinema' in India,[119] which displays serious content, realism and naturalism, with a keen analysis of the socio-political conditions of the times.

'I need to keep making films – it keeps me alive and ticking.'[120]

He grew up in a politically charged atmosphere at home. His works show his understanding of politics and how it affects the lives of people.[121]

Shyam Benegal has the instinctive understanding of a ScorPisces with his deep and empathetic grasp on reality.

Love and Marriage for Him

He loves you till death, truly. This guy is extremely loving, caring, passionate, understanding and loyal, and he demands the same from you. But it would be wrong of you to feel that you can walk all over him. There is an element of ego in him that does not let him be used or abused by anyone. He wants total loyalty and wants to be the most important person in your life.

He understands your every wish, never judges you by your past. He connects with you at the level of the soul. His standards are totally different from the rest of the world. Though he understands the importance of name, fame and money, he works and lives to a different tune altogether. He loves to travel, but to the same places. He wants that sense of déjà vu and wants to feel secure wherever he goes.

There is a possibility of him falling prey to an addiction. The only thing that can get him back is your love. Control, anger or advice will drive him further away. You have to deal with his anger, but the saving grace is, he does realise when he is wrong.

As a father, he is loving and understanding. He may not be interested in the day-to-day activities of his children, as he most likes to spend quality time with them once a week. He can be a little controlling. The Pisces in him knows all the problems they can face and he tries and makes them more aggressive and responsible than he is.

---

[119] http://en.wikipedia.org/wiki/Parallel_Cinema
[120] http://articles.timesofindia.indiatimes.com/2003-09-05/mumbai/27182186_1_shyam-benegal-shyam-benegal-subhash-chandra-bose
[121]

Love and Marriage for Her

Love permeates the room when she is with you. She loves you in such a deep, emotional and spiritual way that you feel truly special when you are with her. No one can love anyone as this girl can and does. She loves from the bottom of her heart and her heart has no bottom. Very few men deserve such honest, devoted and passionate love.

She needs a strong, emotional and sensitive guy. Guys who think only of their ambitions and needs, need not apply for they will never understand her deep-rooted sensitivity and could hurt her deeply with their indifference. She can be a jealous wife who can get vindictive if you cross the line.

She has a tendency to be highly impractical, almost as if she has rose-tinted glasses on. She places you on a pedestal and worships you. She lives in a dream world where anything that happens, happens only for the good. If she has to face the realities of life, she gets shattered. Housework is not her thing but if you want good surroundings, she goes all out to create them for you. Please learn to appreciate her.

As a mother, she is perfectly understanding of her children's needs. She is deeply perceptive of their innermost turmoil. She does not raise her eyebrows at rebellion.

At the Workplace

ScorPisces have deep passion and ambition. Their dreams are very different from the usual and they love to work, not for money, but for the joy of creating something unique. They are not particularly keen on the applause but work hard to gain respect and admiration.

They are extremely loyal to their work and to their organisation. They don't mind gruelling work as long as they know that they will grow from it. They are fast learners and can grasp new ideas with surprising ease. Petty politics is not their domain; yet, they cannot be duped or sidelined.

They are blessed with a highly creative streak due to Piscean imagination and Scorpion perceptiveness. They can become gifted artists, authors and actors who bring life and soul to the characters they create. There is an otherworldly touch to the work they do.

They are also very good at solving mysteries. Analysis comes naturally to them due their highly perceptive nature. Research, too, is a field they can tackle. Jobs that are monotonous are not for them. They can be anything they want and it is as easy to mould them as it is for them to waste their talents.

Spiritual yet vengeful, mysterious yet deceptive, passionate yet unworldly; this double Water sign's charm lies in its contradictions.

Famous ScorPisces Personalities

Einstein, Charles de Gaulle, Mulayam Singh Yadav, Shyam Benegal, Ian Bell, Rohini Hattangadi, Bappi Lahiri, Martin Luther, Tyra Banks, Lisa Ray, Geeta Bali, Mehr Jesia, Warren Beatty, Francis Coppola, Jamie Lee Curtis, Vijay Amritraj, Vince Vaughn, Niharika Singhania, Suhasini Mulay, Anant Neelakantan.

73. SAGITTARIUS–CAPRICORN

The knowledgeable and benevolent Jupiter meets the old and wise Saturn in this extremely ambitious combination. The horse-bodied Centaur has speed, he is super-intelligent and he aims at the sky, but he is not sure why and what is he aiming at. The sure, determined and single-minded mountain Goat when fused with the wandering Archer gives SagCaps a purpose and a clear goal. They chart out their course in life, and are very focused and disciplined.

Capricorn makes them sombre and responsible. The happy-go-lucky ways of Sagittarius are diminished while the Capricornian responsible side comes to the fore. Don't go by the friendly banter and fun; they are very serious from the inside. They amaze you with their maturity during their youth. As they grow older, Jupiter's exuberance overtakes Saturn's old-man attitude and they become quite chilled-out, in another classic case of Capricornian reverse aging.

Extremely intelligent, their minds are like sponges and they are very good at understanding new thoughts and concepts. They are extraordinarily witty and their knowledge leaves you spellbound. They can also be conservative at times. They strike the perfect balance between Capricorn's instinct to go with the tried and tested route and the Sagittarian penchant for experimentation. They always look well groomed. They want to reach the top and believe that the first step to leading is to look like a leader.

The blunt honesty of Sagittarius is softened. SagCaps are able to weigh their words and tread carefully when required. Though they try to be politically correct most of the time, the lack of Water in this combination makes them oblivious to the unstated. They cannot read anyone's heart. They may blurt out things that will make one uncomfortable, and laugh without realising the damage, as they can never judge from your expression that they are being rude. Generous and loyal, they make wonderful friends, despite their insensitivity.

Family is very important to them. The Sagittarian flightiness is quite reduced in them. They may move around the world, due to their ambitions but always remain connected to their families.

Lack of Water and Air may make them appear naïve. They might not be perceptive but they are quite astute and map out the consequences of any action before taking a step. SagCaps are extremely competitive and openly so. They are also shrewd enough to play mind games while climbing the ladder. These are the guys who will throw an open challenge to competitors and then work hard to win. The endearing thing about them is that they tell you frankly that they want to beat you – it has you rooting for them!

They are positive and aggressive but deep inside they have a fear of failure. This may lead to depression. In those moments when they have failed or half-succeeded, or the going gets tough, they may go through dark moods. But very soon the sunny Sagittarian in them wins over old man Saturn and they are back with that cheerful smile. They also love taking up causes and fighting for them, especially if it boosts their CV.

They work hard but they party hard too. They make sure they have the best of both worlds but never let that confuse their decisions. At times, it may seem as if they are two personalities, one solemn and business-oriented and the other ready to party and enjoy. There are a few SagCaps who fritter away opportunities in seeking change as they get bored quickly. There are also a few who are overly dramatic and attention-seeking. But they are very few.

Money is important to them. Stinginess does not afflict them but they surely know the value of things. They can actually save while splurging – an enviable trait! Their anger can be explosive. They will not care what they say to whom when they are angry – they will just say it.

Love will find them playing hard to get. They might marry for their family and hold very traditional and conservative views on marriage, yet their Sagittarian side will propel them towards untested territories too. They will mellow down as they grow older and you can expect them to become quite naughty in their forties!

SagCaps have an extraordinary fighting spirit. They never give up, always looking for that silver lining. Despite all the melancholy, stress and self-deprecation, they show a cheerful face to the world. They can be spiritually inclined as well. Sagittarius is drawn to 'higher' knowledge, while Capricorn reveres tradition. Expect them to have expansive knowledge and beliefs in religion, spirituality, etc.

Sagittarius–Capricorn – Irrfan Khan

'At one point I was bored and almost thought of quitting…I couldn't find my space but I kept myself busy. I realised that I will have to create my own space.'

'For ten years I was fighting fate. But life has its own plans.'

'I hate to build up expectations. I've done enough of that in my life. I used to get these kinds of insecurities early in my life, so I've built up a kind of defence system.'[122]

The Sagittarius fighting spirit and the endurance of Capricorn are evident in Irrfan Khan's statements. His insecurities and failures did not stop him from doggedly pursuing his dreams.

Love and Marriage for Him

He is the provider *par excellence*. This guy wants to create something fabulous for his family and concentrates on achieving his goals. The family-oriented self-sacrificing trait of a Capricorn is present in him. Here the Sagittarian's need for freedom and the Capricorn's love for family are in eternal conflict. He will love his family and do everything for them, yet he will need his time and space.

You need to be the strong, independent one, who understands his needs, can deal with crises, yet be feminine enough to let him be the boss and provider.

Life is an adventure with this guy. He may act traditional but he has a wild heart. He likes to travel to exotic places and is very enthusiastic about adventure sports. His heart may wander, for Capricorn makes him sombre in his youth yet colourful in his middle age while the Sagittarian in him makes him footloose. Do not worry. He comes back; family always pulls him back. He will tell you if he has had a fling.

He is a fun father, but insists on good behaviour and never lets his children run wild. He gives them every opportunity and expects them to have set goals. He is as ambitious for his children as he is for himself.

---

[122] *Verve*, June 2011

Love and Marriage for Her
She is extremely fearless and ever ready to take on a challenge. She is a tomboy at heart and even if she wears a *sari*, do not expect traditional coyness from her. She looks confident and trendy and has strong views. The fact that she cannot read anybody's emotions, or even be sensitive to their thoughts, can make her quite difficult to deal with.

She hates liars and phoneys. But that doesn't make her vulnerable – she is smart enough to know your true worth and will have asked you many uncomfortable questions and uncovered all of the truth before thinking about your proposal.

Family is important to her and she always cares for family members. She is very ambitious. It is extremely necessary for her to work towards her ambitions or she loses her positive enthusiasm and becomes angry and frustrated. She knows how to look after herself and manage work and home. You can easily leave her and go off on long business trips. She can talk insensitively at times and make tactless comments, but those who know her easily forgive her these trespasses.

As a mother, she is amazingly caring. Her children are given a lot of freedom while growing up. She knows how to make them independent while instilling discipline and values in them.

At the Workplace
Extremely ambitious and very intelligent, SagCaps are very hard to beat in the professional arena. From business to sports, they can conquer any field. They are found in professions where hard work bestows money, power and fame. They like all those careers where they can strut their stuff in constant limelight. They work hard to make themselves indispensible and then leave a legacy behind.

They make excellent sports people. Sagittarius is a sporty sign, full of energy and power. Combined with the discipline and focus of Capricorn, they can do wonders. Anger management is an issue with them and they can easily trample on others' egos.

They are able to easily understand the importance of new concepts and are one of the first to implement them. They love explaining things and act as mentors to their subordinates. They make wide sweeps with their hand while talking, to give authority to their views. Their Achilles heel is their tactlessness, though rarely related directly to work. They will be shrewd there, most of the time, but otherwise they can be totally blunt.

Fire and Earth meet in this grounded and fiery sign. Traditional yet adventurous, intelligent yet naïve and enthusiastic proponents of new views, SagCaps are the doers and leaders in their fields.

Famous SagCap Personalities
Irrfan Khan, Vijay Mallya, Darren Lehmann, Imran Khan (actor), K.J. Yesudas, José Mourinho, Denzel Washington, Sienna Miller, Glenn Beck, Hamid Karzai, Prabhu Ganesan, Diane Keaton, Saurabh Tiwary, Rasputin, Mia Farrow, Debbie Allen, Neil Diamond, Edoardo Ponti, Robin Gibb, Donna Summer, Veerappa Moily, Qurratulain Hyder, Bhanupriya, Jaipal Reddy, Abasaheb Garware, Peter May (the cricketer), Biju Menon, Kei Nishikori.

74. SAGITTARIUS–AQUARIUS

Sagittarius and Aquarius cross the most intelligent with the most inventive. Sagittarius is ruled by the knowledgeable and benevolent Jupiter while the maverick and eccentric planet of invention, Uranus, rules Aquarius. SagAquas are intelligent and known for their extraordinary ideas.

SagAquas are outgoing, exuberant and full of energy. When they walk into a room, it resonates with their presence. They create a party atmosphere with their lively voices and deep-throated laughter. They love surprising people and have an insatiable appetite for life. Extremely independent, they can be the best of friends but find it difficult to commit to relationships.

Aquarius hates tradition. Traditions, rituals, conventions and any talk of ancient ideas and values are anathema to them. To this, add Sagittarian independence of spirit and thought and the mix spells rebellion. SagAquas propound free thought and will. Adventure courses through their veins. Sagittarians want to try everything in the world; the more dangerous it sounds the better. While Aquarians love the wacky, eccentric and original; they can never be shocked.

Money has no value for them and they do not strive for it. Aquarians do worry about their old age and keep a little aside. Beyond that, money, savings and investments do not interest them. SagAquas will not work to build an empire or leave a legacy behind. For them, life is today.

However, SagAquas are very ambitious. They dream of doing something so different and innovative that it would be earth shattering. They dream not for personal glory but to benefit people. Aquarius will always want to do something that will bring about a change.

Sagittarius loves to fight for causes. Aquarians always feel for the poor and the marginalised. Expect SagAquas to be the eternal fighter fighting for lost causes. Their humanitarian urges are strong and true. They are never guided by profit or fame – all they want is to see the underdog win.

Both signs are of a scientific bent of mind and motivated by higher ideals. If a SagAquas is a farmer, you can be sure that he farms with a scientific and revolutionary outlook. Whatever they do, they do differently. There is a flip side to these exuberant creatures though; they do not know *exactly* what they want to do. Sagittarius is extremely ambitious and wants to do so *many* things, while Aquarius is so inventive and so curious about *everything* that without some direction, SagAquas can fritter away their abundant energies on insignificant things. They will constantly be excited by new ideas but not work on one thing with determination and focus. The danger is of becoming a jack of all trades and master of none.

The lack of Earth in this combination makes them extremely volatile. Their ideas and thoughts are superb yet sometimes absolutely lacking in practicality. They hate being told what to do. They just can't take advice and turn rebellious when ordered to do things a certain way. You can expect them to mellow down only in their thirties or forties and start listening to advice.

This lack of attention and focus will also be present in their relationships. They can have multiple partners and think nothing of being unfaithful. Both the zodiac signs are highly liberated and free-thinking and shun customs. SagAquas take time to settle down in relationships. Ideals and causes matter more to them than people, relationships or ties.

The absence of Water makes them quite insensitive as well. Though Aquarians have an uncannily perceptive nature and know exactly what you feel, they are too detached to react sensitively. SagAquas will not bother to tone down their voice or be more compassionate if you require care. They believe that you can solve your problems yourself. They will not mind helping you monetarily but don't expect sympathy or caring.

They have a very volatile temper and do not mince words when they are angry. Their anger is as palpable as their laughter but their temper cools down quickly and they hold no grudges. The worst thing you can do to them is to imply that you don't believe them. That affects them deeply for there truly is no one as truthful and honest as they are. Honest to the core, they cannot tell lies or use devious means to earn a living or score over others.

Sagittarius–Aquarius – Elvis Presley
There was a girl on the telephone, who was in the hospital. She had tickets for the show and couldn't come as she had a serious illness. Elvis marched into a room and held up the entire show for fifteen minutes to talk to her.[123]

Famously, Elvis shot out his own TV because Robert Goulet was on the screen. Less famously, he sat beside his pool and ate watermelon while squeezing off rounds with his .22-caliber pistol to blast light bulbs floating in the water.[124]

The King of Rock lived life his own way – with the human touch of Aquarius and the wild brashness of Sagittarius.

Love and Marriage for Him
He is inventive, gregarious, exuberant, volatile and totally enthralling. All that energy and enthusiasm is perfect in a friend but it is very hard to handle 24x7. If you have chosen to be with him then you know what he is and you will have to keep trying to sensitise him. After some time he will learn.

As he matures, he becomes calmer. He needs a woman who is independent and strong. Actually, never let him know that you hold him dear, and never cry for him. Let the tie that binds you two be a subtle one, as he runs away at the smallest hint of possessiveness. He loves his independence and cannot live in a confining relationship. Space and freedom are very important to him. He loves travelling and adventure sports. Keep a suitcase packed for the travelling bug can awaken in him anytime.

It is very difficult to get him to save money, so you need to have a source of income. You should be his opposite in many ways. Be a saver while he will be the spender, be cool and calm while he is adventurous and volatile, be family-oriented while he will hide from his family, be the disciplining force for your children while he will be the fun parent. Of course, he will always acknowledge your efforts. It is just that he is the eternal free bird and will love you if you allow him to be just that.

---

[123] http://www.elvis.com.au/presley/interview_elvis_presley.shtml
[124] http://articles.chicagotribune.com/2008-11-16/news/10-things-elvis-presley_1_jesse-garon-presley-elvis-presley-elvis-crespo

He may have some affairs but his Sagittarian frankness keeps him from being secretive about them. As I said, only cool, strong and independent women need apply – tears and recriminations will drive him away. If you are a romantic and expect roses and mushiness then this guy is not for you; he will never offer his heart on a platter or swear total fidelity to anyone.

He is the most exciting father ever. Grades do not bother him and he encourages his children to think independently.

Love and Marriage for Her
She is definitely not conservative or traditional. Do not expect her to behave like your mother for she shuns the old and looks to the new ways for doing things. Marriage is not an easy decision for her, as she does not like to tie herself down. Strong character and high values matter to her more than money and status.

She has a big network of friends and is connected through parties and causes. Actually, causes rank higher on her list than family.

She prefers a man who believes in equality and does not have an uncontrollable ego. Do not expect the usual feminine traits in her; she is made of rebellious material. She is an intelligent companion, an adventurous fun-loving partner and a woman unlike any other.

As a mother, she ensures that her children learn to fight for rights and values. She does not judge them by their grades or by the way they listen to her. She is happy if they turn out just as independent as her.

At the Workplace
They are highly innovative and come up with out-of-the box ideas. But their brilliant ideas can remain just ideas for they lack the patience and focus to work on them. They are fabulous in high-energy jobs. They love to travel, expound their views and meet new people. Routine and monotony should not be a part of their job descriptions. They are good at marketing, advertising, teaching and anything that is dynamic.

They can also be great at sports with the Sagittarian's natural inclination for it and the Aquarian brilliance at taking decisions in split seconds. You may also find them as leaders fighting for causes. Their outspoken nature and fearlessness make them stand up for others.

As bosses, they are high-energy leaders who expect the best from you and yet are generous. They definitely need help in fine tuning their ideas and making them viable.

Fire and Air combine to make SagAquas humanitarian and adventurous, believers and fighters. Life is more than just living for them – it means fighting for their ideas and filling the world with vitality.

Famous SagAqua Personalities
Elvis Presley, Ricky Ponting, Jyotiraditya Scindia, Govinda, Jennifer Love Hewitt, Rush Limbaugh, Inzamam-ul-Haq, Pravesh Rana, Veena Malik, Christina Ricci, Koena Mitra, Ava Gardner, B. Saroja Devi, Vijay Hazare, Matthew Wade, Kalabhavan Mani, Jack Hobbs, Juliette Binoche, René Redzepi, Kanimozhi Karunanidhi.

75. SAGITTARIUS–PISCES

The knowledgeable and benevolent Jupiter meets the extremely mysterious and philosophical Neptune in SagPisces. Sagittarius and Pisces are poles apart – the former is extremely positive while the latter is filled with unknown fears and phobias. The mingling of the two makes SagPisces a very interesting combination. They are afraid yet drawn to new possibilities and always find a way to conquer their fears.

Sagittarius is the most intelligent and Pisces the wisest. Sagittarius is called the professor of the zodiac while Pisces is the most unworldly. While they have the intelligence to understand the abstract or even specific technicalities, they also possess the wisdom to understand what to use and when. They are founts of knowledge and the fastest learners of the zodiac. They have this uncanny ability to copy things quickly while improving them. They absorb everything that goes on around them; learn, refine, reflect and then teach beautifully to the world.

It is difficult to bind SagPisces to one tradition or thought process. They do not like being bound by family or responsibility. They are fun to be with, though. They have a smile on their lips and are always ready for a prank. They even enjoy it if the joke is on them! There is a happy-go-lucky streak in them that charms their harshest critics. They speak their minds and can be quite politically incorrect in their remarks.

Travel appeals to them. The Sagittarian thrill seeking and the Piscean need for variety will see them backpacking on adventurous trips, performing stunts and exploring exotic places.

SagPisces give a lot to their friends and family without asking for anything in return. While Sagittarius gives them ambition and the fire in the belly to succeed, Pisces understands the transient nature of money, fame and life itself. They have great humility and maturity and an exceptional moral code of conduct due to the honesty of Sagittarius and Piscean personal integrity. Money holds no value for them. They seek glory and ideals and wish to shine, not drown themselves in gold. Even if they turn gladiators in their fight to achieve something, they remain humble, down-to-earth, and soft-spoken, and never become enamoured of the trappings of success.

Sagittarian ambition will surely be present in SagPisces but they will not trample upon anyone to get what they want. Yes, you are also warned here about the Pisces factor, for it can make them manipulative and deceptive. If you are lucky, you will come across the dolphin type of Fish – intelligent, dependable and exacting in habits. Combined with the half-horse, half-human Centaur they can be strong, disciplined and ambitious characters who also know how to have fun. They have a controlled aggression, which they channelise into work rather than words.

Love can find them hard to tame. The Sagittarian desire for freedom battles with the Piscean desire for a soul mate and it takes them a long time to settle down. Pisces will always pull them into a relationship while Sagittarius will pull them towards adventure. They experiment with myriad relationships before settling down and will be quite unconventional in their view of love.

There is a deep spiritual side to SagPisces. They instinctively know and realise the deeper truths of life. They are full of questions and want to examine the deepest mysteries of life and get all the answers. They have a childlike faith in the powers above and have a subconscious belief that everything will turn out fine in the end.

The Sagittarian belief in their luck even in the darkest of times, combined with the Piscean desire to wear rose-tinted glasses, makes them create an illusionary world at times. They can be highly idealistic and can fight for their causes. Or, they might just refuse to look at the negatives around them and refrain from taking any corrective action.

Their desire to search for new ideas makes them hate routine. You can expect the unexpected of them. They find it hard to be disciplined and are rarely punctual. If the contrary is true, then check their background; they probably inculcated these habits in their formative years. When they are young, they sometimes display a rebellious streak.

SagPisces are quite sensitive, but don't easily express their hurt. You can expect them to explode at times, though their anger is always directed at the problem rather than the person. They never carry grudges and are fair to people. Addictions can be a problem due to the Sagittarian desire to experiment and the Piscean tendency of getting hooked to a stimulant. They can also become victim to nagging self-doubts that can drown their energies in insecurities. They need emotional support during those trying times.

They are exceptionally artistic. Pisces can learn quickly and immerse themselves in the beautiful pursuits of life like art, music, dance, etc. and Sagittarius brings in the fearlessness, athleticism and energy to bring an uninhibited, beautiful expression to art and creativity.

Sagittarius–Pisces – Rahul Dravid
Matthew Hayden: 'If you want to see aggression on the cricket field, look into Rahul Dravid's eyes.'[125]
Mahesh Bhupathi: 'He is one of the most down-to-earth and disciplined professionals I've met.'
Rahul is a calm, unassuming gentleman, in typical Piscean fashion. He also has the positive attitude of a Sagittarius. He always fought till the end, though he didn't show any in-your-face aggression. Rahul also kept reinventing himself and learnt the nuances of One-Day and Twenty-20 batting even though he was branded the quintessential test batsman. He is the perfect team man, ready to don any role and sacrifice his interests for the team. Rahul Dravid is the epitome of SagPisces!

Love and Marriage for Him
This is a man to go on an adventure with. He is curious, intelligent, adventurous and always ready for something new. This guy lives life to the fullest. He has many interests and you will see him change continuously over the years.

Dominance does not mean a thing to him and he is happy to let you be the boss if you want. You need to be the more responsible one for he can easily go

---
[125] http://www.crichotline.com/legends-of-the-game-and-other-greats-speak-about-rahul-dravid/

off on an adventure, leaving the bills unpaid. It is better if you take care of the finances too, for he does not know how to save. You cannot bind him to family duties. This man needs his freedom and though he loves you and cares for his family, he also wants frequent breaks from the many responsibilities of family life.

Evaluate his friends carefully for this guy can easily be swayed by malicious people. You will need to add the practical steps to his plans or see that he meets people who can do that.

He is a loving father and his children enjoy his company. He rarely pushes them to do things.

Love and Marriage for Her
This girl is opinionated and quite independent, yet she looks to you for advice. She loves and cares for her family but it is not the only thing that interests her. She actively seeks change in her life. You enjoy travelling with her for she is a no-fuss companion. She is one of those rare girls who enjoy roughing it out.

Her friends' circle is bigger than her smile. She encompasses the whole world with her hugs. She never looks at a person's background before befriending them. She is ambitious and indecisive at the same time and needs encouragement to achieve her goals. Be careful of your words for she gets hurt easily.

As a mother, she is fantastic. She may not want to be a mother early in the relationship but once she has her baby in her arms, she is overjoyed. She is her children's friend and they always share their secrets with her.

At the Workplace
SagPisces are ambitious but want unconventional careers that offer them scope for change. It is very difficult for them to sit in one place for too long. They are individualistic and creative. Sports, acting, dancing and painting interest them, more than nine-to-five jobs.

Pisces is a natural reservoir of ingenuity and has an innate ability for the arts but is shy to express itself. The Sagittarian childlike, unabashed love for the stage and freedom of expression can liberate SagPisces and make them extraordinary performers.

Their spiritual side can also set them on the path of careers dealing with anything from psychology to astrology to alternative healing.

There is a strange confluence in SagPisces: they bring in Sagittarian aggression and energy to softer professions like music and dance, while bringing in Piscean softness and synergy to tougher domains like sports. Though they are strong competitors, they are also fun-loving people. They keep learning throughout their lives. They are extremely malleable and excellent team players. Money has little allure for them. SagPisces would rather experience the joy of doing something original and path-breaking.

They are better followers than leaders. If required they can fit into leadership roles and bring a rare combination of compassion and passion to their leadership.

Fire and Water meet in this exciting yet gentle combination. SagPisces are true to their ideals and desire nothing more than living life according to their kaleidoscopic views.

Famous SagPisces Personalities
Farah Khan, Rahul Dravid, Jeetendra, Prakash Raj, Saakshi Tanwar, Smriti Irani, Mohan Babu, Sarah Jessica Parker, David Letterman, Raju Srivastav, Ramkrishna Dalmia, John Major, Guru Gobind Singh, Diane von Fürstenberg, Mansoor Ali Khan Pataudi, Baba Amte, Prince Albert of Monaco, Mirza Ghalib, Shruti Seth, Drashti Dhami.

76. CAPRICORN–AQUARIUS

A visionary who is innovative yet realistic: that is a CapAqua for you. Old, wise and shrewd Saturn rules Capricorn and gives it a melancholic air and Uranus, the planet of invention and eccentricity, makes it think of wild ideas. Most Aquarians have a faraway look in their eyes and think of impossibly futuristic ideas. On their own, Aquarians usually fritter away their genius but armed with the sure practicality of Capricorn, CapAquas can achieve their wackiest dreams.

The outcome of this combination seems amazing but they are as different as chalk and cheese. While both Capricorn and Aquarius are ambitious and believe in doing something great, Aquarius wants to do it for humanitarian reasons while Capricorn does it for personal greatness, for status, money and fame. Another point of disagreement between the two is that of attitude. Capricorn behaves like a sombre old man – stern, restrictive, focused, disciplined and a slave to his/her ambition. They never do anything new or experimental; they believe in the tried and tested. Aquarians are fun-loving creatures with a wacky sense of humour but a scientific bent of mind; they think fifty years ahead and act in an unconventional manner.

CapAquas incorporate the best of both – they think of innovative ideas and ensure their practical implementation. Hard working and focused but diversified and versatile; tried and tested with new and wacky; old-fox cleverness with the intuitive and penetrative; industriousness and hard work with dexterity and genius – this is an amazing fusion of opposites coming together to make a powerhouse personality.

Aquarians are intensely curious about how people think and feel. They can instinctively sense the deepest thoughts of people. When this intuitive ability meets the shrewd Capricornian desire to succeed, it makes for a person who is good at getting their way by reading minds. The softer, more altruistic heart of Aquarius reduces the ruthlessness and pure ambition of Capricorn. CapAquas usually get their way without harming people.

An Aquarian in love is fun to watch – they become totally strange. They become clumsy and say the weirdest things at the most inopportune times. Capricorns, of course, desire only respectability. They look for status, family approval and an assurance of prosperity. CapAquas combine the two and behave incongruously but veer towards respectability.

Family is very important to them. The detachment of Aquarius to family is conquered by the Capricornian's deep love for the family. They need their family's support and love in all their crucial personal decisions. They are very conscious of money and prefer saving and investing. They have a keen eye for detail too. You cannot fool them with legal terms. New ideas and ventures excite them, but the new ideas they invest in will always be sensible ones.

They are the best school buddies who stay in touch with you for a long time. As they grow older, they start making friends on the basis of value, i.e., they are friends with you if they see potential in you. In one way this is a positive indication of your worth and on the other it is better to be a little careful around them. They are quite capable of using friendly confidences to their own advantage, but make it seem like a win-win situation.

They have a dry sense of humour and they manage to crack a smile in the most difficult of circumstances. However, they definitely bear the Saturnine stamp of melancholy. When these ambitious people feel low, they become intensely pessimistic. Then they work doubly hard and deny themselves the pleasures of life. But the dull and sober colours of Capricorn get the swish of a rainbow due to Aquarian light-heartedness. They manage to break their sobriety and release the maverick in them, especially as they grow older. When they hit their forties and fifties they become more relaxed and exuberant.

CapAquas' genius, extraordinary interests and artistic talents overwhelm people. Their deep perception, intelligence and grace charms everyone. They display a winning persona, which they carefully craft through meticulous planning and relentless hard work.

They perfect the art of doing revolutionary stuff without breaking traditions, stepping on toes, or being stamped as mindless rebels. They are quick to sense which way the wind will blow and align their sails accordingly, in every aspect of life. They are politically astute in every sphere of life. These visionaries can see tomorrow and make it happen today. Follow them. They never go wrong.

Capricorn–Aquarius – Sanjay Leela Bhansali

'I've worked so hard for eighteen years. I haven't gone on any holiday. I've experimented and gone from one difficult film to another. Now I want to relax and produce these films before getting on to directing my own film.'[126]

'I absorb a lot. If I go to a hospital to meet a relative or a friend, my mind absorbs their pain. So I'm a wonderful learner and taker of scenes.'[127]

'I like people… but not all of them. My world is beautiful, I dream… don't want to waste my time in parties.'[128]

Sanjay Leela Bhansali's works reveal the ever-evolving Aquarian mind and his relentless hard work pays tribute to his Capricornian nature.

Love and Marriage for Him

He never stresses you out. Family means everything to him and he loves spending time with you. Of course there are some pre-conditions. When you marry him, you marry his mother, father, brother, sister, dog, etc. It is one big happy family. You party together and have fun together.

He needs a woman who makes him look respectable; so learn cooking, the art of homemaking, and dress and behave with utter decorum. Of course, all this does not mean that he forbids you from having a career. You can do that, only be sure to take care of the other aspects.

He supports you and does not scrimp. Actually, he makes sure that his life is comfortable, if not lavish. He can be very unpredictable and weird while expressing love. It may take you time to understand his clumsiness around you.

---

[126] http://www.hindustantimes.com/News-Feed/Interviews-Cinema/I-have-no-competition-Sanjay-Leela-Bhansali/Article1-759099.aspx
[127] http://www.tehelka.com/story_main50.asp?filename=hu291011Interview.asp
[128] http://www.dailymotion.com/video/xbr1x_aishwarya-rai-interview-9_creation

Career is very important to him, so give him space to work his way up the ladder. He manages to balance work and home. He is a fun guy to be with and knows just what you like to do. He wants to keep you happy and secure. Just do not expect emotions and sentimentality from him.

As a father, he tops the list. Capricorn rules fatherhood and makes him an exceptional one. He is strict yet fair, disciplining yet fun loving and a friend to his children. He wants them to learn things on their own and does not shelter them from reality.

Love and Marriage for Her
If she chose you, you can be sure that she saw potential in you. She is very family-oriented and works to please her family members. She loves the security of a loving family and is not displeased if you send money to your parents or siblings. She wants a career and is happy doing something creative and ambitious. She could sideline her desire to work if your ambitions seem ample to her. More than anything else, she desires social status and security.

She is very conscious of money and spends wisely. An intelligent companion, in conversation she surprises with facts and startling observations. She has the knack of knowing exactly what people think and is shrewd enough to know how to react in difficult circumstances.

She is absolutely lovely as a mother. She knows how to get her children to listen to her without losing her cool and can think of the most original games to keep them occupied for hours. Her children learn to be independent and curious, and she inculcates a love for the unexpected in them.

At the Workplace
They are brilliant at whatever career they choose, and are born to do great things in life. They can start from scratch and climb up. Very aware of potential, you will never find them in fields or organisations that are hopeless. CapAquas find extraordinarily new ways of doing old things and vice versa. They use their inventive magic to add zing to their industrious and diligent nature. CapAquas have the potential to make a small idea revolutionise the world.

Despite their fun-loving and sometimes detached attitude you can be sure that they are completely clued in to the political machinations of the business. They know just how to use circumstances to their advantage without being ruthless. Politics is a natural space for them as they can instinctively grasp how to project themselves in order to reach the top.

They are perfect for the corporate world too. They are also brilliant in systems management. They make extraordinary business leaders. They learn and inculcate every possible trick to reach the top and stay there. Be it speaking with power or power dressing, they develop a cool, calculated style that oozes class and confidence.

Earth and Air combine to give stability and originality which saves Capricorn from becoming stodgy and Aquarius from becoming a loose cannon. They have a mind that is open to ideas yet resists impractical dreams. CapAquas are made to be achievers.

Famous CapAqua Personalities
Sanjay Leela Bhansali, Sashi Tharoor, Neymar, Ashutosh Gowariker, Glenn McGrath, Abraham Lincoln, R.P. Goenka, Benjamin Franklin, Martin Luther King, Charles Darwin, S. Sreesanth, Chaminda Vaas, Jon Bon Jovi, Jennifer Leigh, Mary Pierce, Vinod Mehra, Atif Aslam, Enzo Ferrari, Mike Bloomberg, George Peabody, Marjorie Scardino, Karan Singh Grover, Varun Gandhi, Kim Sharma, Alfred Lowenstein, Solomon Pappaiah, Carrie Underwood.

77. CAPRICORN–PISCES

Ever heard of a goatfish? They have this extraordinary ability to change their coloration depending on their current activity. Also, just like a goat, that seeks anything that is edible, they are extremely focused – they seek anything that achieves their goal. Capricorn is ruled by the shrewd old man Saturn while the all-knowing and mysterious Neptune rules Pisces. Old wisdom is the legacy of this combination.

CapPisces are serious and responsible from a very young age. They act like wise old souls when young, and slowly but steadily break the chain of Saturn and become quite easygoing when they hit their forties. The Capricorn love for tradition and old values is deep-rooted in them. Family is extremely important to them. Elders just love them, for Pisceans have a great respect for age and like being in the company of seniors while Capricorns look upon the old ways as the best.

Creativity is their true nature. Capricorns have hidden talents while Pisceans excel at soft, creative disciplines. An artistic environment is most conducive to the overall growth and wellbeing of a CapPisces. Piscean ingenuity and artistic talent is well-complemented by Capricornian discipline and hard work.

The Piscean quality of compassion, and its talent for listening without judging, makes CapPiscess excellent agony aunts. You can go to them with any problem and they will give you a patient hearing. They are also extremely spiritual and interested in the paranormal sciences. They instinctively understand the deepest mysteries of life and love delving into them.

Capricorns desire to be better than anyone else and use shrewd ideas and manipulative tactics to get ahead, but they lack insight into others. Pisces provides Capricorn with that insightful eye and makes it more sensitive. CapPisces get their way by knowing exactly what to say and when. They can be good when things are good and can turn secretly bad too. You underestimate their deceptive sweetness at your own peril.

Pisces reflects emotions and is very sensitive to its surroundings while Capricorn has a melancholic air and can get disheartened very quickly. This emotional sensitivity makes it essential for CapPisces to be surrounded by goodness. A disturbed or negative family environment cripples them for life. If they get bad vibes or feel slighted, threatened or manipulated they can easily shrug off their Piscean goodness and become deceitful and manipulative. They fight back not by aggression or force but through devious means as they lack the courage to directly face their foes.

Another point of contradiction is discipline. Saturn restricts Capricorn and makes it more focused and disciplined while Pisceans are unfocused and scatter their energies. Things that interest them will hold their attention but they lack the total discipline and control of Capricorn. They are subject to extreme mood swings and depression. They are also highly susceptible to black moods and phobias. They find it hard to forget what affects them. Addictions are another pitfall they need to avoid. They love the escapism that addiction offers and have such a deep inferiority complex that they feel only their addictions help them.

Their unpredictable nature affects money matters as well. If a Capricornian stingy mood attacks them, you may find it very hard to get even a dime out of them but when unworldly Pisces moves through them, they are most casual. They know the inherent value of money and the importance of creating wealth, but may lack the discipline to act in a systematic manner. If they cannot accumulate wealth on their own they would look for opportunities like marriage or other socially accepted means to enhance their wealth. They are also people who forge friendships with people who matter. They instinctively know how to appease and please people with authority and power and they do so with élan!

In love, they are extremely giving and caring. The Capricornian love for family and Piscean sensibility can make them quite self-sacrificing and they keep on giving without expecting anything in return. They can act like doormats at times. I am saying 'act', for if hurt, they never retaliate, they react in the background.

Deep inside, every CapPisces wants to break all the customs and rules and be the ultimate showmen, thrilling people with their antics, art and creativity. But old man Saturn demands discipline and Neptune makes them extremely shy. They are chained by these planets and only gentle nurturing would make them thrive. Love, affection, and emotional and financial security can release the chains of these otherwise lovable souls.

Capricorn–Pisces – Steve McQueen

Steve McQueen had an unusual reputation for demanding free items in bulk from studios when agreeing to do a film. It was later found that McQueen requested these things because he was donating them to the Boy's Republic reformatory school for displaced youth, where he had spent time during his teen years.[129]

'Stardom equals financial success and financial success equals security. I've spent too much of my life feeling insecure. I still have nightmares about being poor; stardom means that can't happen.'[130] Steve McQueen could have easily slid into oblivion, given his troubled youth and addictions, yet the combination of CapPisces made him work for a better life.

Love and Marriage for Him

He is an extremely loving guy and can do anything for his family. You are his weakness and it is you who can push him to success or pull him down into the deepest despair.

His mood swings can be unsettling at times, but you soon learn what to do when the blackness strikes him. All he needs is support and love to feel better. Money is something you need to control and it is a great burden off his shoulders if you, too, decide to work. He is so prone to needless worries that the idea of being the sole breadwinner is quite stressful for him.

He is the most easygoing and loving person to share your life with. He can be very insistent on one issue: conventions and traditions. Personally, he is more open and adaptive to new ideas but prefers that society's conventions are followed in public. You are the love of his life but his mom was the first woman in his life. So it is nice for him if you can live in harmony with her.

---

[129] http://en.wikipedia.org/wiki/Steve_McQueen
[130] http://www.stevemcqueensite.com/stevemcqueenquotes.htm

As a father, he is wonderful. He is very sensitive to his children's needs and realises what they want in life. He is so surrounded by fear that he teaches them to understand fear and live fearlessly, something he cannot do himself.

Love and Marriage for Her
She is lovely and feminine. The Capricorn in her wants the best mate while the Piscean wants nothing more than to share her life with you. She needs a strong man in her life. You have to be strong as well as considerate for she has a bundle of worries and phobias that stress her out.

Home is where her heart is. She is most happy in a happy home and does not want to change a thing. She blends in so well that it seems as if she was born in your family. It will be the rare mother-in-law who is not captivated by her charming and loving ways.

Environment affects CapPisces. So, if people are negative and harsh with her, she retaliates without being obvious. She fulfils her duties to the best of her abilities without being aggressive or domineering. Career is not for her and she instinctively shies away from big positions. The more demanding the job, the more political and shrewd her nature becomes. She is happiest and at peace doing small jobs and helping people.

She is in her element as a mother – loving, caring, nurturing and sensitive. She knows what her children want and care for all their problems. She is the first person they turn to and despite her fears, she knows exactly how to soothe them.

At the Workplace
Arts and the creative fields are the natural abodes of this talented sign. It is in arts that their best qualities shine. The extraordinarily wide range of talents of Pisces, when combined with Capricorn, gets purpose and direction. CapPisces are not just brimming with talent but will also ensure it is noticed and showcased.

You can find them in the corporate sphere too but they tend to lose their brilliance and seem somehow conniving and political there. Most of the time, they are hard working, mind their own business and follow the principle of live and let live. They are good at dealing with people and solving problems for them. Human resources, psychology and the alternative sciences are also subjects that interest them and they excel at.

You need to compliment them and admire their efforts for their deep-rooted inferiority complex makes them desire recommendations from others. If he is your boss, never make the mistake of thinking he can be fooled. He is wise to your follies and flaws. How he treats you depends on how much he values you.

Earth and Water meet in this combination to make it extremely talented yet deeply fearful, unworldly yet filled with desires. More than any other, CapPisces needs a loving environment to shine.

Famous CapPisces Personalities
Steve McQueen, Peyton Manning, Emraan Hashmi, Dilip Vengsarkar, Graeme Swann, Birju Maharaj, Prem Nazir, Garth Brooks, Cheteshwar Pujara, Renuka Shahane, Joseph Pulitzer, Monica Bedi, Mahek Chahal, Shamita Shetty, Chloe Grace Moretz, Princess Eugenie of York, Monica Cruz, Lake Bell.

78. AQUARIUS–PISCES

Aquarius is the most intelligent, scientific and eccentric of all the zodiac signs whereas Pisces is the most compassionate, creative and unworldly. This is an intriguing combination of extraordinary Uranus and deep Neptune.

AquaPisces are original, totally uninhibited and can wear anything, due to Aquarius. Pisces too doesn't care about society or its conventions. You find them sporting different hair dos, walking or talking in a different manner, etc. There will be something about them that screams: 'I am not part of the herd'. Ambition and drive are alien words to them. They are highly evolved and material success does not motivate them. AquaPisces feel happy doing what they love. You can only be sure of one thing – whatever they do, it will be quite apart from the average.

Pisces is a very mature soul. It is said that the Piscean has lived through all the zodiac signs in his previous lives and imbibed the virtues of each. Pisces has the childlike curiosity of Aries without its drive, the calmness of Taurus without its materialistic desires and even the passion of Scorpio without the sting. This combination of the eleventh and twelfth signs knows what life is all about. The inventiveness of Aquarius and the dreamy ideals of Pisces make AquaPisces dream up the extraordinarily unconventional.

Both Aquarius and Pisces are known for their expertise in dealing with people. They both love observing people and Pisceans especially are extremely good at empathising with others. They are curious about others and do not mind listening to their stories, however long-winded. To this, add the fact that Aquarians can pick up on any emotion or thought process that goes through your mind. It is difficult to keep any secrets from them.

AquaPisces believe in equality and fraternity and treat everyone with respect and care. Their deep empathy and understanding make them great psychiatrists and counsellors. They can walk in another's shoes and feel their pain. A killer or a madman, both get a patient hearing without being criticised. They can read your soul, know who you are and never judge you for what you are. They feel for the poor, the old, the sick and the disabled, and genuinely want to make a difference in their lives.

They are extremely lively, original and wacky, and love playing games. They also enjoy it if pranks are played on them. They have the most astonishing of hobbies and interests, which may range from sports to astrology, past-life regression to future progression. Their special research areas could include anything from new theories on orgasms to discovering how colonies can settle in space.

The highly individualistic nature of Aquarius makes them follow their heart without caring for societal rules or norms. The only fear is that if the degree of Pisces is greater, they then do not desire anything and can spend their life drinking and dreaming. This potential laziness, not owning up to responsibility, and extreme abstract thinking can totally destroy the capabilities of a highly intelligent and inventive person. They believe in the natural goodness of people, which can lead them to be used. Many times, they know that they are being taken advantage of, but they let it be.

They excel at generating ideas. Action does not come readily to them. AquaPisces have to be pushed to achieve success. It will take them a while to learn how to make their ideas work. The absent-minded professor completely fits the description of an AquaPisces! Aquarius also adds a touch of clumsiness to them. Add the fact that Pisceans don't walk but glide – these personalities will have an unusual gait.

The sensitivity of AquaPisces can see them giving in to depression and they are quite susceptible to addictions. Pisces needs to hook onto something that gives it a temporary high. Combine that with the Aquarian habit of trying 'everything' at least once and we have a potential hazard. They can easily be lured into a false sense of euphoria or into escapism.

There is a continuous mutability in them. They keep reinventing themselves. Their interests in jobs, hobbies or even people keep changing as they get bored quickly and seek new thrills. There is an innate need for change and sometimes they may seek change, just for the sake of change. This can be constructive or destructive, depending on how they view the process of change.

A potential genius combined with a sensitive artist, AquaPisces would be a dream combination conquering the world by breaking all the rules and conventions. The only missing ingredients are discipline and the urge for action. If added, they are unstoppable!

Aquarius–Pisces – Anupam Kher

Anupam Kher is known for his acting prowess. He broke into the film world by acting as a sixty-year-old-man when he was in his twenties.

'I am a dreamer. That's how I am into films as well; not just because of my talents. Because when you are born in a small town, you only dream.'[131]

'I always wanted to be different.'

'To me, life is about reinventing yourself. You have to keep reinventing. So that's what is important.'[132]

Anupam Kher has the creativity and sensitivity of AquaPisces and the ability to learn and evolve throughout his life.

Love and Marriage for Him

He is very romantic. Life with him is anything but conventional. The amazing thing about this person is that he can change any time. The Piscean in him makes him extremely adaptable.

He is the most sympathetic of husbands and can listen to you for hours. Yet, there are chances that he may wander away mentally. The Aquarian in him may have suddenly thought of some weird idea during his flights of fancy. Gently bring him back to earth and continue the conversation.

His idealistic views and lack of ambition never go away. So, you have to be the realistic one. Do not dictate to him for then he just fades away. What he needs is the support of a practical person who does not take away the beauty of his inventive dreams from him. If ambition, drive and success in a partner are important to you

---

[131] http://www.glamsham.com/movies/interviews/25-anupam-kher-interview-031012.asp
[132] http://lawofsuccess2.blogspot.in/2011/01/interview-with-anupam-kher.html

then this is not your ideal guy. Money holds no importance for him and he does not save.

He may not know exactly what he wants in a relationship. This guy does not settle down early in life, as he is curious about other people and wants to know more about them. Once he knows 'everything' about you and the mystery is solved, he may lose interest. If you are not careful, you may end up being a guinea pig in his 'researches' and then off he will go in search of another 'project' to explore. Overall, there is a distinct possibility of him having many relationships before settling down. The trick is to give him a dose of his own medicine. Do not allow him to know everything about you. Be mysterious. Be sufficiently 'closed', but also be sufficiently 'open', so that he's interested. It's tricky… but you can manage it, can't you?

He is the funniest, quirkiest and most permissive father around. But you need to be the one maintaining the discipline.

Love and Marriage for Her
Aquarian girls are the most beautiful, after Libra, and have beautiful, dreamy, expressive eyes, while Pisces have rounded, liquid eyes. She has a softness about her and her eyes speak volumes. Her style statement is totally individualistic. She does not fit into the mould of an ideal wife with ease. Her lack of ego makes her pliable but do not expect her to take up housework.

If you want her to live with your family, you must make sure that your family is quite broadminded and flexible for she can dress quite unconventionally without meaning to create a stir. She is highly sensitive and has problems expressing her love. She also has the Aquarian habit of changing topics and getting lost during a conversation.

She needs a lot of help in the early years of parenting. You need to sit with her, plan her daily routine and have an hour-by-hour schedule worked out to manage better. She can cook exotic recipes but will require help for the regular days.

At the Workplace
They cannot be pushed into just any field. AquaPisces need to love what they do; only then do their creative juices flow. The Piscean in them makes them good authors and poets and Aquarius adds an individualistic touch. AquaPisces are make great actors and musicians, and even psychologists and counsellors. Do not expect them to work in offices. Routine bores them and they constantly seek change. They often don various roles during their careers.

Money and glory do not excite them. What makes them go on is the belief that they can create something better and completely outstanding. Most of them excel later in life. As bosses, they can be most permissive and understanding. Remember, you can never hide anything from them, so don't even think of fooling them.

This ethereal, sublime and eccentric combination demonstrates that if you are interestingly different, intellectually idiosyncratic and willing to learn discipline, then you will find your place under the sun.

Famous AquaPisces Personalities
Anupam Kher, Michael Clarke, Hugh Hefner, Kesha, Prabhudeva, Zakir Hussein (tabla virtuoso), Rannvijay, Didier Drogba, James Patterson, Rajesh Kumar (writer), Naveen Jindal, Ben Hilfenhaus, Lawrence J. Cadbury, Alka Yagnik, Martin Johnson, Shobana, Savitri Jindal, Khaled, Angela Jonsson, Meera Sanyal, Stephen Fleming, Chitrangada Singh, Prakash Jha, Lucy Lawless, Kenny Chesney, Tanushree Dutta, Devika Rani, Walter Chrysler, Jean Harlow, Chuck Norris, Warner Baxter, Sheila Bair, Hrehaan Roshan, Rex Harrison, Keshav Hedgewar, Eugen Sandow, Jaya Prada, Abraham Maslow, Yo Yo Honey Singh.

79. ARIES–TAURUS–GEMINI

Mars, the violent and powerful god of war, joins the maverick and extremely intelligent Mercury, to impart raw strength and an agile mind. Add to this the calm common sense of Taurus and you have a winning combination of power, thought and mental stability. AriTauGems are born gladiators who fight to the end with all they have. This combination brings out the positives of each zodiac sign.

In AriTauGems, the Arian 'my view first' tendency is diluted due to Taurean calm stability, while maintaining Arian drive and ambition. The Gemini in them makes them think on their feet. They can always think their way out of predicaments. Gemini also gives them the gift of multitasking. AriTauGems are skilled at many different things and are able to work, ideate and act all at once.

The Aries drive, Taurus focus and Gemini talent make them tremendously versatile. AriTauGems are exceptionally creative and full of originality and resourcefulness. They are good at visualising ideas and implementing them logically. Money and power drive them to reach their goals. They need a lot of money and work hard to fulfil their materialistic dreams.

The Gemini-Taurus combination makes them excellent at mind games. 'Mental disintegration' is a special skill of the Taurus-Gemini. AriTauGems slowly get under the skin of the opponent by using words and action and finally the opponent does something stupid and loses the battle. In the entire process, they remain strong and impregnable, while their opponents crumble before they enter the arena. They know the power of words and use them effectively. Where words fail, they use brute strength but that is only as the last option.

They are witty, humorous, sarcastic and intelligent talkers. They are also masters of the one-liner. Expect them to excel in languages and be masters of written and verbal communication. Sociable and genial, they know how to network and maintain relationships. Taurus gives them a pleasant personality and reduces the overdrive trait of Aries.

They will act gentlemanly and know how to camouflage their aggressive warrior aspect. It's a beautiful combination of brain and brawn and a pleasure to watch them in action, bulldozing their way through or decimating their opponents with smart and funny quips. They always have the last word!

Family is extremely important to them. They are always there for their families and strive to improve the family status. But love does not make fools of them. They do not have the Water element and thus aren't overly emotional. AriTauGems never try and fight the world for their love, nor promise the moon to their loved ones. They are extremely commonsensical in their approach to the emotional rollercoaster of love. Practical and sensible as always, they prefer family support and look for a partner who can balance them out.

They can't exactly read into the depths of people's hearts. Gemini adds the knowledge of people without imparting an actual understanding of their souls. So don't expect them to know your deepest fears or your heart's desires. They need to be told what you want.

They also know how to enjoy themselves and love partying. They never spend their time mulling over 'what ifs…' These guys know the importance of living life in the present. They are also adventurous and sporty. They love food and feeding others; food is the highlight of their outings. Whenever they attend a party, they make it a memorable occasion with fun, laughter, pranks and pulling weird faces. And yes; don't believe in all their stories as they do embellish them to make them more interesting for you.

There are chances that you may stumble upon an AriTauGem who has all the negative traits of Aries, Taurus and Gemini: self-centred and materialistic with a dual personality. But they are fairly rare. Hope you get lucky.

AriTauGems are happy, optimistic and strong personalities and carry no emotional baggage to pull them down. They live life with energy and have their sights firmly set on money, status and career advancement. Everything else comes later.

Aries–Taurus–Gemini – Meryl Streep
A hands-on Arian parent, Streep freely admits, 'Lecturing is what I do with my children, not listening. Lecturing, and ordering out.'[133]

Streep is well-known for her ability to imitate foreign and domestic accents from Danish in *Out of Africa*, to English in *Plenty*, Italian in *The Bridges of Madison County*, and the Midwestern dialect in *A Prairie Home Companion*. In *A Cry in the Dark* she coloured Australian English with New Zealand tonalities. Meryl Streep is one of the most versatile actresses to have graced the screen.[134]

She has the Gemini knack of impersonating people along with the well-thought-out nuances she imparts to her roles. She is a true AriTauGem.

Love and Marriage for Him
He is your support system. You can turn to him in times of need and he always helps you out. With him by your side, you can be sure of a rollicking good time. He shows you the sights and makes you travel the world. His ambitions are large and so is his zest for life. He likes to chart his growth path and expects you to support his plans.

He never stops you from chasing your own dreams as long as you take care of his as well. He understands your views once you make them evident to him.

There is one problem with him though. He cannot look into your heart and understand your deepest desires. You need to understand that beneath his intelligent talk and wit lies a man who is childlike. He can only look at his own problems and issues; he cannot see what makes up *your* world. Despite the dilution of the Arian self-centredness, most conversations may veer towards his requirements by the end, which can be very frustrating, especially if you are a strong lady yourself. He may not realise that he is 'me-centric' most of the time. Verbalise your problems and he may listen.

His family is very important to him and he likes to be the man of the house. But expect to handle the small day-to-day emergencies yourself – he simply doesn't think they're worth his while. But he's there to deal with the big ones, so don't worry!

---
[133] http://www.goodhousekeeping.com/family/celebrity-interviews/meryl-streep-interview-2
[134] http://en.wikipedia.org/wiki/Meryl_Streep

Bring on the spice to keep him guessing and interested even after decades of marriage. His Gemini roving eye may cause a few flutters, especially after he settles into achieving his ambitions.

As a father, he is protective and caring. He shows his children how to live like warriors and teaches them to face difficulties with fortitude and well-developed reflexes.

Love and Marriage for Her
She is a forceful personality for sure. Do not expect her to be a traditional wife. She may be less than five feet tall but will be a volcano nonetheless. She wants to prove a point to the world that she is as good as any man. Never tell her that she cannot do something because of her gender, age or status. She has no emotional demands and does not ask you to read her thoughts. She always tells you what she thinks and is the best companion you could ever have.

She needs a man who plays his role effectively. You need to be ambitious and strong if you want her to remain the happy, positive person she is. She is cool and controlled like a Taurean, chirpy like a Gemini, and cheerful and bright like an Arian.

She will do so many things, so well, in such a short span of time, that it will be a wonder to watch her. She is a pillar of strength for the family and knows how to handle problems, from everyday emergencies to major calamities.

She can talk her way out of anything. She can throw verbal volleys at people who offend her and shut them up. You can just leave her to manage everything and concentrate on your career. Money is very important to her, so you need to make sure that her bank balance is good.

As a mother, she is strong and supportive. She does not pamper her children too much. She teaches them new things and trains them to be brave and strong.

At the Workplace
AriTauGems have immense strength, excellent communication skills and are absolutely fearless. They can take on anything, from corporate life to sports. These people are living dynamos who just need to be pointed in the right direction. They have boundless energy, drive, a thirst for victory, plus the inscrutable Taurean mind, with the Gemini ability to think on their feet.

Cardinal, fixed and mutable signs combine in them. This makes them ready to start small and learn along the way, plus dream visionary dreams that they are able to convert into reality. They are excellent team players who strive hard to better themselves. To keep such excellent workers happy, you need to pay them. They want money and always put in more effort for money. Do not forget to appreciate them either.

One day they will want to leave it all and start their own set up. They want to be their own boss and maximise the chance of having in abundance the three things they always want – fame, money and status.

Fire, Earth and Air combine in this exciting combination that is optimistic, level-headed, creative and ambitious, with extreme physical and mental strength.

Famous AriTauGem Personalities
Meryl Streep, Rafael Nadal, Sri Sri Ravishankar, Michael J. Fox, Umar Akmal, E.M.S. Namboodiripad, Kulraj Randhawa, A.M. Rajah, Rajev Paul.

80. ARIES–TAURUS–CANCER

Mars, the violent and powerful lord of war, gets a little respite from being fiery in partnership with the patient and enduring Taurus, and the sensitive Cancer, in AriTauCans. The Aries in them brings in a positivity that is missing in Taurus and Cancer. They try and look beyond their fears and think of all the positive things that could happen. AriTauCans express their passions and ambitions through their expressive eyes.

This is a double cardinal sign – Aries and Cancer. If they pursue something, they won't let it go easily. They definitely know how to lead and do so by first coaxing and cajoling and if that doesn't work, probably by demanding and yelling. AriTauCans have a single aim in life. The high ambition of Aries is fuelled by the exemplary Taurean work ethic and Cancerian tenacity. They never deviate from their path once they make up their minds.

The arrogance and high-handed behaviour of Aries will, thankfully, be quite diluted in them and they come across as warm people. They do think of things beyond themselves and bring a larger perspective to the table. They speak with emotion, sensitivity and practicality. The infusion of logic and drive does wonders to their creativity.

They love a lot, especially their families. They are happiest in the midst of their loved ones. They will do anything for their mothers. They can be the most loving of friends – extremely loyal and very generous. They offer emotional and monetary support without a thought, but are not easy to fool.

Aries desires to be a pioneer while Taurus is extremely creative and enjoys music and art. Cancer adds a heavy dose of talent and imagination to the mix. AriTauCans express their creativity with passion. They have a dry and wry sense of humour and are always ready for a laugh. They prefer being home or in the company of a few good friends to wild nights. They love travelling but carry a memento to remind them of home.

Love is very important to them. Aries desires idealistic love while Cancer makes them very romantic and emotional. Taureans are very sensual lovers too. This is a heady mix. Expect them to be sensitive, volatile and expressive in love. AriTauCans can write heart-rending poems and will never stop being demonstrative of their love. They feel deeply and can hurt deeply too. Love will make them fools, but lovable fools. Once they are in love, expect them to stick to that person and smother them with affection.

Food and music are their twin loves. They love both with a deep passion. They enjoy cooking and eating out, yet their favourite dishes are those that remind them of their childhood and their mother. Music is a great stress-buster for them and they have a deeply emotional connect with music, especially old melodies.

They also have a deep vein of patriotism. They never forget the place that gave them their identities and are very rooted. They can fight for their country and be emotionally connected to it even if they reside far away. They are very nostalgic in general.

They will want their surroundings to be cosy and comfortable – cool modern furniture or interiors are not for them!. They have sharp memories; they can remember things that happened even when they were toddlers. They will remember all the happy moments and will still hurt from the sad ones.

Money is definitely an important part of their lives. They have the Cancerian fear of never having enough, the Taurean materialism and the Arian need to shine. AriTauCans want lots of money and are willing to save rather than splurge. They might be a little tight-fisted but do want luxury and will be ready to bargain for it.

They are afflicted with the Cancerian moodiness. It is not too pronounced due to the level-headed Taurus, but they are prone to mood swings. They sulk when not given attention. They have a temper too, but prefer sulking to let people know of their disappointment. They are also extremely touchy – be careful of your words, they have the habit of reading between the lines and feeling hurt.

AriTauCans love being pampered and looked after. Their family, and especially their partner, needs to be aware of their deep-seated desire for love and approval. They can be extremely stubborn if they feel strongly about something. They can also go into their shells and then it becomes extremely difficult for people to coax them out.

Despite their outward bravado, there is a hidden insecurity in them. They feel they are not good enough, intelligent enough, brave enough, etc. To escape prying eyes and stop themselves from getting hurt, they put up the façade of a toughie but they are gooey-soft inside. They need emotional and financial security to overcome the blues. They need physical expressions of love too. Give them a huge hug and you will see them beaming and regaining the strength to slug it out.

Aries–Taurus–Cancer – Zubin Mehta
Zubin Mehta is a conductor of western classical music.

His mother once shared a memory of how when some people referred to him as a national of their country, Zubin, though honoured, had responded, 'I feel very friendly toward your country, but make no mistake, I'm an Indian first.'[135]

'I cook Italian food mostly and also Indian food. I carry my chillies when I travel.'

In his autobiography, he has mentioned and owned up to his children from outside marriage. 'Otherwise it would be hypocritical... if I am writing about my life... my other children (from outside marriage) are part of my life also.'

Zubin Mehta has the AriTauCans love of music, food and his country, plus its brand of honesty.

Love and Marriage for Him
He loves being entrenched in family life, and if not for his ambitions, would have remained there. He is full of energy and enthusiasm for his chosen profession and has a burning desire to achieve. He will work hard but will still be grounded enough to take time out to spend with you.

Despite his ambitions and enthusiasm, there is a deep vein of insecurity in him. The insecurity will become more apparent when crises loom. He has it in him to battle all odds but will need lots of love and encouragement. He is a sensitive, emotional guy who is quite moody, despite his optimism. You have to understand

---

[135] http://www.littleindia.com/arts-entertainment/1658-zubin-mehta-the-maestro-from-mumbai.html

his different moods and temperaments and work accordingly. He also understands your feelings.

He loves spending time with you. He does not mind long hours spent shopping. He is quite romantic and knows how to woo you. You can expect flowers, candle-light dinners and romantic outings. He loves his mother a lot and wants you to share a warm relationship with her.

He relaxes with music, laughter and food. Actually, food is very important to him.

He is softly dominating; but dominate he does – he will not let you dominate him. Children love him for he is loving and caring. He naturally moves into fatherhood and takes all the responsibilities in his stride. His children love being pampered by him and also know the invisible line they cannot cross.

Love and Marriage for Her
She acts soft and feminine yet her core is stronger than steel. This lady never breaks under pressure; she finds the strength to carry herself and her family through periods of extreme stress. However, she is exceptionally sensitive and emotional, and has strong opinions. Family is important to her and she takes on any burden for their welfare.

She likes to travel but prefers to do it with family. She is ambitious, creative and talented. Capable of achieving a lot of things, she needs you to make her aware of her strengths. She needs a little push at times; do that and see her take the world by storm.

Old memories, food and music will be very dear to her. Her idea of a good time will always have good food in it, especially the kind her mother used to make. She hates wasting food.

Motherhood suits her. She loves nurturing her children and always finds time to be with them. Her children know they can go to her with their problems.

At the Workplace
AriTauCans are born leaders. They are willing to wait and work for success and they reach the pinnacle with their perseverance, endurance and big dreams. They excel in any career, ones that involve routine work or those requiring creative skills. They know how to deal with people and are fabulous team players and leaders.

They are reliable workers. Give them the work and a deadline; if they accept it, they will get it done whatever the situation. Encouragement and money are important to them. They are your most loyal and efficient employees, if treated well. They also want to be their own bosses.

As bosses, they are inspirational leaders – known to be tough taskmasters and tight-fisted, they ensure that the organisation always does well and turns profitable. Their budget management is exemplary.

Fire, Earth and Water combine in AriTauCans. They have the strength and power to overcome their own insecurities and know how to shine bright in the darkest of nights.

Famous AriTauCan Personalities
Zubin Mehta, Cafu, Dave Gahan, Marco Rubio, B.S. Chandrasekhar, Drew Carey.

81. ARIES–TAURUS–LEO

Mars, the violent god of war, meets the calm and patient Taurus, and the royal Apollo, in AriTauLeos. There are three animals in this combination – a Ram, a Bull and a Lion – and their characteristics resemble these tough animals in many ways. They have the forcefulness of the Aries, the doggedness of the Taurus and the pride of the Leo. Just like the Ram, they only look forward in life, undeterred by circumstances, and are extremely goal-oriented. The Bull in them ensures they stay put and the pride of the Lion is at the forefront of all that they do in life.

Looks are very important to them; they dress to impress. The Lion cannot look ordinary. They dream impossible dreams and want to hear thunderous applause. They want to live life king-size and chafe against common existence. They need to be in the spotlight to feel really good about themselves. They like spending time partying and travelling. They swish into the most happening places and love being stared at. They seek attention and are very unhappy if they don't encounter even one admiring glance.

They want and need to be surrounded by luxury – a Taurean need. At the same time, they also invest their money. They want money in abundance to feel happy, secure and satisfied. The Leo and Aries in them also love the 'feel good' factor of expensive purchases and will regularly set out on shopping expeditions to the best outlets in town. The Taurus in them will make sure that they get the best brands and labels at the best prices.

They are artistic and creative. Leo and Taurus add the artistic sheen to them and AriTauLeos want people to notice their talent. They love music and relax by listening to their favourite songs. Expect them to dazzle on the dance floor or croon and mesmerise an adoring audience.

Their needs come first before all else – a typical Arian trait. You may call it self-centred but they feel it's their birthright. They are drawn to danger. They like speed and want to roar down the road. They are full of good cheer and positivity. They have few, but loyal, friends. They push their friends to try out something new and adventurous every day.

Now let's explore the not-so-pleasant traits of these creatures. Have you noticed how a bull refuses to budge when it decides to stay put in the middle of the road? They are also fixed in their opinions. It is quite difficult to change their views and they never think from another's perspective. Both Taurus and Leo are fixed signs and add that stolid immovability to the firebrand Aries. You will have to work around their opinions.

What a combination – the indolent Lion and the slow Bull! Despite their enthusiasm, there is a strong streak of laziness in them. They like relaxing and lounging around. And this is a triple dose! If they have decided they are not going to do something, just forget about it, as the self-interested Aries doesn't want to do it, the Lion's ego won't listen to you and the laidback Bull is just too lazy to do it.

Both Aries and Leo are Fire signs and are prone to insecurities. They will not talk about their fears and be even more aggressive to hide their fears, yet they will be there. Fear is also the reason for their brittle egos. The smallest hint of an opposing view can make them bristle and then they need careful handling. They gain confidence as they achieve success but never say, 'I told you so' when they fail. It destroys their confidence.

They divide the world into two – their near ones and others. They have no time or patience for the others but are generous to the people they love. They are blunt and say what they think to your face. They appreciate it if you also do the same, albeit politely. However, it is important to them that people listen to what they say. They are childishly self-centred without realising it.

AriTauLeos look for love and glamour in their partner. They weigh the monetary repercussions, the effect on status and have a quick check at how you look together before deciding on you as a partner. They look for a partner who can make them look good. Besides, they also need the social acceptance and social security. But once they accept you, they want everlasting, never-ending romance and love. They seek idealistic, copybook love but from the 'right' person.

AriTauLeos contain two Fire signs and these make them spiritually inclined. They definitely believe in a superior power and other esoteric aspects of life. They are proud of their roots and lineage, and the traditional wisdom of their customs and beliefs.

The lack of Water in this combination makes them a bit insensitive to the feelings of others. They do not mind trampling over others or being rude to them. Their anger is fearsome. They shout and scream, and the smallest setback or trespass can result in an angry outburst from them. But if you appeal to their generosity and apologise, they will relent quickly.

Despite all their idiosyncrasies, their biggest strength is the combination of the Ram's inherent energy, the Bull's mental strength and the Lion's brute power. This makes them strong individuals who can move mountains and fight the toughest situations in life admirably. They simply never give up.

Aries–Taurus~Leo – John F. Kennedy
'My fellow Americans, ask not what your country can do for you, ask what you can do for your country.'

'Things do not happen. Things are made to happen.'

'There are risks and costs to action. But they are far less than the long range risks of comfortable inaction.'

'Efforts and courage are not enough without purpose and direction.' 'Let every nation know, whether it wishes us well or ill, that we shall pay any price, bear any burden, meet any hardship, support any friend, oppose any foe to assure the survival and the success of liberty.' J.F.K.'s ambition and courage marked him out as a AriTauLeo worth emulating.

Love and Marriage for Him
He is the lord and master of the house. He loves lazing around and wants everything to be done for him. Please do not ask him to help; it is of no use. Household chores are beneath him.

He is extremely romantic. You can expect flowers, outings and lavish gifts from him. He loves pampering you – if you listen to him. This guy wants a wife who looks good on his arm, and loves to show you off. He loves food and enjoys throwing parties. Be ready to be a superb hostess as he wants his guests impressed.

He is extremely ambitious. This guy dreams big dreams and wants a partner who understands his need to lead. He likes the feeling of being in command, and will allow you to do what you want if you agree to listen to his advice first. His anger is quite spectacular. Feed him well, lie in his arms and look at him with admiration. He can never ever leave you then.

As a father, he is caring and very proud of his children. He loves telling them what to do and is full of advice and commands. They have no option but to obey him.

Love and Marriage for Her
She wants a partner who stands out and is not happy with a person who has modest dreams. Ambition and money count a lot with her and she wants a partner who thinks big and earns well.

She is full of optimism and enthusiasm, especially when she is out to achieve her dreams. Nothing ever stops her. She is also the most fun person at parties. This girl loves to shine wherever she goes and does not tolerate any competition.

She has her own opinions and nothing you say or do can change them. She wants to be heard on every occasion. Housework is not her strong point but she can manage servants well. She loves relaxing and lazing. Her tolerance levels are quite low and any glitch in her plans makes her fume. She loves romantic gestures and wants her love life to be like in the movies, full of dramatic scenes and romantic gifts.

She loves her children, though she may be reluctant to take on such responsibilities at first. Her children are her pride and joy. She also wants to lead them and is a dominating presence in their lives.

At the Workplace
AriTauLeos are born to lead. They have pioneering ideas and are full of enthusiasm to reach their goals. But they need help in finalising their goals for they have many plans and are excited about many things. They want careers where they can lead, advise or create a buzz around themselves.

They are good in artistic fields and love showcasing their talents. They also do well in proprietary businesses where they have to lead.

Money and glory are what they seek. Give them a potful of money and a fancy designation to make them feel good, and they will work harder for you.

Double Fire and Earth meet in this amazingly optimistic combination. AriTauLeos will blaze through life with their audacious dreams, commonsensical solutions and regal air.

Famous AriTauLeo Personalities
J.F.K., Megan Fox, P.T. Usha, Jay Leno, Johan Botha, Aditi Govitrikar, Murali (Tamil actor), Marquis de Sade, N.T. Rama Rao Jr.

82. ARIES–TAURUS–VIRGO

Mars, the often violent and powerful god of war, combines forces with the calm and enduring Taurus, and the perfection-seeking Virgo in AriTauVir. AriTauVirs are quite ambitious but they do not rush headlong into executing new ideas. They are willing to think each step through before acting upon something.

This is an interesting combination of two animals and a human. It is the coming together of the brave and energetic Aries, the Ram, with the dependable and resolute Taurus, the Bull. Add to this, the soft healing touch of the puritanical and fastidious Virgo, the Virgin Maiden. This combination possesses extraordinary idealism, practicality and resourcefulness.

They are super-confident and dependable. When they talk, you hear passion, logic and clarity. They give long and detailed reasons and expound passionately about why their idea is the best. You will find it extremely difficult to counter them when they talk with that conviction. Most of their views are fixed and they do not change them easily. The Taurus in them is quite traditional and conservative but the Aries in them makes them test the limits and break the rules. If they believe in a pioneering idea or cause, or if they form an opinion, they are not afraid to voice it. In fact, they will actively champion their chosen cause.

They have excellent manners. The clinical cleanliness and shining idealistic perfectionism of their minds is reflected in their personal habits. They hate vulgarity, shun unruliness and are idealistic about every aspect of life. They are perfectionists and hygiene freaks.

The glory-seeking pioneering ways of Aries are tempered with the logic of slow and steady Taurus and meticulously calculative Virgo. AriTauVirs are planners and doers. They are very intelligent and have absolute clarity of thought and purpose. They are the flag bearers of logical deduction and the brave whistleblowers and champions of truth and justice. Their phenomenal strength is that they never accept failure and carry on boldly in a structured, logical manner.

Family is extremely important and they feel happy spending time with family members. They are very responsible people in spite of their ambitions. Their words resonate with calm sagacity and you will turn to them in times of crisis for they will seem in control of the situation. Virgo industriousness, combined with the will power of Taurus and the undying zeal and enthusiasm of Aries, makes for an outstanding combination of protector, preserver and nurturer of values, tradition and culture.

AriTauVirs have a definite sense of music. Add the perfectionist Virgo to it and you have meticulously artistic people – from painting, singing to dancing, they do it all perfectly. The reserve of Taurus and Virgo is quite reduced due to the fiery nature of Aries and they are not shy of showcasing their talents. Food is another passion for them. They like cooking and easily whip up mouth-watering delicacies. Expect them to be exacting and fussy about their food preferences, though.

They also like certain things done at certain times. They get agitated if their routine is disturbed. They intuitively understand the effect of various medicines and can give tips for a healthy life to family and friends. The spotlight calls to them and they like being dressed perfectly for every occasion. Money is important and they plan and budget for it. The impulsive nature of Aries is muted in them.

Love will find them faithful. AriTauVirs want a committed and idealistic relationship and might spend a lot of time thinking through the implications of falling in love before actually taking a step. They rarely choose partners who are not accepted by their family.

They do not shout and scream but prefer to think before giving in to their tempers. When they get angry, run for cover for they can get scathingly critical. Though they are excessively critical and scathing in their attacks most of the time, Taurus has a calming effect on them. Some of the more evolved people in this combination master the art of controlled aggression.

Their confidence and optimism hide the characteristic inner insecurity of Fire signs. Though they show a tough exterior, they are unsure within and suffer bouts of anxiety. Virgo makes them virtual nail biters and they have their stressed-out times.

There is no Water or Air element in this combination; therefore insensitivity is their biggest bane. They understand the pain a physical wound can cause and would know how to heal it, but they cannot understand the scars words cause. They can be brutally honest, may not understand the deepest needs of people, and can lack diplomatic language skills.

They are masters of controlled aggression and never give up easily. Although they insist on planned behaviour, they stand tall and strong when emergencies strike and crisis looms large. Despite their tactlessness, occasional thoughtlessness and inconsiderate behaviour, there is a solid dependability, naïve bravery and touching truthfulness about AriTauVirs that makes them truly lovable.

Aries–Taurus–Virgo – Bertrand Russell
Russell was a British philosopher, logician, mathematician, historian, and social critic.

'The intellectual thing I should want to say is this: When you are studying any matter, or considering any philosophy, ask yourself only what are the facts and what is the truth that the facts bear out. Never let yourself be diverted either by what you wish to believe, or by what you think would have beneficent social effects if it were believed.'[136]

'The point of philosophy is to start with something so simple as not to seem worth stating, and to end with something so paradoxical that no one will believe it.'[137]

Bertrand Russell had the pioneering views, deeply incisive mind and courage to speak his mind, of an AriTauVir.

Love and Marriage for Him
He wants to be the master of the house and has fairly conventional views on marriage. He wants to be the provider and works hard for his family. He needs a mate who meets his ideals of perfection. He also expects his wife to take care of the family and actively propagates family values. Don't expect him to be boring just because he is traditional, he will understand humour and be quite romantic too.

---

[136] http://io9.com/5827117/in-1959-mathematician+philosopher-bertrand-russell-had-two-things-he-wanted-to-say-to-people-of-the-future
[137] http://www.brainyquote.com/quotes/quotes/b/bertrandru107179.html

He likes a bit of pampering. Listen to him and let him relax when he comes back from work. He is very particular about how money is spent, so keep a record of your expenses. But he loves luxury; so you both can happily spend money there.

You will know where he is at any given point of time and there will be no rude shocks about him. Don't nag, cry or expect him to understand sighs and hints. He needs clear communication. He tries hard to make you happy. Just tell him what you want.

He is a good father who tries to fulfil all his expected duties. He may not be very good at understanding his children, despite his love for them. He insists on a good education.

Love and Marriage for Her
She is full of energy and concern for her family. This lady prioritises her family, but she also needs financial stability. She is not content managing the home if her family is not financially well off. Work, money and a bit of glory impel her to explore new avenues. She is traditional but may flout conventions if she feels otherwise.

She wants a partner she can look up to. She admires strength and ambition. She is quite romantic and wants passion in her relationship. She is very idealistic in love and deeply sentimental. She expects everything in love and romance to be picture perfect and is a tough lady to please.

Though she is not exactly sensitive to the deep emotions of people around her, she ensures she fulfils her duties. She has a mental and emotional toughness, which makes her a rock for her family in times of crisis. She is often critical of things and people she does not like. The best way to live with this is to respond but not react.

As a mother, she is fun but also demands respect from her children. She loves to play with them and spends ample time with them. She is good at nursing them and caring for their needs.

At the Workplace
AriTauVirs use their energy and drive to accomplish their desires. They are extremely hard-working and never laze around when there is work to be done. They are good planners and doers; also, they are able to think of new ideas.

They are excellent at research and planning. They also find themselves at home in any career related to finance and finance management. They are extremely logical and systematic in their approach. The best thing is they have immensely high energy levels, creativity and staying power and can seamlessly execute their perfectly laid out plans. They are great in business. They can shine in the creative fields as well.

They can be extremely critical and demanding as bosses. They can be penny-pinchers, but highly generous if you listen to their advice and work hard to make their vision come true.

Fire and double Earth meet in this stable yet driven combination and make AriTauVirs shine with positivity while giving them a thinking mind and a caring nature.

Famous AriTauVir Personalities
Bertrand Russell, Mahela Jayawardene, Miuccia Prada, Billy Joel, Pankaj Udhas, Lilette Dubey, King George V of England, Raja Ram Mohan Roy.

83. ARIES–TAURUS–LIBRA

Mars, the god of war, joins forces with the patient and enduring Taurus and the luxury-loving Libra in AriTauLib. The pioneering creativity, energy and zeal of Aries meet the amazing mental strength and sturdiness of Taurus; Libra further enhances the combination with its wit, love, and communication skills. AriTauLib is a coming together of diverse forces to create a powerhouse.

Talking and expressing themselves verbally comes naturally to them. They have fascinating conversation skills and are quite adept at word play with Libran flair and Taurean common sense. They are also quite logical in their speech patterns and are able to state facts in a clear and precise manner without going into Libran overdrive. They are fun people to be with. You are rarely bored in their company for they know the juiciest gossip and the most thrilling anecdotes. They look forward to interesting debates.

They simply love their family. Taureans are extremely protective of their family and Aries is proud of its lineage. AriTauLib are very generous, especially to people they love. They uphold family traditions and are respectful to their elders. Despite a modern upbringing, they have a grounded approach to tradition.

They have a great sense of aesthetics, fashion, music and the arts. Taurus and Libra are wonderfully musical, while Libra is the most fashionable. When combined with forceful Aries, AriTauLibs become fearless in expressing their artistic sensibilities. They are true connoisseurs and patrons of art and creativity. Luxury attracts them. The Libran love for beautiful things, the Taurean desire for delicate sweet-smelling accessories and the Arian affinity for shiny baubles make them buy the most luxurious brands. They are very fashion conscious, and thankfully, the loud and irreverent Aries becomes a little understated, yet very elegant, with the addition of Libra and Taurus.

They can also excel at sports, with the strength, balance and mental stability to do well. Moreover, they are ruthlessly powerful with an exquisite sense of balance. They are always ready for a spot of adventure and are game to try out death-defying stunts.

Love is extremely important to them. They make love an impossible ideal. Sentimental and romantic, you can expect poems, flowers and everything else from AriTauLibs when they are in love. The Arian idealistic love, the sensuousness of Taurus and the Libran desire for eternal love will make them seek a love that is beyond the ordinary. They give their all to a relationship and have high expectations from their partner. Their only problem, if you can call it that, is their inability to read you completely. AriTauLibs need to be told how you feel for them. Please remember to talk to them for talk is essential to them.

They love to travel to new places and discover distant lands but in the lap of luxury. They do not like being alone for long. They want people around them and love partying.

Money is extremely important to them. They spend a lot, without a second thought. They are always on the lookout to earn more rather than save. They will also know how to invest their money and plan for the future. Taurus instinctively knows how to multiply money and when combined with Arian pioneering ideas and clever Libran talk, they will find out more than one avenue to earn money.

AriTauLib is a double cardinal sign and will always seek to lead. They can lead by force, sweet talk or ideas but they will lead for sure. They instinctively know where force will work or where words will turn the key. Expect them to work accordingly.

Anger is not very evident in them, but they have an explosive temper when roused. The immense Taurean patience and the Libran need for peace at all costs will ensure that they can control themselves admirably before the blast.

AriTauLibs are guilty of a little selfishness, especially about their things and views. They are not willing to share things easily till you point out the facts to them. They can also be extremely stubborn. If they decide on a course of action they will stick to it no matter what. However, they will listen to your point of view before they take a decision, so you do have some chance to influence them. The Libran predilection for thinking themselves into circles is present in them, especially on matters which relate to the heart and family. In matters of business and profession, they are much more ruthless.

Did someone call them lazy? Yes, they are. It is one of the most fascinating things about AriTauLibs. While at work, they display the phenomenal energy levels of Aries and are capable of immense hard work like a Taurean. But when at home, they exemplify the laziness of Libra and the indolence of Taurus and don't move a finger.

Aries–Taurus–Libra – Karan Johar
The music- and family-loving Taurus and the stylish and talkative Libra are evident in Johar's exquisitely detailed movies, his attire, and of course, his communication skills.

'*Kuch Kuch Hota Hai* was ridiculously idiotic. I think I made no sense, the film made no sense. *Kabhi Khushi Kabhie Gham* was my tribute to my parents, of course in a melodramatic, over-the-top way. It was filmy.'

'I'm aesthetic. It's the sensibility. I'm born with it. Others don't. I have it. I have the right to exercise it. [About his movies being designer driven.] But that doesn't mean my movies don't have a soul and content.'

'I'm very affected, I get personally very bothered, about this religious bias there is to this entire religion.'

'I had to fight many politicians to get the movie released. Democracy is the biggest hypocrisy in this country.'[138]

Karan Johar is practical, knows to laugh at himself, is non-judgemental, and fearless in voicing his opinion, too. He is a friend to many in an industry rife with rivalry. Karan Johar has perfectly balanced the Fire, Air and Earth in his life, to create the archetypical AriTauLib.

Love and Marriage for Him
He is full of wit and good humour. He likes to lead, but with tact. He expects a lot of love and care. In fact, he expects nothing less than perfection from you. Despite

---
[138] https://www.youtube.com/watch?v=sIyOG_MzkIk

his fun ways and liberal outlook, he wants a partner who fits into the mould of the traditional wife and daughter-in-law. So, plan to charm his parents if you have any long-term plans with him.

He can be quite lazy at home. Please be ready to take on the responsibility of house care. You can be sure of one thing though, when this guy works, he really works. Please learn to save, for he is terrible at it. He is a party animal and is always ready for a good time with his gang. This guy has an eye for décor and he has definite ideas about how his house should look and feel.

He is not sensitive. Despite his caring, protective and friendly ways, he cannot read your heart or emotions. But he makes up for that with his extraordinary sense of partnership and smooth, lovely conversations. Tell him, if you want him to know.

He is a very proud father. He loves splurging on his kids but also wants them to listen to him. He makes them see his point of view with a mixture of guile, logic and aggression.

Love and Marriage for Her
She is sweetly aggressive and knows just how to bat her eyelashes to get you to listen to her. She is extremely talkative and has her own opinions. This lady needs a partner who talks and listens to her. Unappreciative nods and grunts turn her off. She needs to be petted and pampered.

She wants her home to look just perfect and has a keen eye for interiors. She enjoys changing things around in the house to make it look better. But she can also be quite lazy. Don't expect this girl to do the housework; she is happy supervising the help about how exactly they should mop the corners.

She is also ambitious and fearless in thinking of new business ideas. Give her an outlet to experience her ambitions for she is too brilliant to stay at home. She loves spending, especially on fashionable clothes and accessories. Nevertheless, you can be sure that she will compensate by saving and investing money wisely.

As a mother, she is fun. She enjoys playing with her kids and is very proud of them. She knows how to get them to listen to her without being aggressive. They adore her style and love her spirit.

At the Workplace
AriTauLibs make good entrepreneurs and businessmen. They have pioneering ideas, drive, logic, endurance and excellent communication skills to help them through. They are clever at creating something new from old ideas. Money and glory are all they want.

They are extremely creative and know how to take their creativity to the next level. They never shy away from exploring new ideas. They are extremely good at marketing too. They are naturals at artistic careers and fantastic as sports people too. They bring passion and power to softer domains like arts and balance and common sense to powerful domains like sports.

As bosses, they are liberal and generous as long as you are productive. They will pay you exactly what you deserve and give you the appropriate credit.

Fire, Earth and Air meet in AriTauLibs and give them the drive to believe in themselves, the patience to endure and the skill to convince one and all with their ideas.

Famous AriTauLib Personalities
Karan Johar, Brian Lara, Kieron Pollard, Mark Zuckerberg, Tina Fey, Tori Spelling, Henry Fonda, Neelam Sanjiva Reddy, Gail Kelly, Sneha Khanwalkar.

84. ARIES–TAURUS–SCORPIO

Mars, the violent god of war, and Pluto, the powerful dark lord of the underworld, meets the indomitable 'Planet X' in this power-packed combination of AriTauScorps.

Mars endows them with brute force, high energy and extreme restlessness whereas Pluto imbues in them its deep and mysterious strength and magnetic energy. Taurus adds its patience and endurance to this volatile package and makes them ready to face any problem head on. They surprise you with their mental stability and logic in the face of immense crisis and never lose their common sense. AriTauScorps are fearless and full of derring-do. If ever I have to assign an animal to this combination, I would say they are the Tigers of the zodiac.

They will be high-voltage personalities and whatever they do they will give it their all. Scorpio and Aries can make them try dangerous stunts and substances without a second thought. They are willing to try out everything once and can be reckless. Of course, all the three signs have extremely strong willpower, which ensures that AriTauScorps never go overboard with their experiments.

They usually disregard obstacles as they feel that with their passion and drive nothing is impossible to achieve. They can be quite hard to control. They are wilful and do not like to obey all rules. They can be extremely, passionately obstinate. Taurus and Scorpio are both fixed signs and very hard to budge while Aries makes them see things only from their own perspective.

There is also an egotistical streak in them. When they talk passionately you will notice the constant use of 'I, me, myself' in their conversations. They like to put themselves at the centre of the universe and believe that events unfold in a logical pattern around them.

Aries makes them want to take up leading roles and pioneer new ideas while Scorpio gives them the unending passion to pursue their dreams. Taurus also makes them extremely hard working. There is a bubbling vivacity and positivity about them that never turns into frivolity. They are extremely ambitious and passionate about their work and life.

They are fun-loving friends, generous and loyal. But remember, they expect the same loyalty and love from you, too. They want to be the centre of attention of their loved ones and will not tolerate being taken for granted.

Love finds them excessively demanding, too. They want an idealised love imbued with great passion. They can be extremely jealous and possessive of their partner and will see red at the smallest flirtatious glance. It might take them time to find a partner who meets their stringent demands and they would rather spend a lifetime searching than compromise.

Money is extremely important to them. They want lots of it and are cautious about spending. They like to conserve and invest wisely to have the luxurious lifestyle they dream of. They want people to some day look up to them for their tough fight against adversity to achieve all that wealth and glory.

Aries is a deeply insecure sign but portrays a confident façade to outsiders. Similarly, Scorpios feel deeply hurt at the slightest criticism pretend to be unconcerned. AriTauScorps will be deeply sensitive to the remarks of others and will not take kindly to any form of criticism.

Their anger is a thing to fear. Very rarely do they have control over it. They are extremely sensitive and explode at the slightest excuse. In most situations, they prefer exploding to thinking about the problem. Their anger be self-destructive if they refuse to control it. Even if they learn to control their temper, they will never let go of their desire of revenge. AriTauScorps can be deadly enemies and will stop at nothing to put you down.

AriTauScorps are hard to deceive or to argue with, for they have the Scorpio ability to read your deepest secrets. The Taurean ability of making logical deductions enables them to hit the nail on the head. It is very difficult to argue with a AriTauScorp as he will bombard you with verbal volleys passionately and intensely and simply drown you with his words. They may lack empathy, especially if they do not agree with your thinking.

But one thing is sure – expect them to tell you point-blank to your face if they love you or hate you. AriTauScorps never mince their words, especially if they see an opponent in you. They have this habit of dividing the world into 'either you are with me or against me' and can polarise views and invite extreme affection or dislike.

AriTauScorps can be very artistic, as Taurus is naturally good in music and the arts. They put their passion and intensity into even the softest of art forms. This passion imbues all they do. They revel in excesses. They have large appetites for everything from food to sex. They also want to unravel all the mysteries of the world from sex to spirituality. There is a throbbing sexual and magnetic energy about them that seems inviting but challenging too.

Aries~Taurus–Scorpio – Naomi Campbell
Fiery and strong, Naomi Campbell personifies the deep strength and red-hot anger of AriTauScorp.

Throughout her career, Campbell has spoken against the racial bias that exists in the fashion industry. In 1997 she stated, 'There is prejudice. It is a problem and I can't go along any more with brushing it under the carpet. This business is about selling, and blonde and blue-eyed girls are what sell.'[139]

Mike Tyson said: 'She has a great body. And she's scared of nothing.'

The idealistic Aries makes her a very strong believer in human rights and equality and the inherent strength of Scorpio and Taurus gives the resolve to fight. A true AriTauScorp lady!

Love and Marriage for Him
You can have the time of your life with this guy. Join him if you desire to see the heights of ambition and power. Remember, he is the boss even at home. He will look to dominate – be it you, his friends or his empire. He has a very jealous streak in him. He is extremely loyal to you and expects the same in return. Pamper him, love him, think only of him and he puts you on a pedestal forever.

Life with him is exciting, energetic and extremely charged. Parties, adventure, travel to unexplored places make up his life.

---

[139] http://en.wikipedia.org/wiki/Naomi_Campbell

You may see a vulnerable side to him too. Hold his hand and tell him he is right when the whole world doubts him. He needs a loving and encouraging person around him to just tell him that he will be all right. You have to be the more mature and understanding one in the relationship. Be silent and calm when he is in rage.

As a father, he understands his children but may also push them into things they do not want to do. His need for respect can make him harsh but he also loves them a lot and thinks of ways to help them.

Love and Marriage for Her
She is a very strong lady who possesses extraordinary strength and determination even if she seems frail and mild. She demands 100 per cent love and respect from you. She wants you to demand respect from her too.

She does not love easily until she finds the ideal man to arouse love, respect and passion in her. Remember to be extremely loyal to her. Once you sign on the dotted line with her, forgo your desire to ever look at another woman for this lady can be vengeful. She will know you down to your smallest faults and can love you despite them if you gain her love and respect. Do not try and rule her.

She has a lot of ambitions and is ready to make them come true. She will not look to you for support but be happy if you leave her to make her own mark and sincerely applaud her efforts. She wants you in the role of a friend and a passionate lover.

As a mother, she loves and commands her children. Her love for them is absolute. She knows them inside out and is her softest with them. She can also put a lot of pressure on them with her desire to see them succeed.

At the Workplace
Pioneering and strong, AriTauScorps have the ability to develop and create business ideas that take the world by storm. They love to lead and carve out a niche for themselves. Their passion and ideas never run out and they show amazing mental stability to face any challenge that comes their way. They are willing to give everything they have for their dreams and do not mind working under excruciating circumstances to create history.

They can try their hand at creative ventures or business propositions. They are excellent in promoting themselves and their ideas, and are great strategists too. They want something that offers adventure and great rewards. They have a natural talent for understanding finance and are good investors.

They are controlling and commanding as bosses, and generously reward sincerity and effort, but can be harsh too when you are sloppy. You are motivated to outperform just for their intense passion.

Fire, Earth and Water meet in this astoundingly forceful combination. AriTauScorps will be self-driven, motivated, passionate and emotionally strong to take on any role that life throws at them.

Famous AriTauScorp Personalities
Sushil Kumar (the wrestler), Paresh Rawal, T. Rajendar, Vilasrao Deshmukh, Saddam Hussein, Katie Price, Naomi Campbell, Balzac, Mehbooba Mufti Sayeed.

85. ARIES–TAURUS–SAGITTARIUS

The power of the violent Mars, the mental stability of the enduring Taurus and the fiery optimism of Jupiter make up this extremely powerful and driven combination of AriTauSags. Their ambition is overpowering. AriTauSags never think small.

Think about it – a Ram, a Bull and a half horse, half man Centaur join in this circus-like combination. They have the vitality, force and power of the animals; you can smell the animal instincts in them. Passion, enthusiasm and a 'can-do' spirit separate them from the crowd. They bubble with Arian energy and Sagittarian vivacity. They never give up and neither do they ever lose hope. This instinctive belief in the positive side of life makes good things happen to them.

The Goat and the Centaur are relentless in their search for the limelight but the steady Taurean Bull adds that extra mileage to them. They will dream their dreams with logic and enduring patience. AriTauSags might want to explode onto the world's radar but the Taurean in them will believe in the attributes of hard work and patience too. They will be willing to work and bide their time but you can be sure that they will be going places and soon.

AriTauSags are normally very powerfully built. Their physical strength can be immense even if they are built like a tent pole. Despite their childlike enthusiasm, there is a commonsensical maturity about them, brought in by Taurus. The double Fire and strong Earth sign ensures that they have great emotional strength and a fire in the belly to put up a fight against any challenge that life throws in. Their intelligence is inferior to none – the Sagittarian professor is the most knowledgeable and is comfortable talking vociferously about everything from genetic engineering to what causes tsunamis.

They have a loud laugh and an even louder voice. They are naturally happy people who attract a lot of folks with their backslapping ways. They love partying. They are likely to jump off airplanes just for the heck of it. Adventure and travel excite them as much as their dreams. They always want to be going somewhere doing something. They like having plans to fulfil and do not waste their time in idle gossip. When they are happy, you find none as generous or as fun loving as them. The only way you can turn them away is by hurting their egos.

Aries cannot hide things and Sagittarians are typically blunt. Taureans don't like to keep track of what they said to whom. Expect them to tell you the honest truth and nothing but the truth. They can also be extremely tactless and can blurt out uncomfortable truths.

Family is important to them. They like spending time with their families and are the first ones to suggest outings for the entire family. Yet they would also want some 'me time' minus the family.

They just love food. Taurus also brings in the love for luxury and all things beautiful and natural. AriTauSags have a creative side to them. They relax with music and enjoy artistic pursuits in their spare time. The Taurean artistic sensibilities will give them a softer touch. The Sagittarian in them loves showing off before an audience and only needs a partial invitation and they can throw a full-blown performance without any hesitation.

Love will be a high-voltage affair with them. AriTauSags take time to settle down. They are not too keen to get bound down too soon, but slowly come round to the desire for a committed relationship. They search for a partner who can live up to their idealistic expectations. They prefer people with an independent streak, who stand out from the rest.

AriTauSag is a double Fire sign and all Fire signs have a deep insecurity in them that they disguise with bravado. This insecurity is extremely high when they are young and have yet to achieve their big dreams. Add to that the ever-doubtful Taurus who likes to pause before acting, and you have a combination that is high on inner insecurity yet never voices its fears. They need people around them who encourage their most positive traits.

They lack Water and Air, and this makes them a little too self-centred. They cannot guess what other people think or want until they are told. They can be extremely insensitive to people and their emotions. They look at the world only from their angle and are puzzled if you showed them any other.

Their anger is not for mere mortals. These guys can explode. They can also rein in their temper at times but, sooner or later, it comes out. The good thing is that they simmer down soon. AriTauSags are not likely to plot and plan your downfall.

There is a strange mix of materialism and spiritualism in AriTauSags. They can be ambitious, acquisitive, have lofty dreams and want to shake the world with their individuality, style and substance. On the other hand, spirituality is also part of these people and they are vocal about their opinions and beliefs. Their greatest ability is to simplify the most complex philosophies and present them in the most palatable fashion.

Aries–Taurus–Sagittarius – Cher

Cher and I are sitting in the grandly proportioned master bedroom of her 14,000-square-foot, $41 million Italianate villa in Malibu. It feels ponderously, ostentatiously self-important. She loves it. 'I wanted to be famous,' she says, 'I wanted this! …And I also enjoy being an entertainer. Even when you're feeling sick, hurting a lot, once you get out there onstage and find everything is working…you know you'll be fine. You feel so big and so tall, like you are in some sort of alternate universe. It's magnificent! As long as I can do it and people still come to see me, I don't want to quit working. It's magic.'[140]

Cher has the ambition, undying optimism and enduring quality of an AriTauSag.

Love and Marriage for Him

He wants a partner who can take his exuberance and vitality without getting carried away by it. Nor should you belittle his ideas or his vast ambitions.

He is a complete foodie. The way to his heart is through his stomach. He loves to travel and takes you along for his adventure-filled trips. He wants a lot of money and works hard for it. But he can lose it too, especially in gambling. You need to keep an eye on his habits

His honesty is his strength and his weakness. He is blunt, especially when family and relations are concerned. He will tell you if he is attracted to some young girl he met while mountaineering. He says things as he sees them and he is not

---

[140] http://www.cherworld.com/cher-burlesque-movie/cher-famous-people-pay-a-price-parade-interview/

sensitive enough to get subtle hints. Tears are not the way to make him understand either. Just tell him what you feel.

Do not nag this man or put negative thoughts in his head. When things go wrong, he needs someone to motivate him. Despite his alpha male tendencies, he never insists that you leave your career and sit at home. He likes it if you are as independent as him, but wants a little pampering at home.

As a father, he is dominating but loves to have fun with his kids, too. He needs you to help him understand them better. He may ignore them in the midst of his ambitions.

Love and Marriage for Her
Outspoken and independent, she has a mind of her own. She is bubbly, vivacious, full of dreams and ambitions, and stands out in a crowd. She can be a wild tomboy or a hell-raising activist. This girl prides herself on being blunt and honest.

You have to do something to make her proud for she will not spend her life with someone who cannot do anything that gets a WOW out of her. Though she loves good food, this girl has too many dreams to spend her life in the kitchen.

She loves her family but is not tied down to conventions. If you want to live peacefully, live as a nuclear family. Joint families will not suit her for she has too many opinions to listen to anybody else's.

She takes time to feel ready for motherhood but she surprises you when she does. Despite her loud ways, she has a maternal streak in her. She loves pampering her children with food and toys but needs a little help in the sensitivity department.

At the Workplace
AriTauSags want to be pioneers in their field. They think of new and innovative ideas and know how to market them as well. The Arian forcefulness and the Sagittarian desire to shine in the limelight will be enhanced by the Taurean mental stability and calm in moments of crisis. They love showbiz and are a natural in any profession that puts them in spotlight.

Their temper can cause hell in an organisation if they feel slighted. Be ready to tackle those issues when they work for you. They want glory and money, and also growth and learning opportunities. They want careers where they can travel. If they feel appreciated, they work harder.

As bosses, they are brilliant at motivating people and know how to get their work done. Mentoring roles appeal to them.

Double Fire and Earth meet in AriTauSags to give them strength, vitality and an amazing power to rewrite history in their own words.

Famous AriTauSag Personalities
Cher, Jiddu Krishnamurti, Girish Karnad, Adele, Anatoly Karpov, Sam Pitroda, Tom Sayers, Bharathidasan.

86. ARIES–TAURUS–CAPRICORN

Mars, the violent and powerful planet of war, Taurus, the enduring and stable, and the old man Saturn meet in this extremely strong and commanding combination of AriTauCaps.

You get a fair idea of what you can expect of these people from the animals in their combination: the Ram, the Bull and the Goat! Now that is a phenomenal mix. They combine the fierceness and brute strength of Aries with the dependability and immense emotional stability of Taurus and the ambition and supreme self-control of Capricorn.

On meeting them, you can feel their power. There is nothing frivolous about them. Serious, grounded, responsible and strong, they seem to barge through every opposition by the might of their thoughts. They have physical, emotional and mental control and mastery. Sensitive, touchy, nervous, emotional, confused, fearful are words that have no meaning for them.

AriTauCaps will never be followers. Aries and Capricorn are two cardinal signs and destined to lead whereas Taurus is a fixed sign and is very stubborn. AriTauCaps will never listen to contrary views and if you want to be with them, you will have to listen to them or you can march off.

Capricorn makes them extremely responsible at a very young age. As children, they do not talk the way you think children should. Capricorn and Aries give them the burning ambition to succeed and Taurus gives them the mental strength to withstand any problem. They never barge in without thinking as Arians do but think, plan and then conquer. Even their seemingly impulsive statements have been thought out earlier, for they never leave anything to chance.

The shining optimism of Aries rubs off on the otherwise Taurean hesitant nature and the Capricornian melancholic outlook. They have a balanced outlook in life with the common sense of Taurus, rationality of Capricorn and the sheer force of Aries. AriTauCaps never give up: they will never stop attacking or thinking of plans to attack and therein lies their strength. Defeat will only spur them on.

They bowl you over with their energy and verve for life. They love partying and are very good at networking too. They personify the Arian electric energy and with it come the Taurean love of slapstick and a boisterous sense of humour.

They do not waste their emotions on anyone but their families. They are willing to sacrifice a lot for their loved ones without a second thought. They are very protective about their families.

Love is quite important to them but there is a risk that they will neglect it for their career. Aries makes them demand an ideal partner who can rivet their attention. AriTauCaps are comfortable accepting a spouse chosen by their family but they will insist on a say in the choice. They want a partner who brings respectability and status and will not make themselves fools for love.

Food is their weak point. They also like to dress well. Elegant, well-tailored clothes are their obvious choice. They are also surprisingly blessed with artistic faculties. Taurus naturally excels in music and arts and Capricorn has some hidden creative talents. Arts, music and creativity are the only soft expressions of these otherwise hard-nosed people.

Money is very important to them: they see it as a hallmark of success. They want to earn a lot, and save without being too stingy. They are fantastic in money management. They know all the avenues of investment and have a traditional approach towards wealth creation. They are keen on accumulating phenomenal wealth and assets.

Aries and Capricorn are the most self-centred amongst all zodiac signs. They are commanding and expect their will to be law. The sturdy and conservative Taurus only adds to their bull-headedness. These people can be stubborn, selfish, power-hungry, gluttonous and controlling.

They are also quite traditional and conservative. The fiery rebellion of Aries might show up in their youth but they will revert to their family ways soon. As elders in a family, they are very controlling. They can be extremely cruel and heartless. As there is no Water sign in them, AriTauCaps lack the sensitivity to see from another's perspective. There are also no Air signs in the combination; hence, they do not listen to reason or logic once their minds are made up. Plus, once they get into the habit of command you will find it difficult to have an argument with them for they will either turn ballistic or stonewall you.

As they grow older some of their restraint and command will wear off. All Fire signs mellow as they age and Capricorn exhibits a reverse aging syndrome that makes them act younger after their thirties. They will still be in command but their fiery control will become more manageable. They would now be naughtier and funnier.

Spirituality interests them as they grow older. They can move towards rituals or can believe in ideologies. Whatever they do, they believe in it wholeheartedly and never doubt the existence of a greater force in life.

Aries–Taurus–Capricorn – David Beckham
'I feel safest out on the pitch as I'm confident in my own ability, without being arrogant or big-headed, I'm confident on the pitch.'

'Our priority is the children. We respect our careers and love what they've given us and the countries we've been able to see but the children are our priority whether I'm playing for England at one side of world and Victoria at the other. We always make sure one of us is with the boys. It's very important to us.'[141]

David Beckham shows his confidence and love for family – all integral parts of an AriTauCap make-up.

Love and Marriage for Him
He is conservative and traditional, especially about family matters. This guy is the boss and you have to give him the crown whether you like it or not.

---
[141] http://www.mirrorfootball.co.uk/news/David-Beckham-interview-Fabio-Capello-England-World-Cup-flops-Victoria-Beckham-first-kiss-and-more-read-the-full-transcript-here-article527491.html

He is extremely driven and ambitious. Please remember the fact that his career will always be more important to him. He will dream, plan and work relentlessly for his spot in the sun and you will have to be his support. Don't cling to him for emotional sustenance, as it is not his forte. He will do his job well and expect you to do yours.

He finds it easier to exhibit his love through responsible ways rather than sweet words. He will definitely want to be in control. Whether he shouts or is cool about it, his decision is final. When troubles strike, he will be the anchor for the family. There have been tough times you have never known about because he was always in control.

Good food, soothing interiors and music make him relax. He likes old songs and melodies and is a guy who prefers the relaxing aura of the old to the new.

Fatherhood suits him perfectly as Capricorn rules it and Taurus loves being entrenched in family life. His children love and respect him although they know that his word is law. He loves pampering them but can be extremely strict if they act rebellious.

Love and Marriage for Her
She is definitely ambitious but can quite happily live the life of a contented housewife, provided you can provide all that her heart desires – money, status and respect.

She can be a rock to her family; all she needs are your respect and love. She follows conventions and traditions. She might listen to you if you win her respect, but at home, she will rule. She can easily be the matriarch of a family, for she has excellent money management skills and can manage everything and everyone. .

She is fearless, jealous and extremely loving. She does not understand harmless flirting but will not tolerate possessiveness from you. She needs to feel in control.

As a mother, she is caring and loving. Her children are always better dressed than their friends. She teaches them the values of hard work and ambition. She knows how to command their respect. She might need a little help in understanding them, especially if their views clash with hers.

At the Workplace
AriTauCaps want nothing but the topmost positions. They are ready to wait and work but you have to recognise that they have it in them to reach the top. They are never deterred by problems but plan and work their way through them. They can do anything they set their minds to. From creative fields to sports to the corporate world, they shine wherever they go. They work so well that they make themselves indispensable.

They are a double cardinal sign and capable of leadership roles. They have the ability to turn a small idea into a large-scale project. They are phenomenal in cost control and budgeting. They are very good at delegating and overseeing work. They know how to bring in the best talent and get desired results. They will be extremely demanding, but will be extraordinarily generous if you make them succeed. Politics too is a field that opens naturally to them. They want it all – power, prestige and money.

Double Earth and Fire meet in AriTauCaps and endow them with strength, perseverance and a mental stability engineered to beat all odds.

Famous AriTauCap Personalities
David Beckham, Sunil Dutt, Pierce Brosnan, T.N. Seshan, Henry Cavill, Daniel Christian, Henry J. Kaiser, Sumitranandan Pant, George Lucas, Franz Mesmer, Dilip Doshi, Trisha Krishnan, George Best, Christina Hendricks.

87. ARIES–TAURUS–AQUARIUS

Mars, the violent and powerful god of war, Taurus, the calm and enduring, and the intelligently eccentric Uranus meet in AriTauAquas. The drive of Aries, the mental stability of Taurus and humanitarian views of Aquarius make this a very interesting combination.

The fiery and pioneering Aries and the futuristic genius Aquarius have a solid foundation steeped in realism with the steady Taurus. Aquarius adds another dimension to the drive of Aries and stability of Taurus. It makes AriTauAquas think out of the box and be unconventional. Yet they never go wild either. Their unconventional ideas, though different, are logical.

While Aquarius makes them freethinking and curious about ideas that run counter to tradition, Aries makes them bursting with ideas and innovation, Taurus helps them to make things simple, grounded and practical. The extraordinary intelligence of Aquarius and individualistic brazenness of Aries is complimented by the focused Taurus and helps them take their unique ideas to their logical fruition.

They are definitely ambitious. While Aries wants to make a mark in the world and Aquarius wants to gift a unique idea to the world, the Taurean in them ensures that they don't die paupers. They work towards creating and executing a unique idea that will be financially rewarding. The ambition of Aries is retained without making it unthinking. Taurus ensures that their drive doesn't fizzle out midway and AriTauAquas work relentlessly hard to achieve what they desire.

They have a phenomenal memory. The Taurean elephantine memory never lets them forget the most inane conversations and the Aquarian gift of remembering the most quirky things rarely lets them forget anything.

The Arian selfishness and myopic 'me' view is quite reduced due to the stable and practical Taurus and the friendly Aquarius. They are extremely loyal friends who are full of fun, laughter, a thousand jokes and songs. They also help their friends a lot.

AriTauAquas enjoy the outdoors and love speed. They have unique hobbies and interests. While the arts, creativity and fashion do attract them, they are also interested in unearthing the mysteries of the world. From dance to drama, fashion to capitalism, yoga to astrology, all interests them. They have a remarkable way of blending tradition with an ultramodern outlook in anything they do. They have a spiritual bent of mind and believe in a power greater than them.

They want an idealistic, passionate and sensual love yet want to be left alone at times. AriTauAqua is devoid of a Water sign and they are not very sensitive to your deeper feelings. In fact, the Aquarian in them can choose to remain detached despite reading the feelings of people and the Arian self-centredness can be a deterrent too, so they can simply read things but not necessarily act on the knowledge.

Money is quite important to them. AriTauAquas have the Arian desire for pots of money and the Taurean materialistic outlook. Thus, though they think of everyone, they never recklessly blow away their fortunes in philanthropy. Their family will be well cared for and they will work towards their stability and financial security. They are very good at investing and growing their money too. Luxurious living beckons them and they like to own things of lasting use and value.

AriTauAquas use their abundant drive and optimism for the good of people around them and for their own good. They know how to share their goodness and derive maximum benefit from it. They can also take up social causes and can become fighters against injustice or discrimination. They fear no one and can be extremely caustic and direct in voicing their opinions.

Their anger can be explosive. Their egos are easily hurt and they never mince words when they are angry. The double fixed signs of Taurus and Aquarius may make them extremely stubborn when they have made up their mind and one may find it simply impossible to change it.

There can be much insecurity about them. Arians show a tough exterior to hide their inner vulnerabilities, while Taurus can turn pessimistic, world-weary or melancholic when things go against them. They can be possessive, controlling, over-concerned with money, security and future, brooding and pessimistic, or confrontational and provocative, too.

There is also a constant mental tussle between choosing the realistic over the unknown. The futuristic Aquarius and the ever-hopeful Aries re-ignites the fire in them, when the safety-first Taurus retreats. There is a strong tenacity to them because of the mentally tough Aries, emotionally tough Taurus and spiritually detached Aquarius. Once they make up their minds to do something, nothing in the world can stop them.

Aries–Taurus–Aquarius – Audrey Hepburn

Audrey Hepburn was an actress, fashion icon, a proficient ballet dancer and, above all, an ardent humanitarian. She was appointed UNICEF's goodwill ambassador and dedicated the rest of her life to impoverished children in the poorest nations.

'I was too fat, or maybe too tall, or maybe just plain too ugly...you can say my definiteness stems from underlying feelings of insecurity and inferiority. I couldn't conquer these feelings by acting indecisive. I found the only way to get the better of them was by adopting a forceful, concentrated drive.'[142]

Audrey Hepburn had the hard exterior, the soft heart, the giving nature and love for humanity so evident in AriTauAquas.

Love and Marriage for Him

He is the rock of the family and works hard to give a stable future to all. He loves and adores you, but very often, his mind is elsewhere. This guy dreams extraordinary things and works hard to make them come true. Don't nag and cling; he knows his responsibilities. But his ideas and career matter a lot to him too. Give him some space and be ready to live your life independently. Nagging and crying will only push him away.

Occasionally, he likes to command. Usually he is happy letting you take charge of home matters and will excuse himself from the day-to-day running of

---

[142] http://en.wikipedia.org/wiki/Audrey_Hepburn

the house and family decisions. He understands your complaints and knows how you feel, but can often seem selfish and think only of his own needs.

He is a genius at work and the larger issues of society occupy his mind-space. His heart is definitely with you though he seems lost elsewhere most of the time. It is up to you to keep the spark alive in the relationship, as he won't make much of an effort if things go awry. Also, his personal habits can be irritating with his lazy and disengaged ways.

He loves the outdoors and is always ready for some fun and adventure. He also has a huge gang of friends and likes to go out with them frequently. Once in a while, he likes to be by himself.

As a father, he enjoys his kids and likes to be an essential part of their lives despite his hectic schedule. He has certain ideas about what they should do and, if they think differently, they will have to convince him of their point of view.

Love and Marriage for Her
She does not desire to fit herself into conventional roles or to mother you. The Arian optimism, Aquarian unconventionality and Taurean desire to be productive will never allow her to stay at home for long. She is full of opinions and ideas of things to do, and pursues them through all the ups and downs in her life. Her dreams add vitality and vigour to her.

She is the perfect partner if you seek to see life with new eyes, for old ideas spur her on to new ideals. She does not break down easily. Every problem is an opportunity for her. Aggression is not alien to her and she will fight for her beliefs. She has nerves of steel and has an extraordinary mind to match, too.

Music, the outdoors and parties rejuvenate her. She enjoys interesting and intelligent conversation. She slops around in her most comfortable clothes at home but transforms into a fashion diva for the parties. Despite her strong individuality, she is a romantic at heart and wants to be wooed by her man. She goes weak in her knees and loses her characteristic clarity of thought when she is in love.

As a mother, at first she is a little hesitant about trading her dreams for motherhood, but surprises you with her ability to take care of children. She is their friend and confidant, who teaches them to reach for their dreams, and to be comfortable in their own skin.

At the Workplace
AriTauAquas bring in new ideas and are vociferous in their desire for change. Routine jobs kill them. They prefer to travel, think and voice opinions. The best thing about AriTauAquas is their ability to think differently yet rationally.

They want money and the glory of introducing the world to a new idea. They do not respond well to authority and prefer positions where they are free to implement their ideas. They work better as freelancers than as employees.

Business, creative arts, scientific research and fields that allow them to think differently attract them more. They are quite good in sports due to the Arian ruthless power, the Taurean mental stability and the Aquarian eccentric genius.

As bosses, they are extraordinary mentors and are superb pioneers too. They lead from the front with ruthless energy and ambition.

Fire, Earth and Air give AriTauAquas the drive to excel, the logic to think and the unconventionality to cross boundaries without crashing reason.

Famous AriTauAqua Personalities
Audrey Hepburn, Rajdeep Sardesai, Maharani Gayatri Devi, Princess Maxima of Netherlands, Gagan Narang, Morgan Freeman, Deve Gowda, W.V. Raman, Raphael Saadiq, Adrianne Palicki.

88. ARIES–TAURUS–PISCES

Mars, the violent and powerful god of war, and Neptune, the deep and mysterious lord of the seas, join the calm and rooted sign of Taurus. The high energy level of Aries drives the Taurean to great heights and makes even the laid-back Piscean to perform.

This combination – Aries, Taurus and Pisces – has three different elements – Fire, Earth and Water; three different creatures – a Ram, a Bull and a Fish; and three different types – cardinal, fixed and mutable, to form a unique combination. They have extraordinary flexibility of varied responses to choose from their repertoire. They can be leaders, followers or executors of ideas. They have the extraordinary pioneering ideas of Aries, the great emotional strength of Taurus and the malleability, flexibility and learning ability of Pisces.

The distinctive combination ensures that they retain the best of all the zodiac signs while reducing the negative traits. They have the fearlessness, drive and passion of Aries, without its dominance, arrogance and selfishness. They possess the forbearance and rootedness of Taurus without its passivity. They possess the compassion and wisdom of Pisces without its laziness.

AriTauPisces have high levels of empathy. They can read people easily, are tuned into others' emotions and act upon them too. They are very family-oriented. You can expect high levels of devotion, love and care from them. They are the kind of people the elders love to talk to. The Taurean mental stability also makes them extremely strong in dealing with any difficulty. They neither give in to problems nor get flustered at the sight of obstacles.

They are sensible in money matters, despite the Piscean lack of monetary discipline and the Arian spendthrift attitude. The Taurus need for financial stability makes them conservative in their finances. These guys like to follow tried and tested paths rather than shake the world with outrageous and unconventional dreams.

Anger, the Arian trademark, is under control with the Taurean measured thought and the Piscean passivity. However, this does not mean that you can walk over them. Despite their calm and collected ways, it is not easy to dictate your terms to them. They can be extremely stubborn.

The common thread between Pisces and Taurus is their artistic inclination. Pisces have inborn creative sensibilities, while Taureans love music. Expect them to be good dancers, singers and artists. The power of Aries will add strength, stamina and a zing to their artistic abilities, and can release them from the Piscean fear allowing them to exhibit themselves confidently. But it will take some time, though. They will learn, slowly but surely.

Expect them to be born romantics also; Aries long for the ideal love, while Taureans are soft die-hard romantics and Pisceans live and breathe love. You can expect AriTauPisces to be mushy in matters of the heart. A typical AriTauPisces can just let himself flow in love.

In their formative years, communication may not be their strong point. They are not good at initiating conversations and find it difficult to express themselves in words. Their actions speak for them. However, Pisceans have a sponge-like ability to learn everything they are exposed to. So, if a typical AriTauPisces is exposed to people or circumstances where he has to communicate a lot, he will learn that ability too, as he will any skill of life.

There is another extreme case, which is possible in this combination. They can have all the destructive traits of each sign. They can display the Arian dominance without learning from failure and live in Taurean isolation with the Piscean escapist tendency. This mixture can make them brilliant escape artists and commitment-phobics who are never there for anyone, least of all themselves. They can also become excessively indolent, develop some addictions like a Piscean and, combined with Aries, become deviously scheming or victims of jealousy and arrogance.

Periods of laziness and the desire to pass the buck can overwhelm them at times and you will find them delegating and resting. Their biggest enemy is the inner demon of nagging insecurities. If they slay this goblin and retain all the positives of this fabulous combination then they can spread their strength, sunshine and dreams to the world.

There is a strange contradiction in them. With their deep wisdom of Pisces and Taurean understanding, they can simply know and give you the sanest advice to help you come out of your troubles, but they themselves can wallow in self-pity and can be victims of irritating habits and lack control in certain aspects of their lives.

They are highly evolved, spiritually, but never sneer at the bounty of materialism. They are scheming and ruthless when their path to gold is impeded. People in this combination can be shy and do not like to be in the lime light until dire necessity forces them into the public gaze. If they overcome their shyness and willingly step into the limelight, you know that they have finally conquered their inner devils.

Aries–Taurus–Pisces – Enrique Iglesias
Enrique did not want his famous surname to help advance his career. He borrowed money from his family nanny and recorded a demo cassette tape.[143]

'When I'm in Miami the couch is my favourite place. Whenever I come home, it's usually from a long trip for work and I like staying home. But I loooove being able to get away, like on the boat, going water skiing.'[144]

'And people coming up asking for autographs, there's only one time when it kind of bothers me: when I'm eating.'

'I'm a good person, but with many defects.'[145]

Creative, laid-back, food loving, philosophical, with a desire to be self-made, Enrique is a true AriTauPisces.

Love and Marriage for Him
You have got yourself a gem. Considerate, understanding and sensitive, this guy is everything women want. He likes being the man of the house, but is not overbearing in his attitude. Calm and collected, this guy is a steady and solid influence in your life. He is very flexible and you will see various hues of emotions in him which

---
[143] http://en.wikipedia.org/wiki/Enrique_Iglesias
[144] http://www.macdirectory.com/component/option,com_exclusive_news/task,viewDetail/news_id,2781/
[145] www.brainyquote.com/quotes/authors/e/enrique_iglesias.html#Jdjj7cvzLdrsRbVi.99

range from being caring, sentimental and protective to being deeply passionate too.

His attitude is conservative and family always comes first for him. He appreciates a partner who shares these values. Do not expect him to be overactive at home. He is sensitive and moody and can go into deep sulks at times. He can be extremely stubborn at times. Learn to know what makes him so and avoid those situations.

He loves luxury and ensures that he has things that let him relax in style. Money-smart and financially strong, he takes the right decisions in finance and does not give in to spending sprees.

He makes an excellent father and is a friend and companion to his children.

Love and Marriage for Her
She is the quintessential woman, artistic and soulful, with a delightful practical bent of mind. She loves creating happiness around her and shies away from ruffling any feathers.

Calm and collected, she seems totally at ease no matter what life throws at her. Nothing can make her lose her cool. She is a peaceful haven after your stressful day. Tell her your problems. Loyal, caring and sensitive, she is your dedicated companion.

Her high levels of energy make it seem that she loves doing everything, but it would be great if you take over some of her chores and let her fulfil her artistic urges. Creatively intelligent, she needs an outlet for her artistic sensibilities.

This lady can turn domineering and manipulative if she does not feel that her life is going the way she envisaged. It is not flattery and compliments that she craves; just give her financial and emotional security. When she turns lazy, doesn't try to look her best or seems very distracted and irritated, take those as warning signals and rectify the situation.

Her children are her pride and she is very protective of them. She is more permissive than strict but empowers them and motivates them to face the tough challenges of life head on and fearlessly.

At the Workplace
They should choose a career that has artistic possibilities. They can shine in any field but only if it matches their passions. They put their energies into something that gives them a creative outlet along with financial stability. They can be good as dance directors, and music and film directors. Self-effacing to a great degree, they let their actions speak for themselves. But they can become masters of self-promotion too if the situation demands.

Extremely hard working, they are totally consumed by their work and do not rest till they achieve what they desire. The Arian energy drives them to work on their dreams with a deep-rooted passion and conviction. They can leave an organisation if they feel that their efforts are not being appreciated and financially compensated.

As bosses, they are masters of situational leadership. The mix of three different behavioural types, cardinal, fixed and mutable, gives them the flexibility to instinctively choose the right response to situations. They are master strategists, fabulous delegators, and excellent independent contributors too.

Fire, Water and Earth combine in them, and can make them delve into dark depths of insecurity and laziness or rise to great heights with drive, insight and common sense. Both worlds are open to them.

Famous AriTauPisces Personalities
Enrique Iglesias, Muttiah Muralitharan, Ness Wadia, Raghu Ram, Aditya Chopra, Janet Jackson, Ashish Nehra, Nizhalgal Ravi, Manna Dey, Geet Sethi, Vayalar Ravi, Ewan McGregor, Isadora Duncan, Bert Van Marwijk, Zarine Khan, Sarah Class, Robert Browning, Sonal Chauhan, Casey Donovan (singer), Salvador Dali.

89. ARIES–GEMINI–CANCER

Mars, the violent and powerful god of war, gives strength; Mercury, the messenger of the gods, gives vibrant ideas; and the sensitive Moon adds emotions to this extremely volatile and exuberant combination of AriGemCan.

The first thing that you notice about them is the beauty with which they communicate. They are unmatched wordsmiths. The measured and sensitive expounding of Cancer, the word play of Gemini and the clarity of Aries, keep the listener spellbound. They love talking. If they are ever quiet, it indicates anger more than a desire for solitude.

AriGemCans are extremely positive personalities. The sad moodiness of Cancer is hidden by the fiery vitality of Aries and the happy charm of Gemini. They spread good cheer amongst friends and are the first ones to suggest outings or parties to liven things up. They can't sit still for long. The multi-tasking nature of Gemini makes them want to do ten things at once. They are full of ideas, opinions and views.

They like to make a style statement that is highly individualistic. They have their own views on conventions, and are quite rebellious when they are young. As they age, the fire of Aries is subdued but you can still expect interesting times and opinions from them. Both Aries and Cancer are cardinal signs, so AriGemCans will definitely lead. They can lead with the loud-mouthed aggression of Aries or the soft, cajoling ways of Cancer; either way they will never be content being ignored. Expect to receive a lot of advice from these people.

Their mothers are very important to them. They revere their mother and idolise her.

There is a deep emotional side to them too. They carry their emotional baggage wherever they go, and wear their hearts on their sleeves. Cancerians are extremely emotional and touchy and when combined with the childlike Arians, they live, touch, and feel every experience of life, with the Gemini in them giving a running commentary. Reminiscing about past glories is also a part of their emotional landscape. They like remembering their past and think about it as a happy time despite the turbulences, if any, they faced then.

Their anger is as evident as their views. They can go quiet or give you a barrage; it all depends on how you rank in their list. When they are in the mood for long-winded monologues, you better run for cover.

Love is extremely important to AriGemCans. For them, it is all or nothing in love. The Arian desire for the perfect mate, plus the Gemini feeling of there being a better one just around the corner, spurs them to search for a love who matches their ideals. Rather than hold on to a withering love, they will cut ties and move on. There is a strange contradiction in their quest for love; while they are liberal about their own moral ethics, they expect their partners to be idealistic with high moral values.

They are extremely generous and giving to the people they love. They are wonderful children and make amazing parents. They enjoy the small details of parenting and each moment of parenthood, and relive their childhood with their children.

Money is extremely important to them. They need money to feel powerful and secure. They know how to save and invest. The danger also exists that the impulsive Aries and distracted Gemini in them can blow up their entire savings in a day.

They sometimes seem to be multiple personalities with their exuberant ideals, deep emotions and expressive views. Consistency is not their strong point. AriGemCans will have too many views and the Gemini maverick's habit of changing ideas without a moment's notice will surely afflict them. They also have deep inner Cancerian insecurities and fears that haunt them from time to time. They work even harder to keep those fears from haunting them.

They have a wild side to them. They love adventure and speed in their lives. They hate monotony and maximise every day and live life to the fullest. They can seek thrills by indulging in interesting and colourful pursuits. They want to experience everything and then reminisce about it later.

They can also be afflicted with Cancerian mood swings and Geminian boredom. In a lifetime they can range from total atheists to complete believers; but they have some kind of a relationship with spirituality. They will explore and form their own opinions and ideas on spirituality.

They think a lot, feel a lot and talk a lot. They have a deep desire for applause and appreciation. They have abundant creativity and with their original productive thinking and ground-breaking ideas, they would love to create things that would help generations to come. Love, recognition and applause are their deepest desires.

Aries–Gemini–Cancer – Dennis Lillee

Dennis was hugely popular with his fans for his gold necklaces and green-and-yellow headbands. The Arian desire to shine and the wild Gemini ways surely had a lot to do with his dress sense![146]

'The psychology of fear is an important ingredient in fast bowling.'[147]

'Since I was 23, I've been involved in business. At this stage, we run an office full-time. We run a variety of businesses which keep us more than busy.'[148]

The Cancerian desire for reminiscing and the Gemini love for telling a story led Lillee to pen two autobiographies. You can see the love for speed, the quicksilver mind and the insight of an AriGemCan in him.

Love and Marriage for Him

He wants to be the most important person in your life. He also desires immense adulation. He needs you to be intelligent enough to engage him in a conversation. He is quite possessive, although flirts himself. Of course, his flirting is quite harmless, but keep an eye on him, for he is easy to impress with ideas and

---

[146] http://www.espncricinfo.com/wctimeline/content/story/137025.html
[147] http://www.espncricinfo.com/australia/content/story/73779.html
[148] http://www.tylershineon.org/2007/08/interview-australian-cricket-legend-dennis-lillee/

attitude. If he is unhappy at home, he is one of those types who can seek solace outside and be absolutely nonchalant and open about it, too.

He likes an independent woman who does not take the spotlight away off him. He enjoys your ideas as long as they are not too aggressive. Though he enjoys intelligence and is a great conversationalist, he will always want to have the last word.

He is quite sensitive too and it is good if you recognise the signs and take preventive measures. A dose of praise always comes in handy; rub in some encouragement as well. He enjoys change and wants adventure in his life. Keep your bags packed for he will like venturing where few have dared.

As a father, he is exuberant. He is extremely proud of his children and looks for ways to pamper them. He is extremely caring, too, and is his best with them. He can be a little clinging and not know when to treat them as adults.

Love and Marriage for Her
She is the most entrancing person in your life. She needs a lot of praise and love to feel good with you. You will never get bored with her. She keeps changing and will keep you interested. Moreover, she will do anything to keep you happy and satisfied. Lucky you!

She desires an ideal love and is willing to put you up on a pedestal. She does not want to see your weaknesses. She wants a partner who sweeps her off her feet and is a strong, stable person in her life. Her ideas and adventures liven up your days, making for exuberant times together. Take care of her emotions for she is quite sensitive. She has changing moods, and needs you to respond to them.

Take active part in conversations if you love her, for she does not like talking to a person sitting behind a newspaper. Let her win arguments, it is essential for her to do so and good for your peace of mind. It is great if you can keep your ego in check and let her say the final word too.

As a mother, she insists on spoiling her children. She wants to pamper their whims and loves to cook for them. She wants to insulate her children from all the problems of life and refuses to let them handle their own problems.

At the Workplace
Energetic and communicative, imaginative and sensible, these people bring in a lot as employees. Once they realise what exactly they want to do, they stick to it with tenacity and work hard to make their dreams come true.

They have pioneering ideas and never shy away from implementing them. They are able to think through small details and implement their ideas wonderfully well. The Gemini's skill at writing and talking combined with the exuberance of Aries can make them great orators and writers. Their fertile Cancerian imagination combined with the innovative thinking of Aries and adroitness of Gemini makes them shine in show business. They are fabulous storytellers, actors or directors.

AriGemCans are fabulous at communicating their ideas and also have a flair for leading. They are fabulous coaches and mentors and as bosses, love being father figures to their teams. But they are very demanding and uncompromising on the results.

Fire, Air and Water mix together in this amazingly vibrant combination, which has a unique blend of opinion, action and sentiment.

Famous AriGemCan Personalities
Dennis Lillee, Bharathiraja, Lindsay Lohan, Alfredo Di Stéfano, Barbara Cartland, Doug Bollinger, Carl Jung, Kannadasan, Nicole Scherzinger, Jim Corbett, Aamna Sharif, Natasha Poly, Yul Brynner, Laurent Gaude.

90. ARIES–GEMINI–PISCES

Mars, the violent god of destruction, joins hands with the highly communicative and complex Mercury and the deeply mysterious Neptune. This sign is riddled with innumerable complexities and interesting dimensions.

Pisces is one Water sign in the zodiac that behaves like water – it can act any way and take any form to merge with its surroundings. When Pisces meets Gemini, the result is a complex mix, for Gemini adds versatility to AriGemPisces. Add to that the strong views and impulsive nature of Aries and you have a person with oodles of energy, excellent communication skills, and a vivid and wild imagination.

They amaze you with their erudition and powers of elucidation. They can put the most complex views and thoughts into simple words. But more than just talking, they respond beautifully to their environment. They pick up emotions and thoughts the minute they enter a room. There is an element of drama in them due to Aries and Gemini. When AriGemPisces talk, they like to add extra colour to their thoughts and ideas and will speak with such panache that you will find it hard to disbelieve their words.

You will find them to be extremely intelligent and vivacious. They are fast learners and easily pick up new concepts and ideas. Change is an integral part of their personality. They change their views as they meet different people. It makes them unreliable at times; you will be amazed at the change in their opinions from the last time you spoke to them. You will also find their responses very unnerving for they can give a variety of responses to the same statement.

The problem with them is that they want to look good to everybody and, as it is difficult to please everyone, they say different things to different people. The fact is that this combination has the undeniable potential to achieve outstanding results but can also damage everything they aspire for due to their ego and duplicity.

The Pisces tendency of self-undoing can also rear its head in AriGemPisces as they will decide to leave relationships and views after fighting ardently for them. There is a deep-seated need for variety and after winning over something or someone, it isn't elusive anymore, and loses attraction. They know the repercussions of their wrong steps but take them anyhow. There is also a deep-seated self-doubt in both Aries and Pisces, which can drive them to act exactly the opposite – brave and brash.

AriGemPisces need a lot of love, understanding and support to glow their brightest. They need to be told over and over again that they are special and mean a lot to their loved ones. Words mean a lot to them; despite the instinctive Piscean understanding of heartfelt actions, they need verbal expressions. They need external assurances to overcome their inner self-doubts.

Confusingly, they can give everything in love yet they can also walk away from it. The Pisces desire for soulful love and the Arian need for idealistic love makes them love wholeheartedly; but if the Gemini aspect in them is strong they will leave all that for a new love they think might be better. Till they learn to control their Gemini desires, they find stability lacking in their lives.

They can be very moody too and their sensitivity makes them wallow in sorrow at times. They get hurt easily and can lash out without giving the other person a chance to defend himself. The anger of AriGemPisces can sometimes be really bad. When they are offended, the typical Arian is rude and yells the loudest, the Piscean tells you what hurts the most, and the Geminian is sarcastic. They can do anything when they are overcome by strong emotions.

Pisces makes them prone to addictions and, with the Gemini and Arian desire to try new things, they can turn things horribly wrong with their lives if they decide to walk down that path.

AriGemPisces have communication skills, artistic talent and even pioneering ability; yet they need a lot of support to achieve their full potential. If they can somehow shed the Aries selfishness, Piscean quickness to get hurt and the Geminian duality, then the deep understanding of Pisces, the brilliant intelligence of Gemini and enterprising spirit of Aries can make them extraordinary individuals who would be loved truly by one and all – the one thing that they deeply desire.

Aries–Gemini–Pisces – Moon Moon Sen
'I wanted my children to be independent and to live life on their own terms. Not be a slave to some man just because they were married to him.'[149]

Sen said she would bare all even at 70: 'Age is not important, the attitude is. In fact, I wouldn't mind myself if the shoot is done aesthetically and with taste.'[150]

Moon Moon Sen has the ever-youthful look of a Gemini and Pisces adds softness to it. None can doubt her skill with words and her intelligence even as she speaks to shock. The Arian comes out in her decisions to be herself.

Love and Marriage for Him
This guy can love you a lot but can also give you a lot of grief. You have to be certain before getting into a relationship with him and if by the age of twenty-five he does not really know where he wants to go, it is better you let him find that out first.

Observing his family and friends gives you an idea about what he's like. If you find any negatives in his environment, you can be sure that they are reflected in him to a certain extent. He needs a lot of love and care. You need to be the strong and stable person in the relationship.

Please keep the tabs on money for he does not know how to save or invest. You truly have to be the one who wears the pants around the house but do it tactfully or he may slip out of your grasp. He loves change and travel tops his list. He prefers luxury travel to roughing it out. He makes you see so many sides of life that there is never a dull moment with him.

As a father, he is fun and excitement. He rarely bosses around his children and prefers to let them experience their lives. He may not be there for all the major events but makes it up with his charm and enthusiasm when he is with them.

Love and Marriage for Her
This girl is an impressive package – she is intelligent, sexy, independent, loving, impulsive and extremely different from any one you have ever met before. It can even be intimidating to some people who cannot handle such extraversion.

---

[149] http://www.ratedesi.com/video/v/rGo7jRRxnZQ/Raima-Sen-and-Moon-Moon-Sen-talk-about-their-Relationship-II
[150] http://en.wikipedia.org/wiki/Moon_Moon_Sen

She loves talking and being talked to. You need to pamper and love this girl for her to be with you. She has many moods and can be crabby one minute and smiling the next. She loves to flirt too. Possessiveness may excite her in the beginning but it drives her away if you persist in such behaviour. She knows how to be sensual with a lot of intelligence. There is a youthfulness about her. She has an admirable ability to adapt and change according to her circumstances and be a girl at heart even at sixty.

She can blast you in anger when disappointed. She needs a stable, comforting presence at that time so that she feels secure and soothed or her anger can become even more devastating. Budgeting is an art that is beyond her. She loves to live in luxury and rarely pays bills on time unless taught to do so. Please handle all mundane and dreary matters on your own and let this bundle of energy and vitality live life her way, full of happiness.

As a mother, she spoils her children with love and abundance. She understands them and never tries to discipline them, or try to make them change their views. She is one mother who can never be scandalised or shocked. She is always there for her children when they need her and stays away when they do not.

At the Workplace
AriGemPisces have amazing communication skills and fabulous artistic talents. A life of routine and monotony is not for them. They prefer careers where they can learn and have fun at the same time. They are masters of self-promotion and pursue an idea with passion and assurance.

Do not expect them to follow schedules or live regulated lives. They are adept at multitasking and see the positives of any problem. They can be excellent writers, poets, singers and even do well in human relations. More than money or fame, they need to be challenged to do something good. They want a job where they get to learn and adapt every day. They crave appreciation – don't be stingy in that area, and you will be rewarded with great results.

As bosses they can be extremely demanding and expect you to look up to them. They will be very generous if you go to them for advice, value their smart ideas and truly believe in their greatness. If they feel that you are not appreciative of their superior intelligence they can sense it and make life hell for you.

Fire, Air and Water combine to give AriGemPisces drive, speech and thought. Creative and emotional, they can make or break their destiny with words and deeds; especially words that they don't say and deeds that they don't do.

Famous AriGemPisces Personalities
Moon Moon Sen, Johan Cruyff, K.L. Sehgal, Dr Najma Heptullah, Emma Thompson.

91. ARIES–CANCER–LEO

Mars, the violent god of war, joins the deeply emotional Moon and the proud Sun to create the passionate, sensitive and stylish AriCanLeos. The combination has three fascinating creatures – the proud Lion, the untameable Ram and the hard-shelled Crab that has a tough exterior but a soft interior. Let's explore the different shades to their persona.

The Aries passion and energy is extremely evident in them. They will light up any conversation with their determined ideas, and AriCanLeos have a flair about them. Whatever they say or do is with an enthusiasm, energy and flamboyance that overshadows everyone else. Both Aries and Leo love standing out. Individualistic style, elegance and regal splendour are their trademark.

The key characteristic of AriCanLeos is youthfulness. Aries is the baby of the zodiac, Leos are the adolescents and Cancerians love being babied forever. AriCanLeos seem never to age, and are forever exuberant and eager to perform. The Arian loves taking initiative, Leo is a natural leader and Cancer is a cardinal sign too. They are the cynosure of all eyes, and inspire love in the people they meet. Arian energy and innovativeness combines with the dazzling brightness of Leo to create a stylish, sunny and outgoing personality.

The Leo in them will make AriCanLeos generous and extremely caring. Cancer adds its nurturing touch. They love their families above everything else and can make great sacrifices for the family. They love their mothers and take up family responsibilities, behaving like responsible elder siblings even if they are the youngest. Watch them when there is an emergency – these people can handle calamities like hardened warriors.

AriCanLeos are very sensitive people: Cancerians go into a shell when teased and Leos sulk as well; add the explosive Arian and Leonine anger and ego to it and you have a person who is easily offended and needs a lot of cajoling, love and appreciation to be mollified. This same sensitivity will make them understand others, problems and make them fight for the rights of the disadvantaged.

They are extremely demanding in love. Aries gives them an idealistic view of love and they want their love to be the best of all. It will put tremendous pressure on their partner to always shine and match the AriCanLeo's glitter. Their Leonine side makes them extremely romantic and dramatic in love. Cancer makes them highly sentimental and sensitive. They expect you to be as passionate, and it will be a long time before the pressure is off, for these people mellow and calm down very slowly.

They are extremely spiritual and maybe even ritualistic. They believe in the power above and are proud of their belief systems. They never take a no for an answer. Once they determine they want something, they go for it. They live, breathe and dream only of that object of desire and work hard towards achieving it.

They do not make friends easily. They have strict criteria by which they judge others. They love, hate, hurt and pine with such theatrical flair that you think no one feels as much as them.

There is also a bit of stinginess, for Cancerians just hate parting with money. Introduce Aries selfishness to the mix and you have people who can be the soul of generosity to their loved ones but indifferent to others. Deep-seated insecurities also lie hidden in them, stemming from all three signs. Cancer is always uncertain and afraid of the future while Fire signs have a niggling insecurity that they try and hide with their air of confidence. You might think that such positive signs are self-starters – they are, but they also need lots of appreciation to make them feel good.

Despite their insecurities, they come across as arrogant and rude at times, especially towards people who do not matter to them. Leo and Aries have this brash style that seems to look down on certain people, while their moody Cancerian temperament can make their moodiness a primary feature in their dealings. They are complex creatures, but there is a way to handle them – give them respect, love and admiration and they are yours.

Anger is their hallmark. AriCanLeos can really lose it. They shout, scream and create a massive scene. They take a long time to recover, brooding over insults and sulking. Insult them and they will never forget it for a lifetime and you may have to pay one day. The exuberance, youthfulness and childlikeness of these people and their blind belief in their invincibility induce them to make mistakes, especially when young, that they rue forever. They want to achieve things too much too soon, which could be their undoing. What they want is love, love and more love, and huge unconditional adoration, just like a baby!

Aries–Cancer–Leo – Bill Clinton
'Sometime in my sixteenth year, I decided I wanted to be in public life. I loved music and thought I could be very good, but I knew I would never be John Coltrane or Stan Getz. I was interested in medicine and thought I could be a fine doctor, but I knew I would never be Michael DeBakey. But I knew I could be great in public service.'[151]

Mr Clinton concedes that he was voted out as governor (of Arkansas) after just one term because he tried to do too much too fast.[152]

Bill Clinton has the energy, the desire to do something different and the zeal of an AriCanLeo.

Love and Marriage for Him
He is extremely generous and would love a chance to splurge on you. You just need to appreciate him. He feels hurt at the minutest barbs or if ignored. Understand that he is a child at heart and he is your first baby. Baby him, adore him and he will do anything for you. But the big plus, of course, is that he is a die-hard romantic and no one can woo and conquer a girl with as much style and chutzpah.

He comes with huge emotional baggage. There is high drama in his love and he wants you to be the best of all mates. The minute he walks in through the door, you have to focus on him. He wants your attention and you can easily become a doormat to his demands. Set some ground rules in the beginning for it can be difficult to assert yourself later.

This man seems invincible but is actually fragile. You need to be his confidence-booster and never let him give in to his pessimistic streak. Despite his outward courage, he is insecure inside. You should be aware of that and handle him accordingly.

---

[151] http://en.wikipedia.org/wiki/Bill_Clinton
[152] http://www.cbsnews.com/stories/2004/06/18/60minutes/main624880.shtml?tag=contentMain;contentBody

He is a fabulous father. He knows how to nurture his children. He tries to control them and this can be a source of friction between him and his brood. He is generous and caring.

Love and Marriage for Her

She is amazingly stylish. You can congratulate yourself on getting a diva for all eyes turn to her when she walks in with you. Her amazing energy and positivity charm everyone. She also has it in her to be caring and loving. Her generosity for her family is limitless and she will do anything to ensure their happiness.

She can be a big help to you in your work. She is born to be a queen or the consort of a king. She can help you achieve your highest ambitions with her desire to succeed. Command and control come naturally to her and she can deal with more than mere household emergencies with ease; the perfect wife for a businessman or a politician.

This girl needs lots of money and compliments to keep her happy. She craves drama and excitement. Do not expect her to save, though she desperately wants to. But she is extremely good in getting the best bargains and value for money.

It is amazing how this diva can instantly turn into a caring mother. Her children are her pride and joy, and she loves pampering them. She can even let her ambitions take a break for them.

At the Workplace

AriCanLeo is a combination of two cardinal signs (Aries and Cancer) and the dramatic Leo, which loves taking up responsibilities too. They want to start directly at the top and are impatient to achieve coveted positions. They simply dream big and with the Arian energy and Cancerian tenacity, they just hang in there and ensure their dream reaches its logical conclusion. They have fantastic ideating skills, grand plans and superb finishing skills.

AriCanLeos are made for glory. They thrive on adulation and give everything for their success. If you have them by your side, you can never lose. They are self-starters and extremely hardworking. They do not need to be supervised.

Money does excite them but glory counts for more. They work for laurels and applause; the money will come as a byproduct. Their egos can come in their way at times and they are definitely not good at conflict management.

You can expect loyalty from them. All three signs are known for their loyalty. They do not part ways so long as you recognise and publicly applaud their achievements, and pay them well. They are a natural as bosses, flamboyant and stylish. They prefer making the bold brush-strokes of a project and leaving the details for you to complete. You will have a lot of work to do.

Pioneering and applause seeking, loving and extremely demanding, creative yet logical – AriCanLeos are dramatic achievers.

Famous AriCanLeo Personalities

Bill Clinton, Pete Sampras, Mario Balotelli, Cameron Diaz, Phoolan Devi, Edmund Hillary, Kobe Bryant, Marco Materazzi, Mette-Marit (Crown Princess of Norway), Demi Lovato, Morten Olsen.

92. ARIES–CANCER–PISCES

Mars, the ruthless god of war, meets two gentler companions – the emotional and sensitive Moon and the deep and mysterious Neptune. AriCanPisces is inherently tender, sensitive and highly emotional; but they have a steely determination too. An interesting soft and hard combination!

Three diverse sets of creatures form this combination – one that lives only on land – the Ram, another only in water – the Fish, and the third with amphibious qualities – the Crab. While this makes them extremely flexible, with the ability to survive in all situations, it also gives them many more interesting aspects.

The Arian fearlessness becomes an invisible armour for these unlikely warriors. They are gentle, docile, deeply sensitive and highly empathetic. They are extremely warm and wonderful people. The Arian selfishness gets diluted due to the other two generous signs. AriCanPisces have understanding and empathy but think for themselves.

Family is important to them. However far they go, they will never forget the place they grew up. Mother, her cooking, and the days of childhood are etched in their minds forever, and often recalled. They give much more than they receive in love with people in their lives. They care, protect, nurture and are pillars of rock for their loved ones and families. The values that they imbibe at an impressionable age are very important as Pisces holds on to them and Cancer nurtures them all their life.

Expect them to know the deepest thoughts that run inside your mind. If they are positive towards them, they are all smiles and very happy to reciprocate. On the contrary, if your thoughts are not so positive, they somehow detect that too, and be morose around you. They also have a habit of reading between the lines and getting upset; so clarify if you do not mean any harm.

Love comes naturally to them. Pisces have a deep need to love, while Cancer wants a mate and Aries looks for an ideal love. With so much thought on love, they are absolutely committed to their love, and are very emotionally demanding. They look for their mamma's love in their mates. In fact, they need love, care, understanding and sensitivity from everyone around them.

Both Cancer and Pisces are highly creative signs. They possess the amazingly fertile imagination of Cancer and the deep artistic abilities of Pisces, especially if raised in such an environment. Aries chips in with the much-needed energy, sizzle and vitality to their performances. The fearless Aries lets the creative ability shine through brightly.

Travel excites them. Wihin the AriCanPisces, there is ever the urge to see new places and visit new destinations. They are always ready to explore the world, but they like company in travel. After initial caution and fear, they jump in to enjoy whole-heartedly all activities that involve adventure and dare devilry. Money matters find them quite alert. They can be a little stingy and prefer saving to squandering money.

Anger is not their way. They sulk, cry and crib rather than explode. It can be a bit trying for they never shout and scream but disappear into a black cloud. It takes a lot of words and time to get them back.

Emotions rule this combination. Cancer is highly sensitive and deeply insecure. Like Pisces, it is also highly imaginative. Both these signs tend to be a little pessimistic too. The changing phases of the Moon can make them cranky and Piscean duality can make them moody as well. AriCanPisces do not know how to be truly and absolutely happy. No matter how happy they are, they find a gloomy thought to darken their sunniest hour. You may find them arrogant, rude or snooty at times. Do not worry. This is the mask they need to wear if they feel they have been trampled upon.

Cancerians suffer from all kinds of fears – of losing their loved ones to losing all the money they possess. They also fear change – they need constancy in everything in life. Thankfully, the change-loving Fish and the truly pioneering Aries will forcefully take the timorous Crab out of its shelter and into new territory. All these conflicting ideologies in the three zodiac signs will keep pulling them in different directions. But eventually AriCanPisces will move in a constructive direction with the determination of Cancer and fearlessness of Aries.

All three zodiac signs have inferiority complexes. Aries shows a brave face to the world while it secretly trembles, as does Cancer, who is not self-confident. The Fish, in any case, does not want to assert itself. If hurt, angry, betrayed, feeling inadequate or feeling lonely, AriCanPisces simply wallow in self-pity. They sulk, go into their shells, cry, swim around in circles and take some time before coming out. They need to be a bit careful about alcohol and other such substances. The Aries in them can lose direction and Pisces is prone to addiction if they are not careful.

Some AriCanPisces can also exhibit the worst qualities of this combination. The Cancerian insecurities, jealousies and secretiveness combine with the chameleonic and elusive deceptiveness of Pisces and the Arian selfishness, to make them the meanest and wiliest of people, if forced by circumstances.

AriCanPisces show that out of our deepest fears come our greatest strengths. They may take time to overcome their fears, but once they do that they will be unstoppable. They have within themselves the power to transform dramatically. They can bring in the tenacity of the Crab, the changeability of the Fish and the forcefulness of the Ram, to rise above self-pity and self-induced obstacles and rise to meet the toughest challenges of life.

Aries–Cancer–Pisces – Aung San Suu Kyi
Aung San Suu Kyi's father was a much-revered freedom fighter in Burma and his aura surely rubbed off on the Piscean in her. Her Arian idealism and Cancerian perseverance added to her strengths.

'I could not, as my father's daughter, remain indifferent to all that was going on.'[153]

'When people ask me, "Do you want to be the next president of Burma?" I say no. The object of this exercise is that you have president after president after president.'

Idealistic, courageous, philosophical and humble, Suu Kyi is a heroic blend of AriCanPisces.

---

[153] http://www.ft.com/cms/s/2/8fd74dd6-29b4-11e0-bb9b-00144feab49a.html#axzz1rhypOPGX

Love and Marriage for Him
He is caring, loving and extremely emotional. He understands you and knows just how to talk to you when you are feeling low, and expects the same from you. He loves to take you out, especially to try different cuisines, and is a very good cook himself.

He is prone to mood swings. It is good if you understand them and provide balance by not being as emotional as him. You need to be the strong one in the relationship and be ready to prop him up when he is fighting his inner demons.

A word of advice – avoid clashing with his mother; he loves and worships her.

He is a wonderful father. Fatherhood fulfils his urge to care, protect and nurture. He does not mind the nappy stage and is good at dealing with all the emergencies of childhood. He can be a bit paranoid about his children and finds it difficult to let go as they grow older.

Love and Marriage for Her
She is highly emotional and sensitive, a true woman. You need to be sensitive too or you can make her withdraw into a shell. Timing is essential here. If you meet her before she gains her strength and determination, you may find her fearful and immature, but she surprises you when she finds her balance. Her moodiness can be a trial. This girl can have dark mood swings. You need to really love her. She needs a lot of emotional support and cannot deal with itif you want your own space. You always come first for her and she loves planning her life around you.

She is an extremely creative and artistic person. She would be a happier person if you allow her to get immersed in her passions. Domination is not her agenda. She is quite happy letting you lead if you assure her that she is the one. She responds beautifully to love – love is her all-consuming need. She is capable of meeting every need you have from a woman.

As a mother, she is in her element. Her children are abundantly pampered, loved and nurtured. She is always there for them and when they are older, finds it hard to let go.

At the Workplace
Cancer and Pisces make AriCanPisces extremely creative, imaginative and artistic. Their hearts are in creative pursuits – but those that provide adequate monetary compensation. They will not give up everything for the sake of their art. They can be brilliant in careers ranging from advertising to hairstyling, and even acting and sports.

They are prone to indiscipline and laziness, and need to be inspired and encouraged. They need good mentors to guide them. Do not expect them to work well in routine jobs or those demand long hours. They need professions that provide variety and give them time with their families too.

Both Aries and Cancer are cardinal signs with extremely different leadership styles. AriCanPisces know how to lead and make good leaders. They can cajole or command (the former is more likely). As bosses, they are full of life and ideas, understanding of your needs, and treat employees as family.

AriCanPisces are full of emotions and insecurities yet they hold the key to success deep within them.

Famous AriCanPisces Personalities
Aung San Suu Kyi, Ajith Kumar, Lara Dutta, Ghanshyam Das Birla, Kofi Annan, Queen Elizabeth II, Domenico Fioravanti, Carmen Electra, Narayani Shastri.

93. ARIES–LEO–VIRGO

This is one fiery combination. It has Aries, fiery and pioneering, combined with the domineering and regal Leo and the hardworking and diligent Virgo. You can expect extremely high standards of work and play from AriLeoVirgos.

They have a forcefulness that cannot be denied. When an Aries puts forward his unique views, people stop and listen. Add to that the charm of a Leo and the diligence of a Virgo who makes sure that the words carry substance, and you have a person who is very hard to ignore. Aries and Leo are fired by high ideals and love applause. AriLeoVirgos don't just pioneer ideas but provide detailed roadmaps too. Applauding such effort is not hard, is it?

This combination strives for perfection. The Virgo in them can detect the smallest loophole in any project proposal. Their eyes catch the flaws first and the better aspects later. When they are satisfied, they roll out the project in grand Leo scale and present it in a unique manner in typical Arian style. Everything in life is classy, large-scale or perfect with these people!

They are undeniably generous. The Virgo thriftiness is greatly reduced by the Aries and Leo extravagance. They spend not only on themselves, but also on friends and colleagues.

AriLeoVirgos have the Virgo passion for healthy food. They like to dabble in medicine as well, and have an instinctive knowledge for healing. They are also spiritual and may have the Virgo fondness for rituals. Their high standards apply to everything they do and feel. They are very selective while choosing their friends, but once they are friends with you, they will be your passionate champions.

When they fall in love, it has to be to their near-impossible high standards. The Virgo's refined tastes mingle with the royal demands of Leo and the ideals of Aries – it might be very difficult for them to find someone who meets their exacting criteria. Imperfections drive them away and they can be hurt while they try to come to terms with their partner's more human standards. If that happens then they will sorrow for some time and then look again for another perfect mate.

With all the fire, fury and some earthy tones in them, you do not find sensitivity or understanding. They find it very difficult to understand someone else's point of view. They see things in black and white – you are either with them or against them. They are neither tactful nor diplomatic. They tend to talk a lot about themselves, and in their naïveté, they forget that they are being self-centred. 'My needs, my standards, my ego' come first. But they don't have a mean bone in them; they are not intentionally bad.

It is frightening to watch them in a battle of wills, with the Leo roar, the Aries dominating demeanour and the Virgo propensity to criticise. They can flare up and they shout, rave and rant so much that you find it almost impossible to defend yourself. Only large doses of flattery can calm them down. Their huge egos can lead them astray.

The Aries' blind belief in people and the Virgo's naïveté about others' deeper feelings inevitably leads the AriLeoVir to feel let down by people at some point in life. AriLeoVirs take things at face value and are easily duped by con artists. When this happens, they react by becoming extremely self-centred and counting every penny they spend on people other than family.

All Fire signs are extremely positive and seem incapable of fear, but deep within them is self-doubt. AriLeoVirgos do not admit it even to themselves but they do fear failure. Anyone who understands that basic fear in them can win their love by expressing solidarity during their times of crisis. Never forget that they make the most loyal and generous of friends. They may seem arrogant and rude and even seem self-absorbed, but they are trusting, childlike souls who have an interesting purity about them which is very endearing.

Aries–Leo–Virgo – Hugh Grant
Eric Felner: 'He really thinks about every single aspect of every prop, every set, every line, every interaction, and he works it and works it and works it until he feels it's absolutely perfect.'

'I'm so tense and pernickety and perfectionist.'[154]

A few months before firing his agent, he said, 'They've known for years that I have total control. I've never taken any advice on anything.'

'There is at least as much of Hugh that is charismatic, intellectual, and whose tongue is maybe too clever for its own good, as there is of him that's gorgeous and kind of woolly and flubsy,' according to Mike Newell.

Hugh Grant is a perfectionist and has the high standards, ethics and pride of an AriLeoVir.

Love and Marriage for Him
He is The Man. Understand and absorb the fact. He needs to be respected. If you have a desire to control as strong as his, it is impossible for you to live with him. He needs someone a little submissive and adulating. However, submission does not mean that you have to look meek and mousy. He wants a partner who shines on his arm. Perfect standards are what he desires, be it in dressing or talking. He wants a wife who outclasses everybody.

He is extremely involved in his career and does not spend much time at home. Of course he would have gone all out during the courtship period to woo you for the Leo in him is highly romantic but he will take up the role of a dutiful provider after marriage. He worries a lot; ensure that he doesn't need to worry about home. You need to support his dreams and be there to hold his hand when the going gets tough.

He is very generous when it comes to family. So when he actually says it is time to start saving and investing for the children's future and your retirement, just go ahead and cut down on luxuries. There is only one way you can get your way with him: appeal to his generosity. Nagging, criticising or getting angry never work. Tell him that your life is a dream with him. To top this, look your best whenever he is around.

As a father, too, he needs to be treated as the boss. He is very proud of his children's achievements and love to talk about them. They have to listen to his long-winded talks on life and it is best if they do so with a dutiful nod.

---

[154] http://jeffdawsonblog.blogspot.in/2011/07/hugh-grant.html

Love and Marriage for Her

She has very high standards. It is going to be extremely difficult for normal men to meet her exacting requirements. She is well dressed with impeccable style. She has the refined tastes of Virgo and the expensive demands of Leo, mixed with the individuality of an Aries. She always stands out in a crowd. Her tastes are royal and unique, so nothing ordinary or common is ever right for her. So even if she shops very little she spends a lot when she does.

Marriage frightens her with its responsibilities and needs. So, if you managed to get her, she must have seen something really good in you. But if you try to deceive her or fall badly short of her expectations at a later stage, she has the courage to cut off ties completely.

If the Virgo in her is strong, she is very dutiful about her home and work. But she will need help – do not expect her to stoop to doing menial chores. She needs to have a career and is very good at it. She is fiercely competitive and it is a good outlet for her natural aggression. If she does not have a career she will probably take up causes and fight for them, armed with faultless details and vociferous arguments.

She is very blunt in her criticism. If she doesn't like something, she will tell you without mincing her words. You need not fear coy deception from her! She loves throwing and attending parties for she loves attention. Despite her apparent self-confidence, she has a deep sense of inadequacy within. Hold her in your arms and give her strength. There is a soft naïveté about her despite her bravado, which you will love.

She is a dominating and controlling mother. She makes sure her children do exactly what she tells them. You have to be the one more sensitive to their needs for she lacks the soft touch.

At the Workplace

Excellence, hard work and idealism are their mantra and they live and die by this. They can motivate people towards distinction with their drive and commitment. Planning and commanding come naturally to them. Their fiery and pioneering nature is best suited to business. They are delighted to start from scratch. They cannot under someone else because of their blunt tongues.

AriLeoVir excel in any profession that requires research and pioneering ideas. They take pride in doling out perfection everytime they go to work. They are perfectionists who follow high standards in work ethics.

They make generous bosses. Their one weakness is flattery. If you know how to use it well, they can be extremely partial to you. Never make the mistake of acting smarter than them. It puts them off completely.

Earth with double Fire and gives AriLeoVirs stability with dynamism. They have a will to succeed and they back it up with excruciating hard work.

Famous AriLeoVir Personalities

Hugh Grant, Khushboo Sundar, George Bailey, Lasith Malinga, T. Subbarami Reddy, Maneka Gandhi, Guy Ritchie, Naval Tata, O. Henry, Vanessa Gusmeroli, Nick Jonas, Greta Garbo, Lauren Bacall, Amala Akkineni, Murali Kartik.

94. ARIES–LEO–PISCES

Mars, the violent and powerful god of war, exudes the regal grace of Apollo, while the deep and mysterious Neptune creates a soft mystique in AriLeoPisces. This is a very interesting combination: two fiery animals – the Lion and the Ram, merged with the elusive Fish. There are some amazing shades to their persona.

AriLeoPisces are full of life and vitality. The fire blazes true and strong in this double Fire combination. They are hard to ignore. They love being well-dressed and want to make a style statement; they aspire to the best brands. Their Arian childlike curiosity and Piscean sponge-like ability to learn new things ensures they never age mentally.

Ambition is strong and there's always a touch of drama about them. Aries always wants to pioneer and Leo desires only to lead; with these two leaders, the timid Pisces becomes more confident and AriLeoPisces will want to lead and to be heard. They love to proclaim their activities to the whole world. They love exaggerating their emotions and want to be the centre of attention.

Family and friends are extremely important to them. While Pisces looks upon the whole world with love, AriLeoPisces draw a line between their loved ones and others. AriLeoPisces are very loving, generous and sensitive to their family's needs. The only thing they need from people they help is respect; they want to be looked up to and can show their explosive temper if they are ignored.

The most remarkable thing about them is the fusion of Fire of Aries and Leo with the Water of Pisces. They may be exuberant, idealistic and proud, but also have the compassion, sensitivity and deep power to look into your soul. As they can read your mind easily, they cannot be fooled by flattery.

Romance will loom large on their horizon. AriLeoPisces are die-hard romantics and will want to be wooed and courted in style. If you love them, give in to their wide-eyed charm and romance them with elegance and emotion. They seek a love that is idealistic and strong. AriLeoPisces wants someone special in their lives but they will not think twice about walking out if their desires are not met.

All three signs are highly creative and this gives AriLeoPisces a definite edge in all things creative and imaginative. Aries likes to pioneer new thoughts and ideas, while Leo is never shy of showing off its talents to an adoring public and the soft Pisces is endowed with great creative energies. AriLeoPisces will surely have a creative bent of mind and will be able to utilise their creative potential to the hilt.

While Aries is the baby of the zodiac, Leo is the adolescent and Pisces can either behave with the maturity of a wise old man or wear rose-coloured glasses and escape from reality. Rebellion and adventure will surely mark them out in the early stages of youth. They are game for any adventure and rarely hold back at the sight of excitement. They can be really lazy at times.

They are prone to lose their temper. They regret their harsh words the next day but are also quick to apologise. AriLeoPisces find it difficult to hold on to money. They rarely understand the concept of saving and would rather earn more than save for a distant future.

AriLeoPisces rarely practise tact and diplomacy except when really necessary. It is hard to make them soften their opinions and views, and they love to advise. They are good at listening too – but not for long. The best thing about them is that they are quite free of malice.

The Piscean susceptibility to addictions and the Arian predilection for novelty can lead them to some abysmal lows in life. The deceptive Pisces combined with the self-centred but single-minded Aries and flashy Leo can also make a spectacular con artist. Here, all the negative traits of the three zodiac signs are manifest – deception, ruthlessness and the desire to win at all costs. Such cases are few and far between, but cannot be ruled out completely.

All the spectacle, action, vanity, ego and drama in their life are just in search of true love, admiration and applause. If they get these in full measure they can mend their ways and be the nicest people around.

Spirituality will also attract them. All the three signs understand the meaning of spirituality and are drawn to it at some point. They will be attracted to religion and search for a deeper meaning to life.

The lack of Earth is very evident in this combination for they lack stability in their views and ideas. AriLeoPisces need people in their lives who bind them to reality and make them see the world as it is, not as they think it is. Despite all their bravado, deep inside they have doubts; they fear that they may not be able to pull off the stunts that they claim. So when they really do it, you know that they have slain their internal demons, and triumphed. Give them a big thumbs up for that… it's not that easy!

Aries–Leo–Pisces – Michelle Pfeiffer
The AriLeoPisces actress displayed more than her share of Arian rebellion and Leo pride by being the most rebellious of all her siblings.

It was a mark of her vulnerability that shortly after her arrival she fell under the sway of a murky quasi-religious cult dedicated, as she puts it, to 'vegetarianism and metaphysics' that attempted to take control of her life.

She happily admits to having been in therapy for many years: 'I'm really over-analysed.'

The insecurity inherent in all three signs is evident in her struggles yet she battled on with the daredevilry of Aries and the Leo determination to make it big.[155]

Love and Marriage for Him
He wants to be the boss. He wants to have the first and the last word in any discussion and does not take kindly to opposition. The easiest way to deal with him is to show him that you respect his views. He never denies you anything as long as you tell him that he is the best. He shares your troubles and knows when you feel sad. Despite his boisterous ways, he has a soft heart, which is especially soft for his family.

He wants to shine at family gatherings, so please do not criticise him in public. You will push him into being cunning, self-centred and deceptive if he does not feel loved and respected. Look at him with adoring eyes and he returns your love with loyalty and love. He has deep insecurities and only your love can build up his inner confidence.

---
[155] http://www.telegraph.co.uk/culture/film/starsandstories/5158069/Michelle-Pfeiffer-interview.html

You can be sure of exciting times when he is with you. He dreams big and has great ambitions for himself and his family. He loves travelling but probably you will have to do all the planning. He is a generous husband, but you should take control of finances, as money runs through his fingers quickly.

He loves to pamper his children. He also loves to advise and control them.

Love and Marriage for Her
She glows with confidence and affection. This lady makes heads turn. Enjoy her company and be proud that you have a striking mate. In turn, she wants to be pampered and needs to feel that you love her. She wants it all, from loving glances to expensive presents.

Her family is extremely important to her and she wants it to be outstanding. She is extremely generous and loving. She is unlikely to be content being just your wife even if you are very successful. Ambition drives her. This lady is too energetic and adventurous to remain bound to housewifely duties for long.

Pay attention to her needs and be appreciative of all the little things she does to make you happy. She needs lots of love and appreciation. She can be moody, sulk, brood and whine if unloved. If you do not make her the centre of your universe, she will be disappointed and disillusioned, and may walk out of your life.

As a mother, she truly excels. She leads, dominates and loves her children. She is very ambitious for them and knows when to push them. She understands their moods and helps them overcome their difficulties.

At the Workplace
AriLeoPisces people are extremely ambitious and optimistic. They are always full of big ideas and dreams. It is quite hard for them to live and work in someone else's shadow and they prefer going out on their own to strive for success.

It may take them some time to decide on what they want to do. They are often guilty of starting things with a big bang and then leaving halfway when things get tough. They need a lot of praise and push to keep on trying. Harsh words demoralise them.

Creative, determined and pioneering, they excel in artistic pursuits. They hate routine and are not made for nine to five jobs. Glory and the feeling of achievement matter more to them than money. They want status and respect in society and to be looked at with awe and wonder. As bosses, they can be controlling and demanding and have a soft corner for those who flatter them.

Double Fire and Water make AriLeoPisces generous, opinionated and very much in your face, and they combine the vitality of Fire with the loving sensitivity of Water.

Famous AriLeoPisces Personalities
Michelle Pfeiffer, Michael Fassbender, Mary Pickford, Babita, Shirley MacLaine, S. Venkataraghavan, Charles Sobhraj, Adrien Brody.

95. ARIES–VIRGO–LIBRA

Mars, the fierce god of war, meets the meticulous perfectionist Virgo, and Venus, the planet of beauty and grace. This makes AriVirLibs have everything – drive, ambition, focus and charm.

They are very passionate, intense and ambitious, and know where they want to go. On meeting them for the first time, you may think that they are not really passionate or ambitious. This is due to the Virgo and Libran tendency of putting other people first. But the more you know them, the more you realise the burning desire within them to achieve their dreams.

Their ideals mark them out as special. Aries is a very idealistic sign, which makes them work towards actualising superlative ideas. Add the Virgo purity of thought, and these guys will never think of taking shortcuts in life. They want to do something big and want people to look up to them. They are able to communicate with clarity. Virgo will add depth and analysis to their thoughts while Libra puts their thoughts across brilliantly: you never leave a conversation with them feeling confused. They imbue everyone with motivation and zeal. They are very intelligent too.

Despite their obvious intelligence and desire to lead, there is a certain naïveté in them. Aries is the first sign of the zodiac and has many childlike characteristics – they are impetuous and can be naïvely self-centred, they have the purity of thought of a Virgo and like a Libra, will rarely manipulate or understand manipulation.

Virgo's power of analysis will make them study a subject with great attention to detail. They will know everything there is to know about their work and interests. You will never catch them off guard. They are orderly in everything, from their food habits to how they dress to sleep patterns. They like cleanliness and hate to live in mess. They like to organise their rooms and have each thing in its place.

AriVirLibs are idealistic in love too. They demand a partner who fits into the ideal mould and want their beloved to be exceptional. They are slow deciding on their love, as the Libra in them gets confused between love and friendship and will need time to figure it out. You can expect a lot of love, loyalty and passion from them. They can also sacrifice a lot for their love.

AriVirLibs are both fun-loving and idealistic but will never mix work and play. They love partying and meeting friends but never lose track of their work. They unwind with music. Music and arts appeal to them, and when they take up either they bring perfection and passion to them.

They are not very emotional or sensitive. This will be hotly contradicted by AriVirLibs, for they will say that they are emotional, as Aries do things from their heart and Libra can think from others' perspective; but due to Virgo's realistic analytical mind they will usually act from their heads rather than their hearts. They are not too emotional but are caring, loving and understanding. There is a difference! Also, it is necessary that you communicate your thoughts to them. They are not sensitive enough to really read between the lines.

They are often misunderstood, as they can appear rude, snobbish and intense, like a typical Arian. The truth is that they have an inner core that is tender and pure, the essence of a true Virgo, Aries and Libra. They do not lose their temper often, but when they do, it is best to run for cover. They can also be highly critical when they want. Their anger is directed at the situation and not the person. They hold no malice towards anyone.

They worry a lot. The Virgo predilection for deep analysis and Libran habit of weighing options from every angle will results in their having a tough time making decisions. But finally, the fiery Aries in them propels them to spring into action with renewed vigour and determination.

They are very spiritual. They give a thing their best shot and then put their faith in the almighty to take it forward.

Aries–Virgo–Libra – Gautam Gambhir

'I could be the most worried and nervous person in the dugout…ask the boys. They play playstation and music to keep me cool.'[156]

His wife Natasha: 'His game is so flamboyant that one would think that he is an aggressive person but that's reserved for the field… He is calm, chilled out.'[157]

'The feeling is 'mission accomplished'. It's always about us, not about me… a captain is as good as his team. It's not about individuals; everyone played their role.'[158]

Idealistic, a natural leader, dedicated, relaxed at home, with an understated sense of humour, a perfectionist and a great team-man, Gautam Gambhir makes a true AriVirLib.

Love and Marriage for Him

He has a passion in life and follows it with enthusiasm and energy. But he makes sure he gives equal attention to his home too. He wants his love to be idealistic and is a dependable and romantic mate. He loves being leaned on and is willing to carry out all the duties expected of him.

He is fun loving but not reckless and likes everything from fast cars to roller coasters provided they fulfil the safety norms.

He does not mean to carry work home but he needs a sounding board in you. He is one of those rare husbands who will talk to you about work and you will always know how he is faring at work. He doesn't want your advice; he just needs to share. Speaking is therapeutic for him and you need to let him unburden himself often.

You have to verbalise your feelings to him for it is hard for him to pick up signals. Often, he may seem preoccupied or tense, and you have to lighten his moods with laughter. He likes routine and prefers certain kinds of food. He likes you to be independent in your views – so long as you do not overshadow his thoughts and ideas. He is a child at heart, with few demands; meet those with a smile and he is happy with you.

As a father, he is fun loving yet strict. He insists on discipline at certain times. He expects academic excellence from his children and plans their future keeping their views in mind.

---

[156] Post-match chat after the Delhi Daredevils–Kolkata Knight Riders match, 7 May 2012 –Sony SetMax
[157] *People*, December 2, 2011
[158] Post-match, after KKR won IPL-V –Sony SetMax

Love and Marriage for Her
Give yourself a pat on the back for you have found a mate who is intelligent, smart, idealistic and very loving. Her love is of the highest order and she will sacrifice much for it. She will do everything and more that you ever wanted from a woman and always be ready to amuse and pamper you. In return, she wants to be the love of your life. Do not let her down.

This lady is great for boosting your confidence and knows just how to motivate you to achieve your best. She has her own ambitions, so do not restrain her. She can also be an ideal business partner and will bring a great positivity to your business besides her undeniable skills.

She knows how to lead albeit in a feminine way. There are no lazy moods in her and she is cheerfully hard working. She creates a beautiful home that reflects her positivity and artistic desires. Music helps her relax.

All that is great but you too have to put in effort in this relationship. The Aries in her can easily make her jealous and suspicious of your smallest move and her Virgo habit of nagging can be a trial. She loves with her heart but is no fool in love and demands the same attention she gives you.

As a mother, she is at ease. She knows exactly what to do when her children cry and is rarely flustered by their different demands. She disciplines with a smile and they learn the right values from her.

At the Workplace
AriVirLibs are extremely focused and hardworking in their careers. They bring dynamism and enthusiasm to whatever they do and work with idealistic dreams. They neither play politics at work, nor understand its workings. They just go about their work diligently, perfectly and passionately.

Analytical and logical, they solve problems by going into the very details. They do not waste time wallowing in problems – they find solutions. They can be good in any career, from science to sports and even acting. The best part is that they are not put off by routine. They bring zest and commitment in equal measure to their work.

They excel as leaders in their chosen professions. The double cardinal sign in this combination makes it easy for them to lead. They excel as great individual contributors and are perfect managers too. They lead from the front, always ready to put their neck on line, take calculated risks, are very fair and are great motivators.

Fire, Earth and Air combine to give drive, stability and ability to AriVirLibs. They are passionately driven yet do not lose their humour and positivity in the most trying circumstances.

Famous AriVirLib Personalities
Gautam Gambhir, A.P.J. Abdul Kalam, Farooq Abdullah, Ronit Roy, Danny Boyle, Enrico Fermi.

96. ARIES–VIRGO–PISCES

Mars, the violent and powerful lord of war, meets the perfection-conscious Virgo and the deeply mysterious Neptune in AriVirPisces. They combine strength, ambition and diligence with a highly sensitive soul.

The Virgo and Pisces in them combine to give them the qualities of the mermaid of Hans Christian Andersen's beautiful tale – loving, self-sacrificing, perfectionist, spiritually evolved, and more. But when Aries enters the picture, they can use their amazing qualities without being unnecessarily self-sacrificial and with a positive vibration, energy and passion. A mermaid with horns, probably!

Aries adds enthusiasm and a certain drive to AriVirPisces. Both Virgo and Pisces prefer to live in the background and don't like pushing themselves into the limelight. Aries are friendly and enjoy basking in glory. The Arian self-love makes them rise above being mere victims in life and push themselves towards achieving respect and status.

The Piscean ability to learn new things and its innate desire to keep on learning mixes well with the Virgo ability to go deep into the details of any subject; add the Arian desire to pioneer new ideas and concepts and you get a very enterprising mix. They think of wildly innovative ideas and have the diligence and drive to make them work. They are extremely successful when they get over their phases of self-doubt.

They are generally happy souls. But when they are feeling low, the deeply sensitive Piscean sees only the negatives in everything, and it makes them feel worse. Thankfully, it lasts only a little while, before the Arian positivity rears its head again. They are survivors. They might cry and brood a bit but they will again straighten their clothes and march off into the battlefield. They are flexible and ready to change with the times. This ability to change, learn and renew themselves stops them from being diminished.

Despite their ambition, AriVirPisces think about others and are not willing to trample on them to get ahead. There is a certain softness in them, so they understand the deepest pains of people. They try to be as good as they can without diluting their self-esteem.

Creative and artistic, AriVirPisces are full of talent. The creative talent of Pisces gets a big boost due to the perfectionism and diligence of Virgo and the enthusiasm of Aries. They can learn and copy a thing quickly and improve on it too. Add liberal doses of enthusiasm to the mix and you have some riveting performers.

Love makes them think a lot, love a lot and cry a lot. They want an idealistic love and a soul mate. AriVirPisces love deeply but they will not live in bad relationships for long. Both Virgo and Aries will snap bonds that don't hold tight and true. They might cry of heartbreak but will soon pick themselves up and look for another more worthy partner.

The Virgo health-consciousness makes them look after themselves well. They also prefer routine if it is good for them. Piscean carelessness results in the occasional lapse at times but they will start over again. They love luxury and are always well dressed. The Piscean disregard for neatness will thankfully be absent in them, especially when they are in the public's eye.

Money is important to them. Once they have enough to spend, they start saving. They are quite generous, especially to people close to them. They do not have a long list of acquaintances but a few really close friends they like being with. Spirituality and religion interest them. They find it easy to understand the deeper ideas of theology.

This is an extraordinary union of the most methodical and punctilious Virgo, the most emotional and intuitive Pisces and the most passionate and relentless Aries. This mix can liberate Pisces of its shyness while retaining its sensitivity, pushes Virgo not just to rehearse for life but also live it and gives compassion and patience to the tactless and brash Aries.

The AriVirPisces combination can be manifest as brilliantly positive attributes or can be absolutely negative too. The Arian selfishness when combined with the fastidiousness of Virgo can make them self-absorbed and appear narcissistic at times. They can also have the Piscean tendency of escapism and living in an alternate reality. The Arian self-centredness and ruthlessness, the Virgo acting talent and Piscean capacity for deception, can combine to produce extraordinary con artists or talented individuals using their talent for all the wrong purposes.

All three zodiac signs suffer deep insecurities. Aries secretly feels it can't live up to its claims, Pisces would rather live in a dream world than make things happen and Virgo fears it is not good enough. Despite all their insecurities, they can still make their dream come true as their combination of assorted characteristics can work wonders. The dreams of Pisces can be perfected industriously by Virgo and when the power and ruthlessness of Aries is added, no dream is unachievable.

Aries–Virgo–Pisces – Kapil Sharma
'You pick up things from where you grew up. I lived in police quarters. I developed some characters based on my experiences from there. My sense of humour is from my mother.'

'I'm a little moody in real life.'

'I don't have any aim in life. If you aim for something and you don't achieve it, you feel sad.'

'I believe in people very easily. I'm very emotional. I cry a lot.'[159]

He definitely has Piscean traits; he impersonates people amazingly, doesn't think too much ahead and is very emotional. The Virgoan and Piscean qualities of perfectionism and extraordinary talent are brought out effectively by the fearless Aries.

Love and Marriage for Him
He makes a very good husband, for Aries concentrates on 'my family and me', Virgo is conscientious about duty and responsibility and Pisces is very sensitive to its spouse's needs. Life with him is an adventure trip – minus the wild part. He would love you to share his interests and converse with him on diverse topics.

---
[159] The Anupam Kher Show 'Kuch bhi ho sakta hai', 17 August, 2014, Colors

He is very romantic and goes all out to find ways to express his love for you. This guy loves deeply and surely but is anxious whether it is returned and can walk away if he feels rejected. Don't criticise his plans too harshly or say, 'I told you so' to him, for he can easily read it as lack of love and start worrying again.

He needs a partner who does not dominate him. He may not seem very authoritarian but he may surprise you by his rigidity when he decides on something. He will not share his fears with you; instead, you have to be perceptive enough to understand them.

He is a proud father. The Pisces in him makes him instinctively understand his kids' needs. He worries about them and works very hard to be a responsible parent. He is a friend and philosopher to them.

Love and Marriage for Her
She is independent, strong, sure and responsible. She has an instinctive understanding of how you feel just by looking at you. She is highly idealistic and needs a person who fits her vision of the ideal. Romance and love rank high in her needs and she wants you to be nothing less than her soul mate.

She is a real lady and has a dignified manner despite her childlike smile. She can talk like a woman of experience and then surprise you with her naïve belief in people's goodness. She has amazing energy levels. She works relentlessly keeping the home immaculate and fulfilling all her duties. She has a lot of home remedies for medical problems. She likes time for herself: be it spending long hours thinking about and delving into arcane subjects, or perfecting her dancing or painting skills, or just at the beauty salon.

Adventurous, and even rebellious, she can surprise you with her soft heart and sensitive ways. She is a bundle of opposites: you might be pardoned for thinking that you are dealing with different personalities. She will slowly lose that wild edge in her and become more mellow and soft as the years go by, but will always retain that spark.

She may take her time before taking on the responsibility of motherhood due to Virgo's reluctance about taking on new responsibilities. Once a mother, she makes an excellent one.

At the Workplace
Their ambitions are not sky-high but they worry about getting wherever they want to. The Aries in them wants to pioneer ideas while Virgo makes them think through all the minor details and hitches. You can be sure that when they do something they do it perfectly with an instinctive understanding and a flair for ideas.

The Piscean hatred for figures can affect them but they can learn anything from aeronautical engineering to the intricacies of finance jargon if they have good teachers, and are taught interestingly. They learn quickly and implement things fast, so a strong mentor is needed to rein them in. In fact, they can become extraordinary coaches and mentors themselves. They prefer to travel and move around when they work and are excellent marketers and planners. They are good in creative fields too, with a method in their madness. They make fantastic actors, singers, mimics, dancers and directors.

As bosses, they are flexible and understanding. They prefer to lead quietly but can flare up when things go wrong. They can also be extraordinarily creative and innovative but can be very critical and acerbic too.

Fire, Earth and Water makes AriVirPisces think pessimistically but they will ultimately try and conquer their fears to lay the foundations of their success.

Famous AriVirPisces Personalities
Kristen Stewart, Lily Allen, Akon, Gloria Swanson, Craig McDermott, Sarah Coyte, Kapil Sharma.

97. ARIES–LIBRA–SCORPIO

This strong combination has Mars, the lord of war, and Pluto, the lord of the underworld, with Venus, the planet of love and beauty. The animal magnetism of Scorpio, the sweet charm of Libra and the sprightly enthusiasm of Aries makes them turn heads wherever they go.

The first thing you notice about them is their phenomenal communication skills. AriLibsScorps bowl you over with their clarity of thought and beauty of expression. They make the most mundane topics sparkle. They can speak in velvety-soft voices or with intense passion, depending on the occasion, but will always leave a lasting impression.

Strong, opinionated and very passionate, AriLibScorps are able to hide their simmering ambition under a pleasant demeanour but are rarely distracted from their aim. They can land a killer punch if you pick a fight with them and then give a disarming smile. They are a unique combination of balance, poise, style and aggression. They have passion and ambition, with a steely determination that drives them to reach their aim. They want to rise above situations and are never content with the status quo.

They have only a few friends but stand by them through thick and thin; they are always ready to help their friends and loved ones. It is hard to restrain their adventurous spirits. Adventure looms large on their horizon. They are keen to try something new every day. They love the outdoors and are happy doing something wild!

They are speed demons, love adrenaline-pumping activities and love doing anything where there is opportunity to win. Winning is very important to them: losing even in little things hurts AriLibScorps. Try arguing with them. You can never win against their compelling, intense and logical deductions. They have an insatiable thirst for experimenting and rarely follow conventions. Rebellion, too, differentiates them from the herd.

They metamorphose and keep changing gradually. They are always driven, energetic and positive; the Libra laziness is missing. They have a deep perception of emotions. They easily read people and are hard to fool.

Love rules for AriLibScorps. The Arian desire of finding an ideal partner merges with the extreme romantic notions of Libra and the passionate love of Scorpio. They love truly and completely and want a partner who responds in kind. If you love them, show your emotions and be deep in your affections, for they want to be inseparable from your life and dreams.

Family is very important to them. They like to be surrounded by their families and, though they occasionally want their own space, they never let ambition take precedence. AriLibScorps keep their priorities straight. They find it easy to compartmentalise their life and live happily with their decisions.

Anger is quite strong in them. They feel very deeply and this makes them lose their temper often. And when they are angry, they don't keep quiet! Let them shout it out as it brings down their anger. The Ram's horns, when combined with the revenge-seeking, seething Scorpio, are something to be avoided.

Expect them to delve deep into the profoundest mysteries of life and retrieve some gems. They are deeply spiritual too. They have their own strong opinions and ideas about the esoteric aspects of life and love expounding on them.

They have the indecisiveness of Libra: they take time, they think it through, they rationalise. But once they get past the initial Libran way of looking at both sides of an argument, they form strong opinions and see their path clearly. They stick to their decision and rarely spend time brooding over 'what might have been'.

They can also possess the downbeat qualities of the combination, like indulging in excesses: food, love, lust and everything in between. They can be strongly possessed by jealousy, hatred, impulsiveness and ruthlessness, and be power-hungry, opinionated and controlling.

They are amazingly artistic. Libran talents like the arts and creativity are enhanced by the passion of Aries and depth of Scorpio. It is the softer faculties of life that bring in peace and happiness to their lives.

AriLibScorps never say die. They rise like the phoenix from the ashes to win the place they deserve. When victory is sure they overcome the petty, base emotions and soar above the rest.

Aries–Libra–Scorpio – Vijender Singh

After his Olympic win, Vijender became Indian media's latest pin-up boy. When the boxer started modelling on the ramp, it raised a few eyebrows. He explained he wished to 'bring the game [boxing] in the limelight, make it as popular as possible and catapult it to its deserving place at the top.'[160]

'My blood boils when everybody goes gaga over cricket...It is not easy becoming a boxer in a cricket-crazy country...People here think boxers are violent or mad,' says Vijender.[161]

Vijender Singh has the passion, enthusiasm and drive of an AriLibScorp.

Love and Marriage for Him

It is not easy to ignore him. With his irresistible charm, and attractive and forceful personality, he makes women go weak in the knees. Getting him is just the first bit; living happily with him ever after is the tough part. This guy needs to be pampered, loved and indulged. He wants a mate who understands his need for love and gives it unconditionally to him: the only way to keep him. He is a romantic and one of the few men who find it easy to express their emotions. He knows how to surprise you and will expect the same!

He has a fiery temper and can get angry quickly; a sweet apology will cool him down. However, if both of you are strong-headed, his ego and vengefulness can be quite tough to handle. He needs to feel he's the boss; if not, he feels very hurt, even if he hides it with a smile. He loves talking and needs a partner who can hold a conversation with him. This man is witty and fun with a lot of daredevilry. He is very happy if you partner him in his adventures.

He is ambitious and he works tirelessly to achieve his aims. But his Libran sense of balance makes him want to give equal time to his family. Remember the key to dealing with him is soft persuasion; never go for aggression – he will walk away.

---

[160] http://sports.ndtv.com/boxing/news/66800-vijender-hopes-modelling-will-promote-boxing
[161] http://news.bbc.co.uk/2/hi/south_asia/7482661.stm

He is a good father, caring and loving, though he may not be very handy at baby care. He makes his children think and experience life as an adventure. They like his positive attitude and feel that life is a journey worth experiencing.

Love and Marriage for Her

She is intensely loyal and can lay down her life for the man of her life. But she expects the same intensity from you. She will sulk and brood if your passion for her dims. She can look into your eyes and read your deepest thoughts. Her passion for life and her man is unabated. Only take her on if you are ready to be her devoted and passionate lover even in your eighties.

She is charming, loving and utterly romantic. You are the centre of her life. She wants a partner with whom she can talk, joke and discuss her life. She is not a home-centric person – she has many interests outside it. She is independent and is not afraid of trying new things.

She can be very argumentative and also gets easily hurt. Be careful dealing with her: never commit the mistake of insulting or abusing her. She is also extremely jealous and possessive and will either wreak revenge or leave you if you have been disloyal. This bundle of energy needs something productive to channel some of her attention or you will have a full-time job on your hands.

As a mother, she is in her element. She loves looking after her children and knows how to have fun with them without losing command over them. They respect and obey her.

At the Workplace

Intensity, aggression and passion are part of their DNA, and are carried into their careers too. They possess powerful communication skills that mesmerise and motivate you. They excel in professions that require extreme skills – they revel in living on the edge. Routine jobs rarely appeal to them and they want to do too many different things to be called conventional.

It might take them time to decide on their career for they find many things that interest them. They can be lawyers fighting for new laws or artists exuding creativity and passion or boxers knocking down opponents. They have the pioneering ability, and extraordinary execution skills. They look at the larger picture, and go ahead and achieve it. Whatever they do, you can be sure that they will do it with absolute clarity of vision, forcefulness and undying enthusiasm.

AriLibScorp is a double cardinal sign that always aims to lead. They find it difficult to remain in subservient positions for long. They are passionate speakers who force you into action with their speech. You can expect them to lead the troops. They can strategise and plan, keeping both sides in view, and are very good at arguing their cases.

AriLibScorps are driven, positive, full of ideas and quite opinionated. They fill their hours with work and passion and never let a dull moment enter their lives.

Famous AriLibScorp Personalities

Vijender Singh, Rani Laxmibai, Ciara Hanna, Shalini Ajith, Nayantara, Rupa Ganguly, Walchand Hirachand, Abdul Razzaq, Capt G.R. Gopinath.

98. ARIES–LIBRA–PISCES

Mars, the often violent god of war, meets two soft signs in AriLibPisces. Venus, the planet of grace, beauty and luxury, rules Libra and Neptune, the mysterious god of the seas, rules Pisces. Despite the softness of Libra and Pisces, do not forget that AriLibPisces is a double cardinal sign.

What a combination of opposites! Librans always put themselves into the other person's shoes and understand. Pisces is the highest embodiment of empathy. They will even forgive people who tried to kill them. Both are soft, sweet, sympathetic zodiac signs. Now fuse these two with the fiercest and the most self-centred amongst them – Aries – and that creates an interesting type of person.

AriLibPisces are not only highly empathetic but also have the Arian courage to do something about it; however, they will not be foolhardy or taken for ride by people. They are assertive and stand by their views, without being rigid. They have a knack of seeing the other person's point of view, which stops them from being judgemental.

They talk a lot. They have a very vivid imagination and are good at expressing their thoughts. They are excellent communicators and can talk gracefully and even forcefully if needed. Thankfully, many of them also know how to listen, due to Pisces, and can be charming listeners. They understand you and empathise.

They are very generous to the people they love. They may lose their temper occasionally but are too generous to ever hold a grudge. They are quite idealistic too. They are fun friends and you can be sure of a good time when you are with them.

They want things of beauty and luxury around them and wilt in an environment of routine and monotony. They work hard to make things look beautiful and harmonious around them. The creative instincts of Libra and Pisces get a boost due to Aries. They are superbly artistic. The balance and the fashion sense of Libra, the creativity and imagination of Pisces, when combined with the extraordinary energy levels and originality of Aries, creates wonderful dancers, artists – or fashionistas.

Aries adds great positivity to this combination. Libra can kill itself with over-analysis while Pisces can be subject to phobias and fears. Aries adds a sense of derring-do to AriLibPisces and makes them happily accept challenges. They are forceful and highly dynamic when required and are not content to live in their comfort zones.

Love is top of the list of important things for AriLibPisces. A Libran without love is incomplete, Piscean hearts overflow with love and a typical Arian would kill for true unadulterated love and admiration. The Arian desire for an ideal mate and the Libran need to be in love can make the knowing Pisces love blindly. Even if the mate turns out to be less than perfect, AriLibPisces still adore them to the hilt. They never let the fire of romance die.

AriLibPisces are not good at saving money: none of the three signs are known for their saving or budgeting abilities. They love travelling, and though they may like adventure, they do not like roughing it out for too long. They like peace and calm. They are honest, frank souls who do not like subterfuge. They can be rash at times but it is not a habit.

Both Aries and Libra lead, but in different ways – while Aries leads by commanding, Libra leads through diplomacy. AriLibPisces lead by persuasive talk, then gently nudge you into doing things their way.

Don't disturb them or push them to take decisions, especially when they seem confused and at sea. The Libra in them wants to take a rational, informed and fair decision and they are best allowed their moments of indecision.

Love is the essence of life for Venus, Mars and Neptune. They can become addicted to intense love, become self-sacrificing or lovelorn fools and lost in their own world. The Piscean risk of addiction and Libran love of luxury can lead them into another world of delusions too. Despite their evident good cheer, they can be quite afraid deep down and can suffer with their highly imaginative fears. AriLibPisces lack the stabilising influence of Earth. They need people around them who bring solidity to their dreamy, unstructured ambitions.

Some AriLibPisces are unambitious and live in a dream world. They are contented and happy with their status quo and wouldn't change it for anything. Also expect some of them to grow spiritually inclined and interested in the esoteric principles of life. They can see and feel vibrations and visions that most of us are never be able to.

Aries–Libra–Pisces – Sam Walton
'Sam' Walton was the founder of Walmart and Sam's Club. His leadership style:
'We're all working together; that's the secret.'
'I have always been driven to buck the system, to innovate, to take things beyond where they've been.'
'You can learn from everybody.'
'I've never been one to dwell on reverses, and I didn't do so then... maybe I became a little more wary of just how tough the world can be... But I didn't dwell on my disappointment.'[162]

He combined the pioneering spirit and unbounded enthusiasm of Aries, the soft leadership of Libra and the learning capacity of Pisces. He exemplified the best in AriLibPisces.

Love and Marriage for Him
This man truly loves you. He wants nothing more than a wife who loves and looks up to him. He is your friend and the most interesting person to talk to. He is an inveterate talker. He is deeply philosophical, too.

He is very optimistic and courageous but you will know his fears. Never let him know that you can see his fear; just hold his hand and say you are with him. He is often indecisive about things: help him arrive at a conclusion but do it subtly.

He has big dreams and, although very caring, is mostly out of the house pursuing his ambitions. You need to be the stable one, the one who saves and budgets. Though he might not tidy up after himself, yet he likes a neat, clean

---
[162] http://www.brainyquote.com/quotes/authors/s/sam_walton.html

room. Keep his working areas well lit and clean to keep his creative ideas running.

He is a fabulous father. He showers his children with love and affection. He wants them to dream big. He does not force his ideas on them.

Love and Marriage for Her
No one can love as passionately, as intensely and as romantically as her. She has a soft heart and longs for the ideal love. She puts her man above everything else in life and will be deeply disappointed if you don't match up to those ideals. The best way you can show that you love her is to listen to her when she talks and respond accordingly. She needs you to argue with her, fight with her and sometimes even win over her. She is a fabulous partner but you have to love her, and show it too.

This girl is known for her intelligent thoughts and dynamic ways. She has a strong creative streak in her. Encourage her. This girl needs a man who appreciates her. She loves travelling too. She is a fun companion who wants to live life to the fullest. She has a temper and really loses it at times although she cools off pretty soon. She apologises when she realises it's her mistake, but don't bully her.

She is very loving and caring but is not the typical submissive daughter-in-law; a nuclear family might be more suitable for her. She readily tries her hand at household tasks but it is not really her forte. She has her fears too, but does not show them. Just let her know that you stand by her decisions, and see her fly high! You need to be the stable and calm person in the relationship.

As a mother, she surprises you with her care and concern. Of course, she needs help with the daily chores of parenting. She teaches her children to be independent yet caring and endows them with a sense of adventure about the world.

At the Workplace
AriLibPisces want to do something different. They are very creative and do not want to waste time in routine jobs. Expect them to be superbly artistic and fabulous communicators. They are also highly empathetic and good team players. They are very good learners and easily adapt to new techniques. It takes them some time to know what they want to do but they learn along the way and treat each experience as a stepping-stone. Any careers to do with communication, human resources, music, arts, creativity and even sports see them excel.

Money is not the reason for their hard work. Glory and a sense of achievement matter more to them than all the bank balances in the world. AriLibPisces is a double cardinal sign, so you can be sure that they know how to lead. As bosses, they are ready to experiment and try new things. They are very caring and practise leadership through partnership.

Fire, Air and Water meet in AriLibPisces to make them driven yet sensitive, creative yet analytical, and restrained yet optimistic people.

Famous AriLibPisces Personalities
Sam Walton, Linda Goodman, Hayden Christensen, Charlie Chaplin, Bhanu Athaiya, Eric Clapton, Meira Kumar, Shannen Doherty, Ravi Bopara, Nafisa Joseph.

99. ARIES–SCORPIO–SAGITTARIUS

Mars, the violent lord of war, with Pluto, the powerful lord of the underworld, and Jupiter, the wise and knowledgeable, makes an explosive combination in AriScorpSags. Raw energy meets pulsating power and deep strength to make them almost invincible. When AriScorpSags decide on anything, consider it done, for no power on earth can ever stop them.

What a combination! The untameable Ram combined with the Centaur's horsepower, and complete with a venomous sting! They are extremely fearless. All the three signs are known for their power to overcome fears of any kind. There is a restlessness about them and they are not comfortable till they are up and about doing something. They can actually be faulted for extreme enthusiasm and drive – it makes their more complacent counterparts feel quite harried while in their company.

The super intelligence of Sagittarius and the deep perceptiveness of Scorpio makes them *know* everything. They just look at people and things and can comprehend a lot. Some of them are strong and silent; you can feel their raw power, even if they don't speak much. AriScorpSags find it a little difficult to put their passion in words. Of course, you will guess their intensity by just looking deep into their eyes. You can see their awe-inspiring intelligence and spine-chilling will power.

They fight to their last breath for their dreams and aspirations. Scorpio adds immense passion in them. While both Aries and Sagittarius dream of making it big, they lack the single-minded obsession of Scorpio. With the conjugation of Scorpio, they are extremely difficult to distract. They think, live and breathe their goals.

They are extremely positive, too. Both Aries and Sagittarius are Fire signs and Fire signs don't give in to depressive thoughts: rather, they always look at the silver lining in every cloud. This helps dilute the Scorpio's obsessively dark thoughts and makes them shine with optimism and a can-do attitude. They are all for change, progression and a new way of looking at things. The past only serves as a benchmark to propel them forward. They prefer to think unconventionally rather than traditionally.

Their positive attitude attracts a lot of friends though they are very close to only a few. They are outgoing personalities, especially when they want to have fun. They seek adventure and thrills, but mostly in their youth. Don't be surprised to see them trying their hand at dangerous sports. They will want to take their life to the next level of excitement by indulging in dangerous expeditions and nail-biting quests. They love winning and would be ready to gamble in any aspect of life to win big. They live life at the extremes.

As with all their emotions, love too is a deep sentiment in them. AriScorpSags idealise love and expect a lot from their partner. It is no mean task to be their soul mate, for you have to love as intensely and romantically as them or they will be heartbroken. They are extremely jealous too and are very possessive of their love. Flirtatious glances at others while you are with them will definitely not bode well for you.

Scorpio gives AriScorpSags its ability to read people. They know your deepest secrets. It is hard to deceive them and the consequences of such deception will never be good. Money attracts them, but they are spenders not savers. They are impulsive buyers and generous to friends. If money is short, they would rather earn more than save. They are foodies too. They enjoy having the good things in life.

They are emotional, and can be deeply hurt, but they have the knack of hiding their deepest hurts. They can be extremely sensitive to people who doubt their abilities and can harbour grudges for a long time. They are self-centred, and focus on their own feelings, so at times they can be uncaring of others' feelings, especially if their own interests are involved. They can fly into rages, which can be quite frightening. They are also vengeful. If you apologise for your trespasses, they will forgive – but don't expect them to forget.

Spirituality attracts them. All the three signs believe in the existence of a greater omnipresent force in nature. Their beliefs can follow non-traditional lines. They are not ritualistic.

Despite their bravado, they have the Aries self-doubt and insecurity within. But they are good at hiding their fears and never admit to them. There is a naïve bravado about them, which is endearing. The Aries in them is capable of being extremely fearless, Sagittarius is extremely positive and with the phoenix-like ability of Scorpio to rise above their inner fears, they are capable of rising to transform into the highest form of evolved Scorpio, rise above petty passions or vindictiveness and soar.

Aries–Scorpio–Saggitarius – John Abraham
'Biking is more than a passion to me. It's a way of life.'[163]

'I like going into unexplored territory…I'm constantly looking for challenging scripts. The only way I could grow was to go beyond my comfort zone.'[164]

On Simi Garewal's show (*India's Most Desirable*): 'I am very intuitive.

We both [Bipasha and he] are very headstrong people.'

John Abraham is intense and passionate, is a speed demon, and loves to explore new avenues to grow in life, like a typical AriScorpSag.

Love and Marriage for Him
This is no ordinary man. Get ready for an exhilarating time with him. He takes you to the depths of passion and the heights of ambition. He is extremely adventurous and does not think twice before going on risky ventures.

He needs somebody he can control, and is ready to hand the reins to him. He loves you passionately, idolises you and wants you to be the one for him. He wants you to have the best of everything and is most considerate when you are unwell. He understands your deepest emotions.

He has a very sensitive side to him and only you are privy to it. He wants a partner who understands and loves him unconditionally. Never make the mistake of hurting his ego – he has a big one. He is very thin-skinned despite his bravado. Though he never hurts people whom he loves, he can sulk and brood and remain incommunicado if you don't give him the respect and importance he expects.

---

[163] http://www.johnabraham.com/#wheels
[164] I like going into unexplored territory: John Abraham
[Interview by Subhash K. Jha] Tuesday, March 22, 2005 (http://www.indiaglitz.com/channels/hindi/interview/6283.html)

He can be an extremely dominating father but he knows what his children want. He is caring and loving. This guy relaxes in their company and feels comforted by their childish talk.

Love and Marriage for Her
She is exceptionally strong. She does not bow to pressure by anything or anybody. The only thing that makes her listen is love. She wants a partner whom she can truly love and respect. She is extremely ambitious and passionate. This lady does not merely stay at home looking after her children.

This woman needs a man who loves her for her strength and never tries to put her down. She is full of exuberance and ideas and does not want a man who thinks negatively. She loves adventure and wants to live life to the fullest. She is bored and unhappy if she doesn't have exciting things to do.

She has a commanding nature but is sensuous, too. She knows your smallest faults, but if she loves you, she can ignore them and think only of you. She has certain deep fears in her heart and comes running to you when people hurt her for her exuberance. Despite her knowledge of people, she has a certain naïveté about her. She will show her weak side only to you and puts up a brave front for the world. Just a few doses of encouragement would help her a lot as she is capable of great bravery with her deep inner strength. But remember that she will destroy you if you lie to her or deceive her.

She loves her children but is also a commanding figure in their lives. She understands them and plays with them too. She teaches them the value of ambition and gives the strength of passion to their dreams.

At the Workplace
AriScorpSags never think small. They work with passion, zeal and an optimism that is infectious. You see them often as leaders in whatever field they are. It takes them some time to realise what they want but once they do, you can be sure of their single-minded dedication. Money, glory and passion are what they seek and they never return empty-handed from their missions.

They are great pioneers and executors. They are always on the lookout for new ventures and ideas to grow. They are great gamblers. They want the biggest and the best in life. Life is a game for them and they want to win at any cost. They love racing, on the tracks and in life too. High risk leading to high returns is always their motto.

They are blunt and forthright in their opinions and rarely mask their views. They prefer careers that allow them to travel and move around for they hate being confined to desks. Their passion, aggression and single-mindedness makes them extraordinary sportspeople. There is no question about their ability to lead. They are dominating, commanding and visionary leaders. They are generous to people who help them and be extremely dangerous to people who don't.

Double Fire and Water endow AriScorpSags with incredible strength, zeal and a spirit that can never be broken.

Famous AriScorpSag Personalities
Jim Morrison, Magnus Carlsen, Mark Boucher, Mita Vashisht, Milind Deora, James Blake, Christina Aguilera, B.K.S. Iyengar, Conrad Hilton, Katrina Law, John Abraham.

100. ARIES–SCORPIO–PISCES

Mars, the violent god of war, meets Pluto, the ruthless and extremely powerful lord of the underworld. These two alone make this combination extremely violent and aggressive. On top of that, the deep and mysterious Neptune adds another dimension.

Probably the most complex amongst all zodiac combinations, at no point can you feel that you know everything about them. This combination can bring out the extraordinary hues and colours of the complex Fish. It can entertain like a dolphin, or can become ferocious and destroy or gobble everything in its way… like a tiger shark! It is the Fish at its best or worst!

AriScorPisces is an extraordinary combination where fearlessness meets passion, with an inherent knowledge of the mysteries of the world. Nothing can be hidden from them: they know both vices and virtues. They try everything, from drugs to sex, from a very young age. The Aries childlike curiosity is heightened by the Scorpio desire to penetrate any mystery. They experiment in a more adult fashion: they know what they are getting into and why they are doing it. Brought up in the right atmosphere, they can do great good and turn their energies to positive ways of life. They can be saints or sinners, for AriScorPisces can delve into the deepest abyss or reach for the highest star, depending upon their formative years.

Scorpio and Pisces give this combination great empathy. They easily feel the emotions of others and are excellent at reading people. The Aries and Scorpio in them act on that information, while Pisces would be happy just knowing and wouldn't use its knowledge. Unlike the typical Piscean who bows down to the wishes of people around them, AriScorPisces is canny enough to know its own mind and doesn't get used, all without offending people who matter. Their ability to divine the ulterior motives of people helps prevent their being manipulated, and choose their own path. This sense of purpose lifts them out of any situation. Determination, courage and empathy can make them an unbeatable combination.

They are very generous and never forget anyone who helps them. Both Scorpio and Aries have this trait of repaying every kindness and you can expect AriScorPisces to remember and recompense everyone who helped them along the way.

The love of AriScorPisces is not trifling. They love with a deep, intense passion that tests the very limits of love. Love is their weakness, though they will be manipulated by it. AriScorPisces can read people and they completely know the person they love so it will be very difficult to betray them. If someone tries it he/she will have to contend with their Arian anger and Scorpio vengefulness. Their love is all consuming and very idealistic; though they can understand and forgive a past, they will never forgive any future transgressions. They are deeply possessive and controlling in love. They give and expect to receive passionate, all-encompassing, and no-holds-barred love. A passion or a profession that further enriches their life can make them a little easier to love, as their intensity will find another vent.

Their anger is not pleasant to watch. It is violent, brutal and furious. An AriScorPisces can be the kindest person in the world, or the most cruel and selfish. The violence of Aries and vengefulness of a Scorpio can make them extremely dangerous. The Pisces tendency to deceive can also make them cunning and deceitful. They make the best of friends and the worst of enemies.

Money means nothing to them. It does not excite or motivate them. What they really seek are happiness and pleasure. Their deep passions demand something more satisfying than money or glory. AriScorPisces need a lot of love, care and affection to feel really worthwhile. If they learn to rise above their distractions then they can conquer anything and be anyone.

Some AriScorPisces display all the downbeat qualities of the combination. The combination can make for the slyest person around with cruelty and cunning added: all-consuming, all-devouring sharks who win over love and amass wealth through deceit and unscrupulous means. They can be reservoirs of vices, which no one would suspect and can also be addicted to excesses of all kinds of carnal and other pleasures. They may even dabble in the darker side of life from drugs to even black magic.

The biggest plus of this combination is its ability to rise above all vices. They can leave everything behind and rise like a phoenix or an eagle, another variant of the Scorpio in them. The awesome inner strength of Scorpio can help them pull through any problem or circumstance, however messy it is. Deep spirituality marks them. Both Scorpio and Pisces tend to look beyond religion; they make AriScorPiscess look towards spirituality to discern the mysteries of life. They can use this strength to benefit humanity.

Aries–Scorpio–Pisces – Al Pacino
He started smoking at age nine, drinking and casual marijuana use at age thirteen, but never took hard drugs. Growing up in the Bronx, he got into occasional fights and was something of a troublemaker at school.[165]

On being asked whether he sees Shylock in *Merchant of Venice* as good or bad:
'Because I see good and bad in all of us, I can't answer that question. I have to say a good-bad man.'[166]

On the effort he puts into his roles: 'The actor becomes an emotional athlete. The process is painful – my personal life suffers.'[167]

Al Pacino has the fearlessness, intensity and sensitivity of an AriScorPisces.

Love and Marriage for Him
He loves you deeply and expects the same in return. But the fact remains that no matter how much you love him, you never really know him.

He can either take you down a path of glory or make you walk to the gallows with him. There is no middle path. He has so many shades and so many secrets to him that you won't know about his many lives till the very end. You have to be independent and strong without being aggressive and loudmouthed.

---

[165] http://en.wikipedia.org/wiki/Al_Pacino
[166] http://www.guardian.co.uk/film/2004/dec/03/2
[167] http://www.thebiographychannel.co.uk/biographies/al-pacino/quotes.html;jsessionid=7D78DDFEA1481E8393
2B80D2FAE8B1C

He needs a wife who fulfils her duties and does not eternally cling to him for support.

This is one guy with whom you can have long conversations. He can talk interestingly on almost any topic. He loves to travel and seeks adventure wherever he goes. Money is something that you have to deal with. He can make money but saving and investing are not for him.

As a father, he is there for his children but do not expect him to attend every school function. He teaches them to live life by their own rules and never makes them bend to conventions unless they desire so.

Love and Marriage for Her
She is certainly not an easy wife. You cannot cheat on her for she sees through you. Only a man who is very confident about himself and strong in his determination can take her on for she respects a superior will. She is a very strong lady with the Arian directness, Scorpio sensuality and the Piscean childlikeness. You would wonder at her myriad personalities that make her a woman, a child, a teenager and a seductress at different times.

She is no traditional perfect wife and her views can be shocking for some feeble-hearted relatives. Household duties do not interest her. Get domestic help and set her free. This girl needs to feel free in marriage. She wants love, not rules.

Money does not entice her and she may not calculate every penny she spends. She is a very emotional person but may not express everything she feels. You are expected to understand her and if you look into her deep eyes you will. Her sulks can be bad. If you don't reciprocate her all-consuming, passionate and intense adulating love, she will find someone who will. You will have no inkling, while she continues to be the sweet, demure wife your relatives adore.

As a mother, she allows her children to experiment and explore the world. This mother is very hard to shock; in fact, she can shock them. She teaches them to conquer their inner fears and demons.

At the Workplace
AriScorPisces are explosive material that you can mould to your own specifications. These guys can be programmed for destructive use or for creative tasks. It all depends on their mentor. They can be groomed to do any job. They are the fastest learners of the zodiac.

When they set out to conquer, AriScorPisces don't make blueprints or plan in detail. They build a picture in their minds and set about accomplishing it with passion and intensity. They need to be motivated. Their focus can wander at times; work must excite them enough to forget all distractions. Only then do they deliver their best. From arts and creativity to science and inventions, from psychology to sports to human resources: they can do anything. They just need to be taught.

If they are fascinated enough, they can go into the depth of the subject and bring about the greatest invention or discovery, or give a new dimension to old thinking. They are revolutionary pioneers. As bosses, they simply know all the mistakes you can make, all your weaknesses and pitfalls, as they have been there themselves and mastered them all.

Double Water and Fire combine in them to give AriScorPisces profound intensity and a deep desire for excitement. Passion, drive, sensitivity and an unquenchable need to be loved defines them.

Famous AriScorPisces Personalities
Al Pacino, Thomas Jefferson, Raphael, Leonardo da Vinci, Garry Kasparov, Suchitra Sen, Pete Rose.

101. ARIES–SAGITTARIUS–CAPRICORN

Mars, the violent and powerful god of war, gets a fillip by joining the knowledgeable Jupiter and the wise old Saturn in AriSagCaps. For all their occasional arrogance and nonchalance, and apparent egocentricity, they are extremely honest.

Look at the animals that constitute the combination – a Ram, a Goat and a Centaur, which is half horse, half man. They definitely have the quickness of the Ram, the stability of the Goat, along with the horsepower of the Centaur! Aries gives them power and passion, Sagittarius makes them daredevils; Capricorn gives much-needed maturity to this otherwise fiery combination.

They don't walk; they gallop. These guys are stylish and enthusiastic. They seem to be on a mission and look set to take over everything on their way. Their infectious smile, their eagerness, their wry sense of humour, their dynamism and clear body language that says they are here to conquer, all tend to make you give way to them. Despite their candour, pluck and, sometimes, arrogance, there is an aura of innocence that hangs on them that is endearing.

They say things one may not like to hear. They are blunt and speak up for what they feel is right. They value tradition and customs – when they are older. Interestingly, despite having been unruly, adventurous and rebellious in their youth, they find it difficult to understand the rebelliousness and new thinking of the young. They are not exactly spoilsports but feel that no one could be as good as they were. They look at any situation in life from their own perspective.

These guys are highly intelligent. They surprise you with amazing, in-depth knowledge on myriad subjects. They are not just brilliant speakers; their thirst for knowledge ensures they learn with every experience and store it up, to make them reservoirs of wisdom. They share this knowledge with those whom they feel it would benefit.

Ambition is deeply embedded in them as all the three signs are known for it. They want to shine before everybody. The pioneering Aries and the attention-seeking Sagittarius make AriSagCaps venture fearlessly to new ideas. The Capricorn in them is the moderating factor and bestows maturity on them and makes them stable, smart and sensible. They know how to be in the good books of people who matter and always are found at the right place at the right time. Capricorn loses its meekness here and they are never shy in declaring their ambitions openly.

In fact they do everything openly, including their relationships. While the Capricorn wants a partner who is accepted by family and society, the Aries wants a fantastic, enviable one. But Sagittarius hates settling down too soon and fears responsibilities. AriSagCaps might settle down to a compatible relationship after going through several. They want an ideal life partner and as they always seek to be larger than life they admire a partner who shows more restraint!

You can never match their energy levels. They sizzle with enthusiasm and retain a zest for life even at sixty. The reverse-aging process of Capricorn makes them more eager for adventure as they grow older. Their immense enthusiasm, nonchalance and flamboyance can be mistaken for arrogance. AriSagCaps love speed and anything to do with adventure. You won't find them sitting still for long. Their stamina, brute force and adventurousness make them shine on the sports field.

They have a rebellious streak in them; however, Capricorn adds the love for family. They want to do everything to increase their family's status, and their own too. Money is extremely important to them and they want lots of it. They spend money wisely, as they have the Capricornian saving instinct without the usual stinginess. They are more interested in investing and earning rather than just hoarding money under their mattress. They also like to dress well and draw admiring glances.

They are fun loving and enjoy partying. They like all activities that give an adrenaline rush. They try their hand at everything. Gambling and risk-taking is part and parcel of life; they just go for it! They live life king size. They can get very angry very quickly. But they also cool down as quickly. Their anger is never directed towards a person, nor do they hate anyone. There is no malice in them at all.

It is very difficult for them to understand the emotions of others. There are no Water signs in them and the most self-centric zodiac signs, Aries and Capricorn, only make matters worse. AriSagCaps need to be told if you feel bad about anything they said or did for they will never realise it on their own. The Arian and Sagittarian childlike selfishness will be evident in them, even when they are fifty. It will be extremely difficult to make them see from your point of view and you normally resign with helplessness and allow them to go on.

They take to spirituality in a big way. Sagittarius and Aries believe in the power above while Capricorns revere all things traditional. They will be flamboyantly spiritual.

They have their vices – brutally frank, rebels without a cause, temperamental, alternating between traditional and modern, insensitive, unplanned, emotionally charged and self-centred. But their sweet innocence, naïveté, love for family, bravery and dependability in crisis more than makes up for that.

Aries–Sagittarius–Capricorn – Syed Kirmani
India's legendary wicket-keeper, reputed to have a heart as big as the outdoors, was known as the quintessential team man.

'I believe in being transparent in what I say. I know the truth always hurts, but you cannot make it go away.'[168]

'Why not try to match the performances of those great men instead of just aping their mannerisms? It all boils down to good grooming, which players today lack. I hope these basic problems are set right soon, and that we will be able to turn out capable and performing Indian cricket teams with good wicket-keepers.'[169]

Syed Kirmani has the flamboyance, blunt honesty and reverence for the past of a typical AriSagCap.

Love and Marriage for Him
He is extremely ambitious and wants a partner who shares his ambition. However, this guy wants to be looked up to and heard. He needs to be the boss despite the

---

[168] http://www.rediff.com/sports/2000/feb/08kiri.htm
[169] http://www.rediff.com/sports/2000/feb/08kiri1.htm

air of lightheartedness and he will be happy with you only if you accept him as The One.

He loves going out. Be ready to share his love of the outdoors and adventure for it is a big part of his life. He finds parties hard to resist, too. You need to be the one who looks after the details and ensures everything works just right. He likes moving around, trying out new things, finding ways to earn even more while the household responsibilities rest on you.

You also need to be the one slow to anger. He needs a more tranquil partner than him or ego wars can escalate to destructive levels. He needs mature handling as he cannot handle emotional scenes: be sure to keep your tears in check while talking or he will just run away!

You keep wondering if he is modern or traditional. Interestingly, he can be both to the extreme, and you ask yourself if he dons the role according to his convenience.

He enjoys a father's role. He loves guiding them, travelling with them and, of course, bonding with them over sports. He sets the rules for them. They consider him the best dad ever.

Love and Marriage for Her
She wants a friend for a partner. This lady has her own opinions and views. Her honesty can surprise you at times for she does not believe in sparing the truth.

Her ambitions are too high and dreams too lofty to be held in abeyance. This lady deserves to fly high and there is no way you will be able to stop her from doing so. Occasionally the Sagittarian in her wants to get away from everything. Let her be: she will feel claustrophobic if you tie her down to responsibilities. Parties and outings cheer her up more than a daily dose of sweet talk. Adventure is what she craves: she enjoys jumping off planes and deep sea diving.

She isn't exactly sensitive to your needs and may wonder why you get hurt by her honest remarks. Behind her naïve tactlessness there is an honest soul that seeks acceptance and love. Give her the confidence that she lacks, she has the guts to take it forward.

As a mother, she is full of fun and enthusiasm. She may resist being one for some time as she worries about the responsibilities and needs a lot of help during the baby years.

At the Workplace
This is a mind-blowing combination. AriSagCaps think differently, are creatively intelligent and extremely ambitious. They are excellent at visualising and implementing their ideas. They are trailblazers and pioneers with abundant energy and unmatched industriousness and organising capabilities. They like to work on their own and can be good at anything from business to sports to careers in creative fields.

They can be very aggressive if they do not get what they want. Their absolute candour can ruffle a few feathers. Their aggressive self-promotion and eagerness to reach the top may not go down well with a few. AriSagCaps hate to work under supervision and feel they can manage it all, which they normally do.

They love leading from the front and are natural leaders who are highly motivating. They love mentoring people and guiding them, though they are controlling and authoritarian too.

Double Fire and Earth makes this a totally explosive combination. AriSagCaps live life on their own terms and are optimistic even in the face of defeat.

Famous AriSagCap Personalities
Syed Kirmani, Pritish Nandy, Ajay Jadeja.

102. ARIES–SAGITTARIUS–PISCES

This combination is ruled by Mars, the violent and powerful god of war, Jupiter, the planet of knowledge and luck, and Neptune, the deep and mysterious god of the seas. They give AriSagPisces a commanding air, ambition, strength and power along with humility, compassion and a loving nature.

Intelligence, wisdom and idealism merge in this unworldly combination. Sagittarians are the most intelligent amongst all zodiac signs and called the professors of the zodiac, while Pisces is the wisest. Aries is very idealistic and devoid of any guile. These people can be your fountains of knowledge, highly evolved and intensely passionate about causes but free of any materialistic ambitions.

This is a double Fire sign with a Water element. Fire signs are not known for their sensitivity and understanding. They cannot see through deceptive moves nor are they discreet or tactful. Pisces makes AriSagPisces calm despite the raging double Fires within. They are not too dominating or controlling except during times when it matters. AriSagPisces retain the best of Piscean wisdom, intuitiveness and sensitivity without becoming moody or depressive. The double Fire also helps fight the fears and insecurities of Pisces and lets the Piscean talents flourish.

The Piscean humility also makes them give due respect to age. They lack the arrogance of the Fire signs. They desire love and attention to feel secure. There is also a possibility that the AriSagPisces show an outward ruthlessness and arrogance just to hide their inner insecurities and to ensure no one takes advantage of their vulnerabilities.

All the three signs are keen on food and are likely to be food connoisseurs. They are big patrons of music, arts and anything to do with creativity. Their optimism attracts a lot of people. They like having lots of friends, enjoy partying and playing pranks, and are extremely good at mimicking people. They love pomp and show, and being the centre of attention when they are showing off their talents.

Routines and rules are a casualty with this combination. Aries is hard to confine while Sagittarians love flouting rules. Pisces, despite being the most peace loving, is also the most elusive of all the signs and loves the distraction of new experiences. It will not be easy to put AriSagPisces into a routine; they lack the discipline to do the same thing over and over again. If you see the contrary in them, it could be due to the inculcating of disciplined behaviour at a young age: they do not forget things learnt at an impressionable age. Besides, the fire within them to succeed ensures that they discipline themselves.

Pisces is the most sensitive of all the signs and the most riddled by fears. All Fire signs too have inner fears and insecurities: Aries and Sagittarius as well. AriSagPisces have this nagging feeling that they may not be able to do well when it matters. But they derive strength from the fearlessness of Aries and positivity of Sagittarius to overcome their fears. They need to constantly fight their inner demons to become victorious. They initially feign fearlessness and with practice become masters at controlling their nerves. You will never notice their inner jitters when they pose confidently.

AriSagPisces cannot understand the language of money. These guys cannot understand that to get a debit you need to increase your credits first. Pisces can make them deceptive about money matters. Aries and Sagittarius makes them very generous with their money.

Aries and Sagittarius have a wild uncontrollable anger, which is subdued to a large extent by Pisces. But it is advisable to be careful while uttering words that may hurt them.

Some AriSagPisces can acquire all the downbeat qualities of the combination. Then they will exhibit the Arian self-centredness with the Sagittarian carelessness and Piscean deceptiveness. They can submerge themselves in pleasures of all kinds and become escape artists, and lead a nomadic life of irresponsibility.

The combination of two Fire signs, which are anyway spiritually inclined, with the wisdom-filled Pisces makes them deeply spiritual. They understand the transient nature of all worldly things.

Aries–Sagittarius–Pisces – Sachin Tendulkar

Dr B.P. Bam, sports psychologist: 'Tendulkar has the enthusiasm of a child, the skills and fitness of an adult and the wisdom of a very old man.'[170]

M.S. Dhoni: 'His schoolboy-like enthusiasm for the game is something I envy and admire.'[171]

Pravin Amre: 'His humility is amazing. I have seen Sachin carry drinks for the junior-most, much to the embarrassment of the youngster.'[172]

Tendulkar is an ardent devotee of Sathya Sai Baba of Puttaparthi. He sponsors 200 underprivileged children every year through Apnalaya.[173]

Dr Bam's description explains the Tendulkar phenomenon: His enthusiasm comes from Sagittarius, his skills from Aries and wisdom from Pisces. He also has the humility, spiritual inclination and philanthropic nature of AriSagPisces.

Love and Marriage for Him

If you are with him, please keep a speech in hand for you can be called up one day to share your experiences with him. This guy achieves the glory and success he dreams of. This also means that his career is foremost in his life. So, he likes a partner who is independent and strong.

You have to take care of everything else: his home, money and children. Of course, he does not expect you to sit at home all the time and is more than happy to know that you love your job; but is unable to help out at home. Money is not something he understands. It is up to you to manage it.

The best part is that despite his aggression in his career, he is the most easy-to-live-with guy at home. He does have an ego and a temper but, most of the time, he vents them at his workplace and brings home his nicer self. He needs you to be his friend. Remember that nagging does not work with him. He needs you to hold his hand and support him whole-heartedly. Thankfully, he has some sensitivity to recognise your feelings.

---

[170] *DNA*, JBM edition, 17 November, 2013, page 7
[171] http://www.telegraph.co.uk/sport/cricket/international/india/10445798/Sachin-Tendulkar-what-they-say-I-have-seen-God.-And-he-bats-at-No-4-for-India.html
[172] http://sachinandcritics.com/quotes_on_sachin.php
[173] http://en.wikipedia.org/wiki/Sachin_Tendulkar

As a father, he is extremely proud of his children and wants them to excel. The Piscean sensitivity makes him less controlling and he likes them to go for their dreams. He does not know what to do with them when they are small; but as soon as he can have intelligent conversations with them, he gladly takes on the role of their friend and mentor.

Love and Marriage for Her
She has her own dreams and ambitions. Do not expect her to be the traditional wife and or to change. She is neither commanding nor controlling. Be her friend, hold her hand when the going gets tough and support her views. She can be brutally honest. She tells you what she feels and expects the same in return. She is not manipulative.

She is a fun companion and no situation can ever make her lose her positivity. Remember that she needs attention, care and the freedom to do what she wills. Give her that and you are the partner of a woman with rare talents. Give her space in the relationship and also take her out on adventure trips. She gets bored easily and needs change.

She will find it difficult to conform to the traditional ideals of a daughter-in-law, and to settle in the lap of matrimony. Aries women are not very interested in settling down early in life nor are Sagittarians attracted to family life. Most probably she will like to start a family later and concentrate on her career first.

Do not expect her to be a hands-on mother. She prefers to leave the routine care to able helpers and is more than happy in developing her children's talents through activities and classes. She teaches them to be honest and outspoken.

At the Workplace
They are misfits for the corporate world. Their aggression, passion and sensitivity can make the artistic, sports, business or even spiritual world come alive. They find strict structures and confinement stifling. They excel in professions that have no time boundaries, no restrictions for dreams, and the entire world to conquer.

Whatever they do, they do it competitively and also dream the extraordinary. It is a pleasure to see them achieve the impossible. Routine jobs may find them quitting to pursue their fantastic dreams. It is ideal if their jobs involve travelling for they find it enervating to be in one place for long.

If they do work, they love to create a difference and have idealistic views. Money is the last thing on their minds. They love the entire process of learning, preparing, and finally the thrill and satisfaction of winning against all odds.

They are wonderful in sports. They are fearless, enthusiastic, speed-driven and ambitious. The ruthlessness of Aries and the childlike enthusiasm of Sagittarius combine to make an absolute warrior who will fight till his/her last breath. Pisces adds an element of wisdom, cunning and intuitiveness to their combat style.

If they are your bosses, be ready with grand plans and help them win. They need to win at all costs. They will be extraordinarily generous and understanding, and are great mentors; but they need some help in breaking up their idealistic ideas into workable parts

AriSagPisces are fearless, strong and wisdom-filled yet they are instinctively modest and respectful.

Famous AriSagPisces Personalities
Sachin Tendulkar, Dwayne Johnson, Joe Hart, Maria Sharapova, Mario Miranda, King Mswati III, Arshad Warsi, Jyoti Randhawa, Vinoo Mankad, Waseem Ahmad, Curt Kissinger, Irene Rosenfeld, Giorgio Moroder, Rosie Huntington-Whiteley.

103. ARIES–CAPRICORN–AQUARIUS

Mars, the violent god of war, joins forces with the wise old man Saturn, and the wildly eccentric Aquarius in this highly driven and a trifle wild combination.

What an extraordinary combination: the fiery, domineering, joyful, assertive Aries; the ruthless, cold, calculative and persuasive Capricorn; combining with the generous, flexible, humanitarian genius Aquarius. AriCapAquas dream massively huge dreams and stand apart from the crowd with their magnificent ambitions. Nothing small or average can ever do for them. They are the pioneers who dream of wild and wonderful things, plan meticulously, work hard and ensure that they come true.

The Arian wildness and the Aquarian desire to shock people is apparent in them. They can be speed demons or bungee-jumping aficionados. They dazzle you with their energy and their out-of-the-box thinking. They always seem poised for action and rarely sit still for long. The same rebelliousness of Aquarius and the high-octane power of Aries can make them extremely unmanageable in their teenage years. These wild kids do turn mellow, albeit a little later in life.

They are fun people. They love to laugh and enjoy life, and have a big appetite for jokes and adventure. They love spreading their warmth, cheer, and sometimes-wild energy around. They are open to everything in life. The Capricornian family love is evident in them and despite their wild ways they will always be there for their family.

They want to do something unique. They want to leave a legacy. They do not want to lead a normal life. You can see them searching desperately for that one idea, that one moment that will make them great. They have ideals too and are willing to fight for them. They have the drive to push these forward and make everyone listen to their views.

Honesty is their most positive trait. They will say what they think, in no uncertain terms. However, the innate Capricornian ability of controlling their speech when things go wrong stops them from shooting off without a thought. They know whom they can be brutally honest with.

They can read people very easily. The Aquarian antennae are designed to sift information that doesn't meet the eye. Expect them to be interested in everything from spirituality to the deepest mysteries of the world. They make great conversationalists too, with their extraordinary intelligence, infectious Arian energy levels and the refined, distinguished persona that Capricorn bestows.

AriCapAquas look for an ideal love. They want to be in love with someone who meets their high ideals and also brings status to their lives.

Freedom is very important to them and they are forever caught between their need for relationships and their desire for freedom: so they might be a little detached in love.

The childlike selfishness of Aries will be accentuated by the Capricornian desire to mark out what is theirs and the Aquarian indifference to all else but their own dreams. AriCapAquas draw a line between 'mine' and 'theirs'. They can be quite self-absorbed in their own world and dreams to the exclusion of all else. The ambition of AriCapAqua makes them seem insensitive to others. Family and inner-circle friends are the only set of people who are untouched by their apparent ambition and self-interest.

Anger is very strong in them and they find it hard to remain calm, especially when their dreams are challenged. They can be quite stressed-out at such times and are prone to explosive bursts of anger. Expect them to sober down in later years in all aspects of life. Their ambitions are practical, their drive is controlled and they find more time for family. Expect them to enjoy life and relax much more in their twilight years.

The fact that there is no Water sign in them works to their benefit. While it does make them a little insensitive and self-centric, it also makes them immensely strong and oblivious to tears, pain, or hurts. They do go through a few Capricornian moments of melancholy and depression when the chips are down. But they can quickly jump back to action as no one else can.

Impatient, self-centred, quick to anger, experimentative, distracted, detached, and rebellious are some words you can associate with them as their downbeat qualities. But they more than make up for that with their generosity, enthusiasm, mad-hatter genius, enterpreneurial skills, family-loving nature and humanitarian ideals.

Aries–Capricorn–Aquarius – Matt Dillon

'I've never really taken jobs for the money. I have to be true to myself and f--- what anybody else thinks.'

'Let's just say I smoked cigarettes and experimented with drugs from a young age. I was a little wild but I had good parents, hard-working people. I got along with my parents but was just so rebellious that I didn't care what they said.'[174]

'I had direction in my life at a young age. Some guys around me were a little lost and some paid the price for it.'[175]

Matt Dillon has the honesty and rebelliousness combined with the family love and responsibility of an AriCapAqua.

Love and Marriage for Him

He wants to be your man and is quite a romantic. Expect flowers and surprises. He wants you to be his ideal love and see people's admiration for your grace and intelligence. He knows your weaknesses but expects you to be his ideal despite them. He wants a partner who has style: in clothes, speech, and manner. He chose you for this, and because, probably, he saw you would make an excellent mother and get along well with his family. He is a family man who will make any sacrifice for the family.

His ambition and passion keep him going. You have to make space in your relationship for his dreams. He needs you to back him in his dreams and think of them as your dreams too. Sometimes, he also needs his own space.

With him, you will see sights you only dreamed of before. Speed and wild exploits attract him. Times with him will be vibrant and fun. Put your crash helmet on and learn to laugh in the rushing wind for your life will rarely be sedentary with him.

---

[174] http://www.totalfilm.com/features/the-total-film-interview-matt-dillon

[175] http://www.cigaraficionado.com/webfeatures/show/id/Rebel-with-a-Cause_6010/p/2

Emotions find him unimpressed. It is not that he does not understand; he does, but he cannot act emotional or deal with tears. Try logic and reasoning, and you may just get your way.

As a father, he is brilliant. Exciting, adventurous, stern and full of ideas, he makes his children toe the line but enjoy life. He wants them to excel and also wants to leave a legacy that they can be proud of.

Love and Marriage for Her
Ambition, intelligence and that extra 'zing' make her someone special. This lady is one of the most exhilarating and unconventional women you can ever meet.

She is willing to make her ambition secondary to yours only if you have one worthy of her dreams. She wants a guy who is above her in everything – intelligence, ambition, status and ideals. She needs to do something of her own, even if your ambitions fulfil both your needs. She is too talented, opinionated, intelligent and driven to be a stay-at-home mom. She needs constant excitement in life and is easily bored: keep her adequately stimulated.

Please learn to praise her. She needs appreciation and forgives your many slips if you learn to comment on her positives. She also needs time for herself. Her moments of solitude and detachment are the times she thinks the best. She does not need you to be by her side every hour. She loves her family and wants the best for them. She can really fight for her family's happiness.

As a mother, she is full of fun and enthusiasm. She plans trips and shouts herself hoarse at school matches. Her children love her vibrancy and fall in line when she commands. She rarely pushes them to do anything they do not like as long as they make their dislikes evident.

At the Workplace
AriCapAquas want everything – glory, money and power. They are willing to work hard for their dreams. The fact is that their dreams and ideals may not seem conventional to you. The Aquarian futuristic views and the Arian pioneering ideas make their dreams sound risky. But believe in them, for despite all their wildness they have thought things through.

Yes – they do get a little distracted if things do not work out as quickly as they planned. But once they know their goal, they follow it with diligence. They have such immense energy levels, fierce work ethics, extraordinary intuition and sparkling intelligence going for them that it almost seems magical when they pull off those improbable victories.

Routine is not for them. They want to be in the limelight. From actors to high-flying businessmen and politicians with promise, you find them making a mark and leaving a trail of blazing glory. They can be activists too. They are demanding and controlling bosses, but full of vision, ideals and dynamism; they're fatherly too.

Fire, Earth and Air meet in AriCapAquas to endow them with passion, logic, dreams and lot of adrenalin. They work hard, party harder and dream with undimmed vision.

Famous AriCapAqua Personalities
Matt Dillon, Gina Rinehart, Floyd Mayweather Jr., Bernard Arnault, Eusébio, Jemima Khan, Pandit Bhimsen Joshi, Neelam Kothari, Natasha St-Pier, Ravindra Jain.

104. ARIES–CAPRICORN–PISCES

Mars, the violent lord of war, meets the old man Saturn and the deeply mysterious Neptune in AriCapPisces. Powerful, forceful, industrious and very deep, AriCapPisces is a force to reckon with.

What you see may not be what you get, with these people. The Capricorns have the ability to ooze class and be prim and proper in public. Pisceans are the sweetest and humblest souls you ever met. Arians are very enthusiastic and dynamic, and extremely friendly.

What they hide inside is the determined, goal-oriented Capricorn, the self-centred and ruthless Aries and the deceptive and cunning Pisces. They have the chameleon ability to change colours depending on situations. They can be mean and ruthless if they see danger in you. They can sweet and loving and generous if they see a friend in you. Not unfair, wouldn't you say?

Family and career are the twin themes of this combination. AriCapPisces are quite ambitious as both Aries and Capricorn desire to lead. Family is the mainstay of this sign. They are capable of great sacrifices for their families. They never scrimp on anything for their loved ones.

They are extremely passionate and driven about certain things in life. AriCapPisces can astound you with their do-or-die approach; they will go through immense hardships to reach their goal. Aries and Capricorn will never allow them to bow down to failure. They always find a way out and have the ability to be in the right place at the right time. AriCapPisces can also use the Piscean talent for deception and the Capricornian urge to manipulate in order to sort things out to their satisfaction.

They are excellent at mind games. They easily sense the secrets of people. Pisces gives them its distinctive power to read through words and facial expressions to reach the crux of the issue. Capricorn is good at making the most of anything and they use the intuitive powers of Pisces to productive use. It will be very hard to deceive them.

They are friendly but do not have a large group of friends. They are extremely generous to their friends but are rarely taken for a ride by sob stories. They are extremely perceptive of the real motives.

AriCapPisces love deeply. They want a partner who matches up to their ideals and loves family as much as them. They can be highly poetic and romantic in love and can truly sweep you off your feet. It might take them some time to settle down or they might even go in for an early marriage if they find a soul mate. They are committed once they make up their minds, at least till they hit their forties.

Money is quite important to them. They are not ready to live on dreams alone. They may be a little reckless and impulsive in their spending, especially for their families and loved ones, but they know how to conserve money.

Respect for elders is deeply ingrained in them and they prefer the company of older and more experienced people to restless young ones.

They are riddled with insecurities and extremely sensitive. All the three signs have their share of fears. Aries tries to hide it in confident talk, but Capricorn exhibits a melancholic temperament and Pisces prefers to live in daydreams to evade its fears. Their fears are deep enough to cripple them. The only ray of hope is the Arian bluster. AriCapPisces need some encouragement and love to get over their insecurities. They are high-strung people and are extremely sensitive too.

They can be mean, selfish, cunning and deceptive too, if required. These qualities come to the fore when they see that their basic honesty and goodness bears no fruit or if they have been deceived by unscrupulous people. The trouble with Pisces is that it learns everything quickly – the good things, and the bad ones too.

AriCapPisces are prone to addictions too. It can be anything, from food to substances. The attention-seeking trait of the combination can find solace in addiction. The Pisces in them is ever ready to try out new things and become addicted while the wild Aries does not mind going off-track for a while. But Capricorn can help them move away from life-threatening addictions. Love is one addiction that can cure them too. They need that in abundance.

They are deeply spiritual and have an unshakeable belief in a greater power that affects them. The Piscean deep mystical thoughts, with the Capricornian traditional views and the Arian belief, make them strong believers in their religion. They may also be ready to think beyond religions and ideologies to a more universal form of spirituality.

Aries–Capricorn–Pisces – Russell Crowe
Crowe is content...'I feel whole again...I missed the family, I always do, but they're here now, so all is good'...In reality, he's far more complex: funny, passionate, kind, interesting, ferociously bright and yes, at times, demanding and direct...' That's one of the things about ambition, you have to make sure it's above what you think is reasonable – otherwise it's not really being ambitious.'[176]

In June 2005, Crowe was arrested and charged with second-degree assault by New York City police, after he threw a telephone at an employee of the Mercer Hotel who refused to help him place a call.[177]

His ambition, desire to excel, temper, family values and sensitive philosophy make him an AriCapPisces.

Love and Marriage for Him
Family is extremely important to him. He wants to be respected and loved by his family members and does not like to hear anyone speak ill of them. He is quite status-conscious too. He has a surfeit of only one thing – ambition. He does not like to think beyond it and is very dedicated to his career. He needs some space to carry out his dreams.

He needs a partner who loves family values and is stable enough to handle him when he goes off the deep end. He can get easily depressed or look at life through rose-tinted glasses. Help him see the middle path and he is grateful. Do not fill his head with negative thoughts for this guy can turn really downbeat. His addictions and depression can take him down a different path if he does not have your love and support.

---

[176] http://www.totalfilm.com/features/the-total-film-interview-russell-crowe
[177] http://en.wikipedia.org/wiki/Russell_Crowe

His brash façade hides his deep sensitivity and he wants you to understand him. He seems difficult to understand but it's simple, actually: this man needs a lot of love and attention. He positively glows when he is adored, and sulks when he doesn't get attention and importance. He can read and understand you completely but sometimes his love is a little selfish. Watch out for him when he hits his forties – he can philander when he has become successful and self-assured.

He is a very loving and understanding father. He loves playing with his children and is always ready to spend time with them. He also knows how to get their respect.

Love and Marriage for Her
She is extremely romantic, understands you well and is your soul mate. This girl also wants a partner who stands out in a crowd. She is ambitious and talented, and loves her family too. She can sacrifice a lot for their happiness. She will support you in your ambition, even stay at home if need be, but certainly wants to use her abilities and talent.

She is normally chirpy, happy and is the glue that binds the family. But she can also be easily depressed and her black moods can be terrible. She has numerous fears, despite her abilities, and really loves you if you can help her fight her insecurities with encouragement and understanding.

After being a pillar of strength and slogging all her life, if you continue to treat her like dirt, she can walk away from you. If she has no financial support or if it will hurt her children's lives, then she is capable of finding love in her own way. Morals, customs and proper behaviour will now not matter to her but you will never know of her secret life.

As a mother, she is very caring and sensitive to her children. She loves being with them and never judges them harshly. She can try and change her ideas for them but takes time to let go of her values.

At the Workplace
Passion combines with extreme work ethics and deep sensitivity in AriCapPisces. They convert their dreams into reality with lots of hard work – and also a little bit of cunning and politics if required. They are fantastic learners and quickly outdistance you. They are chameleonic and can change according to situations to boost their success. They have the ability to convert small ideas into large-scale businesses. They do not lack organising abilities either. They are very creative. Artistic, sports and offbeat careers appeal to them and see them excel. Politics, too, is a field that opens naturally to them.

They need a lot of encouragement, so be ready to motivate them. They become more controlling as they achieve success and are not willing to trust everyone. They have the ability to think from the perspective of others. As bosses, they are smart in hiring the right people to run the business and delegate things very well while keeping a stern control on things.

Fire, Earth and Water meet in AriCapPisces and give them the conviction to carry out their dreams with logic and a little sensitivity.

Famous AriCapPisces Personalities
Russell Crowe, Atul Kasbekar, Samantha Fox, Colin Powell, Franck Ribery, James McAvoy, Kate Hudson.

105. ARIES–AQUARIUS–PISCES

Mars, the aggressive and violent god of war, the inventive and maverick Uranus and the mysterious, all-knowing Neptune combine forces in this combination.

AriAquaPisces are very different from most people you know. Aquarians are futuristic, very evolved and revolutionary: their thoughts can be miles away from reality; and Pisceans, emotional, sensitive, caring, loving and highly reflective of their environment, are in their dream world. With innovative, ambitious and driven Aries in this mix, we get a person who not only thinks and dreams ideas but is also ambitious enough to strive for them. These exceptional geniuses have the guts, determination and passion to go after their wacky visions on their own quirky terms.

Aquarius and Pisces make them extremely perceptive. But, unlike typical Pisces and Aquarius, who are also empathetic and compassionate, AriAquaPisces are a little more selfish when it comes to emotions. This selfishness is good for it stops them from being self-sacrificing. In turn, the unworldly Pisces and detached Aquarius reduce the domineering and self-absorbed nature of Aries.

The boundless optimism of Aries does away with the fears and phobias of Pisces. Pisces are very talented and creative, yet so full of fears of inadequacy that it takes a strong fire to burn down their ghosts and Aries provides that.

These humble and loving people are pleasant even with strangers. All they want to do is good and make people around them happy. All they want in return is lots of admiration and love.

Money, status and luxury do not count for them. They only need to feel happy and involved in whatever they are doing. They love to work for causes, hear applause and achieve glory rather than live their life as an average Jill/Joe. However, to live for dreams and possibilities requires money. Lack of it can force them to abandon their dreams.

They have excellent dress sense. They are trendsetters with the wacky Aquarian style combined with the attention-seeking Arian fashion statements.

You can expect volcanic eruptions when they are angered. Do not worry, for these lovely souls never hold a grudge. Their anger is directed at the situation, not you. Their sense of humour always kicks in when they are feeling low. They can laugh at themselves and the world with equal ease.

Love will find them idealistic and emotional. They love selflessly and truly without any ulterior motive. The Aries in them desires an ideal in love while the Piscean just wants to belong to somebody. The Aquarian habit of experimentation in love and Piscean irresponsibility might make them a little unreliable in love in the beginning, but when they do love, they seek the highest form of romantic love.

Of course, the combination brings out some negative traits too. All three zodiac signs hate boring and mundane stuff in life. Pisces lives in a dream world, Aries is easily distracted and Aquarius keeps jumping to new ideas. You can't expect them to be punctual, stick to timelines and be focused for long.

Another problem that can surface in this combination is addiction. Aquarius loves trying out new things while Pisces can spend a lifetime wallowing in the dark side. The fearlessness of Aries can act against them here. The danger lurks of the person leading the typical life of a creative soul who does not care what the world thinks and does his/her own thing while giving in to laziness and escapism many times. They prefer roles with low levels of responsibility. They can also be afflicted by indolence for a long time.

The Aries self-centredness, arrogance and ego are deeply submerged in the humanistic hues of Aquarius and Pisces, but can still be present. Some of them can create a parallel reality and obsess with wacky, unworkable ideas. They can become eccentric and quarrelsome, and lose track. Their path to success may be lost due to distractions, indiscipline, or the Arian ego coming in their way. Despite their external bravado, they have lots of self-doubt and insecurities too. They are hounded by feelings of inadequacy, and sometimes can have an inferiority complex, which they hide under rude arrogance.

They have a deep spiritual side too. They also love to give to society. AriAquaPisces are highly empathetic and compassionate and have an altruistic side.

Aries~Aquarius~Pisces – Vikram
Vikram is an award-winning actor.

'People around me don't react to me as a superstar or something; and I love that...I have a gym at home but still go to the local gym...for no other reason than that I hate building walls around myself.'[178]

'I have done and will continue doing films which push me beyond the realm as an actor.'

Vikram didn't abandon his dream of being a movie actor for four bedridden years after a motorbike accident while doctors considered it impossible for him even to walk. His desire to try untested waters, his humility and his never-say-die spirit personify him as a true AriAquaPisces.

Love and Marriage for Him
He is fun loving and exciting. Life with him is an adventure, for this guy refuses to be caged by anything more binding than love. Conventions and routines fly out of the window when he steps in.

He loves experimentation, so you can try your hand at new and exotic dishes, change the furniture around every month and wear the latest in fashion. You will enjoy the unexpected with him and his extremely different world-view will drive the cobwebs out of your mind.

He has high ideals and is focused on the bigger things in life and leave the routine stuff to you. It sounds difficult, but your life will be wonderful with his sense of adventure and loving empathy. He puts you on a pedestal. Do not crush his will or try to dominate him. He can be quite fixed in his ways.

He has a streak of irresponsibility in him. You have to be the more responsible of the two. Get him to focus his energies on a few things rather than scattering them all around. Be his sounding board, cheerleader, money manager and helping hand.

There is one problem though: you never know where he is, mentally (often) or physically (sometimes). The Aquarian in him can be lost in thoughts and take a while to come back to earth and be with you. It will be nice if you like having his family

---
[178] *Cine Blitz*, August 2010

around for you can then be the glue that holds him and his relatives together. He doesn't see the need to follow certain customs just to keep society happy.

As a father, he is absolutely fun. He bonds with his children and does not boss them around in the Arian fashion. Grades do not matter to him as much as passion. He lets them choose their own paths in life.

Love and Marriage for Her
She is feminine, but not the sort to lose herself in housework and family. She does her duties but is very distracted at times. She is fun and exciting as a companion. With her, every day is a new beginning with huge possibilities. It will be nice if you share her love for the unexpected and can dream like her.

She is a bundle of raw energy. She is impulsive, can give in to her whims and fancies and can be ruthless when she demands certain things to be done in a certain way. Remember that there is a child within her that continuously seeks attention and she is not as self-centred and heartless as she seems. However, do not ignore the Aries in her, for if she is mistreated or unappreciated, she will rebel.

She is intelligent, and driven when she finds her passion. She excels in creative fields and she loves doing things differently. She needs a lot of encouragement and love to reach her métier. You must be her support system. You have to maintain the budget and be sure of the finances because she lacks control over money matters.

As a mother, she is not very demanding or disciplining. She feels a little guilty at times that she is not the perfect mom. Her controlling Arian streak might pop up a few times when she will yell at the kids. The Piscean in her makes her caring and nurturing.

At the Workplace
AriAquaPisces work best in creative and artistic fields where they are not burdened by timelines and sales. They are full of original and creative ideas and cannot live by routine monotonous work. They are great as artists, psychiatrists, spiritual practitioners and in parasciences. They can even do well as designers and architects – anything that allows them to think beyond the ordinary and does not tie them to a desk. They are fast learners and anything inculcated in them from a young age leaves a deep impression on them.

Give them flexible hours and long deadlines and they are happy. Though money does not rank very high on their list of must-haves, they realise that they cannot do without it. Hence, monetary compensation should be adequate. Applause, however, is always welcome. As bosses, they are thought leaders and path-breaking pioneers. They are very generous too. They love flattery but feign not noticing it.

Fire, Air and Water mix in this combination to give drive to unworldly desires and compassion to passions.

Famous AriAquaPisces Personalities
Vikram, Victoria Beckham, Sir Elton John, David Belle, David Blaine, Varun Dhawan, Celine Dion, Sharman Joshi, Unmukt Chand, William Shakespeare, Puneeth Rajkumar, Eva Longoria, Vincent Kompany, Yana Gupta, Ayesha Takia, Tamia, Rupali Ganguly, Mataji Nirmala Devi, Yashwantrao Chavan, Raul Meireles, Joyce Banda, Humpy Koneru, Anandji (Kalyanji), Sanjeev Kapoor.

106. TAURUS–GEMINI–CANCER

The strong and resilient Taurus loses its extremely stubborn views and gains a sensitive outlook in TauGemCans. Mercury, which invokes lightning thoughts, and Moon, the planet of emotion, add a new dimension to the patient, plodding Taurean.

This is the perfect blend of the old and the new, the traditional and the modern, conventional wisdom and maverick ideas. The Gemini in them is restless, nonconformist and brimming with bright new ideas; but they go about executing those in a stolid fashion, while keeping track of ground reality and knowing their exact limitations.

Taurus provides mental stability, Cancer adds perseverance, while Gemini provides the glow and wit. Determination and perseverance characterise all their actions, and will never let them move away from their goal. Taurus also makes them extremely hard working and dependable. TauGemCans are able to endure everything with fortitude.

Logic and rationality loom large in their decisions. These guys think and talk with uncommon common sense. They master the art of conversation combining reason with sharp wit and humour, without putting anyone down. The Gemini tendency of adding spice to stories will be evident in a positive way with them. They often talk about the 'good old days" with interesting titbits drawn out from their nostalgic memories. Their sense of humour cheers everyone around them. TauGemCans sparkle, making them favourites at any party. They also have an impressive memory: they remember everything you said or did in the past.

Family matters a lot to them. They are happiest spending time at home with their families and loved ones. They are especially close to their mother, and love being pampered by her. Food holds a special connotation for them and their mother's cooking symbolises the best in food and affection. They love eating and also have a flair for cooking.

Love will definitely rank high in their life. TauGemCans will tone down the highly flirtatious and carefree love of Gemini and make it more stable and sensitive. Once they decide to make you a part of their lives they will stand by you and never look elsewhere.

Money is very important to them. They want to make a pile and save it. With the Taurean fine sense of moneymaking, these people are smart and savvy money managers and investors.

TauGemCans have a creative streak as well. They like music and can be very good singers. They instinctively appreciate creative and artistic talent in others and imbibe it in themselves as well.

They are STUBBORN! Their mild nature, charming conversation and misty smile may hide this fact, but beware. On those occasions, only soft persuasion and perseverance can induce them to look at the other viewpoint.

These loving, caring and vibrant people also have an emotional facet. They have mood swings and can get ruffled by opinions that clash with theirs. They like harmony around them and can be very sensitive to negative remarks. Sometimes they read between the lines and hurt themselves even more. They may forgive but their deep memories never let them forget. They retreat into their shells when in a bad mood; if you gently help them come out, they will be thankful to you.

Their insecurities centre round money and family. They will work excessively to insure themselves against an imagined future of financial ruin or lonely death. When they get angry, they rarely blow their tops. Instead, they sulk. You will be able to make out when they are unhappy for their expressive faces will never be able to hide their feelings. They sometimes respond with sarcastic comments.

They simply endure. They have this soft but tough-as-steel staying power; they can simply out-last anything with their ability to stay put and offer stubborn resistance. They are made of solid Taurean Earth that can withstand any calamity, and the strong claws of Cancer offer extraordinary tenacity. If they learn to control the Geminian restlessness and channelise its amazing dexterity, they will be versatile, creative yet practical and resourceful.

Taurus–Gemini–Cancer – Priyanka Chopra
'I didn't think I had too much talent. I don't think I have much of it even now. But I worked hard on it.'[179]

'I am afraid of loneliness, and being without a friend.'[180]

'I just have to be surprised. I hate the whole boring flowers, cards and cake. Take me diving or something.'[181]

Priyanka Chopra has the tenacity and stability of Taurus and Cancer. Her Taurean qualities led to the release of her music album.

Romantic, earthy, a little insecure, and adventurous despite a conservative streak, Priyanka Chopra combines the best of Taurus, Cancer and Gemini.

Love and Marriage for Him
This guy never lets you down. He provides for you, thinks for you and is there with you always. Family means a lot to him. You must love his mother or decide not to say anything bad about her for he is truly a mamma's boy.

He knows how to make you laugh. Sensitive and understanding, he is very easy to talk to. You are able to discuss your hopes and ambitions with him and get sane advice. He can never be egoistic or unchivalrous.

This guy loves saving money and it hurts him to see it spent unnecessarily on clothes and accessories. Count your blessings: he is that one guy who is capable of cooking delicious food for you and waking you up with aromatic tea on a lazy morning. He is extremely expressive in love.

He can sulk, though. Be ready with the pampering for he needs to be lovingly brought back to his cheerful self. He will have an emotional and touchy side and will need sensitive handling. He will very easily adapt to change but will be the rock of your life. This guy will never blink in times of crisis and be the strongest

---
[179] http://www.filmfare.com/articles/priyanka-chopra-i-think-kareena-doesnt-like-me-2090.html
[180] http://www.rediff.com/movies/2005/nov/07priyanka.htm
[181] *People*, July 30, 2010

support in your life. Even if he has the Geminian roving eye, he will never be irresponsible and rock his family.

He is an ideal father who knows how to show his love for his children. He nurtures them and is always there for them. He loves playing with them and can while away hours in family games.

Love and Marriage for Her
She is loving and nurturing. Loyal and steadfast, this girl is happiest when surrounded by the people she loves. She is emotional and highly sensitive. You need to be the person who understands her feelings.

Though she loves home, she is also bored by routine. She needs a bit of change to make her love her home even more. She has a creative streak as well and you would be surprised by the way she develops new interesting hobbies. She loves to flirt and does it delightfully, but always longs for a stable, long-term relationship. She is deeply romantic and loves to keep the spark alive in the relationship, and wants her man to flirt with her even if it is their sixtieth anniversary. She has many insecurities, from her looks to her family. You will need lots of patience while handling them. Watch what you say to her. Ensure that she needs to worry less.

She can pack a lot into a few hours and will relax only when it is time to sleep. She is a fabulous host who will cook up a storm for a whole battalion at a few hours' notice. She will also regale the guests with her witty anecdotes and charming smile.

Money is very important to her. A personal bank account makes her feel secure. This very feminine lady will be a rock for her family in times of crisis. She has high levels of endurance and resilience. She leads, but with feminine charm and lots of smiles.

Motherhood suits her perfectly. She knows what to do when her children cry and is never frazzled by their demands. She is willing to quit her job to take care of them.

At the Workplace
TauGemCans may take time to realise what they want to do, but once they decide, they work tirelessly to fulfil their dreams. Obstacles motivate them to try harder. They are always ready to learn and inject new ideas into their work. They love finding innovative ways to do the same old thing. TauGemCans are the most loyal workers if you understand their worth and pay them for it.

From finance to creative pursuits – these guys can try their hand at anything. They need a career where they can grow and change with time. They can also be very good artists and singers and have a flair for mimicry too. These versatile linguists and fabulous communicators are also smart enough to explore different avenues and ensure a double income source.

The cardinal sign of Cancer gives them the ability to lead. They are excellent team leaders and treat their team members as part of their extended family. A TauGemCan boss is charming, caring and loving, but clear about his priorities. He keeps excellent control of budgets and is very resourceful.

Earth, Air and Water combine in this creative and determined combination. Persevering, stable, intelligent and sensitive, they know the value of work, money and family.

Famous TauGemCan Personalities
Priyanka Chopra, Saurav Ganguly, Subrata Roy, Tom Cruise, Laloo Prasad Yadav, Sonakshi Sinha, Paul McCartney, Stephanie Rice, Amrita Rao, John D. Rockefeller, George Bernard Shaw, Gurbaksh Chahal, Vasantrao Naik, Jade Goody, Neena Gupta, Czar Peter the Great, Angelo Mathews, Anuj Saxena, Karthik Raja, Lord Mountbatten, Sarah Siddons.

107. TAURUS–GEMINI–LEO

The patient and enduring Taurus gets an injection of optimism from the effervescent Mercury and the regal Apollo in TauGemLeos.

Imagine an animal with the brute strength of the Bull and the power and roar of a Lion. Now have the Twins with wings perched on top of this immensely strong animal! However hard the Twins try, the animal won't fly. But it will certainly sing and dance, sparkle and shine.

You can sense the immense strength behind their disarming smile. Taurus makes them solid, unflustered and dependable. Leo gives them a regal air and they stride majestically. The combination makes them responsible, calm and brave enough to face any calamity that life can throw at them. TauGemLeos have their feet firmly planted on the ground. Taurus makes them down-to-earth and practical, while Leos are responsible people.

Both Taurus and Leo are fixed signs and this makes TauGemLeos prefer the old ways of doing work. Gemini adds a whiff of fresh air to their attitude so though they do think of changes they will not do anything drastic. They follow the slow and steady route to change and bring it in gradually in their lives.

Taureans speak little, but whenever they do, it is common sense. Geminians naturally have a way with words and Leos speak with style. So expect TauGemLeos to have captivating communication skills. They speak with the right intonations and effects, using sparse words with amazing use of pauses and tonality.

TauGemLeos are fun loving but only with a few people who are close to them. Leo makes them wary of playing the fool and Taurus has an inhibitive nature. Despite the easy-going ways of Gemini, there will always be a reserve that will keep unwanted people at bay. As they grow older and achieve success, the initial restraint slowly wears off.

Leo gives them a strong sense of pride in themselves. They love being looked up to and strive hard for a highly regarded place in society. Their regal bearing and demeanour is such that you wouldn't guess even if they had humble beginnings. They love being pampered and cared for, and to be treated with respect.

Family is the cornerstone of their existence. They are very loving towards their families. They relax in a family atmosphere. You can expect a lot of advice from them. They are not rebellious. They like to follow their family's rules. Tradition and strong values matter to them. They love good food and are excellent hosts too.

Money is quite important to them. Taurus has a materialistic streak while Gemini makes them smart about money and Leo needs the sheen that money can buy. They want to earn enough to afford all the luxuries they desire. They would want to earn quick and retire rich as soon as possible. They look out for all possible options to increase their income and try their hand at various ventures. They are good at investing it without being stingy: they prefer to spend it on luxury items and good investments rather than keeping it under lock and key. They have a natural flair for business and know how to make money grow.

TauGemLeos are extremely artistic too. The Taurean love for music and art, the Gemini felicity with words and the Leo desire to be the centre of attention make them take to the stage with ease. They have many hidden talents and excel in everything including singing, dancing, mimicry, compering and acting.

TauGemLeos are not restrained, when it comes to love. Leo's natural romanticism and the deep sensuous nature of Taurus, combined with the Geminian ability to whisper sweet nothings, can be quite a heady mix. Gemini's flirtatious nature, Leo's choosiness and Taurus's practicality will make them take their time before settling down but they ultimately commit to a relationship and remain quite loyal too. TauGemLeos love the idea of a family and even if they occasionally indulge in a little harmless flirting, they rarely think about rocking the boat if their partner gives them no cause to complain.

Taurus and Leo also give them an indolence, especially when they are at home. Don't expect TauGemLeos to run around doing chores. But never underestimate their strength, either mentally or physically. When emergencies strike or when intense, excruciating situations rise, they are the ones who stand tall. They have this ability to bear tough situations with a smile.

The double fixed signs of Taurus and Leo make them quite stubborn about their decisions. Once they decide something, or if they are hurt for some reason, it's difficult to get them to come round. Gemini does give a window of hope. They take time to decide so your only chance is to convince them before they make up their mind.

TauGemLeos do not have any Water sign in the combination. This makes them lack sensitivity towards people. They cannot exactly see into you and feel your emotions. They are deeply sentimental in love and have great warmth for family, but towards the rest of the universe, they lack empathy. Some people in this combination can also be haughty, ruthlessly materialistic, insensitive and fickle-minded.

They are believers. Despite a wandering Geminian mind, the Leonine belief in the power above and the Taurean endurance gives them the ability to endure, whatever the situation, like a rock.

Taurus~Gemini~Leo – Kumaramangalam Birla
'The Birlas are very conscious about punctuality. We are not ostentatious. We have a great sense of family. We are taught to respect older people. Good manners and regard for other people are considered very important.'

'I think my father was more hands-on. My style is much more to give people freedom to do their own thing. As long as they deliver, I don't like to get involved. I am available if they need me and I will hold them accountable but I will not interfere needlessly.'[182]

Family figures high in the way he conducts himself, yet he is also confident enough to set his own rules. Kumaramangalam Birla is undoubtedly a TauGemLeo.

---
[182] http://virsanghvi.com/interview-detail.aspx?ID=7

Love and Marriage for Him
He is a charming companion. He never stops being a fun-loving friend and likes to entertain you with his witty remarks. He likes being pampered while you handle the responsibilities at home. His ego needs to be handled delicately or he can sulk.

His mind can be active but he is a lazybones. Allow him to rest at home with his favourite music on and lots of good food to munch on. He is very sensible, but not very sensitive. Don't expect him to understand all your feminine hints. Tell him clearly, what you want. He will be his generous best if you understand his need for space and 'me' time.

He wants to play a strong role in his family and likes advising. Listen to him for he is logical and smart about his decisions. He likes travelling – but in luxury. His idea of a good time is booking himself into a resort with family and friends.

As a father, he is there for his children and is very proud of them. He enjoys watching them grow up and likes to teach them a few things himself. His views are fixed and he sets standards of behaviour.

Love and Marriage for Her
She is stable and grounded, and speaks with a certain flair. She can be elegant and charming, and even an alluring siren, when she wants. She loves talking and expressing opinions. Be ready to converse with her. She gets bored with mundane routine stuff – keep her interested. She likes to be treated as your equal and will never tolerate insults, anger or abuse.

Although she has a restless mind, she really likes resting and lazing around. She needs household help and manages them well. Her multitasking abilities mean she can handle many responsibilities without getting flustered. Remember to compliment her, too. She needs a lot of pampering when she feels low.

She can manage finances but can't resist when big brands display their wares. She loves excitement, drama, travel and socialising. She is talented and likes showing off her singing or dancing skills to her adoring friends. She is a live wire at office, home or parties and the centre of attention with her interesting conversation and regal bearing.

As a mother, she pampers her children and does not like anyone finding fault with them. Academics are very important to her and she wants them to be as smart as her. Her views are slightly traditional but she is open to discussions.

At the Workplace
TauGemLeos have agile minds and are well suited for careers that require intelligence and communication skills. Though they have the capacity to work hard they would rather work smart. They do not mind unconventional careers if they are rewarding. They are extraordinary in creative fields. Music, arts and drama appeal to their Leo fondness of the limelight. Their deepest need is to lead, but they need the money too. So just pats on the back won't suffice.

Gemini makes them very good at picking up languages and in careers dealing with people: they can be brilliant in marketing. The best careers for them are those that involve words; they enjoy travel too. They make teachers and coaches.

As bosses, though conservative, they are open to new ideas. But they will not jump into risky propositions at the drop of a hat. They are excellent mentors.

Earth, Air and Fire meet in TauGemLeos to give them stability of purpose, a way with words and an optimistic outlook.

Famous TauGemLeo Personalities
Kumaramangalam Birla, Natalie Portman, Anoushka Shankar, Anna Kournikova, Misbah-ul-Haq, Venkaiah Naidu, Sherpa Tenzing, Mary-Kate Olsen, Ashley Olsen, Jayanthi Natarajan.

108. TAURUS–GEMINI–VIRGO

At first glance, this seems a very stable combination despite the airy Gemini. The two stable Earth signs of Taurus and Virgo lend enough foundation for the Gemini to stand still.

TauGemVirs are extremely intelligent, as Gemini, the cleverest of the zodiac, and Virgo, the most intelligent and diligent, join forces. They are always calm due to the extremely grounded and slow-moving Taurus.

Both Gemini and Virgo are very good with words. Gemini knows how to talk and orate descriptively and eloquently with the right pauses and perfect emphasis. They are also linguists and likely to speak at least three languages as fluently as their mother tongue. Virgos on the other hand are masters of the written word. Nobody can write, draft, spell-check and even check the lacunae like a Virgo. Conversely, Taureans don't believe in communication. They mumble and eat up their words and nod or wave in lieu of talking. But when they do talk it is all common sense. TauGemVirs talk and write beautifully well with a good dose of common sense and practicality. They are also masters in drafting and planning.

All three signs are loners at heart. Taurus opens very slowly to strangers and is more comfortable with old friends and colleagues. Geminis can light up a room with their vivacious talk, but the Air sign makes them detached; and Virgos are born loners. This quality will make them seem very withdrawn at times, yet at the slightest provocation, they can burst into brilliant speech. Don't take their silence for meekness.

They like to work silently and prefer to stay in the background. The lack of Fire and the stability of double Earth make them shun ostentatious behaviour. TauGemVirs prefer genuine work and talent to grand gestures and impassioned exchanges. They bring the Virgo purity of purpose to everything they do.

They will also find it difficult to get into relationships despite their ability to talk and flirt easily. The loner attitude plus the low comfort levels of Virgo and Taurus with the opposite sex makes it difficult for them to open up their heart easily. But once they get into relationships they remain committed; the Gemini love for philandering gets toned down considerably. When they are in a relationship, they will have the sensuality of a Taurean and the sizzle of a Gemini, which will lighten up the stolid virtue of Virgo. They author exquisite love notes and romantic one-liners when they are in the mood for love. They will not be passionate and possessive lovelorn romantics but will have the self-sacrificing nature of Virgos.

Food is another sphere that is very important to them. The Taurus in them loves food, right from cooking to eating, while Virgo is very health-conscious. You can expect them to cook and serve healthy, non-greasy food. They can be a little fussy about their choice of food.

Money is very dear to them as Taureans need material possessions and Virgos are very careful in money matters. They know all about investments. They like investing in safe funds, gold, jewellery and real estate, and have a healthy bank balance. The one luxury that they desire is to travel in peace and comfort. While Gemini makes them open to ideas, Taurus is traditional and Virgo is conservative. There is a strange paradox in them. They appear, talk and behave in the most modern way, but make no mistake: they are traditionalists at heart.

They are good friends who love to help, even financially. But they are they are no fools and know whom to trust with their money. The Gemini wit and the Taurean sense of humour make them fun companions whose jokes don't make anyone uncomfortable. TauGemVirs are essentially good people. They are humble, kind, loving, caring and intelligent, with a fun streak that saves them from being nice but boring.

Never underestimate them just because they are uncomplicated folks who don't charge at you passionately. With the steely determination of Taurus and single-minded dedication of Virgo, they are capable of moving mountains and create seemingly improbable miracles in their quiet unassuming way.

Taurus~Gemini~Virgo – P.V. Sindhu

The fact that she reports on time at the coaching camps daily, travelling a distance of 56 km from her residence, is perhaps a reflection of her willingness to fulfil her desire to be a good badminton player with the required hard work and commitment. For a player of her age, she shows remarkable stamina. 'This is one of the most significant aspects of her game and should take her a long way,' says her coach Pullela Gopichand.[183]

P. Vijaya (her mother): 'She has reached the level where she is owing to sheer determination.'[184]

Sindhu has the quiet, steely determination and stamina of Taurus, dexterity of Gemini and the meticulousness of Virgo.

Love and Marriage for Him

You can congratulate yourself, if you haven't already, for this guy is good. He is dutiful, caring, dependable and more! He worries about everyone and plans out your future beautifully. You can fall sick without a worry for he cares for you like an angel and takes care of the children too.

He loves to travel and likes change, even in the household. You can expect him to lend a helping hand. He may try his hand at different cuisines. He loves to party but will always be gentlemanly and well behaved and never get drunk.

There is one thing to remember about him – sleep is sacred. He needs his eight hours of slumber. While Gemini and Virgo make for increased mental prowess and Taurus in him works extremely hard to deliver results – he also needs time to cool down and relax.

When angry, he can get quite cranky: he'll complain and criticise. He may even insist on taking on all the work, including yours. He doesn't mind if you are not as particular as him, but don't burden the poor soul by being lax in your basic responsibilities.

He has his foibles, though. He worries constantly. Despite his love and care, he is not very emotional or sensitive. You have to speak your mind to him so he understands. It may also be difficult to get money out of him for shopping sprees.

---

[183] http://www.hindu.com/mp/2008/04/10/stories/2008041050140300.htm
[184] http://www.dnaindia.com/sport/report-pv-sindhus-parents-dedicate-her-feat-to-coach-pullela-gopichand-1872318

As a father, he is extremely good. He helps his children in their activities and is a hands-on dad when they are babies. As they grow older, he likes playing quizzes and having long discussions with them about the state of the world and politics.

Love and Marriage for Her
She is outstandingly duty-conscious. You are one lucky guy for she spends all her free time worrying and caring for you. She is extremely hard working and industrious. She actually finds it very difficult to relax. Do ensure that she gets adequate rest. Gift her spa time or any 'me' time. No one deserves rest more than her.

She loves change and enjoys travelling. She is a fabulous career woman too and is capable of taking care of both her home and work. She has no problem adjusting to circumstances; things may not be to her liking but she does not stop, instead she fights them out. She will avoid a fight as long as she can, preferring solitude and silence to voicing her views. But if things do not settle down, her absolutely brilliant and brutally honest speech is heard.

Money is important to her and she needs to feel secure. She needs to have a bank balance and some investments for her peace of mind.

As a mother, she is brilliant. She is caring without being smothering. She insists on good education and looks through all the courses and institutes to find the one best suited to her children's needs. She is absolutely geared to take care of growing minds. They learn to live life intelligently and zestfully.

At the Workplace
With their unsurpassed communication skills and extensive knowledge, they are a boon to the workplace. You will never find them making baseless statements or being petty – they are too involved with work to spend time playing politics.

They possess the creative talent and sensibility of Taurus and the expressive ability of Gemini and Virgo. They can really put their ideas in beautiful words that captivate. They can be marketing whiz kids working on catchy one-liners or even poets. In fact, these guys can write beautifully on any subject on earth. They will do well in any profession where communication skills, both written and verbal, are needed.

Give them work that is not monotonous, allow them to travel and let them employ their skills. Their extreme hard work and penchant for details, added to their retiring nature, make them excel as the number two or three at work. Just give them money and a car to take them around and they are happy.

They give proper shape to your ideas and plug up the holes in your plans. They have an amazing eye for detail and can plan events to great accuracy. They can excel as business leaders.

If this combination is your boss, do not ever make the mistake of opening your mouth without solid facts to back you up. They are stringent on accuracy and expect hard work rather than flattery from their subordinates.

Double Earth and Air combine to give stability yet flexibility to this combination. Intelligent, hard working, practical and sincere, TauGemVirs will shine wherever you put them.

Famous TauGemVir Personalities
P.V. Sindhu, Sunil Narine, Suraiya, Alois Alzheimer, Isabelle Adjani.

109. TAURUS–GEMINI–LIBRA

The calm and patient Taurus meets the extremely vibrant and hyperactive Gemini and the luxury-loving romantic Libra in TauGemLibs.

Gemini and Libra make excellent communicators. Together they make the world's best salesmen – no one can resist their selling pitch. They make the logical yet curt Taurus speak out with assurance. TauGemLibs never struggle for words, and captivate people with their intelligent and vibrant conversation. When they are around, the ideas keep coming. They think on their feet and are great problem solvers. They have an uncanny facility for new languages.

Optimism is their trademark. They are fun to be with and are rarely in blue moods. They keep you in fits of laughter and they know all the good jokes and the best gossip. They are great mimics and can liven up boring lectures with their talent for observing and replicating the peculiar details of the teacher's mannerisms. They have amazing skills of networking and know instinctively to make long-lasting bonds.

They attract people with their happiness and have many friends and acquaintances. Travel appeals to them, but they miss their families when they are away. Family is important to them. They want happy faces around them and work hard to erase any negative feelings. Family holidays are essential for them as they like bonding over new places.

If there were no Taurus in this combination, they would have too many ideas and be too distracted to make anything of them. Taurus adds stability to Gemini and Libra and makes TauGemLibs stick to their ideas longer. They do take some time to decide, for they spend a long time analysing and thinking through, but soon manage to untangle problems, if any.

They are quick learners who never stop learning. Their childlike curiosity in every new thing imparts a youthful look to them. They see and absorb so many things that they evolve as they grow. They are phenomenally adaptable. Librans love learning new cultures, for Geminians change is oxygen, and Taureans have the wonderful ability to compartmentalise without being troubled by the past. They are at home wherever they go.

Food interests them. They experiment with new cuisines. They are marvellous hosts and love throwing parties.

TauGemLibs will take their time to find their true love. Both Taurus and Libra are extremely committed partners. Taurus loves being nurtured and nurturing others, while Librans are incomplete in life without love. This makes TauGemLibs very loving and caring, yet they will take time to commit due to Gemini. Gemini wants to remain footloose and fancy-free forever; Libra always thinks that the perfect mate awaits them just round the corner; also they see good points in every candidate and this makes it hard to choose! But once smitten, TauGemLibs will be extremely romantic, wax eloquent and pen a thousand poems. Yes, the Geminian roving eye will rove less, but will still be there.

They do not lose their temper much. They have an amazing tolerance level and do not react immediately. Money and luxuries are important to them. They hate living frugally and want all possible comforts at home. They love spending, but are also smart enough to save and invest. In fact, they have immense patience and are ready to wait till all the emotional, financial and intellectual investments that they have made bear fruit.

Creative ideas and artistic abilities are characteristic of TauGemLibs. Taurus is a natural fountain of art and Venusians ooze with unbelievable artistic talents. When combined with the ever-creative and versatile Gemini, TauGemLibs are bound to have some form of talent.

Despite their seemingly empathetic and kind words, they definitely lack the innate ability to sense things due the absence of Water signs. You sometimes wonder why they can't just understand you and why you need to explain things to them in so many words.

The two Air signs definitely slow them down while making decisions. In matters close to the heart the vacillations increase. They are also prone to try too many things at once or need constant variety in their environment to summon interest in mundane tasks. Taurus sometimes makes them extremely stubborn when they are unable to see the other's viewpoint. The laziness of Libra and Taurus can afflict them too, when they would prefer to sit around listening to music, especially before or after doing an important project. Well, they need those breaks to recharge their batteries.

The biggest positive (or occasionally negative) fact about them is that they are absolutely practical and down-to-earth despite their external gregariousness, flair and endless chatter. They have some old-world virtues and cannot be fooled easily. They are hardened, and have the staying power that will not wilt and has the capacity to weather any storm.

Taurus–Gemini–Libra – Nandan Nilekani

'Deconstruction is the ability to press a 'reset' button at periodic intervals. From Bangalore to Dharwad, and when I went from Dharwad to the IIT, and then on to my professional career – it was another reset button and now this work is the latest reset in my life.'[185]

'Going to the IIT was a huge thing. Academically, I didn't do too well. But, socially I did very well – I became the General Secretary, I networked well.'

'I have a huge capacity to postpone gratification. I think that is very critical if you want any substantive rewards.'

In Nandan Nilekani, you see the communication skills, adaptability and endurance that mark out a TauGemLib.

Love and Marriage for Him

He is your friend. This man does not want to rule with an iron rod. He would rather debate and espouse the virtues of free speech. You have to be quite independent and not rely on him for small things, for his mind is usually caught up in different ideas: he rarely has time to worry about details. He understands what is happening around him and even knows why you feel low when you do. That does not make him extra considerate, all the same.

---

[185] http://ibnlive.in.com/news/i-just-do-what-i-need-to-and-i-do-not-worry/111124-7.html

He is definitely not sombre and boring. He thinks a lot and needs a partner who helps him sort out the ideas in his head. He relaxes at home and works energetically while out. His home is his castle and he likes to let go of his busy schedule and just indulge in 'me' time at home. Give him a break before asking him to help and he will surely appreciate that.

This man is the life and soul of parties and he is not above a bit of flirting. He enjoys life and living too much to give in to sad thoughts for long. He needs a partner who keeps him intellectually engaged. He adores a vibrant mind more than pretty clothes.

As a father, he is always there. He enjoys spending time with his children especially as they grow up and start talking intelligently. He has few opinions about how things should be and is willing to listen to their side too. He opens their eyes to the wonderful world around them and makes them see possibilities in everything.

Love and Marriage for Her
She is vibrant, fun, intelligent and very loving. This woman can talk beautifully for hours but hates one-sided conversations: you have to be ready to talk with her. This lady is great at multi-tasking and astounds you with her knowledge of things beyond her domain. Aggression and domination drive her away.

Romance tops her list and she loves receiving flowers and chocolates from you. She loves change too and loves redecorating the home. She enjoys travelling and feels liberated and energised if she is out of the house at least once a day.

She enjoys buying new things and has her own brand of creativity. This lady also has tons of endurance and rarely crumbles. She knows how to tackle each situation and you never find her at a loss for words or solutions.

As a mother, she is absolute fun. She loves organising kiddie parties and does not mind filling her home with her children's friends. She is also great at creating new games and is always full of new and exciting ideas. She imparts her positivity to them and makes them see the wonders of the world.

At the Workplace
TauGemLibs have brilliant ideas. They are master strategists and fabulous at communicating their ideas. These vibrant people can never sit in one place for long and love moving about, dispensing views and clearing doubts. They are full of enthusiasm and energy but never leave their common sense behind. They astound you with their ability to learn and grasp new ideas with amazing speed. They are not just good at ideating as leaders but are also dependable enough to be entrusted with large-scale projects, which they will execute beautifully and take them to successful conclusion.

They are great at sales and marketing too. They will need to work in areas that are dynamic for they quickly get bored by the same old thing. They excel in careers that challenge them. Of course, they need to be paid well!

Libra is a cardinal sign and leads by talking and communicating, and that is how TauGemLibs lead. They are rarely dictatorial and listen to everyone, analyse, decide and then do what they think is right.

Double Air and Earth meet up in this exciting and intelligent combination. TauGemLibs will be positive yet realistic, creative yet smart and extremely good at whatever they decide to do.

Famous TauGemLib Personalities
Nandan Nilekani, Johnny Hallyday, Tigran Petrosian, Phil Mickelson, Adriana Lima, Junaid Khan.

110. TAURUS–GEMINI–SCORPIO

The calm and powerful Taurus meets the multifaceted Mercury and the deeply intense Pluto in this extremely amazing combination. Both Taurus and Scorpio are fixed signs and very powerful while Gemini is an intelligent sign. TauGemScorps bridge the gap between brutal strength and mysterious powers with an abundance of versatility and intelligence.

Taureans don't talk much but when they do, they talk plain common sense. Scorpios speaks with a measured tone while Geminis just can't stop talking. TauGemScorps speak well, with commonsensical logic. They can say much in a few words, and say it with force, beauty and substance. They are very fun loving and cheery, with a talent for impersonation.

They possess razor-sharp intelligence. While Geminis possess multitudinal ways to think through things, Taureans have the ability to make anything sound simple. Scorpios see through the deepest designs in anything: you have a person who simply cannot be fooled. But he can choose to be a master con artist or master strategist if he wants to.

The Scorpio resilience joins hands with the deep emotional stability of Taurus to give them unshakeable calm. TauGemScorps are never bothered by what people say or do. They ponder on their problems and arrive at a decision without giving in to fears and suspicions. They have a strength that cannot be destroyed by words, thoughts or deeds. They are able to read people and situations with an ease that seems akin to witchcraft. It is amazing to see them sniff out the real causes behind every problem.

They have the ability to re-invent themselves. While Gemini makes them very willing to learn new ideas and concepts, Scorpio is the sign that gives them the ability to metamorphose according to their situation. Tough times see them take on new roles. They change because of circumstances, not because they want to.

They have the Taurean love for money. TauGemScorps will drive hard bargains and know exactly how much everything costs. They can be great businessmen and will always be intent on saving and investing money to increase their power and prestige.

The Taurean sensuality, the Geminian longing for mental union, and the extraordinary passion of Scorpio combine to make them ideal lovers. TauGemScorps have one deep, passionate love in their life and can take some time finding it. Both Taurus and Scorpio make them totally committed once they find their soul mate. They need to love on an emotional, physical and spiritual level and will demand the same intensity from their partners. It will not be easy loving them and matching up to their dreams.

Stubbornness can be their most problematic trait. They are so strong mentally and emotionally that they may just refuse to see the writing on the wall. But they never show their inner fears to the world. They have the ability to look unshaken and calm in the face of difficulties. This misleads their opponents. Another thing that can win them the war is their ability at mind wars. They are brilliant in launching verbal warfare and know how to get under the skin of their opponent.

TauGemScorps are versatile and have many talents. They have at least five different ways of doing the same thing. They can also pick up languages very quickly. They are interested in arts and music. They relax to the accompaniment of rhythms and melodies.

The Scorpio vengefulness is their greatest fault. They fume and erupt when insulted or wronged. Then Taurus will wait patiently and when the tide is in their favour, Scorpio will strike with the ingenuity of Gemini. There is no getting away if you make an enemy out of them.

Their other negative traits could be indecision, obstinacy, fickleness, vacillation, getting easily bored and needing constant change and stimulus, starting something with a bang and then losing interest, cunning, and reading and manipulating people. Some of them can also be extremely money-minded, leading to greed and avarice.

TauGemScorps might take time but they soon decide where to focus their energies. This is their biggest strength. They become a force to reckon with once they identify the one thing to focus on. When they channelise their immense energies, their intense passion and stubborn ruthlessness into that goal, it no longer remains a pipe dream.

Taurus~Gemini~Scorpio – Saina Nehwal
'When I was nine, I had to wake up at 4am, take the bus, go 25 km to the stadium and then come home and go to school and then again go 25 km in the evening and sleep at ten at night. I did this (for) two years.'[186]

'I cannot sleep at night! I keep on thinking about the reasons behind losing a game.'[187]

'A champion has to be disciplined by practising regularly in the right manner, respect coaches and, most importantly, ought to have self-belief.'[188]

Saina Nehwal has the Taurean determination, Scorpio passion and the Geminian ability to speak her mind with clarity.

Love and Marriage for Him
He loves you with a deep intensity and is quite possessive about you. He wants to be everything you desire and is your lover, friend and husband, all rolled into one. Feminine virtues attract him. He is quite traditional in his views and expects you to take care of the family: he is happy to see you grow in your career provided you take care of the family's needs

This guy has a passion and goes after it single-mindedly. You have to accept this and act as a catalyst in his journey to success. He is the boss of the house even though he acts cool. Aggression is absent in his rule. He prefers a partner who can talk intelligently and hold his attention with her views.

He stands like a rock for his family. Tough times bring out the best in him. He is very fun loving, a riot of laughs and a master of one-liners. He may not tell the truth all the time and with his penchant for playing with words, you will have

---
[186] http://www.moneycontrol.com/news/features/saina-nehwal-what-dedication-can-do_505899.html
[187] http://zeenews.india.com/news/exclusive/there-are-no-sharapovas-in-badminton-saina-nehwal_546306.html
[188] http://mybadmintonbook.blogspot.in/2011/04/badminton-quotes.html

a hard time segregating the truth from the concocted. If he is bored and you don't keep the passion ignited and his interest alive, he may wander, seeking variety. But he will never let the home disintegrate.

At home, he is generally laid-back and lazy. As a father, he is loving, kind and extremely caring. He broadens his children's minds with his views.

Love and Marriage for Her
There are many shades to her personality and she is surely not frail at heart. She is a mountain of strength and reliability. She has the ability to turn tough when rough times come calling. You can always count on her. She is capable of immense sacrifices for her family. She needs a partner who understands her and is strong enough to handle her. She is never an easy girl to deal with and domination never appealed to her. She does not like being told what to do but neither does she want a partner who is extremely soft and laid back. Your passions must match hers.

You can expect energy and passion in her. This lady wants to do something in life. Whatever she does, she does it with such focus and intensity that she makes it a success. She has a creative and artistic side to her. She does a lot of things and is not content with only one path.

She has many moods too and may sometimes seem detached. Listen to her views and never brush off her suggestions, especially in public. Do not try and fool this lady for she can read your mind. She can really retaliate in ways you would never dream of. You incite her anger at your own peril. If she is capable of intense loyalty, she can also be an avenging Fury, after giving you ample chances and being endlessly patient.

As a mother, she is very good. Despite her ambitions and dreams, she has the ability to be a good homemaker. She not only dotes on her children but demands respect from them too.

At the Workplace
You have hit the jackpot with TauGemScorps. They are extremely good organisers. They work more smartly and efficiently than their peers. These guys can develop on ideas very easily. They are masters in multitasking and simplification.

From sports to the boardroom, TauGemScorps shine with their ability to understand, and deep commitment to make ideas work. Their versatile mind makes them grasp the most complex reasoning and they are able to simplify problems and translate solutions into logical actions. They have an extraordinary sense of money and always look at various ways to multiply, save or invest it. This makes them excellent negotiators or business people too. They definitely know how to get the best bang for your buck.

TauGemScorps never give up once they have a goal in sight. These guys can put in long hours of hard work, even under difficult circumstances that can wilt many. They can soak up any kind of pressure and keep themselves and others going with their goal-orientedness and also their fun-loving manner.

You can expect common sense and practical views from them. Though they speak little, their words carry force and conviction: they can deliver a passionate and intense oration. They are masters at motivating and delegating work. As bosses, they make brilliant generals and they lead with passion and team spirit. They strategise with the right mix of shrewdness and common sense.

Enthusiastic, genial, stable and highly intense, TauGemScorps weather every storm with endurance, passion and sharp ideas.

Famous TauGemScorp Personalities
Donald Trump, Saina Nehwal, Rahul Gandhi, Steven Gerrard, Arvind Swamy, Éleuthère du Pont, Arnold Vosloo.

111. TAURUS–GEMINI–SAGITTARIUS

The calm and placid Taurus gets the immense talking skills of Gemini and the knowledgeable outlook of Sagittarius in TauGemSags. They are extremely intelligent. All three signs are known for their mental abilities. Taurus gives them a logical mind while Gemini makes them excessively curious about new facts and endows them with a quick grasp. Sagittarius makes them understand the most complex ideas with startling ease.

They have unique communication skills. The Gemini power over words, when combined with the matter-of-fact Taurus and the frank and opinionated Sagittarius, makes TauGemSags an impossible combination to beat at rhetoric and declamation. Taurus thinks logically but is not articulate while Sagittarius can be quite terse. The talkative and effusive Gemini adds a touch of brilliance to TauGemSags and makes them communicate their thoughts with precision and beauty. They know exactly how to phrase their words well and are good at talking their way out of predicaments.

These people possess extraordinary mental, physical and emotional strength. Taurus makes them down-to-earth and practical with great stamina and endurance, both mentally and physically. Gemini gives them an agile mind with a silver tongue. Sagittarius makes them explorers and philosophical; it is also the fittest amongst zodiac signs. The absence of Water sign makes them free of emotional hang-ups.

They are ready to think new and unconventional thoughts without bowing down to anyone. They are survivors who endure troubles with a smile. TauGemSags are extremely positive people. They rarely give in to the deep thoughts of Taurus and are ready to be up and doing things. They are also quite ambitious. Their cheerful nature, intelligent conversation, novel ideas and loyal sentiments make them friends for life.

Though they make your day with their funny anecdotes and slapstick comedy and impersonations, don't believe everything they say. They have this funny attitude to truth: they can be extremely deceitful and add spice to cook up an interesting story. But if accused of dishonesty, they flare up angrily. They are extremely blunt and blurt out the truth when angry or provoked. They are capable of sarcastic phrases and cutting words when they are irritated. They forgive easily but do not forget.

TauGemSags are very creative. They will have some artistic talent and won't mind showing it off. They are very good dancers who pick up new steps with ease and perform them with energy and enthusiasm. They have the Taurean love for music and relax to the strains of their favourite melodies. They love the stage and are the happiest when they are under the gaze of an appreciative audience.

Love finds them a little unready for its complications. TauGemSags are having too much fun meeting new people, finding new interests to really settle down early into marital bliss. The Gemini trait of thinking there is someone better round the corner and the Sagittarian fear of responsibilities make them flee commitment for a very long time. They prefer friendship to love.

Money entices them. They want a big bank balance and are willing to gamble on get-rich-quick schemes: as there is no Water in this sign, they easily believe people who talk glibly.

They are quite fearless and adventurous too. They want to travel, explore and discover the whole world. They prefer the joy of backpacking around the world to sitting down and reading about it. Adventure is high on their list of things to do. They are naturals at sports. TauGemSags enjoy the outdoors and revel in showing off their quicksilver thinking, mental agility and endurance. They defy age and remain fit mentally and physically for years.

As there is no Water sign in them, they find it hard to read your mind and emotions. You need to tell them how you feel for they cannot read your soul and nor are they bothered to. They can chatter the day away without realising that they have hurt you in some way or been insensitive to your point of view. Despite intelligence and rationality, they are not necessarily very tactful.

They are strong on spirituality and are very religious. They are very proud of their lineage and traditions too. Expect them to be in the forefront in fighting for causes, especially those that affect the common man. They love their motherland and region and would do anything to protect the pride and honour of their country, land, religion or language.

Taurus–Gemini–Sagittarius – Anna Hazare

His crusade began with a non-violent campaign to resurrect his native village Ralegan Siddhi in Ahmednagar. Hazare steered the villagers towards water conservation. The village, which used to be barren, today has plentiful harvests and has become self-sufficient.[189]

The experiences of wartime, coupled with the poverty from which he had come, affected him. 'I felt that God wanted me to stay alive for some reason. And I decided to dedicate my new life to serving people.'[190] Anna Hazare wants his country to improve, like a true Taurean; has strong beliefs and fights for a cause, like a Sagittarian; and has always voiced his opinions, like a Gemini. He is a true TauGemSag.

Love and Marriage for Him

He wants to be the man in the relationship; at the same time, he is not aggressive and likes to be your friend. His thinking is not bound down by tradition. He wants you to be an independent lady. Though he likes his home, he is not around all the time to take decisions for it.

This guy has ambitions in life and works extremely hard for them. He also supports causes, which he is ready to fight for. He wants adventure, travel, money, status and a lot of excitement in life. Problems never break him and he is ready to face them head-on. You will be surprised at his logical clarity in times of stress.

He can make you laugh with his witty remarks, wild ideas and boundless energy. Food is his weakness. He also loves going out, partying and meeting new people. He is an open book most of the time, but you cannot believe

---

[189] http://indiatoday.intoday.in/story/the-story-of-social-activist-anna-hazare/1/134525.html
[190] http://en.wikipedia.org/wiki/Anna_Hazare

everything he says. He loves embroidering on his stories to make them sound interesting. Do not expect him to be sensitive to your emotions; he can actually be the opposite. Just tell him clearly about what you need from him.

Fatherhood brings calmness into his life but though he loves and protects his children, he does not enjoy nappy-changing roles. He is extremely good once he can hold a conversation with them. He expects them to learn a practical approach to life.

Love and Marriage for Her
She wants a partner who is more of a friend for she is not happy doing anybody's bidding. She surprises you with her ability to stay calm when things go awry. She is always full of strength and solutions. She is the support of her family in times of crisis.

This lady has a mind of her own and does not bow to anyone's strictures on how she should lead her life. She faces a constant conflict between tradition and modernity. The Taurus in her makes her want to be conservative while Gemini and Sagittarius will make her push her boundaries.

Adventurous and fun loving, she definitely loves travelling and meeting new people. She is the most positive and ebullient when she is surrounded by new people or tackling a new situation. She can really flare up or be bitingly sarcastic when she is irritated, though her temper never lasts for long, especially after she gives you a piece of her mind!

She prefers working, thinking different things and reaching out to her ambition. She loves eating and cooking. Food, travel and music are the things that make her smile. While she is very sensuous and earthy, she can also be aggressive and an experimenter in love. She is brutally honest most of the time, but she is clever enough to hide her true self if you are conservative and inconsiderate.

As a mother, she is caring, fun loving and protective. She makes her children think independently and never stops them from following their dreams. She makes them understand the need for ambition.

At the Workplace
Hard working, communicative and ambitious, TauGemSags work to achieve their ambitions of money and luxury, and want to make something big of their ideas. Routine work does not appeal to them and their indomitable enthusiasm is wasted in it. They excel as marketers. They want to do things that challenge them mentally, and even physically. The field of sports is ideal for them.

They have no trouble grasping complex theories and also have creative abilities. They do not let their creative talents go to waste and have the drive and ambition to reach the limelight. They do well in fields like education, travel, law, finance, arts and all careers that are connected to showbiz and any form of communication. If they are in business, they need to resist the temptation to get into highly speculative ventures.

They are also good at managing people without controlling them harshly. As bosses they may send confusing signals or may even lose their temper at times, but they are tough negotiators and have excellent grasp of finance.

Earth, Air and Fire give them mental endurance, the gift of the gab and indomitable spirit. TauGemSags enjoy working their way to the top and make their life an adventure worthy of them.

Famous TauGemSag Personalities
Anna Hazare, Sanath Jayasuriya, Supriya Sule, Mahesh Bhupathi, Balakrishna Nandamuri, Paula Abdul, Kemar Roach, Judy Garland.

112. TAURUS–GEMINI–CAPRICORN

The calm and enduring Taurus, the unpredictable Mercury and the staid old man Capricorn meet in TauGemCaps to give them earthy stolidity, industriousness and a command over speech.

This is a combination of great physical, emotional and mental strength. Taurus blesses them with great stamina and endurance, both physically and mentally; Gemini is mentally quick, with the ability to see all the possible sides of any question; and Capricorn has a cool practicality, the capacity for intense concentration and matchless determination. Even if they look frail they are extremely tough individuals.

Their words have value. They don't make empty talk or gaffes. Gemini makes them interesting conversationalists who are very good at expressing their thoughts and opinions. Taurus brings common sense in speech while Capricorn ensures that there is a certain maturity to their talks. But expect them to be master critics: they cut you with the sharp sarcasm and quick wit of Gemini. They are masters of mental warfare. They use cleverly chosen words to distract, disintegrate and start a panic amongst opposition, while remaining cool and calm themselves.

They also have very inquisitive minds. TauGemCaps are logical, practical and poised. They rarely display youthful folly. Unlike true-blue Taureans and Capricornians they do not mind learning new ideas and even experiment a little. TauGemCaps are quite unpretentious and practical even in their sartorial choices: they don't care for flashy outfits, preferring not to stand out.

Family is extremely important to them. They are home birds. They are affectionate people and like to include even their extended families in their plans. They are capable of sacrificing much for their families. They love feeding people, embrace them in their warmth, and form lasting bonds with people who matter, especially the family.They know how to work their charm in an understated manner and are also reliable as friends. Their sense of humour is down-to-earth. They have the knack of telling the most unpleasant things about you in the most diplomatic way.

Status and respectability are important to TauGemCap. They work extremely hard to reach the heights of which they dream. They are not content till they have a sizeable bank balance. They desire material success and stability and build a solid, long-lasting empire, brick by brick. Gemini ensures that they try their hand at new ventures to increase their earning capacity: they will not be content with only one income stream. They know exactly how to conserve money and not splurge it needlessly. Conserve, save and invest are their mantras. The only place where they spend without thinking is on their family.

Love makes them very committed partners. Chances are, they may have a few flings before they settle down, due to the flirtatious Gemini. But once they do, they make their family and home their priority. Gemini also makes them good at romantic talk and though they are shy and reserved at first, later you see their softer side.

The laziness of Taurus is offset by the strong work ethic of Capricorn and the multitasking ability of Gemini. TauGemCaps are very hard working and will not rest till they reach their goals.

Music and arts appeal to their artistic sensibilities. They prefer the older artists and musicians to the newer breed. TauGemCaps never shy away from exhibiting their artistic talents and know how to make the most of them. They have the knack of turning a simple hobby or artistic pursuit into a moneymaking venture.

Both Taurus and Capricorn have a slightly pessimistic outlook on life. Taurus makes them hesitant in taking the first step and Capricorn will never look at a glass as half full. They always see the negatives in any situation. The only saving grace is the optimistic Gemini who helps them get past their negative ideas. However, if TauGemCaps face a lot of problems, they lose their positivity and can become quite depressed.

They are late bloomers. They take time to open up, may remain secluded from people and may seem unemotional and too self-contained. They are not exactly anti-social but they do not find it easy to let their hair down while duty awaits. When they are more relaxed and meet people with an air of cheerfulness, you know that they have finally broken the self-induced shackles.

They are master strategists. Their stoic silence and black humour conceal a person who desires success more than anyone else. They plot and plan with cold rationality to reach the top of the mountain they have chosen. They are armed with the skills to do just that.

Taurus–Gemini–Capricorn – Tobey Maguire
'All the people throughout my life who were naysayers pissed me off. But they've all given me a fervour — an angry ambition that cannot be stopped...'[191]

'I experienced fame before this but Spider-Man was such an intense thing. I wanted to retreat, I wasn't particularly comfortable with the attention...I've grown to be more comfortable about it.'[192]

Tobey Maguire supplemented his professional earnings at the card table, where his well-practised ability to deadpan helped win hundreds of thousands of dollars at illegal games of high-stakes poker.[193]

Tobey Maguire has the TauGemCap desire to succeed against all odds and has its moneymaking skills too.

Love and Marriage for Him
He is responsible and caring, and never boring. This guy is full of witty humour and laughs, especially when he is with people he loves. He respects tradition. Do not expect him to change easily. His family will be his first love and he will love and respect elders. His ambition will never take him away from his family and he will always find time to spend with his dear ones.

His home is his place for rest and relaxation, a place away from stress. He thinks a lot, especially about his work, and wants it to be the place where he can

---

[191] http://ohnotheydidnt.livejournal.com
[192] www.belfasttelegraph.co.uk/entertainment/film-tv/news/tobey-maguire-eyes-right-for-a-tired-superhero
[193] http://www.independent.co.uk/news/world/americas/tobey-maguire-sued-over-winnings-at-highstakes-poker-matches-2301843.html

leave all his worries behind. Good music, food and the company of his family make him smile.

He understands you but is not interested in your emotions. Be sure to tell him if something bothers you. Express your concerns. He can talk romantic sweet nothings – but not for long. He finds it very difficult to part with his money and will try to insist on partying at home instead of expensive restaurants. But he is a superb host and a master at networking.

Keep a watch on him after he is successful and has earned his stripes or after he turns forty. He has it in him to be naughty and a little carefree after all those younger years that he spent chasing money and status: he may try and compensate for all those lost years.

He is a very good father. He is a friend to his children. He knows how to make them listen to him. He teaches them old values and discipline.

Love and Marriage for Her
She is a bit of a home bird. This lady has a lot of ambition, yet she is willing to look after her family while you pursue your goals. She is the ideal girl to take to your mom. She is a stickler for status. She wants her family to outshine everybody. She will be your support in times of crisis and can help you in your business too.

She is creative and loves dance and music. She wants to help people, especially family members in need, and turns into a benevolent matriarch if required. She is too smart to let people take her for a ride.

But remember, despite her apparent cheerfulness, there is a deep vein of doubt in her. She can be cold, melancholic and turn helpless if things don't work out for her. Her strong spirit gives up when she loses your love. If she becomes quiet, then there is definite trouble. Help her, encourage her and she shines.

If, when she is forty, she realises that after all her sacrifices, life is still not kind, she can set herself free in search of newer pastures. But she will never let her family suffer for her new-found freedom.

She is an unflappable mother. She makes sure that her children look up to her. She knows all the parenting tricks. She does not let her children endanger her family's status in any way.

At the Workplace
TauGemCaps work for the money and deliver results beyond your expectations. They are workaholics. It takes them some time to decide on what they want to do, but once they do, they use the Taurean practicality and endurance, the Capricornian stability and perseverance and the Gemini skill at strategising, to come up with great, achievable ideas. TauGemCaps excel in their careers.

They are masters at networking and know how to communicate well. TauGemCaps are never at a loss for words or ideas and think logically through every problem. Their intelligence is exemplary. They use shrewd and manipulative tactics to get their way if straightforward ones don't give results. They have many ways to do the same thing. You can always count on them to deliver, especially when the chips are down. They can be excellent businessmen with their grasp of finance and smart utilisation of resources. Their intelligence and skills suit a career as a politician too.

As bosses, they are fatherly figures and great mentors. They motivate people with great oratory. They delegate superbly and know how to build a team of people. They are great negotiators and are masters in getting things done at an economical price.

TauGemCaps combine solid ideas and speaking skills to match their endurance and ambitions. They are masters at strategising, planning and organising.

Famous TauGemCap Personalities
Tobey Maguire, Marissa Mayer, Dale Steyn, Prakash Padukone, Russell Hitchcock.

113. TAURUS–GEMINI–AQUARIUS

The patient and enduring Taurus gets a splash of colour with the versatile brilliance of Gemini and the unconventional genius of Aquarius.

The cleverest sign of the zodiac, Gemini, when combined with the most intelligent Aquarius creates absolutely bright and dazzling personalities. But both the signs are also wild and wacky: Taurus adds abundant common sense and practicality to this combination and channelises their intelligence to create something substantial.

TauGemAquas are fun-loving people. The wordsmith and communicator extraordinaire Gemini, combined with the unconventional gregariousness of Aquarius and earthy humour of Taurus, makes them a hit wherever they go. These masters of one-liners and mimicry love being in a crowd and make everyone laugh. There is a positive energy about them that attracts a lot of friends. Their skill at lightening the atmosphere is most valuable during stressful times.

They are fabulous learners and pick up new ideas with startling ease. The Aquarian desire for unconventionality plus the Gemini's quick-thinking ways build on the Taurean stolidity: they can think futuristic and exceptional ideas due to Aquarius and Gemini but the solid Taurean can also make a workable plan and execute it *now*.

They make very good friends who are always ready to help. You can pick up the phone and call them after a five-year gap and they start from where they left without a second thought. The double Air also gives them the ability to understand other people. They understand what drives others and what makes them tick. In fact, they can read through the deepest motives of people. But they are rarely shocked by outrageous views for they can out-think all those outrageous thoughts.

They maintain a calm demeanour in times of crisis. The multiple thoughts suddenly go away, they are able to think clearly and calmly when all around them are losing their heads. They also have the Taurean ability to endure anything – no problem will ever be able to dominate them for long. The Aquarian detachment also enables them to see problems from a neutral perspective.

They are quite changeable. They evolve over the years and seem different every time you meet them. The fact is that these people easily absorb new ideas and conventions and make them their own. Strangely, they can also be very fixed in their views. Aquarius and Gemini are full of ideas to change the world but find it hard to change their personal habits. Do not expect them to practise what they preach all the time.

Their search for love never ends. Gemini makes them think that there is a better person round the corner and Aquarius makes them a bit detached, even in love. TauGemAquas are romantic and know the right words to charm a person yet they will rarely commit early or stay committed for long. It takes them a long time to know what they are seeking and they can spend their life just searching for the right mate.

This is a strange blend of the materialistic Taurus and humanitarian Aquarius. While Taurus wants to accumulate wealth and create dynasties, Aquarius understands their temporal value and wants to lead a meaningful life. They may work initially with a tunnel vision focusing on that one goal of creating wealth but eventually end up upholding values that would help the common good.

There is also a flip side to all their keenness for learning – it is hard for them to settle on any one thing. They are good at many things but lack the patience to master anything: Gemini and Aquarius want change. TauGemAquas are easily bored and do not stick long to one thing until they discover a passion.

The Aquarian tendency to disconnect from reality and retreat into their own world makes them seem lost. They can spend ages thinking of abstract or irrelevant matters and forget to look at the reality around them. The Geminian way of 'adding spice' to make things sound interesting, may not go down well with people who demand the exact truth.

Gemini can be happy just thinking ideas, Taurus can be slow thinking and Aquarius can live too much in the future: they can visualise how the future may unfold and make the mistake of feeling that it is already a reality and be paralysed by inertia. They need to draw from the immense organising abilities of Taurus and work to make it a reality.

TauGemAquas have multifarious talents yet find it hard to achieve what they desire, for they lack the stability and drive to stick to anything. But they have it in them to overcome this shortcoming. The day they can draw upon the calmness and patience of Taurus and rein in the wavering Gemini and the fidgeting Aquarius, they will be on the path to glory.

Taurus–Gemini–Aquarius – Gautam Adani
Gautam Adani is an Indian entrepreneur and self-made billionaire.

He is never ruffled in the face of adversity. 'I am a very calm person. I never lose sleep,' says Adani.[194]

He was in the Taj hotel in Mumbai on 26/11. 'I was the last to move out.'

'I have seen money come and go. Neither are you happy while getting the money nor are you sad while losing it. I believe one should not worry about what is not in one's control. Destiny will decide.'

Gautam Adani has the Geminian gift of the gab, the calmness and financial instincts of Taurus, but the Aquarian in him knows the ephemeral nature of wealth.

Love and Marriage for Him
There are many shades to this guy. He is stable in his own way but is full of so many thoughts, opinions and ideas that you may feel you are dealing with multiple personalities. However, he is a good friend. You can talk of anything under the sun with him. He has no ego hassles but is very fixed in some opinions.

This man needs a partner who is independent and self-sufficient, for he has so many things on his mind that he finds it difficult to attend to moods. The best way to love him is to set him free: he needs a lot of space in his relationship. He will seem dazed and faraway at times, for that is how he is. He is excellent at communication, but he speaks little and seeks peace when he is with you.

He is quite messy in his habits and does not remember to pick up things or tidy up his closet. Don't prod him, call him lazy or tease him. He will become extremely obstinate and you will have a tough time dealing with it. Despite his

---

[194] http://en.wikipedia.org/wiki/Gautam_Adani

quirky habits, he is a genius and you fell for his intelligence in the first place. If you allow him his moments and don't become a nag, he can create magic.

As a father, he is fun. He stays calm even when he hears the most outrageous things from his kids. He likes talking to them and makes them think of things in a different way.

Love and Marriage for Her
This lady is full of life, views, opinions, ideas and everything in between. She finds it hard to sit still for long, though she surprises you with bouts of laziness in between. She always thinks of new things and loves having friends over for any occasion. She is extremely sociable.

She seems lost at times. Relax; she just needs some time to think out some odd ideas. She has some pretty wild ideas and does not easily conform. She is not very keen on housework. She likes having a career, though she is not very ambitious. Her joy lies in learning more things and developing new, interesting hobbies rather than excelling at what she knows.

She wants to save for the future, and needs a bank balance to make her feel good. Ensure that her worries about health, insurance and investments are taken care of, or she will turn into a worrywart. Her ability to get along with any person will amaze you.

As a mother, she is interested in her children but her life does not begin and end with them. She teaches them to think beyond boundaries and always supports their desires. She teaches them to be independent and loves to play with them.

At the Workplace
They are reservoirs of ideas. They can think of outstanding innovations and path-breaking stuff; the best thing is that they have the verve and sustainability to go ahead and execute those ideas too. They cannot settle in conventional careers for long and, if at all they do, they do it unconventionally. They excel in jobs that require extraordinary communication skills with a dash of practicality added to it.

TauGemAquas are good at many things and are interested in so many ideas that it is very hard to get them to focus on just one thing. Routine, monotonous jobs are not for them. They want to be challenged with something new and once they learn (for they learn with ease), they leave it for another.

They are also very good at coming up with seemingly far-fetched ideas on money and creation of wealth. Listen to them; you will thank them some twenty years from now. They can be very interested in social work and reform. They want to change the world to a better place and have revolutionary ideas about living life. They are fun-loving colleagues and unintimidating bosses. They are great teachers who teach you patiently and in a way that you remember for life.

Double Air and Earth meet in TauGemAquas and give them a flair for learning, a desire for change and a need to reinvent themselves throughout their lives.

Famous TauGemAqua Personalities
Gautam Adani, Jaspal Rana, Jodie Fields, Upasana Singh.

114. TAURUS–GEMINI–PISCES

TauGemPisces combines the solid earthiness of Taurus with the airy views of Gemini and the deep Piscean mystery. There are many shades to TauGemPisces and they always astound you with their chameleon-like ability to change.

You can expect them to talk well whenever it is necessary. Taurus will give them lucid simplicity of expression, Gemini will give them wonderful communicative abilities and Pisces will give them deep sensitivity. They are able to tell you how they feel in such a way that you actually feel and live their joys or sorrows.

There is a lot of fun and entertainment when they are around. They love having people around them and are the happiest when they are surrounded by a huge gang, playing harmless pranks on others. They have a 'live and let live' attitude.

TauGemPisces will be extremely artistic and creative. All three signs have a creative flair in them and Gemini adds to their talent by making them very good at expressing their emotions. Pisces is a very deep sign, and it is full of talent and Taurus is full of imagination. They will be original and quite unique in their thought and expression.

Both Taurus and Pisces are fairly subdued signs and are not given to flaunting their talents. They do not actively seek the limelight or take any initiative, but Gemini adds the spark to TauGemPisces. It makes them a little street-smart and gives them the voice to expound on their talents.

TauGemPisces are extremely romantic. The Taurean romantic caring, the Gemini ability to express feelings and the deep Piscean sensitivity makes them excel as lovers. Their soulful look and beautiful words can penetrate the hardest of hearts and they will surely wax poetic in love! These tender people need a lot of understanding and love in return or they will soon drift away. They will also take some time in deciding on their true love for the Gemini heart always thinks there is a better one round the corner: they take time to settle down. Once they decide, there will be none as protective, caring or sensitive as them.

They love learning and never stop evolving. The Piscean desire to learn is added to the quick-learning capacity of Gemini and makes them veritable sponges that will absorb knowledge and ideas anywhere and anytime. They can also be the most versatile people you know.

Gemini and Pisces are zodiac signs characterised by excessive thoughts and emotions respectively. Taurus imparts some stability to these two free-flowing signs. Due to Taurus, TauGemPisces will manage to stabilise their thoughts for a while and achieve something they primarily set out to do. Taurus also adds endurance to them. Yet they can also live in their illusions if not roused in time. They need people around them to help them look beyond the obvious problems.

Pisces and Gemini are dual signs with minds and emotions chasing phantasms. They are not very easy to understand. The Piscean mood swings can be quite alarming and its combination with Gemini can make you think that they are more than one person. They have a deceptiveness about them too, and do not mind changing their words to suit the situation.

Ambition does not rank high on their list. They do not hanker after filling their vaults or seeing their faces in magazines. But Taurus makes them desire monetary stability in life and Pisces loves luxury. If they chance upon it, they are happy, but don't go chasing it single-mindedly. TauGemPisces are quite lazy, too, but then astound you with their sudden bursts of activity. They will usually take life quite easy and work only when faced with a mental challenge.

The Piscean propensity to addiction is present in them. TauGemPisces experiment with new things and find it difficult to let go of some of their habits. The Gemini desire to look for shortcuts and the Piscean love of an easy life can mark them out too. You might find it hard to rely on them for they will be subject to so many contradictory ideas that you will be quite confused about them at times.

The creative genius of Gemini, the sensitive noble soul of Pisces and the solid dependability of Taurus can combine to create the greatest sports people or people connected to creativity. They can also look deep into the abyss of a self-created deceptive world. Both the options are open to them.

Taurus–Gemini–Pisces – Imtiaz Ali
'I am not a US-Iran pipeline that has some direction or flow. I don't plan.'[195]

'I was fascinated by all the different kind of people who came to the show.'[196]

Imtiaz Ali works like a true TauGemPisces, on instinct rather than direction

His knack for observing people, his Taurean music sense, Gemini penchant for crisp dialogue, and Piscean affinity for stories that wring emotions from your heart, are evident in his movies.

The final dialogue in the movie *Rockstar* probably sums up the entire philosophy of a typical TauGemPisces: '*Yahan aur koi nahi hai, koi journalist nahi koi photographer nahi, na society na rules... ye humari duniya hai…sirf hamari.* [Here, there's no one else, no journalist, no photographer; neither society nor rules... this is our world, only ours.]'

They dream of such surreal worlds.

Love and Marriage for Him
He is one of the most amazingly soft-spoken guys you have ever known. He exudes a quiet calm and charm that is unexplainable. He is very down-to-earth and does not have airs about himself. He would be a hit with your father as he would listen patiently to his grandiloquent stories. Your mother would also love him as he is not critical about how she looks or cooks.

Do not enter matrimony lightly with this guy. He is the most romantic of guys but you have to use your judgement to see whether he stands up to the rigours of married life. You have to be the more sensible and grounded one. Of course, he is loving, protective and caring, but do not expect him to remember to pay the bills on time or tidy his own cupboard.

He needs a partner who is sensitive to him and does not dominate him aggressively. He does not mind domination if you do it with tact and sensibility. The best way to manage him is to give him enough freedom to be himself. One thing is for sure – you can never be bored in his company. He loves adventure and is always ready to try something new.

---

[195] http://ibnlive.in.com/news/interview-filmmaker-imtiaz-ali-on-his-love-stories/98232-8.html
[196] http://www.tehelka.com/story_main39.asp?filename=hub170508what_love.asp

Be careful of his susceptibility to addictions, and keep an eye on his friends, for he is affected by the company he keeps. He has some far-fetched and shocking ideas on relationships and he is incomprehensible many times. He has a secret side that you can never perceive; if you can live with that, and love his creativity, then there is no one better for you.

He is a loving father who pampers his children quite a lot. He never forces them into doing anything against their will and is always there to listen to them. He is never shocked by anything outrageous they say or do.

Love and Marriage for Her

She is very feminine and artistic. She lets you rule if you adore her. This lady needs a lot of love and care. She can leave you without notice if she does not get that from you. She loves talking and wants a partner who talks to her.

She loves travel and learning about obscure customs – anything that is different from the humdrum will attract her. She needs you to put some drive in her. She is such a good learner that she soon learns to push herself if you persist. She finds happiness in small things. She does not need to reach great heights to feel good about herself. She is very patient and is a good listener. You can rely on her during the toughest times; she is your pillar of strength.

The only problem is that she gets bored very quickly. She needs to be mentally stimulated to be really happy. Do not expect her to find bliss in housework. Also, understand that she is extremely emotional and sensitive. Be nice to her, and try and understand her.

Her children always get her attention and no task is too difficult for her to do for her little ones. She loves talking to them and is always there for them.

At the Workplace

TauGemPisces do extremely well in careers that have artistic scope and challenges. They want to be in a place that offers constant change. Put them in routine jobs and see all their optimism and joy wither away. They not only want to be paid well but also want to be challenged in what they do.

The Piscean ability to absorb, observe and learn quickly, the Geminian versatility, gift of the gab, power of written and verbal expression, and Taurean natural sense of arts, music and creativity opens up a plethora of options to them. They are good artists, actors, and directors and do well in fields that allow them to travel, see new things and meet new people. They are also extremely good writers and poets, and versatile sports people as well.

They are bosses who will give you a long rope, and are very flexible.. Expect the unexpected from them. They change their plans any time or just go with their gut feelings.

Earth, Air and Water meet in this extremely innovative and original combination. They will need special handling to achieve their full potential.

Famous TauGemPisces Personalities

Ajinkya Rahane, Andrei Arshavin, Helen Hunt, Imtiaz Ali, Kirron Kher, Malaysia Vasudevan, Wally Hammond, Jess Cameron, Erin Osborne, E.M.S. Namboodiripad.

115. TAURUS–CANCER–LEO

The patient and enduring Taurus meets the stylish and regal Leo and gets a dose of emotions and sensitivity from Cancer in TauCanLeos.

They have a calm exterior. The cool, calm, collected, sober and sane person you see is the tip of the iceberg. They are the most peaceful characters around, until you poke or provoke them.

Taurus gives them an innate serenity and calm confidence, which is real. They mind their business and prefer peace to anything else in life. The soft and sweet Cancer in them is deeply emotional and sensitive to other people's behaviour and moods. TauCanLeos will never meddle into your affairs unless you invite them.

What you shouldn't forget is that deep inside them is a self-respecting, proud Lion. Besides the Leo pride, which will not tolerate insults them, Taurus hates being teased and Cancer is extremely touchy and sensitive to others' remarks. So let these soft creatures alone and leave them in peace.

They stand like a rock for their family. Family is sacred for Cancer and they adore their mothers. Taureans like to be with their family. They love their homes and enjoy home-cooked meals. Cancerians love cooking and Taureans love feeding others. Leos love playing magnificent hosts. These people are extremely attached to their families and hate being parted from them.

They have a very sharp memory. They will not wax eloquent but talk succinctly with feeling and logic. They can describe an entire movie in a few words. They also like giving advice.

TauCanLeos definitely like comfort around them and spend their money on making their immediate environment comfortable. They like soft beds and indulge in long baths and love smelling good. They like to dress well but keep an eye open for bargains. Despite their fondness for money, they are not misers. They have a generous streak in them and want to give to people less fortunate than themselves. Family and friends also get their share of the TauCanLeo largesse.

Love will be very important for TauCanLeos. They want to be adored and smothered in love. TauCanLeos are very romantic but find it difficult to express their emotions. But look in their face and you will know exactly what they are feeling. They absolutely melt when in love, and become sentimental softies. All the three zodiac signs are known for their romantic nature. They give a lot in a relationship and are ultra loyal too. But there is a catch – they do not like to commit to a person who is financially unstable and doesn't have a good family background.

TauCanLeos will want to do something big in life. They will not only dream but also work towards that goal and will shine all the brighter when they hear applause. They want glory and money too.

TauCanLeos have a very creative side and can surprise you with their hidden talents, especially in music and arts. They need a little shove to showcase their talent for though they like the stage and the applause, they are a little reserved at first.

There is a finality about everything they say or do and it is very difficult to make them change their minds once they have decided something. TauCanLeos can be quite stubborn: the only time you can change their decision is *before* they decide.

Remember that Cancer makes them hypersensitive. They can read between lines and see imagined slights. The Leo pride, too, doesn't stand being ignored or injured. Do not make fun of them in public. They like to maintain their dignity and are very hurt if people say things against them. These are the times you may see them flare up and display their temper. In the worst cases, they will sulk days.

They are very traditional at heart. Taurus respects custom and tradition; Cancer is always wary of anything new and Leo likes to maintain its honour at all costs. Expect them to uphold conventions and be sceptical of anything modern. Don't go by the sunny Leonine personality they display. They resist and take time to change.

They have much insecurity within them. Cancer worries about the future, of being poor or losing all that they have. It makes them clingy, stingy, moody, edgy and fearful. Despite their outer bravado, Leos have deep-seated fears of inadequacy. They feel that they may not be up to what is required to excel. The TauCanLeo will have all sorts of fears and insecurities about money, future, relationships and their family.

Laziness can also be their bane. Taurus and Leo both are lazy and are rarely enthusiastic about any activity. But when emergencies strike, they stand tall. They can withstand any calamity or problem in their lives with the tough endurance of Taurus and the extraordinary tenacity of Cancer. They know how to deal with the worst situation with grace and firmness. They can get stubborn about many things in life – sometimes extremely so – but when things go wrong, they stubbornly refuse to give up.

Taurus–Cancer–Leo – Sridevi

'I was enjoying every moment of bringing up my daughters...I don't believe in doing both. When I was working, I was totally giving my 100 per cent. When I am with my children, I want to give my 100 per cent to them.'

'When you are watching your movie with your husband and children you should feel proud about it and not ashamed of it.'

Question: Do you cover the eyes of your children when they see kissing scenes?

Sridevi: 'Yes, I do. I do. Now, I don't need to tell them, they automatically do it.'[197]

Sridevi has the extraordinary creative energy, the single-minded purpose, the love for motherhood, and the traditional outlook of a true TauCanLeo.

Love and Marriage for Him

He has a possessive streak and is also quite traditional in his attitude. He is not excessively rigid, though, and is able to understand your views too. He wants your undivided attention when he speaks. He is very emotional and sentimental in love

---
[197] http://www.youtube.com/watch?v=jQoIUOVtytA

but finds it difficult to express himself. Look out for the signs instead. He wants to be treated with respect. Although he is not aggressive, do not laugh at him

He is a provider and a very responsible husband. He wants to build a solid foundation for the financial security of your family. Don't upset his plans and increase his worries by spending more than necessary.

Home is the only place where he puts his feet up, so let him. Music and food are the two things that relax him. He can surprise you with his talents and abilities in both spheres. He loves having his friends over and feeding them.

As a father, he is perfect. He is caring, nurturing, protective and understanding. He gives them a lot of advice but also allows them to take their own decisions.

Love and Marriage for Her
She is a woman of indomitable strength and boundless love. She cares for her family and stands strong as a rock in times of peril. She is an ideal wife who loves her home. It is her top priority despite her ambitions.

She takes care to dress with style and has an added glamour that makes her stand out in a crowd. Do not think that she likes secondary status. She has her views and gets her way with her smile. She loves travelling to places that are near water yet always pines for home when she is away.

Money never passes unaccounted from her hands. This lady knows how to look good and maintain a good bank balance, both at the same time. She can go through extreme black moods if there are monetary worries. Just ensure that you are not the root cause. She loves cooking and can make mouth-watering delicacies, but do not expect her to spend her entire life in the kitchen. She is amazingly creative, especially in art and music.

She can be stubborn too and it is difficult to get her to listen to your views once her mind is made up. She is also quite romantic and wants you to remember all the important dates.

As a mother, she knows just what to do. She wants to be around her children and can let her career take a backseat for them. She teaches them to work hard and strive for their dreams.

At the Workplace
TauCanLeos are able to do anything to which they set themselves. They want money. They are your most loyal workers if you pay them adequately and praise them well. Their loyalty is very high: they usually start and end their careers at the same place. They like working in fields that offer breaks between high stress periods, for despite their ability to work hard for they will not kill themselves with work. They are also exceptional in creative arts and finance. They can excel as smart business people too.

They do not mind starting at the bottom and assiduously work their way to the top. They are the most hard-working employees and affable leaders. They are never aggressive and get their work done by motivating, coaxing and cajoling. They are extremely good at getting maximum work done with minimum budgets. In the beginning, you may think that they could be a bit more modern in their approach, but after a few years you will be stunned by how right they were in their approach and amazed by the way they saved the organisation from going bankrupt.

Earth, Water and Fire combine in this extremely strong and determined combination. TauCanLeos will endure the darkest problems to shine bright.

Famous TauCanLeo Personalities
Sunidhi Chauhan, Sridevi, Narayana Murthy, Sergey Brin, Vijayalakshmi Pandit, Emmanuelle Beart, Kristen Wiig, Jennifer Lawrence, Nathalia Kaur.

116. TAURUS–LEO–VIRGO

Grounded, driven, ambitious and stylish, TauLeoVir combine the calm authority of Taurus with the fiery ambition of Leo and the meticulousness of Virgo. TauLeoVir is a double Earth combination as both Taurus and Virgo are Earth signs, with a strong stabilising effect.

TauLeoVirs speak with plain common sense and are not given to flighty ideas that have no solid basis. They dream of do-able things and don't spend their time thinking extravagant ideas which cannot be accomplished. They are very intelligent. They like to attract attention with their talk and ideas. Logic, common sense and deep analysis mark their decisions. They are given to analysing an issue down to its bare bones; it is hard to fudge facts with them.

There is a fun side to them too. They love a good laugh and are the most easy-going creatures till you step on their pride. They love slapstick comedy and have a great sense of humour but they never lose their dignity. They are loyal friends who are ever ready to help. Duty, love and care are attractively mixed in them. They make a lot of sacrifices for their families.

Their appearance matters to them. The flamboyance of Leo and the fastidiousness of Virgo make them choose their clothes with care. TauLeoVirs want to be perfectly dressed for any occasion. They love everything big – a big car, a big house, a big bank balance, and a big career.

The Taurean love for music and art combines beautifully with the Leo desire to show off its talents and TauLeoVirs do not shy away from displaying their capabilities. They are quite artistic and musical. You can expect the Virgo perfectionism to make itself felt in their appreciation of art and music and their execution of both.

TauLeoVir are certainly receptive to love but don't expect them to change their ways or lose sight of their long-term goals. They take a little time to settle down, for they feel unequal to the responsibilities of commitment; but once they say 'yes' they keep their word. They also want a partner who adds to their prestige and shares their belief in living a life of respectable stability. But don't think they are boring in romance. TauLeoVirs love wooing and being wooed with all the trimmings of love – remember flowers, anniversaries and gifts when you are with them. They are also deeply sensual, but they hide that side of their personality with refined behaviour.

They have their days well planned and their ideas sorted out into neat compartments before they awake. Running wild, being disorganised and arriving late are not traits that you find in them. They adhere to routine with fanatical dedication. But they have their lazy side. They are capable of immense hard work, but they need their beauty sleep too.

Money is important to them, both as a sign of success and as security for the future. They know how to save and invest, and are not happy till they have a bank balance that they feel they can retire on. They have a fondness for comfortable and luxurious living. They revel in aesthetics, pleasures and materialistic comforts. Food is their weakness, but if their Virgo component is strong, it can make them abstain from rich food. They are good hosts. A party with them is a party to remember, with good food and music, and personal attention to the guests.

Their anger is quite controlled. They do not easily lose their cool; they endure problems and calmly look for solutions rather than giving vent to unreasonable anger. Of course, they have a knack for constructive criticism which is hard to counter. They are extremely stubborn. You can move mountains but not change their opinion when they have made up their minds, especially when challenged or angry.

They are not emotional fools. In fact, they are devoid of sensitivity because of the absence of Water signs. They will not be able to read your soul or be perceptive to every emotion, but they more than make up for it with their sound common sense and warm sentiments. In fact, with their sense of duty and love for protecting the weak, they often take up social causes and spread their largesse around.

TauLeoVir are very fixed in their ideas and opinions. They are not open to change and prefer doing things in the conventional manner. They go about taking the safe route and have well-thought-out reasons for doing the things they do. If you want to change their decisions then give your input before they make their final decision – you will get a chance, as they usually take time to decide. They may be subdued in style but they demand and command respect. Respect them for what they are and you will have all doors opening up for you.

Taurus–Leo–Virgo – Claudia Schiffer
Exercise continues to play an important role in her life – from dancing to horseback riding, tennis and skiing. She doesn't wear jewellery, she doesn't drink or smoke and she's proud of never having taken drugs.

'I see anorexic, exhausted models, who in photos look as though they're drugged or shattered by all-night partying. Fashion is beauty, not this.'

'I'd like to be more happy with myself. I've always thought I should be more extroverted – more this, more that. But you have to learn to accept yourself as you are.'[198]

Claudia Schiffer prizes health and is well grounded despite her pride in her habits; a true TauLeoVir indeed.

Love and Marriage for Him
He is the provider. You do not have to worry about unpaid bills or long periods of unemployment with this guy. He is aware of his duties and strives to fulfil them. He is very traditional and wants a partner who is an ideal wife. He also wants a partner who respects him and his ideals.

He has very fixed ideas on certain things. The best part about him is that you know him thoroughly. He likes doing things in certain ways at certain times. His habits are fixed and he rarely surprises you with unknown friends or untold secrets. He loves travelling with his family.

He wants his home to be the place where he relaxes. Do not put emotional stress on him for he finds it very hard to handle emotions. This guy needs to be told if there is some problem for he does not discern much from your sighs. He is very sentimental about his loved ones, but will remain cool and nonchalant and hide it in humour. He expresses his feelings through warm, tight hugs, by feeding you and taking care of you while you are sick. Never tease him or insult him before

---

[198] http://www.vogue.it/en/beauty/beauty-icons/2010/02/claudia-schiffer

others or you will lose him forever. When he gets into that stubborn mood, you will find it extremely difficult to break his stoic silence.

He is a very loving father. He does not mind taking over some of the baby duties. Academics are important to him and he stresses good studying habits.

Love and Marriage for Her
She loves her home and enjoys taking care of it. You can expect well-kept rooms and good food with her around. She does not mind pampering you but please remember to say thank you and tell her how much she means to you.

She is the fulcrum of her family. She likes joint families. She spends her free time sorting out problems, travelling with a wagonful of relatives or advising them on the correct way to do things. She is not content if her bank balance is inadequate. Let her follow a career and see her happy every time she puts in a deposit.

The best way to make her stop her nagging is to take her to a music concert or compliment her well on her care. Give her some time to relax and put her feet up. She needs to laze around and is happier after a good sleep or a massage or aromatherapy session.

As a mother, she excels. She knows which medicine to give for a belly ache and how to sing a disturbed child to sleep. She inculcates good values in them. She may find it hard to understand their unconventional thoughts.

At the Workplace
TauLeoVirs excel in any career. They are ambitious. They have clarity of thought and spot the tiniest of errors. Their stamina and intense concentration at work is awe-inspiring. They also bring in a certain style, flair and substance to their work. They fulfil every job with an extraordinary finesse and ensure its logical completion. They also pride themselves in getting the work done well and at quarter of the cost.

Remember to pay them well. They work their hearts out but will not work at mean-hearted prices. They need the occasional pat on the back too. They positively glow when recognised and appreciated, but will pretend to brush it off nonchalantly.

Finance, research, analysis and creative fields beckon them. They want to work where they do not have to travel much. As bosses, they are good at motivating their subordinates with ideas, opinions and vision. They are also great at delegating. Be truthful, do your homework, be prepared with the relevant figures and be ready to answer some critical questions if you report to them, or you will be in deep water.

Double Earth and Fire combine in this deeply grounded and driven combination. Loving, protective, prudent and generous, TauLeoVir excel at home and work with an emphasis on care.

Famous TauLeoVir Personalities
Claudia Schiffer, Akkineni Nageswara Rao, Dadabhai Naoroji, Mother Teresa, Indu Jain, Ishant Sharma, Vinoba Bhave, Periyar E.V. Ramasamy, Alex Blackwell, Claudette Colbert.

117. TAURUS–VIRGO–LIBRA

The calm and enduring Taurus joins the perfection-seeking Virgo and the beauty-loving Venus in TauVirLibs.

The first thing that you notice about them is their amazing calmness. They seem unruffled, unperturbed, tranquil and serene. Some of them have that brooding intelligent look on them with the forehead crinkled in deep thought. Then they turn on the magic with that soft, touching smile. You find peace around these characters.

You will never suspect the inner turmoil that these people can go through. The Libra in them continuously analyses every situation and the Virgo is stressed about getting everything in perfection and in order. They do get themselves tied up in knots over details and deep analysis of matters under scrutiny. But the Taurus gives them stability and helps find simple solutions to complex problems, after all the mental gymnastics.

They are very intelligent and have a fantastic memory. The simple common sense of Taurus and the clarity of Virgo combine well with the analytical views of Libra to make them very intelligent and sharp. They have a flair for written and verbal communication that will be both precise and beautiful.

They love talking but intersperse their intelligent chatter with periods of silence. You can be sure that their agile minds never rest, even during self-enforced periods of quiet. They do not change their mind once it is made up for they really have thought through all the implications before deciding.

They are quite jovial and have a happy, witty way of talking about people and situations. But do not take their non-aggressive nature for granted for they can really hit back when they are provoked.

Double Earth in Taurus and Virgo makes them very grounded in their ideas. Libra makes them see new ideas, yet they are quite conservative in their approach. They have a deep love for their motherland and are also very traditional in most of their views. They find it easy to divide people into groups of 'us' and 'them' and are very protective of their group. They are good friends: loyal, considerate and very caring. They are not frivolous in their affections.

Waste and vulgarity really irritate them. They mourn any kind of loss, be it monetary or of traditions and values. They love routine: there is a right time for each thing. Libra and Taurus are foodies and naturally food entices them. But the Virgo in them will ensure that they conquer their taste buds and choose healthy food. The Virgo's natural inclination to healing care-giving and Libra's understanding and Taurean dependability makes them very reliable when you are sick or in any case of emergency.

They love pampering themselves with luxurious baths and expensive gifts. Both Taurus and Libra love to surround themselves with luxury. Laziness is part of their makeup. When they work, there is none as hard working as they; but when the time comes to relax, they can remain lying in one place for hours.

They never overspend for they have a fear of losing money. Money is important to them and they plan their earnings and savings. They have an extraordinary sense of investments and will always look for ways to increase their wealth. It's really interesting how these people try – and manage – to get material success without actually having to work too hard.

Love will find them a bit confused in the beginning. The romantic Libra loves to be in love; but the modest Virgo can fear love. They might think that they are not good enough or that the object of their affections can do better with someone else.

TauVirLibs appreciate creativity. They are quite artistic in their own right and love singing and dancing. Music relaxes them and you can be sure to hear them humming a tune when they are happy. They combine the beauty of art with amazing perfection and create masterpieces.

These gentle people can really lose their temper. They are very critical and get angry when they are irritated. TauVirLibs will buzz like angry bees or just explode. Hold back your retorts for you will not be able to counter-argue them.

However modern they look, do not forget that there are two conservative Earth signs in them. They are practical, methodical and slow in their ways and will not be pushed into anything. They can be extremely subborn, especially after they have made their decision after hearing everybody's opinion.

This combination lacks Water and has a double dose of Earth. This makes them a little insensitive despite their caring ways. TauVirLibs cannot guess what lies behind the sighs of their loved one. They can spend a lot of time in hair-splitting analysis and introspection but find it hard to decipher emotions without being told.

If you overlook their occasional laziness, their inability to take quick decisions, their hair-splitting analysis and habit of stressing themselves, or even their stubbornness and certain unbending values, you will find a solid and enduring person who is truly dependable in any kind of stressful situation in life.

Taurus–Virgo–Libra – Hugh Jackman
'I go to the gym in the morning, as much for a state of mind as a physical state.'[199]
'Vegan to me always seemed sort of strange, but I read the book, the benefits and that's when I started to twig that maybe I should have more energy and not kill myself eating that animal protein.'[200]
'I have a terrific marriage, but unlike a lot of relationships where they ebb and flow, no matter what happens, you fall deeper and deeper in love every day. It's kind of the best thing that can happen to you.'[201]
Hugh Jackman is a true TauVirLib – a family man, conscientious, loving and romantic.

Love and Marriage for Him
He is a sweetheart! He is the one you always longed for: loving, caring, romantic, calm, dependable and understanding. He is a fantastic companion: he can talk to

---
[199] http://screencrave.com/2008-11-26/exclusive-interview-hugh-jackman/
[200] http://www.askmen.com/celebs/interview_600/623_hugh-jackman-
[201] http://www.brainyquote.com/quotes/authors/h/hugh_jackman.html

you for hours and he even listens empathetically. But be warned – he cannot read you completely. Don't expect him to look deeply into your eyes and read your soul.

You have to care for the house. This guy just wants to put his feet up and relax. But don't get worried: at work, he is really hard-working. He is quite traditional in his views. He wants to be your friend and to be respected. Do not try and topple his throne for he likes feeling the lord of the manor. He encourages you to work and explore your possibilities as long as you pay attention to him at home.

He is fun too. He knows how to make you laugh and is full of jokes and good cheer. You can be sure of his attention for he responds with views, ideas and opinions. He is your rock in times of stress. He sorts out each problem and does not give up till he wins the battle. Just do not burden him with emotional stress at such times. His worst moods are his overly critical ones.

As a father, he is perfect. Caring, loving and extremely protective of his children, he does not shirk child duties. He will help out at the nappy-changing stage and he can also give impromptu tuitions to his children. He is a chilled-out father who insists on good education.

Love and Marriage for Her
She is a full of good cheer. There are very few things that make her lose her joyfulness. This lady is the happiest looking after her family and also earning some money for herself. She needs to feel financially secure or gets really depressed. Her family is extremely important to her and she loves keeping her house neat and tidy.

She loves talking and giving her opinion. If you see her bad, irritable moods coming on, take her to the spa: she revels in a massage and being surrounded with fragrances. Take her out to eat at her favourite restaurant, too.

She needs you to gently push her when her lazy moods make her give up on her work. But she wants a partner who lets her be herself, for though she is a soft soul, she does not like being dictated to.

Her children are her pride and joy. She enjoys spending time with them. She insists on good behaviour and knows how to make them listen to her while having fun with them. She insists on good education. She deals with them with humour, attention and care.

At the Workplace
TauVirLibs are extremely analytical and are smart about money. They are great negotiators and their excellent communication skills make them adept at striking good bargains. From finance to creative fields, they can dazzle with their wit and capacity to think of every possibility. They are equally adept at mentally or physically challenging work and can soak up high-pressure situations. They also need lots of free time in between hectic hours of work to unwind.

They are loyal workers as long as they get paid adequately for their efforts. They make good lawyers, financial gurus, musicians and actors. They bring perfection into everything they do. They are calm bosses who have a plan and strategy in place. They are very democratic and soft, but will not pay you more than your exact worth. They never keep yes-men around them and are always open for a discussion.

Double Earth and Air makes TauVirLibs intelligent yet lazy, creative yet opinionated, with a deeply ingrained sense of honour and tradition.

Famous TauVirLib Personalities
Hugh Jackman, Vladimir Putin, Roger Moore, Brigitte Bardot, Sivakumar, Julia Gillard, Meghna Reddy, Vadivelu, Arvind Mafatlal, Basil Zaharoff.

118. TAURUS–LIBRA–SCORPIO

The calm and patient Taurus meets the romantic and luxury-loving Libra and the extremely passionate Scorpio in TauLibScorps.

You can feel their deep emotional strength even before they speak. They look like they can take on anything in life head-on with an astonishing impassivity. Taurus blesses them with extraordinary will power and an icy-cool temperament. Scorpios are powerful, instinctual, with a deep penetrating intensity and a seething magnetism. And there is the mesmerising and alluring Venusian smile. An extraordinary package.

TauLibScorps speak beautifully. They speak with Scorpio's intensity, Taurean common sense and unassailable Libran logic. They think carefully and go deep into the roots of an issue. After the analysis, when they look into your eyes and talk about it, you are swept away with the effortless brilliance of their words.

You are assured of a good time with them. They have extremely sunny natures and love laughing out loud. The Taurean sense of humour and the Libran airy ways will make them pleasant companions who care for you and make you laugh too. The plain-speaking groundedness of Taurus and fun-loving and companionship-seeking Libra will help in mellowing the intensity of Scorpio, but it will always be there.

There is also a deep emotional and sensitive side to them. They feel hurt quite easily and may hide it for a long time. Both Taurus and Scorpio give them the ability to face troubles calmly despite their inner turmoils. They are also armed with the Scorpio sting, so beware of injuring them or you might provoke vengeance.

They know how to endure the greatest failures and come out on top. Never underestimate them. TauLibScorps can weather any kind of calamity thanks to their endurance and mental strength. Yet their sensitivity can also make them suffer greatly. They can become very depressed or give in to the Scorpio urge for revenge or self-destruction. As Libra and Taurus are peace-loving signs, the inner turmoil and seething anger of the Scorpio is internalised and can be harmful to them. They need to vent their anger; at least in words. Be with them at such times for they need to see a friend around them.

They have deep love for their families and people close to them. They are rarely untouched by their problems and always try to care for them. They are the emotional rocks of their family.

Ideas and views will abound in them; so will their desire to try new things. TauLibScorps will never be intimidated by the unconventional. But they rarely go overboard in experimentation despite the Scorpio tendency to do so. Libra adds its dose of balanced thought to them and Taurus will add its desire for stability. Hence despite their strong passions and volatile expression, they can control themselvelves admirably.

No one can love as intensely, passionately, completely, madly and unconventionally as TauLibScorps. The Libran love of love and the Scorpio intensity can make them fall hard when they fall in love. They give a lot of themselves and expect the same intense, unconditional, uninhibited, no-holds-barred love from their partners. They can be driven to despair if it doesn't happen that way. The volatility in their nature gives way to extreme expressions of love and hate and can destabilise them for some time till good sense prevails.

There is a creative side to them. Taurus gives them a love of music while Libra has great artistic talent. TauLibScorps will try their hand at something creative and will be good at penning verses. They are also smart enough to make their artistic pursuits pay them as well.

They enjoy travelling and meeting new people. But they like to travel in comfort. They like relaxing and lazing around in comfortable, even luxurious surroundings. They cannot tolerate smells or untidiness. TauLibScorps love perfumes, cosmetics and the rituals of grooming.

They can be quite stubborn. They will out-argue you everytime. When they explain your mistakes point by point, you will have nowhere to hide. Once they have made a decision, they stick to it, come what may. They take a long time to decide, though. They get angry; and beware: they have an explosive temper. When wronged, they will get even with with their smile intact. They have to win at any cost, but they will not lose their cool while doing it.

Money is important and they are good at investing and saving. They want to build a financial empire and retire rich early. They have excellent memory too: especially of hurts and insults.

Their propensity for excess is a weakness – it can be in anything – food, clothes, even love: both the emotional and the physical expressions. When uncontrolled, they can lead to addictions. They can also go through extreme vacillations of the mind, which peak especially before they are craving, or falling in or out of love – the one thing of which they can never get enough.

Taurus–Libra–Scorpio – Sushmita Sen

'I am ambitious but my ambition is not limited to the film world. If I do so, I would be undervaluing myself.'[202]

'I've faced all the hardships in my life as and when they've hit me. Whether it was the sudden spurt of success as Miss Universe at 18 or the battle in the courts to adopt my daughter Renee, or my relationships, failed or successful; they've all been full of turmoil when it happened.

I craved for marriage forever. I've always been a home-lover, in spite of living a very public life.'[203]

Sushmita Sen loves her home, is a true romantic but is also a strong individual, a true TauLibScorp indeed.

Love and Marriage for Him

He is very loving and quite romantic. You won't have to remind him about important dates nor will you have nudge him to get presents. He is good at talking too. You certainly hear a lot of views and opinions from him.

---

[202] http://ww.smashits.com/sush-films-are-not-the-be-all-in-my-life/interview-4240.html
[203] http://entertainment.oneindia.in/bollywood/features/2007/sushmita-sen-290107.html

He is lazy at home. When he works, he works very hard but he hates to be disturbed during his siesta hours. He loves listening to music, and will invest in a good music system. His artistic tastes are quite evident and he will definitely have a say in the house décor.

He likes to lead but is rarely aggressive in his views. He is definitely opinionated but the good thing is that he is rarely judgemental without a good reason and you can always argue the matter with him. He is loyal and always repays kindness with kindness. Do not forget that he is a bundle of emotions within and tread carefully around his ego.

As a father, he is a complete family man. He loves spending time with his family and is very protective about them. He dominates without controlling and his laughter and good cheer spread to the children.

Love and Marriage for Her
She is very sensuous, sensitive and sensible. She knows exactly how to charm a man, talk her way into his heart, love him to death and be as passionate as he could ever desire.

She enjoys being a wife and is quite happy in a nurturing role. She is also very emotional and needs a partner who understands her need for passionate romance. You have to really love her and show her your love in many ways, from flowers to romantic getaways.

Despite her seemingly emotional frailty, she is the rock for her family in times of crisis. No calamity can shake her calm strength. She is very good at reading you. Be good when you are with her for she knows from your body language about the mischief you have been up to. Remember not to break her heart for she rarely forgives and forgets.

She loves being creative and is good at artistic pursuits. Music has a soothing effect on her and she can spend hours listening to her favourite numbers. This lady wants her home to be neat, clean and aesthetically pleasing. She also needs help with housework. She loves buying new things and surrounding herself with luxury. She takes retail therapy quite seriously though she always budgets her spending.

As a mother, she is fabulous. She loves spending time with her children and encourages them. She also dominates them but in such a soft manner that it is pleasing to them.

At the Workplace
TauLibScorps excel in fields that require communication. They are not fond of working in routine jobs and like professions that allow them long periods of rest after strenuous work hours. They are able to work harder than anyone else when required, but do not like a job that has hectic schedules on a daily basis.

They are extremely intelligent and good at finding solutions to problems. They are also very good as writers and artists. They are intensely passionate about their career and go about it seriously. They excel in creative fields, fashion, sports and anything to do with finance. They want money and respect in equal measure.

As bosses, they are great motivators, and fantastic team leaders, leading from the front. They are great at budget control and money management too.

Earth, Air and Water meet in TauLibScorps and fuel them with vivid imagination, commonsensical logic and enough passion to carry their dreams through.

Famous TauLibScorp Personalities
Sushmita Sen, Aditya Vikram Birla, Nani (footballer), Prithviraj Kapoor, Dr. Amartya Sen, Konkana Sen Sharma, Silk Smitha, Aaron Finch, John Keats, Roberto Cavalli, Tina Brown.

119. TAURUS–SCORPIO–SAGITTARIUS

The cool and calm Taurus meets the passionate Scorpio and the knowledgeable Sagittarius in this extremely strong combination. TauScorpSags have a traditional and conservative approach to life. They prefer to appear sensible and responsible rather than fun loving.

Imagine a Bull with the power and speed of a Horse and the venom of a Scorpion! Complete the picture with a sting instead of the tail. Deadly isn't it?

All the three signs are known for their forbearance and calm attitude in times of stress. They are very stable people who never fall prey to emotional storms. They have high levels of endurance and a positive outlook. The fire of Sagittarius does not allow them to stay gloomy for long while the endurance of Taurus and the strong emotional self-control of Scorpio make them pillars of strength for their families.

They are good conversationalists with a great sense of humour. There is a madcap intelligence about them. Sagittarius bestows them an innate ability to understand the most abstract of subjects while Scorpio simply *knows*. Add to it the practical outlook of Taurus and you have a person who is absolutely at home talking intelligently about the most abstruse, the most revolutionary or the most mundane subjects with a touch of wacky humour.

They surprise you with the many shades to their persona. They are the most dependable, logical and sensible people around. They can also be the most adventurous, break parochial conventions and have unorthodox ideas, which they propagate with scorching intensity and honesty.

They always think and weigh the consequences before doing anything different. They also like to gamble, but stop while the going is good. But they never lack the courage to try something new that will lead them closer to their dreams. They don't shy away from adventure.

They are fighters. They simply won't give up on anything. They just hang in there with the endurance of Taurus, the awe-inspiring self-belief of Scorpio and the battle-ready Sagittarian spirit. They are fiercely honest. When they speak out, the truth hits you in the face; but you realise it is nothing but plain, commonsensical truth that you avoided looking at.

They have the Scorpio ability to sense the deepest emotions in people. They can simply read your mind with amazing quickness. While this helps them be sensitive to people close to them, it also helps them while dealing with people they meet everywhere. They deal with any situation in life with superbly finessed defense. They can also go into attack mode if they want, but will avoid it until necessary.

While Taurus is at its sensual best, Scorpio revels in eroticism and Sagittarius loves experimenting. These people can be shockingly honest about their liaisons and experiences. TauScorpSags take some time to decide on their true love but they are committed and loyal once they do. They are very caring and protective of their beloved and expect the same devotion and passion from their partner.

TauScorpSags rarely forget hurts, or forgive them: they have the Taurean memory and the Scorpio thin-skinned reaction to insults. They will remember, wait patiently, and then unleash the sting in their arsenal. Their anger can be hard to withstand, for it is fierce. The good thing is that they have an iron control over it.

There will be a creative side to them too. TauScorpSags love music and art. They relax with their creative pursuits and are good at turning their talent into career options. They are very highly evolved spiritually. Their deep understanding and logical deductions on spiritual subjects, the mysteries of the world, and abstract ideas will perplex you.

The downbeat qualities of this combination are that TauScorpSags can be possessive, materialistic, jingoistic, rebels without a cause, regressive, traditional, controlling, tactless, quarrelsome, and obsessive about winning and succeeding at any cost.

They are extremely stubborn. They cannot be dominated by anger, or controlled. They flare up and become extremely obdurate if forced to do something. Once they decide to do something, it's difficult to make them change their mind. With the passion and intensity of Scorpio, the hope and knowledge of Sagittarius and practical outlook of Taurus, they stay put. Look at this trait positively!

Taurus–Scorpio–Sagittarius – Kirk Douglas

'People say that the old movies were better, that the old actors were so great. All I can say about the old days is that they have passed.'
   'My kids never had the advantage I had. I was born poor.'
   'When you become a star, you don't change. Everyone else does.'
   'I've made a career of playing sons of bitches.'
   'In order to achieve anything you must be brave enough to fail.'[204]
   'I guess I was a bad boy…yes, yes, I've had lots of women in my life.'[205]
   Kirk Douglas has the subtle humour, common sense, candidness, rebelliousness, endurance and passion of a TauScorpSag.

Love and Marriage for Him

He is an ideal provider and protector for the family. He is the rock of the family. He wants you to rely totally on him. He is traditional enough to want a wife to be feminine and a husband to be the boss. He definitely prefers a partner who doesn't rock the boat or creates a sensation with her dress sense for there is a tinge of possessiveness in him, too.

However, he is not very dominating. He is good with money too, neither stingy nor too extravagant. His Sagittarian side makes him a good friend but he likes to have the upper hand. He is his most chilled-out with you around. He relaxes with music and is full of ideas for parties. He is a foodie and loves feeding people. You'll need to have enough ideas to help out here.

He is intensely passionate about every aspect of life. Be ready to share his passions. Though there are many shades to his personality, one good thing

---

[204] http://m.imdb.com/name/nm0000018/quotes
[205] http://www.brainyquote.com/quotes/authors/k/kirk_douglas.html

about him is that he will tell you the truth – always. Though he will never do anything that will affect the family, he will always confess the smallest slip he makes.

As a father, he commands respect, but is fun loving too. He loves going on holidays with his family and likes to have them around him most of the time. He provides such logical solutions that his children always run to him with their problems.

Love and Marriage for Her
She is the strongest link in the family. This lady works for her family's success and wants them to enjoy power and prestige in life. She pursues her ambitions but is willing to take the back seat if her husband is ambitious enough. However, you can be sure that she excels in back-seat driving!

She is the partner for you when times are tough, for nothing ever deters her from securing her aims, and she strives with superhuman endurance. She is a rock, despite her femininity; but she is still vulnerable enough to feel hurt easily. Be good to her for there are very few who can match her endurance or loyalty.

There are many sides to her and she is not easy to decode. She has in her the sunny temperament of Sagittarius, the practical femininity of Taurus and the deep secretive nature of Scorpio. She is very intelligent and is a match for any conversation and any situation. She will surprise you by reading your mind and will also never be too shy to dance the night away. She can don any role and the best part is she can get along with any kind of people in your family.

She is extremely creative too and puts it to good use. Take her out; new places and people interest her, though she soon longs for her own home. She rarely gives way to sadness for she is optimistic. She loves eating out. She is a good cook plus a good host. She loves feeding people.

As a mother, she is extremely caring and protective. She pampers her children but without spoiling them. She teaches them to aim high and plan well, and they benefit from her teachings.

At the Workplace
Passion, intelligence and application, in equal parts, are in them. TauScorpSags work wonders wherever they go. They need to find a passion, and then they excel at it, withstanding any obstacle with their steely resolve and abundant fortitude. Though they are good in any kind of work, they are extraordinary at execution. You can consider the job done once you ideate and give them the outline. Money and power are extremely important to them. They can trample on people and their egos in their quest for both.

They are good with money and can be canny businessmen or investment advisors. They are fabulous negotiators too. They enjoy working with numbers and understand complex theorems with ease. They can also be good at politics. Sports too attract them. The grander the stage, the better, and they revel in it. As bosses, they are absolutely in control, hands-on, and good at dealing with both the aspects of a business – people and money.

Earth, Water and Fire meet in this extremely strong combination to give TauScorpSags amazing endurance, stupendous intelligence and intimidating power.

Famous TauScorpSag Personalities
Ashley Cole, Kirk Douglas, Pratibha Patil, Emperor Akbar, Arun Jaitley, Alyssa Milano, Jennifer Connelly, C. Rajagopalachari, Dr. Rajendra Prasad, Tim Paine, Jonathan Swift, Cheran.

120. TAURUS–SAGITTARIUS–CAPRICORN

The calm and enduring Taurus meets the intelligent Jupiter and the wise old man Saturn to make TauSagCaps extremely intelligent and highly ambitious. The immense physical strength and extraordinary emotional power of these people can be guessed by the three animals that constitute this combination: a Bull, a Goat and a half horse, half man Centaur. Extraordinary! Even if they look matchstick-thin, don't underestimate their physical strength. They are iron-willed too. The Bull gives them the staying power to endure, whatever the situation, the Goat toughens them to climb any mountain and the Centaur blesses them with extreme positivity. Powerhouses indeed!

The double Earth effect of Taurus and Capricorn make them extremely grounded. They have a calmness that belies their drive and ambition. TauSagCaps are extremely responsible too. Capricorn is known for its mature ways in childhood. Add to it the rock-solid enduring qualities of Taurus and you find them mature in their outlook.

Family is very important to them. The Sagittarian aversion to family ties is quite diluted due to the double family-loving signs, Taurus and Capricorn. But do not expect them to submerge themselves in their families.

If, looking at their calm, you think they are boring – think again. The excitement and optimism of Sagittarius is also present in them. They are amazing friends, full of vibrant fun when the time is right. Taurus and Sagittarius will combine to make them great foodies and you will never leave their home without an epicurean delight. Their sense of humour is more veered towards slapstick than understated jokes.

Both Taurus and Capricorn are diligent, hard working and efficient, without any flamboyance. Sagittarius adds panache to them and makes TauSagCaps come out in the open with their opinions. They know how to grab centre-stage and thunder when required. The professor of the zodiac, Sagittarius, makes them very intelligent and they can talk on any arcane subject with the common sense of Taurus and practicality of Capricorn.

TauSagCaps are extremely ambitious and want to be financially independent. Sagittarians need the limelight while Capricorns want to reach the top and Taureans want a bank full of money to relax. TauSagCaps will never be content being average. They want to shine, hear applause and make a mark. They want money, glory and everything that comes in between! They are extremely smart about money management too. Taurus rules money and Capricorn rules career; both of these would be their focal points, besides the family, of course.

There is a creative side to them too. Both Taurus and Capricorn are artistic and love music, but are hesitant to showcase their abilities. Sagittarius erases their inhibitions and they are ready to shine. The drive, optimism and derring-do of Sagittarius is evident in their acts. The reverse-aging syndrome of Capricorn makes them more fun as they age. They will lose some of that extreme responsibility baggage and learn to enjoy life more after they achieve part of their dreams by the mid thirties.

They love travelling and exploring new places, sampling new cuisine and discovering new ideas, but they are just as happy coming back home. The wildness of Sagittarius is quite reduced in them but the brashness pops out every now and then. While they take time to reach decisions, they also find it hard to change them easily. They may seem traditional but they keep us grounded and realistic.

Most of the time, when irritated, they are patient and expect you to understand their displeasure. But if they are tried too far, they can get quite angry. They do not bottle up their opinions and are likely to be blunt: expect to hear the bitter, hard truth when they shout. But, thankfully, they do not lose their temper at the drop of a hat.

It is interesting how many of the Sagittarius-Taurus combinations are fearless fighters. The Sagittarius in them finds a cause and wages an eternal fight. Taureans love their motherland, and you see them in the forefront resisting any force that would oppress their countrymen.

While Taurus is traditional and conventional, Sagittarius is extremely spiritual and Capricorn revers customs. TauSagCaps are followers of old virtues, morals and traditions. They delve deeply into spirituality and other traditional sciences, understand the deeper forces of life and are aware of their influence.

TauSagCaps lack Water and Air and this makes them highly opinionated. They will find it hard to understand another's point of view until they are told. They may not be too sensitive to others' emotions, nor are they diplomatic or sugarcoat their words. But their immense mental, physical and emotional strength is what you depend on in times of uncertainties.

Taurus–Sagittarius–Capricorn – Bal Thackeray

'Balasaheb's hallmark was spontaneity. He liked to make statements that shocked and made headlines, though in private he was a shy and even timid person.'[206]

'He has been a good family man, a traditional husband and a good father to his children. He respected his wife very much. It was his father Keshav Thackeray who mentored him into public life.'[207]

Bal Thackeray had the fearless honesty of Taurus and Sagittarius. The son-of-the-soil views were very Taurean and his love for tradition, family and respect to father, typically Capricorn. He also had the Sagittarian love for the good things in life – he enjoyed his cigar and didn't mind the spotlight.

Love and Marriage for Him

You have a guy who never lets you down and strives for the betterment of his family and status. He ensures that the bills are paid and that his family enjoys success. He is extremely ambitious and appreciates it if you do not cling to him. This man needs a wife who is independent enough to handle home and even her career, if she wants. He likes to be the authority at home but is rarely aggressive. Respect his views and give him a patient hearing. That keeps him happy and contented.

---

[206] http://www.tehelka.com/bal-thackerays-hallmark-was-his-spontaneity-he-liked-to-make-statements-that-shocked-and-made-headlines/2/
[207] http://artoflivingsblog.com/what-is-wrong-with-bal-thackeray/

He is quite conventional, and likes you to follow family traditions and customs. If you are a free spirit who wants to dazzle the world, he may not be the guy for you. He will honour, respect and adore you if you make his family the centre of your universe. He does not understand silence or reproachful looks. Tell him how you feel; he then tries to make you feel better.

He wants to spend the evenings partying with friends or eating out. His mantra is to work hard and party harder. He enjoys music and dance. You will have an exciting time with him and he will show you the world, as he loves travelling. He loves luxury and comforts, so you can make him part with money for those, even if he is unwilling to spend freely elsewhere. He is working towards the financial stability of your family, so is a bit tight-fisted. Don't get him worked up on those matters.

He is a great father. This man knows how to get respect from his children while playing with them. He effortlessly mixes cheer with sternness and they adore him. He does not mind taking time out for them and also listens to their unconventional ideas without losing his cool.

Love and Marriage for Her
This lady loves her family and is rock-solid support for them. She also has her own dreams. Ambition is important to her and, though she may stay at home for some time, do not expect her to give up her life for mere praise: she has the ability to dream big and will work towards it with drive and responsibility. Status is important.

She is able to handle anything life throws at her with cheer and enthusiasm. She is more rational than emotional and tells you whatever she feels. She expects the same from you.

She needs free time to feel good about herself. The best way to bring a smile to her lips is to take her out for a meal or let her spend time at a spa. Food, lovely fragrances and, of course, time out for herself, make her feel rejuvenated. She likes to travel to exotic destinations and does not mind going trekking so long as she is sure of the destination.

As a mother, she excels. She loves doing things for her children and is very content. She teaches them the right values and encourages them to respect traditions. She neither pampers nor dominates them.

At the Workplace
TauSagCaps are extremely ambitious. They are ready to work long and hard for their dreams but do not like being in the background. The dependability of Taurus, the complex code-cracking intelligence of Sagittarius and the extreme maturity and diligence of Capricorn make them favourite employees of tough, demanding bosses. They have extreme physical and mental strength and can work under any kind of circumstances uncomplaininglyt.

They are able to think big and achieve their ambitions. Money, glory and status are all that they want. They can do well in creative arts and thrive in the attention. Their extraordinary knowledge and skills of finance can be a big boon to any organisation. As bosses, they lead from the front, are fiery and temperamental, and brutally honest, but will be father figures and mentors of success.

Double Earth and Fire makes TauSagCaps an unstoppable combination. They will be driven yet grounded, fiery yet logical and extremely persistent in achieving their dreams.

Famous TauSagCap Personalities
Bal Thackeray, Vikram Pandit, Raghuram Rajan, Giancarlo Fisichella, Krishnam Raju, Maria Goretti, Danny Kaye, Seema Biswas.

121. TAURUS–CAPRICORN–AQUARIUS

The calm and enduring Taurus, the old man Saturn and the inventive genius Uranus meet in TauCapAquas to endow them with stability and a sense of purpose along with a streak of inventiveness that is hard to miss.

There is a sense of unruffled calm about TauCapAquas. They rarely hurry into a decision. Rashness of any kind is completely absent in them. Even when they seem impulsive, they really have thought about it for some time. The calm and placid Taurus and the ever-old Saturn give them this talent of always thinking through their actions.

TauCapAquas are extremely focused in life, despite Aquarius's attempts to make them think of many different and unconventional routes. They have a tunnel vision for their ultimate goal. What that goal is might take some time for them to work out but it will definitely involve money and status along with adventure.

Status and respect are extremely important to them. TauCapAquas want to be looked up to and work hard to garner status in their life. But the good thing is that the sparkle of Aquarius and the earthy humour of Taurus stops them from becoming deadly bores about their ambition.

There is a stolid practicality about them. They do not like talking a lot, but when they do, you can be sure to hear some sense. The Aquarian need for rebellion is quite toned down in them, but it is definitely there. Whenever they try and act rebellious, you will rarely be shocked, for they make their rebellion sound like the most reasonable thing to do. These guys can envisage the most outrageous things but know how to make them look logical and practical.

They are responsible from a very young age. They might be the youngest in the family but never seem that, for they speak logically and take on responsibility with such ease that they rarely seem childlike. As they grow older, the reverse-aging process of Capricorn shifts into gear and they seem more chilled-out in their thirties than in their twenties.

Family is extremely important to them. They can sacrifice anything for the happiness of their families. They like to travel with their families and do not like being away from home for too long. Their sense of humour is fantastic. They tell you your faults to your face without sounding hurtful and know how to laugh at themselves.

They have many friends but are close only to a few. There is a constant struggle with friendship as the Aquarian in them wants a large crowd, but their inner core longs to be left alone. TauCapAquas also like networking. The shrewd Capricorn in them knows whom to befriend and why.

They are sensitive to others. Aquarius helps them to understand people and they do not foist themselves on those who do not wish their company. They can read through the deepest needs of people and are smart enough to utilise those instincts to fulfil the needs for mutual benefit. They are adept in showing a win-win situation but you can be sure that *they* are the ones getting the best and biggest share of the pie.

Another interesting area for TauCapAquas is in relationships. The rebel Aquarian in them has a devil-may-care attitude about what society thinks of their affairs. But the traditionalist Capricorn and peace-loving Taurus in them wants the acceptance of their family before finalising a life partner. They would ideally seek a middle path and a win-win for all. TauCapAquas can be very sensuous in love but might find it hard to put their feelings in words. The curiosity of Aquarius and its open-minded, independent views on relationships can also make them try to know more people but they are not serial lovers. They ultimately look for security and respectability.

TauCapAquas have a lot of creative talent too. Taurus is known for its love of music and arts while Capricorn also has hidden talents. Aquarius adds magic to their abilities and enhances their talents with a touch of quirkiness. Once they realise their talent TauCapAquas know how to make the most of it by dint of hard work, planning and very good networking. They are able to give a new twist to an old art and present it in a stunning manner.

Taurus and Aquarius make it a double fixed sign. This means it is difficult to convince them of something different from their way of thinking. These guys take time to make their decisions and don't change their mind easily once it is made up.

There is a melancholic air to them, especially if things do not go as they planned. Taurus makes them a little hesitant and Capricorn can turn despondent if their plans go haywire. Aquarius also makes them quite detached at times. They need loving and understanding people around them to help them move out of their self-inflicted miseries.

They never forget their old values and are courteous, especially in public. They respect the advice of elders. These guys combine old values and beliefs with a slightly new way of thinking – it always gives them an air of being midway between elderly caution and rebellious young thoughts.

Taurus–Capricorn–Aquarius – Durjoy Datta

'People have told me I am selling sex…But that's the kind of people and stories I know. People do sleep around these days and cheat on their partners.'[208]

'These days, love doesn't mean as much as being in a relationship.'[209]

'I like to write books that are entertaining and contemporary. I have no illusions about the fact that the book that I write today may not be in the bookstores fifteen years down the line.'[210]

Engineer by education and writer by passion, he has co-founded a publishing company too. Durjoy is bold and far-sighted, has a practical, commonsensical approach and is a smart entrepreneur – a true TauCapAqua indeed.

Love and Marriage for Him

He is a very good husband. Both Taurus and Capricorn fill him with deep love for his family. He can be full of pranks and jokes with his family and can be a riot of laughs when the mood overtakes him.

He needs and desires financial security and respectability above all else. He needs you to understand his deep ambitions. He also needs some space to think

---

[208] http://www.openthemagazine.com/article/books/the-lovey-dovey-boys
[209] http://www.thehindu.com/life-and-style/nxg/article95535.ece
[210] *Society*, August 2012

his wild ideas. He may bring work home, occasionally, but consciously tries and spends time with his family if you tell him to. Emotional sulks and tears do not work with him.

He wants a partner who doesn't flout traditional values just for the heck of it. He has his wild side and the good thing is that the wild side becomes wilder as he grows older!

This guy will pay all the bills on time and worry for his family in times of crisis. He wants to be the responsible one, though he may not pick up his clothes or tidy his cupboard. He needs a little help there. At home he wants to relax, lie around and listen to music. He doesn't mind handing you the reins of the house if you pamper his lazy ways!

As a father, he is excellent as Capricorn rules fatherhood. Aquarius makes him understand their rebellious nature. He teaches them to be independent.

Love and Marriage for Her
She is an ideal wife. She loves her family and wants to be part of a huge loving group, but without losing her identity. She is quite creative and ambitious yet can sideline her desire to work if your ambitions seem adequate.

More than anything else, she desires social standing and security. She is quite careful about money and does not make impulsive purchases. She needs a little help in the sensitivity department, for though she loves her family, she does not read people very well.

She handles money beautifully. She can work it and make it grow. She is excellent at budgeting. She acts as the glue that binds the family together. She loves holding family meetings and feeding everyone. She is the happiest when she spends time with family, with all the cousins and in-laws thrown in.

As a mother, she is fantastic. She knows how to get her children to do her bidding without losing patience. They adore her for she never lets them down and helps them through every problem.

At the Workplace
The inventive genius of the Aquarius can think of the wackiest ideas ever. The industrious Capricorn will sift the workable inspiration from the imprudent and create a master plan. The practical Taurean will make sure that the entire enterprise is financially viable and bears fruit. These guys are outlandish and far-reaching in their thoughts but have the gift to make them work in the practical world. An Aquarian would have the germ of an idea which can be a practical reality only fifty years from now, but when combined with Taurus and Capricorn, it can happen *now*.

TauCapAquas are brilliant and dedicated workers. They do not mind routine jobs and find a way to do them faster and more productively. They can think out of the box without being impractical and always work to make a success of their lives.

They are good at politics and also the creative arts. They know how to use their circumstances to their best possible advantage. As bosses, they are brilliant ideators and extraordinary executors. They can handle the grandest of projects and make it succeed.

Double Earth and Air make TauCapAquas strongly opinionated, stable, practical and intelligent with ambition to match their quirky thought processes.

Famous TauCapAqua Personalities
Durjoy Datta, Helen Clark, Zoe Cruz, Jessica Biel, Raju Sundaram, Rahul Roy, Bhagyashree Patwardhan, Ghulam Nabi Azad, Annu Kapoor.

122. TAURUS–AQUARIUS–PISCES

The calm and steady Taurus meets the highly intelligent Uranus and the deeply sensitive Pisces. TauAquaPisces combines strength, detached emotions and a philosophical attitude. The three elements, Earth, Water and Air, come together in TauAquaPisces and impart their three different and unique flavours to it – the earthiness and stability of a Taurean, the supreme intelligence and eccentricity of an Aquarian and the sensitivity and poetic nature of a Piscean.

This is an amazing congregation of the ancient wisdom of Pisces, the unconventional, futuristic intelligence of Aquarius and the solid, down-to-earth, logical practicality of Taurus. Their minds are very expansive. They are shockproof and can think and imagine the weirdest to the wildest. But they somehow know how to distill their thoughts and present them in the most palatable way to people as they are extremely perceptive and sensible too.

Pisces and Aquarius make them great at empathising. They can actually feel the depth of your sorrow and the exuberance of your happiness. They are not rigid in their views and never judge you. You can be a murderer or their tormentor; they will be able to put themselves in your shoes. They can never get into a fight or argument wholeheartedly, for they know why you did all that you did.

TauAquaPisces are emotional and sensitive, but don't let emotions rule them. They amaze you with their detached empathy. They are not easily affected by the emotions raging around them. Talkative and fun loving, they have lots of friends, but the twist in the tale is that they like being loners too.

They are traditional. Taurus ensures that they are not flighty or given to extreme wildness. They are levelheaded and mature. This makes them a big hit with their elders. It is only in the company of friends that their wacky irreverence and eccentric ideas surface; for others, they are a model of good behaviour and stability.

The Piscean in them makes them want to belong. They will be soft and loving, but if they feel unfairly treated, they will quietly move out and you will never find them again. The Aquarian aloofness makes it easy for them to tune out emotions they don't want.

TauAquaPisces have a strong creative streak. They like trying out new things. The intelligence of Aquarius and the Taurean capacity to work hard will see them add brain and will to their ideas. Neptune, the fountain of thought, Uranus the lover of invention and the steadfast Taurus give a logical outcome to their imaginative ideas.

Money is a confusing thing to them. The Pisces in them is absolutely non-materialistic but loves the luxury that money brings; Aquarius, too, doesn't want it now but worries for the future; but the Taurean knows the value of money and needs it. They want to live the classic life of a poet in a garret, with wonderful ideas – but usually also strive to make and save money as well. Some of the TauAquaPisces can be at the other extreme too. They can be super-smart in money management and have a perfect plan in place for early retirement.

They have one irritating habit though, thanks to the Aquarian in them. They get easily distracted during a serious conversation and interrupt it with the most unrelated gossip. You may start wondering whether you had their attention in the first place. Of course, they heard you, but too much of anything bores them.

They are always willing to try new ideas and not stay confined to one thought, but once they make up their minds they are very stubborn about it. They suffer from bouts of uncertainty. They think that their talents are not good enough, which stops them from achieving their true potential. You have to push them gently to make them realise their strengths.

They can also become excessively nonconformist, as well as pessimistic, irrational and brooding, especially when things don't go their way. Some of them can also become moody, withdrawn or reclusive and have unfounded fears and phobias. They can get angry, though they are usually calm, and suddenly fly into a rage. They are emotionally stronger than people who may merely look commanding. These soft-looking people are able to endure big problems with a cheerful countenance.

They may fall prey to the vice of addictions and revelling in sensual and other pleasures. Pisces hates routine and Aquarius is super-inquisitive about everything in life; when it combines with the Taurean love for food and sensual pleasures, TauAquaPisces can become escapists who shun responsibility and immerse themselves in time-wasting activities, and may even turn hedonistic or avaricious.

Aquarius and Pisces make for a high spiritual quotient. In fact, they are intrigued by any esoteric life science. Past life regression to future life progression to alternate healing methods – all appeal to them. Once they overcome their inadequacies and are well settled, they will always look for ways to give back to the society. They are humanitarians and understand the transient nature of everything in the world.

Taurus–Aquarius–Pisces – Jackie Chan
'I want to do charity, I don't know how many people I can help, but it makes me happy.'

'I always travel around the world to speak to young children. First, work hard then only think about money. When you have money, return to society, pay back. I poor, now become rich, I give back [sic].'[211]

Jackie Chan, actor, action choreographer, comedian, director, producer, martial artist, screenwriter, entrepreneur, singer and stunt performer, is a fine example of the potential of a TauAquaPisces. He is also a keen philanthropist and a UNICEF Goodwill Ambassador. Jackie Chan personifies the good-heartedness of TauAquaPisces.

Love and Marriage for Him
He is a soft and emotional guy. He is neither aggressive nor does he expect you to be docile just because you are a woman. Women with independent ideas do not faze him, but do not try and get aggressive with him. He cannot be submissive for long.

His extreme dedication to his work and desire to strive for a better life make him work long hours and spend a lot of time at home, thinking about his plans. He

---
[211] http://www.nationmultimedia.com/entertainment/Full-interview-with-Jackie-Chan-30120657.html

gets hurt easily, so you have to be sensitive to his ambitions and dreams. Sometimes he may look lost and spaced out. Allow him those moments – they are therapeutic to him.

He may not be very clean. You really have to try hard to keep the house neat and tidy. He is lazy too. Just control the urge to shout at him when you see him lie in that cozy corner doing nothing except listening to music and demanding good food. Have you any wacky, outstanding, amazing or adventurous idea with which to fool around? He will venture out willingly.

As a father, he loves and understands his children. He is their friend rather than a commanding figure and they run to him in times of stress.

Love and Marriage for Her
Totally feminine, this girl is very stable and rooted with the calmness of the Taurean. She is not aggressive or dominating. However, do not take her submission for granted. She is made of steel and can withstand any pressure. If treated unfairly, she responds by walking away without a backward glance.

She also has a passion in life. She may not be ambitious but wants you to understand her need to do something beyond caring for her family.

She needs to be loved and wanted, and shies away from conflict. She is a great companion, but needs constant reassurance; she needs to feel good about herself. Moodiness afflicts her and she needs you to understand those moods.

Space is important to her. She wants love, yet is detached. Let her find her balance and when she wants to be alone doing her own thing, let her. Remember that she has the Taurean stubbornness too. She will be the most flexible of creatures, but once she digs in her heels, it will be very hard to make her change her mind.

As a mother, she is not bothered about marks or grades. She understands that children need to be happy and do things they like rather than what society demands.

At the Workplace
TauAquaPisces do not abide by routine. They would rather work where creativity flows and where every day brings a new way! It takes them time to know what they really want to do, but once they know what they want, they pursue their dreams. Hard working and reliable, they do not let go of their ambitions without trying really hard.

They want money and work harder for an assured amount. Power and prestige do not usually excite them as much as the chance of doing something new. They are fast learners; they will speak your line of thought within days of interaction.

They can be good psychologists. Any field that deals with people or ideas attracts them. The intelligence of the Aquarian and creativity of a Piscean will ensure that their ideas will be unique. It will also make them turn their creative ideas into viable enterprises.

They are also good at acting, music, and even human relations. In fact any venture related to creativity will see them at their best. As bosses, they maintain the perfect balance between ideas and business. They are open to any new idea that is pioneering but are also keen on it raking in the profits.

Conservative yet creative, loving yet detached; TauAquaPisces will surely create a new way but without treading on toes or squashing any egos.

Famous TauAquPisces Personalities
Jackie Chan, Ajit Wadekar, Lothar Matthaus, Bette Davis, Reba McEntire.

123. GEMINI–CANCER–LEO

Mercury, the messenger of the gods, the sensitive Moon and the regal Apollo come together in GemCanLeos to impart the gift of speech, creativity and a sunny assurance. GemCanLeos have a beaming smile and an optimistic demeanour during the best of times. These positive and energetic people come with many facets to their personality.

Gemini gives them the gift of the gab. They delight you with their talk, ideas and thoughts. They are able to think of a thousand amazing things in a moment, thanks to Cancer's fertile imagination. There is never a dull moment in their vivacious conversations. They are always ready with some witty remark or wild jokes to liven up the moment. The Gemini in them can add some creativity to the story and colour the truth a little. Don't fret: it's their way of making things more interesting.

They like style, and are often the style icons of their group or community. They also have a flair for learning new things, especially languages, and do not like to spend their life doing only one thing. GemCanLeos are always ready for a bit of fun and frolic. These vibrant people like to be outdoors or with a lot of people around them.

They love their homes and families. They consciously try and make time for family trips even if they are extremely busy at work. You see a very loving and sensitive side to them when they are surrounded by their favourite people. GemCanLeos love being pampered and looked after: they become almost childlike in the vicinity of their mother. In turn, they act like a big brother or sister to younger people, and are very caring and protective of people they love.

GemCanLeos are very romantic and sensitive in love. They say and do the right things: they know what makes a good romance! GemCanLeos can fall in love more than once. Gemini's flirtatious nature and Leo's romantic leanings make them go through a few relationships, but sooner or later their heart will be trapped and they will be willing to settle down with one love. But they feel claustrophobic when smothered by over-possessive people. GemCanLeos like the idea of freedom yet are happy with one person too. But if things don't go well they won't stick on for life, for better or for worse, like a typical Cancerian would. They have the capability to move on and try their luck again.

Cancer and Leo make them very good with food. GemCanLeos like trying out different cuisines and are good at creating new dishes too. They are excellent hosts. GemCanLeos have the Gemini trait of multitasking. They are very smart about money. They know how to save and invest without being stingy. However, they tend to make impulsive purchases and worry about the expenses later.

GemCanLeos are very creative: all three signs hold creative powers, and they do not let their talent go unnoticed. Leo makes them want to take to the centre stage and Gemini makes them smart enough to grab the opportunities to showcase their talent.

They hide the sensitive Cancerian side and prefer to show only their luminous Leo smiles to the world. They are liable to feel hurt by thoughtless remarks, even if they don't show it. They can be quite insecure deep within, which only to their closest friends and family members know. They worry about their fallibility, and emotional and financial stability.

They can sulk, and if not handled properly, can explode into full-blown temper tantrums. They need to be cajoled into a good mood. If rubbed the wrong way, they can be bitingly sarcastic. Beware of getting into verbal duels with them – you will emerge badly bruised. They will tell you unpleasant home truths you'd rather not hear. If they are not given the love or importance they crave, or if insulted, they hit back with a volley of verbal missiles.

They have a deeply spiritual side to them. Both Cancer and Leo believe in a force greater than themselves. They will shed a few secret tears but show their brave face to the world and march on with the faith that everything will be fine one day. They love being leaned upon and being pillars of strength. They do it just by being there – for eternity.

Gemini–Cancer–Leo – Nagarjuna

'I believe acting is not the be-all and end-all of life. I take Sundays off. After my shoot finishes, I immediately head off to my home and enjoy quality time with my family. I also go to the Maldives regularly for scuba diving.'[212]

'I am very conscious about the way I look. It pays off. Health is something I work very hard at.'[213]

'I enjoy acting as it's ever-changing. In six months you are doing something different, getting into a new character.'[214]

Nagarjuna combines the versatility of a Gemini with the Leo love of style and the Cancerian tenderness towards family.

Love and Marriage for Him

He wants to be your most loved, respected and adored person. This guy does not mind talking about his emotions and need for love. There is no way you can feign ignorance about his deep desire to be loved and cared for. Independent women do not put him off. He sees you more as a friend. This guy is sensitive and, though he is not aggressive, do not walk all over him as Leo makes him egoistic too.

He does a lot for the family and you are always his top priority, so it is not hard for you to love him. He loves his mother too and wants you to have a cordial and loving relationship with her.

He likes surprising you with gifts and knick-knacks. More than anything else, he loves the look of surprise on your face. This guy will rarely forget important dates and will be good at planning something special for each one of them. Be ready to think of some ideas for him too for he does not mind being pampered. He loves any excuse to party and invite his huge gang of friends. Be ready to feed friends and family on short notice.

As a father, he is wonderful. His children always seem the most brilliant and the most talented to him and he loves pampering them. He talks to them, tries and understands them and is very nurturing too. He only demands respect from them. He finds it hard to let go when they grow older.

---

[212] http://www.telugucinema.com/c/publish/stars/nagarjuna_new.php
[213] http://www.idlebrain.com/celeb/interview/nagarjuna.html
[214] *People*, April 8, 2011

Love and Marriage for Her

Grace, sensitivity and charm come naturally to her. Heads turn and necks crane when she enters the room and it is not only for her style but also for her wit. She knows how to talk beautifully and sensitively. She is a natural agony aunt and wraps her adoring fans in the cocoon of her attention. Vanity and concern are the two extremes of her personality; it is amazing how both work in tandem to create her unique style.

She is very romantic and expects you to remember important dates. Do not act unconcerned when she sheds tears but rush to offer solace. She needs tons of attention and lots of love. She likes to have a career and financial independence. She is a hostess extraordinaire and has superb culinary skills to showcase too. Never make the mistake of trying to make her a doormat – she will put you firmly in your place.

She loves ruling over people. Drama and melodrama are her forte. She does not mind gossiping either. She loses her temper rarely, but if people deliberately cross the line, insult or ridicule her, she can be caustic, or spout fire. No one can dream of winning an argument with her. Despite her brave dramatic front, she has many insecurities, including over money and love. You will have her love for life if you can keep her secure and reassured.

She is an ideal mother. She is ready to play games, tell stories and kiss away tears. She loves to spend on her kids and always encourages them. She wants respect too and can be a strict mother, if needed.

At the Workplace

Creative, communicative and ready to take charge, GemCanLeos are good at whatever they do. They have a formidable imagination. Routine work does not interest them as much as work that requires them to think. They have three basic needs – respect, appreciation and money. Give them these three and they will never let you down. They are loyal so long as you realise their worth.

They can take creativity to new levels and add zing to it. They need applause and space to build on their creative thoughts and are natural delegators. They can work hard but prefer to work smart. They are good at jobs that need a lot of talking and guiding from the front. They are savvy marketers and add drama to sales. They can be good leaders, who use persuasion to lead. They are expressive, nurturing and fun loving as bosses, but never cross that invisible line between the boss and you.

Air, Water and Fire mix in GemCanLeos, and give them energy, imagination and a regal flair. They want to be respected and pampered and know how to reciprocate with love and emotions.

Famous GemCanLeo Personalities

Nagarjuna Akkineni, Uddhav Thackeray, Shiv Nadar, Urvashi Dholakia, Steve Wozniak, Vijayashanti, Geeta Kapoor, Meg Whitman, Ramakrishna Hegde, Guillermo Vilas, Gina Lollobrigida, Sean Penn, Robin Van Persie, David Headley, Evonne Goolagong, Chinni Jayanth.

124. GEMINI–CANCER–VIRGO

Mercury, the changeable and intelligent messenger of the gods, meets the highly emotional Moon and the inherently perfect Virgo in GemCanVirs.

Identifying these people shouldn't be very tough. They have this worried, intelligent look, as if they are forever analysing something. They have a measured smile, and rarely laugh out loud.

GemCanVirs are very intelligent. The Gemini's quick grasp of different ideas, aided with the Virgo's intense and detailed analysis, makes them experts on everything they speak about; their thoughts are always fully researched ideas. They love talking, and pepper their talk with anecdotes and witty observations. The Virgo's perfect command over language, the Gemini's ability to communicate beautifully, and the emotional quotient of Cancer ensures they are riveting speakers. Interestingly, despite this love of talking, they also like periods of solitude.

They are smart. GemCanVirs can easily read into the ulterior motives of others. They know when they are being used and rarely allow it to happen. They also have a very sharp memory. They remember faces, facts and even emotions. Their Gemini creativity can also lend colour to their imagination or make them colour facts to suit their needs. But they colour it so seamlessly that you cannot distinguish it.

Family holds a special place in their lives. The Cancerian in them will revere their homes and mothers and Virgos can be extremely self-sacrificing in their responsibilities towards home. They also make excellent parents themselves. They love reminiscing about their childhood and past homes. They are deeply conscientious and responsible.

They are very talented and know how to best utilise their talents. There's not a lazy bone in a GemCanVir. They are always busy working away at an idea or thinking of something different. They amaze you with their Geminian ability to do more than two things at one time, and do them with perfection.

They also like to keep themselves healthy and fit. They eat right and exercise well. They also stick to certain routines. They are natty dressers and prefer clean, immaculate lines to expensive brands. They generally like their environment to be spick and span. Messy untidiness makes them drop everything else to create a more organised space, for it really bothers them. Wastage of any kind is abhorrent to them and they like holding on to their money.

Love finds them at their sensitive and analytical best. They like a partner with whom they can converse and who is interested in new ideas. GemCanVirs are very nurturing and emotionally attached to their love. Once they are committed, they usually remain so. Gemini can also make them harmless flirts but usually their heart will be in the right place. If they cheat, you have no chance to catch them: they do it with the Virgoan perfection. But the Virgo would actually prefer to cut ties and move on than stick to a dead relationship. At times, the Gemini desire for change can be strong in them and they can keep wondering if there is a better love waiting somewhere.

They are very emotional and sensitive. Do not be fooled by their cheerful, talkative exteriors: they can get hurt. Their Virgo aloofness can make them hide their tears, and they can go into a shell, or prefer a bout of solitude to get their smile back. Only their families and close friends know of their innate sensitivity. However, they do not allow themselves to be hassled by others. They think through their problems without giving way to emotional stress.

When they are angry, they can be highly critical and sarcastic. You had better plug your ears, for once they start discussing your negative points, they can really get carried away by their oratory powers. It is a distinct rumble rather than an explosion.

The Cancerian insecurities about money, relationships and everything in between can afflict them. They can also be cranky or subject to black moods. The constantly analysing Virgo and the Gemini mind running over a hundred possibilities can also result in their constantly analysing, thinking, and worrying, with the mind permanently in a whirl.

They seem like softies, but they have a spine of steel: if they decide on doing something, they plan meticulously, just hang in there, and after a soul-scorching, hard-fought battle, they triumph. It isn't easy, as they do it most of the time alone, all by themselves.

Gemini–Cancer–Virgo – Arjun Kapoor

'I'm very shy and reserved; I'm not the guy who would like to be at the centre of focus at a party.'

'I am finicky like my father: food and things the way they should be. My understanding, dealing with situations is a lot like my mom's.'[215]

'I'd sell my soul to get my mother [Mona Kapoor] back.'

'I have been having no-strings-attached affairs for the last eight years.'[216]

Arjun is shy and is also finicky like a Virgo, is emotional and worships his mother like a Cancerian, and is articulate and doesn't mind unattached escapades like a Gemini – a true GemCanVir.

Love and Marriage for Him

You can rely on this man. He plans out his family's future and works towards his goals, staying cheerful all the while. You can relax with this guy for he takes on all the problems. Your bills are paid on time and holidays are planned at least a month in advance. Despite all his love for planning and organising, he also has an inventive streak so you will never be too tied down by plans. Just don't leave all the managing to him, or he can get very stressed out.

He wants a partner who understands his varying moods and is intelligent enough to comprehend his agile mind. The guy has a tough time sorting the hundred things that run through his mind: either help him out or leave him alone.

He is your friend and companion. Aggression does not work with him, but he prefers a friendly argument to a submissive nod. The only things that he insists on are routine and diet. He wants to do certain things at certain times and

---

[215] *DNA*, 'After Hrs', Mumbai, 11 December, 2013
[216] *Filmfare*, 11 June 2014

if you can accommodate him there, it will make for a contented man! He can be a nag. The Cancerian in him has put his mother on a pedestal, and looks for shades of his mother in you. He feels that no one can love him like his mother: not even you.

As a father, he is exemplary. This man loves looking after his children and has a deeply nurturing side to him. He does not mind changing nappies or even cooking for them. Of course, he insists on good grades.

Love and Marriage for Her

She is intelligent and active. This lady thinks of everything and is super efficient. You can leave all the parties and trips in her highly organised hands. She loves chatting and spreading cheer. There is a gentle charm about her.

She has a serious side too. Be attentive to her emotional needs for she can get deeply hurt if her emotions are ignored. She has a whole set of moods, ranging from vivacious to morose. She can be hurt by the smallest of things. So, while she needs conversation, you must be careful of your choice of words. You can make or break her day by what you say or how you listen to her.

Travel cheers her up. She needs a little change in her surroundings to feel alive. Seeing the same old things every day makes her lose her joie de vivre. Take her out and stimulate her mind with lively topics to revive her. She likes neatness around her and does not tolerate messy habits. She can be highly critical and deliver bitingly true comments when provoked.

She is extremely conscientious of her roles as daughter, mother, wife and employee, and dons all the roles perfectly. She worries, thinks a lot, her mind is always working, thinking of her commitments. Don't add to her burden. She gives her all to the relationship and everything else. If she still doesn't get reciprocation, she can cut off ties absolutely to leave for good. It will be extremely painful to her but she can take that call.

As a mother, she is in her element. She may be a little hesitant in becoming a mother for she knows that it entails a lot of responsibilities, but once she does, she is the perfect mother. She plays a big role in sharpening their minds.

At the Workplace

GemCanVirs are brilliant as planners and organisers. They are able to communicate their thoughts beautifully and are extremely analytical too. They have a way with words and excel in any profession that needs speaking or writing. They are creative.

Money is very important to them. They also want to be challenged with ideas rather than live with hollow titles. They can be excellent researchers, scientists, writers and even mentors. They like learning new things and applying new thought to old ideas. They can do the same thing in ten different ways.

They are not aggressive leaders, but persistent ones. Never go to them with half-baked ideas or castles in the air. GemCanVirs know what they are talking about and are not impressed by mere words. As leaders, they can envision an idea and work towards its realisation.

Air, Water and Earth meet in this meticulous and intelligent combination. GemCanVirs will be systematic but creative, analytical yet original, and talkative yet loners.

Famous GemCanVir Personalities

Harsha Bhogle, Ingmar Bergman, Arjun Kapoor, Benazir Bhutto, George Bush Jr., Ram Vilas Paswan, Alexandre Dumas, Kailash Kher, Gauri Shinde, Katrina Kaif, Barbara Stanwyck, Jeh Wadia.

125. GEMINI–CANCER–LIBRA

Mercury, the messenger of the gods, the sensitive Moon, and Venus, the planet of love, beauty and luxury, meet in GemCanLibs to give them grace, emotions and the gift of good speech.

GemCanLibs are communicators par excellence. The Gemini power over words meets the beautifully formed sentences of Libra and gives them great grace and tact while talking – and they just love talking. Both Gemini and Libra are Air signs and have lots of thoughts and opinions, for their minds like to think of new and novel things to discuss.

They portray emotions beautifully. The Cancerian sensitivity will add a more loving side to them. They are extremely attached to their families, especially their mothers. Food entices them. They love trying out new cuisines but their favourite foods are the ones cooked by their moms. Travel, too, excites them. They like having people around them and are full of fun and laughter. They love entertaining their friends with wit, humour and mimicry.

Gemini and Libra also make them great at learning new things with amazing speed. GemCanLibs are very good at picking up new skills and ideas. The two Air signs also give them the gift of languages. GemCanLibs learn new languages with ease and usually know at least four languages.

They also love doing a lot of things at one time. Their periods of intense activity are thankfully interspersed with interludes of deep thought and lassitide. They do not remain the same throughout their lives but alter in appearance and attitude. They keep re-inventing themselves almost throughout their lives. They never remain entrenched in one idea or one reality.

Creativity will be an intrinsic part of their nature. Both Libra and Cancer are extremely artistic and imaginative. The versatility of Gemini further arms their talent and gives them the ability to make use of their creative ideas. Cancer bestows the tenacity to pursue their dreams. Once they decide on a line of action, they will not leave it till they have accomplished it. The Gemini and Libra habit of leaving things halfway will not be theirs. GemCanLibs will worry and work their way through and will not rest till they have achieved what they set out to.

Cancer and Libra are cardinal signs and they give GemCanLibs the ability to lead. In any life situation, they lead without aggression or dominance but with kind words, solicitude and a sprinkling of emotional blackmail!

The idea of romance is extremely important to them. The Gemini's wandering eye gets a rest due to the commitment-seeking Cancer and extremely affectionate Libra. Libra is in love with the idea of love. GemCanLibs will be very romantic: they want their love embellished with beautiful poems, loving glances, sweet nothings and an abundance of feelings. Love finds them at their emotional best but they might go through certain periods of dejection in their search for love. GemCanLibs take time to find 'the one' who will define love for them and they may wander around for some time but they will eventually decide and be happy in that decision.

The Cancerian moodiness and despondency afflict them. They have the Cancerian ability to drown you in their emotions. They can have fears of various kinds and also get hurt quickly; sometimes the hurts can be imaginary. The good thing is that the fertile minds of Libra and Gemini help them see the brighter side of life. They wear charming smiles despite their inner insecurities and moods. They are very expressive and rarely hide their anger or disappointment, but sulk rather than get explosively angry. They are also quite good at sarcastic remarks.

There is a lot of positivity in this combination but the Libran indecisiveness and the Gemini fickleness can play havoc with them. GemCanLibs find it extremely difficult to take decisions and stick to them. They prefer postponing things or keep plenty of options open simultaneously. With the double Air signs, Gemini and Libra, they have the danger of becoming fickle-minded, excessively talkative and sometimes tend to take shortcuts in life.

They lack Earth and this makes them a little impractical. They always think through their decisions yet fail to look realistically at an issue. The lack of a Fire sign means they lack intense ambition. There will be initial hiccups, for they lack the force to drive them forward, especially due to the Gemini and Libra predilections to distraction. But on the brighter side, if expressed positively, they also have the chance to become versatile with a multitude of creative talents.

Gemini–Cancer–Libra – R.D. Burman
'Pancham [R.D.] was shy, self-effacing and locked.' –Asha Bhosale

R.D. was, as Gulzar says, as much a craftsman as he was a musician. He picked the sounds for his songs from very ingenious sources. In *'Chura liya'*, he used the sound of a spoon hitting a glass. Once to get the sound of raindrops, he spent a whole rainy night on his house's balcony recording the sound. During the recording of *'Hum dono do premee'* (*Ajnabee*) the musicians were on strike. So he improvised the song with emptied-out musical interludes![217]

The abundant creative talent of GemCanLib and its inventiveness marked R.D. Burman as one of the most inspired and inspiring composers.

Love and Marriage for Him
He understands and knows everything about you. He is not averse to long conversations: you can wake him up any time for a chat. Family is important to him. He never shirks his duties and is there whenever you need him. He is caring, but is sometimes detached too. He may seem lost in his thoughts. Time management is not his trademark either.

This guy can woo and talk round any girl he wants with his extraordinary communication skills and sensitivity; sometimes just for the pleasure of the chase. You should be aware that a relationship with him is not necessarily secure. The Gemini wandering mind makes him get bored very quickly, and the Libran desire to evaluate every interesting woman he meets can render him slightly unstable in relationships.

No matter how long you stay with him, you find something new. He likes to change his ideas and appearance, but thanks to Cancer, the change is never drastic.

---
[217] http://www.panchamonline.com/

Double Air signs also make him detached. He may not quite like to be smothered in love and needs his 'private' moments. You will never own this guy completely; give him his space and be your own woman.

For him, his family also means his mother. He adores her and wants you to do the same.

He is a good father and does not mind helping out in the nursery or playing around with his children. You can easily leave him with them and go for a girls' night out; just keep a check by calling on him for he can get a little distracted.

Love and Marriage for Her
She is sweet and truly feminine. But she knows how to get her work done, too. She talks, emotes and lovingly pushes you into decisions that you (in all your foolishness) thought were yours!

She is full of a thousand different ideas and always seems to have a new hobby. This lady never looks old, for her mind always remains young. She loves talking. You need some conversational skills if you want to keep her interested. At the same time, she is quite indecisive about even simple things in life like deciding what dress to wear or what to have for dinner.

She is extremely loving and caring, and is good at understanding you, but prefers you to talk and let her know your problems. She desperately wants to save money and thinks of ways to do it. However, she can't resist all the luxury brands in the stores. She has a few deep-rooted insecurities and she spends sleepless nights worrying about financial security; ensure she can sleep peacefully.

As a mother, she is loving, caring and great fun. She tells her children what to do. She makes them see the wisdom of her ways without raising her voice and they never feel as if she has decided for them.

At the Workplace
You can expect them to take a long time deciding what they really want to do. These intelligent people are too talented to select a profession easily. They get bored fast and want to do something that is challenging. They need a lot of appreciation to feel secure in their position. They do not demand praise but positively glow when they get it. If there is also enough scope to improve their income slowly but steadily, they will stay on for a long time; or off they go.

They are extremely adaptable and versatile, and love it if their work is dynamic and flexible. They are good in fields that require good communication skills and a mastery over many subjects. They can be good lawyers and negotiators, with their analytical skills and innate sense of justice. They can handle their own business with the Cancerian shrewdness and thrift combined with the Libran communication skills. Languages and travel also interest them and they can skillfully turn them into their vocations.

GemCanLibs are great at communicating and leading. They are charming bosses and know smart ways to get their work done quickly and efficiently.

Double Air and Water combine in GemCanLibs to give them unusual ideas, creative views, a penchant for small talk and a desire to lead with love.

Famous GemCanLib Personalities
R.D. Burman, Rakesh Jhunjhunwala, Sylvester Stallone, Gisele Bundchen, Vin Diesel, Minka Kelly, Julian Assange, Ramnaresh Sarwan, Rohinton Mistry, Suman Ranganathan.

126. GEMINI–CANCER–SCORPIO

Mercury, the messenger of the gods, the emotional Moon, and the secretive lord of the underworld, Pluto, join in this extremely sensitive and passionate combination with a tinge of fickleness. GemCanScorps have a childlike quality about them. Each incident in their lives is a big deal. They love with their entire being and the smallest hint of deceit crushes them.

They have the passion of Scorpio, the tenacity of Cancer and the smartness of Gemini. They appear super-confident and cocky but also seem to be brimming with emotions. When you get past that façade of confidence that they portray to keep unwanted people at bay, you see a soft heart quivering inside. The Cancerian in them is highly emotional and sensitive. They get hurt by the mindless jibes of people. The Scorpio too is thin-skinned and ready to get into an attack mode at the smallest barbs. They show their vulnerable side to you only if they believe in you; otherwise, you get a cold shoulder, sneers and scathing rebuttals.

GemCanScorps' deep desire is to be pampered and loved unconditionally, made the centre of your world, just as mama would do. The Cancerian in them never forgets their mother and misses her, whichever corner of the world they are. They miss the food she used to cook and the way she used to sacrifice things for them. They love and remember their families even when they are far away; they call home daily and send money to help their family members. They want to be caregivers to the people they love.

They are extremely competitive. They cannot lose. They love the thrill of winning. They work, practise and make themselves stronger in every possible way to fight against all odds. The Cancerian desire for money and the Scorpio need to earn respect make them see the importance of financial independence. They want to have enough money and are conservative in their spending.

Cancer blesses them with extraordinarily photographic memories. They also possess vivid imagination in colourful hues. When they talk with eloquence and unbridled intensity, you are mesmerised. Never mind the fact that they may have the Geminian way of peppering those events with some figments of imagination, which they genuinely believe are real. They certainly sound extraordinarily interesting.

They react to any hurt by fighting or going deep into themselves. If you are important to them, they may just sulk. You will never know what exactly they have in mind; they have the Gemini's deceptiveness, the Cancer's secretiveness and Scorpio's vindictiveness too. It is unwise to make enemies of them. They will frustrate you by keeping you guessing about their next moves. They have a seething, intense passion to succeed. They can trample over anyone who comes in their path to success and glory, by will power or even brute force, for they have to win at all costs.

Love sends them running around in circles. When GemCanScorps are in love, they think, dream and talk only of their partner. Their love goes deep and they desire the same kind of love in return. Gemini will make them speak of their love and you will know what they want; but it can be very demanding too. They need a soul mate with whom to spend their life. The flirtatious Gemini will be toned down if they find 'The One'; if they don't, they keep seeking till they do.

GemCanScorps feel hurt at the slightest rudeness of tone, if your smile is a fraction smaller, or if you hold their hand a moment shorter than the previous day. These guys can get hurt at the slightest provocation. This is their eccentricity. They love a lot, hate a lot and cry a lot. They do not trust people easily.

They have deeply ingrained insecurities that drive them crazy. They are insecure about their looks, their careers, the possibility of becoming poor or losing mom's love. They always crave more money, love, genuine praise, and mom's food and love. They also have the dream to own a nice, spacious, beautiful place that they can call home, every corner of which they have meticulously planned and visualised.

They can fall prey to addictions too. The Scorpio in them likes experimenting with the dark side of life while Gemini is never averse to trying something new. They can try out dangerous drugs and even habits but are also able to shake them off if they come in conflict with their love or careers. Depression, too, can take hold of them.

They need people who love and understand them for they can really go round the bend, especially when they face setbacks in love or in their profession. They have a do-or-die attitude and whenever they face defeat, they think they have fallen in a deep dark pit with no rescue team near. They are not exactly fearless but they overcome their inner demons with their intense desire to win. They definitely have it in them to overcome the Geminian distractedness and forge ahead with the persistence of Cancer and fervour of Scorpio.

Gemini–Cancer–Scorpio – Michael Phelps
Bob Bowman (his trainer) describes Phelps as 'a solitary man' with a 'rigid focus': 'He's unbelievably kind-hearted,' he says, recounting Phelps's interaction with young children after practices.[218]

'He's the best I've ever seen in terms of visualisation,' says Bowman. 'He'll see [what he's up against] sitting in the stands, and then he'll see it in the water. And then he will go through scenarios – what if things, don't go well? Like if his suit rips or his goggles break... And then he has this database, so that when he swims the race he's already programmed his nervous system to do one of those.'[219]

Michael's personality aptly fits the imagination and mental strength of a GemCanScorp.

Love and Marriage for Him
He is a maverick who thinks and dreams on his own terms. Family is extremely important to him and he is physically, emotionally and even spiritually there for you.

His love overflows and he expects the same from you. If you are not one of those who really desire to be 'loved' then you might feel suffocated with his constant vocalisation of his love and care. He is deeply possessive. He can also be a little controlling and uses either anger or emotions to make you do what he wants. He needs a partner who understands his deep emotional needs.

He is extremely sensitive and sentimental. It can be good or bad depending on how he utilises his emotions. Due to his swinging moods people will view him

---
[218] http://en.wikipedia.org/wiki/Michael_Phelps
[219] http://www.businessinsider.com/the-mental-strategies-michael-phelps-uses-to-dominate-the-competition-2012-6

as cranky and grumpy – but you will know that he is just a little kid at heart and wants desperately to be loved, adored and cared for.

Despite his intense passion and love, he is not above board in matters of loyalty. The Geminian in him has a roving eye and coupled with the intense passion of Scorpio, there are always chances for some slip-ups. But he will never rock the family boat.

He is a very emotional and loving father. He thinks of his children whenever he is away from home and they are always a part of his life. He clicks their pictures and records their gurgles to keep with him forever. He wants minute-by-minute reporting and is not happy until he is with them.

Love and Marriage for Her
She is extremely good at getting things done and is emotional and sensitive. She does not have a lazy bone in her and actively works on ten different demands from different family members at one time. Family is her major concern and she thinks of ways to help and nurture them.

She takes care of your every need, but remember – she needs pampering too. Thankfully, she tells you how she feels and what you can do to cheer her up. You need to be sensitive to her needs and her myriad moods. Her tears, fears and emotions are all genuine and you should understand that emotions define her.

Insecurities and terrors about her appearance, bank account and love plague her. Reassurance and love help her battle them. Her mother is very important to her and you have to love her too. Mother-in-law jokes are taboo. If you are not catering to her financial insecurities or not heeding to her need for a burning, intense love, she is perfectly capable of making alternative arrangements.

As a mom, she is wonderful. She is extremely involved and teaches her children everything she knows. She does not know how to let go when they grow up and you may have to help her with that.

At the Workplace
GemCanScorps are talkers, thinkers and doers. They tenaciously stick to their ambitions and do not let them go even if they face a hundred failures along the way. They are passionate, loyal and can be bitingly sarcastic of people who do not respect them. Money and growth are important to them.

They can excel in almost any field with their intensity and commitment. They can be particularly good in fields related to communication, sports, media, or even food. They understand people very well and are good at helping them overcome their problems. Finance too is a good profession for them to pursue.

They can be excellent at managing people and teams, and you can be sure that their teams love them as father figures.

Double Water and Air make GemCanScorps deep thinkers, passionate creators and extremely volatile personalities. They love a lot, hate a lot and talk a lot!

Famous GemCanScorp Personalities
Michael Phelps, Mike Tyson, Uday Kiran, Sangeeta Bijlani.

127. GEMINI–CANCER–SAGITTARIUS

Mercury, the messenger of the gods, joins the emotionally sensitive Moon and the highly knowledgeable Jupiter in GemCanSags.

The happy-go-lucky, intelligent and positive Sagittarius, combined with the fun-loving, mischievous and maverick Gemini, manages to conceal the butter-soft, sensitive and emotional inner core of the GemCanSags. Well, almost!

The first thing you notice about GemCanSags is their positivity. They love talking, and do it with emotion. Conversations with them are rarely dull: they are always full of exhilarating ideas. They know how to create drama and add an impish touch to the most serious gatherings with their impulse to laughter and skill at word play or even mimicry.

They are extremely fun loving and ready for any adventure. They love the outdoors and want to travel. They are always ready to take risks. They are exciting friends too. They will surprise you with their knowledge about obscure places and customs.

Cancer adds its touch of family love to the two wandering souls of Gemini and Sagittarius. GemCanSags love their families but are not too keen on spending every waking hour with them. They are also attached to their mothers but are not tied to their apron strings for long; the wanderlust is too strong in them. Sagittarius and Cancer are both big foodies: GemCanSags love eating and cooking good food.

GemCanSags are quite ambitious and want to shine in everyone's eyes. The Gemini communication skills and ability to make friends add to their strength and makes them very good at networking. Cancer adds its persistence. GemCanSags dream big and work relentlessly hard to turn their dream into a reality. Roadblocks will rarely frighten them away and they carry on with the Gemini smartness in finding solutions and the fighting spirit of Sagittarius. They believe in the power above and are spiritually very evolved. Their positivity stems from their belief systems.

GemCanSags are as adventurous in love as in the rest of their life. Cancer ensures that they seek commitment and put themselves in a family setting but the Gemini desire to look for someone better and the Sagittarian love of freedom can make them take wayward steps. They are trapped between the two extremes and find a way out by trying their hand at both. It will take them time to realise what they want and will be more stable as they age.

The Gemini smartness is combined with the Sagittarian naïveté in GemCanSags. They can blurt out some uncomfortable facts at times and shock people; they seem unable to stop themselves from putting their foot in the mouth sometimes.

They are also good learners who better themselves over the years. The Gemini flair of evolving is evident in them. The Sagittarius is enamoured of new thoughts and doesn't want to live life the same old way. They are not stingy about money, though they aspire to own lots of it. Money is their weakness for they are very insecure if they do not have a good bank balance.

The fickleness of Gemini will be evident for they don't mind changing their position to suit the times. Their 'facts' are quite changeable and they will give different versions of the same thing at different times. They also love gossiping and adding further embellishments to the stories they hear – don't take everything they say at face value.

Sagittarius and Cancer bring contradictions in the GemCanSags character: Sagittarius loves freedom while Cancer wants family. GemCanSags fear the responsibility of having children and put it off as long as they can but once they become parents they will be very loving and caring, like true Cancerians.

The anger of GemCanSags can manifest as volcanic eruptions or deep sulks. These outgoing creatures can feel very hurt if they are ill treated. Of course, you can expect to hear of their agonies, for they do not hide them from the world. There is a sensitive side to them despite their smart talk and swagger. There are deep insecurities in them and they secretly fear failure. Gemini is torn between various possibilities and Sagittarius is always looking for something new. At their worst, they are a confused emotional wreck and wayward genius gone wrong.

GemCanSags want to be pampered and want to be the centre of attention. Gemini remains a teenager forever, Sagittarius craves for applause even at sixty and Cancer will always be a grown-up baby. If you look deep inside them, you will see a child; and just like a child, they only want love and adoration!

Gemini–Cancer–Sagittarius – Kevin Pietersen

Pietersen is portrayed in the media as self-assured, described by Geoffrey Boycott as 'cocky and confident'. Michael Vaughan counters this, saying, 'KP is not a confident person. He obviously has great belief in his ability, but I know KP wants to be loved. I text him and talk to him often because I know he is insecure.'[220]

Kevin's controversial tweets ousted him from the English cricket team for a while. Like a typical Gemini, he loves playing with words (tweets, mobile texting), but like a Sagittarian without tact, he blurted certain things which shouldn't be disclosed in public. His deep-felt Cancerian hurt was also out in the open when he disclosed in his autobiography, his not-so-pleasant experiences with the English team.

Courageous but brash, outspoken and insecure, Pietersen has the instincts and emotions of a GemCanSag.

Love and Marriage for Him

He is a fun guy to be with. He loves laughing and joking, and is more of your friend than a dominating presence in your life. He is also very ambitious. You have to be more independent and ready to take on the responsibilities of the house without his help for he concentrates his energies on reaching high. Of course, he is there when required. Despite his good intentions, he might forget to do certain things. He will also surprise you with his bloopers; there is a clumsiness to him that makes him lovable.

He is very close to his mother and loves mom's cooking. Don't try and compete with her. No point.

He loves wandering and travelling around, meeting new people. He misses his family when he is out and his travels when he is at home. He wants a partner

---

[220] http://en.wikipedia.org/wiki/Kevin_Pietersen

who understands his need for freedom and lets him wander around a bit. Relax; he always comes back to you. He is also prone to mood swings. He needs an overdose of pampering during those times or they can grow into full-blown sulks.

His life transforms when he becomes a father. It will be amazing to see this rock star, wandering hippie become a loving, caring and doting father. He is always around emotionally and physically for his children. He is capable of any sacrifice for his children. He also comes very close to family after the birth of his children. He allows them to go forward on their own with a little concern from his side.

Love and Marriage for Her
This lady is full of life and good cheer. She never refrains from trying something new and changes herself over the years. She is extremely intelligent and knows a lot about diverse things.

She is quite good at talking too, but sometimes surprises you with her clumsy retorts. The idea of travel makes her eyes sparkle. She gets bored quickly and needs new experiences. Give her the freedom to pick up those myriad hobbies that she wants, leave her at her mom's place every now and then, and she will be eternally happy with you. She loves cracking jokes and is the cynosure of every party. She is a bundle of energy and you will be amazed at her talent for doing so many things in so little time. She can cook for a battalion at short notice. She is also very ambitious and wants a bank balance of her own. She is quite sensitive too and needs a lot of support and love from you.

As a mother, she is enchanting. Of course, she worries about the responsibility and keeps wondering if she is up to it but once she has children, she adores them. This lady is a fun mom and loves laughing and playing with her children.

At the Workplace
GemCanSags take time to realise what they want to do, but once they do, you find it hard to shake them off their decided paths. They work with amazing perseverance. They know how to work hard and smart. They are notorious for being candid at the most inopportune moments. But their enthusiasm and honesty will be valued by organisations.

They are good at networking and people skills, and instinctively know how to word their thoughts in a beautiful manner. They prefer a career in which they get to move around and meet new people. They do well in careers that involve communication skills. They can also be good as writers, journalists, TV anchors, politicians, lawyers, financial consultants, teachers and scientists. As bosses, they love spreading their cheer and become father figures to employees. They have multiple plans and may change plans at the last moment.

Air, Water and Fire meet in this amazingly versatile and driven combination. GemCanSags will think differently, act tenaciously and live adventurously.

Famous GemCanSag Personalities
Arnold Schwarzenegger, Kevin Pieterson, Ashley Tisdale, Jyoti Basu, Vishal Bhardwaj, Hilary Swank, Sanjay Manjrekar, Manoj Tiwari (actor), Faf du Plessis.

128. GEMINI–CANCER–CAPRICORN

Mercurial Gemini adds the power of speech to old man Saturn and emotional Moon in GemCanCaps. Only two things dominate their interests – family and career. GemCanCaps think, plan and worry for them. They are emotionally attached to their family and always work to enhance their status. They are capable of sacrificing a lot for their families.

Cancer rules the mother, everything to do with home and its surroundings, Capricorn rules the father and career. No other explanation is needed for their loving care and sensitivity towards family and their ruthless practicality towards their career. They are two different people at home and work.

GemCanCaps have a deep, serious side and are willing to take on a lot of stress. The reverse-aging syndrome of Capricorn makes them serious in their youthful years and more chilled out as they age.

Thankfully, they are saved from being standoffish, aloof or cold because of the presence of Gemini. Gemini will liberate them from their inherent shyness, make them outgoing, and bless them with good communication skills. Their seriousness gets some style and they are open to ideas. They just need to feel comfortable to bring out their funny side, and once they start, they can keep you in splits with their wisecracks drawn from observations in daily life. Gemini also blesses them with the ability to learn languages and be exceptional mimics. Their best ability is to express their thoughts in a beautiful way.

Both Cancer and Capricorn are cardinal signs and this makes GemCanCaps willing leaders. The confluence of Cancer and Capricorn also makes them very tenacious and persistent in their goals. The distracted mind of Gemini finds some calm and endows GemCanCaps with an ability to think out of the box. They know how to use tradition in a modern manner and they are ready to think of new ways to do things.They have the Gemini ability to multitask and the Cancer-Capricorn tendency to overwork; so they enjoy doing as much as they can in as little time as possible. They are well-organised and good time managers.

Love finds them quite emotional, yet they also have the Gemini trait of not knowing what they want. It takes them some time and even an emotional roller coaster ride to know their true feelings. Cancer and Capricorn makes them very committed and they seek permanency in a relationship, while Gemini adds its flavour of indiscreetness to them. They like flirting and do more of it as they grow older, as Capricorn turns fun loving over time. The flirting can be harmless if they are in an emotionally fulfilling relationship, and they will always think a hundred times before breaking family ties.

Nostalgia is always present in them. Mother and her home-made delicacies, their carefree childhood, school friends, puppy love, teachers – they love reminiscing about all those things. They have excellent memories, too.

Anything old is sacred to them. They toe the line and think a hundred times before breaking traditions. They love networking and have an astounding number of acquaintances. They know whom to call in times of stress and do so without any compunction. They are good at manipulating people and situations to suit themselves.

Cancerians fear loss of any sort, especially their money and loved ones. They have deep inner fears and sometimes behave strangely to overcome those. They are extremely touchy and sensitive, too. Capricorn loses sleep over things going wrong, especially in career, and plots and plans to keep things going right, and can turn melancholic if they don't. Most of the negative qualities of GemCanCaps stem from these insecurities. They can fill their hours with imagined grievances.

This, combined with the devious Gemini, means they can go to any extent to protect themselves, their finances, career and family. Money is extremely important for them and they are obsessed by the thought of making more. They can be stingy for they only spend on their families. They are quite emotional and get hurt easily, and they know when to express their displeasure, often by sulking. GemCanCaps need a lot of help and hand-holding to get out of their self-created torture chambers.

Some of their downbeat qualities are extreme sensitivity, excessive attachment to home, capriciousness, being cold and calculating, and manipulating situations to get their way. They can be ruthless in their pursuit of money and career.

They never shrug off their duties as parents. As responsible children, they have the capacity to sacrifice their career for their family's happiness or to care for an ailing parent.

Gemini–Cancer–Capricorn – Suriya

'He is the ideal husband; took care of me during my pregnancy for six months without shooting.'[221]

Suriya runs the Agaram Foundation to help children who drop out of school.

Suriya changes his physique according to the requirements of his character. From a college student to an old man, he's portrayed every kind of role with élan.

Suriya's versatility in acting skills, connectivity with audience, respect for family values and philanthropy for childen makes him an ideal GemCanCap.

Love and Marriage for Him

As I said earlier, family is extremely important to him. He is definitely a provider and wants nothing more than elevating his family's status. He is a fun companion with a caring streak. He loves jokes and is full of witty rejoinders, but has his sensitive side. Do not poke fun at him or he is very upset.

He likes to lead, and if you too like leading, it can lead to an impasse for he does not like to let go of his desire to dominate. He can be quite miserly about money but readily spends on things that add to his status.

He wants to be pampered and cared for. Add him to your list of children to hug and he will be quite happy. You also need to love his family as your own. He wants his entire family by his side, so be sure that you are ready to fit into the good daughter-in-law mode. He reveres his parents and will never leave their side for anyone – not even you.

---

[221] http://articles.timesofindia.indiatimes.com/2009-04-14/news-interviews/28052653_1_surya-overseas-market-audiences

One thing that you need not worry about is when you have to leave him and go to your mom's place in an emergency. He can take care of himself very well and cook a meal on his own. In fact he may be a great cook and make your Sunday or anniversary special by cooking a delicious meal for you. He is a soft romantic and his way of expressions and love will only get better with every passing year.

As a father, he is very caring and loving. He enjoys spending time with his children. He enjoys family holidays and will plan trips to places they know well. He is stern about inculcating values in them.

Love and Marriage for Her
She is the perfect daughter-in-law. This lady wants to maintain the old traditions of the family as much as possible. She is everything your mom could ask for and does not mind having your mother with her. She can cook for a battalion, take control of all the activities of a large family and even manage an entire wedding on her own, while regaling the guests with her funny anecdotes.

She is very talented and quite ambitious. She can take care of home and career simultaneously. She wants to achieve big things and is easily depressed if she does not get them as planned.

Emotional, sensitive and quite talkative, she lets you know how she feels. She needs a person with whom to share her thoughts. She worries about her looks, her bank balance, her parents' illnesses, her siblings' careers and her family's security. Understand and allay those fears.

She is very moody and changeable. She can also add spice to stories to make them interesting. Understand her fear of not missing out anything in life or possibly losing out on everything in life. She is just being prepared, not being manipulative.

As a mother, she is fabulous. Mothering comes naturally to her and she knows how to get her children to respect her while playing around with them. She is a fun mother who instils discipline in them.

At the Workplace
Cancerians are hard workers and Capricorns are diligent, industrious and workaholic. The Gemini adds versatility to the stable Cancer and Capricorn. They are great in ideating, with brilliant ideas. They are fantastic planners, delegators and implementers of ideas.

They take their time in deciding their career paths. But once they do, they stick around till eternity. They grow just by being there, staying on and not leaving. Loyalty is bred into them. They need security in their job and want avenues to grow too. Money is extremely important to them and they need regular but assured increases in income. If there is scope for growth and intellectual stimulation too, then they will never leave your organisation.

From finance to careers in creative fields, they do well as long as they get a chance to communicate and think. As bosses, they treat everyone as family, but are cautious with raises and may be a little old-fashioned, too. They have exceptional skills at managing large organisations, projects, and so on. Deep within, every

GemCanCap wants to run his own business. He may leave you once he is financially sound, to take a calculated risk.

Air, Water and Earth meet in GemCanCaps to endow them with intelligence, a gift of the gab, emotional sensitivity, perseverance and sheer determination to succeed against all odds.

Famous GemCanCap Personalities
Suriya, Sultan of Brunei, Stuart Broad, George Eastman, Sumona Chakravarti, Alyson Annan, Ryan ten Doeschate, Rahul Mahajan, Angela Merkel, Wilma Rudolph.

129. GEMINI–CANCER–AQUARIUS

GemCanAquas are as freedom loving and deep as the Air and Water of which they are made. Mercury, the messenger of the gods, the emotional and sensitive Moon and the inventive genius of Aquarius make them think beyond traditional boundaries and emotions.

There is an amazing contradiction in them. If at first, they appear flighty, fidgety, careless, wandering and irresponsible you need to think again. If they appear emotional, sensitive, touchy, high-strung or detached, you need to think again too. It's difficult to understand them, despite knowing them. This is a fascinating combination of interesting traits.

Speech and communication are their strong points. GemCanAquas talk well and are very good at expressing their emotions. They are extremely friendly people. They attract others with their cheeriness and conversation. They can talk with anyone and never shy away from making new friends and acquaintances. There is a youthfulness about GemCanAquas. Their ability to learn new things with ease and their good humour make them seem younger than they actually are.

They love freedom and will say so. The unconventional Aquarius gives them views that are fifty years ahead of their time and they do not want to live mired in tradition. Despite their desire for unconventionality, they are never shockingly outrageous. They seem to evolve and change over the years, not only in their appearance but also in their attitude. They know how to re-invent themselves.

Do not take their chatty friendliness to mean that they can be pushed around; they are strong without being aggressive due to the cardinal sign of Cancer and the fixed Aquarius. The sensitive Cancer and the ever-curious Aquarius also help them understand people: to scan and read their deepest thoughts. Family, their childhood and especially their mothers, all these hold a special place in their hearts. They are always there for their family.

GemCanAquas are thinkers. They are full of ideas and new ways to do things. You will rarely find them sitting or lazing around. The GemCanAqua idea of work can leave you bedazzled, for they have the Gemini ability to multitask. They love travelling, meeting new people and learning new languages. They hate being confined to a single place and are the happiest roaming around the world.

They can be extremely flirtatious and casual to begin with – they are searching for that elusive perfect partner or even experimenting at relationships! This is the quirkiness of this combination: despite deep emotional needs they can be detached and even deceptive. Still, Cancer adds stability to them and slowly they reconcile themselves to the idea of a single person for they eventually want a family structure around them. Once they are deeply in love, GemCanAqua will relinquish anything for it, even if it means defying a lot of people as Aquarius doesn't bother about convention and Cancer will perish without love.

GemCanAquas have a definite creative streak and love the outdoors. They are extremely talented and sporty too. The Gemini quick thinking and the Cancerian creativity combine well with the Aquarian inventive genius and whatever they do or think will never be common. GemCanAquas are almost shockproof due to the convention-hating Aquarius and the wild-thinking Gemini.

There is one flaw in them, though. Despite their earnest quest to change the world's thinking, they find it impossible to change some of their own self-defeating quirks. They can be quite difficult to understand for they can easily change their views without informing others and can be quite detached too. That's the irony – even when they can understand your deepest needs, sometimes they are too distant to be responsive.

They have deep emotions. They are touched when shown kindness and love, and moved to tears by sufferings of people and poverty. They get hurt quickly and can go into a shell. It takes a lot of coaxing to get them out. They cry buckets, even the males, if hurt deeply. The moodiness and melancholy of Cancer may afflict them at times, but such feelings rarely last for long. If they are angry, they express it with either a brooding sulk or a direct explosion.

It is hard for them to decide on a particular course of action as they see innumerable possibilities in every situation. Yes, they have their flaws and inconsistencies, their flirtatiousness and capability of deception, their detachment and experimentation, their insecurities and rebelliousness; but their deep emotional sensitivity and humanitarian nature, smothering love and caring can make you overlook all their idiosyncrasies.

Gemini–Cancer–Aquarius – Ranveer Singh

'I'm a born flirt…I get taken in by attractive women. I just can't help it.'[222]

'I am a nervous kind of guy! I've learnt how to channelise them and make them a positive energy.'

'When Aditya Chopra said, 'Ranveer, we're going with you,' I just sank to the ground and started crying.'

'I was meeting students, to see how they speak, what their tastes are, where they come from.'[223]

'During my teenage years I two- and three-timed girls, but that's a thing of the past.'[224]

Ranveer Singh has the Gemini's way with words and of charming women. He also has the Cancerian emotional side and the Aquarian knack of dissecting people and their characteristics.

Love and Marriage for Him

He prefers an independent partner. He has a caring streak in him but his mind is full of too many ideas and thoughts to be sympathetic to you all the time. Do not expect him to be by your side always. You have to live and enjoy life on your own too. Daily chores and household duties do not attract him.

He is never judgemental. He does not expect you to behave in a certain way just because you are a woman. He is a tolerant guy who is willing to listen to your divergent views. He is also very moody. His moods can go from detached to

---

[222] http://articles.timesofindia.indiatimes.com/2011-08-12/news-interviews/29876842_1_ranveer-singh-first-film-karan-johar
[223] http://www.glamsham.com/movies/interviews/09-ranveer-singh-interview-121014.asp
[224] http://www.bollywoodlife.com/news-gossip/ranveer-singh-i-was-a-casanova/

witty and you will have to fine-tune to know how to respond to them. He is quite sensitive, too; sometimes even to the tone of your voice.

He has a flirtatious way about him when he is happy and you have to deal with it without acting too possessive or he wanders away. He loves his mother and wants you to share the same regard. For him, his mother is never wrong.

He is very smart with his money and knows how to use it well. He may be a little cautious but can be extravagant on family and friends and, when in the mood, can blow it all up.

He loves being a father and is always ready to spend time with his children. He is their friend and confidant rather than a commanding presence. He understands their point of view and does not force them into things they do not like.

Love and Marriage for Her
She mothers you and cares for you like a typical Cancer. She has a sensitive nurturing side and a highly distracted one too. She can be emotional one moment and then completely change into a chatty mood: she is sensitive but finds it hard to concentrate on one emotion or thought for too long. This lady can think of the most amazing things. Her only problem is that she thinks too many of them to be interested in just one.

She likes some conventions but is not bound to all of them. She loves her family but her thoughts are more than just that. It is hard to decipher her. Do not try and dominate her for though she is gentle and sweet, she does not bow to ideas that do not suit her.

She needs a partner with whom she can discuss anything in this world. Be ready to talk to her for she does not like a silent companion. Interestingly, despite her need for togetherness, she also needs 'me' time. You have to give her enough space in the relationship.

She loves to save money and goes for long-term investments that prevent its use for the present. But she can still be an impulsive buyer, especially if there is a good bargain. Her dress sense will be strongly individualistic.

She can startle you with her maternal sense. She is a loving mother who is ready to hear her children's side every time. She is rarely shocked by anything they do and likes helping them through their problems with unconventional solutions.

At the Workplace
GemCanAquas take a long time to decide what they really want to do. You can expect them to try out various careers before finally settling on one. Money is important to them but they never limit themselves to just that. They do not mind working for a smaller amount if the job offers them scope to use their minds and promises to be interesting.

They have the ability to communicate their thoughts wonderfully and are quite imaginative too. Creative fields suit them, and those that offer new learning every day. They are open to new ideas and thoughts and very good in making others understand the complex theories that they instinctively grasp. They are people-oriented and do well in careers related to people.

They are not commanding or controlling as bosses but prefer to treat their teams as family and friends.

Double Air and Water meet in GemCanAquas to endow them with emotional intelligence and a flair for talk.

Famous GemCanAqua Personalities
Ranveer Singh, Harbhajan Singh, Guru Dutt, Revathi, King Edward VIII, Helen Keller, Syama Prasad Mookerjee, Juliette Lewis, Carson Daly, Olivia Munn, Ginger Rogers.

130. GEMINI–CANCER–PISCES

The innately changeable Mercury, the highly emotional Moon and the deep and mysterious Neptune make this an unusual combination of wit, sensitivity and empathy.

There are various dimensions to this combination. The cleverest, the most sentimental and the wisest combine in this. While the most emotional of all – Cancer and Pisces – make up this combo, it also contains the most malleable signs in Gemini and Pisces. The fact that Gemini and Pisces are dual signs also adds to the unbelievable depth and breadth to this combination.

GemCanPisces are rarely at a loss for words. They can interpret mundane events into beautiful-sounding situations. When they are happy, their chatter and bright views keep you entertained; but when the blues set in then they feel nothing will ever be right again. They know how to surprise you with their expressions and attitudes.

Highly imaginative and very talkative, it is very difficult to keep pace with the mind of a GemCanPisces. They can think ten different solutions to a problem and are never wary of trying out new ideas. They are very intelligent and are able to quickly grasp new theories and comprehend different emotions.

An outstanding trait is their ability to learn fast: all three signs are quick learners and are always open to new experiences. Sensitive and empathetic, they are able to read people's minds and desires with great ease. Of course, they are smart enough to use this talent well and people find it very difficult to outsmart them.

Mothers and memories rank high with GemCanPisces. They love and admire their mothers and remain close to them. They reminisce nostalgically of the good old days. They have the Cancerian aptitude for cooking, love for food and anything to do with home. They can make any sacrifice for the family.

Travel brings them alive and they are always ready to try out new places – without getting too adventurous or rash. They prefer travelling with friends and loved ones. Routine and monotony bore them.

Love is a necessity for this combination. Both Pisces and Cancer love truly and deeply, with sensitivity and emotion generosity. But the Gemini's fickleness and desire for many options, and Piscean escapism, can make them very deceptive in love. That is the strange contradiction: while they desire eternal, true love, they themselves are susceptible to drifting away, especially if they don't get the true love they are seeking. They need lots of love to be able to pour love out selflessly.

They are reservoirs of talent. With the Piscean ability to copy, Geminian sense of improvisation and Cancerian imagination, they can learn, master, apply and excel in any creative work, art form, sport or venture. They can change with chameleonic ease, sparkle as a solitaire or merge with the environment, depending upon the need of the endeavour. They like to keep busy and be productive.

They are not practical or realistic. Sensitive, caring, and emotional, they may find it hard to solve problems logically unless they live around practical people. They need a lot of help to get over their insecurities too. Both Cancer and Pisces afflict them with nameless fears, which they have to learn to overcome. Their Gemini side can make them look for shortcuts to problems.

They can get mired in emotions. Due to Cancer, GemCanPisces can be very moody and sensitive. Pisces adds fuel to the fire where emotions are concerned and makes them jump through hoops for their sentiments. They love being attached to people, friends and family, and creating relationships. The myriad attachments and the ensuing emotional roller-coaster rides can be taxing, but they seem to revel in it. They veer between extreme happiness and extreme sadness – it will take them time to discover the middle ground.

It is not easy for GemCanPisces to save money. They are not the people with whom you can leave money and expect it back. They can be a little untruthful about monetary dealings. Addictions can afflict them too. Both Gemini and Pisces make them like experimenting with different substances. This combination can truly live a dual life without letting anyone get the least bit suspicious.

Gemini Twins, and Pisces Fishes swimming in opposite directions, make four personas and together with Cancer, it is like five persons packed into one. It makes this combination difficult to predict for they have so many ways of reacting to specific situations that it will be difficult to really know them. This also imparts some deceptiveness to the combination. They have lots of talent, communication skills and versatility, but all of that needs to be channelised. They have numerous Geminian distractions and Piscean traps. If they overcome their internal demons they can outdo anyone. Cancer can bring them out of the abyss if they choose, as it gives the ability to stick on to something forever. But they need to will it first!

Gemini–Cancer–Pisces – Louis Armstrong
Armstrong kept a strong connection throughout his life to the cooking of New Orleans, always signing his letters, 'Red beans and ricely yours...'[225]

He avidly typed or wrote on whatever stationery was at hand, recording instant takes on music, sex, food, childhood memories, his heavy 'medicinal' marijuana use – and even his bowel movements, which he gleefully described.

Armstrong incorporated influences into his performances from blues to the arrangements of Guy Lombardo, to Latin American folksongs, to classical symphonies and opera, sometimes to the bewilderment of fans who wanted him to stay in convenient narrow categories.[226]

Adept at words and music, Louis Armstrong was a true GemCanPisces with his ability to learn and evolve as he grew.

Love and Marriage for Him
Environment moulds his abilities. If his family has a positive effect on him, he is responsible and you can breathe a sigh of relief. If he is thirty, and still undecided

---
[225] http://www.npr.org/blogs/ablogsupreme/2011/08/04/138991954/red-beans-and-ricely-yours-the-culinary-habits-of-louis-armstrong
[226] http://en.wikipedia.org/wiki/Louis_Armstrong

or irresponsible, your love should be stronger than his frailties for they can surely try your relationship.

As a partner, he is very loving and caring. He is sensitive to your feelings. This is a guy who is comfortable talking and expressing his softer emotions. Of course, you have to tend to the practical side of life.

Ego hassles and aggression are not expected of him and he is the easiest of all guys to live with. But he is not very organised and needs your help here. Mood swings can bring him low. Give him lots of love and care when he is in his depressed moods for only that can save him.

His mother is his first love. You have to be gracious enough to accept that. As a plus, he is one of those rare men who do not run away at the sight of their mother-in-law, but welcome her with big smiles.

He is an extremely loving and caring father. His children flock to him for his kind words and understanding ways. He lets them decide their ways and never dictates his views. He is protective without being clingy.

Love and Marriage for Her
She is talkative and bright. Her views change fast and you may have a tough time keeping up with her inventive mind. She focuses all her love and energy on her family.

Despite all the laughter and fizz in her, she has a deep emotional and sensitive side. She needs you to be sensitive yet strong. Never laugh at her insecurities. She can go into a shell and then it is very difficult to get that smile back on her face.

She is the most loving person in your life and adjusts easily. Her adaptability is her strong point, but do not push her hard. She loves with all her soul. Her greatest need in life is to belong to someone heart and soul. It would be heartless to treat such a treasure without the care it deserves. In such a scenario, she cannot be blamed if she decides to lead a double life and find her joys elsewhere while seeming true to you.

Her children hold the key to her heart. She loves, pampers and nurtures them and takes joy in their every stride. She can be a little possessive about them and finds it difficult to let go, but she never hampers their growth with her demands.

At the Workplace
GemCanPisces are extremely intelligent and versatile people. They hate being bound to routine and flourish in surroundings that promise deep thinking and diverse views. They prefer creatively satisfying occupations. They might also wander for some time before settling down. They do well in fields that can exploit their extraordinary communication skills, their relationship-building abilities, and deep understanding and empathy.

They love challenges and are always ready to use their inventive minds to create something extraordinary. They need strong mentors to shape them in their early years. Their imagination and gift of words make them amazing poets and writers. They can even write children's books for they are extremely nostalgic about their childhood.

As bosses, they are very protective of their teams and understand when you have family commitments. They may not clearly state their game plan and sometimes it can send confusing signals to people.

Air and double Water make GemCanPisces emotional and inventive. Imaginative and sensitive, they are gentle souls who need support and understanding to reach their goals.

Famous GemCanPisces Personalities
Louis Armstrong, Hans Rosling, Rahul Bose, Lokmanya Tilak, Neetu Singh, Madhu Sapre, Peggy Fleming.

131. GEMINI–LEO–VIRGO

Mercury, the messenger of the gods, meets Apollo, the regal Sun god, and the perfection-seeking Virgo in this intelligent and royal combination.

The Geminis soar in the ether of abstractions, ideas, and most of all, words. The fiery and majestic Leos live to perform and create on a grand scale. Enter the practical Virgo; with its innate refinement and fastidious industriousness, it ensures that the dream of a GemLeoVir has a concrete path to glory and that the grandeur and flamboyance has a basis in truth.

GemLeoVirs talk a lot. The Gemini's untiring tongue and the Leo desire to hear itself will make them expound, explain, advise and guide with aplomb. They bring such detail and analysis into their discussions that it is hard to refute them.

The Gemini versatile mind and the Virgo adherence to perfect language give them wonderful communication skills. They not only learn languages easily but they are able to motivate and inspire people with their skill in words. They are also very quick at grasping new facts and easily absorb details.

They are fun loving and can be quite boisterous and loud. They love surrounding themselves with an adoring crowd. They use their humour and wit to great advantage. They are also excellent mimics. They are master storytellers, with funny rejoinders and killer one-liners, and always have the last word.

They definitely are smart. Gemini multitasking and mental agility gives them an edge over others; add to this the Leo trait of delegating work and basking in glory. GemLeoVirs are never your silent workers. They work smart and know how to get the right reviews. The self-effacing aspect of Virgo is absent in GemLeoVirs. They can tackle anything. With the Geminian dexterity, Leonine ability to 'fix up' things and Virgo's meticulous perfection, they can get anything right, however badly it has gone wrong. The perfectionism of Virgo gets the backing of Leo's audacity and Gemini's gregariousness. Everything that they do has to be stylish, perfect and different from what normal people would do.

Appearance is important to them. They dress well and to suit the occasion. They take care of their diet and make sure they exercise enough, for health is always on their mind. They like to stick to specific routines, especially regarding diet and exercise. Family is very important to them. GemLeoVirs do their duty by their family.

GemLeoVirs are multitalented and though they like doing a lot of things, they do them all in a planned manner. They do not rush into situations without thinking. They are quite good with money too. They know where to invest to grow their money, and manage to save without becoming stingy, and have a portion kept aside for their accessories and favourite brands.

Disrespect is the one thing that can mar their sunniness. They want people to look up to them. They can tell highly imaginative stories to get attention.

They definitely have an ego. The ego stems from their belief that they are perfect and can do no wrong, and when added with the Leo arrogance, can be difficult to handle. They flare up if anyone criticises them or finds fault in them. Their sarcasm and criticism can be cutting. Their anger can be scary. The best thing to do when they are angry is to leave the room.

They have lots of opinions. The most confusing thing is that they change their opinions quite easily. Also, you can't believe everything they say as the Geminian can play with words and take different sides at different times. They are changeable, mercurial, can be bored quickly but also will stick to their guns, as they believe that whatever they say is right.

They lack Water in their combination; hence, they may not be very sensitive to your emotions. Though they realise how you feel, they do not care if you are hurt. The only people they really care for are their families and friends who adore them. You have to give them credit though, as there is no one who is as perfectionist, multitalented, versatile, industrious and stylish as them.

Gemini–Leo–Virgo – Sunita Williams
While in space, Williams participated in the Boston Marathon, the first time an entrant has competed in the race from orbit. She also cut her long flowing hair, while in orbit, to donate to Locks of Love, a non-profit organisation that provides hairpieces to children suffering long-term hair loss due to medical issues.[227]

Sunita Williams does a triathlon in space, sends Diwali wishes from space, and talks to kids fluently in regional languages. She even tackles an international space station coolant leak and fixes it up.[228]

Sunita Williams is a true GemLeoVir – loves what she does, keeps experimenting and takes up new challenges in work and life. She has supreme fitness levels and good communication skills, too.

Love and Marriage for Him
He talks a lot and needs a woman who listens to him, adores him and is intelligent enough to hold a conversation with him. He makes you laugh and tells you witty stories. The only thing he does not provide is emotional understanding. He wants you to handle your emotions on your own and not cling to him. The only way to handle him is to show him that you love him without being too submissive to his views.

Act as though you haven't noticed or grin and bear it when he turns on his charm offensive with women. He is just perfecting his flirting skills. Hopefully, there is nothing more to it, though you cannot rule out anything with the Gemini in him. He will never leave you if you lean on him and admire him.

He is very ambitious and may turn finicky or critical while at home because that is his way of venting the anger and frustrations of work. Help him leave his work behind, but softly and gently. He makes many plans but finds it difficult to stick to them.

He cannot bear sloppy dressing, so you'll need to ensure his clothes are immaculate. You definitely get a helping hand from him but do not rely on it for he

---

[227] http://www.space.com/17221-sunita-williams-astronaut-biography.html

[228] http://www.ndtv.com/article/world/sunita-williams-finishes-triathlon-in-space-268672

has too many tasks in hand to help you out with chores. He loves throwing parties and enjoys meeting people. He does not like being alone for long.

As a father, he likes to pitch in and help with the children but is too busy to be around all the time. He insists on good education. He also teaches them to be exuberant and inquisitive about life.

Love and Marriage for Her
She is the life of your family. This lady sparkles with wit, humour and joy. Her ideas never end and she always has something to say.

You can be sure that everyone turns to look when she walks in. Her clothes and her laugh always draw attention. You need to be an easy-going person and not given to fits of jealousy, for she loves to flirt. Her desire for flirting is usually harmless till you give her cause to be more serious. A word of advice – do not get carried away by her views on people. She likes adding a little spice to her talk and may not stick to the truth while describing events.

She does a lot for her family and is very generous with her time and money. She loves spreading her sunshine and warmth around and wants to be appreciated for her untiring care. She also has many ideas and hobbies that she pursues. If you can't encourage her at least don't douse her enthusiasm. She is a queen at heart and an intelligent one too. Never try to treat her as a doormat. She will just cut ties and leave you.

As a mother, she is fascinating. She does so many things for her children that other mothers feel unequal in her presence. She is also strict and ensures discipline, especially in matters of education, but also pampers them. She also teaches them to respect her views and never tires of advising them.

At the Workplace
Virgos are blessed with superb manual skills and are very industrious, hard working, meticulous and intelligent. Gemini makes them clever and street-smart, brimming with brilliant ideas and ten different ways of doing something. When you add the quality-consciousness and superior and stylish working attitude of Leo, they are simply unbeatable at any work!

GemLeoVirs are excellent communicators who do not shy away from the spotlight. They have a firm grasp of numbers, and are smart and savvy workers. They create big plans and have the ability to work towards them. They are fantastic problem solvers and have at least three ways to solve one problem. Man to machine, everything seems to listen to them and dance to their tune.

The only problem with them is their inability to focus, especially in the beginning. They take time to realise what they want to do. They invest the most strenuous work with fun. Give them money and appreciate their work in full view of others. They need both to feel satisfied. High-sounding titles also make them swell up with pride!

As bosses, they are good organisers and delegators. They command their team well and can talk to them and motivate them beautifully, too. They always have plans and back-up plans for everything.

Air, Fire and Earth meet in this extremely energetic combination. GemLeoVirs will be positive yet grounded, creative yet detail-oriented, and extremely dynamic in view and action.

Famous GemLeoVir Personalities
Sunita Williams, Salujja Firodia, Karthik Muthuraman, Sri Mulyani Indrawati, Shriya Saran, Kavya Madhavan, Manoj Bharathiraja, Urvashi.

132. GEMINI–VIRGO–LIBRA

Eloquence and style mark them. GemVirLibs astound you with their impeccable language and stylish manners. Their air of geniality and laughter immediately puts you at ease. However, they also seem elusive. They may look as if forever thinking and deeply analytical when you meet them. There is more to them.

Mercury for the maverick fun-loving side, 'Planet Y' for the deeply analytical thoughts, and Venus for the love of beauty and grace, form the trident that supports this combination. Virgo adds perfection and analysis to their speech and gives them substance. Libra adds balance and a love for all the good things in life.

There is no chance of saying 'no' to their views for they talk so well that it seems rude to contradict. The problem, however, is that they never stick to their views. You cannot hold them responsible for that as the fickle and fast-moving Gemini mind finds new opinions as quickly as a magnet finds a pin. Please learn not to trust everything you hear them say.

You can't make a person a great talker and expect him or her not to use that ability for personal gain. They know how to use their words and even actions to get what they want. You can call it unfair and even unethical at times, but you cannot deny their absolute advantage over others. Words, words and more words! They simply have a mastery over them.

GemVirLib have a knack for looking good. They have excellent fashion sense and even the men can give women tips on how to dress. These people know how to use their words and body language to impress. Their whole persona exudes confidence.

GenVirLibs have a gift for languages. GemVirLibs are fast learners and even have a flair for understanding numbers – a Virgo blessing. There is no concept too difficult for them to grasp with their quick mind and analytical understanding. They are masters of the one-liner and are very good mimics.

Love is an adventure for them. The Gemini in them finds different things to please them in different people while the Libran tries to be fair to each one and not break anyone's heart. This person has a difficult time settling down to one person. The Virgo sense of perfection makes them know exactly how to woo each one of their different loves and they are excellent in the game of love – for it will be a game for them till they find a person to whom they truly commit. The Virgo fidelity can set in at any time in their love life and make them responsible and devoted.

GemVirLibs are extraordinarily talented. The spoken word is just one aspect, you can expect them to be good at myriad artistic and creative pursuits and the best part is that unlike plain Virgos they do not hide their talents. They are more than willing to display their evident skills.

They like to spend too. Despite the stingy Virgo, they are not uptight about money. GemVirLibs do not mind spending and, sometimes, with the wicked Gemini ways, they can make you spend for them too! You can get a dose of sarcastic, critically analytical remarks if you get on their wrong side. They do not lose their cool easily but if they do, you can expect scathing remarks.

What they truly lack are sensitivity and emotional understanding, as they do not have any Water element in them. So do not expect them to understand how you feel, and though they dispense gladness and joy about them, they do not like being around unhappy faces. They just hate tears. Another thing that you need to cope with is their indecisiveness.

The Gemini and Libra pull them in opposite directions while Virgo's nit-picking targets all the possibilities. There is a peculiar restlessness about them; their mind is always ticking. They also get easily distracted and bored. They see a hundred ways to do a simple thing and are great at complicating small things into big problems. For all their excellence in communication and evident confidence, they can be manipulative.

Gemini–Virgo–Libra – R.K. Narayan

'I've always written without any strain whatever, you know, without any deliberate effort.'[229]

As a young student, at a rather severe missionary school in Madras, R.K. Narayan first encountered the English language, and was immediately bewildered... The fact that he grew out of his bewilderment over English, a foreign language, and became a much sought after writer in the same language, says a lot about the Gemini-Libra gift of languages.[230]

Despite many astrological and financial obstacles, Narayan managed to gain permission from Rajam's father and married her.[231]

R.K. Narayan showed the Gemini flair for communication, the Virgo power over words and the Libran love for romance.

Love and Marriage for Him

You two surely look like a magazine-cover couple, for he is good-looking, and if he has chosen you, then so are you. Personal grooming is a sacred duty for him due to the Libran love of beautiful things and the Virgo attention to detail. He wants you to treat it as such too.

He wants a wife who can hold the fort on her own and look good while she does it. He gives you a free hand and lets you decide on the children's education, the colour scheme of the rooms, and how you want to spend your day. Just do not cry or create emotional scenes for he does not know how to handle them and they make him scurry away from you.

He likes poking fun at people and sometimes can get personal about relatives, even you. You have to have a thick skin, for he is very surprised if you take it as anything but a joke. Understanding people and their emotions requires time and that is one thing he never has. Travel is high on his cards.

Create a beautiful home for him with pretty knick-knacks, keep the food light and healthy, try out new looks and keep the conversation breezy. These make him very happy. He does exaggerate a little bit. You will know when he is doing that after being with him for some time.

---

[229] http://hindu.com/fline/fl2701/stories/20100115270116400.htm
[230] http://www.nybooks.com/articles/archives/2001/feb/22/the-great-narayan/?pagination=false
[231] http://en.wikipedia.org/wiki/R._K._Narayan

As a father, he is duty-conscious, but do not expect him to change nappies or spend time making mud pies with his children. His interesting talk and informative views help them form an expansive and cultured outlook.

Love and Marriage for Her
She is too airy and light to be pulled down by sadness. Actually, it is a shame to waste such buoyant spirits on negative thoughts. Learn to be happy and joyful when you are with her and do not expect her to understand deep emotional needs. If you have any such needs, then she is the wrong girl for you.

She is the woman to have if you like being the cynosure of all eyes, for she draws attention to you with her lovely looks and delightful smile. Possessiveness does not impress her and she demands freedom from such stifling attitudes. The best part about her is that she is independent and allows you to be, too. Insecurities never bother her. However, do not think that you can fool her into believing lies; this girl is far too smart to fall for dishonesty. She might not have penetrating emotional skills but she definitely knows when things are not what they seem, due to the clarity of Virgo.

She can surprise you with her meticulousness about certain things and then totally astound you by not caring about others. Take money for example; it flows from her hands – yet, that does not dissuade her from maintaining an account and diligently writing how much she spent each day.

You find her talking easily to everyone. She has the knack of making everyone feel at ease and it makes her a fabulous hostess. Don't take every tale she tells at face value for she has a habit of making the good sound better and the wild sound outrageous.

She can also be a great help in your work. She hates routine and loves travel: try and keep that in mind when planning a surprise for her.

As a mother, she works hard to fulfil her duties but do not expect her to tie her children to her apron strings. She teaches them to be independent and makes them well-rounded individuals.

At the Workplace
GemVirLibs are known for their communication skills. No one will be able to deliver a presentation with such skill or take apart long-winded documents with such clarity. They talk so well that sometimes you need to be wary of the things you might agree to when you are with them, for these guys are smart and know how to bend words to get their work done. These guys are made for elucidating abstract facts with ease. They're good at multitasking and are talented. It seems as if nature has endowed them with beauty and talent indiscriminately.

They are light and flighty but when they work, you see a different person: they are very dedicated and diligent in their duties.

They make good mentors, educators and artists. They also make excellent sales personnel for they are never dissuaded by a 'no'. Any profession that allows freedom of thought and is not mechanical in nature interests them. As bosses, they are extremely nit-picking and critical. Go to them well prepared but you will still end up with surprises. Expect them to change their plans without keeping you informed.

Air, Earth and another Air combine to make GemVirLibs light, vital and fun with a streak of duty that is pleasing.

Famous GemVirLib Personalities
R.K. Narayan, Asha Parekh, Robert Clive, Ayotollah Khomeini, Stuart Clark.

133. GEMINI–LIBRA–SCORPIO

Mercury, the messenger of the gods, adds complexity to Venus, the lover of all the good things in life. Add to this the Scorpio intensity and passion and we have GemLibScorps.

The first thing you notice about them is their language. They talk exceedingly well. GemLibScorps easily grasp different languages and have excellent linguistic skills. Do not get into an argument with them or you come out not knowing what you were fighting about; they confuse, out-think and out-talk you. However, despite their marathon talking sessions, they also like silence.

They are very intelligent and absorb ideas, theories and complex views without trying very hard. You can have a lot of fun when they are around. They have a wicked and witty sense of humour. They can mimic very well too.

GemLibScorps are fabulous at multitasking. They can do the work of three people and do it with a smile. They also like adding colour to their stories. Don't believe everything they say at face value, they do not mind adding their own version to the commentary.

Traditions do not bind them. They like to live life on their own terms and do not listen to rules. They can be extremely rebellious as children, and fight for the freedom to think and act for themselves. They evolve over time and seem changed over the years.

Travel is high on their list of must-haves. GemLibScorps need to travel; they feel stifled otherwise. New places, people and views are essential for their survival.

Their tendency to analyse and see all probabilities can make it difficult for them to reach decisions quickly. They mull over and analyse their problems from every possible angle to reach a solution. At times, the solutions may not last for long. However, they are very passionate and driven about certain things.

It will be very difficult to cage them in a specific idea or relationship for long without their consent. The Gemini fickleness and Libran ability to empathise with everyone, meets the all-knowing attitude of Scorpio and makes them easily change their views and loves.

There is an emotional side to them despite their airy ways and they easily get upset over seemingly innocuous things. They can get really angry. They never forget an insult and never take things lying down. You can expect snide remarks and furious looks when they get angry. To start with, they will satisfy themselves with cutting jibes and verbally finish you off. They have the Scorpio desire for revenge: be very careful if you take them on as an enemy for they stop at nothing, to get even.

Love will find them very confused. GemLibScorps want passionate, committed love but they can be very fickle, too. They want a partner with whom they can talk and be on an equal footing. If you try to cling to them, they will resist and leave; but if you let them be themselves and overlook their inconsistencies, they will happily stay with you. The Geminian in them can look for experimentation in love and that can turn tricky. But once they are committed they remain so. Mostly.

They are very creative and artistic. With the ingenuity and variations of Gemini, the superb communication skills and diction of Libra, and passion and perceptiveness of Scorpio, they can excel in everything from drama to music and arts to mimicry, with amazing versatility.

On the other hand, their high degree of intelligence can also make them excel as con artists. They can have all the downbeat qualities of the combination: being jealous, cunning, ruthless, scheming, conniving, vacillating, extremely changeable, unreliable and even addicted to vices.

They want change in life. Doing the same things day in and day out is not for them. GemLibScorps will never be satisfied with the status quo and will not mind rocking the boat to create a sense of excitement.

Gemini–Libra–Scorpio – Arundhati Roy
'I thank God that I had none of the conditioning that a normal, middle-class Indian girl would have. I had no father, no presence of this man telling us that he would look after us and beat us occasionally in exchange. I didn't have a caste, I didn't have a class, I had no religion, no traditional blinkers, which are very hard to shrug off. When I see a bride, it gives me a rash. I find it so frightening to see this totally decorated, bejewelled creature who, as I wrote in *The God of Small Things*, is 'polishing firewood'.'[232]

Words, opinions and views, with a heady dose of passion, just pour out of this GemLibScorp.

Love and Marriage for Him
He is a fun guy to be with. He makes you laugh and think, but do not think that you own him. He wants to be his own man even if he loves you. This guy needs a woman who can have a conversation with him and not bind him to emotions.

He gets bored of household chores, so do not expect him to help out at home. You also have to see that the bills are paid on time for he can be too lost in his myriad activities to care of these small details.

This guy is passionate to achieve something and is not happy just going with the flow. His views, opinions and ideas are liable to change, so do not try to remind him of what he said earlier. History does not interest him, especially if it contradicts his current opinions.

You also need to be fairly thick-skinned for he has a way of saying hurtful things when he is in a bad mood. He also knows how to sweet-talk you. He can make you do what he wants by saying it the way you want to hear it.

He needs you to be calm, sensible and, above all, unflappable. You must bring stability into his life, and a love for home. You have to be the one who cares for the family and spends time doing the routine tasks, for though he likes his family he also desires the freedom to think and do what he wants.

As a father, he teaches his children to think beyond the ordinary. He does not like forcing them into what they do not want and is good at realising their needs. He is not a hands-on father and is often caught up in his own world; but when he

---
[232] http://www.progressive.org/intv0401.html

is with them, he makes them laugh. He is a better father when his children start understanding what he says.

Love and Marriage for Her
Talkative and very intelligent, this woman knows her mind and speaks it too: it is just that her mind changes many times; but that is the most refreshing thing about her. She is your friend and mate. Do not expect her to be subservient.

Housework is not for her. This lady simply cannot be confined to the house. She needs to explore and do so many things that one place is not enough for her. She can multitask and multithink with great ease and needs a man with whom she can talk and argue things out. She is very creative and needs an outlet for her artistic talents. Watch her grow and evolve, and marvel at her fast learning.

She loves surprises and is good at springing parties and surprises at a moment's notice. She is the most fun girl you will ever know. Some things can make her rave and rant, though. She also stuns you with her emotional outbursts at times and can be quite sarcastic when angered. She needs a lot of love. She may not state her need for your affections but walks away hurt if you do not exhibit your interest in her. She definitely looks younger than her age: the secret lies in her agile mind. She never thinks herself into a rut and is always ready for new ideas. Don't laugh at her new obsessions for she takes them quite seriously.

As a mother, she is untiringly caring. Initially though, she needs help during the baby days. She loves playing with her children and is full of enthusiasm. She is the mother who organises get-togethers, parties and fun getaways without losing sleep or getting tired. She teaches them to be curious and interested in the world around them and trains them to use their minds rather than rely on others' views.

At the Workplace
GemLibScorps need careers that evolve with time. Routine and monotonous tasks are not for them. They are good in any profession that brings passion to learning. They can be excellent writers, orators and even lawyers with their flair for language and ability to think from every possible perspective. They are also good at learning from others.

They do not know what they seek when they start off, but move from one profession to another seeking, creating and evolving. They bring passion and energy to mundane work and make it more interesting. They are fantastic problem solvers and arrive at five different solutions to one problem.

Libra is a cardinal sign and makes them good at visualising and communicating their ideas. GemLibScorps can be good leaders and be more democratic than most. But remember, they are extremely smart and can see through you. Never try to fool them.

Double Air and Water make GemLibScorps creative and talented with an inexhaustible store of energy; they will astound you with their ideas.

Famous GemLibScorp Personalities
Alviro Petersen, Arundhati Roy, Cécilia Attias, Diana Penty, John Hastings, Manoj Tiwary (cricketer), Rituparna Sengupta, Pele, Monali Thakur, Drake, Bhairavi Goswami.

134. GEMINI–SCORPIO–SAGITTARIUS

Mercury, the messenger of the gods, gives this sign a mind that thinks of dozens of things at one time. Pluto, the lord of the underworld, adds passion and Jupiter adds knowledge and luck into this thinking mix of GemScorpSag.

These people are extremely quick at understanding even the most complex theorems. They find it very easy to understand the inner complexities of almost every strategy and idea. The quicksilver mind of Gemini meets the deep-thinking ways of Scorpio and the sharp brain of Sagittarius to endow them with an ease of understanding that leaves many gasping.

Action and adventure, in thought and deeds, propel them forward. They have a fun-loving streak too. They love speed and can be speed demons on the road or live it up by bungee jumping and whitewater rafting.

Ambition is very strong in them. They always dream of doing something big. Scorpio makes them extremely intense about making a strong impression while Sagittarius makes them long for a big stage to showcase their talents and hear applause. However, it takes them time to know what they want. They are rebellious as teenagers.

Once they decide to do something, they are unstoppable. They do not want to go against people's opinions and try and explain their stance. GemScorpSags have the Gemini ability to think and do multiple things at one time, while the Sagittarian desire for adventure makes them try out many things as well. They will rarely be interested in only one thing at a time.

They have a very positive outlook for life. They are rarely stressed out by problems for they see ten solutions for each. The Sagittarian happy-go-lucky spirit also adds to their good cheer. You can spend hours in their company, laughing and talking, for they have the Sagittarian zest for life and the Gemini quick tongue to tell long tales, mimic and laugh at jokes. GemScorpSags have a natural ability to talk well and make good orators with their gift of the gab and instinctive love of the limelight. They learn languages easily and can communicate their thoughts and ideas in interesting ways.

They love the outdoors. The Sagittarian love for sports is apparent in them. They are the biggest pranksters of their team. They are excellent impersonators and slapstick comedy experts who keep people in splits with their joking ways.

They are not afraid of expressing their love. They will go through a number of relationships before they decide on a single one. GemScorpSags will be committed to the one who can induce passion and intensity in them; if not, they move from one relationship to another, always seeking and never finding. Gemini has the tendency of always thinking that the next person will fulfil their dreams while Sagittarius is too free to want to be tied down to one person. Scorpio is the only sign in this combination that actively seeks a partner with whom to share its dreams and passions and is the only one that can keep them from straying – perhaps.

They are very good at sensing the undercurrents in any situation. The Scorpio ability to understand the hidden depths of human nature and the Gemini inquisitiveness make them adept in the art of analysing people. They can also don a façade to hide their true intentions. This goes on to another trait: they do have this habit of adding spice to stories to make them interesting. You will never know if they are telling the truth or not. While you can never accuse them of dishonesty, they mix truth and fiction to keep themselves amused, too.

They appear fun loving, adventurous: almost carefree. But there is a deep sensitivity to them. They are thin-skinned and can get get hurt quickly. They will never forget insults or jibes. Though most of the time they retaliate with a smart, cutting rebuttal, the anger can seethe deep inside. The Scorpio sting can make them very vengeful if you cross their paths with malicious intent. They can plot and plan ways to destroy an opponent while appearing cool and harmless. They can be dangerous. Though Sagittarius shows anger openly, GemScorpSags do not lose their cool when it can be harmful to their own cause.

Somewhere down the line they sober down and you have the wisest person in your friend. Sagittarus is the most intelligent and spiritual sign while Scorpio explores and unravels the deepest mysteries of life. Expect them to be highly evolved spiritually over time.

The possible shortcoming of this combination is flightiness. They may not stick to one thing for long and keep on experimenting with things in life. Their experimentations and the habit of looking for shortcuts in life, can be a heady mix. They are blessed with extraordinary talents: when coupled with deep intuition and knowledge, it becomes a double-edged sword – they can fly high or get into unnecessary entanglements.

Gemini–Scorpio–Sagittarius – Taylor Swift
'Most of the time, songs that I write end up being finished in thirty minutes or less.'[233]

'Everything that happens to me gets put into a song.'[234]

'I remember when I was a little kid and I used to think about how lucky I would be if someday I was just walking through the mall and saw some little girl walking by with my face on her t-shirt...When you spend so much time daydreaming about things like that, when that actually happens you don't ever complain about it.'[235]

Taylor Swift has the GemScorpSag need to shine, its honesty and its talent for putting thoughts on paper.

Love and Marriage for Him
If this guy has chosen you, you surely have brains, for he is not the sort to stay interested for long in just a pretty face. This man is full of opinions, ideas and views and likes a companion with whom he can talk and discuss all that enters his head. He knows a hundred ways to keep you amused and happy. He can think of another hundred ways to express his love for you.

He is full of vitality. Adventure is in his blood. He enjoys living life in the fast lane. Getting him hooked on you is not so easy. He can drift away very quickly. The easiest way to turn him off is to think and act in the same manner year after year. He wants change and likes a partner who can handle the effects of time with charm and intelligence.

---
[233] http://www.time.com/time/magazine/article/0,9171,1893502,00.html#ixzz1zXpWlVqW
[234] http://www.glamour.com/sex-love-life/2010/10/taylor-swift-talks#ixzz1zXv1q327
[235] http://www.marieclaire.com/celebrity-lifestyle/celebrities/taylor-swift-interview

He has the tendency to flirt and indulge in harmless chit-chat with members of the opposite sex. But he won't be pleased if you try out the same tactics: he is quite possessive and loves with Scorpio's intensity.

As a father, he is indulgent and fun loving. He rewards curiosity in his children and makes them adventurous. They enjoy his company. He ensures that they respect him.

Love and Marriage for Her

She is hard to pin down. Do not expect her to stay at home and cook for you. Her views are too many, her ideas too immense and her spirit too free to be confined to the house. Her laughter and chatter can fill your life with pleasant feelings if you let her. Do not act stuffy with this girl. She needs a person who can talk and also go scuba-diving with her. She is full of fun and adventure.

She is very ambitious and finds ways to make her ambitions come true. This is a partner you should take on only if you have are unafraid of being overshadowed. Support her in following her dreams for she is truly different from the others.

She evolves as she ages, and despite her age, there is a youthfulness about her. She is a harmless flirt – well, almost! Beware of her anger. She never takes things lying down if she can help it. She can really lose her cool and be quite sarcastic too.

As a mother, she is fun. She loves telling tales of far away places and enacting stories. Her children have a lovely time with her and learn to be curious and interested about the world.

At the Workplace

GemScorpSags excel in careers that offer them opportunities to change, learn and grow with time. They are a little impatient and not willing to wait too long for things to develop and learn patience only if the job interests them. It takes them time to decide what they want, but once they do, they stick to it and work on it with passion, intensity and ambition. They are very original and can think of astounding ideas to enhance productivity or solve problems. They are masters in handling emergencies.

They do well in jobs that allow them to talk and express their views. They do not mind travelling either. They can be great sportspersons with the versatility of Gemini, the passion of Scorpio and the sheer strength of Sagittarius. Money and glory are what they seek and you can be sure that they will find them. They are definitely your smart workers and the fastest by far.

They have fun at work and do things with a certain flair. They have the habit of playing with words and you can't always sure of what they say. As bosses, they aim for the skies and have countless ways to reach there.

GemScorpSags have the ability to talk, and the passion and the exuberance to live life to its fullest.

Famous GemScorpSag Personalities

Taylor Swift, Manny Pacquiao, Riteish Deshmukh, Javed Jaffrey, Rohit Khosla, Udham Singh, Asghar Farhadi, Keki Dadiseth, Ann Patchett, Prem Rawat, Lilian Thuram, Richa Chadda, Ragini Khanna.

135. GEMINI–SAGITTARIUS–CAPRICORN

Mercury, the often changeable and highly intelligent messenger of the gods, joins hands with the extremely knowledgeable and ambitious Jupiter, and the wise old Saturn.

GemSagCaps are very ambitious. Both Sagittarius and Capricorn make them strive for their dreams. They think big and want to shine on the world stage. Applause, appreciation and lots of money with glory are all they dream of. Gemini and Capricorn make them good at talking and getting their way.

They can be highly unconventional, too. Gemini makes them think of wild ideas and they can out-think anyone. Add to it the Sagittarius's devil-may-care attitude and you have a combination that does not care about societal norms or rigid beliefs. The Capricorn's conservative thinking is diluted in GemSagCaps, though they are happy to receive the approval of those who matter.

GemSagCaps are happy people. They spread cheer and goodwill wherever they go. Expect them to light up conversations with their cheer and wit. They can work magic with words. The Gemini command over language and Sagittarian clown in them will make them good talkers, pranksters, mischief-mongers and linguists as well.

Adventure and travel are high on their list of wants. They love roughing it out just to see new things and notch up new adventures. Expect them to learn all about different customs and cuisines, and pick up new languages. You should travel with them to really know how to travel adventurously. They can set new trends with their desire to try everything once. They are party animals. Food definitely entices them and their parties come with fabulous food.

Family is very important to them. They are extremely close to their parents, especially their father: most Capricorns are. Capricorn also makes them feel responsible for their family always. They somehow manage their activities in such a way they don't impact their family members.

The Sagittarian integrity also makes them honest people with noble intentions. Sagittarians will fight for a cause, especially something that has larger repercussions for society. Sagittarian childlike enthusiasm, when combined with Gemini gregariousness and Capricorn leadership, makes them excellent at sports, too. Even if they are not seriously involved in sports, they still enjoy them enthusiastically.

Love is about experience rather than true commitment for them. These loving creatures are always ready for new adventures and find it hard to settle down. Gemini's search for a better partner and the Sagittarian fear of commitment will combine to make them extremely wary of settling down for good. The only thing you can say with certainty is that their partners will always be very intelligent. GemSagCaps are attracted to bright minds and can't spend any length of time with a person who hangs on to just one idea. Their ability to multitask in love can let them flirt with four different people at the same time without anyone the wiser. Love gurus, indeed!

Whatever they do, you can be sure that they don't really try to hide it for long, including their numerous affairs or wild ideas.

They blast others with anger occasionally. They know how to use their tongues with deadly intent and can be quite sarcastic. Gemini and Capricorn also add devious smartness to them. If they know your weakness, they have no compunctions about using it for their personal gains. Sagittarian honesty makes them say exactly what they are up to; yet they have the ability to convince the people who matter, about their unconventional stance. Their disdain for societal norms grows as they age, for even the old-fashioned Capricorn starts the process of reverse aging and becomes more open to new ideas.

The Gemini lack of focus can afflict them at times. GemSagCaps are so good at different things and so easily grasp the most complex facts that their interests often wander. Their talent and originality can sometimes not attain its rightful reward for they are not able to sustain their interest for long. Their driving ambition and high intelligence can make them try their hand at various things without staying engrossed for long.

The sad part about this extremely intelligent combination is that they are never able to realise when they are truly happy. Only when they lose that happiness for a reckless adventure does the realisation strike them. GemSagCaps are eternal seekers and might never be able to truly find what they seek.

Even though they try very hard, they are not able to hold on to money for long either. The Capricornian instinct to save faces a losing battle with Sagittarian recklessness.

They understand and talk about spiritual matters. They believe in an omnipresent force but are not religious. They may talk about some divine experiences, which may not make perfect sense to you but they believe in it and their faith shines through.

Gemini–Sagittarius–Capricorn – Kabir Bedi

'I was drawn to people who thought unconventionally…we experimented with various substances, our lifestyles, our marriage…that was part of our rebellion too. We challenged many social norms.'[236]

A true wandering GemSagCap, his career has spanned three continents, including India, the United States and many European countries in three mediums: film, television and theatre. He is best known in Europe for playing the pirate Sandokan in the highly popular TV mini series and for his role as the villainous Gobinda in the 1983 James Bond film Octopussy. He is very popular in Italy in particular, and is fluent in Italian. In 2010, he was knighted by the Italian government.[237]

Love and Marriage for Him

This guy is definitely not a reliable husband. If you love him, be happy as long as he is with you for you never know what the future holds. You need to be strongly individualistic and self-sufficient if you want to try out a relationship with him. He may understand your emotions but do not expect him to be besotted. This guy does

---

[236] *Hello!* August 2010

[237] HTTP://EN.WIKIPEDIA.ORG/WIKI/KABIR_BEDI

not listen to logic or emotions. The best way to treat him is to be as cool as him. Do not try and hold on to him or rely on him.

He cannot hold on to money for long, so you need a separate bank account to cater to your needs. He is the guy to be with if you want life as an adventure without getting emotionally involved. He loves travelling and it will be great if you enjoy it too. Though I am not sure that he will take you out on every trip!

He saves and cares for the children. Fatherhood can sober him down; but, even then, do not expect him to become a normal house-bound husband. He wants his children to be individuals in their own right. He is a fun father who can also make them respect him. Fatherhood is one relationship he truly treasures.

Love and Marriage for Her
She is lovely and charming and seems absolutely different from any other girl you have ever met. Her ideas, views and intelligence set her apart. She cannot be a traditional wife. This girl is too individualistic to fit into a joint family or a conservative idea. She can never listen to orders. She is extremely ambitious, and though a corporate life may not excite her, she tries her hand at different options. Do not try to stop her. Her mind and body can never be caged.

Fun loving and adventurous, she seeks out new experiences in life. You can never get bored with this girl for she has many ideas and a lovely wit to keep you engrossed for hours.

You need to provide household help. Though she can easily manage more than two tasks at a time, housework is not for her. She is extremely bad at conserving money and can run wild in shopping malls.

As a mother, she definitely works overtime. Her children have fun with her and also respect her. Motherhood can tone down her wild, childish ways and make her more responsible, but do not expect her to change completely. She teaches her children to stand up for themselves and their views.

At the Workplace
Ambitious, energetic and driven, GemSagCaps work overtime to achieve their dreams. The only problem is that they may have problems about what their dreams actually are in the beginning. Their excellent communication skills and extremely intelligent views can make them grasp complex facts and explain them with ease. This makes them excellent mentors and philosophers.

This combination also works well in sports. They are naturally inclined towards athletic pursuits. They are master storytellers, writers and authors, and excel in creative pursuits or intellectual fields. More than money, they need mental stimulation to keep them happy and contented in a profession.

They need a big stage. They want to shine and listen to applause, and can never work in the background. They need to be in professions where they can keep on re-inventing themselves.

They are known to work well and smart. They are fun loving and jovial bosses and are very good at delegating their work to the right people. Don't hang on to their every word as gospel as they can change their mind anytime if they find a better way of doing things.

Air, Fire and Earth meet in this sparkling combination of wit, intelligence and ambition. Nothing will ever hold them back from living a life full of exciting twists and turns.

Famous GemSagCap Personalities
Kabir Bedi, Catherine Middleton, Jeff Skoll, Michael Schumacher, K. Bhagyaraj, Dolly Bindra, Anusha Dandekar, Christy Turlington.

136. GEMINI–CAPRICORN–AQUARIUS

The versatile Mercury, the old man Saturn and the inventive genius Uranus meet to create GemCapAquas. They are full of ideas and views. Both Gemini and Aquarius endow them with a talent for thought. They are able to think of the most outrageous things, talk of the wildest ideas and always seem to be thinking something different. While Gemini makes them absorb new ideas at lightning speed, Aquarius gives them the gift of being original. Capricorn gives shape and solidity to those zillion thoughts.

Conversations with them are rarely boring. They are witty, sensible and fun to talk to. They are fabulous as friends. GemCapAquas love people. They are sociable creatures who enjoy having a lot of people around them. They are also good at observing. The double Air sign helps them in understanding people.

Their highly inventive minds and the Gemini ability to think of ten new things make them think of solutions more than problems. Rebelliousness marks them out. They do not like to think conventionally, especially as they become older. They prefer freedom over anything else – freedom to think and talk as they wish.

GemCapAquas have a natural affinity for languages. They understand at least four languages and are always be keen to learn new things. GemCapAquas surprise you by showing a detached side to their intelligent and articulate personality. They like being alone at times and will think their most fruitful thoughts during their detached phases.

Their inner core is unshakeable despite their frivolous ways. They never lose direction though they wander now and then. The Capricorn Earth element makes them stable despite the wild thoughts of Gemini and Aquarius. Capricorn imparts industriousness to them and reduces the flightiness of Gemini and Aquarius. It channelises the Aquarian genius to create value from their ideas and sobers Gemini from its adolescent behaviour. The complex mix retains the best of the three zodiacs.

The Gemini's flirtatious love and the Aquarian's clumsiness with emotions make them prefer a lot of entanglements to actual commitment. They might be unable to hold on to their love for long before getting attracted to others: Gemini makes them think that there is another more promising partner just round the corner. But they will be faithful once they reconcile themselves to what they have. Capricorn desires a partner who brings respectability to them. So they may settle into marriage early but may wander in their forties as Capricorn blooms later.

Family is important to them. The Capricornian desire for a happy family life makes itself felt in them, despite their unconventional attitudes. Money is important to them too, though it is never the focus of their lives. Despite the lack of stinginess, the street-smart Gemini and the money-conscious Capricorn make sure that they save some for themselves and their families and do not splurge everything.

They also have hidden creative and artistic talents. Gemini gives them the gift of words and Aquarius adds creativity. Capricorn makes sure that their ideas are never run-of-the-mill. The good thing is that they are too smart to waste it. They are very enterprising; they are good in creating business empires out of smart ideas. If not an empire, they would at least have a second serious income.

GemCapAquas are never truly satisfied by what they achieve. Glory matters to them of course, but more than that, they will always want to feel motivated and interested in what they do. They seek to overcome challenges rather than resting on their laurels. They always have the itch to do something else, go a little further and explore a little more. They think a lot about the future and want to leave a legacy that benefits the world at large. They are humanitarians at heart and do the smart thing of leaving behind a viable opportunity that helps people but benefits society too.

The Saturnine dark moods and depression do afflict them at times. However, the forward thinking Aquarius and gregarious Gemini empower them to come out of their moods quicker than typical Capricorns.

They can be plagued by too many thoughts and ideas and always feel that the other idea was better. There is a danger of dissipation of their energies, as they are not focused on one. They find it difficult to stick to one idea, thing or person for long. They prefer having multiple options. They run the risk of being a jack-of-all-trades and master of none.

They are also people with the habit of telling you more than what meets the eye and adding spice to a simple tale to make it interesting. Loyalty is one factor that can be missing in them. They can be scheming, plotting and heavily political, if needed, to get what they want.

They are interested in spirituality as well. The earthy Capricorn and the curious Aquarius make them delve into spiritual matters. Though they never follow traditions, they are interested in learning more about the world and its myriad secrets.

Gemini–Capricorn–Aquarius – Urmila Matondkar

'I have covered most genres of film and ventured into areas that people even today would hesitate to step into.'[238]

'I am full of passion for life and I don't do anything just for the heck of it...I am very traditional at heart and believe in the institution of marriage. But I also believe that one should not rush into things because somebody else is getting married. I don't understand what the phrase 'to settle down' means. One needs to settle in one's mind first.'[239]

Urmila has the ability to pursue her goals without being led away by traditional viewpoints and has an optimistic take on life like a GemCapAqua.

Love and Marriage for Him

He likes being a part of the family despite his lively mind. He is the most relaxed and cheerful in a family setting. Hs wittiness ensures he is never dull.

He loves travelling and moving around. Both Gemini and Aquarius fill him with the desire to meet new people and go to new places. He needs an independent partner. He is ready to leave the reins in your hands as long as you know what he wants. You can have a career but must care for the family too. He also wants a partner with whom he can talk and discuss his varying views. Intelligence is the first thing that he looks for. You also have to be the one in charge of daily routines.

---

[238] http://www.bollywoodlife.com/news-gossip/urmila-matondkar-celluloid-will-always-be-my-first-love/
[239] http://www.rediff.com/movies/2003/may/29urmila.htm

He can be a little flirtatious, especially as he grows older. This man needs his independence and runs away if stifled in a relationship. When angry, he can sulk and make sarcastic comments.

Capricorn rules fatherhood and makes him a good father. He likes spending time with his children and is full of fun ideas. He teaches them to think for themselves and appreciates an independent spirit in them.

Love and Marriage for Her
She wants to be a homemaker, but her distracted mind makes her drop tasks midway. She definitely needs help with everyday tasks. You need to love conversations if you want this girl in your life. She is smart with money and does not indulge in impulsive shopping. She wants to save for the future and has her priorities right.

She is very affectionate and loving and has lots of friends. She wants to be a problem-solver. She is also quite ambitious. This lady can do almost anything once she sets her mind to it. Her only fault is that she gets easily distracted. She can be an extraordinary partner in your business. She can take control of things easily but still will be a charming and vivacious presence.

She does everything possible to keep family members happy and contented. If, despite her efforts, some people refuse to acknowledge her worth, her sarcastic tongue tears them to shreds. If you don't value her, she will make alternate arrangements to have her quota of fun to make up fort all those years lost looking after your home. She will look and behave like a teen in her forties: you must keep her happy or lose her forever.

She is the ideal mother who laughs and plays with her children. She teaches them the value of independent thoughts. She is their best friend.

At the Workplace
GemCapAquas take time to decide what they want and change quite a few professions before settling down in one. Once they decide, they work their way to the top with their brilliant ideas and solutions.

They are smart talkers and friendly too. They excel in fields that require communication and inventive ideas. Media, the creative fields and careers that require dealing with people suit them well. They can also be inventors and scientists of repute. The Gemini flair for writing sees them excel in written communication. They also have a flair for languages and are usually multi-lingual. They are geniuses at work and do well in all fields that require brains more than brawn.

They need to reign in their tendency to get bored and jump professions, if they want to scale the heights of which they dream. The smart thing to do would be to find a profession that is very dynamic and still offers a chance to grow. As bosses, they are fun and inventive. They know how to lead without making enemies.

Double Air and Earth combine in GemCapAquas to empower them with brilliant intelligence. GemCapAquas have the ability to pull their ideas through with diligence and smartness.

Famous GemCapAqua Personalities
Urmila Matondkar, Franklin D. Roosevelt, Drew Barrymore, Jagjit Singh, Shaun Tait, Jim Laker, Shalmali Kholgade.

137. GEMINI–AQUARIUS–PISCES

Mercury, the messenger of the gods, joins forces with the eccentrically inventive Uranus and the deeply mysterious Neptune in GemAquaPisces.

The first thing that strikes you about GemAquaPisces is their extreme creativity. You can also be sure that whatever they do involves some form of communication as it involves two Air signs, Gemini and Aquarius. They have the Gemini gift of talking and expressing themselves beautifully. Aquarius makes them inventive, original and wacky and Pisces turns them into highly evolved personalities.

The only problem with Pisces is that it reflects its environment. This can be an advantage or a disadvantage. If their environment pushes them to achieve excellence and teaches them discipline, they mirror it and if it is veered towards deception and laziness, GemAquaPisces reflect those.

GemAquaPisces live in their minds. All three signs tend to think a lot. Gemini can think of a thousand things in a second, while Aquarius can think of the wildest and most futuristic ideas and Pisces loves living in a dream world. This heavy emphasis on the mind makes GemAquPisces thinkers and dreamers. They astound you with their original ideas and unconventional views.

They are excellent friends who never think twice before coming to help and are rarely affected by their friends' contrary opinions. If they like you, they understand your motives and forgive your faults. Fun and laughter walk hand in hand with them: they drive away despair. The Gemini witticisms and the Piscean mimicry match the Aquarian wacky humour to make them cheery people to meet. Of course, they have their mood swings too, but the blues rarely last long.

Unconventionality characterises them, as none of the three signs are known for their love for tradition. GemAquaPisces will never be saddled by society's notions of what is right or wrong. They have the Aquarian revolutionary thought processes, with the out-of-the-box mind of the Gemini. Pisces is fluidic and makes them extremely changeable and malleable. These are extraordinarily different people.

They are always ready for love. GemAquaPisces find it hard to settle down with someone special, especially in their early years. They always look for the elusive perfect partner and are afflicted by the Gemini problem of thinking that the next corner hides the perfect one. It takes them time to realise what they mean by perfect. Aquarius, too, is bored after they know you inside out and keeps experimenting with relationships. They rarely hold grudges against their previous loves and prefer parting on amicable terms.

They evolve over the years. They have an uncanny ability to look different every time you meet them. It is not just their appearance that changes but their thought processes and ideologies, too.

All the three signs love to learn. GemAquaPisces are always learning and absorbing new ideas throughout their lives. Gemini is the most intelligent, Aquarius is a genius and Pisces is the wisest. They are an extraordinary mix of intelligence and wisdom.

There is a deep spiritual side to them as well. Pisces and Aquarius make them intensely involved in deciphering the deepest and most unique mysteries of the world. They are also quite philanthropic.

Handling money is not one of their strong points. They may try and save for the future but their present can be riddled with debts if nobody restricts their expensive ways.

GemAquaPisces lack the stability of Earth and the drive of Fire. They can easily spend hours dreaming and conjuring up an alternative reality without working towards it. Don't expect punctual and disciplined behaviour from them unless it has been inculcated in them from childhood. GemAquaPisces can think of wondrous ways to change the world and be full of ideals yet will always be quite sloppy in their personal habits.

GemAquaPisces do not aim to conquer the world. They lack ambition and need to be pushed and encouraged from time to time. If they are failures and waste their immense talents there is only one person who can be blamed – they themselves.

Addictions can be a problem. They love experimenting and can end up getting addicted to substances. They also need to be very careful about the company they keep for they can easily pick up bad habits.

They are 'not quite there' at times. The Aquarian detachment is quite evident in them. The Piscean love of daydreaming also makes them seem unresponsive to their realities. The fact is that they are aware of reality but try and think otherwise.

GemAquaPisces are thinkers of wild ideas yet sensitive enough to cry at movies. They have a heart that never says no and a tankful of talent to help them live life at their own terms. They need to make their priorities and then need help in planning and driving their way to success.

Gemini–Aquarius–Pisces – Sam Manekshaw
During World War II, a surgeon attending on his bullet-riddled body asked him what had happened. He replied that he was 'kicked by a donkey'.

'I wonder whether those of our political masters who have been put in charge of the defence of the country can distinguish a mortar from a motor; a gun from a howitzer; a guerrilla from a gorilla, although a great many resemble the latter.'

On being asked by Indira Gandhi if he was ready to fight on the eve of the Indo-Pakistani War of 1971: 'I am always ready, sweetie.'[240]

Sam Manekshaw represented the best in GemAquaPisces with his eloquence, bravery and outspokenness.

Love and Marriage for Him
Look closely before settling down with him, for though he is sweet and knows how to make you laugh, he is rarely ready for serious responsibilities. This man can escape like water through your fingers.

---
[240] http://en.wikipedia.org/wiki/Sam_Manekshaw

You will have to be the responsible and stable one to anchor him. This guy has no ego hassles about letting you lead, but don't try to dominate him aggressively, for he may slip out of your grasp. You have to look after the money for it does not stay long with him.

He is full of fun and jokes, and knows enough anecdotes to fill a storybook. But his mind is rarely still and he is always thinking. He needs you to keep him sane and grounded. Do not be negative around him; instead, talk to him sensibly and encourage him to use his creativity positively. He is very sensitive and easily gets hurt. Also, keep the mystery alive in your relationship. He likes the mental gymnastics and can wander off to tackle new interests outside if he is bored at home.

As a father, he is extremely loving and caring. He is a friend to his children, pampers them and rarely disciplines them. He encourages them to think for themselves and always stands by their decisions.

Love and Marriage for Her
If you dream of a traditional wife, she is definitely not the one for you. This lady is too free-willed and unconventional to worry about traditions. Housework rarely interests her. She wants a partner who is a friend, not a dominating presence. You have to think over her views and ideas before responding or she gets very hurt. It will be an added advantage if you are intelligent and interested in a myriad of projects and marvel at the various mysteries of the world.

Help her look after her money and guide her in her investments for she is quite lost with numbers. Words and music appeal more to her and she likes to spend her time talking, singing or involved in some unusual hobby or creating something unique. Her mind needs continuous stimulation or she will be bored and sad.

As a mother, she is fun. She doesn't impose discipline and routine means nothing to her. She loves playing with her children and can be a child with them. She definitely needs some help in bringing them up or she can let them run wild. She understands their smallest desires and they hide nothing from her.

At the Workplace
GemAquaPisces are artistic and creative. They do extremely well in careers that require creative inputs and inventive minds. They are never bound by routine. They are extraordinarily versatile. They have the capacity to create and gift the world something unique, wacky, original, and pathbreaking. The only thing that can work against them is that they bore of things very quickly and need to learn the art of perseverance.

They can do well in professions that are dynamic, unstructured and need abstract thinking. They excel in professions that have to do with communication in any form. They are also experts in all professions that need empathy and a human touch.

More than money or glory, they seek the thrill of doing something different. They do extraordinarily well in extraordinary professions. They are cut out for the most creative professions in the world. They need a lot of encouragement, for despite their creative talents, they lack the drive and stability to stay in their professions. They need people who can guide and monitor them to achieve the desired results.

They can be the most creative and humane boss you could hope for. Just be ready for a new adventure or sudden changes in plans periodically.

Double Air and Water meet in GemAquaPisces and give them excellent communication skills and extraordinary thought processes. They will rarely be average and will astound everyone with their talent and ideas yet they will need help in maintaining their equilibrium for daily life.

Famous GemAquaPisces Personalities
Sam Manekshaw, Theo Walcott, Shreya Ghosal, O.J. Simpson, Sir Alec Guinness, Liza Minnelli, Aretha Franklin.

138. CANCER–LEO–VIRGO

The highly emotional and sensitive Moon meets the proud and generous Leo and the meticulously perfect Virgo in this strong yet insecure combination. CanLeoVirs have the tenacity of Cancer, the focused, ethical nature of Virgo and the majesty of Leo.

CanLeoVirs like being well groomed and exude a confidence that is never overbearing. They project a sense of clean perfection. Discipline and routine are a part of their lives. They have neat and clean habits and hate to be surrounded by mess.

They take time analysing and thinking things out, and don't make rash, untimely decisions. They are emotional and sensitive. They have a sentimental aspect and are often nostalgic: usually a golden glow bathes their past. At times, they can be a bit too emotional but that side is reserved for their intimate friends and family.

Family is extremely important and means everything to them. They love and adore their mothers. They make their family the centre of their lives and seek to provide them with every happiness. Financial and emotional security rank high on their list of priorities and they work hard to ensure that for their family. Every CanLeoVir dreams of building a large, beautiful home for their family, having planned the interiors and details to the last brick.

They are extremely loving and caring. The tenderness with which they treat everyone is charming. They are generous, but with care. They scorn at wastage of any kind but give freely for anything that involves family, financial security, children, parents or the underprivileged. They are the champions and mother figures for the marginalised.

They are very conscientious, and fulfil every role perfectly. CanLeoVirs can astound you with their different personas for different people – they are loving children, stern yet caring parents, fun friends, diligent workers and perfectionist bosses. Love, care and generosity would be common aspects in all the roles that they play.

They are deeply sensitive and perceptive. They can sense people's emotions and thoughts. They don't just understand you but also go out of their way to help you.

They also have their Leo pride and ego. Though their affection, love and generosity are true, they love demonstrating them when people are watching. They like to dramatise and are romantic, but aren't excessively narcissistic like true Leos. Their pride is more about their work, their family, their ethics, their language, their belief systems and their culture.

They are interested in health and are good at understanding medicines. They love food but try and make it as healthy as possible. They also love cooking and serving delicacies to friends and family. Their anger can explode at times, though rarely. They usually show their anger by being irritable and hard to please. They can sulk for hours so be ready to soothe them.

They love very deeply and truly. CanLeoVirs take their time deciding on a partner but once they find you true, they are truly loyal. They like to be treated with love and respect.

Money and status are their twin ambitions. Money is very important to them and they work to save and secure it. They need to have a fat bank balance to get a peaceful night's sleep. They also want to be respected and appreciated. They worry about their social status and what people think of them. They work extra hard to improve their status.

They stick by their moral codes and are not driven by the herd. They try and raise their voice against injustice. Their moral sense and confidence to speak out only increase as the years go by. The Leo desire to protect the weak and the Virgo desire to do the right thing ensure they never withdraw from a fight between right and wrong.

Do not leave your CanLeoVir friends to fight the battle alone. They need support: despite their bravery, they can easily crumble if people around them do not appreciate their work. They are generous and friendly too. Their imagination and sense of drama are evident when they are out with friends and they regale them with amusing stories. They need love and appreciation to achieve their true worth.

They are prey to insecurities and doubts. Despite their own high standards, they may still feel they are not good enough as parents, children or employees and can worry too much about little things. Cancer's extreme sensitivity and tendency to read between the lines can be compounded by Leo's ego, and they can be angered by trifles.

They can be highly critical and acidic in speech when they are hurt. They push themselves hard towards unrealistic perfectionist standards and can hurt themselves and others too. They have mood swings with periods of deep depression and need to be cared for during those times. These loving creatures need their families to stand by them like they do for their families.

Cancer–Leo–Virgo – Vijayakanth
'While heroes and heroines were treated to sumptuous food and fruit juices, we were served only sambar-rice or curd-rice and tea. The rage that was seething inside made me resolve that I would start my own production company one day and treat everyone alike. Today, all those working in my company get the same food,' he says.[241]

Vijayakanth says that during the past twenty-five years, he has spent much of his income from films on charitable work.[242]

'In my films, heroines are treated with dignity. You will never come across vulgar dance movements, embarrassingly intimate love scenes or double entendres.'[243]

Vijayakanth has the creative energy and generosity, compassion and graciousness of a CanLeoVir.

---
[241] http://articles.timesofindia.indiatimes.com/2008-06-22/chennai/27784132_1_vijayakanth-dmdk-winnable-seats
[242] http://www.asiantribune.com/news/2010/08/26/actor-vijayakanth-hits-back-black-money-issue-karunanidhis-remarks-made-out-jealousy
[243] http://www.reocities.com/Hollywood/Set/1876/inde.htm

Love and Marriage for Him

He works to provide you with what you desire. This man fulfils all his duties and never tires of his responsibilities. He even does odd jobs at home with a smile. All he wants is appreciation and to be treated with respect.

Pet and pamper him, for he needs that. He loves his mum's cooking, so don't try and compete, but be generous enough to allow him his quirks. He understands you and is truly sensitive to your needs. Do follow his various routines and schedules as he can panic when he is not in control. His obsession for perfection can be unnerving. But his love, care and generosity will keep you going.

There can be times when you find him pensive and feeling quite low. Do not let him stay that way for long or he can let himself get really down in the dumps. He needs you to cheer him up at those times: a partner who is understanding and sensitive. Loud and aggressive women will never do for him.

As a father, he is strict yet caring. He makes his children follow a high moral code and is extremely protective of them. He insists on good education.

Love and Marriage for Her

Loving, caring, nurturing; this lady can be the air beneath your wings if you shower her with love and trust. You can easily leave her to take care of the minute details and manage things but remember to thank her for her care. Do not take her help for granted or you lose a valuable friend and loyal mate.

She is very strict about maintaining cleanliness and following certain routines. You need not have any worries when she handles money for she is more intent on saving and investing than splurging. Her appearance is usually as immaculate as her house. She loves cooking for people but does not like to be tied up with the kitchen all the time.

This lady has the potential to become a strong individual in her own right. Hard times see a stronger and more confident side of her. Though she is prone to depression, she always puts on a brave face and tries to fight her demons. She needs a man who can be her friend. Do not try and dominate her, for though she may look meek, she has enough strength to stand up for her beliefs.

As a mother, she is wonderful. She wants to nurture and protect her children but without spoiling them. She teaches them the right values and insists on good behaviour. She urges them to be responsible adults and trains them accordingly.

At the Workplace

CanLeoVirs are happy taking one small step at a time. They are content in careers that grow slowly but steadily. Once you hire them, they never leave you midway. Loyalty is their motto and they work exceedingly hard to prove their worth.

They can be great in creative fields and also excel in the boardroom. They know how to talk well and impress others with their clarity and flair. They like to plan and look at all the minute details before deciding on something. They are always prepared for an eventuality.

A seamless mix of cardinal, fixed and mutable signs, they are open to learning, are good at execution and ideate very well. You find it difficult to find faults in their preparation or execution and they would be deeply upset if you do. Though they may not admit it, they love appreciation; be generous with it.

As bosses, they insist on step-by-step learning and are very process-oriented. They look at the cost factor and know how to get work done economically. They are caring and generous, and treat their employees as family.

Soft yet strong, CanLeoVirs are creative, sensitive, honest, courageous and always true to their moral code.

Famous CanLeoVir Personalities
Vijayakanth, Pankaj Advani, Amar Upadhyay, Jesse Randhawa, Suhasini Maniratnam, Giovanni Agnelli Sr., Gilmar, Bob Beamon, Maha Vajiralongkorn, Emmanuel Petit, Klaas-Jan Huntelaar.

139. CANCER–LEO–LIBRA

The sentimental Moon, the regal Apollo and the ever-romantic Venus meet in CanLeoLibs. Emotion is a major part of their personality. They are soft-spoken people who are hurt at the smallest word of criticism. However, do not expect them to be so soft that you can trample on them.

Cancer is a highly emotional sign and makes its people desire excessive love and affection. Leo too has a need to be pampered, loved and adulated, while Libra just loves love. The combination of these three makes CanLeoLibs need and desire love of the deepest kind. Family, friends and partners need to be sensitive to their emotions or they inadvertently hurt them. They are very loving friends who never let you down.

Family is extremely important to them. They have the Cancerian adoration for their mothers. If they do not get their mother's love, they can turn against their family. They do not like living alone but want to be surrounded by their family, friends and dear ones. They are ultra-loyal, not just to life partners but also in friendships, family and work.

They are very creative and expressive. The Cancerian imagination blends well with the Libran ability to express itself beautifully. CanLeoLibs have a knack of saying the right thing albeit slightly emotionally. Leo adds showmanship to the creativity of Cancer and Libra. CanLeoLibs are not too shy to express their creativity. Expect them to revel in every kind of art – acting, singing, dancing – and to have amazing skills for speech and writing.

They are full of good humour and pranks, but never hurt anyone. They can turn quite philosophical too. They have an elephantine memory. They can describe explain in great detail incidents that happened decades ago. They have amazing empathy. Extreme sensitivity to their environment and to what others want or need makes them the favourite of everyone. They don't just understand the innermost needs and feelings of people but go all out to fulfil them or make others happy, especially their loved ones.

Food is one of their loves. They find cooking and eating the most relaxing of activities. Libra and Leo make them lazy at times. Whatever work they do, they do outside home, where they prefer taking the backseat but pepper it up with lots of advice and counsel.

Money is quite important to them and the Cancerian fear of being penniless makes them want to save. Yet, there can be times when they are unable to stop themselves from spending impulsively. Though they love sporting the latest fashion in their own style, they are good bargain hunters too.

CanLeoLibs have an innate sense of what is right and what should be done. They want to be fair always, and if you ever want them to rethink their decisions, just tell them that they are being biased, to make them rethink. They fret, argue and ponder on their decisions for a long time.

Love is an important theme in their life. They are never content till they are loved truly and adoringly. They idolise romance and want their love to be romantic, a little melodramatic and very, very sensitive. Emotions and tears are a great part of their love and they are apt to burst into tears at happy moments and sad ones. If these sensitive people they don't find love, they are heartbroken.

They are full of fears. The Cancerian phobias and fears plus the inner insecurity of Leo make them fear a lot of things in life, though they may not show it. Cancer adds mood swings while Leo makes them sulk a lot when they are upset. They need delicate handling and people who understand their many moods. An inflated ego, sulking for attention, being judgemental, imagined hurts are some of the negative characteristics of this combination. They can also be flamboyant, talkative and vain.

They think too much, especially about the various people in their lives. They worry for their parents and partners. They go through the mental gymnastics of a Libran while deciding things in life; the indecisiveness is worse if it involves their loved ones. They go through extreme emotional upheavals in love. They place a premium on relationships, and wring out every emotion that is connected to anyone they love. They are nostalgic. Strangely, they even savour the sadness that accompanies a heartbreak or separation.

Spirituality, and belief in a power greater than them, are evident. They like to think about and expound on the nature of God, religion and the metaphysical world. They are very generous, especially in love and for family. For the people in their lives, they can sacrifice anything. No one loves the idea of love like a CanLeoLib. No one can protect the weak and fight for social justice like them either. The only thing that they want from you is love, affection and some gratitude.

Cancer–Leo–Libra – Amrita Pritam
'*Maan suche Ishq da hai, hunar da daava nahin…*[I am proud of my pure dedication and I make no claims to artistry]'.[244]

Loneliness led her to writing at a very young age. Falling desperately in love with poet Sahir Ludhianvi, she left her husband. When the relationship with Sahir did not work out – he apparently had another woman in his life — Amrita found comfort with painter Imroze. It was this relationship that sustained Amrita for the last forty years of her life.[245]

Her poetry was emotional and sensitive, it brought feelings to the fore – much like her life. Amrita Pritam possessed deep sensitivity and a romantic disposition, which is the hallmark of a CanLeoLib.

Love and Marriage for Him
He is an absolutely fabulous husband if you know how to handle him the right way. Remember one thing – you cannot win arguments with him. Give him all the attention he desires, adore him, tell him that he is the best and he is happy… and so will you be.

He is quite emotional and sensitive, especially about his ego. If you want him to do anything for you, talk emotionally and appeal to his generosity. It works. There is a lot of insecurity in him and he wants a partner who understands it.

---
[244] http://www.apnaorg.com/articles/amrita/
[245] http://www.asianage.com/arts/poet-amrita-pritam-s-life-enacted-stage-252

You have to tell him about your feelings if he seems unaware. The moment you tell him your problems, he dismisses everything else to take care of them. His family, especially his mother, is very important to him. Food is very important to him too.

As a father, he is very loving and nurturing but needs respect from his children. He gives long lectures and advises them exactly on how to behave. He spends a lot of his time with them. He loves to show off their abilities.

Love and Marriage for Her

She is extremely loving and caring and expects the same from you. She is a true woman but with various moods. You have to be a sensitive person to be happy with her, for her moods and emotions are important to her and she does not like anybody making fun of them.

Grace and beauty come naturally to her. She loves dressing up and takes great care of her appearance. She talks with love and emotion, and her soft nature makes people turn to her for comfort. She also has a very lazy streak in her. It is hard to get her to do many things despite her evident talent, as she does not like to push herself to work. Encourage her and tell her how good it is for her bank balance.

She needs lots of attention. Talk to her, spend a lot of time with her, understand and praise her, be attentive to her needs and be romantic. Be ready for tears or sulks. She is quite possessive and will make your life hell, and hers too, if you like flirting. The best thing about her is the balance that she manages in every aspect of her life. She beautifully manages office, her parents and your family while also managing the cooking at home.

As a mother, she is fun, gregarious, generous and exciting. She instinctively knows how to care for children. Food is one of her ways of showing her love. She wants to be a part of their lives and can have trouble letting go as they grow older.

At the Workplace

CanLeoLibs are very artistic and love showing off their talent. They need a lot of encouragement initially, but once they get started, they never stop excelling. They are also good in careers that involve meeting and communicating with people or even finance or law. Careers dealing with children also attract them for they are always good with children. They do not mind waiting for their chance but cannot accept menial positions. They also need money, fancy titles and the opportunity to use their communication skills.

They are do well in positions where they can teach. They love telling people what to do and are excellent in passing on their learning in an interesting fashion to people.

They are good at delegating and teamwork. They know how to lead with emotions and make everyone a part of their team. Their subordinates need to remember that they need respect. Do not step on their emotions or egos. They are excellent leaders and motivators who can use words to magical effect.

Air, Fire and Air meet in CanLeoLibs to give them a high emotional quotient, great love of talk and a desire to shine bright despite all odds.

Famous CanLeoLib Personalities

Amrita Pritam, Mila Kunis, Shoaib Akhtar, Sir Alfred Hitchcock, Dada Khondke, Preeti Jhangiani, Sunil Chhetri, Mae West, Kirupanandha Variyar.

140. CANCER–LEO–SCORPIO

Moon, the ruler of emotions, Sun, the generous and proud giver, and Pluto, the secretive and powerful lord of the underworld, all rule this combination. CanLeoScorps are a mixture of two fixed signs (Leo and Scorpio) and one cardinal sign (Cancer); they are leaders, and truly strong and powerful personalities.

Lion, Scorpion and Crab! One is the king of the jungle, another can survive even a nuclear holocaust and the last one can hold on tenaciously for as long as it takes. You are meeting power, perpetuity and perseverance. Just beware!

There is style, attitude and assuredness when they walk in. You feel you are talking to someone very important whilst in their company. When they talk in passionate but measured tones, their intense eyes looking deep into yours, you are mesmerised by their magnetic personality.

The double Water in this combination makes CanLeoScorps very sensitive. They are extremely good at reading people. You have to be careful of what you think in front of them.

The Leo leads majestically and expects others to obey while Scorpio commands respect. There is no mutable sign in CanLeoScorps to let them follow anyone's ideas but their own. CanLeoScorps prefer to command, but when the situation demands they can turn on their charm offensive. They will cajole and coax their way into your head, even use tears as a weapon. A CanLeoScorp who sheds tears is unusual; they are too strong to weep.

They are pillars of strength to their families. They are very generous to their families who see the Leo's funny side too. They adore their mothers and are ready to lay down their lives for her. They act very responsible from the time they hit their teens.

Some CanLeoScorps realise the effect their intensity has on people and mask it with a happy-go-lucky and funny personality. Don't take jokes too far with them: one never steps on a Lion's tail or challenges the Scorpion's sting. Revenge is a compulsive reaction of a Scorpio and when combined with the Leo ego and Cancerian sensitivity, it can be life altering – for the one who crosses them.

Love is deep and enduring with them. Cancer's emotions don't get scattered and Leos are great romantics. You can expect them to start a little slow but if they get the encouragement, they will unleash their romantic self. The passion and sensuousness of Scorpio and the deep love of Cancer makes them fabulous, committed partners. Theirs is high-octane love, full of drama and special effects!

Now, we come to money and it is interesting to see how they use it. They love show and flamboyance, yet they go for economic bargains. They are generous to the people they love and there, you see the Leo magnificence and generosity of spirit. However, these guys are too smart to be used in any way.

Though CanLeoScorps have the Leo in them, they rarely roar. These guys smilingly expect submission and you can choose to be irritated by it or submit to it, they are not bothered. They just want to get their way. It is better to make them your friends rather than enemies. Remember, the Scorpio in them is very dangerous.

Of course, they are also very sensitive and fear rejection. They are very soft inside and use bravado as a defence against getting hurt; a stern and forbidding exterior keeps unwanted attention at bay. They can also read too much between the lines and imagine slights. Some poor souls with no malicious intent can be victims of this extra sensitivity.

The Fire sign of Leo also has a deep feeling of vulnerability, which it masks with its majestic posturing; this combined with the insecurities and mood swings of Cancer and vindictiveness of Scorpio makes them hate and fear competition. As they become more successful, they lose their fears and become more confident. It is then that they face their biggest challenge, for overconfidence can be their downfall. Once they have tasted success, they become either magnanimous like Leos or vindictive like Scorpios.

They also have a deeply religious side with the Leo love of religion and the Scorpio desire to delve into the mysteries of life. You can expect them to be flamboyant about their religious practices. They never give up. They don't know what defeat is and can never accept defeat as the final verdict. They shed a few secret tears but soon collect themselves and then go back to the fight. They just keep going till they achieve what they set out for.

Cancer–Leo–Scorp – Ben Affleck
Ben Affleck's story is one of the great rags-to-riches tales. Together with his childhood buddy, Matt Damon, he fought back. Bucking the system, they wrote their own screenplay, attracted their own finance, and produced and starred in their own movie. What really made Affleck's tale fascinating came later when, having squired pop star actress Jennifer Lopez and hit the absolute heights of tabloid fame, his offscreen life took centre stage, his career collapsed in ruins, and a second struggle for success was necessary. And this time he was on his own. He'd made it to the top twice.[246]

The creative talent, the deep passion for his work and his tenacity of purpose make him an ideal CanLeoScorp.

Love and Marriage for Him
He is a very good husband but needs an 'understanding' wife who is not too independent, aggressive or ambitious. He is totally for his family and works for his family's betterment. He wants his family to grow in status. Remember, according to him, his mother is the best cook in this world. Cancerians literally build shrines to their mothers. No point in competing with her.

He is very passionate and driven about his career. You are left holding the fort but keep him informed and take advice from him. He loves telling you how to do things. The wise way of get your way is to make him think it's his idea. There is a lot of ego in this guy and it is important that you respect it. He needs lots and lots of love.

As a father, he is very controlling. His children need to respect his views and follow his advice. Fatherhood is the only role where he does not mind his

---
[246] http://www.talktalk.co.uk/entertainment/film/biography/artist/ben-affleck/biography/6

ego taking a beating at times. Though he is controlling, there are times when his generous spirit and pride in his children let them get their way with him. He is delighted if they take his blessings every day.

Love and Marriage for Her
She is a very dignified lady. People find it very hard to get close to her at first. The fact is that this girl is so soft underneath that she has to protect herself by acting the part of a tough lady. It is only her enchanted circle of close family and friends who see her love and playfulness shine through.

This lady does not love easily, but when she does, she won't give up readily. She is one of those rare people who give their all in love. She loves with her whole heart, passionately, truly and benevolently. She is extremely loyal and loving. There is nothing you do that escapes her eagle eye, so do not try to act smart. The only way to get her attention is to love her truly and deeply.

She is extremely capable and strong, and she knows it. She needs neither your hand to hold nor your strong shoulders to lean on. What she wants is that you stand by her and keep the faith. Despite the dignified look, she can really let down her hair when the time comes to play. She will laugh loudly and play with the enthusiasm of a child.

As a mother, she is extremely loving and ambitious for her children. She plays, nurses, and looks after them with a fierce protectiveness. She can sacrifice a lot, including her ambitions, for them. She also wants her children to listen to her views. She is truly hurt if they choose a path very different from what she desires.

At the Workplace
These guys are extremely ambitious and dream of nothing less than world rule. They want to be acknowledged as the best in their profession and can be fiercely competitive. They know their strengths and weaknesses well. They work hard for success and want everything – money, status and power. If a CanLeoScorp is your subordinate, a pat on the back and the words, 'your best is yet to come', work wonders.

They can do well in any chosen career path with their intensity, passion, style and tenacity. They just hang in there till they succeed. Adversity brings out the best in them. They handle emergencies with maturity and finesse. They love taking on responsibilities and love being leaned upon. They are the leaders people esteem. As a boss, a CanLeoScorp is demanding. Keep his ego in mind. If you don't like him, he will simply know! He can also sniff out the faintest hint of deceit.

Water, Fire and Water combine to give the sign an overriding ambition and deep emotions, a big ego and a deep enduring strength to move on.

Famous CanLeoScorp Personalities
Ben Affleck, Melinda Gates, Pervez Musharraf, Johny Lever, Ranvir Shorey, Krishnan Nair (Jayan), Jesse Ryder, Barry Richards, John Howard.

141. CANCER–LEO–SAGITTARIUS

The extremely sensitive Moon joins the proud and generous Apollo and the highly intelligent Jupiter in this sensitive yet fiery combination. CanLeoSags want to be adored and loved. They want to be the centre of attention all the time. The Cancerian need for love, the Leo desire to be respected and the Sagittarian need for applause makes them suckers for the limelight.

Think of the symbol of Sagittarius – the Centaur: the body of a horse with human face, arms and torso, aiming an arrow at the sky. Now change the face into that of Lion's and have the body encased in a protective shell. Complex? Well, not really.

These people have an outward show of exuberance, pageantry and drama. They have the regal and dignified bearing of a Leo and exude all the charm and playfulness of Sagittarius. But deep inside, they are sensitive souls who can be deeply hurt when ignored or unloved. They may mask their behaviour either by extra cockiness or by putting up a tough exterior, but they are quivering soft inside.

They are very intelligent. Sagittarius is the professor of the zodiac, with profound knowledge, and loves to explore, mentally as well as literally. Leo shines bright, with its ability as problem-solver. When combined with Cancer, which learns lessons from life and stores each and every piece of valuable data in its deep memory, you have people who impress you with practical knowledge.

Their most endearing, and also their most detested, trait, is their blunt honesty. CanLeoSags pride themselves on saying it as it is. Other than that, they are fun to be with. They enliven parties with their laughter and sense of fun. They are highly individualistic and freedom loving, yet want to be tied to the people they love. The fact is they will find it a perpetual struggle to reconcile their Cancerian desire for home and the Sagittarian need for freedom.

CanLeoSags are very creative. They are creative artists who do not hide in the background. Cancer makes them highly imaginative, and Leo and Sagittarius make them want to showcase their talent.

They adore their mother and are heartbroken if she does not treat them with the same unadulterated love. They like looking after their parents and are very respectful to them. They can drown themselves in nostalgia.

They love travel and adventure, though in comfort. Do not expect them to happily trudge miles with just a rucksack for company. They like to travel with friends and have fun while they go.

Love is extremely important to them and they want to be loved and adored by their mate. They want all the accessories and emotions of love. Their love is full of drama, excitement and passion. The Sagittarian desire for freedom makes them a bit confused at times and they can demand space in a relationship while demanding a lot of love too!

Food is very important to them. They like throwing impromptu parties and are wonderful hosts. Money is very important to them but, though they always want to save, they may not be able to stop themselves from spending recklessly.

They may act stern or present strong and silent exteriors but their hearts often suffer. The Cancerian touchiness combines with the extremely vulnerable Leonine ego to make them bleed at the smallest of pricks. They can be very moody. They can sulk for hours and need a lot of care to get back into their sunny groove. They can either sulk in anger or throw a huge fit.

You can expect them to take up cudgels to defend the downtrodden. They always want to help people less fortunate than themselves. There is a brave, courageous soul inside them and it comes to the fore when faced with emergencies or painful situations.

They love things on a grand scale. They have an amazing exuberance and love performing in full public glare. You know that they have won over their Cancerian timidity if they shine bright; it is their coming of age and is good for them. But they can also be quick to confront, challenge authority or break conventions if it doesn't go with their idealogy.

For all their tall Leo talk and Cancerian maturity, there is that specal Sagittarian innocence that hangs about them, which melts hearts. They believe in people's goodness and give their worst enemies the benefit of doubt, truly showing their large hearts. There is a deep spiritual side to them too. They easily understand the deeper concepts of life and are also attracted to religious practices.

For all their pomp, show, ego, hurts, melodrama and love for spotlight, there is a quivering heart inside that seeks love and acceptance. That is the only thing they need from not just people who are close to them, but anyone they meet in life. Allow them to shine and you can bask in ther reflected glory too.

Cancer–Leo–Sagittarius – Ernest Hemingway

Hemingway kept the piece of shrapnel [which had wounded him] along with a small handful of other 'charms', including a ring set with a bullet fragment.

The war also led him to meet and fall in love with a Red Cross nurse; a romance that led him to write *A Farewell to Arms*, a tale of love and war.

He suffered from mood swings and could go from being rambunctious to withdrawn.[247]

Despite his fear and wounds, he carried an Italian soldier to safety under heavy mortar fire, for which he received the Italian Silver Medal of Bravery.[248]

The abundance of emotion, the collection of memorabilia, the need for love, plus his love for adventure, singles him out as a CanLeoSag.

Love and Marriage for Him

You have to truly love and adore him to live with him. He likes an intelligent woman who does not point out his faults. If you say anything other than words of praise, he is very hurt. He has many varying moods and you can face a lot of melodrama in your love. He can have fits of jealousy and be very possessive of you while flirting with other women himself. You have to learn to turn a blind eye to his flirting.

Keep an eye on the money for he does not know how to control it despite his best intentions. He loves lazing around at home. Do not expect him to help

---

[247] http://www.archives.gov/publications/prologue/2006/spring/hemingway.html
[248] http://en.wikipedia.org/wiki/Ernest_Hemingway

out with household tasks. He has occasional mood swings and also bouts of anger; know exactly what irks him.

Despite his apparent childlikeness and need to be mothered, he is extremely generous and has a soft heart. You need to appeal to his vanity to get things done. He is brilliant, adventurous company, if you need a good time.

As a father, he loves giving advice to his children on how to plan their lives. He is an easygoing father if they treat him with respect and adoration.

Love and Marriage for Her

If you meet her when she is young, you will love the sweet innocence that defines her. You can see that she has no malicious intent for anybody and speaks the truth always. She would be the first person to tell you if she is confused whether she is in love with you or not.

She looks like a million dollars and acts like that too, with her highly sensitive ways. She wants to be respected and adored by you. Never appreciate other women in her presence. This lady has views of her own. She prefers an independent reign over her house and does not like to be in a joint family.

She is very loving and generous to her family and friends. She is known for her large-hearted ways and wants to include everyone in her bear hug. Parties, fun and adventure rule when she is around for she is the queen of good times.

She wants to travel and enjoy herself. This girl wants to live life large and not bothered by questions about money. You have to be the more balanced and rational one of the two. She loves the limelight and has a creative streak. Applaud her and praise her beauty, for she needs that like a fish needs water.

As a mother, she is all love and bustle. She loves doing things for her children who are her pride and joy. She is commanding but does pamper them too.

At the Workplace

Extremely ambitious and fearless fighters, CanLeoSags never show the slightest hesitation before jumping into a fight. They plan big and are very tenacious about their dreams. Of course, they may change track along the way but you can expect them to give 110 per cent to whatever they do.

They want to do things that involve travelling, thinking and talking. You cannot chain them to a desk and expect them to work regular hours. They are creatively talented and are natural sportsmen. They need jobs that propel them into the limelight.

Give them grand titles and lots of money. If you ever have to criticise them, talk to them in private, and in case of praise, just shout it out across the hall so that everyone hears it! They are always ready to lead and make very motivational leaders. They know how to delegate without shirking their responsibilities.

CanLeoSags will be full of optimism and dare devilry yet they will also be very sensitive. Creative, outspoken, fiery and very, very individualistic – CanLeoSags will always live life their way.

Famous CanLeoSag Personalities

Ernest Hemingway, Neil Armstrong, Madhavi (actress), Alan Shearer, Agostino Abbagnale, Jeff Gordon.

142. CANCER–LEO–CAPRICORN

Moon, the ruler of emotions, Apollo, the regal Sun god, and the wise old Saturn rule this extremely emotional, dignified and ambitious combination. Ambition is the common thread in all these signs.

While Capricorn makes them silently ambitious, Cancer, too, likes to rule without talking about it and the Leo in them ensures that CanLeoCaps want to do something big in their life. CanLeoCaps have a goal in life and work towards it with determination. At times, they can even swallow their Leo ego to gain their desire.

Another thing common in Capricorn and Leo is the need to look good. Capricorn always wants to reach the top and believes that looking like a boss is the first step to becoming a boss and Leos have that majestic aura about them that makes people look in awe. CanLeoCaps are always well turned-out, no matter where they come from. Their clothes will echo their ambition and the Leo swagger will mark their walk.

There is a fun element in them too. These guys just love drama and excitement. They are fun companions with the wit and energy of Leo and the imagination of Cancer. They love the limelight and attention in true Leo fashion.

Family is very dear to them. Cancer loves family ties and Capricorn is ready to sacrifice anything for their families. They love to talk about their families and are proud of their lineage and achievements.

They are very mature and take on responsibilities at an early age. They are extremely responsible in their views. They adore their parents and really believe in them. Cancer makes them love their mothers and Capricorn influences them to respect their fathers. They can also get very nostalgic and like keeping mementos and collecting antiques.

CanLeoCaps will have an enormous admiration for those who have preceded them to the top, and who have laid down the laws. They will court success but respect authority and honour tradition.

The Leonine tendency to dramatise love and the Cancerian emotional and sensitive needs make CanLeoCaps very romantic. They will wander and fall in and out of love till they find the right mate. Of course, Cancer and Capricorn stabilise their Leo need for adulation by adding responsibility and feelings to their quest. Once they decide on a partner, they will be stable. The Capricornian shrewdness comes in too; so you can expect them to prefer a partner whose virtues they can flaunt – be it money, looks or lineage. You will have to be someone to catch their eye!

CanLeoCaps prefer social acceptance to unorthodox rebellion. They want to keep a very royal bearing and hate public scenes and displays of passion. Anger is an emotion that is absent in them. They sulk and crib rather than blow up. If ever they do blow their top, you can be sure that it does not last for long.

They are fabulous friends: loyal, steadfast and always ready to help. The Leo generosity and desire to protect make them ideal protectors. They never shirk their duties. They love being leaned upon.

Money is essential. Despite their swagger and style, they prefer saving wealth than squandering it. They are very businesslike in their approach to spending and expend where they think maximum returns are generated.

Insecurity and pessimism also run through all three signs. Cancer is a highly insecure sign and makes its children imagine the worst scenarios, Leo, too, has a deep insecurity that it hides with its dazzle and Capricorn has an inclination towards pessimistic thoughts. When things don't go their way, you can expect CanLeoCaps to spin down a black whirlpool of despondency. They have dark mood swings and if you ever hurt their ego, they will go off in a sulk.

CanLeoCaps are never be truly satisfied or feel secure with the money or power in their lives – they will always want more and work hard to get them, to drive away those imaginary fears. But they do it in style and without letting you suspect their fears.

Cancer–Leo–Capricorn – Saif Ali Khan
'It's a beautiful feeling to have a company with people employed, it's not unlike running an empire, almost like being Bonaparte on the sets.'

(Incidently Bonaparte was also a CanLeoCap!)

'I think I am a good son. I have never asked my parents for money. I am royal in very subtle ways, like the cuff links – I used to have my family name and crest embossed on them. So it's there, but it's not seen.'

'I think life is about supporting people you love and doing whatever they want you to do.'[249]

The royal and dramatic Leo, the emotional Cancer and the realistic Capricorn, make themselves felt in Saif's words – a true CanLeoCap.

Love and Marriage for Him
Generous and giving, he is a wonderful partner who adds romance and glamour to the relationship. He has a bright sunny smile and an engaging manner. His wit and intelligence are admired amongst family and friends. He is never at a loss for words and is the life of parties with his style and humour.

You can do your own thing. The Leo tendencies to command and demand attention all the time are diluted in him. But he does not like aggressive or brash behaviour from you. He is always well turned-out and politically correct and expects the same from you. You will be able to rely on him and he will always place his family first.

He likes to be the lord of his manor but a sensitive and loving one. You have to adore his parents. He will hear no disparaging remark about them nor will he ever utter such blasphemous words. He can travel all over the world for his ambition but his heart will always long to be with his parents.

He is sensitive and finds it easy to understand and empathise with your problems. You need not spell out your desires to him: he understands. But you have to read into his words. There is a secretive side to him. He keeps his hurt and grief deep inside him. Of course, he also needs a lot of love and care. You have to watch out for his dark moods and be his support.

As a father, he is in the right groove. He combines the Leo love for fun and desire to discipline with the strict and fatherly behaviour of a Capricorn and the intuitive love of a Cancer. An excellent and loving father, he ensures that he takes out time for his family. He is an integral part of his children's lives.

---
[249] *Hi! Blitz*, 2011

Love and Marriage for Her
She is the power behind you. Her soft looks and stylish clothes do not mean a lack of intelligence. She is worthy of being a queen or the wife of a very powerful man.

Despite her ambition and desire to lead, family is the most important thing in her life. She does everything for her family and nothing is ever too good for them. She is an extremely loyal and loving wife. Lack of love can break her soul and mar her generosity. She is even-tempered and calm, yet her mind is always in turmoil. There are lots of insecurities and fears swirling within her and she needs a mate who can be responsible and understanding enough to let her sort out her problems.

Ambition is important for her and if you decide to take life easy, you have to give her the chance to reach for her own stars for she is not content living an easy life. Money and love are the two deep insecurities in her life. She never thinks that she has enough of either.

She will love and admire her parents and will never need to be told to listen to elders. She is traditional in an untraditional way and tries to keep alive all the customs of her family. She loves cooking for everyone. She knows how to throw parties and loves being a hostess: a generous and glowing one.

She loves motherhood. She loves her children and lavishes affection on them but knows where to draw the line and instil discipline. 'Mother knows best' is her motto. She is fiercely proud of their accomplishments and also teaches them to respect elders.

At the Workplace
They look every inch the boss. Cancer and Capricorn are cardinal signs, and Leo loves to lead: CanLeoCaps lead everywhere. If you are their boss, you may not be that for long! Their need is to be in any profession where they can reach the top and be there forever. Remember one thing: always praise their efforts in front of everybody. They do not appreciate silent applause. Leo makes them want to shine in the public gaze.

Politically correct and highly astute, CanLeoCaps make very good business leaders and politicians. They can be nice guys, but will do business in a businesslike manner and won't let emotions cloud their judgment. The creative imagination of Cancer and the love of limelight can make them turn to a more creative medium too. They need money, power and prestige, and are never satisfied with what they have. And yes, they would want to leave a proud legacy.

Water, Fire and Earth make an inherently vital mix in CanLeoCaps. They are emotional without letting it cloud their reason, extravagant without being thoughtless about money and ambitious without forsaking their family.

Famous CanLeoCap Personalities
Saif Ali Khan, Azim Premji, Naresh Goyal, Manisha Koirala, Sandra Bullock, Napoleon Bonaparte, Jimmy Connors, Audrey Tautou, Viola Davis, Rod Laver, Priya Dutt, Enid Blyton, Melanie Griffith, Daler Mehndi, Rakhi Gulzar, Rameez Raja, Pattukkottai Prabakar.

143. CANCER–LEO–AQUARIUS

The emotional Moon, the regal Apollo, and the inventive Uranus meet in CanLeoAquas. Creativity and an inventive mind are their strengths. The highly imaginative Cancer and the out-of-the-box thinker Aquarius make them think of something new and very original. Plus, the Leonine flair for showcasing its talents ensures that they get noticed.

Their first impression will leave you impressed. When they meet you, the self-assured royal air of Leo and the uniquely intelligent Aquarian brightness shines through. Their wacky sense of humour, which can vary from being restrained to being loud and over-the-top adds to the aura too.

Every CanLeoAqua has a passionate dream. The dream is unique, outstanding, trailblazing and trendsetting. It can have the potential to simplify things, make the world a better place to live in or can just add another aid to manage our daily chores. With their extraordinary Cancerian imagination, coupled with the Aquarian ability to envisage the future, they create something that can benefit human race. The idea will be on a grand scale, as Leos do nothing small. Every CanLeoAqua will not turn out to be a scientist but will bring his uniqueness to the most mundane job in the world.

They have a strong rebellious stage in their lives. Their rebelliousness takes the shape of strong views that they are loath to give up. Both Leo and Aquarius are fixed signs and more difficult to change while Aquarius adds touches of futuristic ideas to them. They think differently from the herd. The good thing about this combination is that they use both their emotional and intelligence quotients to think, so their thought processes are always people-friendly and sensitive.

They are extremely loving, especially to their close friends and families. They are very generous with their time and money to a selected few. They are good at comforting, empathising and advising. There are no better friends than them. They are loyal, generous and full of good cheer. They are friends you can call up even after years and you rarely hear a 'no'.

Do not think that they are capable only of deep emotions. The light side of life interests them too. They surprise you with their ability to always see the silver lining. However, they can be quite sensitive as well. They do not like anyone trampling on their egos. They have an extraordinary sense of humour – they have you in splits from their observations on simple things in life.

They speak their minds, without being the least impudent or nasty. They have their own moral codes of conduct. They have the Leo desire to protect the weak and the Aquarian humanitarian values. They have the common good in mind while doing things.

CanLeoAquas are natural leaders. Cancer is a cardinal sign and desires nothing more than to lead (though it never says so) and Leo can never stay in the shade: it wants to rule. They make good leaders and lead with sensitivity, ideals and a regal flair. They take the lead in all aspects of life.

Love is extremely important to them. Cancer needs a person all its own and desires commitment above all else. This desire for commitment will reduce the wandering ways of Aquarius and the lazy Leo will follow suit. CanLeoAquas are at their most sensitive and emotional in love, and you can expect them to be rebellious too. They are ready to fight for the one they love and do not let society dictate terms to them.

Food interests them and they love trying new delicacies or even cooking up new menus. They enjoy throwing parties for family and friends and are extremely good hosts. You never leave their company without good food or a good laugh.

They want to save and do not spend much. However, they are not too stingy either. They sometimes give in to impulsive buys and want to pamper themselves with good clothes and luxuries. But despite it all they will never spend beyond a certain limit and have enough to save and invest.

They also have a strong sense of adventure. They do not mind trying out new and dangerous things just for a thrill. They are intelligent, inquisitive and scientifically aware.

CanLeoAquas are quite sensitive. Their ego cannot bear critcism and they see everything in a negative light, especially when they are feeling low. Cancer gives them a plethora of emotions and Leo adds its angry roar whenever it feels hurt. CanLeoAquas will do everything with emotion: both work and play. Of course, the Aquarian detachment will come in but it will never stop them from feeling things deeply.

Cancerians are naturally fearful yet they fight their fears every time. Similarly, Leo is full of fears deep inside but it uses its roar to mask it. Once they decide to do something, they will do it with a tenacious will that will silence all their fears. They need to be encouraged, for victory lies within their grasp.

They have a spiritual side and believe in a stronger force. All three signs lead them to think on spiritual rather than religious lines, and their beliefs may not follow conventional rules every time. Home and family are extremely important to them. They relax in the confines of their homes.

Cancer–Leo–Aquarius – J.R.D. Tata
When Tata studied hard, his sister Rodabeh pleaded, 'Why don't you rest Jeh, you are tired and unwell.' J.R.D. replied, 'I want to be worthy of the Tatas.'

Flying was a passion with J.R.D. 'When you are on your own in that plane, at the controls without an instructor, and the plane speeds on the runway and finally takes off – you know you are in the air on you own.'[250]

He firmly believed in employee welfare and espoused the principles of an eight-hour working day, free medical aid, workers' provident scheme, etc., which were later adopted as statutory requirements in India. [251]

J.R.D. Tata embodied the perseverance, generosity, adventurous spirit and humanitarian views of a CanLeoAqua.

---

[250] http://www.newindiadigest.com/lala.htm
[251] http://en.wikipedia.org/wiki/J._R._D._Tata

Love and Marriage for Him
He is the most loving of husbands. He knows you, understands you and is the one who shares all you secrets. This guy wants to be a part of your life.

He loves his family and is very attached to his parents. He wants your relationship with them to be cordial. This man adores his mother. Let him be pampered by her. Though he loves travelling, he misses his home when he is away.

He seeks a partner who not only understands and loves him but also makes intelligent conversation with him.

As a father, he is extremely loving and caring. He not only delights in his children but also understands their need for independence. He takes pride in their achievements, worries when they wander and gives them sage advice when they need it.

Love and Marriage for Her
She enjoys her home but also needs to do something for herself. She is quite individualistic in her opinions and has a strong charitable side. She is the person her friends turn to in times of trouble.

She loves her home but won't waste her time doing all the chores herself. She is a fantastic host, impressing guests with her extraordinary culinary skills and hospitality, which she manages beautifully within budget. There is an air of royalty about her and everything that she does has a style and flair that is unmistakable.

Her idea of a good time at home does not include dealing with domestic issues. She has varied interests and has a flair for creativity. These, along with her imagination and intelligence, mark her out as special. She loves travelling with her family.

Her mood swings can be quite complicated. Indulge her a little, listen to her and understand what she asks of you. This lady needs a supportive partner. However, despite her occasional weeping moods, she is anything but weak. She can surmount any difficulty.

As a mother, she truly excels. She can pamper her children and be a doting, caring mother.

At the Workplace
CanLeoAquas are visionaries. They may have a wacky original idea that initially shocks, but changes the world for better. They are extremely tenacious and rarely give up. The only criterion for their careers should be that it interests them. Routine jobs are not for them. They need to be in careers where they can think, and, of course, delegate. Ever-changing, dynamic careers greatly interest them. From science to business to the arts, they are good wherever they find their calling. They are very creative.

They may lack patience to look into the fine details. They are masters of grandeur, the pomp and show. They do an awe-inspiring job and also ensure that the job is finished thoroughly. They love the excitement, the recognition, and the adrenalin rush that comes with a job well done. They are self-motivated. The flightiness of Aquarius is greatly reduced by the tenacity of Cancer.

They can be good leaders who are quite democratic in their views. They are masters in ideating and direction, and will give the bold strokes and expect you to fill in the detailing. They are very generous and include the families of their employees when planning for welfare.

Water, Fire and Air meet in CanLeoAquas and give them sensitivity, drive and a curiosity about life. They are individualistic in their opinions and generous in their thoughts.

Famous CanLeoAqua Personalities
J.R.D. Tata, M.S. Swaminathan, Usain Bolt, Vikram Sarabhai, Tansen, Cyrus Broacha, Norma Shearer, Percy B. Shelley, Govind Nihalani, Manyata Dutt, Sheila Mello, Dr D. Subbarao.

144. CANCER–LEO–PISCES

The highly emotional Moon meets the glowingly generous Apollo and the mysterious Neptune in this soft yet strong combination.

Get a nice sweet, large, dolphin-like Fish. Get it fitted with the face of a Lion and add protective armour made of shell round its body. That should give an idea what to expect in this interesting combination. They slowly glide and move around the world, spreading their unique charm, making people happy.

CanLeoPisces are very creative. There is the deep reservoir of talent of Pisces, including everything from acting, singing, to mimicking, and Cancer's ability to learn by absorbing and keeping every experience stored for future reference. Now add the bright exuberance, style and pomp of Leo to this personality and you have someone who turns heads wherever they go. Leo will give a definite push to the artistic inclinations of this combination, and will make CanLeoPisces dream big.

The Leo ego gives strength to this soft combination. They also have the Cancerian tenacious love for their families – but within limits. They do not kill themselves over ungrateful people and know when to draw the line between loving care and subservience. Both Cancer and Pisces lack self-assurance but Leo is an extremely positive sign. Leo adds to their confidence without being arrogantly optimistic.

CanLeoPisces walk with a regal air but do not tread unthinkingly on many toes. While they maintain their self-respect and pride in all they do, with a touch of regality, still they are not arrogant or rude. They have a quiet confidence about them. They need the limelight and desperately seek it, but aren't be too blatant about it. You see a positive glow on their face when they are applauded and appreciated. Don't let their dignified presence stop you from paying your compliments to them.

Love is very important to them. They love a lot, and deeply. They want drama, love and passion in their lives, and are very giving. They want partners who understand their need for romance. They need a lot of emotional sensitivity and persist in loving despite all the wrongs done to them, but after a point they will not tolerate more pain. They do not flirt once they are committed and will be loyal partners as long as their mates remember their vows.

Money makes them feel secure, yet they are unable to hold on to it for long. Cancer is the one sign in this combination that loves to save while the other two do not mind spending. CanLeoPisces love to spend on accessories and luxuries.

Family is extremely important to them and they are capable of immense sacrifices for their loved ones. They don't have the heart to deny them anything. Their mothers are the most important persons in their lives.

They love being agony aunts. The Cancerian desire to nurture, the Leo wish to advise and the Piscean ability to listen, will make them excel as friends to turn to for advice and understanding. Don't forget that they need the same care, too, when they go through rough spots!

Food is very important to them. They love cooking and feel satisfied watching their guests eat well. They are generous hosts. The Piscean love for addictions can surface in them. They are extremely soft and sensitive and can use addictions to drown their sorrows.

CanLeoPisces are very emotional and sensitive because all three signs are sensitive. Cancer can use its imaginative powers to see a whole conspiracy behind a friend's stifled laugh. Leo too is very thin-skinned, especially in matters regarding its ego, while Pisces can fill itself with self-pity if given the slightest chance. Be very nice to these gentle souls for they bear no malice and can remain hurt for days due to one insensitive remark.

Problems stem from their deep emotional needs. They are insecure in their darkest moments and can give others a lot of power over themselves. They need people who calm down their fears and add a dose of steadiness in their views. They can even be addicted to attention, love or substances. They get lost in their own dreamy escape world if they do not get the love and attention they seek.

Behind that self-assured demeanour and cool attitude, lies a gentle soul with many vulnerabilities. If you understand that and reassure them about the pool of talents they possess they will elevate your position in their private rankings. They will be a little insecure about their abilities in the beginning but will soon gain confidence with success.

Spirituality and religion attract them. They understand the deep philosophies of life, which can be a strong stabilising force in their lives. They never judge people by their faith. They instinctively understand the laws of *karma* and past lives. They can also be extra sensitive to paranormal activities. Expect them to regale you with some spine-chilling stories.

Cancer–Leo–Pisces – Whitney Houston

'To me, my dad was just perfect in the way he treated us and the way he treated Mom. When you get older you realise that you're never going to find a man like your father.'[252]

I ask Whitney where she sees herself years down the road. 'I'm going to be on a porch somewhere rocking with my husband and my grandchildren.'[253]

Family meant more to her than anything else. Whitney Houston had the creative talent evident in all three signs, but she also had the deep emotional sensitivity of Cancer. Her Piscean addictions went out of hand and became the reason for her sudden death.

Love and Marriage for Him

He loves you a lot and wants to be the centre of your universe. He wants intense pampering. He is very sensitive and has varying moods. You need to be the sensible one in the relationship. He finds it impossible to bear physical pain and can make a fuss over a small bruise.

He is your friend and companion. The Leonine egoistic ways are diluted in him. He has a very expressive face that shows exactly what he thinks. He can sulk when upset. You have to be his mother, wife, friend and companion, all rolled into one!

---

[252] http://www.classicwhitney.com/interview/ebony_june1990.htm
[253] http://www.classicwhitney.com/interview/essence_july2003.htm

He is not of much help at home and is not bothered by mess and clutter. He only cares about his own appearance. Take care of the money too. You have to be the one who sticks to budgets for he is prone to overspending.

He is a fabulous father. This guy is nurturing, loving and extremely caring. He does not mind changing nappies or cooking for the kids. He spends all the time after work with his family and likes to travel with them too. He makes his children realise the importance of family and never forces them to do what they do not want to. He can be a little possessive about them and cannot let go easily.

Love and Marriage for Her
She has an expressive face that reveals her deepest secrets. This girl is fun, too, and can make you double up with laughter with her knack of imitating people. Her dress sense is fabulous and she knows how to make heads turn without being flamboyant. She is extremely feminine, but the Leo leadership is evident in her. There will be strength deep within her despite her inherent softness and she will never be a pushover.

She is extremely loving and caring. She pampers you, loves you, cares for you and has fun with you. Commitment is important and she does not leave you till you give her enough cause to do so. You must realise her deep need for love and care, and never give this soft, sensitive woman a reason to cry. She is very emotional in her needs.

She wants to have a bank balance of her own, which makes her feel secure. She does not think twice before spending on luxuries. She is a fabulous cook. But do not imprison her in the kitchen for she is highly creative and talented.

As a mother, she is in her element. Her children are always cared for with the utmost attention and love. She takes pride in them and is the most understanding and loving mother around. Her only problem is her extreme love for them. She can sometimes keep mothering them, even when they reach their thirties.

At the Workplace
CanLeoPisces is an extremely creative combination. They can excel in artistic fields. They know how to make their art a success and are not content staying in the background. They are extremely imaginative and when coupled with the beautiful sensitivity of Cancer and style and oomph of Leo, they can be mesmerising dancers, singers, actors or painters. They want to reach the top without being aggressive about it.

They are very persevering. Money is quite important for them, but more so, admiration. They need lots of appreciation. They can brood over negative remarks and take them to heart, so you should try and push them positively. Cancer is a cardinal sign and it gives them the ability to visualise and lead. They are good as team managers too. They are fantastic mentors and teachers. They have a deep understanding of people and coach you after getting a deep insight into your personality.

Double Water and Fire make CanLeoPisces a very emotional yet strong combination. They wallow in sentiment but can call upon their innate optimism and belief to help them tide over difficulties.

Famous CanLeoPisces Personalities
Whitney Houston, Khali, Tom Brady, Bhoomika Chawla, Mark Knopfler.

145. CANCER–VIRGO–LIBRA

All the three signs in CanVirLib are mild and mature. Cancer is ruled by the gentle Moon and is compassionate, caring and emotional, with deep and abiding love. Virgo is meticulous, practical, hardworking, pure, soft and a perfectionist. The Venus of Libra makes it peace loving and an excellent communicator.

Cancer is ruled by emotions, while Virgo embraces routine and Libra appreciates beauty. There is no anger or volatility in this combination. It is pure, peaceful and loving, and has an inner strength and sense of purpose that underlies its actions.

CanVirLibs are love personified in all its positive traits. They are loving, giving, expressive, understanding, compassionate and sacrificing. It is very difficult to reciprocate their feelings adequately. It is love in its purest form, like that of a mother for her child. Three people are most important in their lives – mother, spouse and child. For the happiness of these three, they can do anything!

This loving tenderness is not restricted to their family alone. They are soft to all people they meet. They mother all children and act as elder brother or sister to anyone younger to them. You are touched by their kind and soft-spoken ways. They are also very fair and just. They never shy away from raising their voices (kindly, though) against any kind of discrimination. They are moved by poverty and the distress of children and old people.

Food is important, too. Cancer loves feeding people, Libra loves food, while Virgo makes them highly accomplished cooks. Healthy food is always on their menu. Money is a touchy topic with them. The Libra love of beautiful things is overshadowed by the stingy habits of Cancer and the careful ways of Virgo. They love investing in funds that offer low but assured returns and spend only on their homes, spouses, children, parents and food. Everything else is termed as waste. Except for one thing – photography. They will spend their money and time on it.

Despite the Libran lightness, they have very few friends; they are old friends with whom they like to reminisce about the good old days. CanVirLibs are soft and easy to be with, but there is a catch in this loving combination: it is very difficult to handle them, due to the double cardinal signs of Cancer and Libra. You can be sure that in any relationship or situation they will have the last word and decide the outcome.

The Virgo in them makes them highly critical and analytical. Combined with the Libran softness, they talk mildly but with such deep penetration and analysis that you learn to dread their argument sessions. If, despite all these efforts, you remain unconvinced of their views, they will look at you in such a way that you feel miserable for having hurt the feelings of such a tender soul. Either way you cannot win an argument against them.

Despite their apparent softness, they have a spine of steel. They meticulously plan their duties, have an alternative back-up plan for everything, and then go about doing the work slowly but surely. They don't show off or brag about their achievements, but put in more hard work than the average Joe. Their focus, meticulousness, concentration and dedication to duty ensure they complete everything they take up.

Their perfectionism can also turn to nitpicking and make them worrywarts. Virgo's analysing enhances Libra's vacillation and they can be extremely critical of anyone who is against their ideas. The moodiness of Cancer can afflict them too. When hurt, they turn depressive or cranky and look and feel miserable. They can go into a shell and lose contact with humanity if deeply hurt. The Cancer insecurity and feeling of inadequacy also plays its part in their complex psyche. If they are insecure about their relationship with you, they smother you with love and care; as they start feeling secure they stop acting so obsessive about you.

Venus ensures they have fantastic artistic skills and abilities. When combined with the perfectionist Virgo, they can fine-tune their art with such dedication and skill that it would be pointless to compete with them. But the best thing about them is that they are not competitive despite their double cardinal signs. Music and other arts help liberate them from their self-induced worries. They just love the process and enjoy it – they know that winning or losing is ephemeral. What is permanent is inherent goodness, of which they are symbols.

Cancer–Virgo–Libra – Shweta Tiwari

'I'm here today because of my mother.'[254]

'I was missing my daughter so much (while participating in a reality show) that I talked only about her all the time.'

'I am a person who is rooted to cultural values and marriage holds a lot of significance to me. That is the reason why I did not want to end my marriage and I tolerated Raja for eight long years.'[255]

Shweta Tiwari embodies CanVirLibs, who can suffer a lot for their loved ones; but they also know how to cut the thread once a relationship is completely frayed. Shweta's emotional strength saw her through without resorting to aggression. That is the strength of a CanVirLib.

Love and Marriage for Him

He is your love, support system, one-man cheerleader, the only guy in the whole world who understands you: a soul mate. These are the good things; and now, the not-so-good things about him: his sensitivity is as great as a woman's. You need to be careful about what you say, and how you say it. He is extremely sensitive, can shred your opinion to bits in his mild unassuming manner, smothers you in his love and possessiveness, and can make you feel miserable by going into a sulk.

He is extremely committed. He can sacrifice himself without a fuss and be there for you whenever you need, cook for you, nurse you and be everything you desire. Duties and responsibilities are what he lives for. He makes sure he meets all his family's needs. Life with him is happy and contented, if not extravagant and lavish. However, it is wrong if you think that he is a doormat. If you like to dominate and to get your way, this guy is not for you. Where money is concerned, he can be a terror for he does not like extravagance or waste of any sort.

---

[254] *People*, March 11, 2011
[255] http://forum.santabanta.com/showthread.htm?95702-Shweta-Tiwari-s-Emotional-Outburst-In-a-Bare-it-All-Interview-!

His fatherly instincts are excellent. He likes to be involved in every facet of his children's growth. He insists on good education and guides them.

Love and Marriage for Her
If you want lots and lots of loving care, she is the one for you. She loves you and respects your views. Her life revolves around you. Despite all that love that makes her seem submissive, she is not! She gently moves you to match her views. She allows you to roar and stamp your presence in the house, but others in the house know that her wishes carry weight and they listen to her command. The Libran in her believes in love and and she can stick to something forever with a Cancerian tenacity: especially a flawed marriage. But remember, there is a Virgo in her too, which will not tolerate being a doormat and will cut all ties with the precision of a surgeon and walk away, although with a heavy heart and after giving umpteen chances.

Her cooking skills are noteworthy. She loves to cook healthy food for her family. She loves worrying too. Money tops her list of worries, so learn to save. She knows how to look good in the least expensive manner. Her house is always immaculate and full of memorabilia. She can also be very jealous and possessive.

She is in her element as a mother. She makes her children her world and does not think of anything else when they are around. Over-possessiveness can spoil this love if she feels insecure in any way. Her love becomes smothering and sends them scurrying away from her.

At the Workplace
CanVirLibs are the most hard-working and diligent workers. The Virgo in them doesn't let go till the work is perfect and complete in every respect, while Libra communicates ideas and thoughts beautifully and Cancer works with tenacity and a sense of purpose that never lets up till the goal is won.

They work so well that you cannot but appreciate them. The appreciation need not be in front of others, though. Nevertheless, they need it, for they are so riddled with insecurities and fears that despite all the hard work they feel that they are not good enough.

They do not mind starting at the bottom but are ambitious enough to aim for the top. All they want is security in the form of money, and time with family. Give them family holidays, offer trips with spouses and an expected raise every year. This will keep them happy.

They have a sarcastic wit and can use it on subordinates who think they can get away with less work and more talk. CanVirLibs know how to be politically correct and not barge in with their opinions. They always have the final say in decisions, though. If a CanVirLib is your boss, never go to him without doing your homework.

CanVirLibs are soft souls who are fair despite being cranky, justice-oriented despite their vacillations and are conscientious, hard working and persistent.

Famous CanVirLib Personalities
Shweta Tiwari, Mahatma Gandhi, Catherine Deneuve, Bruno Mars, Marion Cotillard, Neil Harvey, S.T. Coleridge, Stacy Keibler.

146. CANCER–LIBRA–SCORPIO

Moon, the controller of emotions, Venus, the planet of love, luxury and art, and Pluto, the ruthless lord of the underworld, combine in this highly intense and extremely complex combination. When you tackle a CanLibScorp, you take on more emotions than you can understand.

They have the deep sensitivity and extreme insecurity of Cancer, the excellent communication skills and love for luxury of Libra and the intense passion and deep dedication of Scorpio. They want to win at all costs, and they are willing to put in the hard work. They are dedicated to their work and and can withstand anything to improve their status in life. They just hang in there and stay put.

These high-strung people overflow with emotions, which have no boundaries. They are intense, passionate, motherly (even the men); they are possessive, vulnerable, can turn jealous, can be tender, loving, caring, receptive, romantic, erotic, depressed or aggressive. Mood swings and emotional upheavals characterise them.

CanLibScorps are excellent orators and can use language very effectively. They can talk about anything with great understanding and wit. They talk with the intensity and passion of Scorpio and the deep understanding and perceptiveness of Cancer. The Libran logic flows in smooth words. They give almost a running commentary on their emotional upheavals. They can either show hurt clearly on their face, accusing you, or look stony-faced, stupefied with grief.

They have a deep-seated need for approval. They get hurt easily. Many a time the hurts could be imaginary, from reading too much between the lines. When hurt they withdraw into a shell. The Scorpio tendency of seething anger will seek revenge and they can turn deadly. Even if the motherly Cancer and peaceful Libra in them forgive your sins, they will never forget. They have the facility to put up a façade and a brave front. They can act silent and unconcerned, with the Scorpio ability to act poker-faced, even when they are seething inside. They then create a wall to ensure that they are not hurt in future by anyone.

Love finds them all charged up and passionate. They fall intensely, passionately and whole-heartedly in love. Cancer can love till death and Scorpio also add its passions to the deep loyalty of Cancer. The Libran desire to be eternally in love makes them loyal, caring, sensitive and high-strung in love. You can expect the love of ten people from them. Go for them only if you are ready to submerge yourself in love for they cannot tone down their emotions or their passions. They pamper and mother their loved ones and expect no less from them.

You can expect CanLibScorps to lead. Both Cancer and Libra are cardinal signs and lead excellently without coercing. They lead by talking, expressing and creating opinions that you can't refute; and when all else fails you can expect them to cajole with an intensity that is hard to reject. Their personality has shades ranging from forceful determination to sensitive softness.

CanLibScorps certainly have a sense of purpose. Scorpio makes them goal-oriented. You can expect them to work very hard and withstand any hardship to reach their goal. The Scorpio in them also reduces the shallowness and indecisiveness of Libra, while Libra's charm reduces the extreme intensity of Scorpio and makes the combination more approachable and balanced.

Money is very dear to them. They do not spend easily and try to spend very little and still look good. They also like to hold on to memorabilia. The reasons might range from nostalgia to economy. CanLibScorps have few friends; they are extremely loyal to them.

They are drawn to the mysteries of life. They seek meaning and spirituality in an attempt to understand life and their own fears. They have so many fears that only by delving deep into themselves can they find a cure. Cancer is an extremely pessimistic sign, but it also lends this combination its tenacity of purpose.

They can go through terrible mood swings due to the changing phases of the Moon and extreme mental vacillations due to Libra. They need patient, calm people around them who can soothe their fears, understand their sensitivities and encourage them to reach out for their goals. After they conquer their inner fears and self-doubts, they soar like an eagle in true Scorpio fashion, assisted with the persistency of Cancer and finesse of Libra.

Caner–Libra–Scorpio – Boris Becker

Whenever he considered himself to be playing badly, he often swore at himself and occasionally smashed his rackets.[256]

'I used to prepare for tennis matches by playing chess; it would get my mind stimulated and focused...The fifth set is not about tennis, it's about nerves.'[257]

'When you are thrown onto the stage at seventeen in such an enormous way, it becomes living on the edge. And it became, for me, life or death.'[258]

'Girls had never been important. I'd had a girlfriend or two and had liked them a lot but it wasn't love, because my first love was tennis.'[259]

Boris Becker has the deep emotions, passion and amazing analytical skills of a CanLibScorp.

Love and Marriage for Him

If you want love that lasts and passion that endures, this is the guy for you. He loves you, cares for you and does everything for you. He talks and listens to you, tells you funny stories and makes you feel like a million dollars.

But before you jump for joy, know that this guy requires a lot of care and love in return. He doesn't mind being smothered in love – he just can't get enough of it! If you desire space and independence in life then leave this guy alone or you will end up hurting both of you. His emotional needs are very great. He may be prone to black moods and deep depressions too. He is actually a bundle of nerves. You have to be his sanity and reason. He is extremely sensitive and can get hurt even at some innocent remarks.

---

[256] http://en.wikipedia.org/wiki/Boris_Becker
[257] http://uk.eurosport.yahoo.com/06122011/58/becker-key-tennis-success-chess.html
[258] http://www.searchquotes.com/quotation/So_this_is_it._Match_point_for_eternity./57986/
[259] http://www.brainyquote.com/quotes/authors/b/boris_becker

You have to love his mother too, for she is perfect in his eyes. He gives a lot of importance to *his* family and is hurt if you don't. The big bonus is that he loves being with *your* family too. If you have expensive tastes, please reconsider your decision, for he does not part with money easily.

As a father, he is exceptional. He jumps into action from the first day, making you feel blessed for having such a caring mate. He is as protective and nurturing as a mother. He treasures his children.

Love and Marriage for Her
She loves you a lot. This lady's love is extreme. It is not for the faint-hearted, for she demands total commitment. Her family is her priority. She is warm and humorous and intelligent. She is an excellent companion. She can make herself a doormat if you are aggressive, but it may not last long for soon her cardinal tendencies emerge.

She needs a lot of emotional and financial security: pamper her. She has her mood swings. Her fears can overpower her and she needs your support in overcoming her troubles. No problem will be too small for her and she worries herself over each doubt. You truly have to be her calming force for she can lose herself in her fears and distort her potential with her insecurities.

Nostalgia and memories are extremely precious to her. She keeps all her old photographs and knickknacks. Everything is possible with this girl who is absolutely goofy about love. She needs only five things in life – a great love and companion, nice soft music, good home-cooked food, financial security and a child to shower all her love on.

As a mother, she is unbeatable. This lady is born to be a mother and is immensely caring. She strives to give her children everything they want.

At the Workplace
Imaginative, creative, passionate, determined and extremely competitive, CanLibScorps can survive and reach the summit of any profession. They can succeed, if they overcome their insecurities. They are born leaders but need a mentor to make them reach their potential.

No one can stand in their way once their minds are made up. They can talk their way out of anything. Their communication skills combine with their passion and sensitivity to give them a winning edge over others. They have an amazing sense of aesthetics, art and fashion. With their tremendous staying power, extraordinary competitiveness and phenomenal sense of balance, they do superbly well in sports and politics too.

Money and power motivate them to succeed. They do not require adulation; just remember to appreciate their work. They work very hard to reach that unassailable position that they long for. They are unbeatable, as they are not just competing with others but also with themselves. They do not rest till they reach the summit.

They are very demanding bosses who will not be easy to fool. They want you to work as hard as they do. But they transform into kind, soft and fatherly figures if you look up to them and respect them.

CanLibScorps have depth, intensity and many shades and emotions coursing through them. Love and appreciation is what they crave; give them that and they will achieve the impossible.

Famous CanLibScorp Personalities
Boris Becker, Gary Kirsten, Jawaharlal Nehru, David Warner, Brian Weiss, K.V. Kamath, Saroj Khan, Pullela Gopichand, R. Parthiepan, Naga Chaitanya, Jaspinder Narula, Evo Morales, Shakuntala Devi, Brad Paisley.

147. CANCER–SCORPIO–SAGITTARIUS

Moon, the ruler of emotions, Pluto, the ruthless lord of the underworld, and the knowledgeable Jupiter, all combine in this one emotional and passionate mix up. You can expect them to be highly idealistic. Scorpio makes them passionate, and combined with Sagittarius's high ideals, CanScorpSags are passionate about doing the right thing and living the right way. Moreover, Cancer adds perseverance to these high ideals.

Imagine a Crab with a soft interior and a hard shell. Make it more interesting – besides the claws, it also possesses a poisonous sting. Now add the power of a horse to this unique Crab and you should get the point.

They have a passion – every Scorpio has one – an intense, burning passion for which they will lay down their lives. Sagittarius adds intelligence and exuberance to them. When combined with the tenacity of purpose of Cancer, these people will not just start work with pomp and show but will ensure its completion and showcase it with lots of drama and action.

Their emotional quotient is very high due to the presence of two Water signs, Scorpio and Cancer. They have deep and abiding emotions and are rarely happy till someone reciprocates those feelings. They wear their hearts on their sleeves. They present all their Sagittarian clown acts with the childlike attention-seeking habit of Cancer. They seek love and affection from everyone they meet.

The best thing about this combination is that it brings out the positives of each sign. Therefore, CanScorpSags retain the positivity and intelligence of Sagittarius while doing away with its reckless convention-defying nature and changeable opinions. The ambition, perseverance and loving, caring nature of Cancer is combined with the force of Saggitarius and passion of Scorpio.

They eulogise their mothers, to whom they are extremely attached. Of course, the rest of the family matters too, but in their youth the influence of their mother is unequalled. Food has a special connotation for them. It is more than sustenance: they adore, admire and talk about food. They love to cook for friends and acquaintances at home and are ever ready to try out new cusines. They bond over food.

They are not reckless though they like to visit exciting places, try out new things and are always ready for adventure. They try and find a mean and their whole life is spent balancing these two opposite forces: the pull of orthodox family values and the attraction of uncharted territories.

Love is extremely essential in their lives. CanScorpSags love with their heart and soul. They are very possessive and demand to be the centre of their loved ones' universe. They want their love to be around them all the time, babying them.

The Scorpio vengefulness gets a rest here – though they get hurt easily, they are not vengeful. However, Scorpio makes them understand people's deepest desires and read into their souls. Sadly, the Cancerian insecurity slightly warps their understanding, for it makes them read messages into every gesture – from a flick of the hand to a lopsided smile. Be very cautious around them, because despite their seemingly firm looks, they are easily hurt.

The Cancer mood swings can make them go through dark periods for no apparent reason. Do not ever mistake their emotional love for a weakness. This very strong combination can withstand any problem with rock-like fortitude.

Sagittarius and Scorpio alone would have given CanScorpSags passion, energy and loads of positivity. The addition of Cancer to this combination develops their insecurity. They have to brave their inherent doubts to reach out to the positive strains within them. That is their struggle.

One feels the absence of the element of Air in them. This deficiency makes them unable to communicate their thoughts very well. They find it hard to verbalise their thoughts, especially their hurts. They look sad, sulk or act despondent, but do not state the facts. You have to ask and question to get some responses.

They behave differently at different times when money is involved. They can be extremely stingy, yet very generous too. The Scorpio in them makes them spend wisely, but sometimes extravagantly, on their family. Cancer makes them extremely stingy on all matters other than food and family, and Sagittarius makes them splurge without thinking at times. They spend, but save and invest more.

They have the capacity to unearth the deepest mysteries of life. They love exploring everything – from life to death, sex to childhood, past life to future progression, and have a great inner understanding of spirituality and alternative sciences.

CanScorpSags need their partner around them but are quite self-sufficient on their own. They can hold back their tears and drama when they are alone and get on with their work. Actually, due to Cancer and Scorpio, they have the ability to lead a double life – full of emotions when they are around their loved ones and focused on their work when they are on their own.

Cancer–Scorpio–Sagittarius – Raj Kapoor

'He used to sit with the *sabziwali* (vegetable vendor) outside his home. There was a woman who was quite similar to the banana seller character in *Awara* which was played by Lalita Pawar.'[260]

It is said that *Mera Naam Joker* was more or less Raj's autobiography as he depicted the deep pain and anguish of a man who had to keep smiling for the entertainment of others even while facing great separations and setbacks in life.[261]

Raj Kapoor transferred his deeply felt personal experiences onto celluloid. His creative energy, intensity of emotions and ambition as a showman marked him as a CanScorpSag.

Love and Marriage for Him

He is the provider and nurturer. He is always there for his family, ready to listen, empathise, and sympathise with your views. Pamper him, take care of his needs and be sure to baby him at times. He needs that smothering love to feel good. Be sure to get along well with his mother too.

He likes you to be with him when he is at home. You have to be ready to give him a lot of time. He may not dominate but is always in command. Of course, his

---

[260] http://www.outlookindia.com/article.aspx?229798
[261] http://www.tribuneindia.com/2005/20050529/spectrum/main8.htm

moods can have you running in circles. He often sulks. Also, remember that he is not very good when it comes to communicating. You may have to ask him to know what he feels. This man needs a lot of understanding. His relationship and emotional needs are very high.

He definitely broadens your horizon. This guy is so intelligent and well informed about so many diverse things that he makes you think beyond your world.

Fatherhood finds him in his element. He never runs away at the thought of looking after his kids and wants to spend time with them. He likes to teach them, have fun with them and be there for them at all times.

Love and Marriage for Her
She is definitely not a simpleton. This lady has passion, romance, emotions and anger. She is highly temperamental and is extremely expressive. She is as easy to read as a book – and equally difficult to understand, if you are devoid of emotions.

She loves cooking for you and pampers your every need. If you like playing around, she is definitely not for you for she is very possessive. She can kill you for your transgressions.

Despite her strong individuality, she loves the family structure. She is the glue that binds the family together. The family would encompass hers and yours too. She loves to excel in all roles – daughter, wife and daughter-in-law.

Her mood swings are quite strong and she may often sulk in a corner. Talk to her to find out the reason. It may be as innocuous as her dismay at not receiving a broad smile from you. She needs attention and love – she can never get enough of that. She is madly in love and will immerse you in an extreme love that only she is capable of. You are either ucky or unlucky – it depends from which angle you look.

As a mother, she is fantastic. Loving, caring, nurturing and deeply concerned about her children, she wraps herself around them. She loves spending time with them, helps them with their homework and has fun with them. However, she has to learn to let go, as they grow older.

At the Workplace
CanScorpSags need passions to fire them up and their perseverance ensures that these passions are realised. They are extremely creative and intelligent workers. The Sagittarius in them likes the limelight. Their tenacity makes them carry on when everyone else leaves the bandwagon. This tenacity is their greatest strength in times of adversity.

They should be in fields that require creativity and oodles of hard work for they are always ready for challenges and think out of the box. Do not expect them to present their ideas well. They need some help in communicating their views; however, their actions speak loud enough. They love doing things on a large scale, especially if it involves someone else's money! Do not worry, for they are careful. They need lots of appreciation. Monetary rewards also motivate them.

They are loving and caring bosses, but are tough taskmasters. Follow their passion and make it yours; do it sincerely, and they appreciate you.

CanScorpSags are sensitive, creative, insightful and idealistic, with deep emotional demands and a loving heart.

Famous CanScorpSag Personalities
Raj Kapoor, Mao Zedong, Katie Holmes, Vanessa Paradis, Lal (Paul Michael), Diane Sawyer, Bharat Chhetri, Ankita Lokhande.

148. CANCER–SAGITTARIUS–CAPRICORN

The highly emotional Moon meets the spiritual and knowledgeable Jupiter and the wise old Saturn in CanSagCaps. A Crab, a Centaur and a mountain Goat – interesting mix of creatures, indeed. The touchy Crab gets a good deal of strength from the horsey Sagittarius and the implacable Goat. But they are touchy, still.

CanSagCap is a double cardinal sign and all the three signs want to make something of their lives. Cancer is soft yet determined and very tenacious in its ambitions; Sagittarius always dreams big and Capricorn makes them work assiduously and diligently to reach the top. They want to achieve success and not be distracted in their quest for fame and fortune.

Family is extremely important to them. The Sagittarian indifference and fear of ties are diluted due to Cancer and Capricorn's family love. CanSagCaps like spending time with their families. They hate being alone for long. They feel secure wrapped up in their family. They idolise their mothers, but if their mothers do not return their affection, they can get very deeply hurt and that love turns to hate.

Memory is their special gift. They remember events that happened decades ago. CanSagCaps are also extremely imaginative and creative. They easily tilt towards artistic expression and do not mind displaying their talents. The Sagittarian desire to shine on the stage will make them seek adulation rather than run away from it.

They are very intelligent and find it easy to understand complex theories. If Sagittarius is strong in this combination, they can be very adventurous. Otherwise, they are a little more conservative in their approach. Cancer seems timid but never gives up once it decides to do something and Capricorn makes them work hard at turning a seemingly harebrained plan into a viable proposition. They have imaginative ideas and try hard to make them a success. They never give up and are always ready to slog their way to success.

They have a circle of friends with whom they like to be. It takes time for them to feel comfortable with strangers and they do not open up immediately. But once they decide to trust you, they are fun people to be with. They love food and fun. Food speaks to them. Both Cancer and Sagittarius give them an insatiable delight in epicurean ventures.

Money is extremely important to them. Cancer needs money to feel secure while Capricorn wants nothing less than creating a solid empire and Sagittarius cares only for the applause. Hence, money and glory are both important to them. They are extremely insecure about money and can have funny ways to save it. Though they do have the habit of throwing away their lifetime savings on a single night, especially on people they love a lot, still, they would rather save than splurge. They fear a rainy day, even calamities.

Love is very important to them. CanSagCaps want to have a person to love and care for them. They are not happy living alone. The emotional needs of Cancer exist but they might not express them well.

They love their family and are ready to sacrifice their desires and loves for them. Yet Sagittarius gives them an element of desire for freedom too and though they might nearly kill themselves over their family, they will stop short of committing hara-kiri.

The frankness of Sagittarius is reduced in this combination but they still surprise you at times with their forthright remarks. They can explode in anger or sulk for long hours when they feel slighted, especially with those they know very well.

They are very positive, yet suffer from bouts of melancholy as well. The Cancerian sensitivity and the Capricornian predilection for misery can hide their sunniness at times. They need lots of comfort and encouragement to recover from these bouts and shine again. However, despite their occasional melancholia and depression, they stay strong and courageous.

Many of them put up façades. They may act tough on the outside but are soft inside. They need to feel safe before they put aside their brittle Cancerian exteriors, Capricorn's loneliness and Sagittarian's love for attention. All three signs love being in love and work towards appreciation and acceptance. But they are wary, defensive and quick to withdraw into their shells if not loved enough.

They are spiritual too and are interested in exploring this facet of life. Their views are not rigid and change with time. The Capricornian reverse-aging syndrome makes them act younger as they grow older. Capricorn's sombre ways and Cancer's insecurities reduce as they age and grow in wealth and experience.

Cancer–Sagittarius–Capricorn – Shakira

At the age of eight, Shakira wrote her first song, titled 'Us gafas oscuras' (Your dark glasses), which was inspired by her father, who for years wore dark glasses, to hide his grief [over the death of her half-brother].[262]

'Over the course of our meeting, she will quote Socrates ("a life without examination is a life that's not worth living"), openly discuss the fact that she's in therapy.'[263]

Nobel Prize winning author Gabriel Garcia Marques says, 'No one can sing or dance like her, with such an innocent sensuality.'[264]

Shakira has the family love and dedication of a Capricorn, the emotional sensitivity of a Cancer and the frankness, innocence and showmanship of a Sagittarius.

Love and Marriage for Him

You can rest easy with this guy. He is responsible, caring and very comfortable with household duties. He is all for his family and loves spending time with his extended family too. He is fun and good company but also needs lots of positivity around him. He can easily shift from happy to morose and you have to bring his spirits up when the blues strike him. He does not communicate his feelings easily. He is a little conservative in his thought processes and wants a traditional wife. He loves being the centre of attention at home.

---

[262] http://en.wikipedia.org/wiki/Shakira
[263] http://www.guardian.co.uk/music/2009/oct/15/shakira-interview
[264] http://www.fazeteen.com/issue07/shakira.html

His ambition is the driving force of his life and you need to understand this. Extend your support and understanding when he strives for his dreams. Despite his good intentions of handling money, he has the Sagittarian gambling instincts. Do not fear for he only gambles when he is absolutely sure of winning.

As a father, he is wonderful. This man loves fatherhood and is the perfect father – loving, doting, protective and fun loving. His children instinctively turn to him. You can expect a helping hand even during nappy changing. He can also make their tantrums disappear in record time.

Love and Marriage for Her
Loving, caring and very emotional, she is the perfect wife who knows how to get her way without charging at you. This lady cares for her house and family and works selflessly for everyone. But do not take her for granted, for she knows how to make herself heard. She is the daughter-in-law everyone praises. She knows how to budget and cook mouth-watering dishes at minimum cost.

She is quite conservative in her dress sense and prefers traditional and comfortable wear to luxury brands. You can expect her to go trekking in *salwar kameez* and a pair of sturdy shoes. Money is important to her and she worries a lot if there is any shortfall. She can easily handle problems. Despite her self-assuredness, there is an endearing innocence about her.

She is a great help if you have a business or are into politics. Her organising abilities can make you reach the top. This lady can be the power behind the throne but wants some of the applause too. She can be blunt at times too and will speak her mind but she always speaks sense. Take care of her and pay attention to her needs for she likes pampering at times.

She is a wonderful mother who knows when to have fun and when to discipline. Her children always find her near them. Her only failing is her desire to protect her children even when they grow up.

At the Workplace
CanSagCaps can be in anything from finance to the stage; they prefer professions that give glory and money. They don't mind starting small and want to shine through their efforts. They are tenacious in their careers and never give up without a fight – in fact, they never give up. Praise them and pay them well and they will never let you down.

CanSagCaps are extremely intelligent and easily understand abstract ideas. They also have a very creative side and know how turn their creativity into a money-spinning career. They never shy away from displaying their talents, though you might have to push them initially. They can be celebrated artists, actors and singers.

They are very ambitious and will always stick to careers that offer them opportunities for growth. You will never find them in a failing industry – the hardy Capricorn in them knows which rocks to climb to reach the mountaintop. As bosses, they are very caring and protective of their employees. They have phenomenal control on budgets.

Water, Fire and Earth make them inimitable in their drive, ambition and focus. CanSagCaps know how to utilise their talents and create enduring legacies during their lifetime.

Famous CanSagCap Personalities
Shakira, Omi Vaidya, Lord Byron, Dinkar Deodhar, Princess Charlene of Monaco.

149. CANCER–CAPRICORN–AQUARIUS

The emotional Moon adds a touch of sensitivity to the old man Saturn and the wild and wacky Uranus. Love, family, nostalgia, ideals and money are what CanCapAquas dream of. Advanced humanitarian ideals, without unthinking rebellion, mark them out as doers with a heart and mind.

Cancerians revel in the past, Capricornians are practical and live in today while Aquarians are dreamy eyed about the future. CanCapAquas have the phenomenal ability to balance and leverage all the three paradigms of life – the past, the present and the future.

Aquarius adds laughter to the melancholic duo of Cancer and Capricorn. It makes them see the lighter side of life and stops them from being completely forlorn. It also makes them think differently by adding unconventionality to their dreams. They live life according to their own terms albeit without any aggressive ways.

They have very expressive faces, thanks to Cancer. They show their emotions, especially to the ones near them, and it is very easy to make out when they are hurt. They are very sensitive and need sensitive people around them. CanCapAquas are also very good at knowing how people feel. The sensitivity of Cancer and the curiosity of Aquarius merge well with Capricornian logic to accurately piece together the reasons for a person's particular behaviour. They are quite intuitive.

Family is extremely important. CanCapAquas have Cancer's desire to be surrounded by the people they love and Capricorn's desire for family ties. Cancer can make them Mother's pet. Love is crucial for them, both for emotional reasons and the desire for family support. They want a partner who not only understands and loves them but also provides them with status and respectability. Career is their second love.

CanCapAquas want to succeed and are willing to wait and work to get their desired results. Capricorn's need to succeed and Cancer's perseverance mark them out as ambitious. They have a plan and stick to it despite the Aquarian desire for change. CanCapAquas want to achieve status and respectability in life. They want people to look up at them, though they might not say so; but you see them positively glow on hearing compliments. They always strive for the right status. They do it for themselves and for their family.

Money is important to them. They are very insecure if they do not have a healthy bank balance. They always strive to make more and are not spendthrifts: saving comes naturally to them. They might not mind spending for long-lasting assets and things that add to their social worth but don't expect them to splurge needlessly on small extravagances. Owning a house is very essential for them too.

They are good cooks who like to try their hand at new recipes and family favourites. They can turn to cooking to de-stress. Of course, their favourite food will always be their mother's home-cooked meals.

CanCapAqua is a double cardinal sign, which makes them leaders. CanCapAquas do not lead by aggression or domination; rather they lead by appealing to your emotions and logic.

They have an edge over others with their ability to foresee the future. They have the Aquarian genius of picking up new trends and the capability of working things through with Capricornian perseverance and the Cancerian tenacity. Aquarius also eases the stuffy attitude of Capricorn and makes them more human and humane. The practicality of Capricorn, the 'saving for a rainy day' habit of Cancer and Aquarius's ability to predict what will work in the future make CanCapAqua a deadly combination.

They can also be quite moody. They have myriad mood swings, from melancholic and depressive, to cold and distant. They can spend an inordinate amount of time tormenting themselves about the things that can go wrong without ever thinking of the things that are going well. They need strong faith and loving friends and family to help tide over their fears. The good part is that Aquarius makes them eventually rise above their problems and find unusual solutions. As they age, their fears and anxieties slowly fade. The Capricornian phenomenon of reverse aging makes them more chilled out after their thirties.

Whether they are religious or atheist, whatever they believe, Aquarius makes them believe wholeheartedly. They may also be interested in esoteric sciences and use their intuition to understand people and situations around them better. They are humanitarians at heart and turn philanthropist to give something back to society.

Cancer–Capricorn–Aquarius – Y.C. Deveshwar
'Yogi' Deveshwar is chairman of ITC.

Yogi's colleagues: 'Many would have described the inheritance as a crown of thorns but Deveshwar's commitment to the company never wavered.'[265]

Yogi: 'The obligation is on the Indian businesses to create Indian brands to capture and retain value in India and redeploy it for the Indians.'[266]

E-Choupal is an initiative of ITC to link directly with rural farmers via the Internet for procurement of agricultural and aquaculture products.[267]

Padmabhushan awardee Yogi has transformed the tobacco company into a conglomerate with interests in hotels, FMCG, agribusiness, IT and more.

Yogi has the doggedness of a Cancerian, the shrewd business mind and the capacity to scale up things like a Capricorn and can envisage the future and diversify smartly like an Aquarian.

Love and Marriage for Him
He is extremely caring. This man loves spending time with his family and hates being away for long. Of course, his work occupies him too. He wants to succeed not only for himself but also for his family. If you love him, you have to love his parents and his extended family too.

Be there for him; for, despite his desire to earn money and success, he is a bundle of fears and insecurities. He is extremely emotional and sensitive. There is a very deep side to him and he is hurt easily. Fortunately, he is quite easy to read

---

[265] http://www.rediff.com/money/2005/apr/09spec6.htm
[266] http://articles.economictimes.indiatimes.com/2013-01-25/news/36548086_1_investment-cycle-yc-deveshwar-rate-of-capital-formation/2
[267] http://en.wikipedia.org/wiki/E-Choupal

if you know him well. Keep note of his expressions for they tell you his moods and be extra caring when he seems down.

At times, he can surprise you by being detached. Allow him the freedom of being himself. He uses such moments to think of unusual plans and unheard-of ideas. You need to be a little self-sufficient and not pile your emotions on him.

He ensures that the bank balance is never low. Of course, it is a little difficult to get him to splurge. He frowns on things that are not specifically for the house. Use tact and a little sensibility to get him to agree.

He is a doting father. His children mean the world to him and he makes sure he spends time with them. He is quite indulgent but knows where to draw the line. He never dominates them but makes them change their minds in more subtle ways.

Love and Marriage for Her
She is loving, caring and motherly. She worries about everyone in the family and spends sleepless nights over them. Yet, she also has a streak of individuality and her views rarely seem run-of-the-mill. Though she listens to everyone, she does what she feels is right.

She needs care for her moods change easily. She needs a shoulder to lean on and frequent words of assurance. However, she can surprise you with her inner strength in times of crisis. There is deep strength in her so don't take her tears as proof of her weakness.

She is very creative and thinks of unusual things to do. She knows how to utilise her talents and earn money. Money is quite important to her and she is happy if she has a bank balance she can rely on. She spends only when absolutely necessary. There is a bit of fun in her too and her wild sense of humour can really crack you up. She can be nostalgic at times.

She is the most loving of mothers. Her children are thoroughly pampered by her. However, she maintains discipline as well. Her idea of fun is spending time with her family. It takes her some time to realise that they have grown up.

At the Workplace
CanCapAquas are extremely ambitious but rarely reveal their dreams for fear of blighting them. They are talented and creative. They do well as artists and pioneers. They also know how to innovate logically and make it a success. They have a fertile imagination and will astound you with their maturity and their futuristic but viable ideas.

They are good at anything they try. They have the perseverance and patience to work long and hard, along with the extra genius of thought to carry them forward. They are also good at networking and will not be above using politics to get their goals. They never let you down if you pay them well.

They are good at finance and make very good entrepreneurs too. They have an instinct for saving and know the right people for the right job. They are adept at turning a small idea into a big project and are never intimidated by the scale of their dreams. CanCapAquas can be great leaders and politicians too. They can lead using control and emotion. They are father figures as bosses and care for everyone. Expect them to be in the forefront of activities that are socially relevant and beneficial to all.

Water, Earth and Air meet in CanCapAquas to endow them with emotions, stability and a desire to change things for better.

Famous CanCapAqua Personalities
Y.C. Deveshwar, Gundappa Vishwanath, Gregory van der Wiel, Gordon Brown, Evangeline Adams, Mandolin U. Srinivas.

150. CANCER–AQUARIUS–PISCES

The emotional and moody Moon, inventive and intelligent Uranus and the extremely deep and mysterious Pisces form the backdrop of this sensitive personality. CanAquaPisces are extremely loving and sentimental sweethearts. It is impossible not to love them.

They are empathetic and easily understand your problems without you confiding in them. Do not think that they are uninterested in your problems if they seem distracted in a conversation. It is an Aquarian trait that makes them talk about absolutely unrelated things in the middle of a serious discussion. Do not worry, they have heard and absorbed every word and nuance.

Pisces is the most evolved sign and displays wisdom beyond its age. Also, the Aquarian unconventionality makes CanAquaPisces work for ideals rather than the glitter of gold. Their nonconformity will encompass everything that they do in life, from relationships to career.

They adore their mothers. These guys know just how to care for and appreciate their loved ones. Their families and selected circle of friends are really lucky, for these guys combine responsibility with love and are always protective. They are quite nostalgic about their past. They are fun to be with and can talk very warmly to strangers too. Though they are emotional, they do not burden others with their emotions and can switch off their sadness while talking to strangers. They have an impish sense of humour and joke and play pranks without hurting anyone.

The steadfast Cancer in them ensures that the artistic Piscean imagination, original Aquarian ideas and wild Cancerian imagination all work together and come to a logical conclusion. CanAquaPisces are very focused and for all their artistic thoughts, their ventures are always grounded in reality. This is a wonderful and rare trait in a creative personality. Their artistic ventures (and their ventures are always artistic) will materialise due to their focus. The tight-fisted Cancer also keeps them a bit conservative in their spending. They never think of spending anyone else's money without assessing the returns.

These lovely people, however, have one unattractive trait. They are extremely messy unless trained otherwise right from childhood. They can also be easily tempted into distractions. Addictions to all the pleasures of life can be a big temptation and they can succumb to this if not handled well.

They are very moody people. Both Cancer and Pisces have this trait. They are deeply afflicted by mood swings and don't know why they are suddenly upset or happy. They also get hurt quickly as they read too much between the lines. When hurt or disturbed, they withdraw into a shell. They rarely lose their cool and are never rude or vindictive. The only way they show displeasure and hurt is by cutting themselves off. Their family will have to be very patient and loving when they are in such moods.

They also seem very dazed and detached at times. Let them have their space and be reclusive whenever they want, for one thing is certain, every time they go to the deep side of the ocean, they come back with a gem. Solitude is their 'me' time and makes them think the most amazing ideas.

When CanAquaPisces fall in love, they love with their whole being and soul. These people are very giving and emotional in love. They have the gift of knowing exactly what their partner needs. There might be times when the Aquarian curiosity will overtake their emotions and they want to know more about other people. But usually they will stay committed once they are in a loving relationship.

They can also very timid, shy and introverted to start with. Only with age and experience do they open up. They can also get into deep depressions when things don't go their way. They are acutely sensitive to people's emotions and deep inside themselves are extremely sensitive about everything too. They cry a lot.

They love children and understand their fears and innocence. They are deeply moved by hunger, poverty and crimes against the underprivileged. They want to make a difference to people when they reach positions of strength in their lives.

This wonderful combination is truly a mixture of creative and realistic thoughts. Their ideas may be wild, but are viable and refreshingly new. With their sensitivity and highly evolved sensibility, they live life on their own terms without stepping on anybody's toes or squashing anyone with their ego. Though rebellious, they are deep, perceptive and highly evolved spiritually.They are attracted to values that embody thought rather than materialistic urges.

Cancer–Aquarius–Pisces – Aamir Khan
'I have broken so many rules and not followed conventions.'[268]

'It's a perception people have of me, that I have these grand plans. It's not necessary that I stick to a pre-determined plan. It's a rather incorrect perception.'

'I don't have a bath everyday and Kiran can't understand why.'

Kiran: 'He is immensely patient and understanding of people's problems... When he is upset with me, he goes into a shell and completely shuts me out.'[269]

'I am a shy person...I am lazy and love to sleep...I went through depression after divorce...I cry a lot.'[270]

Aamir Khan is instinctive, creative, inventive, adaptable, extremely emotional, sensitive and surprisingly laid-back, like a true CanAquaPisces. He improvises; he is not a perfectionist.

Love and Marriage for Him
If you are his partner, you are very lucky indeed, for you won't find another as caring and loving. He loves his family and wants to spend a lot of time with them. Of course, his moods remain and you have to work round them, but, otherwise, he is quite an easy-going guy, not given to rigid thoughts and open to new ideas. His only condition is that you are sensitive and intelligent. He is extremely romantic too and is capable of creating some memorable mements that you will cherish for the rest of your life.

---

[268] *Stardust*, August 2010
[269] *Hello!* January 2011
[270] Excerpts from an interview on Zoom tv

The guy is also great at listening. And he is emotional – yes, he is! You will have to be careful of hurting him; he is quite sensitive. Be careful about speaking without thinking. He is expressive and lets you know what is bothering him. You are free to have your own views too. It is very easy to live with him if you can pick up after him for he has messy habits and cannot be routine-oriented. He may be a thorough professional at work but is completely laid-back and even lazy at home.

As a father, he is in tune with his children's thoughts and knows how they feel. He does not judge them by the parameters of outsiders and never forces them to do anything that they do not like. He ensures that his children are not bound by old, traditional ideas and reveals to them new values and thoughts that broaden their views.

Love and Marriage for Her
She is truly a lovely wife and the only thing she asks of you is that you display sensitivity towards her feelings. She is sympathetic and caring, and home is a peaceful abode where you can leave all your worries behind and just relax. She rarely nags, and is soft and compliant to your views. This does not mean that she is a doormat. She never asserts herself but has many opinions and knows how to get them across without resorting to a raised voice.

She can be easily crushed under the load of a big ego and if the burden does not cease, she disappears. She dreads a disturbed, unpleasant family life. Provide her the emotional security that she needs. She is neither materialistic nor a spendthrift. She knows how to save money without being miserly and spends only when the need arises. She has artistic sensibilities and is happy creating something, be it food or a work of art.

You might have to turn a blind eye to the mess in the house at times when she gets engrossed in her work. Either help or get some help – she will need some support in that department.

She is a loving mother. She knows just how to calm crying children and make them laugh with stories and jokes. She lets them live their dreams. She is more of a friend than a mother.

At the Workplace
CanAquaPisces burst with creativity and imagination. They always think of new ideas and ways to do old things. Whatever they do, you can be sure of one thing: they bring something totally new to the table. Spontaneity is what they are all about. Always thinking, evolving, re-thinking – they are never be satisfied with the status quo and truly believe that everything and anything can be improved in a million ways.

They are fabulous artists, great dancers, actors, directors and so on. Their ability to learn quickly and improvise makes them unbeatable in all creative fields. This combination works well for writes, thinkers and philosophers. Their great empathetic skills, their ability to read people and fabulous people skills can also make them extraordinary good teachers, doctors and psychiatrists. Their high knowledge of the esoteric also makes them good healers, spiritual gurus and the like.

If they are your boss, be sure that they will give you a free hand. They are sensitive to your issues and truly understand you. But they can see through phony people and people who play politics.

CanAquaPisces are truly human and not bound by old ideas and traditions. They are motivated by amazing possibilities rather than by money and glory.

Famous CanAquaPisces Personalities
Aamir Khan, Rohit Shetty, Vivian Richards, Remo D'Souza, Queen Latifah, Mustafa Kamil Pasha.

151. LEO–VIRGO–LIBRA

Apollo, the generous and majestic Sun god, the perfectly meticulous Virgo, and Venus, the planet of beauty, grace and love come together in this beautifully majestic mix. LeoVirLib is a very elegant and stylish combination. These guys define style in their own way and are utterly romantic too. This is a mix of fixed (Leo), mutable (Virgo) and cardinal (Libra) signs and it gives them a well-rounded personality. They have the ability to think, visualise and create higher destinaties for their lives. They do so without stepping on many toes or resorting to devious means.

These guys have extraordinary communication skills. Librans are born communicators, Virgos talk with a crystal-clear thought process and Leo adds style to their communication. They speak and you listen. You will notice that subtle softness in their speech. Their tone is rarely high-pitched and they never go in for ugly spats or vulgar displays of emotions.

They have the Leo pride and desire to do something big, without its excessive arrogance. LeoVirLibs are extremely positive and enthusiastic, and infect others with their *joie de vivre*. They are extremely diplomatic, superbly dignified, ooze with panache and restrained sex appeal, are highly cultured, well mannered, and proponents of doing things right.

They are disciplined people. Despite the extremely lazy Leo and Libra, they are not casual in their approach to life and work. They have specific routines. As they grow older, though, the Virgo traits may decrease and make them more moderate in discipline. They are finicky about food and choose healthy food over tasty take-aways.

Extremely artistic and creative, LeoVirLibs are full of imagination, and thanks to the Leo showmanship, they are not shy of showing off their talents. Venus blesses them with the natural ability to understand and flow with music and the arts, Virgo ensures perfection, and Leo takes their creativity to a different plane altogether. It is amazing to watch them in action for they combine Libran grace with Virgo's extreme attention to detail. Dressing-up time is sacrosanct for them. These people want to look elegant. They are flamboyant, but not blindingly so.

LeoVirLibs are extremely romantic. You can expect the abundant Leo indulgence in romance and the Libran desire for companionship. They know just how to talk and act and how to woo and attract attention and adoration. The high standards of Leo make them pick and choose, but at the same time, befuddled Libra makes them very unsure of the status of their love. They need to be in love but can be very confused about how to take it further. You have to give a firm push if you want to settle into matrimony with them. Given a choice, they will keep on thinking forever.

They make excellent friends with their unmatched sense of humour and desire to spread goodwill. They know how to have fun without hurting anyone's feelings. The inherent Leo largesse and desire to protect make them very dependable too. They lend a helping hand to those in need. They are considerate and though they are not able to read your hidden sorrows, they do everything to help once you tell them your problems. Remember to talk and communicate your hopes and hurts for these guys need a little help in decoding people.

Libra and Leo personify laziness and the trait will be prominent in them. LeoVirLibs will work very hard when they have to but don't expect them to move a muscle in their spare time. However, despite being lazy they like their space to be neat and clean. Messy interiors and rooms with no artistic sensibilities put them off.

There is a possibility of analysis-paralysis with these people. They analyse things too much, getting into the details and nuances, and take a long time to take decisions. Procrastination, vacillation, and prolonged states of confusion, can be major irritants about LeoVirLibs. Some of the lesser souls in this combination can also be arrogant, egoistic and hyperbolic; but they are rare.

Expect them to be very spiritual and maybe even ritualistic. Other than the arts, their strained nerves and wobbling minds find peace and solace when they submit to the powers above.

Leo–Virgo–Libra – Akshay Kumar

'I want martial arts to become compulsory in every school because discipline is something the youth requires today.' Akshay Kumar is punctual: so punctual that he arrives ten minutes before time.[271]

'I would rate myself pretty high as a family man.'

'The youth should never believe in powder, steroids or anything artificial. They should have conviction and faith in themselves and should not resort to short cuts.'[272]

'Tina is extremely honest. I'm diplomatic.' (Twinkle Khanna [Tina] is a GemSag.)[273]

Health, fitness and fashion find a good combination in Akshay Kumar. He personifies LeoVirLib with his confidence, discipline and suave charm.

Love and Marriage for Him

He will have taken time to decide before finally plunging into the relationship. He will have analysed in detail the future of the relationship in true Virgo fashion. He will have been confused for a while like a typical Libran and been charming and romantic during courtship like a Lion. But once he ties the knot, he is a dutiful and loving husband.

Forget about his roving eye before marriage: a typical Leo or Libran settles down nicely once he is domesticated. Actually, if you set him free, the Virgo in him makes him extremely responsible. He is one of those guys who become more mature and responsible after marriage. He surprises his family with his newfound sobriety and stability.

He fills your life with excitement. You have to keep pace with him. You too need to look good to match his style but take care not to steal his thunder. He is one of those rare guys who talk their way into a woman's heart. You can talk to him

---

[271] *DNA*, November 16, 2011
[272] http://www.gomolo.com/46/feature-there-is-just-no-competition-between-salman-srk-and-me
[273] *Bombay Times*, pg 6, 13 August, 2013

and, in return, he never tires of talking or expressing his views. He also involves you in decision-making. In spite of his many views, he leaves the final decision in your hands. He rarely insists that you follow his path but his arguments are so logical that you easily find yourself following him.

He has very few demands. His first is that you keep the house neat and clean and the second that you let him live by his rules. He has a set of rules on how to exercise, what to eat and how to medicate himself.

As a father, he is very loving and caring, and also fair and generous in his views. He wants his children to excel in academics and lets them decide their ways. He is not a completely hands-on father in the beginning, but as they grow older, he takes more interest in their upbringing.

Love and Marriage for Her
She is everything and more. This lady is stylish, elegant and disciplined. You sense perfection when you are with her. An added plus is that she is an eternal romantic. Be ready to love her and express your love every day in many romantic ways.

She is extremely dutiful. She effortlessly manages all her activities and never relegates her duties to the back burner. She manages her career and home while looking absolutely stunning.

She does not like doing things on her own. She wants you to be by her side when she is out having fun. And she needs to have fun. She loves shopping, and retail therapy really gets her excited. She also loves talking; her views are intelligent. Communication is extremely important to her.

Despite all the seeming fluff of romance and talk, she is very intelligent and disciplined. She always tries to do the right things and thinks analytically through every decision. This girl is a diva and you have to be ready to accept this aspect of her. Do not be possessive or egoistic with her. You have to be a relaxed and charming person to deserve her.

As a mother, she is definitely caring. She is good at nursing her children and fulfils all her duties as a mother. She expects academic excellence and helps them achieve distinction in life.

At the Workplace
LeoVirLibs shine in every field. They can be excellent salespersons and marketers, and do well in creative professions as well. They do not like to work very hard all the time, so professions where work is interspersed with free time really appeal to them.

They are disciplined workers who work very hard. They are also very artistic and can do well as actors, designers, painters and musicians. Any profession that requires discipline and ideation is perfect for them. They make good number crunchers too. Their analytical and extraordinary communication skills make them excel in presentations and discussions.

They want a pat on their backs and work harder after being praised. They love to take their ideas to a greater level and bask in the spotlight.

They take to leadership with élan and do a fabulous job with panache and a smile. If they are your bosses, be prepared with numbers and be ready for a lot of advice and scrutiny.

Fire, Earth and Air mix to make them optimistic yet rational, routine-addicted yet fun loving, and fair yet opinionated. They are driven, focused, and stylish, combined with substance.

Famous LeoVirLib Personalities
Akshay Kumar, Beyonce Knowles, Serena Williams, , Margaret Thatcher, Deborah Kerr, Ram Jethmalani, Brendon McCullum, Pete Cashmore, Kader Khan, Sabyasachi Chakraborty, Raj Kundra, Cho Ramaswamy.

152. LEO–VIRGO–SCORPIO

The proud and generous Apollo combines with the perfect and meticulous Virgo and the passionate Scorpio to create a powerhouse. LeoVirScorps are not only focused on being the best but also have the passion and drive to see their dreams come true. The Leo in them loves setting high standards. LeoVirScorps are truly impressed by supremacy and love impressing too.

LeoVirScorp is a true combination of flair, focus and passion. They are ready to work and slog with passion, and hate coming second. They want to succeed and be at the front of every race. If they ever hear a comment doubting their ability, their Leo ego is badly punctured. Then Virgo's need for perfection and Scorpio's intensity take over and they will not rest till they achieve their aim and they stand tall. Applaud them for there is no better role model for determination.

Irrespective of their looks, they command respect and whenever you meet them, you feel that you are in the company of 'somebody'. The Leo flamboyance and style, Virgo's refined perfection and the mysterious aura of Scorpio, make a heady mix for a magnetic personality.

The Scorpio ability to read people makes it very hard to fool them. Add to it the Virgo clarity of thought and these people know your strengths and weaknesses without you telling them. Though they like to hear praises, they have the sense to know when they are being taken for a ride.

They work very hard to maintain that style and poise. They have put their heart and soul into reaching those lofty standards and have earned their right to be in the spotlight, by their work or by their looks. They have the Virgo eye for detail and are great critics, but do not criticise them. You can do that only if you are part of their hallowed group and, even then, use tact.

Only before their family and those they have found to be true, do LeoVirScorps give way to the Leo desire to be loud, boisterous and playful. They love throwing parties and organising lavish get-togethers. Here, the key word is organising. They are not the ones cooking and cleaning, if they can help it. Their parties have a sense of drama and they are always fabulously dressed.

Money has no allure for them. They do not work solely to gain money. LeoVirScorps want to stand out, to be applauded and to achieve glory. They want to achieve a position that people will admire and want to emulate. The Leo melodrama may be subdued in them, but the pride and ego is intact. When combined with the intelligent Virgo and deeply fierce Scorpio, they become the ultimate planners and executors of any vision.

LeoVirScorps never like or dislike anyone – they usually love or hate people. Their feelings are rarely middling. They are ready to fall in love, yet they are highly analytical before letting the virus overtake them. Romantic and passionate, they want an ideal to fall for and are highly selective of their partner. They know the right words and know how to charm, and the intense look in their eyes will make them perfectly romantic! They can be committed if they find the love and adoration they desire. Partners who show insensitivity to their views or act differently after marriage can make them rethink their vows.

The Scorpio revenge tendency exists in them and the moment they get a whiff of manipulative moves from you, your life changes for the worse. They are fabulous friends and equally dangerous enemies. They are definitely not above base emotions like jealousy and possessiveness. They can really make life hard for their foes. Conversely, they are extremely generous and loyal to people they love. People who get into their good books will witness their amazing generosity. They stand tall for people who need them and love being leaned upon.

As they grow older, their spiritual leanings grow too. They believe in a power above and do not mind talking about it.

There is one secret about them that they will never tell you. The most important thing that they desire in life is love and admiration. But they have this nagging self-doubt about themselves, which the Leo in them conceals with a false bravado. However, the immensely brave and ruthlessly passionate Scorpio combines with the Virgo meticulousness to keep that insecurity at bay. This force drives them to keep going on. A time arrives when they rise above these inner restrictions and soar like eagles. Then they become forgiving, generous and champions of the underprivileged.

Leo–Virgo–Scorpio – Shabana Azmi

Javed Akhtar: 'Shabana is a perfectionist. She is extremely picky and choosy about her work. If she reads a hundred scripts, she says no to all except maybe three or four!...She takes her role very seriously and goes into small details to get the role right...she perfects everything!...Even in personal life Shabana is 'perfection personified'...Whether wife, daughter, sister or friend...she goes out of her way to make people feel special.'[274]

Moved deeply by the plight of slum-dwellers of glittering Mumbai, Shabana took up their cause. In the aftermath of the Babri Mosque tragedy, she tirelessly fought religious extremism and communalism.[275]

Shabana has the fire, zeal and desire for perfection of a LeoVirScorp.

Love and Marriage for Him

He may seem lazy and regal, but when crisis strikes, this man never fails you. His lazy looks hide a mind that can analyse and plan all possibilities and an endurance level that never gives up.

He can be rebellious too. He walks his own path. He needs a stable woman to handle him. His moods and passions are varied and a calm partner can do much to soothe his uneven temperament. He can be loud and boisterous or soft and reclusive. You need to understand when to compliment him and when to leave him alone. He knows how to criticise and can be quite a nitpicker at times. His passions are the reason for his enthusiasm.

As a father, he dotes on his children. He loves taking care of them and is very good at nursing them when they are sick. He is their friend who expects them to respect him.

---

[274] Filmitown.com, 11 Dec 2011
[275] http://www.drishtipat.org/activists/shabana.html

Love and Marriage for Her
If she has chosen you as a partner, you are lucky for she only chooses someone who is a cut above the rest. This girl sets very high standards.

However, to make the relationship work, you have to know how to compliment her for she loves sincere compliments. She works very hard to please your mother, to impress your guests with that extraordinary menu of food that she toiled hard to create, and she has just collected a fortune for her favourite organisation. She wants to share all those details with you and wants you to to look up to her in admiration. If you are not a good listener, she may end up sulking for days. Yes, she does spend a bomb on managing her alluring good looks, but she will prefer working and spending her own money than depending on you.

Cheap jokes and vulgarity are not tolerated by her. She wants a partner of whom she can be proud and who can command her without being aggressive. She admires ideals and stands by you if you choose an idealistic path. Her endurance and courage are remarkable and she can face any challenge in life.

She is bound to have some passion in life and it does the relationship good if she indulges in it. This lady loves to become a crusader and is very good at motivating people to stand up against injustice.

She may not initially be very eager to be a mother, but once she is one, she is exceptional. It mellows her down slightly. Of course, she is controlling. She indulges the children but is strict, too. Strangers are never allowed to criticise her brood.

At the Workplace
Passionate and intense, LeoVirScorps are very ambitious. Their Leonine need for name and recognition drives them to work extremely hard to gain their desires. Virgo makes them workaholics. The Scorpio's heart dies a bit if it loses. Even being number two is not enough. They do not rest till they succeed, and put all their passion and energy to drive themselves relentlessly to achieve the high standards they have set for themselves.

LeoVirScorps shine bright in a corporate set up. Their logical Virgo minds are great at devising plans and charting courses of action. They are great at visualising the applause on success and actually work backwards estimating the amount of work and stress involved, and then let their perfection-seeking hard work do the rest. They are brilliant at crunching numbers and perfectly suited for research-oriented functions or any work that needs deep analysis, meticulous perfection and intense hard work.

If they work for you, you are lucky. Never undermine, ridicule or be stingy in recognition of their talents, and they will work doubly hard to make you proud. There are no better subordinates than them and no worse bosses! As bosses, they are so demanding and so scrutinising that no error escapes them. But they will be extraordinarily generous if you make them proud and don't play politics with them.

Fire, Water and Earth combine in this dedicated, loyal, courageous, generous and passionate combination. LeoVirScorps are made for success and always strive to deliver more than expected.

Famous LeoVirScorp Personalities
Shabana Azmi, Warren Buffet, Richard Gere, Javagal Srinath, Vishnuvardhan, Lucky Ali, Anjali Gopalan, Mumtaz Mahal.

153. LEO–VIRGO–SAGITTARIUS

This is one confident and bubbly combination. It has the generous and majestic Leo, the pure and disciplined Virgo, and the enthusiastic and highly ambitious Sagittarius. LeoVirSags are the most vital and energetic people you will ever meet. Intelligence is the hallmark of this combination.

Leos are intelligent and smart, despite their loud talk, while Virgo is blessed with clarity of thought and a deeply analytical mind. Sagittarius complements the two with its instinctive knowledge of the abstract and spiritual. There are two types of LeoVirSag – the brooding and intelligent types or the bubbly, talkative, enthusiastic and intelligent types. LeoVirSags are never boring. Their faces display energy and intellectual charm.

Ambition is a big part of LeoVirSags. Leos dream of creating magic and bowing to applause, while Sagittarians have soaring ambition. The diligent and conscientious spirit of Virgo guides them to work and focus their abundant energies on specific things. Talking big is something they just cannot avoid, but their conversations are sensible, with details and facts. Winning is an exhilarating feeling and they just love winning races – all kinds.

You get what you see with them. There is no malice or manipulative manoeuvring in their DNA. They speak frankly and do not care about the consequences. These guys are also very generous and giving. Money is something that Leos and Sagittarians have no control over, while Virgo is very adept at managing and budgeting. LeoVirSags know how to plan and budget their monetary needs and spend without being stingy.

LeoVirSags are easy to read when in love. They are very romantic and like to woo in style. Despite their evident romantic streak, LeoVirSags are likely to defer marriage for some time for the Sagittarius in them is wary of ties. It needs space to breathe and gets claustrophobic at the idea of accumulating a crowd of affectionate in-laws. The Virgo in them is scared of the responsibilities of marriage.

Food is high on their agenda; Leo loves food and hosting extravagant parties while Sagittarius also loves good food. But Virgo ensures that they prefer healthy eating habits. These people love partying but are careful not to go overboard in their search for excitement. But you know who is the centre of attraction, strumming his guitar and everyone swaying to his tunes, right? They love leading, whatever the situation, wherever they are.

They can blurt out unpleasant truths when angry. Their anger is stormy till they calm down, but they are not vindictive. The lack of Water in this combination makes them insensitive to the moods and views of others, and they find it hard to understand your sentiments.

Some of them live life on the edge, love showing off, are extremely adventurous, and have no qualms about their erratic lifestyle, or multiple relationships. They ensure they have their distractions and fun, but without affecting work or duties at home.

They have one secret that you should know. All their ebullience is to cover their secret inferiority complex, common to all Fire signs. Their demeanour and behaviour never show it but they are afraid of failure. They may work very hard or display that verve just to hide their insecurities. They also sulk if not accorded importance. They can become angry, proud creatures who either go silent or constantly criticise, if they feel unappreciated.

Spirituality is important to them. Fire signs are known for their inclination towards the spiritual and LeoVirSags show interest in the deeper aspects of life and religion.

They want to do something big, and shine. They work hard for that with a meticulous plan. No one can discount their intelligence, poise and style. They want to reach the stars but enjoy the journey too.

Leo–Virgo–Sagittarius – Michael Douglas

His former wife Diandra: 'The other women were difficult to deal with.'

'I was always just Kirk Douglas's son,' he once recalled. 'I had to fight for my own identity.'[276]

'Producing is fun for all the adult kinds of things you do. You deal in business, you deal with the creative forces. As an adult who continues to get older, you like the adult risks. It's flying without a net, taking chances and learning. I was never good in economics or business – had no business background, you know, and I like it.'[277]

Michael lives life on the edge, but is keen to learn and shape his own destiny like a LeoVirSag.

Love and Marriage for Him

He is your friend. This guy is cool and has very few ego hassles; but it is better to treat him with a little respect or the Leo might just roar to get your attention. He is fun, adventurous and an exciting companion whose idea of private time is not to lounge in front of the TV. He may take you out trekking or spend quality time in meditation with you.

Career is very important to him. It may make him forget his romantic nature of the courtship days. Nagging and crying at such times make him run away for he is not sensitive enough to handle emotions. The ways of his youth, when he was a nomad in romance, may ease off after he is married and domesticated, and responsibilities take over. It is good if he has worries, because if he is successful and carefree, he will still run wild and seek casual encounters just for the thrill.

You need to be strong and independent and voice your opinions without using wiles to get him to listen. The Virgo in him is attendant to duties, so give him tasks that he cannot refuse, like going to the parent–teacher meeting, attending weddings and going on annual holidays. He is there for you if ever there is a problem but routine and tedious chores are not for him.

He is meticulous and expects you to understand his obsession with good food. He likes to be surprised at mealtimes and is usually very health-conscious.

---

[276] http://www.independent.co.uk/life-style/profile-michael-douglas--this-man-is-not-a-sex-addict-1102843.html
[277] http://en.wikipedia.org/wiki/Michael_Douglas

He may not be too sensitive to your deepest needs and many a time you wish he could read your heart. He can't. Read your mind? He can!

As a father, he loves to have fun with his children. He enjoys giving them lectures on success. He insists on quality education. The best way for them to handle him is to show him respect and listen to his views.

Love and Marriage for Her
She is independent and fiery. She has the pride of Leo and ambition of Sagittarius that are hard to contain at home. She needs a career or an interest to utilise her abundant ebullient energy. Though she loves food, the kitchen is not her domain. She is a fabulous friend to you, with her infectious energy, sane advice and unrestrained laughter. She loves to travel and try out new adventures, with or without you.

She has her own personality and has no compunction in following her will. If you are as ambitious and independent as her, she is a great support system. But if the man in her life is irresponsible or philandering, she is capable of cutting off all ties and living a separate life.

Although she likes routine and rules, she finds it very difficult to stick to them. Tell her to relax and take life as it comes. It is better if you invest in a home away from parental pressures, for she is not a conventional daughter-in-law. She likes to do things her way and gets claustrophobic during family events. She is duty-conscious and will do everything expected of her as a daughter and daughter-in-law. Do not expect her to go beyond that.

Money management is not her strong point though she always looks for bargains. Her instinctive taste for luxury can often make her forget her good intentions. She is capable of taking you apart with her accurate and blunt criticism. She may also be insensitive to your feelings or offend a family member, but she never means it and will apologise if she was wrong.

She is ambitious for her children and pushes them to excel. She also spoils them with her generosity at times. The Virgo in her makes her an excellent nurse when they are sick.

At the Workplace
Career is the focal point of their lives. These people are very ambitious and love to overperform. Planning is their strong point; they work very systematically. They are excellent promoters and love all the details and theatre that goes with marketing. They are also good at number crunching and love scale and magnitude in projects. They are perfectionists and hate sloppiness in any job.

They are too focused and straightforward to be bothered by politics in the workplace. But their lack of sensitivity and love of flattery can make them easy pawns in the games of others. They are good team leaders who do not desire the entire limelight but generously include all of their team in their hour of glory. As bosses, they can be very demanding and expect their subordinates to be well versed in the details. Go to them prepared or you can be in for some scathing critical comments, or worse. They make very stylish, confident bosses who love telling you how to do things.

Double Fire and Earth make LeoVirSags driven yet stable and adventurous yet practical, and possess a solidity under all that excitement.

Famous LeoVirSag Personalities
Michael Douglas, Andrew Garfield, Aarav Akshay Kumar, Vivek Oberoi, P. Chidambaram, Ursula Burns, Louis C. K., Queen Elizabeth I, LeAnn Rimes, Manish Pandey.

154. LEO–VIRGO–CAPRICORN

Apollo, the proud Sun god, meets the perfection-seeking Virgo and the saturnine Capricorn in this extremely grounded yet volatile combination. LeoVirCaps are extremely responsible and stable personalities. You can be sure that they work relentlessly to fulfil their duties. Virgo makes them duty-conscious and so does Capricorn. Leo spurs them with ambition to go for their goals.

They are proud and impeccable. The Leo in them is proud of their lineage, while the Capricorn wants to hold their family traditions high. The Virgo in them is very conscientious and always toes the line. They are extremely prim and proper. They never falter in their responsibilities, especially those to their family. They are fiercely protective of their family values and do everything to keep up the family name and tradition. They are the pillars of the family: the keepers of tradition and upholders of customs.

They love planning and organising details. You can pass on those arduous tasks which require a great deal of precision and care to them. They enjoy discovering and highlighting minute details. Just remember to praise them well, especially in front of a crowd – they positively glow after that!

Leo adds flamboyance, though not excessive, and style, to their precise nature. LeoVirCaps take pride in their appearance. They know how to dress with understated elegance. They are very status-conscious too. They may come across as snobbish at times.

LeoVirCaps are well aware of their own importance. The Leo in them ensures that the self-effacing Virgo and melancholic Capricorn are a little diluted. Hence, LeoVirCaps do not mind talking about themselves. They also like to advise and guide. Their views are well thought out and logical. They can be a bit clannish: they tend to divide the world into two sectors – their own and others. They work and worry for their own and do not bother about others.

You know they are ambitious. The Capricorn Goat will soon find a mountain to climb, the Lion wants to roar after reaching the top and the Virgin has a plan for every step of the climb. Their nonchalance, their minding their own business, their industriousness and meticulousness, all manifest their ambition. They are very cool about it. They support their ambitions with extreme hard work. They can sacrifice anything in their quest for success. Any distraction, anything that interferes in their path to gold is scorned and avoided.

They are bound by routine and order. They like doing certain things at certain times and are very careful about their health. You can expect them to work out and eat sensibly. They like having a medicine chest at hand and their desire for cleanliness can become irritating. They are also very spiritual, and may be fond of ritual. Anything old and customary is sacred for them.

Love finds them ready but cautious. They rarely fall headlong in love. LeoVirCaps want a mate who adds to their social status and acceptability. Don't expect them to have romantic ideals. They do not easily understand deep-rooted emotions and sentiments. You need to tell them how you feel to get them to understand you. Even the romantic Leo in this combination can sacrifice love and romance if it interferes with family values or career.

The reverse-aging syndrome of Capricorn can make them more amenable to adventure as they grow older. Once they achieve a part of their ambitions, you can expect to see a lighter side to them.

They are the stingiest Leos you can ever meet. Both Virgo and Capricorn drastically affect their spending abilities. LeoVirCaps are unable to spend without counting pennies and looking for cheaper alternatives. But they do not mind spending on things that make people look at them with awe.

They have a temper and lose it royally, too. They are prone to irritability. They really know how to nag and be over-analytical in their extreme criticism. Of course, they know when to get angry and at whom.

Their desire to succeed and their inherent ambitions make them quite melancholic too. They are often stressed out and never see life as a happy venture. It is all about working hard and reaching somewhere. They slog all their lives for their pride. They despise themselves if they allow themselves an occasional lapse or laziness. They set the highest and often impossible standards for others to follow. The day they take it easy, you know that they have reached their destination.

Leo–Virgo–Capricorn – Phil Jackson

Jackson cites Robert Pirsig's book *Zen and the Art of Motorcycle Maintenance* as one of the major guiding forces in his life. He also applies Native American spiritual practices.[278]

'My father was the superintendent of the churches in the state of Montana. He was truly a man of peace. I think that my carriage and my demeanour are very much what the image of my father was like.'[279]

Phil prefers a more moral and spiritual stance than loud aggression. This has gained him the nickname Zen Master. He has the Leo regard for spirituality, the Capricornian reverence of his father and the Virgo desire to delve deep into his beliefs.

Love and Marriage for Him

He is definitely a responsible provider. Ambitious, hard working and grounded, he does not forget his duties. You can expect to see the bills paid on time and the future planned in detail. Provide the cheer and laughter in the relationship. It helps reduce the enormous strain he undergoes. He does not see life as a beautiful adventure at all.

He likes to be in command but that does not mean that you need to be subservient. Do your thing without rocking his boat and he is fine. His ego is evident and you have to pander to his whims and views. He sticks to routine and wants his room and food in specific ways. His family is also important to him and he desires a conservative attitude in his wife.

---

[278] http://en.wikipedia.org/wiki/Phil_Jackson
[279] Interview with Phil Jackson - Esquire http://www.esquire.com/features/what-ive-learned/phil-jackson

Money is a major issue, if you like spending. He takes a dim view of it, unless it is expenditure for his personal use: where it impresses people or enhances his reputation and status. His ambition is foremost in his mind. Do not stress him with emotional needs and sensitivity. He is not a very perceptive person. He may be more ready to help if you tell him what bothers you. The best thing about this guy is his ability to nurse you during sickness. He can be quite chilled out as he crosses his forties and has tasted success. Watch out, as he can get naughty in his forties.

As a father, he really cares for his children and likes to brag about them. He may not be the most understanding of fathers and demands their respect. He insists on good education.

Love and Marriage for Her
She is the wife who looks after home and work with a stern zeal. She needs a partner who provides her with status and security and cannot be content if you are not as ambitious as her. She is very loving towards her family but do not expect her to easily understand their different views. She needs to be told. She may not be very sensitive, but she is supremely sensible.

Her house is always spick and span. She loves showing off her virtues and takes care never to put the wrong foot forward, especially in public. She dresses perfectly too. Expect her to be conservative and traditional in her views. Praise her and tell her how good she is; a few good words can make her smile for a long time.

She has her pride too; never mistake her conventionality for meekness. If you continually illtreat her, she can either cut off ties and leave without looking back, or even find an alternative solution for herself while she plays the part of a perfect wife and mother. You ignore or mistreat her at your own risk.

She is a fabulous mother. Her children are her priority and she loves caring for them. Her love does not dilute her discipline, though. She knows how to get them to respect and listen to her. She insists on good behaviour and education. They learn to follow tradition too.

At the Workplace
You can never find fault in their work. They hate it if anyone does. They are their own worst critic. In fact, with their meticulousness and hard work, and the high standards they set themselves, you would be really brave to criticise them.

LeoVirCaps need money and glory, and are willing to work hard and smart for them. They are good in any field that requires analysis and intelligence. They have mastery over design, tools and machines. Their organising and delegating abilities let their talents shine. They easily understand numbers too. All three signs have creative talent, and Leo, especially, enjoys the spotlight. LeoVirCaps can be good actors and artists.

They really need to feel important. They can be quite rigid in their views and expect adulation as they grow in position. Praise them, but make sure you do it in front of a large crowd, and give them many assistants to boss over and feel important. These go a long way in making them contented. Also, do not forget the money. They are naturals as bosses, fabulous at ideating, dynamic executors, and always in control, anticipating and prepared for surprises.

Hard working, meticulous, organised, yet vibrant – LeoCirCaps strive to gain respect and power.

Famous LeoVirCap Personalities
Ramya Krishnan, Aleksandr Medved, Meena, Phil Jackson, John McCain, Kirka Babitzin.

155. LEO–VIRGO–AQUARIUS

Sun, the generous and proud giver, Virgo, the pure and disciplined, and Uranus, the unconventional thinker, all combine in the colourful combination of LeoVirgAqua. They have a flair about them. Their walk, style and talk are truly unique. You can expect strong, independent and intelligent views from them. There is also a strain of wildness in them, especially in their younger years. They do not listen to advice easily and like to do their own thing.

They sparkle with intelligence. The Leonine habit of knowing everything from carpentry to luxury cars, the Virgoan perfectionism and research orientedness with the touch of the Aquarian madcap genius can make their intelligence rise several octaves above the normal and make a heady mix of a personality. If you see them with a pleased smile and a distant look, that faraway look on their face is an indication that they are shaping their next project.

Aquarius lives in the future, many light years ahead of the rest of us. It lends vivid colours to their dreams while Leo makes them dream big. Virgo perfects the dream and systematically ensures that the dream coalesces into something concrete, and adds stable analytical intelligence to their armoury of wits.

They are strongly individualistic. They like to map out their own route rather than follow on the success of their illustrious forebears. The best way to let them flourish is to let them decide on their own path and not force them to follow your plans, however well laid out. They have a very scientific bent of mind. Though the Aquarius in them gets sudden jolts of Uranian brain waves, they scrutinise the facts, research the matter and then give shape to their grand dreams.

You can expect them to be idealistic too – especially about their work. They never take shortcuts and prefer working on big ideas with relentless pursuit. LeoVirAquas have pride; you won't find them lying or twisting facts to suit their convenience.

LeoVirgAquas are the most reliable of friends. Their optimism lights up even the gloomiest room. They are always ready to have fun. But, despite their bright and airy views, they are fastidious about a few things. They are not only very careful about their clothes but also love rules and regulations in matters of food and diet. Cleanliness, too, is a special area of concern for them. They hate messy places.

Love will never make them maudlin. LeoVirAquas know how to love with cheer and fizz. You can expect them to be wild in the beginning and try out many people, from sheer curiosity. Yet when they do love, it will not be a random bolt but after thoroughly analysing the whole affair. They take informed decisions in love and career and then commit. But if things don't work out well, they don't hesitate in making a clean break from the relationship. They will never suffer in silence or bind themselves to you for infinity.

They can be shockingly blunt. Do not expect the Virgo side of their personality to make them bow down to your views. They revel in thinking and acting differently and spare no words to express their disdain of the old ways. When angry, they may shout for a few minutes and then explain your errors to you. Aquarius makes it very easy for them to read the minds of people. They may not be sensitive or emotional, but do know exactly what makes you tick.

They need money for their style, but rarely spend it recklessly. You can expect them to do a complete analysis before investing any substantial amount on assets.

They have a colourful side to them. They are adventurous, fun loving and love being the centre of attraction. They are speed demons. They love doing stunts to shock and impress people. They are also very spiritual, sometimes even ritualistic. They understand the deepest mysteries of the world and are interested in learning about all kinds of alternative sciences and esoteric principles of life.

The downbeat traits of these three zodiac signs can afflict them too. The Leo style can transgress into rudeness and arrogance, the Aquarian originality can dissipate into a rebel without a cause, and the Virgo perfectionism can turn to nitpicking and strictness.

There is no Water sign in this combination and though Aquarius can read the emotions expressed even by your eyebrows, they prefer to remain detached; Virgo, too, is a loner and Leo can often be narcissistic. Some of them can be too experimentative, too far removed from reality, egoistic, arrogant, nitpicking, complaining, critical and too changeable.

They have a few flaws as do most humans but they are the best humanitarians you can find. They are large hearted and are moved when they see the sufferings of people who are less privileged. They do whatever is in their capacity for the general upliftment of society.

Leo–Virgo–Aquarius – Rakesh Roshan
Hrithik: 'When my dad comes out of the shower in a towel suddenly, it means he has a mind-blowing idea.'[280]

'I had worked for one and a half years on a script for *Krishh-3* and then dropped it as I was unsure of the content. I was extremely nervous and my hands were cold when I started shooting...I try to be a perfectionist. No one should say that my movie was not well made.'[281]

'I could have shot *Kaho Na Pyar Hai* on a mud island. But I did it in New Zealand and Phuket. I gave bigness to the film. I had to mortgage my house for that.'

Rakesh Roshan has the perfectionism, huge vision and unusualness of a LeoVirgAqua.

Love and Marriage for Him
You have a winner! This guy is a responsible and caring husband. He is dutiful, and ready with a plan for every emergency. You do not need to care about details when

---

[280] http://www.youtube.com/watch?v=oMDTdKk6y1s
[281] http://www.youtube.com/watch?v=rCfLvc9liyk

you are with him for he carries all the worries on his able shoulders. He knows when to spend and when to save, without being stingy.

It is your job to ensure that his food and clothes match up to his demands. Thankfully, due to the influence of Virgo and Aquarius, the ego and aggression of Leo is quite diluted in him, so he does not expect a doormat. He lets you do what you desire as long as you do it without stepping on his toes.

He needs space in the relationship. Let him be, at times. It helps him think and return with better ideas. He can be a little detached and aloof at times too. Clinging, emotional scenes make him run the other way. He may not understand your deepest fears until you tell him. At most times, he is full of energy. His wit and humour is unmatched and though he is prone to speak plainly, he does not make gaffes.

As a father, he is perfect. He encourages intellectual activities. You may not see much of him during nappy-changing times but he certainly likes to be around his children. He protects them and motivates them to achieve their desires.

Love and Marriage for Her
She is a stylish and extremely intelligent companion. She always speaks her mind and doesn't suffer mindless customs just to fit in. But on the other hand, she cares for you, takes all your worries on herself, nurses you like an angel, ensures your travel plans are perfectly in place and is a conscientious wife. Just expect her to be lost in her thoughts and aloof at times.

The best part about this girl is that she can fit into any role. However, it is foolish to try and expect this go-getter to be satisfied in the role of a housewife: it would be a sheer waste of her talent, ability and abundant energies. She can easily manage a home and career together. She can be a great companion to a businessman or a politician for she helps to think differently and is able to put her plans into action on a large scale.

As a mother, she encourages her children to reach for their dreams. She makes them independent. They learn how to take charge of their lives and remain positive during challenges.

At the Workplace
They are inventive and analytical, and need to do something big. All these abilities make them stand out in their careers. They will do anything so long as they get the applause they desire. These excellent workers do not work for money alone. They are delighted if they are in charge of innovative projects and don't mind some glory too. Only a job well done, exactly per plan, meeting their own high standards, satisfies them. They are their own critics and do not get deterred by others' opinions.

Hard working and extremely diligent, they are excellent planners and researchers. They can simplify complex things and are good with numbers. They innovate but implement realistically. They need to guard themselves against the habit of getting bored quickly and moving on to the next project too soon, or over-analysing and getting stuck in something for too long. As bosses, they are fussy, finicky perfectionists but are generous and permissive.

LeoVirAquas combine style, intelligence and substance with an eye for detail. They will be curious yet detached, inventive yet analytical and optimistic without being foolhardy.

Famous LeoVirAqua Personalities
Mohinder Amarnath, Rakesh Roshan, Heidi Montag, Divya Dutta, Siddharth Trivedi, H.G. Wells, Soundarya Rajinikanth, Paul Walker, Evan Rachel Wood, Sushil Kumar Shinde.

156. LEO–VIRGO–PISCES

Apollo, the Sun god, meets the perfection-seeking Virgo and the soulful Pisces in LeoVirPisces. It is the perfect combination of style, substance and sensitivity. LeoVirPisces carry themselves with assurance. They have a benevolent, regal air and know how to quietly command.

Pisces understands and knows things. It believes in the temporal nature of things yet lives in a world of fantasy and make-believe. Virgo is the exact opposite of Pisces. It believes that life is a constant struggle and works hard to prove it. This basic difference characterises the elemental conflict between Pisces and Virgo in LeoVirPisces. They fear that life is difficult yet also daydream about the beauty of life.

They have the pride of Leo without its extreme egotism. Both Virgo and Pisces prefer to stay in the background and rarely trumpet their good points. LeoVirPisces want to be looked up to and respected. They work hard and dream of great things, but when the day comes for them to accept their reward, you can expect them to be quite modest about it and include everyone in the applause.

Leo adds the spark to them. On their own, both Virgo and Pisces lack the drive and energy to start anything new. They would have been mere followers if it were not for Leo. Leo gives them the adrenalin rush to start something and the positivity to pull them through. They have the ambition but they need a push in the beginning.

LeoVirPisces are responsible people. They perform their duties not merely out obligation but from a desire to help everyone around them. The generosity of Leo is heightened by the non-materialistic urges of Pisces and they go out of their way to help people in trouble. They are very loving and kind. They understand the sadness behind your smile and do anything for the underprivileged. They instinctively protect and preserve rather than destroy anyone or anything. You cannot find more loyal or more concerned friends than them. They always try and help their friends, and are great fun to be with. They never criticise without hearing your point of view. Of course, they have their mood swings and like to be left alone at times. But the shadows soon lift and they are their happy selves again.

LeoVirPisces are very romantic. Leo loves romance and its love is garbed in melodramatic colours, while Pisces loves deeply and soulfully and Virgos love with gentle consideration. LeoVirPisces know how to romance and you can expect everything from midnight dinners to heart-touching poetry from them. They love with a deep commitment. When in love they do not bother about the norms of society.

They love food and can be great cooks. Of course, they do not like perspiring in the kitchen all the time: just for memorable events. They love spending money. Although they desperately try to keep tabs on their spending, they usually give in to their impulses. They sound quite contradictory in many aspects but that is due to the fact that Pisces and Virgo are completely opposite signs and both of them together lead to many conflicting traits.

They have the Virgo love for routine though they are never as routine-bound as they would like. Despite their desire to work, LeoVirPisces are quite lazy. They procrastinate and take quite long to do certain things. They love learning new things, and their grasp of a subject is exceptional; they like going into the details and know it to its core. They like expounding on what they learnt: expect long conversations!

These loving creatures can get angry too and sulk a lot. They are quite sensitive and get hurt very easily, especially when their pride is pricked. But they rarely hold grudges. They usually tell you how they feel or you can tell from their behaviour. Their self-respect matters a lot to them and are hurt and sulk if ignored, unloved or denied importance. They are extremely intuitive and almost read your emotions and feelings as their own.

All the three zodiac signs have deep-rooted insecurities in them. They may be hesitant, confused and diffident in the beginning. But the Pisces in them believes that all things happen for good and all things also end well. The Leo positivity, enthusiasm and ambition to sparkle rub off on them too. With the dedication, sincerity and discipline of Virgo, they are ready to fight and put life back on the winning track.

There are always chances of them becoming loud, self-proclaiming, know-it-alls. They can live in the Piscean world of make believe where everything is beautiful, perfect and big. They can be footloose, not knowing what exactly they are up to, revelling in every kind of escapism that gives a temporary high.

They are quite spiritual. Both Leo and Pisces have deep beliefs. They can be quite religious too. They like practising rituals. Even spirituality they pursue in style. Spirituality helps them find themselves.

Leo–Virgo–Pisces – Sir Richard Attenborough

Attenborough's love for his mother was matched by his enormous respect for his father. In fact, his desire for his father's approval was to drive a large part of his life.

'Throughout my life, I always remember that consideration of people who were less fortunate than we. We lived in an atmosphere of awareness and we certainly did not live a life whereby we ignored, or felt that we could ignore which was in evidence around us.'[282]

Sir Richard Attenborough's *Gandhi* won multiple Oscars and he famously wept while accepting them. Emotional, generous and a visionary, he was the quintessential LeoVirPisces.

Love and Marriage for Him

This man is too good to be ignored. He is loving, caring, kind and loves listening to you. He understands you completely and is able to gauge your moods by looking at you. There is also an added plus – he is extremely romantic. He is always well groomed. Crumpled shirts and unwashed collars can irritate him. He likes travelling but in luxury. He will impress your family and friends with his artistic abilities.

---

[282] http://www.scotsman.com/news/triumph_of_the_spirit_sir_richard_attenborough_interview_1_1437268

If you want more ambition in him, you just need to gently prod him a bit. Do not get aggressive with him, for though he does not mind listening to you, he does not want the whole world to know it.

You need to keep tabs on the company he keeps, without intruding. He can splurge unnecessarily on them or can pick up some unwanted habits too. Appeal to his vanity and generosity to get things done. A little bit of appreciation and lots of love can do wonders with him.

As a father, he is extremely good. He does not mind taking over nappy duty and is quite good in the sick room. Education means a lot to him and he loves talking about his children's achievements.

Love and Marriage for Her
She is a lovely wife who can carry herself with grace. She has gentle caring ways. This lady likes dressing well. She is also very intelligent. Her mind is sharp and picks up new ideas with ease. She performs her family duties well and with great sensitivity. Her home and family are of paramount importance to her and she does not like to let either one down. Her home is always clean and organised but she needs help in doing that and prefers supervising rather than doing all the chores herself.

You have to really love and care for her for she needs to feel a part of your life. Take her out to the fanciest restaurant, go for a walk with her on a moonlit night, and she is the most romantic person ever. She is also talented. This girl knows how to sing, dance, paint or write well. Help her pursue her dreams for she has a lot of them.

You can throw a lot of parties with her around for she loves playing the role of the perfect hostess and charms everyone with her smile and warmth. She is also good in advising others when they are in trouble.

As a mother, she is divine. She knows just what to do in every emergency and does it with grace and love. She is proud of them and encourages them to lead their lives with positivity.

At the Workplace
They excel in creative works and arts. They can be extraordinary artists, interior decorators, actors, dancers, singers or designers. They bring soulfulness and perfectionism to their work and brighten things up with their exuberance. If they are in sports, they have a flair about them and crush opponents with their accuracy and deception.

They need a little push and encouragement to start and want short periods of rest interspersed with work. They are very good with numbers and are able to calculate in their heads with ease. They look into even the smallest details. They rarely leave their work unfinished. They know their worth and can talk tough during negotiations; but once they decide to work for you, they are extremely loyal and dedicated.

They need lots of applause and recognition for their work. Provide it in plenty and they are the happiest. They also know how to delegate their work. They ideate beautifully in large strokes, then plan meticulously, and then give you full freedom in completing the task. They are generous and understanding bosses, but won't tolerate sloppy work.

Fire, Earth and Water meet in LeoVirPisces and they think big but stay humble, plan well but procrastinate and are generous to all whom they love.

Famous LeoVirPisces Personalities
Sudha Chandran, Richard Attenborough, Fabio Cannavaro, Jerry Bruckheimer.

157. LEO–LIBRA–SCORPIO

Leo, ruled by the optimistic and proud Sun, Libra, ruled by the beauty and grace of Venus, and Scorpio, dominated by the passionate and powerful Pluto, combine in this sign. This person displays exuberance, charm, vitality, energy and passion. Along with these positive traits, he also exhibits the rudeness and arrogance of Leo, the indecisiveness and laziness of Libra and the ruthless and vengeful nature of Scorpio. In short, a very strong personality!

The king of the jungle combining with the venomous arachnid is a potent mix. What you may see on the surface though, could just be the sweet charm of sugary Libra. Don't be fooled, as there is more depth to their intense personality.

It is very hard to resist their charm. They love talking and are the cynosure of all eyes wherever they go. Though the flashiness of Leo may be subdued by the natural elegance of Libra, they always manage to have their own style. They make a good first impression and can enamour anyone with their communication skills and intelligence. But somewhere along the third or fourth meeting, you may start wondering if you will get the chance to speak your mind. So either people shut up in their presence or become highly argumentative, while LeoLibScorps just go on spouting their wisdom.

The passion of Scorpio shines through whatever they do or think and that's what makes up for all the big talk and brazen 'look at me' attitude. It is that passion that makes people realise that this person is not just hot air.

LeoLibScorps desire success more than anything else. The Leo in them wants to dominate and control, and Scorpio too desires power; also, though Libra is soft, it is a cardinal sign and likes to lead. They are extremely ambitious and passionate, but they can also be the laziest and most indolent people ever. Let them be; when the time is right, they act, and live up to their talk and exuberance. These periods of sheer laziness are very necessary for them to get recharged.

Both Scorpio and Leo are fixed signs while Libra is a cardinal one. Therefore, they are quite obstinate. Once they make up their mind, it is very hard to get them to change it. Remember, these people love to talk, so if they don't, it means that something is wrong. Scorpio's vengefulness is a very big part of them. If you ever get on the wrong side of them, be fully armed and well prepared, for you must be ready for war.

Their desire to succeed is matched by their total fearlessness. They easily take on things that lesser mortals will not dare. They love to work for greater glory and honour. They also hate injustice and love to protect the weak. They can fight against any power, opposing discrimination and inequality. They are also extremely generous. They will part with anything they have if you appeal to them for a favour. However, they can tell if you are bluffing: nothing escapes their eye. They can read to the very souls of people.

Money doesn't rank very high with them; it is power and the desire to dominate that makes them chart their glory. No matter how much or how little they have, they behave like royalty. The pride of the Lion shines through in their walk and posture.

These people have their own personal caste systems. The Scorpio ability of sizing people up and knowing exactly what they think make them very good at evaluating others. Despite being talkative, they have an aura of aloofness around them and allow within their charmed circle only those privileged members who they deem fit to be their friends. They are immensely attracted by the deepest mysteries of life and spirituality. They have their own ideas on these and are not influenced in any way.

They would rather die than admit that they have niggling self-doubts. They keep wondering if they really have the guts and skills that can take them on the path to glory. It is this sense of inadequacy that makes them argue and impress their superiority on others whenever possible. But they also possess the Scorpion ability to overcome their insecurities and rise like a phoenix or an eagle above the base emotions of greed, hatred or jealousy. And yes – Lions don't roar unless it is absolutely necessary.

Leo–Libra–Scorpio – Sir Winston Churchill

Churchill is the only British Prime Minister to have received the Nobel Prize for Literature.[283]

Winston Churchill was an accomplished artist and took great pleasure in painting. He found a haven in art to overcome the spells of depression, or as he termed it, his 'Black Dog'. Despite his lifelong fame and upper-class origins, Churchill always struggled to keep his income at a level that would fund his extravagant lifestyle.

His speeches and writings motivated a generation burdened by war, his unfailing courage and determination in the face of danger earned him his reputation as a leader. He exemplified the pride of Leo, the communication skills of Libra and the willpower of Scorpio.

Love and Marriage for Him

When you decide to marry him, you must leave your ego behind, for he has enough for both! To put it mildly, he is one of the most difficult men to live with if you are used to getting your own way. The Leo in him makes him desire almost continuous adulation and the Scorpio vindictiveness jumps in whenever he does not receive recognition.

When he is in a jovial mood, he keeps you totally entertained. He can be the most caring husband and loving father when surrounded by people who love and admire him. Miserliness is not his trait. Even during courtship, he is as free with his money as with his words. The regal air of Leo makes him want to act in a kingly fashion and shower gifts on all whom he loves. Leo makes him highly romantic, too. The Scorpio sensitivity makes him aware exactly how you think, but if that does not gel with what he wants, he does not care about it. His ambition and need for power make him push himself very hard and sometimes you are ignored. If you love him, let him reach for the stars while you manage the ground realities.

When angry, he can be sulky and petulant. If you do not pay him special attention during this stage, there is danger of him turning vindictive. He can then be sarcastic and even verbally abusive. You'll have to be the one to say sorry first,

---

[283] http://en.wikipedia.org/wiki/Winston_Churchill

whereupon he then gets off his pedestal and apologises too. Do not expect to tame or change him.

His continuous self-centredness and need for attention can get quite irritating and only someone who truly loves him can stay and blossom at his side. If you like your man to have the final say and don't have any burning ambition, then he is your man; but if you are independent and like taking your own decisions, then this guy holds no joy for you.

As a father, he wants the best for his children. He wants them to shine, be the best in their field so that he can be proud of them. He clearly has control, is a strict disciplinarian, but works hard to leave behind a legacy for his children.

Love and Marriage for Her
She is an unshakeable force. Extremely romantic and passionate, she needs to be adored. Never criticise her; praise her lavishly. Highly talkative and extremely elegant, she is not a person who is easy to approach. If she has allowed you to become entangled with her dazzling personality, it only means that she has found something worthy in you.

She makes her own decisions, and they are final: nothing will change them. There is nobody who can talk and think as she does – tell her so: everytime. She is flamboyant and loves creating a stir wherever she goes.

She can be quite sarcastic. Her verbal barrage can shake the Eiffel Tower so do not think of ever doing anything wrong. She is also one of the most generous souls around and loves showering her friends and family with gifts. Highly independent and strong, she does not like asking for favours, but if she ever accepts one from you, she repays it a million times over.

She is a permissive mother. She is controlling too, but will launch a blistering attack on anyone who dares to criticise her children.

At the Workplace
These people are highly ambitious and crave fame and glory. They love displaying their dominance and aggression too, so, you can expect enormous ego clashes at work. They want to stay in leadership positions. Even as subordinates, their energy levels are such that their seniors either resent them or view them as protégés.

These people are fabulous promoters. Give them a small idea and they add their flash and fervour to make it sound amazing. It may have been your idea in the first place, but you need to give them credit for giving new life to that idea.

Their excellent communication skills make them fabulous as representatives of their companies. They can literally sell anything to anyone with their forceful presentation skills. They also love fancy titles, cabins and chauffeur-driven cars. They are controlling as bosses, but are great visionaries and can be extraordinarily generous, too, if you submit to their blinding luminescence.

Famous LeoLibScorp Personalities
Winston Churchill, Dayanidhi Maran, Jack Welch, Toni Collette, Richard Burton (actor), Sœur Emmanuelle, Jenny McCarthy.

158. LEO–SCORPIO–SAGITTARIUS

This combination makes you say WOW! A typical LeoScorpSag believes that nothing in this world is impossible. They just go about it with flamboyance, passion, intelligence and spirituality. They have deep intensity, regal bearing and high ambition to keep them going.

If you see a Lion charging at you, coming at an alarming speed as it also has the power of a horse, and it possesses a huge poisonous sting in its tail: run! You have angered a LeoScorpSag.

When you meet LeoScorpSags, their enthusiasm, exuberance and extreme positivity amazes you. Nothing seems to faze them and they see each problem as a challenge. These guys adore the limelight. The Leo in them loves applause and performs best under a spotlght. Sagittarius loves admiration, too, while Scorpio adds the passionate desire to succeed. Whatever they do, they it is with a sense of fun, adventure and intensity.

LeoScorpSags love to lead. Leo gives them natural grace and regal demeanour, while Scorpio will not stay subservient for long. They never take anything lying down and are always ready to stand up and fight for whatever cause comes their way. Their code of ethics may be different from that of ordinary folks like you and me, but they stick to it relentlessly. There is one commendable thing about them – they are always absolutely sure about what they want in life. They know their minds and are not bothered about your opinion.

Ruthless honesty is their trademark. It is beneath their dignity to tell lies. You can expect some temperamental behaviour from these otherwise cheerful companions. When the doldrums hit them, they become malicious and brooding too, with a terrible temper that lasts for hours. Don't forget that they are one-third Scorpio; revenge compulsion is very much a part of their DNA.

If all this makes you wary of them, relax. Despite the Leo boastfulness and the Scorpio ego, their Sagittarius side makes them very down-to-earth. There is also a deep spiritual streak in them. Scorpio's instinctive knowledge of the esoteric and deeper principles of life makes them desire to know more from a deeper perspective.

They think of themselves as very humorous but their jokes often fall flat. Sagittarius makes them very fun loving; however, they fail to see the joke when it is on them. Sagittarius makes them extremely tactless; they can easily drop verbal bombs without thinking of the possible destruction.

Ambition is a big part of whatever they do. They think and dream on a large scale. They work extremely hard to get what they want. Be ready to applaud them for they want standing ovations and thank-you speeches. There is no defence in the style of a LeoScorpSag: it is attack from the word go! Their ambition and intense desire to achieve something can make them ruthless at times. They need to feel proud of themselves and their successes, only then will the fire in them mellow down to a glowing light.

Don't expect them to be humble or modest. They are flamboyant and stylish and love telling you how good they are. It's not all gas; Sagittarius makes them extremely intelligent and knowledgeable. Scorpio knows the deepest secrets of the universe. LeoScorpSags have immense ego, but true love and admiration can humble them. They bow only before adulation and love, give them that and they will never let you down. The more successful and loved they are, the humbler they become.

They can also be a little clumsy in love; their Sagittarian side is not known to express love in sublime tones. You can expect them to declare their love from the tallest rooftops. You will be loved with passion and style – who could ask for more?

They are extremely generous and might find money matters a little difficult to manage. Their Leonine tendency to spend lavishly and the Sagittarian happy-go-lucky attitude makes saving an issue. Of course, their Scorpio side will make them cautious at times, but usually you will find their hands itching to spend.

All Fire signs hide an element of fear deep within them that makes them glow even brighter to hide this fear from view. LeoScorpSags have two Fire signs (Leo and Sagittarius), so be sure that the fear exists in them though they make themselves stronger to bear it. It is essential that their friends and loved ones realise it and not say things to hurt or undermine their confidence for they neither forgive nor forget insensitive remarks. If they overcome their innermost insecurities, and truly become as fearless and secure in themselves as they portray, the battle is won. They will soar like eagles rising above all base emotions after they win their toughest battle – the one with the self!

Leo–Scorpio–Sagittarius – Psy

'In South Korea...'Gangnam' implies handsome [or sexy]. I know I'm not...You don't call this success. You call this a phenomenon. I didn't do anything. People did it.'[284]

'I dress classy and dance cheesy.'[285]

'I partied hard to celebrate ten million views. I'm the guy...! Katy Perry, Britney Spears, Tom Cruise tweeted my video...I have got lots of offers from France, Germany, Italy, China, every country. I have travelled in four–five months to 20 countries and 50 cities.'[286]

Psy has the inexhaustible energy of the Scorpio, the theatrics and the ability to laugh at self of a Sagittarian and the unabashedly self-promoting but still sunny and dignified self of a Leo.

Love and Marriage for Him

The place lights up when he walks in. You have a guy who dreams of making it big. You are his love, but his eyes are fixed on the final prize, and for that, you have to give him all the space in the world. He needs your support to stand tall and really appreciates it if you let him handle the big game while you handle the home

---

[284] https://www.youtube.com/watch?v=LPMG-Qvl-7E
[285] https://www.youtube.com/watch?v=Vcjns6Di6ZE&src_vid=1GlnlyfZdA4&feature=iv&annotation_id=annotation_857444
[286] https://www.youtube.com/watch?v=wJKjsb_A8M4

and its multifarious affairs. He can be quite lazy at home, but the fact is, he works himself raw and needs to sleep and recuperate.

He needs a lot of love, pampering and care to really shine; it would be unfortunate if his mate too were a very aggressive personality. This is a very volatile guy and needs to be handled with care. You have to look up to him and never sharpen your sarcastic wit on him. Ridicule dampens his spirits. You need to be there for him when the whole world is against him. Do that and he will work wonders.

He is extra generous with money. You need to ensure he is careful with finances. Adventure attracts him and he is always ready to try out new holiday destinations and cuisines. This guy is capable of great things but he needs a person to plan and conceptualise his steps. It would be great teamwork if you add your strength to his dreams.

As a father, he is extremely proud of his children. He is their guide and mentor, and is at his most playful with them. But he wants to be treated with respect.

Love and Marriage for Her
This lady is every feminist's dream! She is sassy, independent, flamboyant, ambitious, proud, temperamental and extremely stylish. This girl never shies away from voicing her opinions, so it is prudent to set up home for just the two of you, lest you are caught in the eternal struggle between your mum and her.

She has big dreams and either achieves them or dies trying. Lack of emotional support from you can turn her temperamental levels to high and be detrimental to your health. Her anger can get the better of her at times. You need to have great negotiating skills to squeeze yourself out of such situations.

She is definitely fun to be with. So, take her out, make her go bungee jumping or surfing, this girl is game for anything. Just never expect her to slog it at home. The best thing about her is that she is totally true and loyal to those who have helped her in her time of need.

As a mother, she wants to be respected and wants her children to listen to her. She is also extremely playful, and though she is strict, they turn to her for advice and guidance.

At the Workplace
LeoScorpSags are always geared to achieve impossible dreams. The Leo in them wants to hear people gasp in wonder while Scorpio is totally committed to its dreams. Due to these two elements, the ambitious but unfocused Sagittarius in them becomes more focused and channelises its energies well. Despite their utter disregard for office politics, they instantly understand when they are being driven in the wrong direction.

Sagittarius makes them excel in sports. They are extremely intelligent and excel in any career that needs strong nerves and can work with the spotlight on constantly. They thrive in challenging situations and face tough situations head on. They need appreciation. Praise makes them feel invincible. You can expect loyalty from them. These guys do not run away when the going gets tough. As bosses, they are totally in command, nothing escapes their eyes, and they are brutally honest but fantastic mentors, and are very generous too. A little bit of flattery and bowing to their bright sunshine will do a lot of good to you.

Double Fire and Water makes LeoScorpSags regal yet realistic, demanding yet loving, and most of all, warrior leaders in the face of adversity.

Famous LeoScorpSag Personalities
Krishnamachari Srikkanth, Princess Srirasm of Thailand, Gopinath Munde, Ajit Agarkar, Psy, N. Srinivasan.

159. LEO–SAGITTARIUS–CAPRICORN

Apollo, the Sun god, shines brilliantly with the benevolent and knowledgeable Jupiter and the wise old man Saturn in LeoSagCaps. The first thing you notice about them is their sheer optimism. They glow with confidence and vitality. They make you feel excited and hopeful every time you meet them. The melancholic world-view of Capricorn is brightened by the double blaze of Leo and Sagittarius.

Look at the animals that make up the combo: a Lion, a half-horse, half-human Centaur and a mountain Goat. While there is no doubt about their immense physical strength, the intelligent Centaur provides mental power too. This is an extraordinarily strong combination – blessed with the great physical strength of Sagittarius, combined with the strong emotional control of Capricorn and tough physicality of both the Fire signs.

They love talking and have an infectious laugh. They advise people and have such reasonable logic that you really like listening to them. They love looking good and revel in getting noticed by everybody. Their style is never understated. They always go for a flamboyantly eye-catching look.

Ambition is blazing in them. All the three signs are ambitious. Leo wants a big stage, Sagittarius is unabashedly go-getting and Capricorn is willing to wait and work for its crown. The ambition of the double Fire gets an Earthy touch with Capricorn, grounded and focused in life. They definitely work towards their dream with a driving force that seems unreal at times due to its high optimism in the face of staggering difficulties.

They are extremely honest and blunt. Their honesty makes you like them all the more, for you can be sure that they rarely hide their true views. Sometimes, it gets them into trouble. They may just say something obnoxious unthinkingly.

LeoSagCaps are extraordinarily intelligent. They easily understand complex theorems and are very logical too. Common sense rubs shoulders with innate intelligence in them and they know what they are talking about. They are also creative and artistically talented and want to show their talents to the whole world. Sports and outdoor activites would be their favourite areas as well. The need for adventure is quite strong in them and they have an insatiable appetite for life and its wonders.

Family is very important to them. The Sagittarian averseness to family ties is diluted here. Though they like their moments of freedom, they also want to be surrounded by their loved ones. They always find time for their families despite their ambitions and like to be present at family functions.

Despite their love for family, they have a rebellious streak in them. They want to try things their way, and love adventure. Their desire for rebellion gets stronger as they age due to the Capricornian reverse-aging syndrome. They are more footloose and fancy-free after they achieve a modicum of success.

Love is important to them and they want a mate who does them proud – but without overshadowing them. They want a person who has some gumption, though they have enough for a dozen! They seek quality in people and want someone outstanding with whom they'll spend their life. They love experimentation too: they have numerous affairs before settling down with one person.

Food is also a favourite. They enjoy eating and are a chef's delight. They love cooking too. A meeting with them is never complete without eating. Generosity defines them, and they only want respect in return. They can also be actively involved with helping people, and even animals. They are quite philanthropic.

Money is something that they want sackfuls of, but find a little hard to hold on to. Capricorn is the only saver in this combination while both Leo and Sagittarius do not think twice before spending on outfits and luxurious necessities. They want to own the most expensive cars and all sorts of status symbols. But more importantly, they want to leave an enduring legacy. It can be in any form — an immortal name, everlasting fame or unending wealth.

Their anger can be quite wild. They shout, roar and blaze, but once they are through with you, they are fine as long as you apologise. Leos have an inner insecurity that they hide with their confidence while Capricorns are naturally suspicious of good luck. LeoSagCaps fear failure but hide it under a bright smile and positive attitude. Remember never to demotivate them for they need support and encouragement to feel good.

They are quite spiritual and believe in a higher force. All three signs believe in something bigger than them that helps them achieve their dreams. They understand the mysterious workings of fate and are faithful to their beliefs. They believe in all things that are traditional and have a history.

They need to dazzle and shine bright. They may put up a Capricorn façade and pretend they are uninterested. But they seek acceptance from the society, they love the glare, the glamour and the glitz. They need to shine. That is their deepest desire. They are blessed with deep intelligence, immense self-control and fabulous talents to explore their fair share of glory under the sun.

Leo–Sagittarius–Capricorn – Nafisa Ali
Nafisa Ali was a national swimming champion, Miss India, a jockey, and actress, and is now a social activist. She dared to let her hair grey and now the look of graceful aging is almost synonymous with her.

'I realised very early in my life that material benefits were not as important as health and family values...If I'm a beautiful woman, I am beautiful in many ways.'[287]

'It's not just a pretty face that has kept me here. It is my commitment to people, my work, my dedication and determination that is known here.'[288]

She has the sunny outlook, the desire to lead and the diligence of a LeoSagCap.

Love and Marriage for Him
He is an exciting guy. Views, opinions and laughter flow from him. Tell him that you love him, adore his ways and praise his work and he is completely yours. He

---
[287] http://www.verveonline.com/26/people/nafisa/full.shtml
[288] http://www.rediff.com/election/2004/may/10einter1.htm

likes a partner who adds to his glory while remaining in the background. Do not steal his thunder.

He cares for his family and wants you to share the same concern. You have to be a part of his family and not pull him away from it. It is wonderful if you are the calmer one for he needs someone who is soft-spoken and understanding of his fiery ways. You definitely have to be the one handling household duties for his attention is always on his ambitions.

His anger can explode at regular intervals. You have to deal with it! The good thing, though, is that he never keeps anything in his heart and is fine after his roar. You have to tell him how you feel in order for him to understand you, not sulk or cry.

As a father, he is super fun. He has a blast with his children. They respect his views. He pampers them with love and gifts.

Love and Marriage for Her
She is an explosion of energy, creativity and vitality. She needs a calm yet strong partner. You can be sure that when she says 'Yes', she means it. She rarely says or does something that is not true to her nature. You have to love and adore her, and tell her that you do so, often.

She loves family, and adopts your family too, but it is advisable if you stay with her separate from the rest of the family, for her strong views can cause a lot of friction. She does not mind housework but it is not one of her most important things. This lady is meant to shine and sparkle. She is more an outdoor person than indoor. She wants to achieve something in life and it is a shame if you try and stop her. Encourage her ambition and motivate her to achieve her dreams.

She loves dressing up. Her infectious laughter and honest views make more friends than enemies. She is definitely very different from all the other women you know.

As a mother, she is fun. She insists on values. She becomes one of them while playing with them and her excitement at childish games is a thrill to watch. She really enjoys motherhood and pampers her children without spoiling them.

At the Workplace
LeoSagCaps need the big stage – the bigger the better! Their ambitions are rarely small and they are able to achieve them too. Routine work does not excite them. They think big things and plan them out well. They are great as delegators and have amazing organising abilities.

They prefer creative careers and are good at promoting themselves. They do not mind staring crowds; rather, they revel in a chance to show off their talents to people. They have varied interests and should take some time to decide what they want to do or they may change tracks midway. But whatever they do, they always shine.

Praise them, show them places where they can win their laurels and encourage them to work towards their dreams. They have the Capricornian knack of being in the right place at the right time. They are absolutely at home as bosses, with fantastic ideating abilities, perfect as task masters, and are every inch a stylish, knowledgeable boss.

Double Fire and yet earthy, LeoSagCaps are adventurous yet grounded, fame-loving yet family-loving, and honestly exuberant souls.

Famous LeoSagCap Personalities
Nafisa Ali, Christine Lagarde, Amy Jackson, Gianluigi Buffon, Aristotle Onassis, Dolly Parton, Melanie C, Kamran Akmal, Christian Marclay.

160. LEO–CAPRICORN–AQUARIUS

This is a mixture of the royal Sun, the wise Saturn and the wild Uranus. When you meet LeoCapAquas, you are mesmerised by their style and aura. They look and speak stylishly and ooze confidence. They sound well educated and cultured, no matter where they come from.

A Lion with the steadiness of a Goat and the genius touch of the Water Bearer! These people are walking, talking dynamite. The Leo in them is ambitious, wants to succeed and bask in glory. Capricorn is shrewd, practical, has well-laid plans and is ready to work hard to achieve its ambition. Aquarius adds magic to the whole thing; whatever they do, they do with their signature uniqueness.

They are dreamers, but their dreams are founded in reality. They are flamboyant and stylish, but they also strive to be the best. Hard work accompanies everything they do. Original, wacky, inventive, are adjectives you use for them: but also practical, determined, meticulous and organised. They know how to do it, and do it in style and dash in to receive the coveted prize. They work smart and hard to achieve their aims and stay focused on their achievements without losing their zest for life.

They love adulation and applause. They expound on their views and give you long-winded discourses on how to run your life. They are also very fun loving and love entertaining people.

LeoCapAquas are extremely gregarious and have hundreds of friends. They know how to get their work done through their network of friends and acquaintances. Of course, they help their friends a lot. In fact, they go out of their way to help, but expect the same in return.

LeoCapAquas maintain their high standards in love too. They want the very best mate, one who complements their looks and style. Leos are highly romantic and know how to show their love in style – you can expect candlelight dinners and delightful surprises from a LeoCapAqua guy, while the girl will expect you to do the same. The Capricorn in them always wants parental approval and if they fall in love then they make sure that their parents agree with their choice.

They love being leaned upon and always act as the elder brother or sister of the family. They are responsible towards family duties from a young age. They want to improve the family status and are proud of their family lineage too.

Both Leo and Aquarius are fixed signs and can be very stubborn in their views. But Capricorn, being a cardinal sign, adds more thought to their ideas. Their egos are rooted in working towards more creative and fruitful goals, rather than in ensuring that their opinions are adhered to. The influence of Capricorn and Aquarius also reduces the arrogance of Leo while retaining its style. Aquarius's humanitarian instincts add a more sensitive side to the other two.

The generosity of Leo is toned down due to the stinginess of Capricorn. They like to spend the least amount of money in getting their work done, except when the spending adds to their magnificence. The Leo in them loves adulation and can spend money on huge parties and events just to get people talking about them.

You can never fool them as the Aquarius in them is extremely perceptive and can look deep into you to know exactly what you are thinking. They seem to be lost in their own world at times but do not assume that they are not there. They find out everything.

They can have downbeat qualities in them too. They can be dreamers with plans that are too futuristic. They may keep changing their plans as something more interesting and exciting catches their eye. They may have the secret fear of failure, which they may not admit. They also go through deep depressions when things don't go their way.

They have a very spiritual side as well, despite their addiction to a lavish lifestyle. All Fire signs are spiritual, and Capricorns too, while Aquarius has a sense of deep understanding of the esoteric. Spirituality in them coexists with their love for a good life.

Leo–Capricorn–Aquarius – AB de Villiers

'I want to be the best. That's why I play cricket. That's my goal.'[289]

'The dreamers of the day are dangerous, for they dream their dreams with open eyes, and make them come true.'[290]

De Villiers wants to be remembered not for the hundreds of runs scored, but rather for specific knocks that win big matches.

'My faith means more to me than playing for my country. It comes first.'[291]

De Villiers and his good friend Ampie du Preez released their first full-length album, *Maak Jou Drome Waar* (Make Your Dreams True).

AB de Villiers has the diligence, belief and ambition of a LeoCapAqua, while having his feet firmly on the ground.

Love and Marriage for Him

He is a friend first. You can expect to have a good time with him. He loves to throw parties. Be ready to rush off in your best clothes at a moment's notice. He likes to take you to the best places in town and show you off. The Capricorn in him may make him a little serious in his early years but he matures like wine and becomes more fun loving and bubbly as he gets older. But ensure that you keep the fires burning and keep him interested.

He loves it if you have a career and are independent, but you have to take care of the Leo ego and not outshine him in any way. He needs to feel that he is the head of the family. He is loving and caring but his attention to household duties and responsibilities varies. He prefers you to take care of them.

Money is not an issue with him. He spends carefully. Investments, too, are safe with him and though he is generous with friends, he also knows how to get the generosity back from them! He likes staying in touch with all his relatives

---

[289] http://www.espncricinfo.com/ipl2009/content/story/403566.html
[290] http://www.espncricinfo.com/magazine/content/story/490550.html
[291] https://www.facebook.com/ABdeVilliers17/info

and likes to play the father figure or genial family head at family gatherings. If relatives and traditions are not your thing, this trait may get hard for you to bear.

Despite his high standards in love, you can expect him to have a few flings. Capricorns are naturally responsible and act mature from a young age but they are susceptible to reverse aging. As they achieve their dreams and fulfil their ambitions, they gain a roving eye. Add the Leo romanticism and the Aquarian love for experimentation, and you have a person who can easily be in and out of relationships.

As a father, he is exceptional. He is loving, friendly, proud and strict. He knows instinctively when to be their friend and when to lead.

Love and Marriage for Her
If this girl has chosen you, you must possess intelligence, money and style, for she never falls for average guys. Substance is very important to her. She needs a partner she can talk to and admire, and who needs something more than just a beautiful trophy wife. She loves attention and you should praise her occasionally. Her basic desire is to be respected.

Family and work are the two essentials for her. This lady can balance them beautifully, so it is a shame if her abundant skills are not utilised fully. If you have a family business, absorb her into it.

She loves dressing up and, despite the showy extravagance of Leo and the wild unconventionality of Aquarius, she knows exactly how to dress for the occasion. She has an innate sense of style and looks regal even if she was born in a cottage.

The Capricorn in her ensures that she does not blow her top in front of people who matter; nevertheless, she can have a temper. Her ego is not submissive either. The Leo laziness does not afflict her to a great degree for she has the Capricorn desire to strive.

As a mother, she is ideal. Even if she works, she knows exactly how to delegate her child's upbringing. She is a fun mother despite being the one who sets the rules.

At the Workplace
Expect them to come out with a brilliant, out-of-the-world idea, and embellish it with their uniqueness, style and drama. When they market it with the grandeur and shrewdness all their own, you are assured of the success of the product.

They are tailor-made for great careers with their fabulous networking skills, hard work, drive, ambition, and, most of all, intelligence. LeoCapAquas are very hard to put down because of their extraordinary social skills, people skills and showmanship. You must never try politics on them for Capricorn makes them master manipulators who know how to get back at you.

You cannot find much to complain of in their work for they strive hard and do not give way to distractions. They also come up with innovative yet practical ideas to solve problems.

If you have a LeoCapAqua as a boss, then please walk up to him and ask for advice. You have to show them respect and flatter them a little to keep them in good spirits. There is no denying the fact that you have to work hard too.

Hard working yet fun loving, creative yet practical, blunt yet diplomatic, and egoistic yet loving – that's what LeoCapAquas are all about.

Famous LeoCapAqua Personalities

AB De Villiers, John Grisham, Michael Slater, Prince Al-Waleed bin Talal, Manmohan Desai, Khushwant Singh, Morarji Desai, Evangeline Adams.

161. LEO–AQUARIUS–PISCES

The generous Sun, the wacky and inventive Uranus and the deep and mysterious Neptune combine in this maverick and charming combination. LeoAquaPisces have charm in abundance. The playful and regal Sun makes them shine their benevolence around while the non-confrontational Pisces just wants love and happiness.

The main thing about this sign is that it is uninterested in monetary pursuits. Of course, they have ambition (you cannot be a Leo without thinking big), but it is ambition to be appreciated for creating something different, innovative, wacky, inventive or original. They just do not bow to conventions and traditions. These people bring about change in thinking, because they simply cannot think the same old thoughts. The Pisces in them has superb imagination and creative ideas that mingle well with the inventive genius of Aquarius to create a cauldron of change.

LeoAquaPisces are extremely broad-minded. They are the true free spirits of the world and not shocked by anybody or anything. LeoAquaPisces are extremely intuitive. They are very good at reading people and can reflect the emotions of their surroundings, a Pisces trait. Aquarius makes them curious about people and they like to learn of the fears and insecurities of everyone they meet. This love for people makes them more approachable than Leo who thinks mainly of himself.

Leo's magnificent romantic views and the Piscean need for a soul mate makes them extremely romantic people. LeoAquaPisces live and breathe romance when they are with their beloved. Thankfully, the detached lover of humanity, Aquarius, stops them from going totally bonkers in love. It makes them want some space in their relationship and they will not be too demanding or clinging.

The double fixed sign makes them extremely obstinate in their views. Once their mind is made up, it is very difficult to change it. They have some bizarre and out-of-the-ordinary belief systems and opinions. You had better respect them or leave them alone.

They are extremely talented and creative. They bring uniqueness to whatever they do. Their talents can be in anything from drama, theatre, arts, singing, dancing and even impersonating others. They learn things very quickly and add to them with their amazing imagination and originality. Then they package it with their style to make it dazzle.

They positively glow when applauded but won't aggressively seek glory. They can be flamboyant and exuberant but are not arrogant, unlike true-blue Leos. They hold money in scant regard and cannot be motivated by it. They demand only creative satisfaction and applause.

Their habits can be quite slovenly at times, with the Piscean disregard for fashion and the Aquarian untamed ways. The Leo in them likes being waited upon, and none of the signs are very good at cleaning up after themselves. Clean, neat and orderly rooms are not their priority though the Leo in them takes care to look good when they walk out in company.

Again, all three signs are disinclined to routine or discipline. LeoAquaPisces are wild and untamed creatures who cannot abide by rules, unless trained while still young. Addiction, too, can be a problem as Pisces is prone to addictions, Aquarius likes experimenting and Leo is fearless in treading where many fear to go. One wrong step can ruin their lives.

LeoAquaPisces have a low sense of duty, as there is no stabilising effect of an Earth sign. They need a steadying influence in life to sober them up and make them work towards achieving the success they dreamed of. Some of them can become self-indulgent and attention-hungry, and try to awe people with extreme showmanship, pretence to genius, flashy dress, stunts and extravaganzas.

Leo and Pisces are both slow starters – Pisces is extremely insecure and fearful and Leo, too, has its share of fears. But with that confident demenour and sometimes even arrogant stance, you wouldn't notice that they are insecure deep inside. This makes LeoAquaPisces progress slowly to their goal. They need a lot of support and love from their loved ones. Indifference or ridicule can seriously harm these soft and inventive souls.

But once they conquer their inner fears, they will not be bothered by people who criticise them. They will be very confident in their own talents and expertise and take pride in their achievements.

There is a deep spiritual side to them. Both Aquarius and Pisces are interested in spirituality, the paranormal, and the study and practice of alternative sciences. They are also very protective of the marginalised and the weak. They are true humanitarians: kind and noble souls.

Leo–Aquarius–Pisces – Abhay Deol
Abhay has resisted market pressures and done what he wanted to do, unlike actors who do what they think they ought to do.[292]

'Seeing stardom since childhood made it less attractive to me. The interviews, the gossip, the rumors...nothing shocks me.'[293]

'And then the whole dance thing; I'm always uncomfortable going up on stage and public speaking is not my strongest point.'[294]

His movies are always different, the heroes closer to real life than the ones we are used to watching on the big screen and he makes their flaws understandable. Abhay walks to his own tune and sets his own pace like a LeoAquaPisces.

Love and Marriage for Him
This is a tricky guy to handle and it all depends on when you meet him. As mentioned before, he is a slow starter. If he is still in search of his path and is lost in his dreams of success, it is best to give him time to prove himself or you may end up looking after him his whole life. He is a nice guy but you have to look at him sensibly before deciding to choose him.

You need to be the strong person in the marriage. This guy requires a strong, independent woman who lets him be himself and loves him despite his inconsistencies. You need to say things gently to him as he has an ego and a thin

---
[292] http://thechasingiamb.blogspot.com/2009/01/interview-with-abhay-deol.html
[293] http://www.desipowerchat.com/bollywoodnews/v88-abhay-deol-in-heart-talk.htm
[294] http://filmiholic.com/2011/09/05/abhay-deol-interview/

skin. He can never be involved in the day-to-day running of the house. But he can write beautiful love notes to you. If you want poetic love, he is the guy for you.

He loves to travel and see new places and people. There is fun and excitement when he is around. He never sticks to one idea or path. The Aquarius and Pisces in him make him incomprehensible at times. He seems irresponsible and beyond worldly cares. Money is for you to handle since saving and investing are terms he can never understand. Besides, his generosity can become a problem if you are not careful. He can be very stubborn about certain things and you need to know what they are. A little bit of praise and pampering will get a lot of things done for you.

As a father, he is permissive and fun. He knows what his children want to do and never tries to control or lead them the other way. This guy realises the importance of living your dreams.

Love and Marriage for Her
She is a very loving wife. She understands your moods and is able to read your mind. She is sensitive, caring, generous and loving, but she is her own person. Controlling her is beyond you for she knows exactly how to live her life her way without getting into confrontations. She knows how to dress like a lady. The Leonine aura gives her a regal air.

There are so many shades to her that you can never truly comprehend her. She is fun loving, adventurous, motherly, romantic, rebellious and traditional. She can be all these and more. She can be sixty and still be a young girl at heart.

She is attracted by the unconventional. Her choices in life stem from her heart and monetary considerations do not weigh her down. She may just hand over all her money to a needy friend. You need to be the stabilising factor in her life. Please note – stabilising and not controlling – for no one can control her.

Housework is not for her. You may find the house in a mess when she is sad. You need to be her support and help her live her dreams. There is great artistic talent within her, just waiting to be tapped.

As a mother, she is wonderful. Her children always run to her for aid and encouragement and she gives both unstintingly. Her generous spirit is never able to deny them anything. But she knows where to draw the line.

At the Workplace
LeoAquaPisces are made for the creative and inventive world. The corporate world holds no dreams for them unless the Pisces in them has been rigorously trained in discipline and routine. But why waste such immense talent in the corporate sector?

The Leo in them just wants to shine. Praise and the feeling that they are making a worthwhile contribution to the world are what keep them going. They need money too as they spend a fortune on their friends and other worthy interests. They are slow starters who need a lot of understanding and support from their families to achieve success.

Their intense enthusiasm and drive motivate them and they strive to achieve success in untested fields. They can innovate trends, infuse style and bring in the sizzle, electricity and vivacity to any stream they decide to devote their lives. They are pioneering bosses who can change the work place for better. They are generous too, especially if you make them look good.

Fire, Air and Water combine to give LeoAquaPisces drive, enthusiasm and creativity. They are extraordinary creative forces and need to be utilised well.

Famous LeoAquaPisces Personalities
Abhay Deol, Akira Kurosawa, Douglas Adams, Farida Jalal, Jayshree Gadkar, Ram Manohar Lohia.

162. VIRGO–LIBRA–SCORPIO

The deeply analytical Virgo meets Venus, the planet of beauty and grace, and Pluto, the ruthless lord of the underworld, to create VirLibScorps. This is a very powerful combination, which brings together the Virgo perfection, Libra balance and Scorpio passion.

VirLibScorps are most attentive to detail. Virgo is known for going into the details of everything while Scorpio makes them masters at deciphering mysteries and people. They also have the clarity of thought of Virgo. They can easily deduce the reason for every obscure happening, true to Libra; and the deep intensity of Scorpio gives them the courage to overcome any crisis. Add the Libran smart talk and you have an unbeatable debater.

You can expect oodles of passion and tons of hard work from these guys. Whatever they do, they do with total intensity and passion. You can't fault them in anything, be it planning, analysis or execution – they are perfect in all three. Virgo is the perfect planner with plans, back-up plans and back-up plans for back-up plans to meet any eventuality while Libra adds its analysis and charm to the execution, which is done with Scorpio passion.

It might take some time to get them talking. But once you get them started you need say nothing while they expound, propound and discuss their views. They can communicate their thoughts and ideas with the brilliance of a Libran and their words convey their passion and intelligence. The Virgo's capacity for research and Scorpio's knowledge of the unknown can help them decode and gain vivid understanding of things, from the mundane to the deepest mysteries of the world.

It's a joy to see them take on any task for they will do it so beautifully and display both perfection and power in equal measure. They are down to earth and practical. They have the Scorpio ability to be calm and composed even in times of pressure.

They like to be fair and philosophical, but the Scorpio in them can sting when wronged. They never forgive a wrong and find ways to get their own back. The fair Libra in them, however, allows them to forgive you if you are genuinely sorry. But they will never forget an insult, especially a deliberate one. They will come back for revenge or will hit you where it hurts most. Their favourite way of revenge would be to work hard, become more powerful than you and then keep you wondering if they will exercise that power against you.

They are very good at reading people and have the ability to see through acts and attitudes, so do not think that you can fool them. Scorpio's knack of knowing the deepest secrets of the soul and Virgo's clarity of thought make them very good at deciphering people.

When in love they are totally passionate and committed. The Libran in them feels life is complete only with love and whenever they fall in love it will be with the romance of a Libran, the passion of a Scorpio and the commitment of a Virgo. Cheap stunts and vulgarity put them off, so be sure to be well spoken and well dressed when you date such a guy or girl.

They just love criticising! Steer clear of them when they are moody for they can shred your ego to bits with their biting disparagement. You cannot argue and say they are wrong simply because they are never wrong. But you need not criticise back: they are great self-critics and constantly keep evaluating themselves critically, and openly so.

Whatever they do for a living, they have a passion for which they would be ready to die. Scorpio makes them extremely intense and focused in their aims, but extreme passion and Libra's tendency to analyse every decision can make them extremely stressed out too. Add to it the Virgo compulsion for perfection and you have someone who at times can tie themselves in knots thinking about solutions and deciding on actions.

They have the Virgo desire to eat right and live right. They are finicky about what they eat and are driven by routines and schedules. They always rise early and go to bed early. Health, fitness and diet are of special importance to them.

Money is important too, but there are times when they give in to their Libran urges and spend without looking at their bank balance. Usually they are conservative spenders and savers of money.

Usually they just don't know how to take life easy, and for them life truly isn't easy because they are forever analysing, deciding and working towards their dream of perfection. They need to learn that life isn't all about being great at what you do but also enjoying what you do – so tell them to take a deep breath, meditate, go for walks, talk to friends, and do nothing at times.

Virgo–Libra–Scorpio – Adam Gilchrist
'Losing the Ashes was intense and emotional. My personal lack of results and contribution through that series played havoc in my mind...It started to allow a little demon in my mind: 'Are you up for it still?' All these little mind games and doubts crept in...I felt like I wasn't doing anything well – I wasn't being a good cricketer, I certainly wasn't being a great husband and I wasn't being the best dad.'[295]

The intense self-criticism of Virgo is apparent in Adam's words. Probably he is the only Australian cricketer who *walks*: a Libran trait. The way he ruthlessly destroyed bowlers was typically Scorpio – a true VirLibScorp indeed!

Love and Marriage for Him
This guy is incredibly good though you must handle him delicately. The excessive tension and stress in him make it imperative that you are the more stable and the calmer of the two. Of course, when a crisis actually looms he will be the most unflappable person around. You also know that he has a passion – don't dishearten him by criticising him or his passion.

Along with a calm personality, you also need to have a very thick skin and a well-developed sense of humour for there can be days when he criticises everything (including you) around him.

The Virgo purity and the Scorpio intensity make him a very committed partner and he prefers to spend time at home rather than party the night away.

As a father, he is always there for his children. He is responsible yet fun loving. He makes sure that he dutifully attends every parent-teacher meeting and

---

[295] http://www.guardian.co.uk/sport/2009/jun/28/adam-gilchrist-ashes-australia-interview

important event in their lives. Of course, he has an opinion on what his child must do, and can be quite harsh and controlling at times.

Love and Marriage for Her
She is a gem who loves you, and cares and worries for you all the time. She has beautiful eyes that reflect her deep love. She is also the perfect daughter-in-law. She is not submissive, though. She knows how to command even in her soft tone. She is always well turned out. Your house, too, displays her love for neatness and cleanliness.

As I said before, this sign is prone to worrying and you have to bear the brunt of her agitated words. Despite her charm and grace, she can get extremely irritated at times and can win awards for nagging. This is her one fault. Take her shopping. Retail therapy does help her though she worries about the bill.

As a mother, she is protective, caring and extremely attentive to her children's needs. This lady knows exactly what to feed them, how to take care of medical emergencies and when to give in to their demands. She is a mother who does not need to read parental help books or scroll through the net, looking for advice. Academic excellence matters to her and she teaches them to persevere and work hard to reach their goals.

At the Workplace
This combination is a very powerful performer. It has the perfection and clarity of Virgo, the fine balance and excellent communication skills of Libra and the passion and intensity of Scorpio. In any profession, be it the corporate or artistic field, these guys bring out every nuance and detail perfectly and effortlessly. They take time to plan and deliberate on different aspects.

Librans are very good at creative art forms too, be it singing, dancing or acting, while Virgos are excellent actors. So VirLibScorps can be good in the arts and acting. They can be totally modest and submissive and talk very diplomatically, but always get their way.

Libra is a cardinal sign while Virgo is mutable and Scorpio is fixed. This combination makes them good subordinates and superiors. They do not mind starting at the bottom and are willing to learn. As they grow in their chosen professions, they learn to lead and manage large teams.

Money and position matter to them. They are realistic, and demand raises accordingly. Treat them well, compliment them at times and provide them with opportunities to grow. They are liberal and democratic bosses who will keep it simple and show you exactly how it is done. They will never steal your thunder.

Earth, Air and Water combine to give them stability, skill and intensity. VirLibScorps will think perfectly, plan analytically, believe passionately and bring integrity, grace and force to whatever they do.

Famous VirLibScorp Personalities
Adam Gilchrist, Amish Tripathy, Brinda Karat, Courtney Walsh, Gulshan Grover, Hilary Duff, Lillian Gish, Malaika Arora Khan, Naomi Watts, Navjot Singh Sidhu, Nauheed Cyrusi, Prateik Babbar, Ritu Kumar, Sathyaraj, Sivaji Ganesan, Simi Garewal, Suresh Raina, Scott Parker, J.J. Valaya, Verghese Kurien, Vikram Phadnis.

163. VIRGO–LIBRA–SAGITTARIUS

The meticulously perfect Virgo teams up with the luxury-loving Venus and the extremely intelligent Jupiter in VirLibSags. You can be sure of an overdose of intelligence in them. They think deeply and analytically. Even their more impulsive decisions are rarely truly off the cuff. They think through their actions and spend a lot of time over their decisions, rethinking them from every angle.

The most evident talent of VirLibSags is their excellent skill of communication. They talk and write beautifully, with great attention to perfect language. They are easily able to convince people with their wit, humour and analysis.

The Sagittarian rebelliousness is toned down due to Virgo and Libra's willingness to talk and listen, but it is still there. They have a few revolutionary ideas, which they do not give up easily. This rebelliousness is surprising, since in most matters they are quite traditional and ready to toe the line.

The Libra smile and the Sagittarian optimism make them great people to hang around with. You can be sure of a heart-melting smile whenever they try to change you over to their views. There is certainly fun and adventure in them. Sagittarius will also make them a little more open to new ideas. Libra will add to their ability to think from another's perspective and they will not be very rigid in their views. They to laugh at jokes and are quite chilled out in their views.

VirLibSags are quite creative as all three signs have creative talents plus Virgo adds its perfectionist ways to the creativity. They know how to mimic well and love the stage. The Sagittarius in them makes them want applause and they always want a big stage to perform, but they are willing to wait and work for it. They might act unconcerned about fame but they really crave it.

They are also quite honest, sometimes brutally so. This usually happens when they are angry. The Virgo trait of criticism makes them opinionated and the Libran analysis has you wishing they did not have such a good memory for your past mistakes. You find many VirLibSags fighting for some cause or the other. It can be as simple as keeping your community clean or as gargantuan as a fight against corruption.

They are a little confused about love. They want their freedom and worry about the responsibilities of being in a relationship while they also dream about being in a loving relationship. The Libran desire for being in love is not as strong in them and they are good at analysing the pros and cons of a relationship before committing to it. Once they commit they are loyal.

They are neat and clean people. The clumsy disorderliness of Sagittarius reduces due to the clean and aesthetic habits of Virgo and Libra. They like doing up their surroundings.

Money matters to them, but they do not kill themselves over it. They prefer a stress-free existence. They love to shop and often give in to their impulses. But they have a plan for the future, and save for it, too. Travel interests them. They want to see the world. They miss home, but love meeting new people and learning new things.

The Virgo tendency to analyse is accentuated by the Libran indecisiveness and fairness. The Sagittarian in them makes them discuss things with everyone to whom they are close. They spend hours and days in analysing, especially when they are in love, just out of love or falling in love. Then one fine day, they decide to give up all the analysis and go on a trek, a yoga session in the mountains or a spiritual club meeting, and come back rejuvenated to restart life once again. They are spiritual and may even follow rituals. They believe that 'everything will be fine one day'.

They take you at face value. They believe what you say and don't try to read between lines. They are not good at deciphering your unsaid words or looking into your soul and reading your deepest thoughts. They can never cheat nor mean any harm to anyone. They don't hold grudges and let you know their displeasure in simple language. They are soft, clean souls who have this sweet but brave naïveté about them. It is their greatest disadvantage and actually the biggest plus too.

Virgo–Libra–Sagittarius – Zoya Akhtar
Honey Irani: 'Zoya is a good writer…As a person, she is temperamental, though she's calmed down a lot. She's so honest that one gets hurt. We ask her to be *thoda sa* diplomatic. But that's not possible.'[296]

Honey Irani: 'Zoya was a responsible child so I could rely on her.'[297]

Zoya started her career in Bollywood as an assistant director and then worked as a casting director, executive producer, storywriter and a director! She says, 'I wanted to learn everything extensively.'[298]

Zoya has the blunt honesty, the magical ability with words and the responsibility and thoroughness of VirLibSag.

Love and Marriage for Him
He is very loving and caring. He is your friend and expects you to be the same. You can be yourself with him. He loves a good conversation at any time of the day. He is responsive too, and his wit and humour make you smile even when you are mad at him. You may get fed up of his deep analyses and thoughts at times. Take care of the daily expenses while he plans for the future. He is a great lover but do not expect him to understand all your unspoken sighs.

He always tries to balance his work and love, and if you ever tell him that you are feeling bad about something, he tries to work it out. He tries to understand your point of view and thinks deeply about your problems to reach a solution.

He is quite conscious about his health and is athletic. He likes to try new diets and maintains his weight. You have to follow his diet chart and timings for those are things about which he is quite particular.

Keep your bags packed and ready for he can be quite impulsive about his travel plans, despite his love for planning. He likes to travel to new destinations and is ready for adventure sports.

---
[296] *Idiva*, 'Shabana and I are not sahelis', 15 June, 2012
[297] http://www.rediff.com/movies/2009/jan/30honey-irani-on-farhan-zoya-akhtar.htm
[298] http://articles.timesofindia.indiatimes.com/2011-08-10/news-interviews/29867802_1_zoya-akhtar-znmd-farhan

As a father, he is full of fun and concern. His children have a grand time for he knows how to make them laugh while making them work. The one thing he really insists on is good education.

Love and Marriage for Her
She is the most fun person you know. However, she has a serious side too. She is your friend and though she loves you a lot, she has her own sense of independence. If you want a girl to boss over, give her a miss for she has her own views and does not conform easily to fixed ideas without a logical basis.

She is very creative too. She likes dabbling in a lot of things and is happiest when learning new skills. Give her the freedom to be herself and you will have a companion whose views are never boring and whose laugh always holds you mesmerised. She needs a push to accomplish her ambitions. She carries out her duties well. Her house is always clean and beautiful and she takes good care of everything around her.

Do not kill her with household routine. She needs space and understanding to be herself and truly happy. The best thing about her is that she will give you space too and not strangle you with excessive emotional demands. Some of her views are quite unconventional. She may need a little help while shopping – despite her good intentions, she may give in to her desire for beautiful things.

As a mother, she is absolute fun. She delights in her children's activities and enjoys their adventures. She knows how to nurse them when they are sick and cheer them up when they are sad. Despite all her fun and frolic, there is also an element of sternness in her. She trains her children to be responsible and independent.

At the Workplace
VirLibSags have a thinking mind and can be good scientists, researchers and even mathematicians. They excel in any profession that needs speaking and hypothesising. They are quite ambitious, as Sagittarius makes them aspire for applause while Libra is a cardinal sign. However, they need a push in the right direction. They are interested in so many things, and so many ideas seem right to them, that they have a hard time deciding what they want.

They prefer careers that offer opportunities for growth, learning, creativity, and travel. They do not tolerate unfairness in the workplace. They voice their unhappiness subtly, initially, and if it persists, strongly. They have excellent communication skills and can be wonderful writers, teachers and even orators. Their creative skills are quite evident and they know how to make their skills work for them.

As bosses, they demand professionalism from you and are fair and extremely honest in their appraisals. You will never have any unpleasant surprises with them.

Earth, Air and Fire meet in this loving combination. VirLibSags will be traditional yet harbour unconventional dreams. They will be exciting, friendly and honest souls who live life with cheer, goodwill and thought.

Famous VirLibSag Personalities
Zoya Akhtar, Simon Cowell, Mitchell Johnson, Samir Soni, Esha Deol, W.E. Boeing, Dileep, Charles G. Koch, Gurudas Kamat.

164. VIRGO–LIBRA–CAPRICORN

Meticulous and analytical Virgo joins Venus, the planet of beauty and love, and Saturn, the wise and capricious, to give VirLibCaps an earthy stability along with grace and wisdom. In them, you have Libra's creativity and talent, Capricorn's determination and Virgo's diligence.

They like to act older than their age. When you meet them in their twenties, you feel like you are talking to mellow middle-aged people. They talk about planning their future and taking the right steps towards their dream objectives. They know what they want and go about trying to achieve it by meeting the right people, going to the right places and, of course, working extremely hard. As children, they study long hours every day while the rest of their friends play.

They are extremely intelligent. Libra gives them the gift of the gab. They talk analytically and logically and are able to convince people easily. They are also able to turn on their charm when required. The fact is that though they seem quite subdued and restrained, they can surprise you with their dry wit and understated eloquence. The Libran smile can charm you when their logic does not.

Duty is first in their value system. They know their responsibilities and like being true to their family's values. The worst thing that can happen to them is an unstable family life. It can break them and turn them against all rules and regulations. They want to be good children to their parents and need elders to look up to. They play their expected roles very well. Shortcuts don't exist for them. They also know exactly what they are and what they can achieve.

Money is important to them and they are quite frugal in their requirements. The only things they spend on are assets of lasting value for their families and themselves. They want security, they want to build assets that last till eternity, and long for durable power and lasting monuments. They plan meticulously, step by step, and slowly but steadily get to the top. They are blessed with superb technical skills too.

They have very finicky habits. They want their food at specific times and are concerned about its quality. They have precise instructions for many things. Cleanliness, too, is one of their favourite fixations. They are perfectionists to the core.

Love never catches them unprepared. VirLibCaps rarely fall blindly and instantly in love. They take their time to understand and work out the dynamics of a relationship before deciding to fall in love. The Libran desire to fall in love will be there, and even if they opt for a romantic 'love marriage', they do so with the blessings of their elders.

Thankfully, they become less tedious as they grow older. The Capricornian reverse-aging syndrome makes them act more freely in their forties and fifties, rather than in their twenties. If their love life hasn't been too satisfactory or their mates have grown apart from them over the years, they look around and are ready for new adventures in their middle age.

They are extraordinarily artistically talented. They can easily win all elocution, singing or dance competitions and can be a fantastic hit with their acting skills too. They are not just talented but are smart enough to showcase their talents at the right places and make a career out of their talents. They are masters of self-promotion but do so unobstrusively. They naturally look like people who will go places in life, without much trying.

Worry consumes them. They seem so preoccupied with ideas of their goals that they rarely have the lightness of spirit to laugh at problems. They are never relaxed. All this worrying can make them melancholic. They are prone to depression, if this tendency is not curbed. Love and family are two things that can affect their mental balance. If either love is lost or family is in disarray, they tend to be lonely and sad. They find it easier to handle career issues than issues of the heart.

There is a strange contradiction, though. They are sentimental but not emotional and caring. They can trample on people's feelings, especially of those who are not family. They are extremely smart using their charm to manipulate things, people and situations to favour them in their career or even in romance. They land up with the best life partner or the best job, simply by perfect planning and execution and little bit of manoeuvring.

Virgo–Libra–Capricorn – Bruce Jenner
'To me, the definition of focus is knowing exactly where you want to be today, next week, next month, next year, then never deviating from your plan...I always felt that my greatest asset was not my physical ability, it was my mental ability.'[299]

Jenner used his popularity after the Olympics to sign up for commercials, promotions, and public appearances. As Greg Garber commented, he 'has made a spectacular living simply being Bruce Jenner.'

'Activity, variety and the next challenge around the bend and my eight kids – keep me excited and inspired.'[300]

The VirLibCap deep focus, ability to make money, excellent communication skills and family orientation are apparent in Bruce Jenner.

Love and Marriage for Him
He is a dutiful and caring husband. His appeal lies in his protective nature. You are never caught unawares by emergencies when you are with him. He has every eventuality planned and accounted for before it actually happens. He is the guy who pays bills on time. You can expect a smooth financial ride with him. He also balances work and family time well.

He is a very private person with a habit of worrying and going over details again and again. Try and calm him down and do not pile problems on him. You need to be the more optimistic and outgoing of the two for he is prone to melancholic spells and prefers solitude to laughter. He prefers your independent nature and ambition to helpless feminine charms.

Family is very important for him and he even makes your family a part of his. He plans family holidays and outings. He is not very adventurous in his choice of locations but tries and takes everyone out together wherever he goes. Romance actually rears its head late in life for before that he is more interested in duties and responsibilities. It is better if you retain your spark as you age, too.

As a father, he is caring, protective, loving and imparts discipline with a sense of fairness. He wants academic excellence in his children and teaches them to aim high and work hard for their dreams.

---

[299] http://www.answers.com/topic/bruce-jenner#ixzz1xk7K56xr
[300] http://biography.yourdictionary.com/bruce-jenner

Love and Marriage for Her
She plays the role of a wife very well, but do not expect her to be just a housewife. This lady has ambitions and is willing to toil for them. If your own ambitions are big enough for the two of you, she helps you out; otherwise, let her be her own mistress in working out her dreams. She has the overpowering need to improve her status. She can be a great business partner for you and helps lighten your burdens.

She is wonderful at maintaining relationships. She wants her family to be close-knit. But she often forgets to relax. You need to constantly remind her to let go of minor irritants and live in the moment. Add energy and zest to her life or she can stay tied to problems. She manages money well and is very good at budgeting.

She is romantic and can balance career and romance beautifully. She blossoms and eases up with age. Be ready to woo her again her forties. If you betray her and make a mockery of all the sacrifices she made for the family, she can cut off all ties and walk off with her children. It will greatly pain her to do so, but she will do it.

As a mother, she teaches her children to work hard. She also insists on discipline while being scrupulously fair and very protective. She relaxes with her children.

At the Workplace
VirLibCaps are dedicated workaholics who never flinch at hard work. They are always willing to go the extra mile. They are extremely focused. Libra's talent, Virgo's hard work and Capricorn's planning and execution, make them brilliant in the workplace.

These guys can be anything they want. From creative arts to corporate finances, they can tackle everything with ease. Their clarity of thought and extraordinary communication skills make them stand out. They are those rare employees who don't just talk but also back it up with indefatigable work. People find it difficult to match the standards set by VirLibCaps. They are also smart enough to network well and use their connections, if necessary, to get things done in their favour.

Patience is also one of their virtues. They are ready to wait and work their way to the top. You need to show them opportunities to grow to attract them to your organisation. These people want to see a path for themselves and remunerations to match.

This combination has two cardinal signs – Libra and Capricorn. These make them great leaders who lead by example. They can delegate and are willing to listen. They motivate their subordinates and extract the best out of them.

Duty-minded, stable and loving, creative and diligent, VirLibCaps will always better their life and work themselves to a higher level.

Famous VirLibCap Personalities
Bruce Jenner, Vinod Khanna, John Lennon, Hrishikesh Mukherjee, Om Puri, Rakshanda Khan, Tony Greig, Candice Swanepoel, Mona Singh, Jayaprakash Narayan, Bilawal Bhutto Zardari, Pramod Mahajan, Abhijeet Sawant, Protima Bedi, Susan Sarandon.

165. VIRGO–LIBRA–AQUARIUS

VirLibAquas have the perfection of Virgo, the conversational skills of Libra and the inventive genius of Aquarius. There is purity in this combination that makes them seem too good to be true at times, but it is true. They think deeply, feel truly and are rarely of the malicious grudging nature.

Both Virgo and Aquarius are known for their intelligence. The Virgo intelligence digs deeper; it needs details and wants to be absolutely sure of everything that concerns them. Aquarius adds sparkle to the Virgo talent of putting everything in order. The Aquarian in VirLibAquas makes them think of futuristic ideas. They dream Utopian dreams and think more inventively than pure Virgos.

VirLibAquas are very duty-conscious. They do what is desired of them. From friends to relatives, all are treated with the same consideration. You can imagine what stress they go through with the Virgo desire to be perfect and the Libran wish to be balanced and fair. They need some breathing space with the number of worries they needlessly accumulate in their lives.

They possess superb communication skills. With Virgo's clarity of thought and the Aquarian knowledge of a thousand subjects, when they expound with the charm, wit and diplomacy of a Libran, you are swept off your feet. They know the minutest details of certain things, which can stun you.

Humanitarian and considerate, they are fabulous friends. If you ever have a problem, you can talk to them about it. You can be sure that they take the trouble to think, analyse and solve it for you.

They like to live in neat and clean surroundings. Mess of any kind makes them feel stressed. The Libran desire for symmetry too makes itself felt in their surroundings. They itch to rearrange the pieces on the mantelpiece and can't rest till they have placed them in perfect harmony. These intelligent chatterboxes sometimes remain silent and prefer solitude. Those are their spaced-out Aquarian moments, when they go fifty years into the future. They will come back soon with some wacky thoughts. The Virgo in them also prefers solitude at times.

They surprise you with their broad-minded views. They do not bind themselves to traditions that have lost their meaning. They question rather than accept meaningless rituals and traditions. They also possess high ideals and humanitarian ideas, and are touched by poverty, inequality and discrimination. They voice their opinions and even fight openly for such causes.

Love is very important to them. The Libra in them needs a partner and feels a void in life without love. Yet despite their seemingly strong desire to be in love, they do not want to be cocooned or smothered in love. The Aquarian need for space and detachment, and the Virgo desire for solitude, might make them seem disinterested at times, but their love is usually too strong to be broken by their need for space. VirLibAquas have a very pure love; they are extremely understanding and do not like to cling or exhibit possessiveness. Their love is more emotional than sentimental. They are very dutiful, idealistic and puritanical in their approach to it.

Their fashion sense is highly developed and individualistic. The Libran sense of high fashion and the Aquarian wackiness combine beautifully with the perfectionist attitude of Virgo. They dress well, and even differently, without being outrageous.

They have a pragmatic approach to money. Their Virgoan practicality and Aquarian desire to save for the future meets the Libran need for balance, making VirLibAquas save without becoming stingy. They plan and invest well, though they may take some time to decide where to invest.

They are usually calm and collected. They are neither bubbling with energy nor do they laze around. They are quite even-tempered, though they may have sudden bursts of anger on rare occasions. They keep experimenting with various wacky ideas. Everything from alternative medicine, to past-life regression to genetic engineering, fascinates and interests them.

Though Virgo makes them do everything with great discipline and rigour, Aquarius makes them dream and think such different thoughts that it will take them quite some time to realise what they actually want to do. Their Libran side also makes them highly indecisive. They spend a lot of time thinking about what they want to do in life but once they are sure they work with great diligence and perseverance.

Actually, they prefer starting on something new every time they master a job. They like change and though they don't allow their life to become unstable, they can't be confined to a single thought. They can keep on reinventing themselves, and do it in a positive way. They grow in thought and knowledge every single day. They are perfectly capable of bringing in dramatic transformations in their personality with great dedication, sustained efforts, innovative thinking and moral courage.

Virgo–Libra–Aquarius – Rekha
'I was called "Ugly Duckling" because of my dark complexion and South-Indian features...I was determined to make it big on sheer merit.'...She started paying attention to her make-up, dress sense, and worked to improve her acting technique and perfect her Hindi-language skills. To lose weight, she followed a nutritious diet, led a disciplined life, and practised yoga...According to Khalid Mohamed, 'The audience was floored when there was a swift change in her screen personality, as well as her style of acting.'[301]

Rekha displays the iron self-control of Virgo, the Libran desire to lead softly and the Aquarian ability to evolve with time.

Love and Marriage for Him
He wants to and tries to be the perfect husband for you. He caters to every demand. He is not only dutiful but also extremely liberal. He is loving and caring and, best of all, he nurses you back to health when you fall sick. But despite his love

---
[301] http://en.wikipedia.org/wiki/Gautam_Adani

and care, he needs space. Give him time to be with himself and his thoughts, and you will find him rejuvenated.

He is an animated companion. This guy has so many interests, knows so many things, and talks so well about them, that it is hard to be bored in his company. He knows what you feel and why you act weird at times. He takes it all in his stride and lets you be yourself.

He may not be as liberal with his wallet as with his views, but it's prudence. Music and arts are a special joy to him. Food, too, is important, but he prefers organic and healthy food to rich delicacies. He is of fastidious habits. Neatness, cleanliness and orderliness are absolute necessities for him.

As a father, he is permissive, though he insists on good education. He does not seek to control but tries to understand and work with his children.

Love and Marriage for Her

This intelligent, bright, talkative and smart girl goes mushy and dumbstruck when in love. She will do anything for her man. She is an extraordinary mix of love, care and sensitivity. She is an ideal wife without resorting to clinging or dramatic scenes. This lady knows that space is essential for a relationship to blossom. Calm and composed most of the time, she may use her beautiful smile and diplomatic talk to get what she wants. There can be a few outbursts of tears, though. She is duty-conscious. Her smile is her biggest asset.

She loves talking and likes it if you actively participate in her conversations. Monologues are not her idea of a discussion. A neat and clean home is her wish and she works hard to make it come true. She takes her time when it comes to household chores. That is the secret to her well-kept home.

She is duty-conscious, but is not satisfied with doing one thing alone. This chirpy girl loves working and thinking of so many different things that change and travel are essential to her. She needs a change of environment to feel recharged. She has myriad hobbies, and experiments with them in her various quests. She is extremely intelligent, bordering on genius; it would be a crime if you didn't allow her to blossom.

As a mother, she works with her children to understand them. She is also concerned about their health. Her love does not smother them but makes them grow into independent and confident people.

At the Workplace

The Libran power over communication skills and the Aquarian desire to know everything combine fabulously with the Virgo trait of going deep into every matter, to make them perfect researchers. VirgLibAquas bring new ideas to the table and help in creating original thoughts.

They need to experiment and create differently as much as they need to breathe. They do not do anything for glory. They bring a lot of good attitude to a team with their penchant for hard work and intelligent converstion.

From the sciences to more creative fields, and everything in between, they can excel in anything with their charm and ready wit combined with their dedication and knowledge. The only jobs they cannot do are those that are monotonous or repetitive in nature. They want to learn and move on. They can be brilliant in software development. They can also be good actors, musicians, singers, physicians, surgeons, architects and doctors: all places where sensibility, creativity and perfection meet. They are ingenious and futuristic as bosses, but have a perfect plan in place to get there.

VirLibAquas are loving yet cool, talkative yet seekers of solitude, and workaholics with a sense of balance.

Famous VirLibAqua Personalities
Rekha, Indra Nooyi, Nusrat Fateh Ali Khan, Raaj Kumar, Parineeti Chopra, Pablo Picasso, Carol Lombard, Arnab Goswami.

166. VIRGO–LIBRA–PISCES

This is a wonderful combination of perfection, balance, art and compassion. VirLibPisces are extremely gentle and kind people. They have an inherent goodness and purity in them that the world's degenerate ways cannot erode or touch. The only thing to watch out for is their environment, for Pisces has the tendency to reflect its surroundings. Therefore, except when bad experiences or bad people mar their worldview, VirLibPisces are beautiful, reflective and sensitive souls.

Libra and Pisces are both very empathetic. The next level of empathy is compassion and they can feel others' pain too. Virgo adds to their ability to sense the pain of others, for it is a healer. VirLibPisces can easily get hurt, so some of them use the superb acting skills of Virgo to wear a mask. They can easily portray themselves as domineering, cool, reclusive or fashionable, just to hide their vulnerable softness.

Artistic and creative talents, and their expression, are intrinsic to them. Pisces is deeply talented and creative and Venus, the ruler of Libra, is the planet of beauty and the arts. They will love, nurture and perfect any art form.

Virgos are known for their systematic planning and methodical steps; they love routines, have back-up plans and are ready to meet every eventuality. All these lessen the lazy, unorganised ways of Pisces and Libra and stop VirLibPisces from wasting their precious talents. Duty, a Virgo trait, gets embedded in the psyche of Pisces and Libra.

They are conscious of their health but may not be able to control themselves as much as a Virgo. You find them adopting healthy diets and organic foods, but giving in at times to their basic cravings. Both Libra and Pisces love food, but Virgo's discipline ensures that whenever they need to look good, they go in for crash diets and exercise to tone up. The Virgo interest in healing and medicine sees them adopt many alternative healing practices.

Librans love luxury while Pisceans love the extraordinary joys of life. VirLibPisces love fashion. The Virgo sense of detail ensures that they are very particular about what they wear and how they look. They have an acute sense of smell. Dirty, smelly and unkempt people turn them off.

VirLibPisces is a sign deeply immersed in love. Libra feels incomplete without a partner while Pisces has a deep-rooted need to belong to someone; Virgo is the only one who can live out a solitary existence filling time with duties and responsibilities. Virgo's capacity for self-sacrifice makes VirLibPisces very giving in love. There will be purity in their love and they can love totally without expectations. For VirLibPisces, nothing matters when they are in love: neither looks nor money; neither status, caste nor creed.

Money is not very important for such selfless and creative souls. Of course, they do love luxury and the good things in life but they just cannot understand the fuss people make about creating and hoarding wealth. Unless the Piscean in them was trained by extremely money-conscious parents or lived in an environment where saving was paramount to existence, they do not have many saving traits except in the last few days of the month when the Virgo discipline steps in.

They are wonderful communicators. They have the Libran skill in speech. The Piscean love of conversation makes them talk nineteen to the dozen, and the Virgo sensibility ensures that their talk has substance. They are excellent companions who know how to have fun without harming or hurting anyone's feelings.

The lack of Fire in this combination makes them lack drive, and also the anger, connected to high passions. Their only way of showing their displeasure is through irritable snapping or criticising. The Piscean in them does not say anything and the Libran makes them sugarcoat their words. You can expect long-winded speeches from them when they are angry, for they do need to vent their feelings occasionally.

They suffer bouts of depression when they are unloved, and extreme vacillations of mind while taking some important decisions; they chew off their nails while doing their deep analyses. But they never let others know of their inner conflicts, and hide them behind a charming smile.

You find deep spirituality in them. They are totally non-judgemental and do not believe in categorising people into generalities. They also like giving to society and donate to charities. Truly amazing souls, indeed!

Virgo–Libra–Pisces – Bill Gates

Bill Gates has confirmed that he plans to give his children a 'minuscule' amount of his fortune. 'They will be given an unbelievable education and certainly anything related to health issues we will take care of. But in terms of their income, they will have to pick a job and go to work.'[302]

'I never took a day off in my twenties. Not one. And I'm still fanatical. I don't want a legacy. If people look and see that childhood deaths dropped from nine million a year to four million because of our investment, then wow!'[303]

The conscientiousness of Virgo, the Libran ability to think from different perspectives and the Piscean empathy, meet beautifully in Bill Gates.

Love and Marriage for Him

You are a very lucky girl indeed to have found a guy who is not only loving and caring but also understands your thoughts. He finds it very easy to forgive your faults and likes your success and independence. He cares for you when you are sick and nurses you back to health.

This guy needs to earn money and concentrate on his career. Do not tie him to yourself for he can get lost in family ties and let his talents go. You need to be his strength and support, for him to do wonders. It is ideal if you can take the monetary decisions and plans in your hands, for though he loves planning for a better tomorrow, his plans always unwind at the first shop he sees.

Though he is very understanding and emotional, he needs an independent and strong partner for only then does he feel that the home is taken care of. He needs to be stress-free to perform well in his work, for the Virgo in him is prone to worry and Pisces can give in easily to fears and phobias. You have to be strong, yet sensitive enough to understand him as much as he understands you.

---

[302] http://www.zdnet.com/blog/btl/new-bill-gates-interview-legacy-is-a-stupid-thing-i-dont-want-a-legacy/50411
[303] http://www.dailymail.co.uk/home/moslive/article-2001697/Microsofts-Bill-Gates-A-rare-remarkable-interview-worlds-second-richest-man.html

This guy is not made for a materialistic and selfish world. His thoughts and ideals are beyond the ordinary. If selflessness is weird for you, and ambition is what drives you, do not choose him.

He is everything that a father should be without being strict or domineering. The only thing he demands is that his children receive a good education. He then allows them to be whatever they want to be.

Love and Marriage for Her
She does everything for you. She worries for you, cares for you and thinks only of you. You are her one and only love. She is one woman who does not want anything from you but your love.

Of course, she does not mind luxury and it is nice if you earn enough to keep her well stocked with perfumes and toiletries. She takes good care of herself.

She can sacrifice herself in love but that does not mean you let her become a martyr to your cause. She needs you to allow her to grow. Her artistic talents and sensibilities must not get crushed while looking after you. Give her space and encouragement to pursue her dreams for she lacks the drive to match up with her ideas.

She needs to be treated well. If you work long hours, and are highly ambitious, make sure that you at least talk to her when you come home. That small token of love and care keeps her going. She is emotional and sensitive. You need to be soft and kind with her. If you want her to understand money matters, go about it with patience. She is a fast learner and soon learns the tricks to save while spending.

As a mother, she is truly lovely. She understands the smallest demands of her children and does not refuse them anything. She can be very permissive at times. However, the Virgo in her ensures discipline, and she instils values, albeit in a loving manner. She becomes a friend who guides them perfectly through the challenges of life.

At the Workplace
Creativity and originality, and the knack of applying these skills in their careers, are their biggest assets. They can be very talented actors, singers and dancers. They hate routine, despite the Virgo in them, and are happy doing things that allow them freedom and movement. They are very intelligent and can talk on any subject with clarity and wit.

In the corporate world, they are good in positions that require them to be in touch with people and solve problems. They are not cut out for sales nor do they enjoy roles where they have to dominate or control. They do not dream of leaving a legacy behind, rather, they dream of helping people. The chameleonic Piscean in them can make them anything from a scientist to a dancer or even a reluctant boss, but with a deep, compassionate soul.

Earth, Air and Water combine beautifully in VirLibPisces to give a methodical mind and a sympathetic heart with a healing touch.

Famous VirLibPisces Personalities
Bill Gates, Hema Malini, Sunny Deol, Mahesh Bhatt, Martina Navratilova, Luciano Pavarotti, Acharya Vidyasagar, Bhairon Singh Shekhawat, Sneha, Heather Locklear, Steve Bhaerman, Ashley Hamilton, Usher.

167. VIRGO–SCORPIO–SAGITTARIUS

This is a combination of perfectionism, passion and intelligence. Virgo is guided by routine and duty, Scorpio is passion personified, while Sagittarius has instinctive wisdom for the abstract and a fun-loving nature. VirScorpSags are extremely intelligent; Virgo adds love of detail, Scorpio gives them the desire to know about everything mysterious, and added to the Sagittarian knowledge of the abstract, these are clever people.

One thing that strikes you about them is their passion. The Scorpio in them needs to be intensely, single-mindedly bound to a .love or mission while the Virgo wants to know everything about their chosen object of desire. The Sagittarian energy makes them work enthusiastically and positively in achieving their passions.

Virgo adds purity to Scorpio and reduces its sting. The high ideals and virginal thoughts of Virgo neutralise the seamy side of Scorpio. Scorpios can experiment in the darkest mysteries of life; the Virgo desire for purity stops this combination from ever walking that path. They have the Sagittarian high ambition, and the intense Scorpio's focus. Sagittarius reduces the highly stressed-out state of Virgo and adds zing to it.

VirScorpSags are extremely health-conscious, and they strive for holistic fitness rather than looks. While Virgos are very conscious of what they eat, the Sagittarian in them finds it difficult to refuse delicious food. They somehow strike a balance, and look good naturally without really fretting over it.

They are enthusiastic and positive people but not total extroverts. They have a deeply private core to them. You do not find them brazenly partying. They always look their best. The well-known Sagittarian sloppiness is missing in them. They insist on neatness and cleanliness, always and everywhere. Sagittarius redeems them from becoming obsessive and fastidious.

Honesty is a virtue and a vice in them. The Sagittarian fearless, outspoken nature meets Scorpio's awesome inner strength and Virgo's clarity of thought to make them honest to a great degree. They tell the truth even when they know that its consequences may not be good for them.

Love is an enduring passion with them. You can expect the Scorpio dedication and the Virgo commitment from them. Sagittarius is the only weak link with its fear of attachments and it is totally outnumbered by the two dedicated signs. Love will never be a hasty decision for them. They take their time to zero in on real love. The Scorpio in them is very good at reading signs and will not be fooled.

VirScorpSags are wise when it comes to money. Sagittarius is again the weak link in this but constrained by Virgo's desire to save and Scorpio's natural stinginess. VirScorpSags save and count their pennies, and spend only on their loved ones. But when they are in the Sagittarian mood, they can blow an entire year's savings in one evening.

They love the adrenalin rush of adventure sports. Of course, they go fully prepared and know the risks involved, and the precision required. Sports come naturally to them and they have all the attributes of good sportspersons – dedication, passion and planning.

The revenge element of Scorpio may be diluted in them, but the sting is still there. More than anything else, they hate dishonesty, cheating and backstabbing. These can make them react with the Sagittarian uncontrollable anger or the Scorpio sting, depending on the gravity of the situation.

They are extremely critical and frankly opinionated. They don't care about the opinions of others but would rather live by their own beliefs. They are their own worst critics and know their own weaknesses. Their negative qualities can be harsh criticism, excessive nervousness, restlessness, revenge compulsion, occasional violent temper. They are also one of the most misunderstood people of the zodiac. Their laughter can be mistaken for carelessness, their quick retorts misconstrued as arrogance, and their enthusiasm misinterpreted as being overfriendly.

They never lose a fight. They are extremely focused and hard working, and defeats and hardships only spur them on. This combination somehow brings in the best features of the three zodiac signs. Virgo retains its naïveté and perfection without being nitpicky. Scorpio retains its eroticism and its capacity to rise from failures, without its jealousy and possessiveness. Sagittarius retains its positivity, integrity and enthusiasm but knows where to aim and shoot.

They are total believers. They intuitively know about the secret mysteries of the world. The Scorpio in them is deeply perceptive, the Sagittarius gives them a higher wisdom and the belief in a power above. The Virgo knows right from wrong. They believe that there is always a better tomorrow and the next day will always be better. Aren't they right?

Virgo–Scorpio–Sagittarius – Vidya Balan
[The correspondent]: I wonder why and what is it that makes her laugh so much.
'On sets too, I find anything and everything funny,' Vidya says.[304]
Vidya: 'My fashion fiasco phase ended the moment I started being myself.'[305]
Priya (Vidya's sister): 'She believes in the power of dreams. Even when she was called a jinx down South, she never lost faith.'[306]
Vidya: 'These characters (in *Parineeta*, *Ishqiya* and *The Dirty Picture*) have inhabited me and my personality. I am neither of them, yet all of them in some ways.'[307]
The Sagittarian laughter and candidness, the Virgo meticulousness and perfectionism, and the Scorpion ability to fight against all odds, are present in Vidya.

Love and Marriage for Him
You have picked one committed guy who can never let you down. He isn't one to shirk his responsibilities and is always there for you. The poor guy stresses himself out trying to be everything to you – the perfect husband, friend, provider and lover. So be ready to love and be loved.

---
[304] *Cine Blitz*, August 2010
[305] *Stardust*, October 2010
[306] *People*, Feb 24, 2012
[306] *Cine Blitz* , January 2012

He is extremely honest and frank, and understands your smallest worries. If you also worry too much, it can be bad, for he loves to take on your problems. Give him a break for he is already stressed out. He feels deeply and gets hurt easily although he may not show it.

He has a fun side too. There is enthusiasm, energy and positivity in him. He loves travel and adventure. He wants a woman who is independent and strong. He is not controlling or aggressive.

You have to take care of one important factor in his life – his health. This guy is very particular about his health right from what he eats to how much he works out. He is also neat and clean in his habits and wants that neatness to be reflected all around him.

As a father, he is loving and caring. He is a firm and disciplined father who wants to teach his children the right values in life. He makes them emulate his hard-working nature.

Love and Marriage for Her
She knows right from wrong and never lets herself brood or speak deceitfully. There is a rare honesty in her that is quite charming. The Scorpio in her makes her all-knowing: you cannot hide anything, good or bad, from her.

She is the opposite of lazy. This lady just does not know how to relax. Lack of focus and purpose in life are anathema to her. Her habits are meticulous and her house is perfect. She is independent and strong, and ambitious too. She knows what she wants to do and goes about doing it without wasting time on fears and insecurities. She has a spine of steel and never takes a 'no' from life. She is very positive that all her hard work will ultimately end in good results. She just keeps doing her duties diligently.

She likes fun but is not impulsive. Her fun times are well planned and she never works at the time of play or vice versa. She plays like a child, has the throaty Sagittarian laughter and lets her hair down when she seeks those adrenaline-pumping momemts. She is always well groomed and looks for that in her mate.

As a mother, she is conscientious and duty-conscious with a love for studies and a flair for fun. She teaches her children the value of education, work and purpose. She is the ideal mother – firm, fun and true.

At the Workplace
VirScorpSags are fabulous in careers. They are hard working, focused, passionate, ambitious and, most of all, enthusiastic about their work. They are the ideal workers who take on all your worries and work nonstop for the company. They are ideal in positions that require meticulous planning, dedication and even physical perfection.

They are loyal and true, but make sure that you give them their due or they move to where their talents are better appreciated. They know exactly how much they are worth and you cannot fool them into believing otherwise. They are workaholics – they never tire and give more than 100 per cent to their work. They are highly conscientious and work is worship for them. You will never find a more intelligent, diligent and focused employee.

They are fantastic problem solvers. They have a knack for numbers and scrutinise data deeply to arrive at solutions. They never lose their positivity in any situation. As bosses, they are very critical and passionate and expect nothing less than 100 per cent effort. They believe that honesty, and integrity and proper adherence to the processes will always give favourable results.

Duty and perfection, passion and determination, enthusiasm and ambition, make them eternal idealists who make the world a better place with their higher values.

Famous VirScorpSag Personalities
Vidya Balan, Kasturbhai Lalbhai, Baichung Bhutia, Jane Austen, Liv Ullmann, Piyush Chawla, Kirti Azad, Tanisha Mukherjee, Quinton de Kock.

168. VIRGO–SAGITTARIUS–CAPRICORN

The extremely analytical and methodical Virgo meets the fiercely ambitious duo of Sagittarius and Capricorn to propel this combination to its highest dreams. The three signs complement each other. Virgo gives extreme diligence, Capricorn puts in the focus and aim, and Sagittarius adds the zing to VirSagCaps.

You cannot find a more intelligent combination. All three signs are intelligent and knowledgeable. While Virgo makes them delve deep into the smaller details and gives them clarity of thought, Sagittarius makes them brilliantly at ease with the most arcane subjects. Capricorn adds practical knowledge to the mix.

Saturn is sombre, self-sufficient and goal oriented, and Virgo is responsible and conscientious. The expressive and outgoing Jupiter reduces the sobriety of these two signs. It also brings its talent as teacher.

VirSagCaps are stable and extremely responsible even at a young age. They are rarely rebels; they want status in society. Saturn, the melancholic old man, imparts some of its wise old ways to them. Sagittarius stops them from becoming dreadfully boring at a young age. They have a spark in them despite their age-old ideas, and do what they want to do with enthusiasm and energy.

They do everything seriously – even having fun. They feel that there is a time for everything and everything has to be timed. They do enjoy fun and games, but their sense of humour is rather basic. The Sagittarian clumsiness can surface in their lighter moments: they forget the need to be politically correct and say what they think. They are usually quite blunt.

Family is very important to them, second only to their burning ambition. They can sacrifice themselves for their families. They want to achieve status and respect for their families and themselves, and strive hard to provide everything for their loved ones. They worry about every single detail. At such times they need a little encouragement from more vivacious friends to come out of their self-inflicted torture sessions. Fortunately, the Sagittarian in them gives them the ability to laugh off their problems when they see the futility of worrying.

They usually have an opinion on everything and are not very flexible. They prefer traditional views to revolutionary ones and have a practical approach to life. Money is important. They are never spendthrifts. VirSagCaps know how to save and invest and multiply material gains.

Love doesn't hit them like a bolt of lightning. Virgo makes them highly idealistic and they can even sacrifice their love for a higher cause, while Capricorn makes them desire a match that will be socially acceptable and add to their prestige. Sagittarius is the odd man out in this respectable mix and can make them go in and out of relationships without getting their heart involved. But once they decide to tie themselves to matrimony they will be the most stable partners. Don't expect romantic nothings and loving gestures from them; their love will be more about providing the necessities and creating a respectable life for themselves and their family.

The possibility of Sagittarius making them hop from one relationship to another can increase as they grow older and achieve all that they set out to achieve.

That is the time the reverse-aging syndrome of Capricorn can hit them hard and they can turn to experimentation.

They like routine and discipline. Any deviation from set patterns may anger them.They prefer to lead by example and also nag a little. Don't expect sensitivity from them; though their extreme intelligence will understand the flow of your ideas but they will never sense the deepest secrets in your heart. VirSagCaps are more practical and unsentimental in their approach to things and ideas.

They are religious, too, and believe in the faith to which they were brought up, rarely diverting from its path. Customs and traditions mean a lot to them.

They can be worrywarts, nitpicky, choosy and can turn depressive, especially when their ambitions don't materialise according to their wishes. Their various insecurities also make them work hard; their inner fears propel them.

Though occasionally they are jovial and fun loving, they can be cold, calculating and remorseless. They are extremely practical, ruthless, penny-pinching and manipulative to reach the pinnacle of the mountain they want to climb.

They need to learn to appreciate the good things of life before it is too late. They do realise it when it is late. But would it be too late by then?

Virgo–Sagittarius–Capricorn – Mel Gibson
'I get pretty dark sometimes, pretty bleak. But that passes. I rarely lose my temper anymore…You've got to get it out. I used to just hang on to it and then some little thing would set it off, which was stupid. You behave like an asshole when you lose it, and you feel like an asshole afterward. It's not healthy.'[308]

Gibson has a reputation for practical jokes, puns, Stooge-inspired physical comedy, and doing outrageous things to shock people. As a director he sometimes breaks the tension on set by having his actors perform serious scenes wearing a red clown nose.[309]

Mel Gibson has the traditional views, insecurities and slapstick humour of a double Earth and Fire combination.

Love and Marriage for Him
He is dutiful and extremely conscious of his role as the provider in the family. He is the guy you can know completely, from the food he wants to the way he plans his day. However, be ready for some surprises. He loves travelling with his family and wants to spend all his free time with them. Of course, his career is extremely important to him but he never leaves his family behind. He needs a mate who understands the value of family just like him.

Do not expect roses all the time. He shows his love by working hard to leave behind a legacy for his family. He does not need negative comments: he is the first one to point out all the flaws in his plan and work towards negating them. Be his support and don't pull him down with prophecies of doom.

He has specific tastes and a set timetable. Of course, you have equal freedom to choose your way but you must not disturb his routine. He may be insensitive at

---

[308] http://denniseearl.wordpress.com/2010/07/18/revealing-quotes-from-mel-gibsons-1995-playboy-interview/
[309]

times and seem ruthless and self-centred, but remember that his inner insecurities about most things in life drive him to be too self-sufficient. He will become more relaxed and even adventurous once he hits the forties. Ensure that you are the one who is with him on his second honeymoon.

This guy is a hands-on father, including nappy changing, and loves taking care of his kids when he is at home. He explains the value of hard work to his children but is ready to have fun with them.

Love and Marriage for Her
This lady loves to work. She does not squander time on pampering herself. All she wants in a partner is love for family, and ambition. She is a prize catch if you want a home bird. She starts her days by planning her day and sleeps well only if she has completed the tasks she set herself.

You can easily make her a joint account holder for she never thinks of spending, but on the other hand, has very good investment ideas. The thought of less money turns her melancholic. Despite her conservative traits, she surprises you at times with an uncharacteristic adventurous streak. This lady has a lot of courage. Despite her duty-consciousness, she gets bored with things easily and needs change in settings frequently. Take her out often to new places to recharge her spirits.

Don't make the mistake of thinking that she is a pushover. She has given up her freedom and overcome her fear of in-laws, to be with your family. She goes out of her way to keep your family and you happy. She does not expect perfection from you, but if you betray her faith she will walk away from you, never to return.

As a mother, she is just right. Caring and loving, with a dash of fun and a dose of discipline, she never lets her children stray. They learn the value of work and ambition, and learn to be better by emulating her.

At the Workplace
Ambitious workaholics, VirSagCaps always want to reach the top and are willing to work, plan and wait for it. These guys can be anything they set their minds on. They bring perfection and diligence to every job, be it in banking, science, politics or sports. Any field that requires planning, great attention to detail, focus and even a bit of manipulation, works for them.

They always have a plan, a back-up plan and an additional plan. They do all the backward calculation and go for it with intense concentration and matchless determination. They never give up till the goal is won. They have a cold rationality about them aand work towards building lasting monuments.

They are loyal. They just stay put and slowly take over the place. They become dependable and irreplaceable and you have no choice but to promote them. As bosses, they have extraordinary managerial skills. They are fantastic coaches and mentors. But they can also be insensitive and cold – they don't empathise with your problems and may think you are avoiding responsibility.

Double Earth and Fire mix in this extremely stable and intelligent combination. VirSagCaps will be family-loving, status-seeking planners who will work their way to their dreams.

Famous VirSagCap Personalities
Mel Gibson, Stephen Hawking, Dalida, Arjen Robben, Veerappan, Kid Rock, Vanessa Redgrave, Sanjay Nirupam, Fred Trueman, Francoise Hardy, Bradley Cooper.

169. VIRGO–CAPRICORN–AQUARIUS

The meticulous Virgo, the wise old man Saturn and the unconventional inventor Uranus, meet in this extremely focused combination. VirCapAquas work with a single aim in mind and work hard to achieve it.

They prefer leading a life of routine and discipline. However, there are times when the wild Aquarius rears its head and they head out to untested zones. The unconventionality of Aquarius can also make them try out different things, but Virgo and Capricorn ensure that whatever they try out, they have clear views and focused ideas. They never waste their talents!

Family is their bedrock. They are extremely family-oriented and treat their families on a par with their aspirations. They work hard for their family's happiness. The Aquarian wacky sense of humour livens them up and adds the spark to the otherwise sedate Virgo and Capricorn.

Aquarian ideals and humanitarian views make them outspoken and forthright. They try to be as honest and as fearless as possible while trying to reach the top. You will rarely detect dishonourable conduct in them. The Capricorn in them knows when to talk and when to keep quiet. They do not take things lying down, so be sure that you treat them with wary respect. They care for the environment and humanitarian issues – this trait, combined with their forthrightness, makes them good spokespersons and advocates for causes dear to them.

They plan well and despite the few detours Aquarius makes them take, they know exactly where they are heading. They have the ability to become somebody from a mere nobody. The Aquarian desire to bring in a new thought process, the Virgo capacity to think out the details and the Capricornian desire to lead can make them leaders in thinking, too.

All three signs are geared for high mental ability – while Virgo makes them methodical and clear in their views, Capricorn makes them mature and responsible and Aquarius adds an element of genius to their innate wisdom. They are able to think through every problem and reach a logical, if slightly unconventional, solution. The Aquarian rebelliousness is toned down and if they do act unconventionally, they give you a solid reason for it.

They are always well dressed. The Capricornian desire to look successful and the Virgo perfectionism make them flawlessly attired with, obviously, an Aquarian individualistic streak. The Aquarian clumsiness is almost eradicated in them.

VirCapAquas are intelligent, well informed, quite opinionated and extremely meticulous, with a touch of the wild child. They want status and respect in society, but even more than that, they want to feel that they have achieved something different. The Aquarian need to think and act their own way makes them want to carve their own separate identity in the world.

They are workaholics. They get into myriad projects and can immerse themselves in them with intense concentration. Their Aquarian scientific temper, the natural ability of Virgo for research and the ability to go to the minutest detail, coupled with the hard-working abilities of Capricorn, are an unbeatable combination. They make something of their lives: probably something pathbreaking, innovative, helpful to mankind.

They will think out all the positives and negatives before tying themselves to a relationship. While this ensures that once thay are hooked, it's for the long term, it will usually take them an *extremely* long time to find someone who really fits their definition of a mate. Aquarius can make them try out various partners before settling down and the reverse aging of Capricorn can make them wander when they reach their forties or fifties if their family life is not satisfactory.

Their desire for status and extreme hardwork can make them loners. They may become too engrossed in their work to even think of anything else. They also tend to worry a lot. They will spend a lot of time thinking of what-if scenarios and can depress themselves with their extremely critical evaluations. They require a loving family to keep them involved. The good thing is that Aquarius will generally step in before Virgo and Capricorn make them truly forlorn, and makes them think of new ways to tackle their problems.

They have the unique facility to envisage the future. The Aquarian ability foresee decades ahead, the Capricornian fundamentals entrenched in deep practicality and the Virgo's ability to separate the wheat from the chaff, gives them the power to see future with clarity. They are prepared; they are never surprised.

Virgo–Capricorn–Aquarius – Preity Zinta
'No matter what, I take the time to work out every single day.'[310]

'You work hard; give 100 per cent; there are no shortcuts to success.'[311]

Priety was reminded of the Bharat Shah case. She received a bravery award for it and was amiably called 'the only man in Bollywood' as most witnesses had turned hostile.

'I want to do something substantial. There are lots of young mothers who can be made aware about hygiene, HIV, etc. My biggest concern is female infanticide.'[312]

Priety Zinta has the focus and industriousness of Virgo and Capricorn, along with the sparkle, fearlessness, humanitarianism and futuristic views of an Aquarius to make her an interesting VirCapAqua.

Love and Marriage for Him
He is a provider. This man dreams of making it big and works relentlessly towards his dreams. It is great if you are equally interested in his dream and do not discourage him from working. The pursuit of his ambitions does not make him forget his family, though.

He is not very sociable. With this guy, there are rarely any surprises in store. He is quite predictable, too. He wants his food done in a specific way and served at exact times, and he is particular about his clothes. Routine and discipline guide his life.

The only thing wanting in this perfect partner is emotional sensitivity. He may know what you are feeling, and why you are feeling so, but cannot be emotionally there for you. Of course, he is always there to nurse, protect and care.

---

[310] *People*, March 26, 2010
[311] http://edition.cnn.com/2005/WORLD/asiapcf/01/11/talkasia.zinta.script/
[312] http://articles.timesofindia.indiatimes.com/2007-10-18/news-interviews/27970598_1_bravery-award-bharat-shah-case-new-face

He likes defining the roles for everyone in the house. He performs his duties well and expects you to do the same.

As a father, he is in his element. You can expect him to care for and protect his children. He is responsible but also fun loving. He deals with them with ease and comfort. He likes nothing better than spending time with them and teaches them the values of hard work and ambition.

Love and Marriage for Her

She is a fantastic homemaker, though her abilities and ambition do not stop at that. This lady has it in her to be the ideal daughter-in-law and the perfect working woman as well. Do not stop her from achieving her dreams.

She is very lady-like in public. She never washes her dirty linen in front of others. She does not like to put her social status in jeopardy. Social respectability is very important to her; never make her look ridiculous in public.

She works very hard to ensure that her home is perfect. There is not a lazy bone in her and she does not stop till she creates the perfect setting for her life. You can safely leave your bank accounts in her care for she is careful in spending.

She worries a lot, too. She is rarely completely satisfied with her work and always drives herself hard. This can burn her out, if you do not see the symptoms early enough to take care of them. Be kind to her and do not expect a lot from her. The thing that hurts her deeply is if things go wrong with family and relationships. She values the entire family structure and finds it hard when it breaks down. She may find it difficult to express her love, though she does show it through her caring, but not smothering, ways. Her detachment may be annoying at times but she is loving, deep inside. She can also cut off all ties and walk off if things don't work out. She doesn't cry over spilt milk – she moves on, after shedding a few tears.

As a mother, she is rarely flustered. She knows how to deal with her children. She is loving, caring and protective, without being overly emotional. She thinks, dreams and works tirelessly for them.

At the Workplace

If you get VirCapAquas to work for you, grab them with both hands and do not let them go. Give them opportunities to prove themselves and move forward. They are the most hard-working, stable, intelligent workers you can ever get. The only thing is that they soon do your work better than you and outpace you! Be their mentor and they remain grateful to you always.

They are ready to wait and do not expect things on a silver platter. Their diligence and extreme clarity of vision make them logical. They always have practical solutions and are never demoralised by problems.

They can be anything from wildlife conservationists, like Steve Irwin, to actors, to business tycoons. They are always ready to learn, expand and develop their world-view in order to gain social respectability and tons of money. They make fantastic, resourceful bosses. They are visionaries with many back-up plans to get their futuristic ventures on track.

Double Earth and Air make VirCapAquas extremely stable and dependable with a humanitarian and rebellious touch and a wit that will take people with surprise.

Famous VirCapAqua Personalities
Preity Zinta, Mary Kom, Steve Irwin, Praful Patel, Azhar Mahmood, Parimarjan Negi.

170. VIRGO–AQUARIUS–PISCES

The analytical Virgo joins hands with the unconventionally intelligent Aquarius and the deeply mysterious Pisces in VirgAquaPisces. Their thought processes are deeply analytical and extremely original. They painstakingly think through every new idea to come up with well-thought-out plans. They come up with logical out-of-the-box ideas.

Aquarius and Pisces combine to make them extremely futuristic in their thoughts. They do not spend time going over their past. During every challenge, they look towards the future and envision a better time. Their focus on the future also makes them plan for it.

The Aquarian madness and Piscean creativity make them truly original. However, they are systematically different, thanks to Virgo. They are very idealistic, humanitarian and compassionate. The extremely rigid and puritanical views of Virgo give way to more flexible thinking. They feel for everybody around them, even strangers. They are extremely giving as well. They have the Piscean empathy and deep sensitivity, with the Virgo rectitude and the Aquarian humanitarianism.

There is a hard-working streak in them. VirgAquaPisces guys don't desire glory or money: they work for their own satisfaction. A job, well done, means more than money or fame to them. However, torn between a disciplined and a casual approach to their work, they try and bring routine and discipline to a few things in their life and are blasé about others.

They are fun loving and can think of the wackiest pranks and tell the most hilarious jokes with a straight face. There isn't a mean bone in them. In fact, they can be accused of being too good to be true. They like to travel and always have a bag packed and ready.

VirAquaPisces are very intelligent. They are very good at understanding complex facts and have an innate curiosity about life and its mysteries. Virgo's clarity of thought and eye for detail combine beautifully with Aquarius's amazing genius and Pisces's intuitive understanding of the world.

The Aquarian clumsiness in love and the Virgo self-sacrificing, idealistic nature make it very difficult for them to settle down easily. The Piscean craving for a soul mate may get diluted with the Aquarian and Virgo desire to put work before love. Virgo and Aquarius, if given a choice, would live a loner's life for as long as they can. While Aquarius and Pisces finds it difficult to be tied up to one person for their entire life, Virgo fears the responsibilities and duties that accompany marriage and similar commitments. Besides, VirAquaPisces find it very hard to be confident in love and always think that their mate will find someone better.

This lack of confidence will also be apparent in other spheres of their life. Although they think unconventionally, they are never too aggressive or focused about their dreams. The Piscean self-sacrificing nature and the Virgo desire to do their duty make them silent performers who shy away from the limelight. Plus, it takes them time to get over the fears and phobias of Pisces. Both Pisces and Virgo disparage their dreams, which can pull VirAquaPisces down. The Piscean self-destructive streak can make them think negatively in times of crisis and they need people who enhance their belief in themselves.

The Virgo habit of criticising makes them very good at finding faults in others and themselves. When they get angry, they keep on nagging and criticising while erupting once in a while. Do not worry; these moods are rare.

The Aquarius in them thinks of the most shockingly unconventional ideas and path-breaking innovations. The conscientious and perfectionist Virgo analyses those thoughts accurately and creates a perfect plan to execute those ideas. But the Pisces in them fears that nothing can materialise as the world doesn't think in the same eccentric fashion as they do. This is their constant inner struggle: to live through a mundane boring life or be a pioneering torch-bearer.

Virgo–Aquarius–Pisces – Akshaye Khanna
'Even today I am hugely lacking in self-confidence.'[313]

'I love being low-profile. I don't like to be in the press all the time.'[314]

'I find it very difficult staying awake after 11:00. None of the parties start before 10:30 and it doesn't suit my body cycle.'

'I am not an interesting person. There are certain actors who make boring interviews and I am one of them.'

'I am only 36. I would get married around 44–45. I enjoy being single. I can spend two weeks all on my own.'[315]

Akshaye Khanna is a reclusive actor despite the awards he has won. He has the diffidence and sensitivity of a VirAquaPisces.

Love and Marriage for Him
It takes him time to realise that you are the one. Do not give up, for he is really worth the wait. Aggression or dominance are not part of his makeup. He is your friend; you can travel to your heart's content and spend hours talking to him. He has spent a lot of time mulling whether it is really worth living with all the idiosyncrasies of another person, besides his own. Make it worthwhile for him. The attention he gives to his duties, as a husband and father, may pleasantly surprise you.

He lets you handle all his plans, but though he is mild, he will not allow himself to be controlled or ruled.

He can get extremely engrossed in his profession at times. Do not expect him to be a hands-on householder. He needs space in the relationship. It may get on your nerves, when you know that he knows you in and out, but still remains detached. Also, there is some part of him which he will share with no one, even you. You need to be independent and cheerful. Be the more responsible one and do not cling on to him.

Fill him with optimism. He spends a lot of time thinking and analysing his work and rarely feels confident about himself. He can be analytical about everything. This guy will rarely shout but he occasionally needs to get rid of the stress and tension, and that's the only way he knows how to.

---

[313] http://www.webindia123.com/movie/interview/in120406.htm
[314] http://movie.webindia123.com/movie/interview/2010/october/AkshayeKhanna.htm?cat_id=2
[315] http://articles.timesofindia.indiatimes.com/2011-12-26/news-interviews/30558240_1_akshaye-khanna-salman-release

As a father, he is definitely fun. He enjoys his children and becomes their friend. Despite his fun ways, he insists on a good education for them. He invests for their future.

Love and Marriage for Her
She is creative and exciting. She sees herself as your friend rather than wife. Do not expect this unconventional woman to spend time in household tasks, though she may surprise you with her penchant for cleanliness. You need to be the more stable one. But don't ever think that you can drown her wild ways with your stodgy thoughts. Her unconventionality is her charm. She likes doing lots of different things. Travel attracts her and she likes immersing herself in new cultures and thoughts. She easily picks up languages and has a charming smile.

She has taken a long time to say yes to you and that should make you realise her need for freedom despite her loving ways. Do not try and cage her mind or put her on the straight and narrow path. This lady will have her own ideas and myriad interests and hobbies to give her the challenge she enjoys.

She can be very sensitive at times and wilts in the face of criticism, but do not expect her to show her despair. She also needs a lot of space in the relationship and does not cling to you. She can be a nag at times and finds it hard to stop criticising.

She may not be able to control money but plans well for the future. She knows how to invest wisely while you take care of the budgeting.

As a mother, she surprises you with her care. She knows how to look after her children and is very good at nursing them, despite her initial doubts of her abilities as a mother. She is a fun mother too. Her children always share their secrets with her. She also insists on good education and wants them to have curious, open minds.

At the Workplace
Creative and analytical, VirAquaPisces do not fit into regular nine-to-five jobs. They want change and get bored with the status quo. Their intelligent minds help them excel as researchers and scientists. They prefer spending time thinking and coming up with absolutely different but logical ideas. They can also make a mark for themselves in creative fields. Whatever they do, they go into the details and bring out every nuance.

They may take time to know what they want. They learn from experience, and prefer learning rather than being know-it-alls. Money and status do not excite them as much as the idea of doing something different and worthwhile. You have to make them believe in themselves, as despite their apparent talents, they constantly feel a lack of something. They are their worst critics, so you need to put in the positive thoughts to push them forward.

As bosses, they are creative and forward thinking and somehow manage to bring in discipline and orderliness despite their erratically intelligent brainwaves.

Earth, Air and Water combine in this unconventional and thinking combination. VirAquaPisces can create radically different realities out of farfetched ideas but will need help in pushing themselves forward.

Famous VirAquaPisces Personalities
Akshaye Khanna, Jill Abramson, Kamala Das, Sandeep Singh, Arjun Atwal, Alexander Graham Bell, Fergie, Parthiv Patel, Sandhya Mridul, Nikolai Gogol, Simone Signoret, Brooklyn Beckham.

171. LIBRA–SCORPIO–SAGITTARIUS

Venus, the planet of grace and beauty, meets Pluto, the ruthless god of the underworld, and Jupiter, the extremely knowledgeable. All the three add to the might of this combination. LibScorpSags are full of grace, intelligence and deep magnetism. This intelligent combination of Air, Water and Fire has the Libran longing for love and companionship, coupled with Scorpio's passion and Sagittarian's love for adventure.

LibScorpSags crackle with charm, vitality, intelligence and energy wherever they go. They bring the house down with their wisecracks, witty one-liners and throaty Sagittarian laughter. LibScorpSags will be chatterboxes, full of wise ideas and wild schemes. Libra endows them with the skills of communication and diplomacy. They talk intelligently on extremely diverse topics. You are never bored in their company. They can actually argue with themselves.

Scorpio's passion ensures that LibScorpSags are intense and focused about whatever they do. They definitely want to win and are ambitious enough to want a bigger stage for their deeds. LibScorpSags need space to shine and are always ready for applause.

They are beautifully artistic. The Libran gift of music and creativity can combine with the overwhelming enthralling force of Scorpio and the extraordinary energy of Sagittarius to produce a spellbinding performance. They are also naturals in sports. They know how to play by the rules and are elegant, while also bringing in the raw power of Scorpio and ruthless energy of Sagittarius.

They are sure to have a rebellious streak in them. They are ready for life and like to live it in top gear. They feel that every emotion needs to be felt and every experience needs to be explored before one rests in the grave. Travel and adventure are high on their list. The Scorpio tendency of experimenting on myriad subjects and their lack of fear can sometimes land them in trouble. But they are good at talking their way out of it.

LibScorpSags tend to confuse love and friendship. Both Libra and Sagittarius are signs that find it difficult to differentiate between the two. The Libran in them loves being in love and makes them believe that every friendship is the love they were looking for. Fortunately, their Scorpio ability to read other people's minds helps them eventually understand the relationship and decide what they want. But once they find their love, they will be quite content.

Interestingly, they are highly spiritual. The Scorpio in them senses a power above all, and Sagittarius is a natural believer. They believe there is a silver lining to every cloud. They have the immense positivity and self-belief of Sagittarius, emotional control and even aggression of Scorpio and Libra's sense of balance, to overcome any turbulence in life.

They are careful about investing their money, but are unable to hold on to cash for long. They just love spending on accessories and are impulsive shoppers.

The Libran tactfulness neutralises the Sagittarian tactless speech, especially for outsiders. Their families and friends may witness the tactless side at times. When they are hurt, all the tactfulness vanishes; they can yell and shout, and give vent to their spleen. No one can destroy you verbally like them. But this is the safe variety of LibScorpSag. If you have hurt them and they just give you a long, hard look and don't say anything, then you really need to be worried.

The secretive nature of Scorpio ensures that they rarely show their true nature to the world. LibScorpSags can be hurting inside but their indomitable will and strength make them smile graciously. It is not only difficult for them to accept defeat but also painful to show it. Don't expect LibScorpSags to look dejected when they lose – the British stiff upper lip with a charming smile will be their look. They can smile and hide their anger too. Be very wary if you have hurt them for they will get back at you.

The Libran indecisiveness and paying too much attention to others' development while ignoring their own, can be their bane. Their constant Sagittarian need for change for the sake of change and the Scorpio's deep purple passions can be the pitfalls that they need to avoid, to soar as the highly intelligent and evolved souls that they are destined to be.

Libra–Scorpio–Sagittarius – Aishwarya Rai Bachchan
Abhishek Bachchan: 'There is something nice about her which is a bit of a contradiction; she is like the epitome of grace, she is very feminine; she is a lady and she gets treated like that, but at heart she is like one of the guys. She just likes to get in there and have fun.'[316]

The magical thing about Aishwarya is her silky smooth finesse and impeccable good manners. People vouch for her perfectionism and professionalism. She gives her all to whatever she undertakes – marriage and movies – strictly in that order.[317]

Aishwarya has the Scorpion depth and Sagittarian tomboyishness beneath her feminine charm and Libran grace, and achieves balance in life with seeming effortlessness.

Love and Marriage for Him
Charming, persuasive and very passionate, he is a class apart. This man loves talking. He often gives a fair hearing to your opinions too. He loves a good argument but does not wash dirty linen in public. He is your best friend who is always ready for a bit of banter. His talk may be frivolous but his feelings are deep. Understand his deep love for you. He expects more understanding from you than others and you must not fail him there.

He competes with you while shopping. This guy likes looking good and is truly metrosexual in his choice of accessories. He loves adventure and travel too, and may want you around when he jumps off a cliff in a glider. Be ready for lots of love, companionship and excitement when you are with him. Independence in a woman attracts him. He wants an unconventional girl.

---

[316] http://www.youtube.com/watch?v=Bh8xZtkcTv4
[317] *Hello!* April 2010

His work is his passion. He is very focused about his career and that is one thing that he rarely jokes about. He needs to be left alone for a while when he plans his big projects.

As a father, he is loads of fun and listens to his children empathatically. He loves to play and enjoy time with his kids but also wants to be respected by them. There is always a thin line that they are not allowed to cross.

Love and Marriage for Her
She has the magnetic personality of a Scorpio and knows how to make heads turn wherever she goes. It is not just her expensive taste in clothes that gets her all the attention, but also her charming smile. She can use this smile to get things done.

As a partner, she is just what you need if you love adventure and excitement. This girl wants more than the security of your presence. She is never content with just family, no matter how much she loves them. Her heart also yearns for adventure and travel. Freedom and companionship are very important to her. You have to talk to her for she does not like long periods of silence.

Her idea of being a good wife does not include the skills of dusting and cooking alone. If you expect her to be bound to household chores, think again. It was her brilliant mind and fun loving nature that attracted you. So, why expect her to be something she is not? She will be very good at using her wiles and use her best smile to get her work done. So beware when she smiles a lot! But take care – you will miss her hearty laughter when she is sighing, brooding and sulking after you have hurt her.

Her spending ability is quite high. She loves indulging herself in clothes and accessories. It is the one thing that she really cannot control! She loves being with people and enjoys the company of her loved ones. However, she needs her space at times. Her work is her passion and she strives to be the leader in whatever she does.

As a mother, she is caring and nurturing and trains her children to be independent. She enjoys their childhood and expects them to be good at what they do. She never burdens them with her choices.

At the Workplace
Libra is a cardinal sign and that ensures that LibScorpSags pursue their ambition to lead. They get their way through with sheer focus, exceptional communication skills and passion. Of course, do not discount their charm. They love to showcase their skills and desire a large canvas and stage. Never be stingy with them in praise or money.

They are able to ideate and work hard to achieve their aims. From creative fields to the corporate ladder, nothing is hard for them. They do not like jobs that are bound by routine and relax for days after hectic bouts of work. They need jobs that satisfy them intellectually.

As bosses, they are great motivators and passionate speakers. They keep their lines of communication clearly open, they are very fair, honest and democratic.

But don't take their fun-loving and gregarious nature as permission for being too friendly.

Air, Water and Fire meet in this highly excitable and optimistic combination. LibScorpSags will be opinionated yet fair, erudite yet fun loving and extremely charming.

Famous LibScorpSag Personalities
Aishwarya Rai, Steven Spielberg, Kelly Brook, Jude Law, Bryan Adams, Andrew Flintoff, Mike Denness, J. Paul Getty, Billy Graham, Ashutosh Rana, Sagarika Ghose, William Herschel, G.K. Vasan, Burt Lancaster, Peter Forrest, Aditya Roy Kapur.

172. LIBRA–SCORPIO–CAPRICORN

Venus, the planet of beauty and grace, meets Pluto, the ruthless god of the underworld, and the old, wise and taciturn Saturn to form LibScorpCaps. Beauty, passion and ambition fuel them to great heights. LibScorpCaps are winners. It is very hard to put them down.

Never underestimate them. When you meet them, you wouldn't guess the deep intensity and burning ambitions of these people. Scorpios love masking their inner core and the Goat doesn't want to be too obvious that it wants to be number one. Both these strong, deep zodiac signs hide their intensity behind the chattering Libra. They have a magnetic quality about them with their fluent communication skills, intense looks and instinctive knowledge of people.

Well-read and suave, they are never at a loss for words. No matter where they come from, they exude charm and elegance. The delicious Libran smile is enough to make half their problems, if any, disappear. You naturally sway to their mesmerising speech and give way to this vital force. They understand the power they have on you and use it to maximum effect. Respectful to elders and the successful, they look up to them for guidance. They prefer tried and tested routes.

They are designed for success. They have Capricorn's extraordinary work ethic, Scorpio's burning ambition and appetite for extreme hard work, and top it up with an ability to work under intense pressure with a disarming Libran smile. They are cool and calculative. Number two is boring, being the number one in their chosen field is their ultimate dream. They work tirelessly to reach that goal. No distractions, no temptations can stop them, and they will make any sacrifice and use any means to get there. They want to leave behind a huge legacy for their family.

They never give way to anger or display displeasure when they face a challenge. Rather, they think it through and can even submerge their egos for greater gains. They are rarely unruly or aggressive for they believe that the best way to win is without antagonising anyone. Family is extremely important. They focus on two things – family and career. However, they do not like to take their work home. Family time is sacred to them.

They are so focused on their careers that they may find it difficult to find time for love. But the Libran in them longs for love and the Scorpio in them can identify their soul mates at first glance. Then they can quickly settle into matrimony and go on to continue to pursue their goals. The Capricorn reverse-aging syndrome will also make its presence felt in their lives. LibScorpCaps need partners who not only love them but also keep them interested, for these people can have a roving eye once they hit their forties.

Money is very important. They do not mind spending but only on things that increase their worth. They want to make lots of money. These guys know how to make a success of any venture with their glib talk, endless energy and organising abilities.

Manipulations are not beyond them. Capricorns can use every method in the book to get where they want to reach. They can invent a few of their own too.

They are masters in manipulating environments and people to suit their needs. Scorpio's baser emotions like jealousy, hatred and envy spur them further and help them plan better. They are ruthless and self-centred and don't mind if a pawn is sacrificed enroute to their victory.

The Scorpio in them does not take easily to criticism. They can act cool while fuming inside, for they prefer winning the race rather than proving their point. But remember they are still one-third a Scorpio; do not think you can get away after doing them a wrong. They can get back at you in a smart and almost undetectable manner. They don't make enemies out of powerful people. In fact, they strive to get into the good books of successful and powerful people. They are grateful to people who helped them along and repay them in a big way.

They can suffer dark Capricorn moods and be melancholic. They suffer deep insecurities, sulk and brood alone, especially when things go wrong, and can imagine the worst. They probably work doubly hard to reach an unassailable position to ensure that those nightmares don't haunt them again.

Libra–Scorpio–Capricorn – Shah Rukh Khan
'If we are competing for a film I'd like to come first. I am not running a race to come second.'[318]

'Oh yes, I was very possessive [as a boyfriend].'[319]

'I really get scared sometimes that I'll lose all that I've got by next morning.'[320]

'I really lose it if anyone messes around with my family'

'Work is oxygen. Work for me is the life-giving force.'[321]

Shah Rukh Khan expresses himself brilliantly with Libran charm. The passionate, possessive and driven Scorpio meets the ambitious, materialistic, family-oriented and some times pessimistic Capricorn in him.

Love and Marriage for Him
He is a considerate and charming husband. Loyal and true, he keeps his commitment to you. The only thing he wants from you is absolute love. Do not hurt his feelings. He makes you laugh with his funny stories and charms you with his philosophising streak. He is ready to talk for hours and is always there to listen to you.

He loves being ensconced in a family atmosphere and enjoys spending time with you. He wants you to do the same. This guy is quite happy to see you work as long as the family does not suffer. He wants his rooms done up in style and hates clutter.

The best part is that he is so good at reading people that he knows instantly how to court you. If you need attention and flowers, they are yours, and to get your parents to approve he convinces them of his sincerity.

His career is his second love, and though he never brings his work home, you have to allow his passion for work take the front seat at times. Do not cling to him. He adores a strong independent woman who can fight a few battles on her own.

---

[318] *Cine Blitz*, March 2007
[319] *Hello!* August 2011
[320] 'Shahrukh Getting Emotional... : An Interview', Courtesy *Stardust magazine* (http://www.pyara.com/shahrukh/article7.htm)
[321] *DNA*, After Hrs, 11 August 2013

To his children, he is a fun-loving father figure. He loves to spend time with them and indulges them. He insists on a basic code of conduct and demands respect. He wants to create an empire for them to carry forward. They give him stronger reasons to aim for success.

Love and Marriage for Her
Bubbly, with an infectious smile, she can talk and laugh for hours. This girl wants a man who listens to her for she has many things to discuss and many thoughts to share. She loves arguing and putting forth a different point of view just to hear yours.

Her lovely smile hides a mind of her own. She is an independent and strong woman. She never remains in obscurity and her talents are too good to remain unused for long. She can become your partner if you are in business or politics for she knows how to talk and delegate. You have to love her ardently and say it quite often. She wants to be treated with the same romantic passion that you used to woo her.

She loves her family and makes it the centre-point of her life. She does not mind giving up her career for it, but if you lack ambition, then let her move around on her own for nothing stifles her more than a life without aim or purpose. She wants status and respect in society. She does an extraordinary balancing act and does justice to all things that matter in her life – her mate, family and career.

As a mother, she is everything children need – loving, firm and understanding. She becomes their friend and is so open to new ideas and so willing to learn new things that she is never too shocked by anything they say or do. Yet, despite that knack of knowing everything, she insists on certain values and wants them to be ambitious and curious.

At the Workplace
LibScorpCaps have an amazing capacity for organising and delegating. They are good at reading people and their decisions regarding them are rarely wrong. Their diligence, perseverance, captivating charm and zeal make them successful.

Expressive and articulate, they communicate their ideas beautifully and are great at convincing others of their plans. Tactful and diplomatic, they hide their passions and focus behind a cool demeanour. They are well groomed and elegant and know how to charm with reason and logic.

No matter how bad the fight, they usually emerge the winners. Their basic desire is to lead, be it anywhere. Even if they are stuck in a lowly position (they cannot be there long though), they lead. Their need for money and status drives them to achieve stupendous success. They cannot rest and once they are through with a goal, find another one. As bosses, they are great motivators, caring and fatherly figures and know everything about each and every employee.

Air, Water and Earth meet in this extremely charming combination. LibScorpCaps will be ambitious but family-oriented, creative yet realistic, and reverberate with passion and energy.

Famous LibScorpCap Personalities
Shah Rukh Khan, Ryan Giggs, Kushal Pal Singh, Andrew Carnegie, Philipp Lahm, Gemini Ganesan, V. Shantaram, Gail Devers, Dara Singh, Padmini Kolhapure, Vivian Leigh, Calista Flockhart, Thomas Cook, Giselli Monteiro, Puneet Issar.

173. LIBRA–SCORPIO–AQUARIUS

Venus, the planet of grace and beauty, rules Libra. To this light, airy, bright and communicative sign are added the intensity and passion of Pluto, the powerful and secretive lord of the underworld, and the eccentric charm and inventive streak of Uranus. They are fun loving and bright. However, do not forget the Scorpio: it adds depth to their airy minds.

People born in this combination are usually very evolved and respond to high ideals; they like to think new revolutionary thoughts and will never be satisfied treading a well-trodden path. Whatever they do, expect to be surprised. With the Scorpio's passion and focus, LibScorpAquas follow wild ideas and make them more plausible.

Their Libran side makes them get along well with people. The communication skills of Libra and the highly intelligent thought processes of Aquarius make them intelligent and fun companions. They can communicate their thoughts and opinions with a dose of humour. They have lots of friends, and know how to enjoy themselves.

They are good at reading people. They love to know what makes them tick but are not prudish and rarely judgemental once they know the details. Despite their gregarious and friendly nature, it is very hard to fool or deceive them. Remember the Scorpio sting!

Fashion is tricky with them, for though they have the Libran knack of dressing well, they do it with the Aquarian wackiness at times. So do not be surprised if you see formal suits coordinated with funky haircuts.

The Pluto–Uranus combination of Scorpio and Aquarius makes them volatile. These guys can get angry at the drop of a hat, especially if you question their ideas and goals. This angry temperament, with the Scorpio vengefulness, is the most negative side of this fun-loving combination.

The Libran in them loves being in love. They are fun-loving, intelligent and magnetic creatures, and attract a lot of friends – a potential hazard. They can get confused between love and friendship and can't do without either. The Aquarian in them needs to find out what makes their partner tick and they love learning more about their loves and decoding them. Once they have done that, they simply lose interest. They move on to new loves, till they find the one who shares their passions and dreams.

Their behaviour in love also depends on which stage in life you met them. The Scorpio in them needs a passion and their Aquarius side motivates them to try out something new. So if you meet them before they realise their passions, they can fall in love and woo you in wildly romantic ways. They will make you the centre of their universe with Libran love and Scorpio passion. Love is a 'wow' experience with them – till they win the object of their passion. The wow can turn to woe if you expect that to carry on forever – they love you but reserve the fireworks for the next new idea. Relax and tell yourself that soon it will pass, for their Libran side always seeks a balance between home and work – but it will be a struggle.

They constantly need to be passionately involved in innovative thoughts, and bring extreme focus to their out-of-the-world ideas. Scorpios and Aquarians share a common passion – unravelling mysteries! Expect these creatures to pull something out of the thin air, a fantastic, wacky idea: something that always existed, unknown, and they deciphered it for you. They may also make a new-age invention that will stir minds and break myths and old ideas.

The Libra in them helps them find a sense of balance or they can lose themselves in their ideas with no time for the world. Libra adds its flair for analytical thought to LibScorpAqua, so their thinking is both innovative and tested. Of course, LibScorpAquas can also go the other way and just tangle themselves in over-analysis. But usually their overriding passions and total focus will make them decide one way or another. Sounds confusing? Well, that's the way they are, but allow them the benefit of doubt, as sooner or later they will do something worthwhile – maybe wacky, but magical.

Libra–Scorpio–Aquarius – Chanda Kochhar

'I have always had a passion to consistently excel in everything I do. I believe that the right balance of vision, strategic intent, hard work and willingness to manage change is necessary in the pursuit of excellence...Keep learning and keep growing – never think that you have learnt all there is to know. Never be afraid of challenges or of stepping into the unknown – those will be your biggest learning experiences and stepping stones to success.'[322]

Chanda Kochhar, always elegant like a Libran, known for the passion she brings to her work, has futuristic views and the determination to succeed in a male-dominated sector, without losing her feminine grace.

Love and Marriage for Him

As a partner, you must expect him to mellow down. He does not get married soon but when he does, it means that he has his goal and wife and needs no other distraction! The Scorpio passion, Libran need for love and the Aquarian need for change all meet if he finds an objective in his life and a wife to share it with. Of course, you really have to understand his ideals. He understands you, realises your needs and yet becomes distant at times – he needs space and may, therefore, seem distracted and aloof. Do not take it to heart for he is back soon. Just do not cling and crib.

Despite his obvious distraction, his deep Scorpio sensitivity understands his family's needs and he will come back from 'outer space' to take his rightful place in the family. He is loyal too. However, it is very important he should realise what he wants to do and that you support him fully and make his ambition yours too.

He is a wonderful but forgetful father who loves to have fun with his children. When he is around, he is totally hands-on and fun loving. With his wild imagination and creativity, he is able to talk to them at their level and they love his happy charm. Of course, he cannot be messed around with. The temper can flare up often, which keeps them in line.

---

[322] *Femina*, June 29, 2011

Love and Marriage for Her
She is a lovely companion. This lady stands out from the rest due to her intelligent conversation. She is never at a loss for words or dreams. You need to let her be free. She has dreams beyond her home and kids.

She has a list of varied friends. You find company presidents, old-age-home retirees and funky teenagers in them. She understands each one perfectly well, even if she does not share their views.

She loves with a passion and devotion that seem at odds with her happy-go-lucky style, but contradictions are what she is about. She is committed and stable though she may seem detached at times. Let her be at such times, for she needs a breath of fresh air and starts feeling claustrophobic if held too close for long.

She may not be the most diligent housewife but makes up with her abundant charm and fabulous smile. Sometimes, this lady can be quite clumsy (because of Aquarius), and that reduces the effect of the Libran grace and Scorpio composure.

As a mother, she is fun loving and caring and tempers it with quiet control. She knows just what her children need and makes them independent and curious thinkers. She knows the value of letting them free at times. She is their friend yet has the final word in their main decisions. A perfect mother, friend and guide!

At the Workplace
They may take a while to settle down in a career. The Aquarian in them is enticed by a hundred different ideas, Libra weighs the pros and cons of all the options before Scorpio zooms on one thing, which later becomes their passion. Till they find their goals and fix their gaze on them, they are not able to utilise the immense capabilities within themselves. Then you can expect some magic with their work – and yes, it may happen anytime!

They can do anything except routine jobs. They need to be excited about new ideas, quirky thoughts and different ways of doing things to be really motivated to perform. From science to advertising, they can try their hand at anything as long as they are passionate about it. It is great if their job involves communicating new ideas for they are totally at ease with expressing views and opinions in an interactive manner.

A typical LibScorpAqua appears to be a confused person to start with. But with their farsighted vision, they see things that you cannot. They may see through a project or an idea's worth even before it is fully conceived.

They are motivated more by their jobs than by money or glory. Of course, money is important, but more than that, they are happy if they feel they are making a worthy contribution. They can lead, too, but are subtle in their leadership rather than aggressive. Once they make up their minds, it is hard to dissuade them.

Double Air and Water give this combination airy dreams and deep thoughts, high ideals and a passionate zeal to achieve. LibScorpAquas need to be intensely involved in ideas to give their best to the world.

Famous LibScorpAqua Personalities
Chanda Kochhar, Maradona, Roman Abramovich, Marie Curie, Gianni Versace, Garrincha, Laura Bush, Alexander Alekhine, Milind Soman, Troy Aikman, Ezio Vendrame, Dougie Payne.

174. LIBRA–SCORPIO–PISCES

Venus, the planet of beauty, grace and luxury, combines forces with Pluto, the dark lord of the underworld, and Neptune, the deeply mysterious lord of the seas, to form LibScorPisces. They have ambition, but it is understated. You only see glimpses of the Scorpio intensity. Libra is a cardinal sign but it likes to lead with an emphasis on co-operation rather than aggression.

They love talking and enjoy expressing their thoughts. Their smiles speak a thousand words. The humour and wit of Libra complement the friendly nature of Pisces and add to their charm as delightful friends and companions.

They find it easy to put themselves in someone else's shoes and think from their perspective. This makes them very understanding people who have very few fixed opinions. They are not judgemental or opinionated and give everyone a fair chance. With Libra's gift of the gab, they argue passionately when they feel they are right.

LibScorPisces are highly creative. Both Libra and Pisces abound in creative abilities while Scorpio adds fervour to their artistic dreams. No one can copy others like a Pisces. Pisceans also have a fabulous sense of humour. Librans are very good at playing with words and have exceptional communication skills. When a LibScorPisces puts up a beautiful act on stage with the sensitivity of the Pisces, the eloquence of the Libra and passion of the Scorpio, you know you have witnessed something extraordinary.

Food is their weakness. They love good food and are very open to trying new tastes and cuisines. Travel is high on their agenda. They love meeting different people and experiencing different cultures. They want the joy of discovering new places and use travel to relax and rejuvenate. They like travelling with people they love. They do not enjoy solitary trips. Luxury definitely appeals to them. LibScorPisces enjoy massages and lying in super-soft beds.

They are extremely loyal in their affections, and expect the same level of commitment from others. They rarely lose their temper. They do not shout or scream; instead, they try and understand the reasons behind each wrong act. The revenge syndrome of Scorpio is reduced in them and they prefer to move away rather than hit back. But do not forget that they have the ability to seek out their enemies if they are deeply wounded, albeit discreetly. If not physically, they will finish you off mentally, jabbing you where it hurts most, with their sharp verbal missiles.

Love finds them at their emotional best and worst. All three signs go deeply for love – Libra loves to be in love, Scorpio is intensely loyal and passionate, while Pisces is inherently romantic and self-sacrificing in love. Their love is of the highest order and involves complete surrender. They want a lot of understanding and sensitivity from their beloved and might ask for more than what is humanly possible. Their love can make or break them.

LibScorPisces are extremely emotional and sensitive. Both Pisces and Scorpio are sensitive. They find it very easy to understand your unspoken thoughts. It is probably a good idea to think only nice things when they are with you. They love analysing people and go over what others had said, time and again, especially when they are unhappy.

When Scorpio combines with Pisces, the person can be either very good or very bad. Libra, of course, tones down the effect, but the truth is that LibScorPisces alternate between the two. They can have the anger and vengefulness of Scorpio combined with the deception of Pisces, or they can act with the passion of Scorpio beautifully mingled with the deep and forgiving understanding of Pisces.

LibScorPisces can fall into deep melancholy and depressive thoughts. They tend to procrastinate. Their minds can be subject to extreme Libran vacillations and Piscean mood swings, too. The Libran wants to be fair, and the Pisces can be timid, unsure and just doesn't want to face the truth. LibScorPisces need to be pushed and guided towards positivity and prodded at times to get back on track and not lose focus.

They are prone to addictions. Scorpio makes them try out things, and if the Piscean predilection for addiction is also strong in them, they can lose themselves in their obsessive cravings. They can also drown their sorrows in food and like to nibble when they are upset. They can be addicted to sex or love and even use the 'high' derived from these distractions to counter the harsh realities of life. Usually, they manage to overcome these with the strong determination of Scorpio.

Spirituality has a definite place in their lives and they believe in a higher force that guides and looks over them. They try to find their own concept of God and do not believe in a religious dogma till it has passed their analytical and inquisitive questions. They also easily understand alternative and occult practices like reiki, meditation, chakra cleansing, etc.

Libra–Scorpio–Pisces – Meg Ryan

Meg Ryan has the lovely Libran smile that just lights up her face. She has been called America's sweetheart for she personifies a charming sweetness. Her sweetness and charm hide her Scorpio passion. On herself:

'I do feel that I've had to fight to be taken seriously, and not just in my career but in general.'[323]

In 2006 Meg adopted a baby from China. On motherhood:

'Motherhood changed me because it is so fundamental, what you're doing for another person.'[324]

Meg Ryan has the light airiness of a Libra-Pisces and the strength of a Scorpio.

Love and Marriage for Him

He fits into a woman's concept of a husband. He is romantic, passionate and extremely caring. He is also a great listener and does not mind chatting till the wee hours of the morning. However, the catch here is that you have to love him as much as he does you. It may be difficult if you are not a deeply sensitive person. You need to understand him as much as he understands you. Do not hurt him for he gets deeply wounded.

---

[323] 'Meg Ryan: A Change of Heart', *Good Housekeeping*, http://www.goodhousekeeping.com/family/celebrity-interviews/meg-ryan-change-apr03_2

[324] http://www.brainyquote.com/quotes/authors/m/meg_ryan.html

This man is your friend. He is not very aggressive or loud and wants you to be the same. You have to take care of the finances: though he wants to save, he is prone to needless expenditure. You should be the one with the saving and investing instinct.

He definitely has a passion in life and appreciates it if you also give him encouragement. You should be his cheerleader and support him when he is dispirited. Also, be very careful of the company he keeps, for he is easily influenced.

He is a very caring father. Fatherhood suits him and he is happy spending time and having fun with his kids. Of course, he wants them to work hard for their goals and encourages them in their passions. He is a very open-minded father who does not force them to do anything against their wishes. He understands their desires and helps them work towards their dreams.

Love and Marriage for Her
She is a charming companion. There is a sweetness about her that dispels your problems. But she needs your help in creating a more stable environment for herself. She is very sensitive; choose her only if you can understand her hopes and fears. An insensitive partner can leave her heartbroken and she eventually gives up on the relationship. You need to be as romantic and loving as she is.

Despite her soft ways, she is individualistic: she is no doormat. She has the most charming smile, which she unhesitatingly uses to get you on her side. You might want to accompany her when she goes shopping or she can buy a whole mall!

Her house is full of beautiful things and she loves surprising you with her cooking, but she hates the routine of chores. New thoughts and ideas occupy her all the time and she has a passion that should be encouraged: she will do great things.

She is a loving mother. Her children are her priority, despite her passion, and she takes good care of them. She knows how to enjoy their childhood and is interested in playing with them. They run to her for everything.

At the Workplace
LibScorPisces are extremely creative people. Artistic fields suit them perfectly. They are also good at thinking and implementing new ideas. They do well in careers that deal with people and their problems and can be good psychiatrists or counsellors. They are great in all the sub-fields of human resource management too, except payroll. They do exceptionally well in all vocations that require creative communication and they even have a flair for more esoteric practices like astrology.

They need encouragement and a push at times to make them achieve their goals. They can be quite lazy, despite their passions, and like to intersperse work with loads of relaxation and family time. Money and glory do not matter to them as much as the need to do something different and defining. They hate routine and excel in work that requires communication and analysis.

They are liberal and articulate bosses who bring passion and energy to work. They portray a tough exterior to overcome their diffidence and keep away people who try to exploit their goodness.

Air and double Water make LibScorPisces an emotional mix. They will be compassionate and helpful and have a passion for love and ideas.

Famous LibScorPisces Personalities
Meg Ryan, Vivek (Tamil movies), Calvin Klein, John Galliano, Linda Evans, Dalip Tahil, Aryan Khan.

175. LIBRA–SAGITTARIUS–CAPRICORN

Venus, the planet of love and luxury, joins the knowledgeable Jupiter and the old man Saturn in LibSagCap. They are very intelligent with the shrewdness of Capricorn and knowledge of Sagittarius. They love arguing their theories and are great at debating and ideating. They are very good at analysing problems and finding logical solutions.

The Libran desire of communicating thoughts and the Sagittarian desire to be the centre of attention make them enjoy talking. They are always full of juicy gossip and interesting comments: sweet talkers with a flair for saying the worst things in the sweetest possible manner. They have the Libran smile, and say the right things to the right people. Though they may be a little clumsy at times and give in to the Sagittarian tendency to put their foot in their mouth, they usually manage to recover their poise just in time.

They are positive people who have a big network of friends and acquaintances. You rarely find them alone. They lose Capricorn's stingy ways and are more giving with their money and time. They want to help their families and friends and are always available to listen to troubles. They love travelling, but in luxury.

They are deeply ambitious. Sagittarius loves the limelight while Capricorn always wants to reach the top. LibSagCaps want applause and their dreams to come true. Libra and Sagittarius make them very vocal about their ambitions, and they mean to be nothing less than a star.

Family is extremely important to LibSagCaps, second only to their careers. The affectionate Libra and the family-conscious Capricorn overcome the freedom-loving ways of Sagittarius. LibSagCaps like being surrounded by their families and are the happiest in their midst. They like going to new places accompanied by their families.

Status is crucial for them: they want people to look up to them. They take extra care to look good in front of others. They have the Libran love for grooming. Their style can be a little unconventional and gaudy due to Sagittarius.

Love is quite important to them and they want a partner who not only loves them but complements them too. They are romantic and love the idea of being with somebody for the rest of their lives, yet their Sagittarian freedom-loving ways always intervene and make them hesitate.

The desire for freedom grows stronger as they age due to the Capricornian reverse-aging syndrome. They become more adventurous after they hit their thirties. Their optimism also increases as they age.

Money is important to them and they want lots of it. They are quite good at throwing it away, though. Of course, they repent later, but are better at earning than saving. Their Capricornian caution makes them think of saving and investing but the luxury-loving ways of Libra and the gambling attitude of Sagittarius make them take big risks. They are attracted to 'get-rich-quick' schemes.

Food is their weakness, and they love good food. The way to their hearts can be through their stomachs. They try out new cuisines and visit unknown restaurants, and can be food critics.

They are quite artistic and creative too. Libra and Capricorn are blessed with creative talents and Sagittarius likes to show them off. They may be excellent singers, fabulous dancers, and good at other art forms, too. They enjoy appreciation and don't mind taking the mike to show off. They are also crusaders of sorts. They believe in equality and hate discrimination. They are vocal about causes and fight against anything that they feel is wrong.

There is no Water sign in this combination and its lack makes them a little insensitive. They do not know how you feel till you tell them, and often, they are too self-absorbed to worry about others. Thankfully, the Libran desire to know more about people makes them listen to you once you tell them your problems.

Anger is not a strong trait in them. They are capable of sarcasm to show their displeasure or may just burst out occasionally, but usually they are ready to argue and sort out differences. They can go through extreme mental vacillations, especially in matters regarding their family and love. They take tough decisions in their career but cannot do the same in personal life. They tend to be melancholic and slip into black moods when they go through the lows of life.

The biggest plus is their love for life and belief in the power above. There is a strange naïveté about them despite their bravado, which helps overcome troubles of life: with their sunny optimism and faith in their own goodness and in the Almighty, they power over their troubles quickly.

Libra–Sagittarius–Capricorn – Silambarasan

'All the films that I have acted so far, I have performed very well…I respect seniors in the industry. I will never on my own quarrel with anybody, but if someone bothers me, I will not keep quiet.'[325]

Interviewer: 'Simbu, your Twitter page reads 'I have said yes to my parents!!! Getting married next year.' Won't you tell us whose the lucky girl is?'

Silambarasan: 'Thank you for the compliment but I'm yet to find the lucky girl. Certainly she has to be very, very pretty because one thing is for sure: I want cute kids.'[326]

Outspoken, creative, talented and a person who never lets modesty suppress his achievements, Silambarasan exhibits the qualities of a LibSagCap.

Love and Marriage for Him

He is always full of plans to reach the top position in his career and, though he likes spending time with his family, he is deeply involved in his work. He wants a partner who can manage the house on her own with a few inputs from him. Emotionally charged women need not apply for he feels caged with them. It is a little confusing to be with him, for though he is very romantic and loving, he wants his space.

This man is full of fun, laughter and jokes but there is also a serious side to him, which is apparent when he is busy at work or worrying about his family. He works very hard for his family's status and is quite conscious of what people think. Don't do things that embarrass him or put him in socially awkward positions.

He loves travelling and meeting new people. Be ready for exciting times with him. He is quite a metrosexual too, and you two can have a great time shopping

---

[325] http://www.indiaglitz.com/channels/tamil/interview/6255.html
[326] http://www.kollytalk.com/interview/simbu-says-love-anthem-not-a-follow-up-to-kolaveri-interview-56532.html

together. Keep your eye on the bank balance though, for he does not think twice before making impulsive purchases. He enjoys parties and is a good host.

If you have a problem with anything, talk it out with him – he will try and sort it out – but don't sit and sulk, for he is not too good with emotions.

As a father, he is extremely loving and caring. He is much better at it when they start responding to him. He loves playing and bantering with them while making sure that they respect him.

Love and Marriage for Her
She is the most positive person you have ever met. She is full of good cheer and laughter. This lady loves talking and is full of anecdotes. She enjoys the outdoors and she is extremely good in the house too, with a knack for making her house a home. Nevertheless, despite her love of home, she is always itching to do something worthwhile and is quite ambitious in her plans.

She can manage both home and career and does a great job at both. Her creative abilities are quite apparent. Appreciate what she does for there are few as talented and vivacious as her. And despite her ambitions it is you who always comes first to her. This girl is romantic to the core: she is incomplete without love. She wants you beside her when she goes bungee jumping or to meditation camps.

You may find it very hard to say no to her. Her smile is hard to ignore. She is an excellent hostess, who is great at planning menus and exciting activities for her guests.

As a mother, she is very good. She loves her children's company and plays with them, but also enforces discipline. They like going to her with their problems for she always tries to help them out, no matter what they have got into.

At the Workplace
LibSagCaps are very ambitious and want to excel in their professions. They work hard, network, and plan for their success. They prefer careers where they get to think, travel and talk. They are excellent communicators. They balance their lives very well by working hard and partying hard as well. They are those employees who work hard during office hours and are popular during Friday events or the office sports tournaments.

They are quite good in creative careers and know how to use their talents well. Money is as important to them as the joy of working and they want both money and enjoyment in their careers. Advertising, media, journalism, public relations, etc. excite them.

The double cardinal signs of Libra and Capricorn ensure that they lead and they do it well. Their positive energy rubs off on people, who are motivated to give their best.

LibSagCaps combine the love for communication, drive to push themselves forward and the stability to plan their life well.

Famous LibSagCap Personalities
Silambarasan, M.K. Alagiri, Andy Roberts, Richard Levi, Narain Karthikeyan, Princess Caroline of Hanover.

176. LIBRA–CAPRICORN–AQUARIUS

From the start, LibCapAquas are impressive. They talk well and look good. Venus for beauty and art, Saturn for a shrewd mind and relentless ambition, and Uranus for innovative thoughts and intelligence make this combination attractive with an underlying intelligence and ambition. The ambition in LibCapAquas is magnified as both Libra and Capricorn are cardinal signs.

They are stylish. The Libran fashion sense, combined with the Aquarian innovative style, makes them stand out in a crowd, though the Capricorn in them makes sure their fashion style is fairly conventional.

They are charmers; Aquarius and Libra are Air signs and bring intelligence and eloquence to a LibCapAqua besides endowing it with wit and a love for speech. Capricorn, the lone Earth element in it, adds a stable outlook and practical nature. One thing you can be sure of is that they always act older than their age. The Capricornian maturity and responsibility are evident in them from a very young age.

LibCapAquas have the beautiful communication skills of Libra, but due to their confluence with the wild and wacky inventive genius of Aquarius, they become unfathomable, aloof and detached at times: they get lost in thoughts of the future. Don't worry; they will be back soon.

LibCapAqua is the culmination of extraordinary creative forces. Venus bestows them with natural abilities for music, dance or any other creative art form. Capricorns are gifted in classical and traditional art forms. Aquarius adds a dash of uniqueness to their entire creative process. These people have wonderful artistic talents and can bring happiness to millions with their work.

Family is always important for LibCapAquas. Capricornians need to have father figures to respect and are always there for their families. This love overcomes the detachment of Aquarius who is generally not interested in maintaining or appreciating relationships. LibCapAquas always find time for their families and are willing to make sacrifices for their happiness.

Capricorn ensures that wherever they are, they will do well. The wily mountain Goat has the knack of knowing which rock to climb to reach the top. The true-blue Aquarian thinks more than fifty years ahead, but due to the stabilising influence of earthy Capricorn, LibCapAquas dream realistic and practical dreams. Though they take occasional sojourns into the future, they do not forget the present and know what steps to take to reach their final destination.

Librans are exceptionally romantic while Capricorns are soft and caring. The pitfall, though, is that the Libran can keep evaluating every possible person as a potential mate and Aquarians can quickly lose interest in a person after knowing everything that is there to know. LibCapAquas need to work extra hard to keep the passion alive in their relationships. The silver lining is that Capricorns prefer to fall in love with parental approval and desire respect and status in society. So when LibCapAquas fall in love they will be stable and committed partners, especially after the nuptials.

They are always concerned about money, without becoming misers. They love to spend on luxuries but look for value in everything they buy. The Libra appreciation of beauty will find them enjoying spas, branded clothes and indulging in 'me time'.

The lack of Water in this combination makes them less sensitive to others. However, perceptive Aquarius and sympathetic Libra make sure that they understand people and their motives. They may not always be empathetic or compassionate for fear of being vulnerable to others.

The Libran indecisiveness can afflict them often, especially in matters of the heart. They worry about how to take things forward in their love lives and how it will affect their family and future. The deep Capricornian black moods do afflict them, especially when they hit a low in their careers or they are away from their families. Their feelings of inadequacy fuel this. Most of their decisions depend on worrying about the future. They need to learn that today has already become the future of yesterday and just allow things to take care of themselves.

Libra–Capricorn–Aquarius – Shahid Kapoor

'I am a major workaholic.'[327]

'I love dancing. I can dance all night and beat every dude.'

'I saw normalcy in my life when I started getting to know dad and becoming a part of his family.'[328]

'I take a little time to decide. The most difficult thing in my life is to say no.'[329]

'I'm a romantic and I'd want to hold my girlfriend's hand and walk.'[330]

Focused, artistic, romantic, fair and family-centred, Shahid displays LibCapAqua traits in his life and words.

Love and Marriage for Him

He is a fantastic husband. This guy knows how to balance his two loves, career and romance, and gives equal attention to both. If, at times, you find his attention dwindling, do not hesitate to let him know. He pulls his act together soon.

Family, including parents, is extremely important to him. He loves to follow the family traditions without being rigid. He wants his family to enjoy respect and status in society and works hard to uphold its name and honour. He is liberated without being irresponsible. He takes care of your every need and is never domineering or aggressive. He is the rock you can depend on in any circumstance.

The Aquarian absentmindedness afflicts him at times. Libra's lazy ways, too, make him love to indulge in sleepathons and long relaxing days. You have to keep the house in order. Do not expect him to help in chores, as home is his retreat to rest and relax.

---

[327] *Hi! Blitz*, August 2009
[328] *People*, 23 September, 2011
[329] 'The pain of Kareena's leaving has receded', Shahid Kapoor by Subhash K. Jha, *Bollywoodhungama*, Saturday, 3 January, 2009, 12:53 [IST] (http://entertainment.oneindia.in/bollywood/fe tures/2009/shahid-kapoor-interview-030109.html)
[330] *People*, 23 September, 2011

He loves to spend on good clothes and luxury but can also display a stingy streak at times. You may need to make the expense sound important and shroud it in the garb of investment for family or future, if this streak becomes prominent.

As a father, he is truly wonderful. His life has been a preparation for this role. He is understanding, yet impressive. He is the guide and friend who encourages his children to think independently, but lays down some basic rules.

Love and Marriage for Her
She is smart and lovely. Her sweet smile hides a strong mind. This lady knows how to use her abundant feminine charms and graces to get you to do her bidding! She has very high standards and needs a guy who satisfies them. She uses both her head and heart when in love and demands respect and admiration from her guy. You cannot walk all over her.

She can warm your mother's heart for she loves to talk to elderly people with respect and decorum. Cultured and warm, she is the charming wife who can 'wow' your friends, and even your crabby old aunt, into loving her. However, she has a wild side too and does not like to be holed up in her house for long. Take her out. She becomes moody and cranky if left in one place for long. Actually, it is great if she has a career for her passion for achievement is too strong to be contained at home.

She loves pampering herself and the spa is her relaxation lounge. Style and substance combine in her and make her a timeless beauty.

Her children are her pride and joy, and she knows how to care for them perfectly. She is a fun mother who loves playing with them, but, at the same time, she educates them on their values and ambitions. She wants her children to think for themselves and not be interested in being spoon-fed ideas.

At the Workplace
The dual cardinal signs of Libra and Capricorn ensure that LibCapAquas are leaders and ideators. They do not lead with aggression but in a more democratic and people-friendly way. They understand politics and are politically correct at all times. They have the art of giving the hardest blows in the softest ways. They have fantastic corporate communication skills and the right language and say the right things. They can sweet-talk or even manipulate things if required. However, they will always put in extreme hard work first and only then back it up with talk.

The Libran creative faculties and Capricornian natural aptitude for soft skills can see them naturally blessed with awe-inspiring artistic talents. Besides, they add their unique Aquarian signature stamp to their art. The best part is, besides doing things extraordinarily differently, they also know how to market themselves. Even if they work in a corporate set up, they nurture some creative hobbies.

You can choose them to represent the organisation in high-powered meetings and they are the ones you can depend on during emergencies. They are extraordinary in negotiations and work supremely well under challenging situations. It does not take long before they reach the highest position in an organisation. Later they leave to pursue the most astonishing dreams and convert them into practical realities.

As bosses, they keep the lines of communication open and insist on written and verbal communication procedures. They take everyone's opinion before making a final decision. They are systematic and planned in their approach. They instinctively pick the right people for the right job. Their ability to delegate is superb.

Double Air and Earth makes LibCapAquas light yet stable, creative yet practical, and ambitious without losing the human touch.

Famous LibCapAqua Personalities
Shahid Kapoor, Justin Bieber, George Harrison, Sarojini Naidu, M.K. Thyagaraja Bhagavathar, Priya Sachdev Chatwal, Nusli Wadia, Gurmeet Choudhary, Jules Verne, Hank Aaron.

177. LIBRA–AQUARIUS–PISCES

Venus, the planet of love and luxury, meets the eccentric genius of Uranus and the soft mystery of Neptune in LibAquaPisces. Conventions do not mean much to them. They are strongly individualistic, without being aggressive. They live in their own world and follow their own rules but do it without deliberately stepping on anyone's toes.

LibAquaPisces are easy-going, fun-loving people. Very few things stress them out. You can spend happy hours laughing and talking with them. They have the Libran gift of talking beautifully and the Piscean charm of listening. They make you feel completely at ease with their ability to match your feelings and comprehend exactly what you did not say!

They are very good at understanding people and are rarely harsh in their judgments. They follow the policy of 'live and let live' and are tolerant of every flaw. They are friends who stand the test of time. They believe in compassion, never seek revenge and are not maliciously vindictive.

Family and friends are very important to them. Unlike the detached Aquarius, who can forget everything and everybody in the excitement of their passion, they retain the loving and caring nature of Libra and Pisces. They like having their friends and family members around and are concerned about them.

They are very intelligent. Theirs is an uncommon intelligence with ideas that seem unlikely to most people. They also have an instinctive grasp of concepts. Despite this faculty, they take a long time to reach a decision. They love to analyse every point. They are good at arguing their view and can defeat many with their debating skills.

They like to dress well, though perhaps outlandishly if the influence of Aquarius is strong. They are sure to mix colours and designs and still look good.

LibAquaPisces will have a dream in life. It might take them a while to know what it is, but once they do, they pursue it with single-minded devotion and an unconventional style.

Love is extremely important to them. While Libra makes them place love above all else, Pisces eternally longs for a soul mate. The Aquarian clumsiness in love is much reduced. They might spend some time analysing but once they do fall in love, neither conventions nor traditions will bind them. LibAquaPisces want a partner who is sensitive and caring. They will be highly emotional in love and deeply sentimental. But there are also a few of them who are extremely experimental in love and keep moving from one relationship to another, as they have the Aquarian fondness for mental games or simply got bored of the person.

Money does not mean much to them except as a source of all good things. They find it very easy to spend and are rarely able to save. The only thing that worries them is old age and they may invest a bit for that. Beyond that, they use their money for charity. They want to give to the world and do not look for fame while doing so. They are genuinely interested in helping people less fortunate than them.

Travel lures them. They want to travel and see the world, though they may not be very adventurous. They prefer luxurious modes of travel to hiking boots.

LibAquaPisces lack Earth and Fire in their combination. Though they are passionate about the things they want to do, they need to be pushed and prodded. There is an element of laziness in them and the lack of Fire reduces their drive. They work for their love of the cause rather than glory or money, so there will be times when they are distracted.

Earth gives stability and that is missing in LibAquaPisces. They are extremely creative and think extraordinary things but also dream impossible ideas that are not in touch with reality. They also constantly seek change just for the sake of change and variety. Stickability may be an issue with them. Some of them can also be eccentric and wild just to be different, but they are rare.

Addictions can be a problem with them. Aquarius does not mind trying anything new, while Pisces can easily fall into the trap of addiction. Libra loves luxury and food in excess. LibAquaPisces need strong people around to help them get rid of their self-inflicted difficulties.

They are very spiritual. They may not believe in traditional religions and set out to find their own version of God. But one thing is certain, they believe in a higher good. They may also have a preference for occult studies and mysticism. These are nice souls and nicer human beings. Nothing shocks them; they are empathetic to all the human foibles. They have been there and done it all; they are beyond malice towards anyone and have great love for fellow humans.

Libra–Aquarius–Pisces – Lady Gaga
She wore a dress that exploded fake blood, she rises from a wheelchair to walk after removing her leg braces ('Paparazzi') and smokes in bed next to a skeleton ('Bad Romance')...She had a period of what she considers addictive cocaine use, but she stopped with help from her family.[331]

On a list of Gaga's passions, there's music, then fame and, somewhere lower, material comfort and cash...She did not take a shower for days while she, her mom and sister took turns beside her dad's hospital bed.[332]

Artistic and original, Lady Gaga personifies LibAquaPisces with her love for music, her innate creativity, her refusal to follow rules and her loving care towards her family.

Love and Marriage for Him
He is your friend. This man does not want to rule over you but just wants to be the one for you. He is extremely romantic and never ceases talking of love. He enjoys talking, laughing, and telling witty stories and anecdotes. He understands your sighs and knows the deepest secrets of your heart. You will never meet a man who is as understanding as him.

Of course, you have to be the more grounded one for he really gives in to flights of fancy. You need to be the stabilising influence in his life without dampening his joy. Be inquisitive and curious like him.

---
[331] http://www.elle.com/Pop-Culture/Cover-Shoots/Lady-Gaga
[332] http://www.harpersbazaar.com/magazine/feature-articles/lady-gaga-born-this-way

There will be times when he is withdrawn or detached: allow him that 'me' time when he goes into his Aquarian journeys into future.

He wants a partner with whom he can discuss the things closest to his heart. Be ready to patiently listen to and gasp at ideas drastically different from the usual. He values your judgement.

You have to keep a check on his friends. He can easily fall prey to bad company. You must also keep an eye on money for it usually disappears from his hands.

He is ready for fun and games, and is a wonderful father. His children love confiding in him, safe in the knowledge that nothing can ever shock him. He never forces them to do anything against their will, rather he makes sure they live their dreams.

Love and Marriage for Her
Loving, caring, sensitive and highly individualistic, this lady is your best friend and your romance, all rolled into one. She likes an intelligent mate; be willing to learn new things and discuss and debate with her.

She is creative. She likes doing many different things and has an inquiring mind. Push her to do the things she likes best. She loves dressing up though her style statement may not always be conventionally acceptable. Do not expect her to revel in housework. Her mind is too full of airy ideas to be grounded by the harsh reality of dusting. Get her some domestic help.

She can love you despite all your faults and expects the same from you. She can understand your mood swings and angry outbursts. The only thing that discourages her is lack of emotional sensitivity. She can slowly fade away from your life rather than force you to acknowledge her. If you realise her worth, start being nice to her.

This lady is a very loving mother. She truly enjoys her children's childhood and is ready for joyful pranks. She is their confidante. She may find it hard to enforce discipline.

At the Workplace
LibAquaPisces settle in careers that offer opportunities for learning and change. They cannot be bound to routines or ideas and like to be in professions that allow them the opportunity to learn, ideate, create and invent. They are also quite good at talking and expressing their views. They can be scientists, artists, musicians or even teachers.

These people are extremely versatile and extraordinarily original. They have some pathbreaking, earth-shattering and sometimes wacky ideas. You just need to sort them into workable ideas for today. It takes them time to realise what they want to do with their lives, but once they find a purpose, they stick to it for a long time.

They have a deep understanding of spirituality and occult sciences, and can be involved in healing. They can be good philosophers and psychologists. Their compassionate and understanding nature helps them do well in professions that deal with people, such as public relations and human resource management. They just hate the idea of bossing others. But once in the role, they are the friendliest and most understanding boss around. You will love to work for them.

Forward thinking yet generous, wild yet sensitive, and compulsively original; LibAquaPisces live life in their own way and work to make the world a more loving place.

Famous LibAquaPisces Personalities
Lady Gaga, Mohit Chauhan, Ivar Kreuger, Harry Houdini, Ajantha Mendis, Eddie Murphy, Nancy Pelosi.

178. SCORPIO–SAGITTARIUS–CAPRICORN

Pluto, the ruthless god of the underworld, joins forces with two highly ambitious signs in ScorpSagCaps. The knowledgeable and spiritual Jupiter and the wise old man Saturn combine to give it immense strength.

The three animals that constitute the combination should give an idea of their power. The horsepower of the Centaur combines with the wily steadfastness of the mountain Goat and the survival instincts of the Scorpion. They are powerhouses, with unbelievable emotional, mental and physical strength. While Scorpio makes them deeply penetrative and gives a magnetic aura, Sagittarius makes them tremendously intelligent. Capricorn adds a grim and gothic side to them so they seem frighteningly powerful.

ScorpSagCaps have focus in life. Though they may take some time to know what they want, nothing distracts them from achieving their aims once they set goals for themselves. The best thing about them is that they know how to utilise their strengths. Scorpio's awesome inner strength and Capricorn's focus do not allow them to give up on their dreams. They are able to fight insurmountable odds to achieve their aims. They can be temperamental at times, and missing in action too, but soon get their act together. There is a maturity about them despite their wild ways.

They are intelligent and can comprehend people. They easily know what you mean apart from what you say. Nevertheless, it may not make them sensitive to your needs unless you are a part of their hallowed circle of family and friends.

Experiences affect them. They have the Scorpio tendency to metamorphose and change themselves according to events. Combined with the Capricornian ability to manoeuvre situations to their favour, ScorpSagCaps are very difficult to undermine. They can change themselves to suit the situation, and this is their greatest talent if used positively.

They are optimistic people. They have a fun side, too. The Sagittarian fun-loving quotient and the Scorpio loyalty make them friends who stay with you through thick and thin. They are adventurous and never fear trying out anything new. Blunt and brash in their views, they have few friends who understand them. During their youth, they are rebellious. They like to do their own thing and do not generally follow conventions if they do not match their views.

If they fall in love, it will be after they feel secure in their ambitions. They are passionate and quite possessive in love. ScorpSagCaps definitely want to be 'the one' in their partner's life. But if a matter of the heart goes awry and doesn't materialise, they won't behave as if they have lost their world. It will take some time and a lot of brooding and black moods, but they get their focus back to their full-time passion – doing something worthwhile in life!

They want tons of money. They know how to save and make it grow despite their tendency to splurge. They are quite materialistic and want things that denote power and status. They want people to look up to them and to reach positions that spell power and success. They simply want to rule the world. Their ambitions are sky high. With their fierceness, intelligence, focus, determination and sacrifice, they can achieve anything that they set their eyes on.

Anger is extremely strong in them. They may become impassive and not let people know the depth of their feelings but get angry very quickly. They can also blast off in volcanic rages that destroy everything before them. They deal with anger in two ways: they either shout in honest rage or keep it to themselves and take revenge later.

But if things go horribly wrong, they turn all that positive energy into a dark force to become vengeful and malicious. They are also prone to brooding, especially when things do not go according to their wishes. With age and success, they mellow down and become very spiritual and grounded.

They are usually quite spiritual. They believe in a power above them and understand religious views. The Scorpio love of the mystical and the Sagittarian spiritual nature make them bow to a higher law.

Scorpio–Sagittarius–Capricorn – Rajinikanth

When asked what he would have been if not an actor, he famously said that he would have been a goon.[333]

'One day before the release of the movie *Chandramukhi*, I celebrated the Silver Jubilee. I was very sure. I'm not an elephant – I'm a horse. I will stand up immediately. I got up...but you fans made me run.'[334]

'I'm not doing anything. It's God who is playing through me. All the producers, directors are all those who made me.'[335]

'Superstar' Rajinikanth has the strong will power and self-belief of the Scorpio, he trusts in the power above like a Sagittarian, but respects tradition and is down to earth like a Capricorn.

Love and Marriage for Him

He is the boss in the relationship and you have to listen to him. He wants a woman who is feminine and takes care of the family for he knows that he cannot do it alone. He loves praise. His Scorpio sensitivity makes it very hard for him to bear criticism. However, do not be very mild for he seeks a partner who can relate to his strong personality.

His first love is definitely his career and you have to accept secondary status in his life. You can be sure of his love if he has chosen you. Passion, intensity and possessiveness characterise his love. You clearly need to be a very calm and balanced person to live with him for he needs that calm, cool approach to mitigate the emergencies caused by his extreme views. You also need to be intelligent enough to recognise his various moods and deal with them with grace.

His anger is his worst trait. Let him rant and shout in his angry moods – his silence is worse than his outbursts for both of you. Keep a watch on him after he has started achieving success. Capricorns work hard all their youth and start enjoying what they missed out after their hard work starts paying off. He may develop a roving eye in his forties and fifties.

---

[333] *Cine Blitz*, December 2010
[334] https://www.youtube.com/watch?v=ql2y3x9pS94
[335] https://www.youtube.com/watch?v=iOL6jdxXOs4

As a father, he knows how to play with his children while maintaining discipline. His children may not find it easy to overrule his views. They must be respectful and strong in their opinions for him to listen to them.

Love and Marriage for Her
This girl is strong, ambitious and very driven. If you want a wife who can stand tall and show the world her strength, go for her. This girl is individualistic too. Consider these facts before wooing her.

Her ambitions for her family can be extremely strong. She is an admirable companion if you are in business or politics. She soon becomes the power behind you. But if your ambitions do not soar high, let her take control and she confidently steers you to a higher destiny. She can manage her family duties while working on her ambitions.

She needs a friend in you. You have to stand by her and be her loyalist. This lady suffers no disparaging remarks or sarcastic comments, especially about her work. You need to be her companion and not her master. Her emotions are always strong: she either loves or hates things. Although she shows a moderate nature to the world, you know her true self. With such strong emotions, she needs a guy who can understand and sternly soften her views. She wants a partner whose abilities she can admire and who complements her strong brashness.

Family is extremely dear to her. They witness her softer side more. Of course, friends do too. Her parents are especially close to her and she likes being in constant touch with them.

Adventure and travel excite her. She wants to travel around the world. It is also a way for her to relax. Take her rock climbing, white water rafting and bungee jumping.

Honest, encouraging, exciting and very demanding – these are her traits as a mother. She expects a lot from her children; at the same time, she knows what they are capable of. She encourages them to reach for the stars. She is her softest best with them while ensuring proper discipline.

At the Workplace
Focus, determination and fierce ambition mark them out as potential winners. ScorpSagCaps have no difficulty spelling out their ambitions and are willing to work extremely hard to get their way. Their positivity makes them seem unfazed by hurdles that come their way. They can also be very good at plotting and planning their way to success.

Money and power appeal to them. They want to be respected by their colleagues and desire a big stage to flaunt their talents. They never work in obscurity and know how to get attention. They are indifferent to obstacles or privations and rarely swayed by the opinions of others.

The only hurdle in their ambitious and hard-working path is their uncontrollable temper. They can ruin their chances with their uncontrolled outbursts and take time to learn lessons in self-control.

As bosses, they are extraordinarily intelligent, passionate leaders who motivate troops with their unmatched vision and ambition. They are in control, they overlook nothing and never accept defeat.

Water, Fire and Earth combine in this highly explosive bundle of energy and passion. ScorpSagCaps are determined to court success and create a trail of glory.

Famous ScorpSagCap Personalities
Rajinikanth, Kalki Koechlin, Tiger Woods, Alastair Cook, Kashmira Shah, Jimmy Shergill, Rasputin, Angad Bedi, Jackky Bhagnani, Minissha Lamba, Randy Rhoads, Preeti Shenoy, Teri Hatcher, Jessica Lall, Sidharth Malhotra.

179. SCORPIO–SAGITTARIUS–AQUARIUS

Pluto, the most powerful planet of the zodiac, meets the highly intelligent and ambitious Jupiter and the eccentric genius Uranus. ScorpSagAquas are truly a combustible combination as none of the three are bothered by conventions or traditions. This is the sign of a born rebel. Water, Fire and Air come together in this extremely volatile combination.

There is no stabilising effect of Earth, so do not expect this bundle of energy to be staid and laid-back. Calmness does not exist in them. They embody the strong passion of Scorpio, extreme independence of Sagittarius and wild unconventionality of Aquarius.

Scorpio makes them intensely perceptive and no one can bamboozle them into believing anything without a valid reason. The Aquarius in them makes them question every rule they encounter, which they easily break to test their sense of infallibility. Sagittarius runs away from traditions. They are free birds who are impossible to chain to anything.

They like to stand out in everything they do. From the way they look to the paths they choose for themselves, they are never like the rest of the herd. They are passionate, honest and full of interesting ideas and different possibilities.

They can be a genius with their penetrating mind and different thoughts but the destructive streak of breaking rules and trying out everything under the sun can lead these potential world-changers down another path. There is a thin line between genius and eccentricity and that is the line they tread.

Frank and totally outspoken, they speak their minds, despite knowing the discomfort it causes. Indeed, they are hell-bent on telling the truth. They believe that truth is more important than sentimental white lies. One cannot lie to them either.

There is nothing that scares them and they react to aggression with more aggression. They can erupt into violence and destruction at the slightest provocation and cool down just as fast. They are not prone to mood swings but are unpredictable.

Despite their violent or destructive streak, they can be the most caring people around in times of need. Aquarius makes them have a deep connect with people and the Sagittarius in them cannot stand inequality of any kind. These people are all for a new world where everyone is equal. They truly want to change the world for the better. The only thing that they cannot change is themselves.

Friends love them. They can do anything for their friends. Once someone is a part of their inner circle, whatever be their shortcomings or weird habits, they are accepted. ScorpSagAquas make the worst enemies, too. They are extremely kind-hearted, but if they are wronged, the Scorpio in them may forgive, but will never forget. If goaded to it, they will destroy you and you will cease to exist for them.

Ambitions don't make them manipulative. Their style is honest and forthright. ScorpSagAquas would rather go on gut instinct, and they have no idea how to play politics. They rarely prepare ahead and do not make plans or strategise. They do care about the future, but it is to worry what others would do without them and not about etching a name for themselves. They definitely want to do something to help future generations.

Love is an experiment for them, for though they have the Scorpio passion they lack commitment and can turn love into a game if they don't find their ideal easily. Neither Aquarius nor Sagittarius are known for their fondness for commitment, and with the Scorpio predilection for sensuous pleasures they can find themselves moving from one relationship to another. It will only stop if they find 'the one' or as they mellow down over the years.

Not surprisingly, there are different shades to their persona. They may search and discover some deeper secrets of life on varied topics like sex, spirituality, the cosmos, yoga and past life.

There is a touching humanitarian side to them. They are deeply moved by poverty, old age and human sufferings and would do anything within their means to alleviate them. They can also have some startling ideas about spirituality. Despite all their apparent vices, there is a touching truthfulness and honesty about them that makes your heart flow with love for these noble souls.

Scorpio–Sagittarius–Aquarius – Salman Khan

Farah Khan: 'He means what he says; he has no agenda. If he likes you, he will love you whether you are the president or a spot-boy. If he hates you, he will hate you whether you are the president or the spot-boy. He has that childlike quality. In the industry, there is a lot of ruthlessness and game playing. He is innocent of all that.'[336]

Salman Khan: 'Find one of your own family members who needs the money for education, or to save a life, and give your money to them. That is part of Being Human, you don't always have to give me the money.'[337]

Salman Khan is a true ScorpSagAqua – untameable yet innocent, impulsive yet generous. Calculations do not enter his mind, only relationships do.

Love and Marriage for Him

He is the kind of guy you have probably been warned against. Wild, uncontrollable and with no interest in being tied down! He is not a dream husband. He loves to woo a girl if she acts unattainable, but once he gets her, he loses interest. As an added woe, the Sagittarius in him makes him totally allergic to householder roles and responsibilities. The Aquarius in him does not like settling down and is totally detached at times. Marry him at your risk. Only age can mellow him!

The Scorpio passion, Aquarian experimentation and Sagittarian athleticism make him one of the most satisfying lovers you have ever been with. Remember, he is a marvellous lover only while his interest is held. Variety is the spice of life and he needs it the most. Keep him interested in all ways possible. Be mysterious.

It is not to easy live with him. No matter how sociable he may be, he needs his space. You have to be a strong, independent lady to handle him. Leave him at

---

[336] http://www.telegraphindia.com/1110612/jsp/7days/story_14102957.jsp
[337] *Hello!* April 2011

times, let him do what he wants and be where he wants. This is the only way to keep him.

Again, unpredictable as ever, he can be an excellent father. Fun loving and caring, he enjoys being with his children; maybe because he is like a child himself. He is a totally chilled-out father who takes excellent care of them. You can expect him to allow them to live their lives according to their dreams.

Love and Marriage for Her
She is not the traditional wife and daughter-in-law. Do not ever think that she can change for you. This girl is honest and blunt, much to your discomfiture. You have to be extremely sensible and able to look at the funny side of things when she starts being honest.

Housewifely duties are not for her. She needs continuous change and excitement in life. She may pack her bags and be off on an exciting adventure minutes after she has landed home from her earlier travels. Her friends (she has tons of them) are her life. She likes to help them out whenever they ask. Do not be jealous. It just amuses her. This independent and strong girl needs no male support to feel adequate. She is not frightened of anything and her rather curious mind always helps her by decoding every mystery before it turns into a horror. She has a colourful and vibrant personality.

There is a very spiritual side to her. She likes to learn the mysteries of life without giving in to religious conventions.

As a mother, she needs a lot of help in the first few years. As her children grow older, she is more comfortable with the idea of being a mother and becomes more of a friend. She is rarely shocked by anything they do or say and teaches them to be independent, strong and better human beings.

At the Workplace
ScorpSagAquas will have a totally scientific bent of mind. No matter what they do, their profession can be unscientific but their mental prowess will never be rudimentary. They will have this burning need to innovate, discover and chart out unthought-of ideas and will want to do something different in life.

Routine and monotony are not for ScorpSagAquas. They need flamboyant and adventurous careers. They find ways to live their adventures while working. They are extremely ambitious but lack intense focus as many things distract them. But they definitely have it in them to reach the top. Money does not attract them as much as adventure and power. Creative and scientific fields are their domain.

They lack the guile of a canny businessman. They feel no urge to build an empire that will feed future generations of descendants. But their honesty shouldn't be misconstrued as weakness. Deeply penetrative and powerful, they cannot be sidelined or manipulated. As bosses, they are unpredictable but permissive and generous as long as you are loyal. They can read through your smallest foibles, never try to fool them.

Water, Fire and Air meet to give power, drive and skill to ScorpSagAquas. They will be volatile yet loving, creative yet destructive, driven yet distracted: a flame-bearing pathbreaker who revels in the moment but lives for others.

Famous ScorpSagAqua Personalities
Salman Khan, Janet Napolitano, Jayasudha, Gul Panag, Manvinder Bisla, Grandhi Mallikarjuna Rao, Queenie Singh, Nigel de Jong, Christina Applegate.

180. SCORPIO–SAGITTARIUS–PISCES

This combination is full of magic and possibility, yet it can also fall hard and low. Pluto, the ruthless god of the underworld, sizzles with the highly intelligent Jupiter and the deeply mysterious Neptune. There is passion, wisdom and enthusiasm in ScorpSagPisces.

A Fish combined with a half-human, half-horse Centaur and a Scorpion: the Fish acquires tremendous power here. It can summon the physical and mental strength of the Archer or even unleash the ruthless venom of the Scorpion if required. The transformation can be simply stunning and magical.

The brilliance of their intelligence is phenomenal. Sagittarians are absolutely at home in rare abstract or Vedic mathematics, while Scorpios have the deep penetrative understanding of all that they perceive. Pisces are wise old souls much beyond what their physical age suggests. The combination of the three can take intelligence to another unexplainable level. Pisces is the one sign that also makes them hard to decipher for Pisces always reflects its environment.

It is very hard to fool ScorpSagPisces. Scorpio gives them the ability to look deep into your soul and they can read your unspoken thoughts while Pisces allows them to look at the world through your eyes. ScorpSagPisces can understand the smallest vibrations of your soul, so lying to them is completely pointless.

Ambition and passion mark them out for success. ScorpSagPisces will be able to endure anything in the wake of their ambition. They will not want to do something and become someone for money or status but would like to do it for power or the sheer joy of their passion. They can live a spartan existence on frugal budgets, travel far and wide, sacrifice everything for that one passion that they have. The biggest issue is to find that passion. Once they find it, they never look back.

Learning is their biggest virtue. They can exactly mimic you moments after they meet you. They are constantly exploring – physically and mentally. They keep enriching themselves by observing and absorbing everything they experience.

There are contradictions however. Though ScorpSagPisces know exactly what you think, though they can be ambitious and passionate, they may also be content to live life in a make-believe world. Though there is imagination and intelligence in this combination, there is also the Piscean escapism: they can, at times, just close their eyes to all their potential.

ScorpSagPisces need partners who bring stability and love into their lives, for these two things can help mould them into good success stories. They are very possessive lovers and will need constant reassurances of their partner's love.

There are many layers to ScorpSagPisces. They are very emotional and sensitive. Scorpio's extreme intensity makes them feel the smallest barbs deeply and, though they may smile and seem unconcerned, their hearts bleed. The legendary Scorpio desire for revenge is diluted to some extent here due to the sunny Sagittarian and forgiving Piscean. But it is always advisable not to mess with anyone with Scorpio in them.

ScorpSagPisces believe in a higher power. They may call it by any name based on their environment and may not even acknowledge it as God, but they feel a power behind their acts. They know that they are being guided and helped through life. They become more spiritual as they grow older.

They also have a tendency to addiction. They have a love for experimentation and want to try out everything in life. Both Pisces and Scorpio are drawn to things they cannot control. However, the Scorpio ability to overcome everything can make them overcome their addictions too.

Pisces adds insecurity to them. ScorpSagPisces have to fight themselves to come out stronger – their deep sensitivity and insecure feelings can lead them down a destructive path if they are not able to stop themselves. When combined with the deeply perceptive Scorpio, they can suffer from various phobias, complexes and imagined hurts. They can also revel in excesses or prefer being lonely and irresponsible. They can simply while away their time day dreaming of a perfectly beautiful world and doing nothing about it.

While the combination ensures that they are the most intelligent and the wisest amongst all, it acts as a deterrent too. While Scorpio propels them to trample traditions and bring in revolutions, and Sagittarius helps them deconstruct the most complex of theorems, Pisces wonders about the futility of the whole thing, as deep inside it knows the transient nature of everything. Inaction can be their worst offence.

They can be the sweetest people you've ever known or can be the most dangerous ever witnessed. The Scorpion passion and Sagittarian intelligence can combine with Piscean wisdom, and if channelised positively they can unravel the deepest mysteries of the world or help alleviate human sufferings and can rise above the base emotions of greed, envy, hatred. There is a mystical, magical quality about all three zodiac signs that can push them to great heights.

Scorpio–Sagittarius–Pisces – Ricky Martin
'I said yes to everything because I wanted the entire world – and more than anything the United States – to notice me. The crossover to the American market meant so much to me that I was willing to do anything at all to make it happen.'[338]

When he travelled in India in a spiritual quest, he witnessed poverty in its awful starkness. It resulted in the Ricky Martin Foundation, dedicated to ameliorate the suffering he saw. The Foundation also works to rescue children in Southeast Asia from being sold as sex workers. Ricky Martin displays the Sagittarian spirituality and desire to shine, the Scorpio deep instincts and passion to succeed and the Piscean sensitivity towards people.

Love and Marriage for Him
He is extremely loving and passionate and demands only one thing. He wants you to make him the centre of your universe. You can never walk away from this guy once he holds your hand, for he loves you for life.

He wants to be loved and understood by you: anything less than that seriously disillusions him. A good partner can make him achieve the dreams he is passionate and ambitious about. You need to make his dream yours and only then can he

---
[338] http://www.southfloridagaynews.com/arts-and-entertainment/book-reviews/2718-book-review-me-by-ricky-martin.html

succeed; push him gently and help him get into a routine without nagging him. Let him daydream, it's good for him, but he he needs that extra support and push to go and achieve those dreams.

He puts a brave face to the world: only you can know all the insecurities that gnaw at him. Be strong for his sake and he will never give in to his fears. You must never wash dirty linen in public; let others believe in his infallibility.

He loves travelling with you. This guy loves adventures.

Firm and disciplining, he is a father who sets the rules. He also knows what his children want. He is playful and loving but you have to care for the children when they are younger for he spends a lot of time pursuing his passions.

Love and Marriage for Her
She is definitely a very strong and individualistic lady. Do not be fooled by her soft Piscean charm: she has very strong views. She is a very sensitive and loving partner. She gets hurt easily too. You have a lot of explaining to do in such circumstances. The fact is that she loves you to bits and is very hurt if you do not show the same regard for her. If you want a lady who is ready to fight for you, look no further. She is ready to lay down her life for you. Keep in mind also that if you happen to glance at another woman, she can kill you.

She is very creative and artistic. Let her pursue her creative talents. It helps her vent her emotions and be calmer. Despite her evident abilities, she has a crippling inferiority complex. You have to keep encouraging her.

Money is difficult for her to manage. Though she tries to save, she rarely finds enough in her handbag. She is more impulsive than budget-conscious while spending. She loves travelling and loves going on adventure trips.

As a mother, she loves playing with her children and understands them beautifully. She is their friend and guide. But she is definitely in control of things and never lets them forget that she is the boss.

At the Workplace
ScorpSagPisces can take some time choosing their careers, but once they do, they never leave them till they win the accolades they deserve. They are passionate, ambitious and extremely hard working. But they need sensible mentors to guide them for they can easily falter along the way. Discipline and sticking to a plan are two things that need to be inculcated early. They are fast learners and may even surprise those who taught them, with amazing improvisations.

They do well in creative fields. They can be extraordinary researchers. They easily understand complex theories. They are extremely intelligent and perceptive, and have innovative solutions to most problems. Give them their due applause, for though they never seek it, they glow when they hear praise. They look for glory and applause rather than money. Never say negative things to them.

As bosses, they are innovative, perceptive and controlling. They have mediators to deal with you, as they know that they are deeply emotional and can easily give in to sob stories.

ScorpSagPisces have deep intelligence, high sensitivity and a complex personality. Their fight to rise to the top is only with their self.

Famous ScorpSagPisces Personalities
Ricky Martin, LeBron James, Joseph Stalin, Srinivasa Ramanujan, Gary Cahill, Sheikh Abdullah, Kiefer Sutherland, Roelof van der Merwe.

181. SCORPIO–CAPRICORN–AQUARIUS

Pluto, the dark lord of the underworld, meets the wise old man Saturn and the wild genius Uranus in ScorpCapAqua. ScorpCapAquas have a purpose in life that they follow passionately. Scorpio needs a passion, Capricorn works diligently towards its aim and Aquarius has a deep-seated desire to create something wonderful and different. They give a lot to their passions and are able to bring something totally different into their achievements. The Aquarian ability to think unconventional, different ideas heightens their passions and drive.

There is an alluring magnetism about them. Scorpios are deep and mysterious, Aquarius makes them eccentric but intellectual and Capricorn gives them the natural aura of solemn grace and wisdom. You can't miss them: there is an electric vitality about them. Scorpio is a very intense sign that feels very deeply while Capricorn has an aura of melancholy around it. Aquarius adds airiness and lightness in them and stops ScorpCapAquas from being very sombre.

ScorpCapAquas have a very tender side and always stand up for the weak. They have humanitarian ideals and detest inequality or discrimination. They are loyal friends too. Though their list of friends is not a yard long, they treasure the few friends they have and are ready to fight for them. They have a deep understanding of human nature. They are very good at decoding people and instinctively know their emotions and motives.

Family is extremely dear to ScorpCapAquas. They really care for their families and are responsible family members. They want to spend time with their families, despite their hectic schedules and big dreams. They are responsible siblings who take care of their brothers and sisters even if they happen to be the youngest in the family.

Ambition is very marked in them. ScorpCapAquas hate losing even at board games and always play to win. Intelligence combines with strong will in them. They are wise beyond their years. All three signs are known for their intelligence while the eccentric genius of Aquarius adds zing to their intellect.

They evolve over time. Experiences mould them and they change as they age. The Capricornian reverse-aging syndrome affects them and they seem much more chilled out after their thirties.

Love finds them deeply committed. ScorpCapAquas do not mind looking around before settling down, but once they say yes, they are passionately involved. Though they love deeply, if they are wronged by the people they trust, they find it hard to forgive and forget. Loyalty is extremely important to them and they can turn vengeful if you break faith.

They are exceptionally good with money. They know how to save and rarely squander it on impulsive purchases. Luxury does not matter to them as much as status symbols and they like to spend on things that accentuate their worth. They work diligently and save for their future.

They have strong values and are ready to fight for their beliefs. They can be quite rebellious, especially if customs do not match their idealism. Indeed, they are able to effect change due to their strong views. They stay focused on their ideas and stay in command of their thoughts.

Scorpio's love for mysteries and Aquarius's natural snoopiness beckon them. Scorpio will make them ready to try out anything while Aquarius will be curious about everything. They have a wild side and need freedom and excitement. The deeply cultured Capricorn cautions them and when combined with the reclusive and secretive Scorpio, they can lead double lives filled with experimentation and excitement, without anyone suspecting them.

Their anger can be very explosive but they know when to control it to their advantage. They are constructively critical and stop short of ruining their chances while airing their views. The Scorpion revenge syndrome is altered: the combination with the evolved Aquarius and calculative Capricorn can make them swallow their pride and work harder towards greater success and make their triumph the best revenge against their enemies.

The Aquarian habit of actively seeking change can end up being evolving and liberating or can make them rudderless and eccentric. When combined with the intense Scorpio and disciplined Capricorn, they can become powerhouses of wisdom, knowledge and humanity, or contrarily become self-seeking manipulators with chilling rationality.

If they overcome their inner insecurities they can combine the extraordinary work ethics of Capricorn with the alchemy of Scorpio and genius of Aquarius to gift something unique, extraordinary, pathbreaking and magical to the world. They definitely have the potential of harnessing their individuality to produce trailblazing works for a happy world tomorrow.

Scorpio–Capricorn–Aquarius – Michael Jordan
'My heroes are and were my parents.'

'Yeah, I've gotten myself into situations where I've pushed the envelope.' When Bradley asked him if his gambling ever got to the level where it jeopardised his livelihood or family, Jordan replied, 'No.'

'I've missed more than 9000 shots in my career. Twenty-six times, I've been trusted to take the game-winning shot and missed. I've failed over and over and over again in my life. And that is why I succeed…Obstacles don't have to stop you.'

'My body could stand the crutches but my mind couldn't stand the sideline.' [339]

Love for family, passion and diligence, the ability to think beyond his limitations – Michael Jordan displays the qualities of a true ScorpCapAqua.

Love and Marriage for Him
He is the man in your life! Responsible, caring and extremely loving, he brings passion and intensity, along with a dose of fun, into the relationship. He loves you a lot, but also loves his ambitions. You have to step aside at times for him to achieve his dreams. He needs you to understand their importance and not nag him for more attention.

[339] http://www.brainyquote.com/quotes/authors/m/michael_jordan.html #ZjAshzgTdqJAKQ0y99

Despite his extreme dedication to his ambitions, he does not forget his responsibilities. You can be sure that he pays the bills on time. He needs love, understanding and a lot of space, and, in return, gives a lot of laughter and love. He needs a partner in whose company he can relax. For that, you have to be the calmer person, and be sensitive too, for he gets hurt easily with thoughtless words.

His anger is bad and can simmer for many days. You have to deal with it without shouting back at him. He can be aloof and detached sometimes and seem lost in his world. Remember that you have a genius at home and he is thinking something unique and fabulous for mankind. He needs a more feminine person and is not drawn to highly individualistic or aggressive women. He prefers a slightly conventional outlook. He wants a partner with whom he can discuss his views and get intelligent feedback.

He is very responsible and loving as a father, but not very useful during the baby days and handles the kids better when they are able to converse with him. He is his chilled-out best with them. They automatically respect him.

Love and Marriage for Her
She is extremely grounded and very intelligent. She is a fighter and a survivor. She wants to leave a mark and create something tangible in her life. Support her, for she has the potential to succeed.

She loves her family and wants a secure home for them. Her home is her most restful place and she is unhappy if it is in disarray. Deep emotions run through her. She needs a partner who understands her need for love and achievement.

She understands you and all your dreams. She knows how to make you happy but also needs a lot of praise and love in return. She needs to be the foremost person in your life. Give her importance and do not treat her emotions disrespectfully – take this tip to bring lots of joy into your relationship.

She loves travel and needs it to relax. Take her out to new locales. Such trips rejuvenate her.

As a mother, she is strict and disciplining but has a fun side too. Her children admire her. She teaches them to work hard for their dreams. Her love for her family, and concern for them, makes her very protective of them. She makes them believe in themselves.

At the Workplace
The courageous, aggressive and instinctive Scorpio has combined with the inventive, versatile and extraordinary Aquarius. The potent energies of these diverse zodiac signs are channelised by the practicality and assiduousness of Capricorn. They are assets to any organisation.

ScorpCapAquas are the most hard-working, persevering and intelligent workers. They want to succeed and do not mind waiting and working for their laurels. Passion for their profession drives them ahead. They work imagining their success confidently, and this positivity helps them get what they want. They work hard to create a substantial legacy and are aided in their work by their ideals and unconventional thoughts.

They can do anything, from sports to finance and research to artistic expressions of their passions. They excel in whatever field they choose with their determination and zeal.

Money is extremely important for them. They do not waste their zeal in fields that offer no rewards. They need to be paid well. Praise, too, is welcome for they need it to prove their worth to themselves. As bosses, they are in control. Nothing can escape their eyes and they know smallest bit of information about each employee. They are caring and paternal too.

Water, Earth and Air make ScorpCapAqua an attractive mix of passion and dreams, logic and rebelliousness, tradition and the avant-garde.

Famous ScorpCapAqua Personalities
Michael Jordan, Pran, Somdev Devvarman, Sonya Kitchell.

182. SCORPIO–AQUARIUS–PISCES

Pluto, the secretive and powerful lord of the underworld, Uranus, the eccentric and intelligent planet, and Neptune, the mysterious lord of the seas, rule over ScorpAquaPisces. In this combination, Scorpio's sting is reduced to some degree due to the soft sensitivity of Pisces and the humanitarian views of Aquarius.

ScorpAquaPisces have the need to create something new, maybe start a revolution. Pluto, Neptune and Uranus are the outermost planets in the solar system and are different from the rest. They make ScorpAquaPisces unconventional in thought, work and deed. Prejudices and conventions do not weigh them down.

Daydreams and imaginary worlds enthrall them as children and their predilection for dreams never grows old with them. You may find them sitting in a corner, thinking, reading and wondering. They like to live in their own world. Let them be, it is their spa therapy. They return energised with strong focus and new ideas.

The Piscean powers of empathy and strong intuition, along with the Aquarian love for dissecting and examining each person, and the Scorpio knack of penetrating the soul make ScorpAquaPisces walking, talking X-ray machines. Nothing can evade their perceptive powers.

Noble, kind-hearted and evolved, they are preciously rare. The innate Piscean goodness in them reduces the Scorpio vindictiveness. They can find good in bad. The Piscean ability to empathise makes it very hard for them to judge anybody and the Aquarian ability of thinking of the future makes them easily forgive and forget.

Pisces turns them into highly evolved personalities, as it is the wisest of all signs. However, if their environment pushes them to achieve excellence and teaches them discipline, ScorpAquaPisces mirror it; if it is veered towards deception and laziness, they reflect those, like typical Pisces. They can easily trick and con people too.

They are true friends who never judge you and are the first to defend you. They are passionately aggressive about their friends and are ready to sacrifice anything for them. Their noble and passionate hearts can sometimes be let down by their not-so-considerate friends, though.

Love is a deep and abiding emotion in ScorpAquaPisces. Once they fall in love, they display the passion of Scorpio and the deep sensitivity of Pisces. The Pisces in them yearns for a soul mate and once they find one, they will never look for another. Aquarius can make them seem detached at times, but it does not mean they are uninterested. ScorpAquaPisces are loving and caring but they require some space in their relationship. Their love is highly evolved – who said that you can love only one person? They can love a hundred people, with the same intensity and same passion. They treat everyone as special. Can they be called polygamous? Well, it's much beyond that. You will never be able to understand if you measure them with your rigid moral codes.

These guys can be quite messy at times. They are not known for their love of cleaning at all.

Addictions can cause big problems for them, if they are not careful. The Scorpio ability of indulging in excesses and the Pisces bent for addiction, combined with Aquarius's wild attitude, can easily lead them into addictions of various kinds. They can let their talents and aspirations slip away under a cloud of addictions and eccentricities. They need their friends and family to help them get a grip on themselves. Their tendency to get bored with things quickly and the need for constant excitement can be a trap too.

Money does not matter to them as much as ideas and ideals do. They work and live for them. They don't want to crush a rival or offend anyone, but though they are soft and sweet, they are part-Scorpio and it never bodes well to rub them the wrong way – don't mistake their goodness for weakness. They can summon the immense strength of Pluto and Uranus, and with Neptune's caginess, attack you surreptiously. ScorpAquaPisces, who have been victims of their own goodness, can turn around and become extremely suspicious of everyone, read too much into people's motives and sting at every perceived attack.

They are spiritual rather than religious, and are highly evolved. Scorpio understands the deep mysteries of life, and Pisces has a strong spiritual side, while Aquarius wants to decipher every mystery. Nothing can shock them. They are rebels who question every custom and tradition. They may rebel violently or softly, but rebel they will. They know every vice and virtue, for they have dissected and lived them all.

Scorpio–Aquarius–Pisces – Kangana Ranaut

'I think it is my nature that I dare to try things that others don't. I always experimented with my clothes and looks.'[340]

'There has to be lots of respect in my relationship. And there should be lots of attraction. That makes it passionate.'[341]

'Money has never been important to me, being a part of an exciting project gives me a high.'[342]

Ranaut recounted to Simi's wide-eyed horror how she hurt her parents, rebelled and eventually left home, without, literally, looking back. 'You have to be mad to chase your destiny.'[343]

Kangana Ranaut reveals a creative personality, which is not bound by conventions and dares to think beyond, like a true ScorpAquaPisces.

Love and Marriage for Him

As a partner, he is wonderfully and amazingly tender. If you want a soul mate who understands your deepest desires and empathises every time you become cranky and unreasonable, he is the only guy for you. He will have the fun element of an Aquarian with the deep understanding of a Piscean and the intensity and passion of a Scorpio. He is loyal and loving, and, once he is committed to you, he is there forever. You can be as demanding as you want when a bad mood descends, and he understands.

---

[340] http://www.glamsham.com/movies/interviews/06-kangna-ranaut-interview-010903.asp
[341] http://entertainment.oneindia.in/bollywood/features/2010/kangana-ranaut-interview-300710.html
[342] http://www.cinegoer.com/telugu-cinema/interviews/interview-with-kangana-ranaut.html
[343] http://mumbaiboss.com/2011/09/26/indias-most-desirable-recap-kangna-ranaut/

He is also the one who initiates all the family holidays and outings, and does not throw a tantrum when his mother-in-law comes to stay. He knows how to be in her good books too. Just give him space to work at his own passions and ideals.

You have to be independent and strong, for though he is always there for you, there can be times when he is unavailable due to his dreams and passions. You have to take charge without being bossy. Handle the finances for he really does not care much about money. If money means a lot to you, you have to work for it.

He is a good father, sensitive to his children's needs and caring enough not to be controlling. He never limits their thoughts, rather introduces them to new ideas and expands their horizon. He loves being a child with them and teaches them through play rather than conventional teaching methods.

Love and Marriage for Her
She is lovely and caring. You are her whole world and she loves you deeply. She surrounds you with so much love, care, affection and understanding that you fail to understand why people denigrate marriages. Of course, you have to give her time to dream and think, for she needs that. You have to understand her wild ideas and unconventional views too. She needs you to be her support system for her to focus on and realise her dreams.

Do not treat her like a doormat and do not ever downplay her intelligence. If you want to feel superior to her, it is better that you look elsewhere, for she has a pride that cannot be trampled upon. She has a caustic tongue and a ferocious mind hiding under her sweet exterior, so be careful of how you treat her.

She loves travelling. Her tastes veer to learning than shopping. Take her out to exotic locales and watch her fill her mind with fresh ideas that rejuvenate her.

As a mother, she is exceptional. She teaches her children the value of individuality and trains them to be humane. She never focuses on grades they obtain in school. Instead, she works towards instilling knowledge and empathy in them. She knows what they want to do and lets them do it.

At the Workplace
The passion of Scorpio and creativity of Aquarius and Pisces come together in ScorpAquaPisces. They display deep creativity coupled with passion and vigour. Be it writing poetry, creating music or acting, these guys are great at delving deep into the soul and creating gems with their passion. The Scorpio intensity and focus lend paths to their dreams.

They are not motivated by monetary gain or even the sound of applause. They are driven by ideas. Monotonous work and routine are not for them. These guys need to use their minds and not fall in with conventions. They are extraordinarily talented, multi-faceted geniuses; what they need is focus. There is a constant struggle in them to give in to their Piscean escapism or to rise above all else and soar high like an eagle. They just need to summon the Scorpio power within them to do so.

As bosses, they simply know you. Nothing can be ever hidden from them. They will be kind if they know you mean no harm, they will simply crush you if they feel you are politicking.

Double Water and Air make them spiritual and creative. ScorpAquaPisces are passionate yet soft, intelligent yet humble and perceptive yet detached.

Famous ScorpAquaPisces Personalities
Kangana Ranaut, Sharon Stone, Pt. Ravi Shankar, Nagesh Kukunoor, Shaquille O'Neal, Chester Bennington, Archana Puran Singh, Nicolaus Copernicus, Edmund Kean, Vasundhara Raje, Sadhana Sargam, Joris Mathijsen, Jim Parsons.

183. SAGITTARIUS–CAPRICORN–AQUARIUS

The knowledgeable and benevolent Jupiter, the old and wise Saturn and Uranus, the eccentric planet of invention and science, rule over this combination. In a horoscope, these planets rule the ninth, tenth and eleventh houses. Nine is the house of intellect, ten of practical knowledge and career while eleven guides the heart towards humanity. SagCapAquas have it all – intelligence, practical wisdom and love for others. A truly blessed sign!

SagCapAquas are brilliantly intelligent. They easily grasp abstract facts, and even mathematics, due to Sagittarius. This sign is at ease with such complex topics as molecular physics and Vedic maths. They are also highly inventive and extremely broad-minded due to Aquarius, and practical and diligent due to Capricorn. They are extremely good at thinking futuristic thoughts. They are honest and intelligent, and original in what they do, think and say.

Sagittarius and Aquarius together make a person intelligent, idealistic and highly humanitarian, but they lack purpose and focus in life. Capricorn adds the steadying force to this honest maverick and makes their dreams more realistic. Capricorn will also give them people-management skills and make them good at understanding people and delegating work to them.

They always stand out with their inimitable style and panache. They keep experimenting with their looks, and know how to blend the new and the old. Ambition is an important part of their make up; they want to achieve success and be recognised for their skills.

SagCapAquas guys love to talk. Their conversations are witty, intelligent and slightly wacky. They can be irreverent or dignified: whatever they say grabs your attention. Sagittarius loves to enthrall audiences and likes adventure sports. Aquarius has a wacky sense of humour and enjoys dabbling in various interesting activities. They dip into various sports and numerous hobbies. They also have lots of friends and love to shine in a crowd. They know how to balance fun and seriousness.

Romance will wait; these guys want to achieve success and status before they fall into the embrace of love. Aquarius and Sagittarius make very good friends but are a little out of their depth in love. They don't know how to deal with romantic details. The Sagittarian and Aquarian ambition is too important to be compromised for love, but the Capricorn in them might agree if the loved one's family and status seem worthy. No, they are not gold diggers – quite the opposite – but if they feel the mate will be a support and partner, and not a dependent burden, they will gladly take on the mantle of love.

Family is extremely important to them. They have a high sense of their families' worth. Sagittarius and Aquarius make them a little free-spirited: though they love their families, they do not mind staying away from them. Travel, too, is very important to them. New places, people and ideas rejuvenate them.

As they grow old, the Fire sign in them mellows and the Capricornian reverse-aging process makes them more laid back. You can expect them to be more fun as they grow old. They become more romantic too, as they age.

There is a trap that they need to avoid. Though they have the sternly disciplined Capricorn within them, some of them may be carried away by the overconfidence of Sagittarius. When combined with the eccentric Aquarius they may lose focus in life and can just dissipate their energy and become a jack-of-all-trades and master of none.

They evolve throughout their lives. They can become wiser, more spiritually inclined and become thought leaders, or lead a wasted life full of squandered opportunities. Both options are open to them.

Sagittarius–Capricorn–Aquarius – Abhishek Bachchan

Ashutosh Gowariker: 'Working with Abhishek is one big party. But at the same time there is a professional side to him which is serious, focused and dedicated.'[344]

Abhishek: 'That's the best thing you can do – come home from work and spend time with your family.'

'I was an athlete in school, and captained the basketball team, the ski team and the athletics team.'

'I enjoy people who can stimulate you mentally: educate you with their conversations.'

'I get excited by (story) ideas and decide to do films. I don't ask what's the script, who's editing the film, who's directing it.'[345]

The fun-loving and intelligent Sagittarius meets the humane Aquarius and the rooted Capricorn in Abhishek Bachchan.

Love and Marriage for Him

He is your friend, first and foremost. This guy is the most chilled-out and cool guy you can ever meet. He is also a family man. Family is one of his priorities. Others are his drive and ambition, which lead him to seek success, for which he wants you to be his mate.

He needs an independent and strong woman who is secure in her own worth. The problem is, despite the emotional understanding of Aquarius, he is quite detached from emotions and finds it very difficult to be sensitive and caring. If you want long insightful conversations, deep emotional bonding and loving care, please let this guy go. Neither does he have the time to hold your hand when you are sick nor is he able to express his love romantically. But he does love you.

If you want excitement, adventure and a friend to share your life with, he is the guy for you. He never dictates, but expects you to regard the family as your priority. Beyond that, he lets you do, think and feel whatever you choose.

As an added advantage, he has a balanced view about money. The Capricornian stinginess does not afflict him, nor does the Sagittarian carelessness. He ensures that there is enough to save and to spend.

He needs space in a relationship. He needs to breathe and feel free, so give him that time to himself. Do not worry, he comes, rejuvenated, back to you. Remember one thing though: despite leaving the reins of control in your hands, he is the boss. There is no way you can ride roughshod over him for he is too secure in his wisdom to be dethroned.

---

[344] http://www.youtube.com/watch?v=Bh8xZtkcTv4 (Coffee with Karan-season-3)
[345] *Hello!* August 2011

He is the most caring, yet fun, father to have. He goes out on adventure trips with his kids, goes trekking, deep-sea diving and even yachting. The fabulous thing about him is that, though he is never involved in their day-to-day routine, he knows exactly what they are doing or should do.

Love and Marriage for Her
She is independent, individualistic and steady. There is no flightiness in this girl. She is total substance. She does have an adventurous streak, and 'extrovert' is her middle name, but she never loses herself to mindless follies.

She is a determined and ambitious person. She likes people around her to have fun and loosen up while striving for their goals. She can never sit idle. So why not take the opportunity to make her your business partner? You can then utilise her innovative ideas for mutual gain.

The best part about her is that she is fabulous in whatever role she undertakes. She can be a college girl, wife and daughter-in-law, administrator, business head, and mother. Whatever she does, she does it so well, yet so differently, that everyone is astounded. She is innately intuitive and knows how to use her talents well on people. A very sensible, level-headed person!

She needs space in her relationship and despite her understanding of people, needs to be away from them at times. This is a necessity for her. She is one girl who can truly be friends with her ex. Her love is not so passionate that it withers with your loss. Though she loves you, she can carry on without you. She works at finding solutions to marital problems, if any. But if she feels that it is better to let go, then she lets go.

She is the perfect mother – fun, adventurous, yet firm at times. Her children may get a little embarrassed by her desire to have fun with them, especially in their rebellious teenage years when parents seem outdated. But she is their friend and guide through it all.

At the Workplace
SagCapAquas are extremely ambitious. Their ambitions are all about creating and leaving something of value. They want people to look at their work and shake their heads in amazement. The wackier, fancier, more dynamic and adventurous the profession, the more glued to it they are. They do extremely well in sports, scientific pursuits and showbiz. They understand the effects of their charm and use it to get their way. They are also ready to work hard for their dreams. They also know to how to be dead serious at work irrespective of their otherwise fun-loving, easygoing personality.

This combination has all the signs – fixed, cardinal and mutable. This makes them excel at all levels, from junior, middle, senior, and even to visionary levels. They learn fast and grow at each stage. They are very good at emulating ideas that help them grow. As bosses, they are futurists, forceful fighters, hands-on and generous. But they do need help in the budgeting department.

Fire, Earth and Water combine to give stability to Fire, intuitiveness to Earth and drive to Water. The three diverse signs combine beautifully in SagCapAqua to grow in strength and power.

Famous SagCapAqua Personalities
Abhishek Bachchan, Shobhana Bhartia, Javed Akhtar, Graeme Smith, Vinod Kambli, Mitchell Starc, Jackie Shroff, Ben Kingsley, Waheeda Rehman, Justin Timberlake, Paul Newman, George Washington, Thomas Alva Edison, Lala Lajpat Rai, Michelle Obama, Seal, Gurdas Maan, Amrita Arora, Eddie Cantor, Prakash Karat, Doutzen Kroes, O.P. Nayyar.

184. SAGITTARIUS–CAPRICORN–PISCES

Sagittarius is ruled by the knowledgeable Jupiter, which endows its people with luck and an instinctive wisdom about abstract facts. Capricorn is ruled by the wise and shrewd Saturn, which imparts logic, while the deep and mysterious Neptune rules Pisces. SagCapPisces are full of wisdom and knowledge. They know so much about so many things that they seem too good to be true. But it is not as simple as that: there are many layers to their complex personality.

SagCapPisces are extremely friendly and outgoing people. The exuberance of Sagittarius diminishes the old-man ways of Capricorn to make them fun-loving extroverts. Pisces, too, is a people-friendly sign; SagCapPisces know how to interact animatedly with both old and young. Wise and responsible, the Capricornian in them makes them shoulder responsibilities beyond their age.

They are shockproof. You can tell them anything, but they remain non-judgemental. They, however, try and adhere to social norms themselves. Capricorn desires status and prestige in society and they work towards that.

Money speaks volumes to them. SagCapPisces are extremely ambitious and plan to create wealth and position for themselves.

The Sagittarius tendency to anger is totally diluted due to Capricorn and Pisces. They are more interested in getting the work done. Many a time, the blunt honesty of Sagittarius gets the better of them and they blurt out uncomfortable truths. But the Capricorn in them understands decorum and the Pisces is sensitive to what people want to hear, so they cover up things later nicely.

Family is their focal point. The family-oriented Capricorn reduces the family-averse ways of Sagittarius and makes them loyal and caring to their family. They get restless in one place and love to travel and enjoy new places and sights. Sometimes, the serious Capricorn in them combines business with travel.

Sagittarians are not lifetime lovers; they love to look around and admire all good things! Thankfully, that element is kept largely in check by Capricorn and Pisces who love to be with their family. Also, the Capricornian desire to seem respectable keeps them more or less that way in public. Pisces, too, wants to avoid confrontation at all costs so it means that SagCapPisces will keep their act comparatively clean.

They have the rose-tinted spectacles of Pisces and super optimism of Sagittarius. They dream big and almost practical dreams. The 'practical' comes from Capricorn and 'almost' from Pisces! But Capricorn will ensure they also work hard for it. Their dreams are realistic only if they do not give in to the deceptive moves of Pisces.

Confident and exuberant, they seem so erudite and plausible when you meet them that you feel you have met a real 'somebody'. The problem is that it is virtually impossible for them to continue looking that good. The danger is that they can go back to the indisciplined ways of Sagittarius and Pisces. While the hard-working Capricorn and ambitious Sagittarius will push them to seek higher avenues in life, they always have the danger of falling prey to the easy life of Pisces.

They like all the good things and distractions in life. They are inveterate party animals who never let go of a chance to party, even if it means waking up bleary-eyed for a conference next morning. They may also give in to Piscean addictions to anything from food to love to marijuana. They can subject people to uncomfortable situations due to their erratic habits and even deceptions in money management. The problem is that they are as good at blowing up money as at earning it.

Due to Capricorn, they work hard, and even manipulate their way, if necessary, to success. Pisces can be masters of deception when they are cornered. Many of them are able to circumvent that danger area but a few can fall into the pit by thinking that they can outsmart others. They also have extreme Piscean fears, phobias and deep sensitivity that they manage to camouflage beautifully with their Sagittarian exuberance. Capricorn can get melancholic when things don't go right and the Pisces in them is tempted to give in to easy options at those times.

These are people who know everything about life – all its pitfalls, ups and downs. Their deep wisdom makes them very spiritual, especially in the later part of their life. They can tell you exactly what is right and wrong as they have been there and done it all and learned from all those experiences of life.

Sagittarius–Capricorn–Pisces – Ellen DeGeneres
In 1997 when Ellen revealed that she was gay, her career went into free-fall. 'I naively thought nobody's going to care. It's like, I'm going to just now say, by the way, I'm gay. It's my journey. And it's who I am.'[346]

'I wouldn't stay down, you know. I could've. My feelings were really hurt. I was really sensitive. So part of it is luck and part of it is talent. And part of it is perseverance.'

'I like dancing…I like to try new things because I get bored so easily.'[347]

Ellen is the quintessential SagCapPisces with her honesty, perseverance, sensitivity and her overriding optimism despite the many challenges in her life.

Love and Marriage for Him
Family is always the centre point of his existence. He gives his all for his family and works relentlessly to ensure that they have status in society. Tradition is important to him and even though he lets you be independent, he wants you to follow his family traditions and values. His environment affects him. His parents and experiences combine to make him the man he is. You need to understand his influences.

He is a caring husband but you have to take care of the responsibilities. His career is too important for him to care about the details of family life. You need to be an independent and strong person to live with him for he needs an excellent support system at home.

Money can be an area of concern. You can either take on the responsibility or divert it to a specialist. Either way, you have to make sure that he does not blow up all that he works hard to earn.

---
[346] http://www.msnbc.msn.com/id/6430100/ns/dateline_nbc-newsmakers/t/catching-ellen-degeneres/
[347] http://www.oprah.com/omagazine/Oprah-Interviews-Ellen-DeGeneres-Ellens-O-Magazine-Cover/

As a father, he is exemplary. He wants his children to look up to him and for that he tries to be the ideal dad. He is playful yet stern, loving and responsible, and ensures that they learn the right values. He is not controlling and lets them live their dreams.

Love and Marriage for Her
She is the ideal wife – caring, loving, traditional and totally supportive of her husband. The only thing she demands of her mate is that he has the ambition and drive to make her proud. She needs status and respect. If you are laid back, let her work at it herself.

She does not mind spending time talking to your mom or looking after your family, but the kitchen is not her sole domain. This girl craves excitement and the outdoors. Take her out and plan holidays to different destinations.

She is the ideal career woman; utilise her abundant energy and enthusiasm. She can be an ideal partner in your business and will work hard to help you achieve success and glory.

You need to be adept at understanding her for Capricorn and Pisces make her susceptible to mood swings. She can get terribly depressed. During such times, she needs your understanding and support. Loss and rejection can leave her with feelings of pessimism and inadequacy.

As a mother, she is totally in her element, with Capricornian care and Piscean love. She nurtures and guides her children. She is everything for them – playful, motherly, ambitious and understanding. She is not obsessive about grades, rather she pushes them to live life according to their dreams.

At the Workplace
Ambition and the need to prove themselves are deeply ingrained in them. They are highly intelligent and confident and can be excellent organisers, talkers and ideators. They dream big and new dreams. They work for money and status, so be sure to pay them in cash and kind. They like fancy designations too.

They are great learners. They have the Piscean knack of learning from you, repackage the whole thing into something better in typical Capricorn fashion, and market it by adding their own ingenuity and creativity like Sagittarius. They need good mentors who can groom them when young and inculcate discipline and rigour.

They need to guard themselves against the feeling of invincibility for it is then that they start making mistakes. They can start off really well and succeed, but then fall prey to conceit. They also need to be very careful about keeping the lines of communication open and clear.

As bosses, they like reinventing the old ways of doing things and are very good at motivating people. The Capricornian excellence in delegating makes them choose wisely and the Piscean intuitiveness makes them know how to use people and situations wisely. Their positive attitude and exuberance makes people follow them. But they need to keep their subordinates informed of their plans and learn to trust.

The three elements, Fire, Earth and Water, combine to give them drive, practicality and vision. SagCapPisces are ideators and doers and need an environment that helps them grow positively.

Famous SagCapPisces Personalities
Ellen DeGeneres, Kamal Amrohi, Asa Griggs Candler, Baba Kalyani, Al Capone, Joan of Arc, Daniel Auteuil, Namrata Shirodkar.

185. SAGITTARIUS–AQUARIUS–PISCES

There is a soft charm about SagAquaPisces that makes them instantly likeable wherever they go. They portray intelligence and knowledge without being overtly aggressive about it. The beautiful sensitivity of the Fish, the super intelligence and playfulness of the Centaur and the humanitarian and friendly Aquarius fuse to form what can probably be called the Dolphin of the zodiac.

Jupiter, the knowledgeable and extremely lucky planet, rules Sagittarius and brilliantly meets up with the highly intelligent Uranus in Aquarius and the deep and mysterious Neptune in Pisces. These three planets ensure that SagAquaPisces are deeply knowledgeable and highly intuitive. They never stamp on anyone's toes or like to interfere in anyone's decisions. They believe in 'live and let live' and use their wisdom with humility.

Aquarius aids futuristic thinking while Sagittarius makes SagAquaPisces crack the code on arcane subjects and abstract theorems. Pisces adds the human touch and stops them from turning into mad geniuses. It adds sensitivity and emotional empathy to Sagittarius and Aquarius and makes them more warm and receptive.

SagAquaPisces are the dreamers and thinkers of the world. You can expect them to live in their heads and think distant thoughts while sipping tea with friends. You can never be sure when they have gone on a dreamy trip, leaving reality behind. Of course, they always return rejuvenated, yet you cannot be sure that they heard your list of woes while nodding beatifically at you.

Money is not important to them. They live, think and dream of ideals, values and Utopian thoughts. They desire to do something different that makes the world a better place. Accumulating money never enters their scheme of things. Their ambition is never defined, yet they are ambitious. They take their time in finding a path true to their dreams and ambitions and despite their soft nature, cannot be led into things that don't excite them.

The Pisces in them makes them reflect their environment to a very high degree. Thus, if their parents are disciplined Virgos, SagAquaPisces display a love for routine and doing things perfectly. Travel is very important to them. They need to travel to feel alive. They love meeting new people and discovering diverse cultures.

Aquarius makes them fabulous friends while Pisces adds deep sympathy and sensitivity to them. These guys neither let you down nor ever think of forming friendships for personal gain. You can expect honesty and fair play from them, plus a dash of fun. They are very mischievous but have fun without hurting anyone. They do get angry quickly and blow their top at times. But if they do hurt anyone, they are the first to apologise without any emotional hang-ups.

Learning is always very important to them. They grow and learn throughout their lives: spiritually and emotionally as well. Sagittarius and Pisces are deeply interested in the spiritual and mysterious aspects of life and like to explore that area too.

Love is extremely important for them. The Pisces in them needs a soul mate while Aquarius and Sagittarius pull them towards ideals and ideas, so you might find a disconnect in them at times. They like to be in love but also demand a lot of space in their relationships. SagAquaPisces are also a little irresponsible in love. Aquarius can make them act very weirdly at times and they can give confused signals – it's okay: the weirder and clumsier they act, the deeper they have fallen in love!

SagAquaPisces contains Fire, Air and Water, while it lacks Earth. This makes them less grounded and it can be their most difficult fault. It makes it hard for them to concentrate on one thing for long and they can scatter their energies and obvious talents on meaningless activities. They are impractical. They need guidance in this area.

They can also become aimless missiles or self-pitying introverts with escapist habits. They can tend to laziness and give in to the habit of procrastination. There are those rare SagAquaPisces who can have the extreme downbeat qualities of these otherwise evolved zodiac signs: they can possess the quarrelsomeness of Sagittarius, be rebels with no cause who get angry at trifles, have the explosive temper of Aquarius, and even resort to the mean, devious ways of Pisces in one-upmanship.

Sagittarius–Aquarius–Pisces – Larry Page
'Technology should do the hard work so people can do the things that make them the happiest in life.'

'We should be building great things that don't exist.'

'I'm sure people in the future will think we're just as crazy as we think people in the past were.'

'I encourage non-incremental thinking and a real deep understanding of what you're doing.'

'Yeah, we've had a difficult relationship with Oracle. Money is more important to them than any sort of collaboration.'[348]

Larry Page has the futuristic views, love for abstract details, candidness and people-friendly ideas of SagAquaPisces. He not only created an amazing search engine but also a workplace that is considered a pathbreaking model.

Love and Marriage for Him
You have married your best friend! He is always there for you, even when he looks a bit distracted. This is a guy with whom you can giggle, fight, argue and even philosophise. He is extremely flexible in his views. He does not mind if you work late, or demand that you cook when you come home. His ego is almost subliminal but do not take it for non-existent, for he cannot take aggression.

There is a catch, though. You have to be the more responsible one, the anchor for all his good intentions and the foundation for his flights of fancy. This guy needs a strong, independent woman to handle him and to bring focus and maturity into his life. Money has to be your concern. He does not know when to invest or how to save.

Fun loving and optimistic, there is not much that puts him out of humour. He has an explosive temper that blows up all of a sudden, but it never lingers. Bad moods never afflict him. He is the easiest guy to get along with, if you don't

---
[348] http://www.businessinsider.com/google-io-live-blog-2013-5?IR=T

mind his occasional detachment. Sometimes, he needs to sit and think. Give him the freedom to be himself.

Pisces makes him caring and sensitive to your needs. It can be hard to keep things from him, for though he is not intrusive, he knows the difference between what you think and what you say.

He is a fun father who knows how to enjoy his children's childhood. His immense knowledge and insight broaden their horizons. He teaches them to be non-judgemental and makes them more humane and understanding than their peers. His ambition for them is to find happiness rather than money, and to pursue dreams rather than blend in with the herd.

Love and Marriage for Her
She is unconventional, even when she tries to be conventional. This girl always thinks futuristically. It is extremely difficult to tie her down to a specific role. She can be a homemaker yet seem absolutely at ease with thinking abstract thoughts while stirring her curry. She can be sweet and charming one moment and adventurous the next. There are many shades to her personality.

She is no doormat. This girl has individuality without its related aggression and makes a point without raising her voice unnecessarily. She needs you to be her support and help her find her focus. Her ambitions are high but scattered and she is eternally grateful to you if you help her use her talents in a more deliberate fashion.

Take her out to exotic places and go on adventure treks with her. She loves exploring new facets of life with the curiosity of a child.

As a mother, she is loving, caring, compassionate and fun. She knows how to play with her children and spends hours with them, being a child in their pranks. She wants them to live life their way and not be influenced by society's dictates. She leads by example and never pushes them to realms they do not intend to tread.

At the Workplace
SagAquaPisces are extremely intelligent and ambitious. The only thing they need to learn is focus. It may take them some time to settle in and finally arrive at the jobs they like. Their inherent intelligence and path-breaking ideas make them fabulous as researchers, mathematicians, scientists and engineers. They like to change things and dream impossible dreams. Human resource proves to be a natural abode for them for they are people-friendly.

Money is not important to them: what matters are ideas and thoughts. They can only be motivated if challenged, and look not to accolades but to achievements. Routine and schedules are not for them. There is a dilemma. A SagAquaPisces can be a gifted genius and if luck goes his way, he can make millions. He can turn a passion into a profession, a great intellectual idea into something special that the world cannot live without. But there is also this danger that he can be that eccentric genius who lost his way, is drenched in impracticality, quarrels with everyone and looks for escapism.

As bosses, they scrutinise the souls of people before they recruit them; but after hiring, they are the most permissive bosses around. They are the most flexible, most approachable and most humane, and promote original thinking and groundbreaking ideas.

Fire, Air and Water meet to give energy and optimism, intelligence and curiosity, sensitivity and spirituality to SagAquaPisces, who revel in thinking what seems improbable to others.

Famous SagAquaPisces Personalities
Shakib Al Hasan, Larry Page, Alia Bhatt, Shweta Bachchan Nanda, Reese Witherspoon, Otto von Bismarck, Victor Hugo, Potti Sriramalu.

186. CAPRICORN–AQUARIUS–PISCES

Saturn, the wise and strict ruler of Capricorn, Uranus, the highly unpredictable and wildly inventive planet of Aquarius, and Neptune, the deep and mysterious planet of Pisces, come together in this combination. They are not only soft and gentle but also the most quietly ambitious people you can meet. Silently, using their amazing inventive genius and empathetic skills, they rise. The timid Fish has definite chances to become a whale with the upwardly mobile Capricorn and the forward-thinking Aquarius.

CapAquaPisces just love their families. Capricorns have deep respect for age and authority while Pisceans are soft souls who instinctively feel the suffering of others. The elders of the family feel respected and instinctively veer towards CapAquaPisces. They look after their parents and send money to them even if they are separated by continents.

The Piscean tendency to always look at the positive traits of people and find something good in everyone is very evident in them. They can easily empathise with people and are capable of thinking from another's point of view. People-oriented and friendly, it is easy to be friends with them for they are great at empathising. They know what makes you tick.

Aquarius adds spark to the Piscean wisdom. The Piscean broadmindedness and the Aquarian predilection for eccentricity lighten the sobering effects of Capricorn and save them from becoming fuddy-duddies. Pisces is not well organised and focused, but with the influence of Saturn, these people are organised while being creative. This is a truly difficult balance to achieve.

Intelligent and wise, CapAquaPisces are unsurprised by the wildest facts and take everything in their stride, easily assimilating different ideas as they go along. Capricorn's deep-seated desire to succeed makes them work to reach the top. They think and do things that seem totally unachievable or imaginable. To the usual Aquarian revolutionary ideas add the Capricornian sense of discipline and work ethics, and those wild thoughts suddenly seem realistic. The Capricorn in them needs status. The Aquarian too wants to do something unusual and helpful to people.

They have some amazing talents. From the Piscean mastery in mimicking others, to the Aquarian predilection for wacky hobbies, to Capricorn's inclination to classical arts, they can master some outstanding art form. They are deeply attracted to the abstract, the unknown and the darkest secrets of the world. They go on quests to decipher the deepest mysteries of the world, from sexuality to spirituality.

A normal Piscean might know what people think but not care enough to use that knowledge. But when combined with the wily Capricorn and the non-confirming Aquarius, they can sniff out all your fears and dreams, and use them against you if required. They honestly try their best to succeed by putting in loads of hard work. But if they see a manipulating environment and scheming people around, they are fully capable of moulding themselves according to situations with chameleonic ease.

The intuitiveness of Pisces and the innate sensors of Aquarius can be a double-edged sword. The continuous façades and masquerading to which they subject themselves according to the needs of the people does put a strain on them. They go through some deeply depressing moments when they see deceit and sham around them. Capricorn's fear of failure and the Piscean self-deprecation and diffidence can affect them too, and contribute to the black moods.

The Pisces in them is the most malleable of signs and can melt into any environment. They can be saints, or the opposite, depending on their company. A CapAquaPisces might be a genius who can convert his extraordinary ideas into moneymaking products, and be successful without being flashy. Or he can be a person who gives in to Piscean self-pity and defeatism, a slave to addictions: an unsightly wreck of a potential genius. The danger of the latter eventuality also exists in this combination.

They can also become master criminals, aided by Capricorn's selfish ambition, Piscean deception and the Aquarian genius in finding an amazing solution for every problem. In such cases, they can use their genius and understanding in carrying out scams. One way or the other, they will leave a legacy.

Capricorn–Aquarius–Pisces – Steve Jobs

Cringely says, 'No one expected him to be a family man – and he was! He was an asshole at work, but at home he wasn't.'

In accepting his mortality, Jobs 'began to think about how he would be remembered and how he would be seen by history.'[349]

'Don't let the noise of others' opinions drown out your own inner voice. And, most important, have the courage to follow your heart and intuition.'[350]

Hard-headed businessman or philosopher, Steve Jobs was as unique in his views as in his products. He wanted to leave a legacy like a Capricorn and left it with the style of an Aquarius and the intuitive logic of a Pisces.

Love and Marriage for Him

You have found a gem; do not let it go. He is an amazing son and a doting father. Family ties hold great importance for him. He is the most non-aggressive and understanding guy you can ever meet. Just tell him that once in a while, for he is not very sure of his own charms.

His empathising skills make him the perfect shoulder to cry on. Both Pisces and Capricorn can sacrifice themselves on the family altar, so you can expect him to give up everything for his family's happiness. But this guy is also very ambitious. It is necessary for him to succeed and though he does not ask you to make his dreams your own, a little understanding and space make him far happier.

You must be the more practical of the two for he has phases of dreaminess. He is highly romantic, but sometimes the melancholic Capricorn may take over and make him sound dejected. Hold his hand then and tell him how much you love him. At times, he may be totally self-centred, day dreaming, absent-minded or seem lost on another planet. Let him be, he needs space to think things out for himself.

---

[349] http://mashable.com/2011/11/10/steve-jobs-lost-interview/
[350] http://www.guardian.co.uk/technology/2011/oct/09/steve-jobs-stanford-commencement-address

As a father, he is exemplary and loves to be friends with his children.

They love to share their secrets with him. His easy friendliness and non-authoritarian nature make them turn to him for advice on mending broken hearts or creating new remote-controlled toys.

Love and Marriage for Her
She is the wife who allows you to wear the pants in the house. Domination and aggression are not her style. But don't let that give you the idea that you are the only boss. This girl is not naïve and knows how to get her work done while her head is in the clouds.

She is not ambitious for herself, and not career-driven either, but she still has the ambition to get on in life. Status and respect matter to her and she is very happy if you provide her with these. She looks to a partner who is ambitious and strives to excel. If you do not desire material success or status, she strives to achieve them herself. While chasing her dreams, she can become very self-centred. Give her space but make her realise the importance of family time too.

Sacrificing and unselfish, she can work herself to the bone for her family. Uncomplaining and stoic, she can bear any burden in her journey to see her family through.

She can easily understand what a person means and is an expert at getting her work done without hurting anybody's feelings. She is the most unobtrusive of wives and an easy soul to get along with. This wifely perfection is marred by one messy fact: she may not be the perfect housekeeper.

She is an amazing mother. She will teach her children to marvel at the mysteries of the world and help them unravel them. She will encourage them to dream and urge them to achieve them.

At the Workplace
These people are highly artistic, creative, versatile and inventive. You can expect them to rise to the top wherever they go. They can make their undeniable talents earn money for them. They are the silent, non-flashy workers who manage to catch the boss's eye and make him realise that they are the ones doing the job. They do not stay in junior positions for long and have the capability of becoming your superior.

Their empathising and curious nature makes them great in human resource management. The Piscean sympathy coupled with the Aquarian 'out of the box' thinking makes them adept at finding marvellous solutions to your seemingly impossible problems. They coach you, guide you, and mentor you as bosses and appreciate inventive thinking. But never try to fool or bluff. They are very good at scrutinising and judging people.

This combination has both the manipulative power and the instinctive knowledge of human psychology. They are quite capable of using others' weaknesses to their advantage. They are devious and extremely strong competitors. They plan and smoothly use ingenious tactics to win or dissuade rivals. Counselling, clinical psychology, psychiatric practices, and even the mystic sciences such as astrology, can be good career options for them. If they ever have to retire, they would prefer taking on consultancy roles and mentoring rather than giving up work altogether.

Earth, Air and Water combine to give this sign insight, empathy, outstanding curiosity and spiritual understanding.

Famous CapAquaPisces Personalities
Steve Jobs, Nicolas Sarkozy, Daniel Craig, Biju Patnaik, Desmond Haynes, Rihanna, Ursula Andress, Jiah Khan, Ali Babacan, Alain Prost, Matt Prior, Kunjarani Devi, Joan Crawford, K.D. Singh 'Babu', T.M. Soundararajan, J.P.R. Williams, Nikhil Nanda.

SELECT BIBLIOGRAPHY

Goodman, Linda (1968). *Linda Goodman's Sun Signs.* Taplinger Publishing Co., New York.

Cosmic Connections (Mysteries of the Unknown). Time-Life Books Inc., Hong Kong, 1988. 'Reading the Sun Signs', pp. 80–91.

GLOSSARY OF TERMS

Sun sign: The zodiac sign in which the Sun was transiting at the time of birth of a person.

Mercury sign: The zodiac sign in which the planet Mercury was transiting at the time of birth of a person.

Moon sign: The zodiac sign in which the Moon was transiting at the time of birth of a person.

The ascendant: The ascendant or the rising sign, is the zodiacal sign that was ascending on the eastern horizon at the specific time and location of an event or during the birth of a person.

Astronality: The permutation and combination of the various zodiac signs in which a person's Sun, Mercury and Moon were transiting at the time of birth.

Ruling planet: The planet that exercises its control over a particular zodiac sign is called the ruling planet. The planet's innate characteristics and behaviour pattern reflect fully on the zodiac sign and vice versa. For example, Pluto rules the zodiac sign Scorpio.

The twelve zodiac signs are classified into four different elements – Fire, Earth, Air and Water – based on their basic characteristics.

Fire signs: The zodiac signs Aries, Leo and Sagittarius are called the Fire signs. Fire signs form the first, fifth and the ninth places of a horoscope. They are called Fire signs, as they are expansive and combustible. The strength of Fire signs lies in their positivity, power of belief, ambition, largesse and capacity to motivate others.

Earth signs: The zodiac signs Taurus, Virgo and Capricorn are called the Earth signs. Earth signs form the second, sixth and tenth places of a horoscope. They are called Earth signs, as they are solid and rooted. The strength of Earth signs lie in their steadfastness, industriousness, durability, practicality and dependability.

Air signs: The zodiac signs Gemini, Libra and Aquarius are called the Air signs. Air signs form the third, seventh and eleventh places of a horoscope. They are called Air signs because they are expansive and have no limits. The strength of Air signs lies in their excellent communication skills, power of expression, futuristic thought processes and capacity to work with others.

Water signs: The zodiac signs Cancer, Scorpio and Pisces are called the Water signs. Water signs form the fourth, eighth and twelfth places of a horoscope. They are called Water signs as they are deep and sensitive. The strength of Water signs lies in their perceptiveness, power of imagination, empathy, sensitivity and capacity to understand and nurture others.

A further classification also divides zodiac signs on the basis of their style of functioning.

Cardinal signs: The zodiac signs Aries, Cancer, Libra and Capricorn are called cardinal signs. Cardinal zodiac signs love to lead others into adapting to their ideas. Aries tries to lead others by conviction, Cancer by emotions, Libra by reasoning and Capricorn by strategy.

Fixed signs: The fixed zodiac signs do not like to be led by others. They like to stick to their own ideas and can even be stubborn. It is very difficult for others to change their point of view. The fixed zodiac signs are Taurus, Leo, Scorpio and Aquarius.

Mutable signs: The mutable are the most malleable amongst zodiac signs. They are open to learning and are flexible in their approach. Gemini, Virgo, Sagittarius and Pisces are the mutable signs.

Zodiac signs can be further classified into masculine and feminine on the basis of their emotional quotient.

Masculine signs: Aries, Leo, Libra, Sagittarius and Aquarius are masculine signs. People born under these zodiac signs generally have an optimistic disposition and are extroverts. They are not particularly emotional or sensitive.

Feminine signs: Taurus, Cancer, Virgo, Scorpio, Capricorn and Pisces are feminine signs. People born under these zodiac signs are pessimistic to start with and are mostly introverts. They are emotional and sensitive too.

Gemini is not classified as a masculine or a feminine sign as Geminians have the ability to be either at any given point of time.

Planet X: The yet to be re-discovered planet that rules Taurus. This 'planet' is currently classified as an 'asteroid' by NASA. The author has identified this as the 'missing link' in the solar system and as the real 'planet' that rules the zodiac sign Taurus. This is the planet that rules the second house of a horoscope and is the indicator of wealth, material possessions, etc. The author will reveal more about this planet, its cause and effects, in his future works.

Planet Y: The yet to be re-discovered planet that rules Virgo. This 'planet' is currently classified as an 'asteroid' by NASA. The author has identified this as the final 'missing link' in the solar system and as the real 'planet' that rules the zodiac sign Virgo. This is the planet that rules the sixth house of a horoscope and is the indicator of health, hardships, obstacles, etc. The author will reveal more about this planet, its cause and effects, in his future works.

ACKNOWLEDGEMENTS

This book would never have materialised if Linda Goodman hadn't written her book on sun signs. She is probably the greatest authority on astro-psychology and no work by any author on the subject can escape a bit of Linda's influence. I salute her as the unofficial psychologist to millions.

My heartfelt thanks to my school and college friends, Melwin Fernando, C.S. Narayanan and Nilesh Shah. The long animated discussions I had with them on astrology and psychology have been the genesis of this book. I also thank all those relatives, friends and colleagues who have been guinea pigs in my experiments in exploring the personality traits of different zodiac combinations.

I want to thank Vijay Tagore, Satya Rath and Derek Abraham, who were responsible for my work on astrology getting a wider audience.

A special mention for Adi Rajan, who helped me write better and has been instrumental in cultivating my tolerable English language skills. I'm thankful to Nishka Rathi for her helpful editorial insights during the first draft of the book.

I thank all those 186-people who have read 'their' chapters and given me feedback. They have helped me to tone down or enhance those aspects I had concentrated on too much or missed completely. I also thank all those people whose curiosity, questions and encouragement kept me motivated and helped to manifest thoughts for the book.

My special thanks to Swarup Nanda, CEO of Leadstart Publishing, who had the nerve to pick up a first-time author, that too on a topic challenging conventional wisdom. My gratitude to Fravashi, who put together a beautiful cover with no real input from me. I am awed by the pace, perfectionism and professionalism displayed by the editor of this book, Padmini Smetacek. If the book is crisp and conveys more in less, she is to be thanked. Finally, this book wouldn't have crystallised into its current avatar without the timely advice and inputs by Chandralekha Maitra, Executive Director, Editorial at Leadstart.

Printed in Great Britain
by Amazon